Novels
for Students

National Advisory Board

Novels for Students

Presenting Analysis, Context, and Criticism on Commonly Studied Novels

Volume 12

Elizabeth Thomason, Editor

Foreword by Anne Devereaux Jordan

GALE GROUP

THOMSON LEARNING

Detroit • New York • San Diego • San Francisco
Boston • New Haven, Conn. • Waterville, Maine
London • Munich

Novels for Students

Staff

Editor: Elizabeth Thomason.

Contributing Editors: Reginald Carlton, Anne Marie Hacht, Michael L. LaBlanc, Ira Mark Milne, Jennifer Smith.

Managing Editor, Content: Dwayne D. Hayes.

Managing Editor, Product: David Galens.

Publisher, Literature Product: Mark Scott.

Literature Content Capture: Joyce Nakamura, *Managing Editor*. Sara Constantakis, *Editor*.

Research: Victoria B. Cariappa, *Research Manager*. Cheryl Warnock, *Research Specialist*. Tamara Nott, Tracie A. Richardson, *Research Associates*. Nicodemus Ford, Sarah Genik, Timothy Lehnerer, Ron Morelli, *Research Assistants*.

Permissions: Maria Franklin, *Permissions Manager*. Jacqueline Jones, Julie Juengling, *Permissions Assistants*.

Manufacturing: Mary Beth Trimper, *Manager, Composition and Electronic Prepress*. Evi Seoud, *Assistant Manager, Composition Purchasing and Electronic Prepress*. Stacy Melson, *Buyer*.

Imaging and Multimedia Content Team: Barbara Yarrow, *Manager*. Randy Bassett, *Imaging Supervisor*. Robert Duncan, Dan Newell, *Imaging Specialists*. Pamela A. Reed, *Imaging Coordinator*. Leitha Etheridge-Sims, Mary Grimes, David G. Oblender, *Image Catalogers*. Robyn V. Young, *Project Manager*. Dean Dauphinais, *Senior Image Editor*. Kelly A. Quin, *Image Editor*.

Product Design Team: Kenn Zorn, *Product Design Manager*. Pamela A. E. Galbreath, *Senior Art Director*. Michael Logusz, *Graphic Artist*.

Copyright Notice

ISBN 0-7876-4895-7
ISSN 1094-3552

Printed in the United States of America.

10 9 8 7 6 5 4 3 2 1

Table of Contents

Guest Foreword
"The Informed Dialogue: Interacting with
Literature" by Anne Devereaux Jordan ix

Introduction xi

Literary Chronology xv

Acknowledgments xvii

Contributors .xxi

The Ambassadors (by Henry James) 1
Author Biography 2
Plot Summary .2
Characters 4
Themes 7
Style 9
Historical Context 10
Critical Overview 12
Criticism 14

Animal Dreams (by Barbara Kingsolver) .24
Author Biography 25
Plot Summary 25
Characters 27
Themes 30
Style 31
Historical Context 32
Critical Overview 34
Criticism 35

Bless Me, Ultima (by Rudolfo Anaya) . . .47
  Author Biography 47
  Plot Summary 48
  Characters 50
  Themes .52
  Style 53
  Historical Context 53
  Critical Overview 55
  Criticism 56

The Bride Price (by Buchi Emecheta) . . .65
  Author Biography 66
  Plot Summary 67
  Characters 68
  Themes .71
  Style 74
  Historical Context 75
  Critical Overview 78
  Criticism 79

The Edible Woman
(by Margaret Atwood) 94
  Author Biography 95
  Plot Summary 95
  Characters 97
  Themes .100
  Style 103
  Historical Context 103
  Critical Overview 105
  Criticism 106

Little Women (by Louisa May Alcott) . .116
  Author Biography 117
  Plot Summary 118
  Characters 119
  Themes .122
  Style 124
  Historical Context 125
  Critical Overview 128
  Criticism 129

Mrs. Dalloway (by Virginia Woolf) 148
  Author Biography 149
  Plot Summary 149
  Characters 151
  Themes .153
  Style 155
  Historical Context 155
  Critical Overview 157
  Criticism 158

The Octopus (by Frank Norris) 168
  Author Biography 169
  Plot Summary 169

  Characters 171
  Themes .174
  Style 176
  Historical Context 177
  Critical Overview 179
  Criticism 181

The Painted Bird (by Jerzy Kosinski) . .195
  Author Biography 196
  Plot Summary 196
  Characters 198
  Themes .201
  Style 203
  Historical Context 203
  Critical Overview 205
  Criticism 206

Pilgrims in Aztlán (by Miguel Méndez) 214
  Author Biography 215
  Plot Summary 216
  Characters 217
  Themes .221
  Style 223
  Historical Context 225
  Critical Overview 226
  Criticism 228

Rabbit, Run (by John Updike) 237
  Author Biography 238
  Plot Summary 238
  Characters 239
  Themes .241
  Style 242
  Historical Context 243
  Critical Overview 245
  Criticism 247

Rebecca (by Daphne du Maurier) 256
  Author Biography 257
  Plot Summary 257
  Characters 259
  Themes .262
  Style 264
  Historical Context 265
  Critical Overview 267
  Criticism 268

The Slave Dancer (by Paula Fox) 280
  Author Biography 281
  Plot Summary 281
  Characters 284
  Themes .287
  Style 289
  Historical Context 290

Critical Overview 291
Criticism 292

Too Late the Phalarope
(by Alan Paton) 298
  Author Biography 299
  Plot Summary 299
  Characters 301
  Themes 304
  Style 306
  Historical Context 307
  Critical Overview 308
  Criticism .310

The World According to Garp
(by John Irving) 323
  Author Biography 324

Plot Summary 325
Characters 327
Themes 335
Style 336
Historical Context 337
Critical Overview 338
Criticism 339

Glossary of Literary Terms 349

Cumulative Author/Title Index 361

**Cumulative Nationality/
Ethnicity Index** 365

Subject/Theme Index 369

The Informed Dialogue:
Interacting with Literature

When we pick up a book, we usually do so with the anticipation of pleasure. We hope that by entering the time and place of the novel and sharing the thoughts and actions of the characters, we will find enjoyment. Unfortunately, this is often not the case; we are disappointed. But we should ask, has the author failed us, or have we failed the author?

We establish a dialogue with the author, the book, and with ourselves when we read. Consciously and unconsciously, we ask questions: "Why did the author write this book?" "Why did the author choose that time, place, or character?" "How did the author achieve that effect?" "Why did the character act that way?" "Would I act in the same way?" The answers we receive depend upon how much information about literature in general and about that book specifically we ourselves bring to our reading.

Young children have limited life and literary experiences. Being young, children frequently do not know how to go about exploring a book, nor sometimes, even know the questions to ask of a book. The books they read help them answer questions, the author often coming right out and *telling* young readers the things they are learning or are expected to learn. The perennial classic, *The Little Engine That Could, tells* its readers that, among other things, it is good to help others and brings happiness:

"Hurray, hurray," cried the funny little clown and all the dolls and toys. "The good little boys and girls in the city will be happy because you helped us, kind, Little Blue Engine."

In picture books, messages are often blatant and simple, the dialogue between the author and reader one-sided. Young children are concerned with the end result of a book—the enjoyment gained, the lesson learned—rather than with how that result was obtained. As we grow older and read further, however, we question more. We come to expect that the world within the book will closely mirror the concerns of our world, and that the author will *show* these through the events, descriptions, and conversations within the story, rather than *telling* of them. We are now expected to do the interpreting, carry on our share of the dialogue with the book and author, and glean not only the author's message, but comprehend how that message and the overall affect of the book were achieved. Sometimes, however, we need help to do these things. *Novels for Students* provides that help.

A novel is made up of many parts interacting to create a coherent whole. In reading a novel, the more obvious features can be easily spotted—theme, characters, plot—but we may overlook the more subtle elements that greatly influence how the novel is perceived by the reader: viewpoint, mood and tone, symbolism, or the use of humor. By focusing on both the obvious and more subtle literary elements within a novel, *Novels for Students* aids readers in both analyzing for message and in determining how and why that message is communicated. In the discussion on Harper Lee's *To Kill a Mockingbird* (Vol. 2), for example, the mockingbird as a symbol of innocence is dealt with, among other things, as is the importance of Lee's use of humor which "enlivens a serious plot, adds depth to the characterization, and creates a sense of familiarity and universality." The reader comes to understand the internal elements of each novel discussed—as well as the external influences that help shape it.

"The desire to write greatly," Harold Bloom of Yale University says, "is the desire to be elsewhere, in a time and place of one's own, in an originality that must compound with inheritance, with an anxiety of influence." A writer seeks to create a unique world within a story, but although it is unique, it is not disconnected from our own world. It speaks to us *because* of what the writer brings to the writing from our world: how he or she was raised and educated; his or her likes and dislikes; the events occurring in the real world at the time of the writing, and while the author was growing up. When we know what an author has brought to his or her work, we gain a greater insight into both the "originality" (the world of the book), and the things that "compound" it. This insight enables us to question that created world and find answers more readily. By informing ourselves, we are able to establish a more effective dialogue with both book and author.

Novels for Students, in addition to providing a plot summary and descriptive list of characters—to remind readers of what they have read—also explores the external influences that shaped each book. Each entry includes a discussion of the author's background, and the historical context in which the novel was written. It is vital to know, for instance, that when Ray Bradbury was writing *Fahrenheit 451* (Vol. 1), the threat of Nazi domination had recently ended in Europe, and the McCarthy hearings were taking place in Washington, D.C. This information goes far in answering the question, "Why did he write a story of oppressive government control and book burning?" Similarly,

it is important to know that Harper Lee, author of *To Kill a Mockingbird,* was born and raised in Monroeville, Alabama, and that her father was a lawyer. Readers can now see why she chose the south as a setting for her novel—it is the place with which she was most familiar—and start to comprehend her characters and their actions.

Novels for Students helps readers find the answers they seek when they establish a dialogue with a particular novel. It also aids in the posing of questions by providing the opinions and interpretations of various critics and reviewers, broadening that dialogue. Some reviewers of *To Kill A Mockingbird,* for example, "faulted the novel's climax as melodramatic." This statement leads readers to ask, "Is it, indeed, melodramatic?" "If not, why did some reviewers see it as such?" "If it is, why did Lee choose to make it melodramatic?" "Is melodrama ever justified?" By being spurred to ask these questions, readers not only learn more about the book and its writer, but about the nature of writing itself.

The literature included for discussion in *Novels for Students* has been chosen because it has something vital to say to us. *Of Mice and Men, Catch-22, The Joy Luck Club, My Antonia, A Separate Peace* and the other novels here speak of life and modern sensibility. In addition to their individual, specific messages of prejudice, power, love or hate, living and dying, however, they and all great literature also share a common intent. They force us to *think*—about life, literature, and about others, not just about ourselves. They pry us from the narrow confines of our minds and thrust us outward to confront the world of books and the larger, real world we all share. *Novels for Students* helps us in this confrontation by providing the means of enriching our conversation with literature and the world, by creating an *informed* dialogue, one that brings true pleasure to the personal act of reading.

Sources

Harold Bloom, *The Western Canon, The Books and School of the Ages,* Riverhead Books, 1994.

Watty Piper, *The Little Engine That Could,* Platt & Munk, 1930.

Anne Devereaux Jordan
Senior Editor, TALL
(Teaching and Learning Literature).

Introduction

Purpose of the Book

The purpose of *Novels for Students* (*NfS*) is to provide readers with a guide to understanding, enjoying, and studying novels by giving them easy access to information about the work. Part of Gale's "For Students" Literature line, *NfS* is specifically designed to meet the curricular needs of high school and undergraduate college students and their teachers, as well as the interests of general readers and researchers considering specific novels. While each volume contains entries on "classic" novels frequently studied in classrooms, there are also entries containing hard-to-find information on contemporary novels, including works by multicultural, international, and women novelists.

The information covered in each entry includes an introduction to the novel and the novel's author; a plot summary, to help readers unravel and understand the events in a novel; descriptions of important characters, including explanation of a given character's role in the novel as well as discussion about that character's relationship to other characters in the novel; analysis of important themes in the novel; and an explanation of important literary techniques and movements as they are demonstrated in the novel.

In addition to this material, which helps the readers analyze the novel itself, students are also provided with important information on the literary and historical background informing each work. This includes a historical context essay, a box comparing the time or place the novel was written to modern Western culture, a critical overview essay, and excerpts from critical essays on the novel. A unique feature of *NfS* is a specially commissioned critical essay on each novel, targeted toward the student reader.

To further aid the student in studying and enjoying each novel, information on media adaptations is provided (if available), as well as reading suggestions for works of fiction and nonfiction on similar themes and topics. Classroom aids include ideas for research papers and lists of critical sources that provide additional material on the novel.

Selection Criteria

The titles for each volume of *NfS* were selected by surveying numerous sources on teaching literature and analyzing course curricula for various school districts. Some of the sources surveyed included: literature anthologies; *Reading Lists for College-Bound Students: The Books Most Recommended by America's Top Colleges*; textbooks on teaching the novel; a College Board survey of novels commonly studied in high schools; a National Council of Teachers of English (NCTE) survey of novels commonly studied in high schools; the NCTE's *Teaching Literature in High School: The Novel*; and the Young Adult Library Services Association (YALSA) list of best books for young adults of the past twenty-five years.

Input was also solicited from our advisory board, as well as educators from various areas.

From these discussions, it was determined that each volume should have a mix of "classic" novels (those works commonly taught in literature classes) and contemporary novels for which information is often hard to find. Because of the interest in expanding the canon of literature, an emphasis was also placed on including works by international, multicultural, and women novelists. Our advisory board members—educational professionals—helped pare down the list for each volume. If a work was not selected for the present volume, it was often noted as a possibility for a future volume. As always, the editor welcomes suggestions for titles to be included in future volumes.

How Each Entry Is Organized

Each entry, or chapter, in *NfS* focuses on one novel. Each entry heading lists the full name of the novel, the author's name, and the date of the novel's publication. The following elements are contained in each entry:

- **Introduction:** a brief overview of the novel which provides information about its first appearance, its literary standing, any controversies surrounding the work, and major conflicts or themes within the work.

- **Author Biography:** this section includes basic facts about the author's life, and focuses on events and times in the author's life that inspired the novel in question.

- **Plot Summary:** a factual description of the major events in the novel. Lengthy summaries are broken down with subheads.

- **Characters:** an alphabetical listing of major characters in the novel. Each character name is followed by a brief to an extensive description of the character's role in the novel, as well as discussion of the character's actions, relationships, and possible motivation.

  Characters are listed alphabetically by last name. If a character is unnamed—for instance, the narrator in *Invisible Man*—the character is listed as "The Narrator" and alphabetized as "Narrator." If a character's first name is the only one given, the name will appear alphabetically by that name.

  Variant names are also included for each character. Thus, the full name "Jean Louise Finch" would head the listing for the narrator of *To Kill a Mockingbird*, but listed in a separate cross-reference would be the nickname "Scout Finch."

- **Themes:** a thorough overview of how the major topics, themes, and issues are addressed within the novel. Each theme discussed appears in a separate subhead, and is easily accessed through the boldface entries in the Subject/Theme Index.

- **Style:** this section addresses important style elements of the novel, such as setting, point of view, and narration; important literary devices used, such as imagery, foreshadowing, symbolism; and, if applicable, genres to which the work might have belonged, such as Gothicism or Romanticism. Literary terms are explained within the entry, but can also be found in the Glossary.

- **Historical Context:** this section outlines the social, political, and cultural climate *in which the author lived and the novel was created.* This section may include descriptions of related historical events, pertinent aspects of daily life in the culture, and the artistic and literary sensibilities of the time in which the work was written. If the novel is a historical work, information regarding the time in which the novel is set is also included. Each section is broken down with helpful subheads.

- **Critical Overview:** this section provides background on the critical reputation of the novel, including bannings or any other public controversies surrounding the work. For older works, this section includes a history of how the novel was first received and how perceptions of it may have changed over the years; for more recent novels, direct quotes from early reviews may also be included.

- **Criticism:** an essay commissioned by *NfS* which specifically deals with the novel and is written specifically for the student audience, as well as excerpts from previously published criticism on the work (if available).

- **Sources:** an alphabetical list of critical material used in compiling the entry, with full bibliographical information.

- **Further Reading:** an alphabetical list of other critical sources which may prove useful for the student. It includes full bibliographical information and a brief annotation.

In addition, each entry contains the following highlighted sections, set apart from the main text as sidebars:

- **Media Adaptations:** if available, a list of important film and television adaptations of the novel, including source information. The list also includes stage adaptations, audio recordings, musical adaptations, etc.

- **Topics for Further Study:** a list of potential study questions or research topics dealing with the novel. This section includes questions related to other disciplines the student may be studying, such as American history, world history, science, math, government, business, geography, economics, psychology, etc.

- **Compare and Contrast:** an "at-a-glance" comparison of the cultural and historical differences between the author's time and culture and late twentieth century or early twenty-first century Western culture. This box includes pertinent parallels between the major scientific, political, and cultural movements of the time or place the novel was written, the time or place the novel was set (if a historical work), and modern Western culture. Works written after the mid-1970s may not have this box.

- **What Do I Read Next?:** a list of works that might complement the featured novel or serve as a contrast to it. This includes works by the same author and others, works of fiction and nonfiction, and works from various genres, cultures, and eras.

Other Features

NfS includes "The Informed Dialogue: Interacting with Literature," a foreword by Anne Devereaux Jordan, Senior Editor for *Teaching and Learning Literature (TALL)*, and a founder of the Children's Literature Association. This essay provides an enlightening look at how readers interact with literature and how *Novels for Students* can help teachers show students how to enrich their own reading experiences.

A Cumulative Author/Title Index lists the authors and titles covered in each volume of the *NfS* series.

A Cumulative Nationality/Ethnicity Index breaks down the authors and titles covered in each volume of the *NfS* series by nationality and ethnicity.

A Subject/Theme Index, specific to each volume, provides easy reference for users who may be studying a particular subject or theme rather than a single work. Significant subjects from events to broad themes are included, and the entries pointing to the specific theme discussions in each entry are indicated in **boldface**.

Each entry may include illustrations, including photo of the author, stills from film adaptations (if available), maps, and/or photos of key historical events.

Citing Novels for Students

When writing papers, students who quote directly from any volume of *Novels for Students* may use the following general forms. These examples are based on MLA style; teachers may request that students adhere to a different style, so the following examples may be adapted as needed.

When citing text from *NfS* that is not attributed to a particular author (i.e., the Themes, Style, Historical Context sections, etc.), the following format should be used in the bibliography section:

> "Night." *Novels for Students.* Ed. Marie Rose Napierkowski. Vol. 4. Detroit: Gale, 1998. 34–5.

When quoting the specially commissioned essay from *NfS* (usually the first piece under the "Criticism" subhead), the following format should be used:

> Miller, Tyrus. Essay on "Winesburg, Ohio." *Novels for Students.* Ed. Marie Rose Napierkowski. Vol. 4. Detroit: Gale, 1998. 218–9.

When quoting a journal or newspaper essay that is reprinted in a volume of *NfS,* the following form may be used:

> Malak, Amin. "Margaret Atwood's The Handmaid's Tale' and the Dystopian Tradition." *Canadian Literature* No. 112 (Spring, 1987), 9–16; excerpted and reprinted in *Novels for Students*, Vol. 4, ed. Marie Rose Napierkowski (Detroit: Gale, 1998), pp. 61–64.

When quoting material reprinted from a book that appears in a volume of *NfS,* the following form may be used:

> Adams, Timothy Dow. "Richard Wright: Wearing the Mask,'" in *Telling Lies in Modern American Autobiography.* University of North Carolina Press, 1990. 69–83; excerpted and reprinted in *Novels for Students,* Vol. 5, eds. Sheryl Ciccarelli and Marie Napierkowski (Detroit: Gale, 1999), pp. 59–61.

We Welcome Your Suggestions

The editor of *Novels for Students* welcomes your comments and ideas. Readers who wish to suggest novels to appear in future volumes, or who have other suggestions, are cordially invited to contact the editor. You may contact the editor via e-mail at: **ForStudentsEditors@galegroup.com.** Or write to the editor at:

> Editor, *Novels for Students*
> Gale Group
> 27500 Drake Road
> Farmington Hills, MI 48331–3535

Literary Chronology

1832: Louisa May Alcott is born on November 29, in Germantown, Pennsylvania.

1843: Henry James is born on April 15, in New York City.

1870: Frank Norris is born in Chicago, on March 5.

1868: Louisa May Alcott's *Little Women* is published.

1882: Virginia Woolf is born in London on January 25.

1888: Louisa May Alcott dies on March 6, in Boston.

1901: Frank Norris's *The Octopus* is published.

1902: Frank Norris dies of appendicitis on October 25, in San Francisco.

1903: Henry James's *The Ambassadors* is published.

1903: Alan Paton is born in Pietermaritz, Natal, South Africa, on January 11.

1907: Daphne du Maurier is born in London, on May 13.

1916: Henry James dies in London, on February 28.

1923: Paula Fox is born on April 22, in New York City.

1925: Virginia Woolf's *Mrs. Dalloway* is published.

1930: Miguel Méndez is born on June 15, in Bisbee, Arizona.

1932: John Updike is born in Shillington, Pennsylvania, on March 18.

1933: Jerzy Kosinski is born in Lodz, Poland, on June 14.

1937: Rudolfo Alfonso Anaya is born on October 30, in Pastura, New Mexico.

1938: Daphne du Maurier's *Rebecca* is published.

1939: Margaret Atwood is born in Ottawa, Canada, on November 18.

1941: Virginia Woolf drowns herself on March 28, in Lewes, Sussex, England.

1942: John Irving is born in Exeter, New Hampshire, on March 2.

1944: Buchi Emecheta is born on July 21, in Yaba, a small village near Lagos, Nigeria.

1953: Alan Paton's *Too Late the Phalarope* is published.

1955: Barbara Kingsolver is born on April 5, in Annapolis, Maryland.

1960: John Updike's *Rabbit, Run* is published.

1965: Jerzy Kosinski's *The Painted Bird* is published.

1965: Margaret Atwood's *Edible Woman* is published.

1972: Rudolfo Alfonso Anaya's *Bless Me, Ultima* is published.

1973: Paula Fox's *The Slave Dancer* is published.

1974: Miguel Méndez's *Pilgrims in Aztlán* is published.

1976: Buchi Emecheta's *The Bride Price* is published.

1978: John Irving's *The World according to Garp* is published.

1988: Alan Paton dies from throat cancer on April 12, in Natal, South Africa.

1989: Daphne du Maurier dies on April 19, in Par, Cornwall, England.

1990: Barbara Kingsolver's *Animal Dreams* is published.

1991: Jerzy Kosinski commits suicide on May 3, in New York City.

Acknowledgments

The editors wish to thank the copyright holders of the excerpted criticism included in this volume and the permissions managers of many book and magazine publishing companies for assisting us in securing reproduction rights. We are also grateful to the staffs of the Detroit Public Library, the Library of Congress, the University of Detroit Mercy Library, Wayne State University Purdy/Kresge Library Complex, and the University of Michigan Libraries for making their resources available to us. Following is a list of the copyright holders who have granted us permission to reproduce material in this volume of *Novels for Students (NfS)*. Every effort has been made to trace copyright, but if omissions have been made, please let us know.

COPYRIGHTED EXCERPTS IN *NfS*, VOLUME 12, WERE REPRODUCED FROM THE FOLLOWING PERIODICALS:

The American Spectator, v. 24, July, 1991. Copyright © *The American Spectator* 1991. Reproduced by permission.—*The Atlantic Monthly,* 1979 for a review of "The World According to Garp" by Bryan Griffin. © 1979 by The Atlantic Monthly Company, Boston, Mass. Reproduced by permission of the author.—*Harper's Magazine,* July, 1978. Copyright © 1978 by *Harper's Magazine*. All rights reserved. Reproduced by permission.—*Neophilologus,* v. LXXIV, January, 1990 for "'The Ambassadors': Two Types of Ambiguity" by Dorothea Krook. © 1990 by Wolters-Noordhoff. Reproduced by permission of the publisher.—*The New Republic,* v. 203, December 24, 1990. © 1990 by *The New Republic*, Inc. Reproduced by permission of The New Republic.—*The New York Times Book Review,* April 23, 1978. Copyright © 1978 by The New York Times Company. Reproduced by permission.—*Ploughshares,* v. 4, 1978 for "Magical Strength in the Human Heart" by Carter Wilson. © 1978 by Ploughshares, Inc. Reproduced by permission of the author.—*The Progressive,* v. 12, February, 1996. Copyright © 1996 by *The Progressive*, Inc. Reproduced by permission of The Progressive, 409 East Main Street, Madison, WI 53703.—*The Saturday Review of Literature,* v. XVIII, September 24, 1938. © 1938, renewed 1966 Saturday Review Magazine, © 1979 General Media International, Inc. Reproduced by permission.—*Signs,* v. 15, 1990. © 1990 by The University of Chicago. All rights reserved. Reproduced by permission.—*The Village Voice,* May 22, 1978. Copyright © 1978 V. V. Publishing Corporation. Reproduced by permission of *The Village Voice.*

COPYRIGHTED EXCERPTS IN *NfS*, VOLUME 12, WERE REPRODUCED FROM THE FOLLOWING BOOKS:

Bakerman, Jane S. From *And Then There Were Nine ... More Women of Mystery.* Edited by Jane S. Bakerman. Bowling Green State University Popular Press, 1985. Reproduced by permission.—Bennett, Arnold. From a letter to Virginia Woolf on December 2, 1926, in *Virginia Woolf: The Critical Heritage.* Edited by Robin Majumdar and

Allen McLaurin. Routledge & Kegan Paul, 1975. © Robin Majumdar and Allen McLaurin 1975. Reproduced by permission.—Bensen, Alice R. From "'The Octopus': Overview," in *Reference Guide to American Literature*. Third edition. Edited by Jim Kamp. St. James Press, 1994. The Gale Group.—Callan, Edward. From *Alan Paton*. Twayne Publishers, 1999. The Gale Group.—Candelaria, Cordelia. From "Rudolfo A. Anaya," in *Dictionary of Literary Biography: Chicano Writers*. First Series, Vol. 82. Edited by Francisco A. Lomeli and Carl R. Shirley. The Gale Group, 1989.—del Pino, Salvador Rodriguez. From "Miguel Mendez: The Commitment Continues," in *Miguel Mendez in Aztlan: Two Decades of Literary Production*. Edited by Gary D. Keller. Bilingual Review/Press, 1995. © 1995 by Bilingual Press/Editorial Bilingue, Arizona State University, Temple, AZ. All rights reserved. Reproduced by permission.—del Pino, Salvador Rodriguez. From "'Peregrinos de Aztlan': Overview," in *Reference Guide to American Literature*. Third edition. Edited by Jim Kamp. St. James Press, 1994. The Gale Group.—Elbert, Sarah. From *A Hunger for Home: Louisa May Alcott and "Little Women."* Temple University Press, 1984. © 1984 by Temple University. All rights reserved. Reproduced by permission of the author.—Fishburn, Katherine. From *Reading Buchi Emecheta: Cross-Cultural Conversations*. Greenwood Press, 1995. Copyright © 1995 Katherine Fishburn. All rights reserved. Reproduced by permission of Greenwood Publishing Group, Inc., Westport, CT.—French, Warren. From *Frank Norris*. Twayne Publishers, 1962. The Gale Group.—Howells, Coral Ann. From *Margaret Atwood*. MacMillan Press Ltd, 1996. © Coral Ann Howells 1996. All rights reserved. Reproduced by permission of Palgrave.—Johnson, Manly. From *Virginia Woolf*. Frederick Ungar Publishing Co., 1973. Copyright © 1973 by Frederick Ungar Publishing Co., Inc. Reproduced by permission.—Petersen, Kristen Holst. From "Buchi Emecheta," in *Dictionary of Literary Biography: Twentieth-Century Caribbean and Black African Writers*. Vol. 117. Edited by Bernth Lindfors and Reinhold Sander. Bruccoli, Clark, Lyman, 1992. Reproduced by permission.—Townsend, John Rowe. From *A Sounding of Storytellers: New and Revised Essay on Contemporary Writers for Children*. J. B. Lippincott, 1979, Kestrel Books, 1979. Copyright © 1971, 1979 by John Rowe Townsend. All rights reserved. Reproduced by permission of the author.

PHOTOGRAPHS APPEARING IN *NfS*, VOLUME 12, WERE RECEIVED FROM THE FOLLOWING SOURCES

Alcott, Louisa May, photograph. Corbis-Bettmann. Reproduced by permission.—Alcott House, photograph. Corbis-Bettmann. Reproduced by permission.—Anaya, Rudolfo, photograph by Cynthia Farah. Reproduced by permission of Cynthia Farah.—Anorexia nervosa (young woman holding zipper across her mouth), photograph. © 1995 SPL. Oscar Burriel/Latin Stock/Science Photo Library/Custom Medical Stock Photo, Inc. Reproduced by permission.—Armed Contras on patrol in mountains of Nicaragua, photograph. © Bill Gentile/Corbis. Reproduced by permission.—Atwood, Margaret, photograph. © Jerry Bauer. Reproduced by permission.—Browning, Frederick, with Christian, Flavia and Tessa, and wife Daphne du Maurier, photograph. Hulton-Deutsch Collection/Corbis. Reproduced by permission.—Caan, James, with Carrie Snodgrass in the film, "Rabbit Run," photograph. © John Springer Collection/Corbis. Reproduced by permission.—Dorze bride being ceremonially kidnaped by tribesman, on way to wedding, photograph. © Jim Sugar Photography/Corbis. Reproduced by permission.—Du Maurier, Daphne, photograph. Popperfoto/Archive Photos, Inc. Reproduced by permission.—Earth moving equipment being used in copper mining, photograph. © Craig Aurness/Corbis. Reproduced by permission.—Emecheta, Buchi, photograph. © Jerry Bauer. Reproduced by permission.—First Atom bomb test site near Alamogordo, New Mexico, photograph. Corbis. Reproduced by permission.—Fontaine, Joan, and Laurence Olivier, in the film "Rebecca," 1940, photograph. The Kobal Collection. Reproduced by permission.—Fox, Paula, photograph. © Jerry Bauer. Reproduced by permission.—Guard standing watch over Polish prisoners of war at Nazi concentration camp. Hulton-Deutsch Collection/Corbis. Reproduced by permission.—Howells, William Dean, photograph. Corbis-Bettmann/Newsphotos, Inc. Reproduced by permission.—Ibo girls dancing with woman, 1970, photograph. AP/Wide World Photos. Reproduced by permission.—"In the Garden of Paris," painting by Jean Beraud, at Musee Camavalet, photograph. © Archivo Iconografico, S.A./Corbis. Reproduced by permission.—Irving, John, photograph. AP/Wide World Photos. Reproduced by permission.—James, Henry, photograph. AP/Wide World Photos. Reproduced by permission.—Lithgow, John, as Roberta Muldoon, with Glenn Close as Jenny Fields and Robin Williams as T.S. Garp, in a scene from the film version of John Irving's novel, "The World According to Garp," 1982, photograph. The Kobal Collection. Reproduced by permission.—Kingsolver, Barbara, photograph. AP/Wide World Photos. Reproduced by permission.—Kosinski, Jerzy, photograph. © Jerry Bauer. Reproduced by permission.—Linder, Benjamin Ernest, photograph. Corbis-Bettmann. Reproduced by permission.—Man with newspaper in lap, watching wife and children play in living room, photograph. Archive Photos, Inc. Reproduced by permission.—Mendez, Miguel, photograph. Arte Publico Press. Reproduced by permission. —Mexican farm workers on truck, photograph. UPI/Corbis-Bettmann. Reproduced by permission.—Segregation in South Africa, photograph. Reuters/Corbis-Bettmann. Reproduced by permission.—South African village of Cross Roads, photograph. United Nations. Reproduced by permission.—Southern Pacific Sunset Limited train, photograph. Hulton-Deutsch Collection/Corbis. Reproduced by permission.—Standing, John and Vanessa Redgrave, in the movie "Mrs. Dalloway," 1996, photograph. The Kobal Collection. © 1996 First Look Pictures. Reproduced by permission.—Suffragettes demonstrating in London's Victoria Park, photograph. Hulton-Deutsch Collection/Corbis. Reproduced by permission.—Teenage boys playing high school basketball, photograph. © Shelley Gazin/Corbis. Reproduced by permission.—Trini Alvarado, Susan Sarandon, Clair Danes, Kirsten Dunst and Winona Ryder in a scene from Little Women, photograph. The Kobal Collection. Reproduced by permission.—Updike, John, photograph. AP/Wide World Photos. Reproduced by permission.—Vitamins, photograph. © Stephanie Maze/Corbis. Reproduced by permission.—Wheat field in Wisconsin, photograph. © Layne Kennedy/Corbis. Reproduced by permission.—Women in Farragut Square, have climbed statue of Admiral David G. Farragut, displaying protest signs, photograph. AP/Wide World Photos. Reproduced by permission.—Woolf, Virginia, photograph. AP/Wide World Photos. Reproduced by permission.

Contributors

Don Akers: Akers is a freelance writer whose work has appeared in college journals and educational publications. Entry on *The World according to Garp*.

Bryan Aubrey: Aubrey holds a Ph.D. in English and has published many articles on twentieth-century literature. Entry on *Animal Dreams*. Original essay on *Animal Dreams*.

Jennifer Bussey: Bussey holds a master's degree in interdisciplinary studies and a bachelor's degree in English literature. She is an independent writer specializing in literature. Entries on *Little Women* and *Too Late the Phalarope*. Original essays on *Little Women* and *Too Late the Phalarope*.

Carol Dell'Amico: Dell'Amico is an instructor of English literature and composition at Santa Monica College, California. Enry on *Mrs. Dalloway*. Original essay on *Mrs. Dalloway*.

Joyce Hart: Hart, a former college professor, is a freelance writer and editor who has written books for the study of English as well as nonfiction articles for national magazines. Entries on *The Bride Price*, *The Edible Woman*, and *Pilgrims in Aztlán*. Original essays on *The Bride Price*, *The Edible Woman*, *Pilgrims in Aztlán*, *The World according to Garp*.

Jeremy W. Hubbell: Hubbell has an M.Litt. from the University of Aberdeen, Scotland, and currently seeks a Ph.D. in history at the State University of New York at Stony Brook. Entry on *The Ambassadors*. Original essay on *The Ambassadors*.

David Kelly: Kelly is an instructor of creative writing and literature at several community colleges in Illinois. Entries on *The Octopus* and *Rebecca*. Original essays on *The Octopus* and *Rebecca*.

Wendy Perkins: Perkins is an associate professor of English at Prince George's Community College in Maryland and has published several articles on British and American authors. Entry on *The Painted Bird*. Original essay on *The Painted Bird*.

Emily Smith Riser: Smith Riser has a master's degree in English literature and teaches high school English. Entry on *Bless Me, Ultima*. Original essay on *Bless Me, Ultima*.

Kelly Winters: Winters is a freelance writer and editor and has written for a wide variety of academic and educational publishers. Entries on *Rabbit, Run* and *The Slave Dancer*. Original essays on *Rabbit, Run* and *The Slave Dancer*.

The Ambassadors

Henry James
1903

Henry James, kept out of the Civil War due to a back injury incurred while fighting a stable fire, began writing professionally with the publication of his first short story in 1865. Throughout his career, James, aware of the significance of the Civil War, used his writing to help America arrive at a new sense of self. He did this by reassessing America's relationship with its origins in Europe. James utilized the increasingly efficient transatlantic transportation to capture the true spirit of contemporary Americans in contact with their European peers. In doing so, he showed how the two sides actively engaged each other in an Atlantic community. The best novel of his last period, *The Ambassadors,* neatly resolves this discussion. In this work, Americans enjoy Paris but then return to America where the grit of life is being manufactured.

The Ambassadors remains one of the few novels whose record of origin appears nearly perfect. The novel began from a "germ" that James captured in his notebook on October 31, 1895. There he records how William Dean Howells, standing in the garden of James McNeill Whistler's Parisian home, sermonized to the young Jonathan Sturges that he must live while he was young. Then, in September of 1900, in an article for *Harpers* called "Project of a Novel by Henry James," James laid out the blueprint of the novel. The piece shows how James constructed from Howells' speech, reworked as the speech that Lewis Lambert Strether gives to John Little Bilham, the basis of his novel. The actual writing took seven months and James super-

Henry James

vised the novel's publication process. Published serially in 1903 by the *North American Review* (where Howells was a literary consultant), the novel's reception was guided by James' appraisal of the novel as "the best, 'all round,' of my productions."

Author Biography

Henry James married Mary Robertson Walsh and, on April 15, 1843, the novelist Henry James was born in New York. Months later, the family visited Europe for the first time. The trip was brief, and the family returned to spend the next ten years in New York. In 1855, the family set off again. This time they numbered four boys and one girl. They remained abroad for a few years, and the children went to a succession of schools in Switzerland, France, England, and Germany.

After their return, the family settled in Newport, Rhode Island. Beginning in 1864, under the influence of W. D. Howells, James devoted his life to literature and began publishing criticism and short stories in 1865. His reputation began to grow in 1870, with his stories about the "American Girl," which he modeled on his cousin Minnie Temple—

who died that same year at the age of twenty four. By 1875, he had decided to live abroad.

He planned to live in Paris, but, by 1876, James had settled in London, where he published his first novel, *Roderick Hudson.* James achieved fame and monetary success from *Daisy Miller* in 1878, and *The Portrait of a Lady* in 1881. In 1883, almost two years after his mother's death, the first collected edition of his works appeared in fourteen volumes.

James had success in travel writing, essays, and as a journalist, but his attempt to break into playwriting in the 1890s was humiliating. The audience booed James off the stage after a production of *Guy Domville* in January of 1895. He gave up drama and returned to fiction. During this year, he recorded the "germ" in his notebook that would become *The Ambassadors.*

James continued writing novels and traveling. He made an extensive tour of the United States in 1904 and 1905. He returned to London and found some success with plays until his health began to decline in 1909. He received two honorary degrees from Harvard in 1911 and Oxford in 1912. When the United States did not enter World War I, James registered his protest by becoming a British citizen in 1915. He died on February 28, 1916, in London but not before being awarded the Order of Merit by King George V. His ashes were eventually buried in Cambridge, Massachusetts, and a memorial plaque was placed in the Poets' Corner of Westminster Abbey.

Plot Summary

England

The Ambassadors begins in England. To maintain his social and employment status, Lewis Lambert Strether arrives in Liverpool under orders from his fiancée, Mrs. Newsome. While waiting for his friend, Mr. Waymarsh, who might be of assistance, Strether meets the ever-resourceful Maria Gostrey, who promises undying support. Waymarsh, once he arrives, seems reluctant about helping Strether's project. While on an outing in the Rows in Chester, Waymarsh reveals his "sacred rage" by dashing madly into a jeweler's shop. As he does so, Gostrey and Strether realize they are, in comparison to Waymarsh, unsuccessful in life.

The party journeys to London, where Strether has a fabulous night on the town with Maria. While attending a play, Maria recapitulates Strether's mission as Mrs. Newsome sees it,

Mr. Chad [Newsome] . . . a young man on whose head high hopes are placed at Woollett; a young man a wicked woman has got hold of and whom his family over there have sent you [Strether] out to rescue.

Waymarsh and Strether head for Paris; Maria follows separately.

Arrival in Paris

Strether, who has told Chad he would drop in sometime, seeks out Chad's apartment on the Malesherbes Boulevard. Strether gains his first impression of Chad through an inspection of this apartment and the housesitter, Mr. John Little Bilham. Far from discovering sordid details and evidence of discredit, Chad's abode impresses Strether. The next morning, Strether brings Waymarsh to breakfast with Bilham and another of Chad's friends, Miss Barrace. Afterwards, Waymarsh urges Strether to stop meddling with Chad's affairs and be done with the whole thing.

Maria arrives in Paris and Strether introduces her to Bilham while they tour the Louvre. She pronounces Bilham "one of us" while speculating about Chad. His wonderful apartment and his absence, for the time being, in Cannes indicate good things, for one does not go to Cannes with a common mistress. Something special is going on. Strether takes a box at the theatre for the group but, with minutes remaining before the show's start, Bilham has not yet arrived. Just before the curtain goes up, Chad himself enters and surprises the party.

Negotiations

During the show, Strether dwells on Chad's obvious improvement. After the performance, Strether and Chad adjourn to a café where Mrs. Newsome's arguments in favor of Chad's return to America to take up advertising—the family's business—are laid out. Chad does not refuse to return but hints that he will be detained. Strether, who has been writing detailed letters to Mrs. Newsome about his progress, now writes telling of his success at finding Chad and delivering the message. Somewhat relieved by having fulfilled his duty, Strether begins to enjoy Paris by becoming a "haunter" of Chad's apartment.

Waymarsh increasingly disapproves of Strether's behavior and has Miss Barrace run in-terference—to help Strether focus on helping Chad free himself from whatever binds him. Chad asks that he not be forced to give an answer until after Strether has met the mother and daughter pair that keeps him in Europe. Maria and Strether discuss this situation, and Maria supposes that Chad's affair is not virtuous and, further, that Chad must want to marry the daughter.

Gloriani's Party

The celebrated artist, Gloriani, hosts a party where Chad presents Madame de Vionnet to Strether, Mrs. Newsome's supposed enemy. Strether has hardly spoken with her when they are interrupted, and Strether finds himself on a bench in the garden alone. Bilham joins Strether, who breaks out into the speech that provided the basis for the novel. Strether urges Bilham to take advantage of his youth and live. Strether says this out of regret that he did not do the same; he feels he has wasted his life. The advice endears Strether to Bilham.

Chad reappears to introduce Jeanne de Vionnet, an absolutely stunning young woman. Strether believes that Chad must be pursuing her, and he hardly blames him. But, Jeanne could never possibly live in Woollett and that, Strether believes, is the crux of the issue. Chad takes Jeanne to her mother and Strether quietly departs. He now assumes that Madame de Vionnet will want to plead for Chad to remain in Europe on Jeanne's account. He discusses everything with Maria, who was at the party. Maria is uncomfortable with recent developments. She had promised to support Strether through his errand but did not imagine she would be implicated. She was a classmate of Madame de Vionnet, whose history she tells Strether. Fearing that she might be compromised and approached by Madame de Vionnet, Maria leaves for a while to visit a sick friend.

Chad Surrenders

The morning after the party, Chad "surrenders" to Strether on the condition that Strether puts himself at Madame de Vionnet's disposal for a time. Chad begins to make clear that Madame de Vionnet should be acknowledged as the reason for his transformation. A woman so capable must be made known to Strether and Mrs. Newsome as a wonderful person—not a temptress of a sordid nature. Strether agrees and begins a relationship with Madame de Vionnet. Against his will, he too is enamored with her. For her part, Madame de Vionnet wishes only for Strether to keep Mrs. Newsome patient. She also assures Strether that Chad is more Jeanne's guardian than her lover.

New Ambassadors

Strether, through hints from Miss Barrace and Bilham, realizes that Madame de Vionnet and Chad are having an affair. This changes everything for Strether, who warns Chad not to give up so wonderful a lady. A bit confused, Chad has to agree with Strether's command due to his prior vow of surrender. With the secret out, Strether gets to know Madame de Vionnet better and likes her even more. To help her, Strether writes favorably of her to Mrs. Newsome. He also prevents Chad from visiting America and pleading with Mrs. Newsome directly. When a telegram arrives demanding their return, Strether decides to stall and Chad plays along. Their negative response prompts Mrs. Newsome to send out her daughter.

Sarah and Jim Pocock arrive with his sister, Mamie, to bring Chad to his senses. Waymarsh immediately joins their group, and it is clear that he has been a double agent. Sarah sticks to the business at hand and refuses to see anything but that. Jim opts out of the mess and resolves to enjoy Paris. Mamie sees that Chad has changed for the better and that he is now too refined to be interested in her, a simple woman. Chad does his best to behave as tour guide. Bilham becomes interested in Mamie. Sarah meets Madame de Vionnet but sees nothing impressive about her.

Returning to America

Sarah issues a three-week ultimatum during which time the Pococks travel to other parts of Europe with Waymarsh and Bilham. Strether decides to spend his last days enjoying his vacation and randomly selects a train to take him into the countryside. While happily enjoying the scenery, he bumps into Madame de Vionnet and Chad, who give every indication that theirs is a normal love affair. Strether, still believing in platonic ideals, is saddened by this and surprised that Chad does not offer an explanation. Instead, Chad travels to London for a week to research advertising, which "presented itself thus as the great new force." After seeing Chad, Strether begins preparations for home. He says goodbye to Madame de Vionnet, who knows she has lost, and declines Maria's offer to stay with her. Strether reveals how much has changed in the past five months by telling Maria he cannot possibly marry Mrs. Newsome; he has become a different person who now "sees things"

whereas she remains an invalid who sees what she wants to see.

Miss Barrace

Miss Barrace is a liberated woman who finds amusement in flirting with Waymarsh and who peers at the world through "her long-handled glass." Miss Barrace has the power of "not being" and responds to seriousness with a "crescendo" of "Oh, oh, oh!"

John Little Bilham

Bilham has failed in his original purpose of becoming an artist by studying in Paris. Instead, he has adopted Parisian habits and struggles to stay there, but he has no purpose—he needs saving. Fortunately, Strether appears, and John finds a more appropriate role model than Chad. The relationship between Bilham and Strether builds to the point where Bilham accepts Strether's mission to help Bilham be saved by Mamie. Consequently, Bilham will cease wasting his life and become Mamie's suitor.

Jeanne de Vionnet

Jeanne is "an exquisite case of education," who honors her mother with her beauty and grace. Her mother has raised her to have some American qualities, like "freedom." This perfect representation of French femininity has entrusted herself to the protection of Chad (who eventually finds her a proper husband). Jeanne confuses Strether whenever she gets near to him.

Madame de Vionnet

The presumably horrible woman who keeps Chad from Mrs. Newsome turns out to be the much-adored Madame de Vionnet. In Gloriani's garden, Madame de Vionnet appears "various and multifold." By her genius, she takes all of Strether's "categories by surprise." A few days later, Strether describes her chamber as a series of passageways that he must journey down so as to lay forth the demands of Mrs. Newsome. To his surprise, far from being a monster, Madame de Vionnet shares a fondness for churches with Strether, and they meet at Notre Dame, where they begin a friendship.

Strether comes to admire Madame de Vionnet as a wise woman in possession of artistic and social ideals. He comes to understand that her education of Chad was done out of a great affection but not because of true love. However, Strether eventually learns that though she transformed Chad, she is human. She did it without marriage but not without physical rewards.

Madame de Vionnet knows the part she plays in the imagination of Woollett, and she registers a protest with Mrs. Pocock. As Madame de Vionnet notes, Strether also has profited at the hands of a woman. However, Madame de Vionnet estimates Miss Gostrey as a "really wonderful woman." Madame de Vionnet realizes that she lost because she failed "to seem to [Strether]—well, sublime!"

Gloriani

Chad arranges for Strether to meet Madame de Vionnet and her daughter at a party held at Gloriani's house. This character also appears in James' first novel, *Roderick Hudson*. For Strether, a brush with Gloriani is the nearest thing to a brush with fame itself. Strether doesn't quite make it with the fashionable crowd, "the deep human expertness in Gloriani's charming smile—oh the terrible life behind it!—was flashed upon him as a test of his stuff." Strether fails the test.

Maria Gostrey

To the American readers of Puritan descent in James' time, Europe embodied sinful luxuries. To the more enlightened, Europe linked America with its Old World heritage. Maria Gostrey, an American expatriate, has it upon herself to serve as the expatriates' guide through their time in Europe. Gostrey stalls those precious few who come to experience European life until they no longer need her. She hurries those Puritans, who arrive to condemn Europe, through their tour and quickly sends them home again.

Gostrey figures out that Strether's quest has little to do with a prodigal son giving himself up. She asks him "*will* you give yourself up?" Receiving an affirmative answer, Gostrey becomes Strether's guide. Throughout the story, she is Strether's confidant and helps him sort out his thoughts on people and the general situation. Her devotion to Strether has two effects. Upon discovery that Strether's adversary is an old school mate, Gostrey becomes unavailable so as not to be put in an uncompromising situation. Consequently, she spends most of the novel in seclusion. Secondly, she rarely provides information. She merely helps Strether understand the information he has gathered.

Foreshadowing a tragic end, Strether says that Gostrey reminds him of Mary Stuart, Queen of Scots. That unfortunate woman was idealized after being beheaded by the jealous Queen Elizabeth. He thinks of this after dwelling on the velvet ribbon around her neck rather than what was revealed to him by her "cut down" dress. By the end of the novel, Gostrey has become the ideal woman for Strether for she combines "beauty and knowledge" in ways that he has come to appreciate. Gostrey, for her part, had already selected Strether to be one of her well-kept things, and she offers him the reward of being kept after his service to the Newsomes is done. He declines and "there we are!"

Chadwick Newsome

Chad, the prodigal son, has been having a fling in Europe, where Paris has polished him into an admirable gentleman: "Chad was brown and thick and strong, and of old Chad had been rough." He has spent too much time on this fling, however, and seeks to extricate himself from his affairs to return home. Strether, his mother's suitor, has been sent to expedite this process.

Mrs. Newsome has reserved a prestigious managerial position for Chad, which includes learning the new art of advertisement to grow the family business. James never identifies the article that the Newsome's manufacture, but it is a domestic necessity that has made the family extremely wealthy. The subject of the business provides the one opportunity in the novel for commentary on contemporary society. Chad's future as an advertising guru for the business is accompanied by the idea that advertising is a new science and nearly an art.

Chad is "formed to please," and he shows himself to be an able salesman throughout the novel. He arranges Strether's impressions of Chad himself and the Vionnets. His show, from his first appearance at the theatre to his last nightly stroll with Strether, has been for Strether's benefit. Strether has purchased the entire show although it means giving up his betrothed.

Mrs. Newsome

A wealthy American, Mrs. Newsome only appears in the novel through her letters, referenced by her fiancé Strether.

Jim Pocock

Jim "arrived in a very mild and reasonable frame of mind" because he has no intention of involving himself in his wife's ambassadorial duties. For Strether, he serves as a revelation of Woollett society—which excludes Jim. "He seemed to say that there was a whole side of life on which the perfectly usual *was* for leading Woollett business-men to be out of the question." Strether sees in Jim his fate should he marry Mrs. Newsome—exclusion from "the Good Life." Jim could have been a man who always enjoyed the fullness of life, but marriage and career squashed him into being a "small and fat . . . failure of type." Released from the rat race of business life, Jim wants to binge on Europe as if it were an amusement park. And, bingeing is not Strether's idea of joy.

Mamie Pocock

Jim's sister, Mamie, is "one of the real and the right." An accomplished young lady who appreciates the arts and recognizes the value of a business-minded man, Woollett hopes that Chad will return home and marry her. Accordingly, "she came over with ideas. Those she had got at home." She wants to save Chad by bringing him around to accepting Mrs. Newsome's argument. She is a good catch, but Chad, as Mamie can see for herself, has drastically changed for the better and does not need her. Bilham, however, suits Mamie, and he accompanies her to Switzerland with the Pococks at the end of the novel.

Sarah Pocock

When Strether fails to obey a summons from Mrs. Newsome, Chad's sister, Sarah, and her family are sent to Paris to retrieve Chad; upon Sarah's arrival, Mrs. Newsome's correspondence with Strether ceases. Sarah acts as Mrs. Newsome's surrogate and executioner. Chad and Strether try to determine "what mother thinks" by means of Sarah. As the new ambassador, Sarah stalks Strether's imagination to the point of giving him "fantastic waking dreams."

Sarah has modeled herself after the worst aspects of Mrs. Newsome. Strether describes her as "gracious" and always "affable" but also fat, unattractive, and "unpleasant." Whereas, Mrs. Newsome was never unpleasant but "reserved" and audibly "silent." Mrs. Newsome had also maintained "the girdle of a maid." Mentally, Sarah is no match for her mother. Sarah, like her mother, hates Chad in Paris and, far from seeing a change in the young man, feels that whatever can be done in Paris should be done in Woollett. Sarah's tenacity in achieving her mother's objective allows Strether to forgive her for being blind. They part on good terms, but "her mother's moral pressure" and ideals sustain her. This is a sustenance Strether can no longer tolerate.

Sally

See Sarah Pocock

Lewis Lambert Strether

A man in his mid-fifties from Woollett—a provincial New England town—Strether holds the esteem of his fellow Americans due to his intellectual abilities and his editorship of a Review, "the cover's green—a most lovely shade." His work ought to make Strether proud, but he only sounds tired when he admits the journal belongs to Mrs. Newsome, who provides all the money as "her tribute to the ideal." Strether's attachment to Mrs. Newsome has grown deeper, culminating in their engagement. He subsequently accepts a mission from Mrs. Newsome of bringing her son home "in triumph as a sort of wedding-present." Strether's increasing awareness of himself forms the focus of the novel. In the preface, James calls Strether his hero, but from a psychological viewpoint, he becomes a case study of the imaginative person—too much immersed in literature—whose dull life and mind are forever changed during a trip abroad.

The burdens of life before his trip haunt Strether. Memories of his wife's death make him feel guilty; in his grief, he was incapable of caring for his sickly child—who died alone. In addition, the weight of living up to Mrs. Newsome's demands has left him "dog-tired." She, in fact, is ever present with him in Europe through her letters and the command that Strether not indulge in distraction. Fortunately, Strether meets Maria Gostrey, who helps him without demanding anything in return, unlike Waymarsh, who is more like Mrs. Newsome. Strether naturally prefers the healthy exchange with Gostrey. His journey to self-realization has only begun.

Paris does wonders for Strether. While he was focused on doing his job when he arrived in Europe, he now seeks reasons for delaying a return to Woollett as long as possible. He has, as an old man, learned new tricks and learned how to live. It is this lesson that provided the "germ" for James's novel. Strether regrets the wasted toil of his days and feels he has only begun to live. He shares this realization—a repetition of the carpe diem theme—with Bilham, who he views as the son he has lost:

> It's not too late for you, on any side, and you don't strike me as in danger of missing the train . . . It doesn't so much matter what you do in particular, so long as you live your life . . . It's too late. And it's as if the train had fairly waited at the station for me without my having had the gumption to know it was there. Now I hear the faint receding whistle miles and miles

down the line . . . Do what you like so long as you don't make *my* mistake. For it was a mistake. Live!

His eyes are open. He can now sees things as they really are; what is valuable in life and what is not. His speech foreshadows the final lesson in his education as a man who celebrates life; he does take a train and makes a grand discovery. His new-found identity makes it impossible to marry Mrs. Newsome because she does not see clearly.

Mr. Waymarsh

Waymarsh is an American lawyer from Milrose, Connecticut. He provides a stark contrast to Strether. Mr. Waymarsh matches Strether in age but has been more successful in life. He stands as a stereotypical American man of money who exhibits a "joyless" disposition—he grumbles about the accommodations, refuses to go to plays, and doesn't appreciate European civilization, from Chester's Rows to Parisian streets. If Strether had not counted Waymarsh as a friend, he would have fit into Gostrey's category of persons needing to leave Europe as soon as possible. Waymarsh is incapable of self-realization: "he'll resist even Miss Gostrey."

Waymarsh comes from an older American mold than Strether which, apparently, did not tolerate challenge or question. Milrose "was most in the real tradition" of New England Puritanism. Strether knows what this means and adequately explains Waymarsh's background to Gostrey. Waymarsh has the "sacred rage" of the old-time righteous Americans who despised the luxurious ways of the Europeans, and who glowered in disgust from across the oceans. The maintenance of the "sacred rage" endears him to Miss Barrace as an antique from childhood, "your friend's a type, the grand old American . . . The Hebrew Prophet, Ezekiel, Jeremiah" who used to visit her father. Miss Barrace loves Waymarsh because he doesn't understand, "so grand is it not to understand." This type of American has been outdated, but, for the moment, he acts like a check on Strether who wishes to be a new American—the open-minded, cultured American. Waymarsh does not appear to Strether as the wonderful curmudgeon Mrs. Barrace sees because he sides with the Pococks against Strether.

Themes

Disillusionment

Strether runs a gauntlet of disillusioning circumstances on his journey to wakefulness and clear sight. Strether realizes that "to be right" he must see things as they are. Right things are seen and understood clearly. "The wrong . . . *was* the obscure." In Woollett, this means seeing things according to Mrs. Newsome's definitions. Strether's actual experiences force him to disavow Mrs. Newsome's theories while maintaining the definitions of right and wrong. That means sacrificing all preconceived notions derived from books, paintings, nostalgia, or the theories of his betrothed. It also means solitude. Strether gains the brand of traitor when he tries to share his knowledge. The disillusionment with the narrow-mindedness of Woollett was bound to happen. In the end, events also destroy Strether's belief in perfection.

This last ideal will vanish during an attempt to enjoy views of France made famous by the Impressionists. From a train station, Strether walks through a series of studio-perfect landscapes. His nature viewing reaches a crescendo when he takes a seat by a river. "A boat advancing around the bend" that contains a man rowing a woman with a "pink parasol" caps the experience. What a perfect sight! In a moment, recognition ruins the experience. Although he had felt assured that he could count on Madame de Vionnet and Chad to maintain their perfection as platonic lovers with good judgment, they are the ones he sees on the river "in a boat of their own," having a regular, romantic affair. That "their country could happen to be exactly his" adds to Strether's feelings of disillusionment.

France

The fear of "going native," or of watching someone else do this, reached nearly neurotic proportions in the heady days of the New Imperialism. With racist undercurrents supported by new theories of eugenics (the study of improving hereditary qualities); Europeans regarded nonwhite ethnicity as horrible, and any white person who adopted nonwhite ways was condemned in polite circles. Indeed, the duty of the European was to "civilize" the nonwhite—usually through a conversion to Christianity and white household habits. A corollary to this was the old tension between the English and French. These two nations had been warring over colonial possessions for a long time. Part of their sparring included the English, for example, loathing of French manners and customs. In fact, the English viewed a man who adopted French ways as effeminate.

The Americans inherited this loathing for French ways, and as they fabricated an American identity, they included French mannerisms in their

Topics for Further Study

- Paying particular attention to the women in the two novels, compare Joseph Conrad's *Heart of Darkness* to *The Ambassadors*.

- What psychological theory did the profession of advertising adopt by 1903? How does this relate to the novel?

- Argue for an interpretation of the novel that inverts the normal, positive assessment of Strether. That is, he has been duped by Chad, whose theatrics make him a natural advertising guru, into purchasing a theory of life that ends his engagement to Mrs. Newsome.

- History has changed dramatically in the last generation. National stories have been de-emphasized in favor of themes, such as the Atlantic Community. Reading such scholars as Paul Gilroy, Ned Landsman, and Alfred Crosby, define this term and apply it to the work of James.

- The novel is rife with allusions to paintings. The title itself repeats the title of a painting by Hans Holbein. Research a few such direct references, and relate them to the novel, or research the works of the Impressionists, and compare them to James' "pictures" of the cityscape of Paris or the French countryside.

"don't" book. In *The Ambassadors,* however, Americans eventually succumbed to French ways and feel better for doing so. Waymarsh and the Pococks keep themselves from becoming French, but Chad, Bilham, and Strether have been converted. Bilham suggests the process was more thorough than conversion. "They've simply—the cannibals!—eaten me; converted me if you like, but converted me into food. I'm but the bleached bones of a Christian." In this speech, Bilham alludes to the history of colonialism as well as the lingering disagreement between the Protestants and Catholics. Arts, manners, and food are involved with "going French" but so is the appreciation of

the Catholic air embodied in the gargoyles and cathedrals of Paris, which Strether speaks of as "the great romancer and the great romance."

Materialism

The manufacturing of millions of things that people consume as part of their daily lives describes the state of the world in which this novel is set. But that "vulgar" world, though alluded to under the guise of the mysterious item at the root of the Newsome's wealth, remains outside the novel. In an "age of mechanical reproduction," to use Walter Benjamin's phrase, the original and rare item is given greater value. That is, a society that spends a great deal of its time buying and selling "vulgar" things idealizes those original, often antique, pieces and their possessors. This theme announces itself from the beginning when Waymarsh goes into a jeweler's shop to vent his "sacred rage." As a representative of the Puritan tradition, luxurious items and their wanton consumption are sinful. Strether does not agree, but he doesn't really know what to think about consumption. Things in Paris show Strether "a different scale of relations."

Expensive and rare things are pointed out in the novel and provide Strether with a means of evaluating people. He begins with Maria whose "velvet band somehow added, in her appearance, to the value of every other item." Maria, Chad, and Miss Barrace collect things—expensive things like artwork and antiques. Chad's "charming place . . . full of beautiful and valuable things" backs up the idea that Chad has become a gentleman of taste. Miss Barrace's informed and intense inspection of objects make them seem "to need to be." Chad and Miss Barrace widen Strether's idea about things, but Maria's Parisian apartment, on the other hand, is an "empire of things" and "as brown as a pirate's cave." Though he worries about breaking something in Maria's "little museum," he realizes that she, the human, is the most important object to appreciate. Madame de Vionnet disrupts Strether's newfound appreciation of people by their precious things. Madame de Vionnet does not collect things; rather, her wealth was "founded more on old accumulations" that simply baffle Strether's mind as he tries to calculate her age. Strether realizes he has entered "the air of supreme respectability—that was a strange blank wall for his adventure to have brought him to break his nose against."

Strether respects the accumulation of things, and he has learned that the exercise of taste and value can create truly wonderful collections. No effort of collecting, as American billionaires from

Gould to Rockefeller were doing at the time, could possibly compete with true collections brought together by a family over centuries. Not for the first time, Madame de Vionnet shows she represents, not an "old and abject and hideous" creature but someone with the "right stuff."

Diversity

Using a mechanical metaphor, Strether puts forth a theory about humans made possible by his trip abroad. If he had stayed at home where things were homogenous, the observation would have been impossible. However, sitting in the audience at the theatre and glancing at the other audience members, Strether notices the wide variety possible in humanity but holds that there are only two molds—male and female. Beyond that, "a series of strong stamps had been applied" to create finite diversity. Miss Barrace helps Strether continue believing in this theory when she identifies Waymarsh as a type. This theory cracks during Strether's experience in Paris where many opinions—compared to Woollett's "Three or four"—make him realize that people, however similar they may appear, possess unique minds. From this he graduates to being a critic, in the best sense of the term. "Everything's comparative," he tells Madame de Vionnet. By this he means that people and places, past and present, can be compared and lessons can be drawn from that comparison without having recourse to a system or theory of moral judgement (like Woollett's "Theory of the Horrible"). Strether's mastery of this idea disables his knee-jerk ability to judge, which he had at the beginning of the novel. Comparison wins him admiration. Seeing the benefit he has derived from this lesson, he attempts to encourage Chad and Bilham in the same direction.

Style

The Psychological Novel

The impression that external stimuli and events make on a character or the thoughts and feelings motivating characters are the subjects of this type of fiction. In the novel's earliest days, the psychology of a character was declarative. Thus, the nervous mind of *Robinson Crusoe* was stated, as was the fear of death in *Tristram Shandy*. However, an increased interest in criminal minds brought greater psychological sophistication to the novel. Detective stories in America and Russia delved into

psychological motivation and reflected current scientific theory. As the nineteenth century wore on, George Eliot and Gustave Flaubert produced psychological novels about normal people. In the twentieth century, following James, the psychological novel would reach new heights with James Joyce, William Faulkner, and Virginia Woolf.

James contributed the technique of sustained focus on one mind to this genre. James used a device called *erlebte Rede* or *le style indirect libre,* a technique that plays with indirect speech. A standard narration, which uses indirect speech to focus on the thoughts of a character, would judge a character's thought: "he thought [blank]." In erlebte Rede, however, the narrator leads us to the judgement but without the overtness just shown. In this novel, the narrator generalizes the sentiments of what Strether thinks by cutting through the literary and metaphorical manners Strether himself would use. The reader, however, has to reach the conclusions by him or herself. For example, the narrator does not clue the reader into the obvious irony of the phrase "in the same boat" at the end of the novel. Some things are better left unsaid, and the result is a focus on the workings of an individual mind as it deals with its environment.

Realism

James and his friend Howells introduced to American fiction the nineteenth-century conceit that art could truly represent life. In this novel, James' style shows that realist techniques do not always lead to straightforward understandings. James focused on the psychological experiences of Strether and recorded them in a natural manner. There is no theoretical jargon or explanation of Strether's mind—just a play-by-play description of Strether's mind processing his experiences according to his linguistic base.

Another area where James shows his realism is in conversation. Highly educated and witty characters perform the dialogues. Thus, facts and figures obvious to the characters are never spelled out. Thoughts by one character are completed by another as each tries to beat the other to a speculation. The ability to follow the exchanges as well as the allusions contained in the descriptions of Strether's mind are rewarded by amusement:

> Considering how many pieces had to fit themselves, it all fell, in Strether's brain, into a close, rapid order. He was on the spot what had happened and what probably would yet; and it was all funny enough.

Ficelle

Ficelle comes from the stage and refers to the tricks and devices now called "special effects." James uses this term as a label for characters whose function assists in firming up the structure of the novel. These characters work much in the same way a letter or other evidence in a detective novel would work; they are an opportunity to fill the reader in on elements otherwise unknown, without using an omniscient narrator or employing interior monologue. Thus, Mrs. Newsome is not a ficelle because she never appears. A ficelle must be present because verbal communication with Strether activates him or her. Miss Gostrey is the purest ficelle in the novel although Waymarsh and Bilham act as ficelles from time to time. When Strether invokes the ficelle, the reader gains information while Strether clarifies his thoughts. The ficelle exists, Strether tells Maria, "to see me through . . . the experience."

Point of View

The perfection of the novel depends on the success of using a third-person narrator spliced with one character's point of view: Strether's. James rejects the obvious choice of first person narrative (his reasons are detailed in the novel's preface) to gain the freedom and reliability of third-person narration while creating a concentrated focus on a person's psychology. He also keeps his novel in prose without quoting letters and only alluding to other literary works. James uses many devices to succeed.

First, James alters the device of "central intelligence" so that it becomes the unifying consciousness of the entire work. Prior to this novel, an "intelligence" was simply a viewpoint or a character. In the character of Strether, James develops a viewpoint through which the entire novel is channeled. Information in the novel reveals itself solely through this intelligence. This is admitted within the novel several times. Second, the third-person narration uses "scenes" and "pictures" to aid Strether's viewpoint. A scene involves characters meeting and speaking while pictures relate Strether's thoughts without the drawbacks of soliloquies. For example, Strether's first meeting alone with Madame de Vionnet begins with a scene with Chad, then flows into a picture, and then into a scene with the lady herself. The picture relays Strether's impressions of the inventory of Madame de Vionnet's apartment in the third person. Their conversation scene is interspersed with comments like, "it gave her another pause; which, however,

she happily enough shook off." By these devices, the third-person narrative is grafted into the singular viewpoint of the main character to create a tight unity that becomes Strether's "experience."

As Strether changes, so does the information relayed by the narrator. The day after the rural outing, a picture of Strether is presented to convey the chaos of his feelings. Amidst a series of questions, the narrator suggests Strether asks himself, Strether is described as having "a deliberate hand on his blue missive, crumpling it up rather tenderly than harshly." The details of the note from Madame de Vionnet are relayed without quoting it.

Historical Context

Transatlantic Travel

The days of the speedy Clipper ship were numbered once Robert Fulton launched a successful steamboat in 1807. Steamboats soon revolutionized inland transport and, combined with the construction of canals, led to an era of decreasing shipping prices. Ocean-going vessels began to be fitted with engines in 1819, but they did not pose a significant threat to sail power until the Cunard Line began regular service to Europe in the 1840s. By the 1870s, boiler and propeller improvements led to the triple-expansion steam engine, which did not require huge amounts of fuel. Further improvements in the 1890s, with the adoption of the turbine, brought the travel time between the United States and Europe down to a week. Increasing the speed of transatlantic shipment of goods and people fostered an increase in world commerce.

Industrialization

Industrialization reached a stage of inertia in the late nineteenth century. Whereas heavy industry, like coal mining or iron production (which due to the Bessemer process had all but lost out to steel), had long been brought under the control of large conglomerates like U.S. Steel, other areas of life had also been industrialized. Transportation was no longer by foot or horse but by railroad or, if you were rich enough, a horseless carriage. Flour was made in great milling centers like Minneapolis, while meat was processed in Chicago; both were shipped by rail to department and chain stores. But industrial efficiency and expansion had its problems, especially in the downturn of the world economy between 1873 and 1896. Thus, advertising was the key. Catalogs, roadside billboards, and even pa-

Compare
&
Contrast

- **1903:** Radio is being developed for transmission of news and music.

  Today: The internet is being developed for the transmission of all media formats, including real time audio and visual interpersonal communications.

- **1903:** The record for transatlantic crossing is set by the German ship *Deutschland* at just under six days. Nellie Bly circumnavigates the globe (from New York to New York) in seventy-two days.

  Today: A Concorde jet flies from Paris to New York in three-and-a-half hours. Richard Rutan and Jeanna Yeager circled the world without refueling between December 14 and 23, 1986. A 747 flew over both planetary poles a few years before in fifty-four hours.

- **1903:** Mass advertising and monopolies are new challenges.

  Today: Advertising is ubiquitous and monopolies are illegal due to a belief in commercial competition and consumer benefits.

- **1903:** The French abandoned construction of a Panama Canal because they could not keep down mortality rates among the workers. Unknown to them, the pretty flower pots outside their cottages were ideal breeding grounds for mosquitoes. Discovery of the role of the mosquito in disease transmission and new medicines, combined with the United States-supported secession of Panama from Columbia, allowed American firms to arrive and finish the job.

  Today: The Panama Canal is now owned and operated by Panama. The canal requires a great deal of repair after a century of use, but it is now too small for many of the supertankers and aircraft carriers that compose the U.S. shipping fleets.

- **1903:** The ability to reduce mortality advances the prosperity of developing nations who have begun to erase childhood diseases like cholera, typhoid fever, small box, and rickets. Still the infant mortality rate is high.

  Today: Mortality rates from disease continue to drop in the developed world to about 10 per 1,000. The situation will only improve as the completion of the human genome project makes new drugs possible. Meanwhile, AIDS has ravaged the African continent and the United Nations projects 27 million dead. Economic digression has begun, and some areas may be set back fifty to one hundred years in their development.

---

rades were used to capture the attention of the newly created mass market.

France

France had imperial ambitions, and its manufactures were expanding as well. A mass society was being created, and Paris was the cultural capital of the world. Under the government of the Third Republic, nationwide compulsory schooling put in place in 1885 created a generation of French citizens who studied the same subjects in the same educational setting. In addition, this generation had similar ideas of patriotism due to compulsory military service. Also, as in other industrialized countries, the railroad and the steam-powered rotary printing press enabled an integrated nation state. Into this mixture, two critical events helped polish mass politics and the beginnings of a truly secular society.

First, General Georges Boulanger attempted to overthrow the Third Republic through a sophisticated political campaign that took advantage of the aforementioned developments in French society. By 1886, his name recognition was high and right-wingers, monarchists, and big business supported him. His platform remained unclear, but he had frightened the entrenched power structure by 1889. The Third Republic was never in real danger of collapse, and he fled the country amidst charges of scandal. He left behind a political machine that looks primitive by the standards of late twentieth-century America but was larger than any other mass political effort of the time.

This overtly reactionary machine was ready when the Dreyfus affair broke in 1894. Anti-Semitism remained more virulent in France than anywhere else in Europe until Hitler's rise to power in Germany. Captain Alfred Dreyfus was framed as a spy and sent to Devil's Island in South America after being convicted on a charge of treason. The trial exposed France's anti-Semitism and showcased the ability of the press and grassroots organizations to influence national politics. Dreyfus was eventually cleared of the charge and returned to the army, where he reached the rank of lieutenant colonel.

The New Imperialism

A number of political and technological developments conspired to bring about New Imperialism. Faster ships made the world smaller, better firepower gave the Europeans the advantage (except at Adowa), Quinine made the malarial sting impotent, and a belief in the white man's right to civilize and subdue the earth came together in the second half of the nineteenth century. From 1875 to the eve of WWI, European nations competed with each other in a scramble for Africa. Wealthy Europeans and adventure-seeking men used the world as a playground as they hunted trophies, stole treasure, and gathered scientific data. Their tales, data, and money helped to bolster the idea that Europeans were superior to everyone else.

The Boer War

Britain had the greatest empire, but by the end of the nineteenth century, it had a nervous hold on its possessions. Britain paid special attention to areas of profitability like India (the only colony that ever turned a profit) and areas with abundant natural resources. Afrikaners (descendents of Dutch settlers) were laying claim to the world's largest supply of gold in South Africa, which Britain viewed as its rightful property. This contest grew problematic when Germany, avowedly friendly to the Afrikaners, annexed Namibia in 1884. British capitalists like Cecil Rhodes invested in mines in South Africa and conspired to overthrow the Afrikaners and establish British rule. They failed in their 1895 attempt.

Tensions increased until the Afrikaners declared war on Britain in 1899. Britain sent 350,000 troops to fight 65,000 Afrikaners in a long, drawn out guerilla war. By 1902, after years of high casualties and international criticism, the British accepted the surrender of the Afrikaners, and South Africa was created. The conditions of this peace, however, set the stage for an eventual independent apartheid state run by the Afrikaners.

Critical Overview

In a "Memorandum," H. M. Alden advised his superiors at Harper and Brothers against accepting *The Ambassadors.* He noted, "the scenario is interesting, but it does not promise a popular novel." Alden was correct; the novel has never been a widely read book. But David Lodge was not exaggerating when he summed up the place of James' novel in the English canon. In his *20th Century Literary Criticism,* Lodge wrote, "more than any other single writer, James may be said to have presided over the transformation of the Victorian novel into the modern novel, and at the same time to have laid the foundations of modern criticism of the novel." Gore Vidal agreed, saying that in James's third period of work, "the magician" broke his "Golden Bowl" and reached the height of his powers.

The incredible awe in which James was held before his death checked original critical reception of the novel. Many of the first reviewers were writers themselves, like Joseph Conrad or Virginia Woolf. Most critics followed the novel's preface and praised the book, while those who wrote negatively betrayed a lack of understanding. A singular exception was H. G. Wells, who engaged in a series of misunderstandings with James. In "Of Art, of Literature, of Henry James," Wells explained that he simply disagrees with James' presumptions about the novel. James, said Wells, "wants a novel to be simply and completely *done.* He wants it to have a unity, he demands homogeneity . . . Why *should* a book have that?" Ezra Pound, shortly thereafter, replied, "I am tired of hearing pettiness talked about Henry James's style." For style was indeed the issue of the negative reviews—the book was found to be difficult. Pound, instead, felt James was a champion of individual liberty.

The critical mood of the 1920s, like the culture at large, wanted nothing to do with prewar culture. In America, H. L. Mencken took a shot at James in an essay within his *A Mencken Chrest-*

omathy. He felt James needed to smell reality; "James would have been vastly improved as a novelist by a few whiffs from the Chicago stockyards." Americans were not alone in their negative assessment. E. M. Forster took special notice of *The Ambassadors* in his *Aspects of the Novel.* Forster found that the novel was "pattern triumphant" and "beautifully done, but not worth doing."

Renewed appreciation for James came in the 1930s but was very defensive. Mostly, this criticism followed James' own preface and interpretations laid down by early apologists, like Joseph Warren Beach and Percy Lubbock. In *The Craft of Fiction,* Lubbock revealed the degree to which he was a follower of James by explaining James' working theory of the novel. Lubbock set criticism's focus on the idea that "the point of view is primarily Strether's," which would be the mainstay of approaches to *The Ambassadors* for almost fifty years. In that span of time, a few critics dared to investigate social forces underpinning the novel. Granville Hicks, who noted that few people were interested in James but those that were formed a "kind of James cult," explored James' theme of civilizations clashing in "The Great Tradition." Hicks noted James' divided loyalties as the reason for his "peculiar fitness for the portrayal of the international scene," a skill that he developed between *Roderick Hudson* and *The Ambassadors.*

The scholarly engagement with James didn't really take fire until the centennial of his birth in 1943 and at first differed little Lubbock. In an essay from 1943, R. P. Blackmur's appreciation of James was less defensive. Blackmur detailed the reasons for James' greatness in presenting the idea that "the man fully an artist is the man, short of the saint, most wholly deprived." Another enthusiast, F. O. Matthiessen, returned to Lubbock's theme but goes further. In his *Henry James: The Major Phase,* Matthiessen says James' "principle contribution to the art of the novel," which writers have since taken for granted, is the creation of a center of consciousness as the unifying element in the structure of a novel.

During the 1960s, scholars (like Christof Wegelin, Stephen Spender, and Graham Greene) began to approach James beyond Lubbock's thesis or the clashing of civilizations theme. Scholars began to delve into the complexity of James' symbols and trace elements of ancient myth, reflections of Nietzschean philosophy, and psychological revelation. By far the most expert analysis of this period came from Ian Watt. He concluded his essay,

William Dean Howells, James' editor and friend

"The First Paragraph of *The Ambassadors,*" saying, "the notorious idiosyncrasies of Jamesian prose are directly related to the imperatives which led him to develop a narrative texture as richly complicated and as highly organized as that of poetry." This, in short, explained the high regard for James.

Beginning in the late 1970s, James became a darling of the literary academy as *The Ambassadors* became ripe ground for cutting edge literary theory. Reader response approaches to the novel filled the journals but did not add anything beyond early Lubbock-style analysis. This gave way, however, to an avalanche of postmodernist approaches to James for the rest of the century. During this most recent period, James' novel has been celebrated as pro-feminist and as a case study in hermeneutics (the methodology of interpretation). The novel has been deconstructed and looked at as a spiritual autobiography of James. The gems in this wave of Jamesian criticism are actually old school approaches. Adeline Tintner investigated the novel's sources in her essays written from 1986 to 1993. Daniel M. Fogel worked in a similar style but followed a different direction in *Covert Relations.* There he showed how James influences specific works of modernism by James Joyce and Virginia Woolf.

Criticism

Jeremy W. Hubbell

Hubbell has a M.Litt. from the University of Aberdeen, Scotland, and is currently studying for a Ph.D. in history at the State University of New York at Stony Brook. In the following essay, he investigates "the Theory of the Horrible" as psychological adventure in James' story.

The Ambassadors conjures a story of a man, or men, on a mission who must carry out an errand for a notable personage. Given the time of its publication, the title further suggests an imperial adventure with an American going out to a foreign land to exchange ideas and sympathies. These are not incorrect assumptions, especially in context of what people were hearing and reading about in the closing decades of the nineteenth century. Lectures about primitive peoples or exhibits of dinosaurs were delivered as captivating eyewitness accounts. *The Adventurers of Tom Sawyer,* H. Rider Haggard's *King Solomon's Mines,* and Rudyard Kipling's colonial tales were just a few of the popular adventure tales. These elements of popular culture were intensely peopling the globe with monsters and strange behaviors from living dinosaurs to cannibals. The newly evolved mass media helped ensure everyone heard these tales and, therefore, when serial murderers were on the loose, like Jack the Ripper in London, hysteria was easily generated. The dangers of such adventures came home in the 1890s to scare people in their bedrooms. Ghost stories never disappeared, but terror tales set at the seats of empire became normal. Sherlock Holmes entered the literary scene and was followed by *Dracula* in 1897.

Adventure and danger, of course, lie at the base of the novel, starting with Daniel Defoe's tales of shipwrecks and pirates. The pattern for the early and more recent tales was transparent: a young man defies the warnings (or he is sent out into the world explicitly to lose his innocence) about the monsters and dangers beyond the village and goes out to see the world. His anxieties often make him ill, but he never actually battles dragons or monsters, only people. In the end, he has gained in wisdom and comes home to tell people about what he has seen. His journey has been spiritually and mentally rewarding. Though the change of scenery was an essential trigger, his adventure was psychological; he overcomes his crippling anxieties. People at home can't believe how normal it all sounds so the sto-

ryteller sprinkles his accounts with monsters. *The Ambassadors* fits this pattern.

John Patterson recognized this in 1960. Skipping the title's allusions, Patterson points out that the very language of "low brow" fiction—adventure tales—composes the heart of James' refined language. In *The Language of "Adventure" in Henry James,* Patterson investigates the novel for its rife allusions to adventure. But he also notes how adventure pervades James' writing in general from his letters to such works as *The Beast in the Jungle.* Patterson sites numerous examples, but one will suffice here; Gloriani's party becomes a jungle in Strether's mind and the host appears as "the glossy male tiger, magnificently marked." Taking Patterson further, James' reliance on adventure language makes sense given the psychology under study—Strether's literary mind weaves his experiences into the linguistics of his reading. Thus, Strether's masculine crisis, which begins with Mrs. Newsome's proposal to him, will be resolved when he grapples, like a young man leaving the village, with the sublime or, as it is labeled in the novel, "the Theory of the Horrible."

A cursory definition of the sublime immediately illuminates its place in the novel, especially when matched with the psychological theory that James agreed with—that of his brother, William James. Reality and literature clash over the sublime for whenever that term is defined a literary example is used—as well as examples from everyday life. In short, the sublime is that moment when a mind finds itself in a place where things are obscured and death could be possible. However, and this is essential to understanding the sublime, death never results for the hero. In the eighteenth century, people like Edmund Burke wrote theories of the sublime where they gave everyday examples. For example, on a stormy night the candle is blown out and a noise is heard. The instinct of self-preservation kicks in as paralysis. When the nature of the danger becomes evident, fight or flight occurs. An evil person tries to maintain paralysis as long as possible to enact a kill or domination of the hero's will. Of course, when the light comes back on the noise source is discovered and nerves settle, eventually. The sensations of the body felt during the episode are described in order to transport the reader to a belief in the novel—escapism. For Burke, the greatest example of the sublime comes from Milton's *Paradise Lost,* when Satan journeys to Eden. Along the way he has to face his daughter, Sin, which is frightening in itself. But Satan experiences sublime terror when he senses something more frightening in the obscurity of the shadows. Death reveals himself as Satan's son by Sin. In this episode, Satan faced uncertainty and fear and gained the knowledge of incest's horror. James, who was well versed in this theory, recreates Satan's encounter with Sin in the moment of Chad's appearance. The assumptions about his activity that had the town of Woollett paralyzed vanish in Strether's first look at Chad.

James' novel, as many critics have noted for the last hundred years, concerns the consciousness of, to use James' wording from the preface to the novel, an "imaginative person." The adventure, therefore, is within the mind of Lewis Lambert Strether. Maria Gostrey makes this evident by noticing that *Louis Lambert* is the title of a novel by Honore de Balzac. That novel concerns the fate of a mystic writing a treatise on spirituality when he falls in love. Much like a character in the twentieth-century movie, *The Fisher King,* he falls into a catatonic stupor. When he awakes, he has arrived at a new plain of wisdom and awareness. The parallels with Strether are as follows: he has been sent out from Woollett—whose idea of the world is that it is full of monsters—on a mission. Though he would rather flee, he fights his way through to find not monsters but people. Maria, in fact, summarizes Strether's mission in the melodramatic light of the play she has seen with Strether. That play contains "a bad woman in a yellow frock who made a pleasant weak good-looking young man in perpetual evening dress do the most dreadful things." The ideas that Woollett and Strether have about the world come from similar literature. Strether, therefore, fears he will be made to do dreadful things. Strether's exciting journey becomes the catatonic stupor of his namesake, and, at the end, he is awake. So the novel, in its large movements, mirrors the adventure tale to the point where, Patterson notes, the psychic confrontations take on the metaphors of blood to heighten their importance in accordance with psychological principles.

According to the psychological theory of William James, as laid out in his *The Principles of Psychology,* three sources of anxiety, or fear, prompt the self-preservation instinct in normal people (those not faced with vampires, cannibals, or barbarians). They are "those of *bodily self-seeking,* those of *social self-seeking,* and those of *spiritual self-seeking.*" The first impulse category describes "the material Self in the widest possible sense of the word," or the vulgar worries dogging all Americans in the novel: monetary well-being, job security, and physical comfort. If Strether fails,

> **The pattern for the early and more recent tales was transparent: a young man defies the warnings (or he is sent out into the world explicitly to lose his innocence) about the monsters and dangers beyond the known world of the village and goes out to see the world."**

Maria discovers, he loses "everything." The second can be summarized as the dandy's terror: to be shunned and ridiculed by society. Strether matures beyond this after failing to impress Gloriani. The last impulse comes out of the religious tradition. At its crudest, it is a fear of hell or all things sinful; Waymarsh exemplifies this. At its most enlightened, it is the "impulse towards psychic progress." Strether wants to learn, and he devises a way of staying in Paris just a little longer to continue to learn. Eventually, as Freudians would note about neuroses such as the fear of the unknown paralyzing Woollett, Strether's anxieties disappear upon contact with the source of the anxiety.

As soon as Strether has distanced himself from Woollett, questions begin to mount. It is immediately apparent that the world outside Woollett is wonderful. Once in Britain, he discloses his mission to Maria who, as a good judge of character, finds Strether's blind adherence to the theory of the horrible strange, "are you quite sure she's very bad for him?" "Of course we are," Strether replies; Madame de Vionnet must be an evil person if she has been able to keep Chad in Paris. However, Strether finally meets Madame de Vionnet, "the embodied influence, the definite adversary, who had by a stroke of her own failed him and on a fond theory of whose palpable presence he had, under Mrs. Newsome's inspiration, altogether proceeded." Strether finds her "wonderful." Instead of the "horror" he "must have imagined," he finds in the presence of Madame de Vionnet that "horrors were so little . . . in this robust and reasoning image." Reality for the traveler and scientist proves

What
Do I Read
Next?

- One of James' most popular novels was the story of Isabel Archer, *Portrait of a Lady* (1881). Isabel, James' model of the "American Girl," travels to Europe where she declines marriage proposals from two honest men. Instead, she falls for Gilbert Osmond and, in doing so, she might just suffer enough to see the ghost of Gardencourt.

- Another of James' novels that explores the theme of naïve Americans colliding with sophisticated Europeans is *The Wings of a Dove* (1902). At the beginning of the novel, Kate Croy, a Londoner, and her fiancée, Merton Densher, are ready to marry—though they differ in their approaches to the institution. Kate's fear of becoming her mother leads her to convince Merton to marry a terminally ill and very wealthy American, Milly Theale, so they will be rich. Theale discovers the plot and dies leaving her riches to Densher. Revenge comes sweetly, however, as guilt prevents the smart Europeans from achieving happiness.

- Leon Edel's five-volume biography, *Henry James: A Life,* is an incredible monument to the giant of letters. Late twentieth-century readers who didn't have the patience to read James' nov-

els chose to read Edel's biography—once it was abridged in 1985 into one volume.

- The clash-of-civilizations theme was explored through a story about a white family fleeing from revolutionaries in South Africa. The family finds sanctuary in the primitive village of one of their servants where they steadily succumb to the villager's way of life. Nadine Gordimer's *July's People* (1981) reflects the increasing tensions for whites and blacks living under Apartheid.

- Saul Bellow used very different techniques from James when he approached the problems of worldly success and the theme of *carpe diem,* seizing the day. His novel *Seize the Day* (1956) tells the sad tale of a man who loses his job, wife, and hope by looking at one day in the life of Tommy Wilhelm.

- Karl Baedeker's *Paris,* the giant of late nineteenth century guidebooks, precisely locates the places, cafés, and homes featured in *The Ambassadors.* The 15th edition of 1900 indicates some developments in Paris that Strether ignored but the Pococks probably did not, like the subway and an international Exposition.

---

to be greater than the goblins from childhood tales. Strether can no longer follow his orders, "you've got morally and intellectually to get rid of her." Strether cannot believe in the idea that the world outside Woollett is horrible because his senses tell him otherwise. Thus, he must recreate his idea of the world, which involves recreating his own psychology. The result is that Strether is less anxious about bumps in the night. Mrs. Newsome, who depends on the theory for her hold on Strether, no longer has power over him. By understanding "the Theory of the Horrible," Strether's transformation becomes obvious.

Waymarsh and Sarah attempt to check Strether's investigations. Waymarsh safeguards the

boundaries of Strether's thought and, for this reason, Strether is "in terror of him." If Strether steps out of line, Waymarsh can denigrate him to Mrs. Newsome. Waymarsh, as a threat to Strether's social self-seeking, increasingly finds himself outweighed by Maria and Madame de Vionnet. That is why Sarah is sent out; "she keeps up the theory of the horrible." Sarah petrifies Strether but he faces her and nothing happens. Strether accumulates "notes of freedom" with every successful contact with his fears. He continues to write home about his success at freeing himself from fear. Newsome's "disappointment" in him begins in the letters because Strether has failed to repeat the theory of the horrible and sprinkle his observations with monsters. Those letters home as well as the conversations with Maria are Strether's efforts to understand Newsome's system.

Creating the mind of the normal person as grounds for adventurous investigation was no easy task. James accomplished this in *The Ambassadors* by using the language of "Adventure" as well as "the Theory of the Horrible. The theme of culture clash and the fear of difference were James' favorite themes throughout his career, and when he investigated the underlying psychology of that fear in one particular person, James created a ground breaking case study. Strether has discovered that the goblins with which Woollett had peopled the earth are not real. He wrote his conclusions to Mrs. Newsome, but she would not believe him. Strether comes to understand that people simply have to learn for themselves although, the novelist believes, they can do so vicariously. If the novelist successfully infects the reader with Strether's experience, then James has not wasted his effort to open the eyes of those back home. Short of that, in terms of fiction's evolution, in literature written after *The Ambassadors,* the mind becomes as exciting as an adventure tale.

Source: Jeremy W. Hubbell, Critical Essay on *The Ambassadors,* in *Novels for Students,* The Gale Group, 2001.

Dorothea Krook

In the following essay, Krook examines how James' use of ambiguity in The Ambassadors *leaves the reader with two separate interpretations of the text from which to choose.*

There is scarcely a page in Henry James's *The Ambassadors* (1903) that is not ambiguous in the common loose sense of the word, in which 'ambiguous' means simply obscure, puzzling, mystifying, baffling, and the like. This passage or this sentence could mean this, or that, or something else, we say to ourselves as we gaze at it, often blankly, trying to make out *what* it could reasonably mean. Here is a typical example. It is the last passage in a long colloquy between Strether and Maria Gostrey late in the story, ending the chapter (Book XI, Chapter 2) which is immediately followed by Strether's fateful day in the French countryside (Book XI, Chapter 3). Maria says:

'Mr. Newsome and Madame de Vionnet may, as we were saying, leave town. How long do you think you can bear it without them?'

Strether's reply to this was first another question. 'Do you mean in order to get away from me?'

> **"** Perhaps this passage, among others, ought to be treated as a Jamesian 'crux', analogous to a crux in Shakespeare, which will require time and the cumulative labours of many James scholars to discover its best reading."

Her answer had an abruptness. 'Don't find me rude if I say I should think they'd want to!'

He looked at her hard again—seemed even for an instant to have an intensity of thought under which his colour changed. But he smiled 'You mean after what they've done to me?'

'After what *she* has.'

At this, however, with a laugh, he was all right again. 'Ah but she hasn't done it yet!'

It is James's elliptical, allusive late style that makes the difficulties, of course. The key questions to be answered are: Why should Chad and Madame de Vionnet want to get away from Strether? What is the thought in Strether's mind that makes him change colour? Why, having evidently pushed aside this thought whatever it was, does he smile when he says 'You mean after what they have done to me?' And what *have* they done to him?—what does *he* think they have done to him? And what does Maria mean when she corrects him, saying, No, after what *she* (Madame de Vionnet) has done to him? What *has* 'she' done to him? And why is Strether relieved ('at this . . . he was all right') to think that it's what she has done to him, whatever it is, that makes them want to get away from him? Finally, what does Strether mean when he says 'with a laugh' that she hasn't done it yet—whatever it is she is supposed to have done?

The list of questions is longer than the passage that raises them; but this is not surprising—it takes less space to produce an obscurity than to explain why it is obscure. I give my gloss for what it is worth. Maria is telling Strether that Chad and Madame de Vionnet want to get away from him because they are beginning to find his constant surveillance nerve-racking. The thought that passes

An artist's rendering of a Parisian garden party

through Strether's mind, making him change colour, is that they are finding his surveillance nerve-racking because their 'virtuous attachment' is not virtuous, and they are getting tired of having to conceal this from him. Having pushed this disagreeable thought aside, he takes refuge in an alternative explanation of Maria's cryptic remark: they want to get away from him because it oppresses them to think how they are 'exploiting' him in the interests of maintaining their relationship, and in particular what he has *lost* as a consequence of their 'exploitation' (Mrs Newsome, and all the benefits for him of marrying her). This is what they have 'done' to him; but it is Marie de Vionnet in

particular, Maria reminds him, who had 'done' it, because her need of Chad is greater than his of her (a point already sufficiently established). In that case, Strether's last remark ('Ah but she hasn't done it yet!'), the most cryptic of all, may mean that she hasn't yet caused him to lose all, because he is still within the six-week's period of grace allowed him by Sarah Pocock, and may yet decide to join them (with Chad, of course) at Liverpool for the voyage back to America—in which case 'all losses are restored' and it is paradise regained for Strether.

An alternative reading is to give Maria's words a simpler, less portentous meaning. When she says

'Don't find me rude if I say I should think they'd want to [get away from you]', what she means, and what Strether understands her to mean, is that he is simply becoming a bore to them with his perpetual hanging around them, and they just want to be on their own for a bit. This is the thought that makes Strether change colour: he finds it most disagreeable to suppose that the brilliant pair, and especially of course Marie de Vionnet, are beginning to be bored by him. So he pushes the thought aside, and suggests instead (as on the first reading) that they want to get away from him because of their bad conscience about what they have been the cause of his losing, this being what they have 'done' to him, and she, Madame de Vionnet, in particular. The meaning of Strether's last statement, 'Ah but she hasn't done it yet!', would then be the same as on the previous reading.

These are both possible readings of the passage. But one cannot be *sure* that either is correct—that there may not be another, quite different reading that 'covers' the elusive data at least as well or perhaps better; and it is significant that neither of the readings I have proposed appears to be decisively confirmed by anything—any act or speech—elsewhere in the book. Perhaps this passage, among others, ought to be treated as a Jamesian 'crux', analogous to a crux in Shakespeare, which will require time and the cumulative labours of many James scholars to discover its best reading.

I cite another passage which, as is stands, is equally obscure, baffling, and 'ambiguous'. It is the dialogue in Book IX, Chapter 1 between Strether and Madame de Vionnet in the scene in which she tells him about the marriage that has been 'arranged' for Jeanne. It too comes at the end of the scene, and starts when Madame de Vionnet pronounces the words 'And—willingly, at least—he [Chad] would never hurt *me*'. At this, there flashes upon Strether 'a light, a lead' that, together with the expression of her face, tells him 'her whole story' as never before. The light grows, becoming ever more luminous as the passage proceeds to its close, its revelation apparently reinforced by 'the refined disguised suppressed passion of her face'. What *is* this light, this lead?—you ask yourself. What *is* the momentous revelation Strether has had by it? There is no clue, no hint, in the passage itself, and you gaze at it baffled, wondering whether the answer might be this, or that, or something else, without much confidence in any of your hypotheses.

But in this instance salvation is just round the corner. In the very next chapter, Strether briefly gives Maria Gostrey the gloss we need. Chad had helped to arrange Jeanne's marriage as a proof to Madame de Vionnet of his unwavering 'attachment' to her following her cold treatment by Sarah Pocock: 'The act is his answer to Mrs Newsome's demonstration', he tells Maria; 'she [Madame de Vionnet] asked for a sign, and he thought of that one'. What Strether had seen in Marie de Vionnet's face was presumably the intense happiness and relief it was to her to have had this 'sign' from Chad, and this had been for him the 'light', the 'lead', for understanding the depth of her feeling for Chad and the 'suppressed passion' behind and beneath it.

This is how Strether interprets Madame de Vionnet's presumed happiness and relief, along with the 'the refined disguised suppressed passion of her face'. But the reader, who knows—as Strether doesn't yet—'the deep deep truth' about her relationship with Chad, may legitimately see more in and behind Chad's demonstration. He may, more cynically, see the marrying off of Jeanne as a means also of getting out of the way an unmarried daughter whose presence in the house would be an impediment to the mutual pair's complete freedom to pursue their relationship. And he may even see Jeanne's departure as, in her mother's eyes, the removal of a possible rival, even though Chad had plainly shown that it was the mother not the daughter he wanted. Nevertheless, if in her last scene with Strether Marie de Vionnet can call herself 'old and abject and hideous', even if only in the self-despising mood of that moment, she might well be happy and relieved—in the depths of her subconscious, of course—to have a beautiful young daughter safely removed by marriage from the possible role of temptress to a lover who happened to be closer in age to the daughter than to the mother.

The ambiguity I have so far talked about is mainly a function of James's late style, which deliberately resorts to the cryptic, the elusive, the mystifying for its own special ends. There is however another kind of ambiguity to be considered, where 'ambiguous' has a more precise meaning than just obscure, puzzling, baffling, and so forth. It is to be found in only a limited number of James's works, the paradigms being *The Turn of the Screw* (1898) and *The Sacred Fount* (1901). The remaining works are *The Lesson of the Master* (1892), *The Figure in the Carpet* (1896), and *The Golden Bowl* (1904). But there are patches or 'pockets' of this kind of ambiguity in (for example) *The Aspern Pa-*

pers (1888), *The Spoils of Poynton* (1897) and *The Wings of the Dove* (1902); and, as we shall see, in *The Ambassadors.*

If the paradigm works, everything can be read in two and *only* two ways. The text—meaning, every key episode, dialogue, and even utterance—admits of two alternative and contradictory readings, each self-complete and wholly consistent with all the data. In *The Turn of the Screw,* one of the two possible readings is that of the first-person narrator, the governness. On this reading, the children are being hideously corrupted by the apparitions of the two depraved servants, Peter Quint and Miss Jessel, and the governess is the Jamesian saviour figure trying to redeem them from the evil to which they have succumbed. The alternative and contradictory reading is that the governess is psychically disturbed (from 'sex-repression', or whatever) and has imagined it all; in which case the apparitions are hallucinations of her deranged brain, the children are totally innocent of the depravity she attributes to them, and the governess herself is hideously guilty—of pursuing and harassing the children with her pathological suspicions, leading the girl to a nervous breakdown and the boy to his death. These and only these are the two possible readings of the story; and there is nothing to tilt the balance decisively in favour of one or the other, thus leaving the ambiguity total and unresolved.

In *The Sacred Fount* the ambiguity is of the same kind, though the outcome is not tragic as it is in *The Turn of the Screw.* Either the first-person narrator's observations and explanations are valid, in which case the strange changes he sees in the principals are real and his 'vampire' hypothesis to explain the changes is confirmed. Or the narrator is wholly and pathologically deluded, in which case the supposed changes are imaginary, and the narrator is an unsavoury *voyeur* who deserves his final exposure by the energetic Mrs Brissenden.

The Ambassadors as a whole is by no means ambiguous in this special sense. But it has one great 'pocket' of this kind of ambiguity; and it turns on Chad's transformation. The matter of Chad's transformation is obviously of key importance in Strether's 'process of vision' and his transvaluation of values vis-a-vis Woollett. It is the foundation of his case for betraying his original mission, for pleading with Mrs Newsome to let Chad stay back with the wonderful woman who has wrought the transformation, for pleading with Chad never to abandon the wonderful woman, and for himself suffering the loss of Mrs Newsome and the security,

the affection, the esteem he would have had by marrying her. If Chad was *not* transformed, or even less radically transformed than Strether supposed, all Strether had built on it collapsed—'cracked' and 'crumbled', in his own words.

So it is disconcerting to find the question suddenly arising in Strether's mind: Is Chad's transformation real; or is it a figment of his imagination (which we know to be highly developed)? Is he seeing something that is objectively there to be seen, or is he just 'seeing things'? The momentous and potentially shattering question springs up for him on the day of the Pocock's arrival (Book VIII, Chapter 2), on his drive from the station with Jim Pocock; and his intense reflections on it proceed by three stages.

First, having observed that neither Sarah Pocock nor Jim has remarked on the change in Chad that he himself had found so overwhelming from his first encounter with Chad in the theatre box, he firmly dismisses their 'sightlessness' as a function of their philistine lack of imagination or their bad faith or both:

> It all suddenly bounced back to their being either stupid or wilful. It was more probably on the whole the former; so that would be the drawback of [Sarah's] bridling brightness . . . Their observation would fail; it would be beyond them; they simply wouldn't understand. Of what use would it be then that they had come?—if they weren't to be intelligent up to *that* point.

Immediately, however, in the same breath, the great doubt about his own 'observation' leaps up in his mind, and grows and grows like a spreading fire from the moment he asks himself whether he himself might not be 'utterly deluded and extravagant':

> Was he, on this question of Chad's improvement, fantastic and away from the truth? Did he live in a false world, a world that had grown simply to suit him, and was his present slight irritation—in the face now of Jim's silence in particular—but the alarm of the vain thing menaced by the touch of the real? Was this contribution of the real possibly the mission of the Pococks—had they come to make the work of observation, as he had practised observation, crack and crumble, and to reduce Chad to the plain terms in which honest minds could deal with him? Had they come in short to be sane, where Strether was destined to feel that he himself had only been silly?

Strether's copiousness in drawing out the implications of his moment of self-doubt stands in sharp contrast to the spareness of the governess in *The Turn of the Screw* when, shortly before Miles dies, the terrifying thought crosses her mind that the child may after all be innocent: 'If he *was* innocent, what then on earth was *I?*' she cries to herself. And the narrator in *The Sacred Fount,* when he sees his wonderful 'palace of thought' crack and crumble (Strether's terms exactly fit his case) in his showdown with Mrs Brissenden, is likewise more succinct: 'What if she *should* be right?' he murmurs inwardly. But the point is the same; it is the moment of radical self-doubt and self-misgiving, which is a crucial element in the pattern of the Jamesian ambiguity of the kind I am describing.

The third stage of Strether's process of coping with the frightening thought that he may have been deluded about Chad's transformation is also integral to the pattern. It is the justification, or re-justification, of his own perception by mentally reviewing the witnesses who have confirmed its validity:

> He glanced at such a contingency ['that he himself had only been silly'], but it failed to hold him long when once he had reflected that he would have been silly, in this case, with Maria Gostrey and little Bilham, with Madame de Vionnet and little Jeanne, with Lambert Strether, in fine, and above all with Chad Newsome himself. Wouldn't it be found to have made more for reality to be silly with these persons than sane with Sarah and Jim?

So Strether concludes that he is, must be, 'all right' after all if his vision is supported by such a cloud of distinguished witnesses. But the reader experienced in the subtleties of the Jamesian method of ensuring that the ambiguity shall remain totally unresolved will recognise that Strether's supposed witnesses are either not witnesses at all, or are not 'reliable' because not disinterested witnesses. Maria Gostrey is the first to be struck off Strether's list. Maria never knew Chad before his supposed transformation—so how could she know whether he had or hadn't been transformed? The answer is, she doesn't know; she has only taken Strether's word for it that there *has* been a transformation, and that it is as marvellous as he says. Madame de Vionnet and Chad, being the most interested 'parties' in the case, are *ipso facto* ruled out as objective witnesses. Little Bilham, as a close friend of Chad and wholly committed to his 'cause', is likewise ruled out; and it is surely significant that when he appears to be explicitly confirming the change in Chad, he immediately throws in the qualification: 'But I'm not sure that I didn't like him about as well in his other state'. And later again:

> 'He wasn't so bad before [the transformation] as I seem to have made out that you think—'(says Little Bilham).

'Oh I don't think anything now!' Strether impatiently broke in . . . 'I mean that originally, for her [Madame de Vionnet] to have cared for him—'

'There must have been stuff in him? Oh yes, there was stuff indeed, and much more of it than ever showed, I dare say, at home.'

These may be intended as hints to the reader that the change in Chad is not as great or remarkable as Strether sees it to be, and that little Bilham's honesty obliges him delicately to correct Strether's 'exaggerated' view. Or it may even mean that there is no change at all, and Bilham's seeming confirmation of it is just another 'technical lie' in support of Chad, of a piece with his lie about the 'virtuous attachment'.

As to 'little Jeanne': there is no mention anywhere of her having perceived a change in Chad; and Strether can be drawing on her as a witness only because he assumes that, being Madame de Vionnet's daughter, she must necessarily 'see' what *maman* sees; or, alternatively, because he assumes that, if she is secretly in love with Chad, she could only be in love with him if he *had* been transformed. Finally, there is Mamie Pocock: whom Strether does not include in his list of witnesses because at this point he has not yet had his private meeting with her. The case of Mamie is particularly interesting. Strether tells Madame de Vionnet even before he has had his talk with Mamie that 'she sees him [Chad] as different'. Then, at their meeting in Sarah's hotel salon, he feels he has received all the confirmation he wants of Mamie's 'seeing' what Sarah and Jim have failed to see; and afterwards, in his talk with little Bilham, inspires his young friend to develop his great theory, about Mamie's being unable to be in love with Chad because she came out to 'save' him, but seeing him already 'saved' had nothing to do in that direction. However, when we re-read Strether's long talk with Mamie in search of evidence for his conviction that she 'sees', we discover that Mamie has actually said nothing—not a word—about it. Strether has merely inferred from her behaviour that she must have seen the change in Chad; and is so certain about his inference that he treats it as a fact. But it is *not* a fact; and the disposition of a mind like Strether's to mistake inferences and assumptions for facts *and* convince others of the factuality of the non-facts is exactly one of the psychological phenomena that Henry James cunningly exploits as a device for creating and sustaining his ambiguity.

What we discover, then, is that there is no reliable independent confirmation of Strether's perception of the change in Chad, which is the starting point of his drama of consciousness, and, consequently, that a huge question-mark hangs over the validity of Strether's vision. This does not mean of course that Strether's perception has been proved to be false. On the contrary, his vision of a Chad transformed remains intact as one of the two possible *true* interpretations of the data. The transformation may be exactly as Strether sees it—as radical and portentous; Waymarsh and the Pococks who don't see it may be exactly as 'sightless' as Strether says they are; the cloud of witnesses he invokes (Chad, Madame de Vionnet, little Bilham) may all be speaking the objective truth in confirming his vision; and about those who don't speak (Jeanne and Mamie) his inference that they see the change in Chad may be totally correct. In short, just as in *The Turn of the Screw* the governess' account of what happened at Bly may be completely valid, so may Strether's of what happened to Chad.

This precisely is the design of the Jamesian ambiguity: to leave the reader faced with two and only two interpretations of the data, which are mutually exclusive (meaning, that if one is true, the other is necessarily false—Chad cannot both be and not be transformed); yet each of which is wholly consistent with all the available evidence—in this instance, the evidence of the witnesses, which may be read both ways, as confirming one interpretation (Strether's) and disconfirming the other (the Pocock's), or confirming the Pocock's and disconfirming Strether's. Nor is there a single piece of evidence that decisively tilts the balance in favour of one interpretation or the other; that there shall be none is another basic rule of the Jamesian ambiguity. Consequently, there are no grounds *on the basis of the evidence*—in other words, no 'rational' grounds—for choosing one interpretation as more valid than the other.

If you do choose—as Strether does, as the governess in *The Turn of the Screw* does—you can choose only on the basis of something other than the evidence. You can choose, in a word, only by an act of faith—'blind' faith—in the validity and integrity of your own vision. And this is the deep truth about human experience and human knowledge that the Jamesian ambiguity is designed to dramatise. When in life a crucial act of choice has to be made between two and only two possible lines of action, figured in the two and only two possible interpretations of the Jamesian fiction, and the facts or data constituting the evidence are intractably ambiguous in supporting with equal force and decisiveness *both* of the two and only two alternatives, the crucial choice can only be made by an act of

faith—which in effect by-passes, ignores, and transcends the evidence, leaving you with your lone unsupported vision of things as the sole basis of your choice. . . .

Source: Dorothea Krook, "*The Ambassadors:* Two Types of Ambiguity," in *Neophilologus,* Vol. LXXIV, No. 1, January 1990, pp. 194–97.

Sources

Alden, H. M., "Memorandum on 'Project of a Novel by Henry James,'" in *The Notebooks of Henry James,* edited by F. O. Matthiessen and Kenneth B. Murdock, Oxford University Press, 1947, p. 372.

Blackmur, R. P., "In the Country of the Blue," in *Critiques and Essays on Modern Fiction: 1920–1951,* edited by John W. Aldridge, Ronald Press Company, 1952, pp. 202–18.

Fogel, Daniel M., *Covert Relations: James Joyce, Virginia Woolf, and Henry James,* University Press of Virginia, 1990.

Forster, E. M., *Aspects of the Novel,* Harvest Books, 1954, pp. 153, 164.

Hicks, Granville, *The Great Tradition: An Interpretation of American Literature Since the Civil War,* Macmillan Publishing Company, 1935, pp. 112, 121.

James, William, *The Principles of Psychology,* Vol. I, Harvard University Press, 1981, pp. 293–95.

Lodge, David, *20th Century Literary Criticism,* Longman, 1981.

Lubbock, Percy, *The Craft of Fiction,* Charles Scribner's Sons, 1955, pp. 156–71.

Matthiessen, F. O., *Henry James: The Major Phase,* Oxford University Press, 1944, p. 22.

Mencken, H. L., "Henry James," in *A Mencken Chrestomathy,* Alfred A. Knopf, Inc., 1953, pp. 500–01.

Patterson, John, "The Language of 'Adventure' in Henry James," in *American Literature,* Vol. XXXII, November 1960, pp. 291–301.

Pound, Ezra, "Henry James," in *Literary Essays of Ezra Pound,* edited by T. S. Eliot, New Directions, 1954, pp. 295–338.

Vidal, Gore, "Return to *The Golden Bowl,*" in *New York Review of Books,* Vol. XXX, Nos. 21–22, January 19, 1984, pp. 8–12.

Watt, Ian, "The First Paragraph of *The Ambassadors:* An Explication," in *Essays in Criticism,* Vol. X, July 1960, p. 274.

Wells, H. G., "Of Art, of Literature, of Henry James," in *Henry James and H. G. Wells: A Record of Their Friendship, and Their Quarrel,* edited by Leon Edel and Gordon N. Ray, University of Illinois Press, 1958, pp. 234–60.

For Further Study

Benjamin, Walter, "The Work of Art in the Age of Mechanical Reproduction," in *Illuminations,* edited by Hannah Arendt, New York, Schocken Books, 1968, pp. 217–51.

> Benjamin investigates the cultural ramifications of the ability to reproduce rare works of art thousands of times. Such multiplication gains a work of art more viewers but also questions the value of the original. Benjamin wonders about the meaning of this development.

Burke, Edmund, *A Philosophical Enquiry into the Origin of Our Ideas of the Sublime and Beautiful,* Oxford University Press, 1990.

> Burke crystallizes seventy-five years of writing on the sublime with this treatise. He sums up the current ideas on why stimuli, especially literary and rhetorical, affect humans.

Cowan, Ruth Schwartz, *The Ironies of Household Technology from the Open Hearth to the Microwave,* Basic Books, 1983.

> Cowan was awarded the Dexter Prize from the Society of the History of Technology for this groundbreaking look at the impact of technology on domesticity. She argues that while the masculine gender's responsibilities were industrialized, the female's household duties were expanded, until by the 1930s the idea of enslaved housewife was thought to be natural. Along the way she discovers the reasons why certain innovations that would have freed up the housewife were rejected by society.

Hays, Samuel P., *The Response to Industrialism 1885–1914,* edited by Daniel J. Boorstin, Chicago History of American Civilization series, University of Chicago Press, 1996.

> Hayes examines the positive and negative responses of people to industrialism in America. The focus of the book is the experience of the male worker and the effects of industrialization on skilled labor. He summarizes the robber barons amassment of wealth as well as the formation of the labor movement.

Sussman, Henry, *Psyche and Text: The Sublime and the Grandiose in Literature, Psychopathology, and Culture,* State University of New York Press, 1993.

> Sussman believes that literature is a place where a society works through its ideas about self, others, and relationships. In *Psyche and Text,* Sussman investigates literary characters who reflect societal tensions and explores their significance by relating psychology to literature.

Animal Dreams

Barbara Kingsolver

1990

In Barbara Kingsolver's *Animal Dreams* (1990), Codi Noline, a young woman unsure of her purpose in life, returns to her hometown of Grace, Arizona, to teach high school and care for her father. As the novel unfolds, Codi gradually becomes aware of important political and environmental issues. She also learns that the detached and cynical individualism that has dominated her life is not the best recipe for happiness. Her exposure to Hispanic and Native American culture shows her the value of the communal way of living, which emphasizes deep and lasting ties to family and to the earth. Although her life is blighted by the tragic death of her sister, Hallie, Codi finally finds peace in the knowledge and acceptance of who she is and where she comes from.

Animal Dreams was Kingsolver's second novel. It won high praise for its convincing portrayal of the complex, interconnected web of human life and relationships, and how this web is shaped by time, memory, and culture. The wide scope of the novel, and the way it manages to weave environmental and political issues into the narrative without sounding preachy, was also praised.

The novel contains many of the elements that characterize Kingsolver's work as a whole: a setting in the American southwest, a female protagonist whose way of living is or becomes more cooperative than competitive (which is intended as a contrast between female and male attitudes); a concern for the environment; an admiration of Native

American culture, and opposition to U.S. involvement in the politics of Central America.

Animal Dreams can be placed in the tradition of "eco-feminist" literature, which began in the 1980s and includes work by authors such as Ursula Le Guin, Leslie Marmon Silko, Louise Erdrich, and Alice Walker.

Author Biography

Barbara Kingsolver was born on April 5, 1955, in Annapolis, Maryland, to Virginia and Wendell R. Kingsolver. Her father was a country physician, and Kingsolver grew up in rural Kentucky, where she became aware of the poverty that many people in the area had to endure. As a child, Kingsolver was a voracious reader and wanted to become a writer although she did not believe this to be a realistic goal.

Blessed with musical talent, Kingsolver won a scholarship to study instrumental music at DePauw University in Indiana. It was at DePauw that she became interested in the social and political issues that would later inform her writing. After changing her major from music to biology, which she considered to be a more practical subject for a future career, she graduated magna cum laude with a B.A. in 1977. After graduation, she traveled and worked in Europe for two years before returning to the United States. She went to live in Tucson, Arizona, where she still lives today.

Kingsolver then enrolled in a doctoral program in evolutionary biology and ecology at the University of Arizona. She completed a master's degree in 1981, terminated her academic studies, and took a job as a technical writer for the Office of Arid Lands Studies at the University of Arizona.

Pleased with becoming a professional writer, Kingsolver took on some freelance writing work and at the same time began her own fiction and nonfiction. Much of her own writing concerned political causes (such as human rights in Central and Latin America) and environmental issues. Out of her work during this period came her book, *Holding the Line: Women in the Great Arizona Mine Strike of 1983* (1989), which was sympathetic to the miners' cause.

Kingsolver's first novel was *The Bean Trees* (1988), in which a young woman escapes her limited prospects in rural Kentucky by moving to Tucson, taking in refugees from Central America, and becoming socially and politically aware. Critical

Barbara Kingsolver

response to this autobiographical novel was highly favorable.

Over the next few years, Kingsolver established herself as an important writer in a variety of genres. Her short stories were published in *Homeland and Other Stories* (1989), and this was followed by another novel, *Animal Dreams,* in 1990. Kingsolver broke new ground again in 1991 when her first volume of poetry, *Another America (Otra America),* was published. The poems appeared with Spanish translations alongside them. The novel *Pigs in Heaven* (1993) was a sequel to *The Bean Trees,* and this was followed by *High Tide in Tucson: Essays from Now or Never* (1995). Her fourth novel, *The Poisonwood Bible* (1998), set in the Belgian Congo in 1959, was a national bestseller.

Kingsolver was married to Joseph Hoffmann, a chemist, from 1985 until 1992. They have one child, Camille. In 1995, Kingsolver married Stephen Hopp, an ornithologist and animal behaviorist, with whom she has another daughter, Lily.

Plot Summary

Chapter 1

In the first chapter of *Animal Dreams,* Dr. Homer Noline gazes on his two young daughters,

Cosima and Halimeda, as they sleep curled up close together. It is early November, the Night of All Souls in the Christian liturgical calendar.

Chapter 2

This chapter jumps forward in time and is narrated by Codi, the name by which Cosima is known. After a fourteen-year absence she is returning to her hometown of Grace, Arizona, to work as a schoolteacher and care for her sick father. Previously, she had been living with her boyfriend, Carlo, and her sister, Hallie, in Tucson, Arizona. Soon after Hallie left for war-torn Nicaragua to help develop agriculture, Codi decided to move also. But as she walks the streets of Grace, she feels like a stranger.

Chapter 3

This chapter is told from the point of view of Doc Homer, the name by which Dr. Homer Noline is known. Doc Homer thinks back to a time when Hallie and Codi were young children and were missing during a storm. They were rescued from a washed-open coyote burrow, nursing seven pups they wanted to save.

Chapters 4–7

In Grace, Codi stays with Emelina, her friend from high school, who has five young boys. Codi recalls the last time she saw Hallie and the close relationship they had always enjoyed. She also catches up on all that has happened in Grace over the previous fourteen years. Although the town is full of memories, she still feels like an outsider. She recalls the day her mother died, when Codi was three years old, and her own loss of a baby to a miscarriage when she was fifteen. The father was Loyd Peregrina, a part-Apache, part-Pueblo high school senior.

At a Labor Day weekend party, Codi meets Loyd, who is now a railroad engineer, and listens to a group of old men talking about how Black Mountain Mining Company is polluting the nearby river.

Chapters 8–9

Codi visits her father for the first time in two years. He is in the early stages of Alzheimer's disease. They communicate little, and Doc refuses to discuss his illness.

Codi begins teaching biology at the high school and also discovers the Stitch and Bitch Club, a sewing group who are holding a meeting in Emelina's house. Codi receives a letter from Hal-

lie, mailed from southern Mexico. It is full of characteristically detailed observations. Codi and Loyd begin talking, and Loyd reveals that he had a twin brother, Leander, who died at the age of fifteen. He invites Codi to accompany him on a business trip.

Chapter 10

Doc Homer lies on his examining table in his office in the hospital basement. He is confused and can no longer distinguish between past and present. He thinks of fifteen-year-old Codi, knowing she is pregnant but having no idea of how to talk to her about it.

Chapters 11–12

Codi's trip with Loyd gets postponed, but Codi discovers that one of his interests is cockfighting. Codi sees Loyd frequently but convinces herself their relationship is only a casual one. She takes her students on a field trip to the river, which she finds to be extremely polluted. Viola tells her of Black Mountain's plan to divert the river, so as not to flout Environmental Protection Agency regulations. But, diverting the river will destroy Grace because there will be no water to nourish the orchards.

Loyd takes Codi on a trip to the Apache reservation and then to Kinishba, an eight-hundred-year-old Pueblo stone dwelling that contains two hundred small rooms—a whole village under one roof.

Chapter 13

Doc Homer is again lost in his memories, and his mind slides from the present to the past. He remembers the day Codi suffered a miscarriage. She emerged from the bathroom carrying a bundle wrapped in a black sweater. Doc Homer followed her outside and watched as she disposed of the dead baby. He did not tell her that he had observed her, or even that he knew she was pregnant.

Chapter 14

A pregnant student drops out of school, and Codi teaches her students about birth control. After hearing from a local resident about Doc Homer's failing memory, she asks to take care of him, but he insists he is fine. Codi celebrates Halloween by going trick-or-treating with Emelina's children and then joins the whole community to celebrate the Mexican Day of the Dead, in which everyone converges on the cemetery and tends family graves. Codi finds a grave marked Homero Nolina, and wonders why his name is so similar to her father's since she believes the family came from Illinois.

Chapter 15

Doc Homer is disturbed by a visit from Codi, who asks whether they have relatives in Grace. Doc Homer's mind once again plays tricks on him and drifts back to images of Codi as a child.

Chapters 16–19

Codi speaks to the Stitch and Bitch Club about the pollution of the river, and the women decide to mount a mass demonstration against Black Mountain. Codi receives a distressing letter from Hallie, describing how three girls in Nicaragua were killed by gunfire. Loyd takes Codi to watch cockfights in which his own birds participate, but after Codi protests, he agrees to give up the sport.

In December, Codi travels to Tucson with the Stitch and Bitch Club, who sell their homemade peacock piñatas to raise funds. Codi visits Carlo, who tries to persuade her to move to Colorado with him. She spends Christmas with Loyd on the Navajo reservation, where Loyd shows her an ancient village built into the cliff. In the Jemez Mountains in New Mexico, they bathe in volcanic hot springs, and Loyd takes her to visit his family in a Pueblo village. On Christmas Day, they watch Pueblo dances.

Chapter 20

Doc Homer receives a telephone call informing him that Hallie has been kidnapped in Nicaragua. He is confused and for a while does not understand what has happened.

Chapters 21–23

Distraught at Hallie's kidnapping, Codi gives her students an impassioned lecture about preserving the environment. She also confronts Doc Homer about the origins of his family, but he refuses to acknowledge the truth. Meanwhile, the campaign against Black Mountain by the Stitch and Bitch Club draws media attention.

Hearing nothing from Hallie, Codi desperately writes letters to anyone of importance. Sean Rideheart, an art dealer from Tucson, tells the Stitch and Bitch Club they can save Grace by putting it on the National Register of Historic Places.

Doc Homer's condition deteriorates, but he confesses to Codi the truth about his family. He had covered up his origins because the Nolina family had a bad reputation in the town.

In a dream, Codi learns how to let go of the haunting memory of the child she lost.

Chapters 24–26

Codi is informed that Hallie has been murdered by her kidnappers. Numbed by grief, she decides to leave Grace and rejoin Carlo. She takes a flight to Denver, but the plane has engine trouble and has to return to Tucson. Codi is relieved to get back on the ground. The shock of the flight makes her alter her plans, and she decides to remain in Grace with Loyd.

Chapter 27

Codi buries some of Hallie's things, and Doc Homer's mind goes back to her burial of her baby at the riverbed. Then he thinks that Codi is Alice, his dead wife. Although he seems unable to distinguish between Codi and Hallie, he feels a deep love for both.

Chapter 28

At least two years have elapsed. Doc Homer has died and is buried with the rest of his family. On All Souls Day in November, Viola takes Codi, who is now pregnant by Loyd, to the place where she watched her dead mother taken away by helicopter, over thirty years ago.

Characters

Doña Althea

Doña Althea is one of the formidable ladies of the Stitch and Bitch Club. She is old, silver-haired, and tiny, and she always dresses in black. She is also strong-willed. Codi regards her as "fierce and miniature like a frightening breed of small dog." When the Stitch and Bitch Club fights to save the town, Doña Althea becomes their media spokeswoman and is interviewed by CBS.

Carlo

Carlo was Codi's lover in Tucson, Arizona, before she moved back to Grace. He is an emergency-room doctor, and he met Codi when they were both in medical school. Shy and preferring to avoid company, Carlo never settles long in one place. He and Codi spent a few years together on Crete.

Uda Dell

Uda Dell is a widow who sometimes took care of Codi over a period of about ten years until Codi

Media Adaptations

- *Animal Dreams* has been recorded unabridged on ten audiocassettes, with a total playing time of 13.75 hours. The cassettes were narrated by C. J. Critt, and were published in 1990; they are available from Recorded Books, cassette no. 94253.

was fourteen. At first, Codi does not remember her. Uda helps Codi explore Doc Homer's attic and shares her memories of Codi as a child. Uda is also fond of Doc Homer and tries to take care of him.

Emelina Domingos

Emelina is an old high school friend of Codi, and Codi stays at her guesthouse when she returns to Grace. Emelina married immediately after her high school graduation and has five young sons. She is a practical and capable woman (she slaughters chickens herself) with an earthy sense of humor. She takes to motherhood easily and manages her large family with loving efficiency. She becomes Codi's confidante.

Juan Teobaldo Domingos

J. T. Domingos is Emelina's husband. When he and Codi were toddlers, they were next door neighbors and played together. They also went to the same high school, where J. T. was the captain of the football team. However, they were not friends. J. T. now works on the railroad and is out of town most of the time.

Viola Domingos

An active member of the Stitch and Bitch Club, Viola Domingos is J. T.'s mother. She is a widow and is close to Doña Althea. Viola is proud of her Hispanic cultural heritage and wants her son and daughter-in-law to raise their children to speak Spanish and know their own culture. At the end of the novel, Viola takes Codi to the alfalfa field where Codi as a three-year-old witnessed the helicopter taking her dead mother away.

Doc Homer

See Homer Noline

Codi Noline

See Cosima Noline

Cosima Noline

Cosima (or Codi) Noline is the sister of Hallie and the daughter of Doc Homer. It is she who narrates most of the story. Codi is tall, just under six feet. She is highly intelligent and well educated, having completed medical school. However, she dropped out of medicine near the end of her first year of residency because she lacked confidence in her abilities. Since that time she has done various research jobs, which she had little interest in, and moved around the country with her lover, Carlo. She also spent a few years on Crete.

When the novel opens, Codi is returning to her hometown of Grace, Arizona, from Tucson, where her most recent job was working the night shift at a convenience store.

Codi is close to her younger sister, Hallie, and wonders why they turned out to be so different in temperament and attitude. Hallie is confident, untroubled by doubt, but Codi feels aimless, not knowing what to do with her life. She is often introspective and indulges in self-criticism. Lacking an inner sense of direction, she goes where the wind blows. In the past, this meant that she went wherever Carlo's work as an emergency-room doctor took him. Codi doesn't believe that she fits in anywhere, and she feels timid about approaching life with any gusto. "I feel small and ridiculous and hemmed in on every side by the need to be safe," she writes in a confessional letter to Hallie.

Codi has no confidence that anyone would enjoy or seek out her company. She feels that she does not deserve love and is incapable of showing any. According to her own analysis, this negative self-image was formed early in her life, in response to the deep losses she suffered. Her mother died when she was three, and Cosima lost a baby to a miscarriage when she was fifteen. This has led her to internalize the belief that "Nothing you love will stay."

However, Codi is more competent and well liked than she realizes. She has no difficulty gaining the loyal friendship of Emelina or attracting the romantic interest of handsome Loyd Peregrina. She also turns out to be an excellent high school teacher. By the end of the novel, Codi has found her place in life. Teaching school, living with Loyd and pregnant, she is content to be part of the community in Grace.

Halimeda Noline

Hallie is the younger sister of Codi and the daughter of Doc Homer. She does not appear directly in the novel but is revealed through Codi's memories of her and her letters from Nicaragua, from which Codi quotes extensively.

Like Codi, Hallie is tall, over six feet. She and Codi are extremely close, although Hallie is Codi's opposite. She is purposeful and knows exactly what she wants to do in life, giving herself totally to causes she believes in. She feels other people's pain as if it was her own and wants to do something to alleviate it. She first becomes aware of the political situation in Central America by taking in refugees while she is living in Tucson. Then she travels to Nicaragua to help the development of agriculture, caring nothing about the danger she will be encountering (there is an armed conflict going on).

Although she has a serious attitude toward life, Hallie possesses a lighter side. She is playful, vivacious, and popular, and she knows how to enjoy herself. "She could moonwalk like Michael Jackson," Codi observes. Codi has a boundless admiration for Hallie. She contrasts Hallie's clarity of mind and purpose with her own indecisiveness. According to Codi, Hallie just charges ahead in life, doing the right thing to save the world.

Hallie vehemently denies that she is doing anything as grandiose as saving the world. She explains her far more modest goal in a letter to Codi:

> The very least you can do in your life is to figure out what you hope for. And the most you can do is live inside that hope. Not admire it from a distance but live right in it, under its roof. What I want is so simple I almost can't say it: elementary kindness. Enough to eat, enough to go around. The possibility that kids might one day grow up to be neither the destroyers nor the destroyed.

Hallie has always been lucky. She has walked away from car wrecks and bike wrecks, and refers to herself as "the luckiest person alive." But Hallie's luck runs out in Nicaragua, where she is kidnapped by the Nicaraguan rebels, the contras, who eventually shoot her in the head and leave her body by a roadside.

Hallie Noline

See Halimeda Noline

Homer Noline

Doc Homer, whose full name is Dr. Homer Noline, is the father of Codi and Hallie. For many years he has been Grace's only physician, but at the age of sixty-six, he is showing signs of the early stages of Alzheimer's disease. He forgets easily, and his mind often cannot distinguish between past and present.

Doc Homer is proud of his independence and self-sufficiency and of the fact that he is like no one else. He lives his life with a careful, well-ordered routine. He has always tended to pursue certain notions to the point of obsession, such as requiring Codi and Hallie as children to wear orthopedic shoes so they would not develop fallen arches.

Emotionally, Doc Homer is withdrawn and does not easily reveal his feelings to people, not even his daughters. One reason for this is the devastating loss he suffered when his wife Alice died a few days after giving birth to Hallie. Driven into himself, Doc Homer has never been able to outwardly show his affection for his daughters, although it is clear from his internal monologues that he loves them deeply. However, he is a difficult man to have a conversation with, even when he is lucid and in full possession of his faculties. If he does not wish to discuss something with Codi, he simply acts as if the subject had not been raised.

His hobby is a kind of eccentric photography in which he creates pictures of things that do not look like what they are—landscapes that look like clouds, for example. On the surface, this seems an odd thing to do, and yet it seems appropriate for Doc Homer because part of his life is based on deception. He has spent a lifetime covering up the fact that he is descended on his father's side from the Nolinas family, which was regarded as trash by the inhabitants of Grace. Although he married a woman from a more respectable family (her family opposed the marriage), he felt he had to escape the stigma of his name, so he joined the army and settled in Illinois with his wife. When he returned to Grace, he changed his name to Noline and pretended he was from Illinois, a myth that his two daughters automatically accepted.

Loyd Peregrina

Loyd Peregrina is a mixture of Apache, Pueblo, and Navajo blood. He briefly dated Codi when they were both in high school, where he had a reputation as a ladies' man (he is strikingly handsome) and a heavy drinker. It was Loyd who got

Codi pregnant when she was fifteen, although Codi never told him. Loyd remained in Grace and now works on the railroad. He meets Codi again when she returns to Grace. Their relationship begins in a casual fashion, and Codi is wary of becoming involved with him, but eventually their friendship grows into mutual love. Codi gradually learns that Loyd is a far more admirable man than she would have expected him to be from her memories of their earlier relationship. Loyd himself admits that in high school he was a "jerk," and he regrets having hurt a lot of people.

Loyd is an expert in cockfighting and owns a number of fighting birds. He takes Codi to a cockfight but agrees to give up the sport when Codi and his mother ask him to. Loyd is well grounded in Native American myth and culture. He takes Codi to Native American sacred places and explains their significance to her. It is Loyd who is instrumental in giving Codi a sense of the importance of community and an identity rooted in traditional values and cultural heritage.

Loyd had a twin brother, Leander, who was killed in a bar fight at the age of fifteen. Although they were close (like Codi and Hallie), the loss of his brother did not have the long-term devastating effect on Loyd that the loss of her child did for Codi at the same age. Loyd has a loving extended family, including his mother, sisters, aunt and a niece, and he is secure in the beliefs and traditions of his Native American culture. This gives him an emotional balance that Codi lacks.

Shawn Rideheart

Amusing and charming, Shawn Rideheart is an art dealer from Tucson who tells the ladies of the Stitch and Bitch Club that they can save their town by placing it on the National Register of Historic Places.

Themes

Culture Clash

Underlying the plot in *Animal Dreams* is the notion of a clash between two different cultures, white and Native American. The focus for this is environmental degradation. The ravages of modern industrial society are represented by the Black Mountain Mining Company. Codi thinks of the mine, with its "pile of dead tailings," as "a mountain cannibalizing its own guts and soon to destroy the living trees and home lives of Grace. It was

such an American story." A similar process is going on in the Jemez mountains in New Mexico, which are being mined for pumice. Pumice is required for the manufacture of the "distressed," or stone-washed, denim jeans that are very popular with the young. Codi launches into a tirade against the practice in her classroom:

> They wash them in a big machine with this special kind of gravel they get out of volcanic mountains. The prettiest mountains you ever saw in your life. But they're fragile, like a big pile of sugar. Levi Strauss or whoever goes in there with bulldozers and chainsaws and cuts down the trees and rips the mountainside to hell, so that all of us lucky Americans can wear jeans that look like somebody threw them in the garbage before we got them.

In contrast to this practice of ripping natural substances out of the ground, making them into something unnatural, and then returning the waste products to the earth in an indigestible form—all in the name of economic progress and profit— Kingsolver presents the very different attitude that Native Americans have toward the earth. At first the difference puzzles Codi. She asks Loyd how it can be that a canyon on Navajo tribal land has remained productive for over a thousand years, but Grace is being destroyed after only a century. The difference, as she later learns, is that Native Americans respect the earth as a living being and seek with humility to maintain the ecological balance that the earth needs. They acknowledge that they do not own the earth but try to be responsible guests. This gives Codi a new perspective on her own culture:

> To people who think of themselves as God's houseguests, American enterprise must seem arrogant beyond belief. Or stupid. A nation of amnesiacs, proceeding as if there were no other day but today. Assuming the land could also forget what had been done to it.

Kingsolver is herself an environmentalist, and she commented on this difference between the two cultures in an interview with Lisa See for *Publishers Weekly:*

> We are only as healthy as our food chain and the environment. The Pueblo corn dances say the same things, only spiritually. Whereas in our culture, we think we're it. The Earth was put here as a garden for us to conquer and use. That way of thought was productive for years, but it's beginning to do us in now.

Individualism and Community

The clash between cultures highlights the contrast between individualism and community. The Black Mountain Mining Company relentlessly pursues its own interests despite responsibilities it has to the human community that is adversely affected by mining activities. This theme also operates at a much more personal level, in the life of Codi. When she first arrives in Grace, she feels isolated and detached, and this has been the pattern of her life. Since her mother died when she was three, and her father has been emotionally unavailable, she has lacked the warm family support that would nourish her life. After dropping out of a medical career, she wanders from one job to the next, and one location to the next, never feeling that she has a purpose in life. She acknowledges that she is not good at "nesting," at making a home for herself somewhere. At the beginning of the novel, Codi is essentially rootless.

Codi's aimlessness is in marked contrast to the social activism of her sister, Hallie. Hallie feels strongly about righting the wrongs of the world and boldly goes off to Nicaragua to put her ideals into practice. She never doubts herself or the value of what she is doing. She has no difficulty in identifying with something larger than herself.

But the character who most clearly represents the value of communal life as opposed to the isolation of the individual is Loyd. It is Loyd, with his supportive family and his appreciation of the living essence of Native American culture, who helps steer Codi in the right direction. Eventually, she recovers her sense of belonging. Whereas she never had any confidence in her ability to be a doctor, she slowly discovers that she has a gift for teaching. This links her to her community, a link that is also fostered by her work with the Stitch and Bitch Club to save the town. Furthermore, Codi discovers that far from being outsiders from Illinois—as Doc Homer had taught her—her family has a heritage going back to the early settlers of Grace.

All these things combine to give Codi a sense that she is larger than the boundaries of her own small self. This is particularly apparent in chapter twenty-six, "The Fifty Mothers," when all the women of the town come to the funeral that Codi arranges for her murdered sister and share their memories of her. Codi's grief is great, but she learns that even that can be bearable when there are others to lend their support: "Loyd was standing on one side of me, and Emelina on the other, and whenever I thought I might fall or just cease to exist, the pressure of their shoulders held me there." Finally, she acknowledges that all the women present are in effect her relatives. She remembers "each one of these fifty mothers who'd been stand-

Topics for Further Study

- Research the history of the Nicaraguan contras during the 1980s. Were the contras the evil force described in *Animal Dreams,* or were they freedom fighters opposing communist tyranny as many in the United States believed?

- Research the subject of industrial pollution in the United States and the methods that different communities and environmental groups have used to combat it. What methods are people using today? What is most effective? What is being done to cut down on industrial pollution currently?

- Research the early symptoms of Alzheimer's disease, and show how they are reflected in the character of Doc Homer.

- Some reviewers have argued that the character Loyd Peregrina is too perfect—he is too good to be true—and this is a flaw in the novel. Do you agree with this verdict? Are the male characters in *Animal Dreams* presented as convincingly as the female ones?

- Is Doc Homer a sympathetic character, or is he someone the reader is likely to dislike?

- Which sister, Codi or Hallie, appeals to you the most and why?

ing at the edges of my childhood, ready to make whatever contribution was needed at the time."

Style

Setting

The novel is set mostly in the fictional town of Grace, Arizona, although some scenes take place in the Santa Rosalia Pueblo, also fictional, in New Mexico. Codi's first sight of Grace on her return gives a good picture of its almost idyllic beauty:

> The view from here was orchards: pecan, plum, apple. . . . The trees filled the whole valley floor to the sides of the canyon. Confetti-colored houses perched on the slopes at its edges with their backs to the canyon wall.

An abundance of wild peacocks strut around the orchards, and the whole town exists under a "shamelessly unpolluted sky." The only flaw in the landscape is a man-made one, the old copper mine: "On the cliff overlooking the valley, the smelter's one brick smokestack pointed obscenely to heaven."

Economically, Grace survives by means of its orchards and the railroad, which provides employment for the town's men. Culturally, it is a mixture of Anglo (white) and Mexican American, with a Native American presence there as well. The Baptist Grocery in Grace's small commercial district is an indication of the former Anglo influence, but the predominant flavor of the Grace to which Codi returns is Hispanic. Spanish is still spoken a lot in people's homes, most of the citizens have Hispanic names, Mexican folk and religious customs such as the Day of the Dead (the Mexican equivalent of All Soul's Day) are celebrated, and the close family structures are matriarchal rather than patriarchal.

Like Grace, the Santa Rosalia Pueblo, where Loyd takes Codi at Christmas, is notable for its natural beauty and also for its antiquity and the sense of the sacred it transmits. This is how Codi describes Spider Rock, for example:

> The canyon walls rose straight up on either side of us, ranging from sunset orange to deep rust, mottled with purple. The sandstone had been carved by ice ages and polished by desert eons of sandpaper winds. The place did not so much inspire religion as it seemed to be religion itself.

As they travel further in the canyon, Codi observes that ancient pictures have been carved in the rock, of antelopes, snakes and ducks, and some human figures as well. This human adornment of nature is in marked contrast to the human intervention that has altered the landscape of Grace, producing ugly, polluting mines.

Structure and Point of View

The novel is divided into twenty-eight chapters, most of which are narrated in the first person, by Codi. Each of Codi's chapters is prefaced by her full name, Cosima. The other chapters are told from Doc Homer's point of view, by a third person narrator who has insight into Doc Homer's mind but no one else's.

In Codi's portion of the narration, Kingsolver makes use of flashbacks to Codi's childhood, including significant moments in her relationship with Hallie and Doc Homer. Kingsolver also makes use of Codi's dreams, particularly a recurring one

in which Codi suddenly goes blind and seems to lose herself altogether.

Doc Homer's chapters, which are prefaced by his full first name, Homero, are all short, most of them no more than two pages in length. Unlike Codi's chapters, these narrations are told in the present tense, even though many of the events described took place many years in the past. The significance of this narrative technique is that Doc Homer's failing mind cannot tell the difference between past and present. Traumatic events from the past co-exist in his mind with things that are happening in the present moment.

Image and Metaphor

In the first chapter, Kingsolver uses a powerful image to set the scene for one of the questions the novel seeks to address, which is, why can two people from the same family, exposed to the same influences as children, become so different as adults? Doc Homer gazes at his two young children, Codi and Hallie, as they lie sleeping. They are completely intertwined, almost as one person. It is not possible to see where one body stops and the other begins. When one breathes, they both move; "Their long hair falls together across the sheet, the colors blending, the curled strands curving gently around the straight." The image illustrates the closeness between the two sisters, while foreshadowing the central question.

The same chapter reveals Kingsolver's use of metaphor to create thematic links between the different elements of her plot. Doc Homer feels that a river separates him from his children, and the term is used metaphorically. Thematically, the river image as a metaphor for separation is connected to the riverbed on which Codi later disposes of her baby, and this is in turn linked to the river that is being polluted by Black Mountain Mining—yet another unnatural occurrence, one that separates the human community from the world of nature.

Historical Context

The United States and Nicaragua in the 1980s

Hallie's impassioned letters to Codi about the political situation in Nicaragua reflect a major foreign policy issue of the times. Throughout the 1980s, U.S. policy toward Nicaragua was in the forefront of public debate.

The origins of the controversy go back to 1979 when the Nicaraguan dictator General Anastasio Somoza was overthrown by an insurgency led by Marxist Sandinista guerrillas. Relations between Nicaragua and the U.S., which had supported Somoza, quickly deteriorated. When President Ronald Reagan took office in 1981, he forcefully advocated the cause of the Nicaraguan rebels known as the contras. The justification for the policy was to prevent the Sandinistas from promoting communist revolutions throughout Central America. In support of his views, Reagan produced evidence that the Sandinistas were sending arms to leftist rebels in El Salvador.

Reagan's policy ran into stiff opposition from many Democratic lawmakers who feared it would lead to American troops being sent to Nicaragua. In 1984, Congress voted to cut off U.S. aid to the contras. This was in the wake of excesses by the American Central Intelligence Agency (CIA), which included the blowing up of Nicaraguan oil depots and the mining of Nicaraguan harbors by Latin American commandos under the direction of CIA agents. The latter actions were declared illegal by the International Court of Justice in the Hague.

Congress voted to restore humanitarian aid to the contras in 1985, and in 1986, Congress approved $100 million in military and other aid. The United States also imposed a trade embargo on Nicaragua in 1985 and urged international financial institutions not to approve loans to the Sandinista government.

The result of the U.S. measures was a slump in the Nicaraguan economy. In 1988, inflation skyrocketed, and unemployment was 21 percent.

Peace talks between the warring parties began in 1987. In 1989, a peace agreement, endorsed by five Central American countries, was signed. Under the plan, the contras would be disbanded in exchange for free elections in Nicaragua. Those elections were held in 1990, and the Sandinistas were defeated by a coalition of opposition groups led by Violeta de Chamorro, who became president. As a result of the peace agreement and the election, U.S.-Nicaraguan relations were normalized.

During the eight-year civil war, the contras were sometimes accused of atrocities. Hallie refers to these atrocities in her letters to Codi, and it is apparent that Hallie vehemently opposes the U.S. policy of supporting the contras. The incident referred to in one of Hallie's letters—in which a helicopter piloted by U.S. National Guardsmen is shot down by the Sandinistas, who take one man prisoner—is loosely based on a real incident that occurred in 1986. At the time when U.S. military aid to the contras was banned, a U.S. cargo plane carrying arms supplies to the contras was shot down. The one survivor of the crash, an American citizen, was charged by Nicaragua with terrorism. He was sentenced to thirty years imprisonment but was later released as part of a prisoner exchange agreement. The CIA denied any involvement in the incident, and just as in the novel, the American government claimed that the helicopter pilot was an ex-mercenary and a drug runner, with no ties to the government.

Hallie, who in the novel is killed by the contras, also has a real life model, a young man named Ben Linder. Linder was a hydroelectric engineer from Portland, Oregon, who traveled to Nicaragua for the same purpose as Hallie, to help the Nicaraguan farmers. He was killed by the contras. When Kingsolver dedicated *Animal Dreams* to Linder, she was making it clear that her own views on the contras, and U.S. policy in the region, were close to those expressed by Hallie.

Eco-Feminism

During the 1980s, a new subgenre began to emerge in American literature, and it was sometimes known as eco-feminism. Paul Gray, in his review of *Animal Dreams* in *Time,* sketched the basic elements of eco-feminist literature:

> Women, relying on intuition and one another, mobilize to save the planet, or their immediate neighborhoods, from the ravages—war, pollution, racism, etc.—wrought by white males. This reformation of human nature usually entails the adoption of older, often Native American, ways.

Gray points out that Ursula K. Le Guin's *Always Coming Home* (1985) contains most of the elements of the form.

Eco-feminists believe in the sacredness and interconnectedness of all forms of life. They oppose patriarchal attitudes, which they believe lead to exploitation of the earth's resources without concern for long-term consequences. Many eco-feminists see a link between the way society treats animals and the natural environment and the way it treats women.

Eco-feminist themes are clearly present in *Animal Dreams.* It is the women of Grace, not the men, who organize to save the town from industrial pollution. (In an amusing scene in which Codi addresses a special meeting of the Stitch and Bitch

American engineer Benjamin Linder working in Nicaragua on a hydroelectric project for the Sandinista government.

Club, it is clear that the men are more interested in staying at home and watching the Miss America Pageant on television than in becoming social activists.) The Native American social organization that is presented in such a positive light is matriarchal: "The women are kind of the center of things up here," Loyd says of the Santa Rosalia Pueblo. Hallie's concern for the environment is apparent throughout, and Codi, in addition to her emerging environmental awareness, is horrified by cruelty to animals.

Critical Overview

When first published in 1990, *Animal Dreams* received a highly positive response from reviewers. Many admired the subtle, interlocking complexities of plot and theme, the vividly described southwestern setting, the satisfying development of character, and Kingsolver's compassion and humor. Lisa See, in *Publishers Weekly,* said that Kingsolver had "taken all of her previous themes—Native Americans, U.S. involvement in Nicaragua, environmental issues, parental relationships,

women's taking charge of their own lives—tossed them into a literary pot and created a perfectly constructed novel."

Paul Gray, in *Time,* described the novel as "an entertaining distillation of eco-feminist materials." Although he regarded Codi as too "preachy" at times, he also commented that "There is enough fun in this novel, though, to balance its rather hectoring tone."

High praise came from Carolyn Cooke in the *Nation:*

> *Animal Dreams* . . . is dense and vivid, and makes ever tighter circles around the question of what it means to be alive, how to live rightly and sweetly even as we feel the confining boundaries of the skin, the closing walls of past and present, with memory like a badly wired lamp, spitting sparks and shorting out.

Cooke especially admired the portrait of Doc Homer, in which "Kingsolver brilliantly delineates the quality of a dissolving but wholly practical mind." Although Cooke suggested that the paradisal symbolism of Grace was "heavy-handed," she added that Kingsolver "redeems herself with her clear and original voice, her smart, plucky women, her eye for the nuances of personality and the depth of her social and moral concerns. Kingsolver can help you learn how to live."

For Jane Smiley, in the *New York Times Book Review,* Kingsolver "demonstrates a special gift for the vivid evocation of landscape and of her characters' state of mind." Smiley did comment, however, that Kingsolver was only partially successful in shaping all the issues she covered into a "larger vision." In choosing to concentrate on exploring Codi's despair, rather than the more dramatic plots, such as Hallie's adventures in Nicaragua and the campaign against the Black Mountain mining company,

> Ms. Kingsolver . . . frequently undermines the suspense and the weight of her book. First-person narration can be tricky, and Ms. Kingsolver falls into its trap: Codi comes across too often as a whiner, observant of others but invariably more concerned with her own state of mind.

Rosellen Brown in the *Massachusetts Review* admired the narrative voice of Codi ("amused and amusing, capable of intricate and engaging detail") and declared that *Animal Dreams* was "a rich book, generous in its perceptions and judgments," although she faulted Kingsolver's "tendency to idealize her characters," noticeable especially in Loyd Peregrina and other Native American or Hispanic characters. No such caveats were offered by the reviewer for the *Antioch Review,* who wrote that "Kingsolver has a wonderful way of blending historical facts and myths (Indian lore) with present-day concerns and insights into how children react to the world around them."

Animal Dreams won a PEN fiction prize and the Edward Abbey Ecofiction Award in 1991. Since then, it has been the subject of two articles in scholarly journals that explore Kingsolver's sense of place and community and her environmental themes. And in 1999, Mary Jean DeMarr explored the themes and characters of the novel, and gave it a brief feminist reading, in her book, *Barbara Kingsolver: A Critical Companion.*

In its range of concerns, from the need to engage in political issues and to protect the environment, to the healing value of family and community, *Animal Dreams* is typical of the themes that are important to Kingsolver as a writer. The novel continues to win new readers and critical respect, as Kingsolver's reputation as one of America's most significant contemporary writers continues to grow.

Criticism

Bryan Aubrey

Aubrey holds a Ph.D. in English and has published many articles and reviews about contemporary American fiction. In the following essay, he discusses the search for identity in Kingsolver's novel.

The unifying theme in all the different strands of plot that make up *Animal Dreams* is Codi Noline's recovery of wholeness in her own psyche and in her relationship with her environment, both human and natural. This takes her on an exploration of the nature of memory and its problematic relationship to truth and self-identity, a theme in which her father, Doc Homer, is deeply involved also. Ultimately, Codi learns that the search for individual identity is by itself not enough to grant her the peace, security, and sense of belonging she craves; she must also understand the relationship between human culture and the natural world.

The framework within which Kingsolver traces this journey is in the form of a circle. The novel begins and ends on All Soul's Day, which takes place in the first week of November; it is the Roman Catholic day of commemoration of the

dead. This is significant for Codi because in her life the dead cast a long shadow; the scars left by the early loss of her mother and her miscarriage at the age of fifteen prevent her from living fully in the present. Deceptions engineered by her father about their family origins have had a similarly deleterious effect on Codi's life. In this novel, there are skeletons from the past that need to be confronted and exorcised.

For Codi, however, the very act of remembering the past is fraught with ambiguity. Memory is a minefield. Looking back, the mind distorts, forgets, invents, plays tricks. Codi remembers things that according to others she could not have witnessed, and yet she does not remember other events that are recalled clearly by her sister and by other townsfolk. As she says, "Memory is a complicated thing, a relative to truth but not its twin." Nonetheless, Codi is compelled to delve into the past to find out whether recalling and understanding it can relieve the acute aimlessness and rootlessness that afflict her. Otherwise, she fears she will never possess a solid sense of her own identity.

Indeed, as Codi describes herself during the course of the novel, it is almost as if she is with the dead herself. Like a specter, she lacks definition and substance. She comments that she cannot remember half of what happened to her before the age of fifteen. She knows little about her origins, other than that her family came from Illinois (and even that piece of information later proves to be only a half-truth). "I guess I'm nothing," she says to Loyd, "The Nothing Tribe." This is in contrast to the surety with which Loyd knows his own background. Similarly, Codi laments in a letter to Hallie, "My life is a pitiful, mechanical thing without a past, like a little wind-up car, ready to run in any direction somebody points me in." The word mechanical is significant; Codi's life lacks conscious, organic connection to its roots in family and community, and to nature itself.

It is clear from the extreme language Codi uses to describe herself that she is in mental disarray; there is an emptiness at her core that leaves her perhaps only one traumatic event away from complete disintegration. Subconsciously, she knows and fears this. She has a recurring nightmare in which she suddenly goes blind, and she realizes midway through the novel that this dream is not about losing her vision but about losing "the whole of myself, whatever that was. What you lose in blindness is the space around you, the place where you are,

> For Codi, however, the
> very act of remembering the past
> is fraught with ambiguity.
> Memory is a minefield. Looking
> back, the mind distorts, forgets,
> invents, plays tricks."

and without that you might not exist. You could be nowhere at all."

This fear of nonexistence, of being nothing and existing nowhere, is what drives Codi to recover her memories of the past, hoping they will help her establish just who she is. With this in mind, she questions the women of the town who knew her when she was a child, and there are one or two moments of cathartic release when she is almost overwhelmed by memories as they come flooding back.

But to find the vital ingredient that will in part end her alienation from the society in which she was born and raised, Codi must penetrate the distortions that have been erected by her father, Doc Homer. As urgently as Codi needs to delve into the past, Doc Homer has over the years felt compelled to cover it up.

Doc Homer is a curious character. One of his hobbies is photography, but he does not record things simply as they are. He takes a photograph of one thing and then tinkers with it to make it look like something else—clouds are made to look like animals, for example, or a clump of five cacti comes to resemble a human hand. When Codi first visits him, he is working on an elaborate procedure to make a photograph of two old men sitting on a stone wall look like a stone wall with two extra rocks balanced on top. Later, it transpires that this is Doc Homer's way of preserving his memories. He takes a memory from the past and tries to revive it by concocting a "photograph" of something else that reminds him of it. For example, he photographs a shadow of a cactus because it reminds him of an extremely unusual aerial view of a river in a desert he saw many years ago in wartime. So he tries to construct out of the photograph an illusion that will resemble and call up in his mind that particular river.

Codi does not know what the point of this activity is although she acknowledges there is "a great deal of art" involved in the process. It is ironic that Doc Homer tries so hard in this unorthodox fashion to preserve certain images from the past, whilst so earnestly trying to obscure another, more pertinent fact: he is descended from the Nolinas family, which had such a bad reputation in the town. Perhaps, like all of us, Doc Homer wants to preserve the acceptable memories and screen out the unacceptable ones, but it is curious that both approaches involve a falsification. Doc Homer's photographs look like one thing but are in fact something else. It is clear that they are a metaphor for the idea that the personal histories that humans construct for themselves are more related to their own psychic needs than to anything that may have actually happened in their lives.

The novel implies that this may not of itself be a bad thing. In fact, a similar realization forms a vital part of Codi's final act of self-acceptance. She has always been puzzled by the fact that she remembers the moment when her mother, at the time of her death, was taken away by helicopter. The incident took place when Codi was only three, and others tell her that she was not there, so she could not possibly remember it. However, when Viola takes her to the field at the crest of the canyon where the incident happened, Codi remembers it vividly. Viola tells her it does not matter whether she was actually there or not: "No, if you remember something, then it's true. . . . In the long run, that's what you've got."

This understanding gives Codi comfort and release. Her memory is vindicated and doubt is removed. This is the final incident in the novel, and it takes place, like the first chapter, on All Soul's Day. The wheel has turned full circle. Instead of the fate of her mother being a source of pain to her, Codi now remembers the helicopter, with her mother in it, rising "like a soul," a phrase which suggests ascension to heaven, a religious notion that Codi, who tends to believe that death is final, has not for a moment entertained before.

This, however, is only part of the truth that Codi discovers during the course of the novel. She also learns that to be complete humans must not only understand their personal heritage, they must also align themselves and their communities with the laws, structures, and processes that operate in the natural world. The elusive secret of peace of mind lies in the mysterious congruence between the human and the natural worlds.

What Do I Read Next?

- Kingsolver's nonfiction book, *Holding the Line: Women in the Great Arizona Mine Strike of 1983* (1989), examines the leadership role played by women during the Phelps Dodge Copper Company labor dispute. The small towns described resemble Grace, and the women are the prototypes of the Stitch and Bitch Club in *Animal Dreams.*

- *The Bean Trees* (1988), Kingsolver's first novel, follows Taylor Greer as she sets off from her native Kentucky to find a better, more rewarding life in Tucson, Arizona.

- *The Poisonwood Bible* (1998) is Kingsolver's fourth novel and a runaway bestseller. Set in 1959 at a time of political upheaval in what was then the Belgian Congo, it follows the story of Baptist minister Nathan Price as he arrives with his family in a remote village to preach the gospel.

- *Waste Land: Meditations on a Ravaged Landscape* (1997), by David T. Hanson, is a startling collection of aerial-view photographs of landscapes in America contaminated by industrial pollution.

- *Our Own Backyard: The United States in Central America, 1977–1992* (2000), by William M. Leogrande, gives a very detailed account of U.S. foreign policy toward Nicaragua (as well as El Salvador) during the time period covered in *Animal Dreams.*

- *Tracks* (1988), by Louise Erdrich, recreates the tensions between white and Native American culture in North Dakota from 1912–1924. Kingsolver names Erdrich as one of her favorite writers.

- Another of Kingsolver's favorite writers is Leslie Marmon Silko. In the vast *Almanac of the Dead* (1991), Silko focuses on the struggles of the native populations of the American southwest to reclaim the land that the Europeans have appropriated.

- "Careful What You Let in the Door," Kingsolver's essay in her collection *High Tide in Tucson* (1995), discusses her justification for sometimes including violence in her novels, and includes reference to the kidnapping and murder of Hallie in *Animal Dreams.*

This point is made clear when Codi, accompanied by Loyd, examines the ancient dwellings at the Santa Rosalia Pueblo. She observes that although they are the products of human hands, they can barely be distinguished from nature itself:

> The walls were shaped to fit the curved hole in the cliff, and the building blocks were cut from the same red rock that served as their foundation. I thought of what Loyd had told me about Pueblo architecture, whose object was to build a structure the earth could embrace. This looked more than embraced. It reminded me of cliff-swallow nests, or mud-dauber nests, or crystal gardens sprung from their own matrix: the perfect constructions of nature.

On an earlier visit to another Pueblo sacred place, Codi makes a similar observation as she looks at the stones that make up the building: "There was something familiar about the way they fit together. . . . They looked just like cells under a microscope." She remarks that the dwelling does not even look as if it was built: "It looks like something alive that just *grew* there." Yet within this completely natural-looking structure, an entire human culture flourished.

What these images symbolize is a harmony between human civilization and nature that is the secret of the fuller, more expansive life that often eludes the individual self, preoccupied as it is with trying to alleviate the pain lodged in the vault of memory. It is significant that the patterns discernible in these natural buildings share the same structures as the cellular structure of the human physiology, something that runs far deeper than the transitory content of the individual mind.

A copper mine in Butte, Montana

There is more than a hint of this search for a harmony with nature that would relieve the human experience of pain in Doc Homer's odd hobby. It is as if in his photographs he is trying to merge the human with the natural—the men, for example, become indistinguishable from the stone wall—or to point out that there are forms in nature that are orderly and have the power to give the soul rest. Memories that may be disturbing can be quieted by being absorbed into images of nature's serene permanence.

When Codi finally understands the threefold secret of living—her own family origins and memories; her place in the community of Grace; and the human as a reflection of the natural—she can at last discover who she really is. And she does not have far to look. She points out early in the novel that her full name, Cosima, means order in the cosmos. Most of her life she has regarded this as a joke since she knows how little it resembles the life she has been leading. But by the end, when she is in a committed relationship with Loyd, pregnant with his baby, productive in her community, and knowing how to live in the embrace of nature, she is truly Cosima, a part of the great harmonious whole, taking simple pleasure in being alive.

Source: Bryan Aubrey, Critical Essay on *Animal Dreams,* in *Novels for Students,* The Gale Group, 2001.

Robin Epstein

In the following interview, conducted in December 1995, Kingsolver discusses her background and interaction with other cultures and how her experiences and her political beliefs inform her works.

In a chapter in her new book of wide-ranging essays, *High Tide in Tucson,* Barbara Kingsolver describes a trip to Phoenix's Heard Museum with her daughter, Camille, who was five years old at the time. One of her hopes for the visit, she writes, is that Camille will shed the notion that Native Americans are "people that lived a long time ago," an idea she picked up from the dominant culture even though it contradicted her own experience with Tohono O'odham and Yaqui playmates. Thanks to the museum's mission of appreciation for modern Native American life as well as history, Camille gleans some understanding of Native American reality outside spaghetti westerns. Indians, she tells her mother as they leave the museum, are "people who love the Earth, and like to sing and dance and make a lot of pretty stuff to use." Then she adds, "And I think they like soda pop. Those guys selling the fry bread were drinking a lot of Cokes."

Barbara Kingsolver's work takes readers on a similar journey. It makes real the daily lives lived by people who are seldom presented with all their smarts and sorrows. Among the people we meet in Kingsolver's novels (all published by Harper-Collins) are, in *The Bean Trees,* working-class white women from Appalachia and Central Americans fleeing death squads; in *Animal Dreams,* Mexican-American grandmothers fighting to save the river that nourishes their town's orchards, a garden-pest hotline worker who joins the Sandinistas' agricultural efforts in Nicaragua, and a part-Apache train engineer with a penchant for cockfighting; and in *Pigs in Heaven,* a Cherokee lawyer who tries to resolve a conflict over a child adopted out of the tribe.

Thanks to her gift for creating characters we care about, for giving them voices that situate them firmly in time and place, and for taking them through plots that unfold inside their hearts and minds as well as out in the world, Kingsolver has been nominated three times for the ABBY award, a booksellers' prize that goes to the author they most love to recommend to customers.

She is also the author of *Homeland,* a collection of short stories (HarperCollins again); *Another*

America/Otra America, a book of poems in English and Spanish (Seal Press); and *Holding the Line: Women in the Great Arizona Mine Strike of 1983* (ILR Press), an oral history of the women in three small to towns who for eighteen months sustained a picket against the Phelps Dodge Copper Corporation despite arrests, evictions, and excoriation from some union bosses and some men in their communities who thought they should stick to making tortillas.

In early December, I spent a day with Barbara Kingsolver in Sabino Canyon on the outskirts of Tucson. Though I had only been in Arizona all of two days, I thought I had figured out the weather— hot during the day and cold at night. It was daytime, so I didn't wear many layers. Well, I didn't know from canyons. I shivered as we rode the Forest Service tram that takes you in. Though she had hoped we would stay in the "v" of the mountains, near the running water that reminds her a tiny bit of the landscape of her childhood in Kentucky, Barbara agreed right away to hike a short distance up the slope to where the sun would reach us faster. We found a suitable rock just off the trail and plopped ourselves down to talk. Nourished by good conversation and Barbara's homemade raisin bread, I warmed up in no time.

[Q:] Some of the essays in your new book read like a kind of Feminine Mystique *for a new generation. Were you especially trying to reach women with the information in those essays? I wonder whether they've prompted some heated dining table conversations between women and the men in their lives.*

[Kingsolver:] I think so. I've heard about a few. I've heard from women who said, "I gave this to my husband with underlines." But when I'm writing I don't really think, "Who's going to read this?" I don't feel my books are mainly for women. When students ask, "Is this a chick book?" I say, "*Moby Dick* is a whale book, but I don't think only whales should read it."

You know, John Updike writes about penises and lusting after women, and he's really one of the most male writers that I read. His point of view is so deeply male. And when he's writing, does he think, "Oh, women aren't going to be able to relate to this?" I don't think it crosses his mind. So there's a role model for me, right?

I do think we can learn a much from reading the perspectives of people we are not. I can learn a lot from John Updike. I'm never going to have a penis in my whole life, so I can read John Updike

"You know, John Updike . . . he's really one of the most male writers that I read. His point of view is so deeply male. And when he's writing, does he think, 'Oh, women aren't going to be able to relate to this?' I don't think it crosses his mind. So there's a role model for me, right?"

and I can get some clue. I mean, that's sort of reductionist, but that male ego that's his focus, that's the eye of his storm, is very interesting. It's kind of heady to read it and get a glimpse of what it would be like to live in the eye of that storm instead of dancing around it all the time saying, "Are you OK? Are you OK?"

I grew up learning about women by reading men and becoming convinced at a pretty early age that they were getting a lot of it wrong. I felt usurped by *Lady Chatterley's Lover.* But a lot of people did it right, too. Look at *Anna Karenina;* look at Emma Bovary. So I will never say men have no right to represent women. That would be absurd. What I will say is I think our first responsibility, and also our first treasure as writers, is to represent ourselves. So women are always dead center in my novels. And my novels are about the things women most think about, like keeping our children fed, and how to manage on not very much income. I think it's important to do that, because it's not traditionally been the main stuff of literature. And it needs to be.

A lot of what I also do is tell people, "Look, you're noble. The things you do in your life, from day to day to day, which you have probably never thought of as the stuff of literature, are heroic. And if it's not you, it's your mother, or your neighbor, or your sister. And think about that. Think how wondrous that is." I think it really might be the main thing I do. And that's crossing a new street. It's looking at yourself and looking at heroism in a new way. Forget about Power Rangers, Power Mongers, Power Bombs, Power Suits, for just one minute of your life. All those icons we associate with power are hard to leave behind. It's hard to build a new iconography of heroism, but that's kind of my bailiwick. I owe that to the people I grew up with.

Do you mean your family or your community?

Both. Just to see people survive. Survival itself, in certain circumstances, is heroic. To live through mean times without becoming mean-spirited is heroic. I saw a lot of that.

In the new book, you explore our anti-child policies on the political level, and imply we also have some anti-child practices on the family level.

Kingsolver: The "terrible twos" is an excellent example. I asked all my Latino friends, "How do you translate terrible twos?" "What?" they said. "There's no terrible twos." They didn't even know what I was talking about. Not only is it not in their language, it's not in their thinking. To define individuation from the parent as terrible is an anti-child mindset. Now, I'm not saying it's not difficult to have a two-year-old, but it's a cultural difficulty. We expect our two-year-olds to fit smoothly into adult schedules.

I think the reason that my friend Carmen was baffled when I said "terrible twos" is that the children in her household don't have to trench a clock. They're with her or there's other people in the household. There's this troupe of kids coming in and out, and always adults to take care of them. They don't have to get up, get dressed, eat breakfast, and get strapped into the car seat by 7 o'clock, which is a schedule that would make any two-year-old cranky. Think about if you had to crawl around and play with blocks all day. You'd be cranky; you'd be a terrible whatever-you-are.

And that's not the fault of the parents. Obviously many, many mothers have no choice but to bundle their kids off to daycare, so I'm not blaming them.

What I'm saying is our culture doesn't make allowances for kids; it doesn't give parental leave. Children are an aberration in late capitalism. They're also a liability, because they're not productive. So that's why capitalism treats them like toxic waste.

Where did you get the desire to learn about different cultures?

I went to school with African Americans and whites. It was a segregated town. When I went to first grade, it was an all-white school. Second grade, the kids who had gone to school in the CME church came down to our school. I remember thinking, "They must be so scared," and wanting to ask, but being afraid. Marilyn and Karen were the two African-American kids in my class. I wanted to be friends with them and I didn't know how. I was a little bit scared, not because my parents said, "Stay away," nothing like that. Just that I knew that they came from a different world, and I knew that they were outnumbered.

It impressed me, because I was also an outcast. I think one of the great pluses is that I grew up as a social outsider. And that had to do with being really skinny and really tall, and physically not blending in, which is so important in pre-adolescence and adolescence—it's sort of the main thing.

But also my family was different. My parents just expected me to do things like read books—big, good books—and one day go to college. Nobody else I knew had that sort of expectation. Nobody in my class was going to college. Everybody kind of had the plan. They'd get married and they'd have kids and they'd stay right there. There was something in my training that was telling me, "You're going to go away."

And then you lived for a while in Africa as a kid?

Yes, my dad was a physician, and he wanted to go where he could be extremely useful. So we ended up living in St. Lucia for a while in a convent hospital, and we lived in Central Africa. The people in our village had not seen white kids. I had really long hair that I could sit on, and people didn't think it was hair, because hair doesn't look like that, and they'd try to pull it off. My mom would explain to me, "They're not trying to hurt you. They just think you're wearing something weird on your head and they're trying to get you to quit showing off."

So you were an outsider?

Very much. I got a real extreme look at what it's like to be a minority. It was an enormous adventure that let me know at the age of seven that there's a great big old world out there that I don't know anything about, that I'm going to see, and that I'm going to know if I can.

Was your connection to small-town life one of the things that led you to write Holding the Line: Women in the Great Arizona Mine Strike of 1983, *about the small towns of Morenci, Ajo, and Clifton?*

Yes, even though I didn't grow up in a mining county. Nicholas County is not mining, it's agricultural. It's a tobacco town, so it's deeply depressed. Times have been tough there for as long as I've known about, and I think they're tougher still now that tobacco doesn't have the economic base it did. So, there are all these divisions. There was black and white. There was merchant and farmer. That was a very clear distinction in my school. The popular kids—the ones with new clothes every year—were the merchants' kids, the ones whose parents owned the dime store or the men's clothing store, or were the county attorney. And then all the other kids were farm kids, and they didn't get to wash their hair every night because they didn't necessarily have hot water. They had to walk through mud to get to the school bus, so they had mud on their shoes.

I was in that group, not because we were farmers but because we lived in the country, and my parents didn't believe in new clothes. They didn't value spending lots of money on superficial things, which of course really irritated me when I was fourteen. But I somehow lived through that and learned to appreciate it.

So in high school I learned about class, and I didn't even know the words. I never read Marx until I was about eighteen, but the first time I read *Grundrisse* and *Capital* I said. "I know this stuff. I grew up with this stuff." Kentucky is such a laboratory of class consciousness because you have really oppressed workers shoulder to shoulder with big capital, which is not something you see necessarily in other parts of the country. Maybe the rust belt, maybe the auto belt, though I still don't know if it's as clear as mining bosses and the way they sort of own their workers wholesale. So it's very clear whose side everyone's on. And add to that, Nicholas County is right in between, it's sandwiched.

You see the wealth of Lexington?

It's just one county away. Nicholas County holds a really interesting geographic position between the wealth of Lexington and the poverty of Appalachia, and people define themselves depending on which way they're facing. In our county we didn't have a swimming pool, not in the whole county. And we would go to Lexington once in a while, and pass through these horse farms. And there was a horse farm where—I swear this was true—the horses had a swimming pool. It was for therapy or something. I remember driving by that every time and smashing our faces against the glass of the window and hating those horses for being so rich. It was so unfair.

One thing that comes through so much in your writing is that people, like those you grew up with in Nicholas County, can understand power. I guess some liberal people would say they know that, but they don't really believe it at a gut level.

That's really wrong. That's a huge underestimation. I think certainly in Kentucky people understand class and power relations. And that's why Kentucky—and Arizona, too—has a history of radical class action, and radical labor organizing. And that's of course what drew me to the strike.

My first national publication was in *The Progressive* and it was about the strike. I started going down there with a friend of mine, Jill Fein. We were activists and organizers and we went there in solidarity with the strikers. I figured I'd write about it, but I didn't at first have an assignment. I loved *The Progressive,* so I wrote a query. We wrote the article together and they published it and it was an enormous thrill when it arrived. Seeing it in print was even more important than the check. There it was, with the photograph we'd taken of the women on the picket line. I remember just standing by the mailbox holding it in my hand and thinking, "All over the country people are reading about this." That's the power of being able to get the word out. After bonegrinding years as an activist, a door opened. I got some sense of the possibilities and of the power of this kind of writing. It was really a turning point for me.

Some people criticize your work as being too political. They try to erect a huge wall between art and politics. There's this idea that political art is bad, and that a divider between the two can actually exist. Where does this idea come from?

I'm not sure. My personal theory is it has a lot to do with McCarthyism. Because if you go back before the 1950s you find great political writers like Steinbeck, Walt Whitman, Carl Sandburg, Henry Thoreau. And then that stopped; things just sort of ground to a halt in the 1950s.

I don't know whether it's cause or effect. I don't know whether it was because of McCarthyism, or whether there was some evil humus in this country from which sprang Joe McCarthy and people who supported him and this idea that art and politics should separate themselves. For whatever reason, it's with us now and we haven't recovered from that time.

What can we do about it?

It's being done to us. Artists are losing the minuscule amount of support that we had. The NEA,

I heard Christopher Reeve say when he was in town years ago, gives out each year less money than the money for military band uniforms. So, there wasn't an enormous amount of public or federal support for artists to begin with, and it's dwindling. And there's a hue and cry, and artists are looking around and saying, "Why doesn't the public support us?"

Well, I have a clue about that. Look to some of the poorest countries in Latin America. They revere their poets. Their poets do not starve. They elect their poets to public office. Their poets are talking about important stuff. Their poets have their finger on the pulse of the human-rights situation, the core of economic oppression, where it's going and where it's coming from. They write about power relations and the common good. They write about all of this stuff that in the United States many artists avert their faces from as being too political. Well, if we write and paint and film things that people understand to be vital to their lives, we'll get public support. Any artistic commission that has Jesse Helms on it is scary. Censorship of any kind is scary. But I don't think we're really talking about censorship here. I think we're taking about a responsiveness of artists to their public that's sort of waning.

It's waning, but it has the potential to come back?

I think if artists can speak of things that matter, then they will be supported. I feel like I say stuff that people really don't want to hear. I write about child abuse, and about sexism and racism and illegal immigration laws, and I think, "Nobody's going to read about this," and yet, they do. I think that you can say difficult things, but do it artfully, and you'll be heard.

And the critics may say, "Oh, this is too political," but people are reading the books.

The gatekeepers of art are the ones who are saying this is too political. I don't hear that from many people. One letter in 100, or even less, will say. "I don't think you should be writing about this stuff."

I think we also have in this country a rare phenomenon in which people are very uneducated about art. I think the average African in Africa, let's say the average citizen of Cameroon, understands more about the art of Cameroon than the average Tucsonian understands about the art of Tucson. Understanding and appreciating art is something you learn from other people who do it, and historically it's been part of oral tradition. You appreciate stories because you sit around in groups where peo-

ple tell them. You appreciate dance because you participate. You grow up seeing other people moved to tears by the events, and you learn what that's about.

Do you think the people who criticize your work are people who already know about the issues and have decided they're on the other side? Or are they people who have so much of their personal and professional identities invested in the idea that they don't take stands that they feel threatened by the fact that your characters do?

Both. Usually when people say, "You're too political," what they mean is, "I don't agree with you." In *High Tide in Tucson,* I wrote about that anecdote at the mall, where the managers decided that the people passing out yellow ribbons and We Kick Butt bumper stickers were not political, and the people who were passing out anti-war propaganda were political. That's come to be a significant definition of the word political in this country, and it's something I don't agree with. The people who have panned my work as being political are people who are not on my side, so I feel kind of proud of that.

Do you think the popularity of your fiction speaks to people's hunger for the acknowledgment of the political in their lives, in addition to the fact that they're drawn in by the great stories and great characters?

Yes. I don't think it's necessarily things people would define as political, although sometimes it is, explicitly. I hear from activists who say, "We've been trying and trying to tell people about Nicaragua and finally what a relief to pick up a book that does it, a real book that people are reading."

You've said a novel can move people in a way a newspaper article can't, because it gets in their heart and because they can't switch to the sports pages. But your new book is nonfiction. Did you want to speak in your own voice instead of through your characters?

I've been writing essays all along, but to write a book of them that all added up to something was really wonderful. This is a really scary thing to say, but it has worried me at times that my work is so popular. Sometimes I think, "Are they just reading the love story and didn't notice the part about Guatemala?" I think people do, on some level, understand the politics of my fiction. Even if only to be awakened to the possibility that the government is doing something not right in Central America and maybe they'll be more open to reading stuff

Contras on patrol in the mountains of Nicaragua

that's more explicitly about that subject. Or sort of an attitude about the environment, or an attitude about women that comes through. You can hear on the left sometimes an elitism of unpopularity. I don't know how many times I've heard people say, "Well, I write, but my work will never be popular because it's so political," and I think, "Well, am I chopped liver? Are you saying that I sold out, or what?"

I felt that I did at this point in my life have a chance to be more direct. Everything in *High Tide in Tucson* I think I've said before behind the mask of fiction, but this time I stepped out from behind the mask and said, "I, Barbara Kingsolver, believe this." And it sold more in the first four months than all six of my other books combined in their first four months.

So you're probably reaching people who haven't heard about these issues from your perspective before.

I have to think so. I can't get over that I get to do this. It also comes with a certain responsibility. You know you get handed in your life this chance to go all over the country and talk and talk and talk, and answer and answer and answer questions, and go on *McNeil/Lehrer* and national shows. I would much rather not do that. I would much rather stay

home and bake bread and write another book. That's what I do. That's what I love. And I do have my limits. I'll do it for a few months after a book comes out, and try to make the most of that time.

The reason that I do it at all is that I can still remember how recently it was that I was cranking out leaflets about the Palo Verde Nuclear Generating Plant, or whatever was the crisis of the week in Tucson, Arizona. And I don't mean to demean these crises; they are all very real.

It's very hard to criticize this country, our domestic or our foreign policy, or our attitude, or our Americanism. And so, given the chance to do that, given this strange moment that I have, little old socialist me, to go talk to David Gergen and be in everybody's living room, I have to do it. And I have to do it right. I have to say the important stuff, not just smile and nod and say, "Oh, yes, I have written another book."

I don't imagine you have time to crank the mimeographs anymore.

No, and it wouldn't be a good use of my time. But I'm still involved locally. It used to be I was the one who would organize the events. Now I go to them. Or I'll go and read a poem. They put my name on the list to draw a different crowd. I find that I can be an effective activist in very different ways, but I feel like I still believe exactly the same things I did when I was twenty.

It seems to me that as disparate as they are, all the essays in the new book fit together. What's the unifying theme?

I didn't title the book, *Barbara the Marxist Takes on Life,* but that's what it is. Let's face it. I steered clear of the M word, because people are so ignorant. Even though we're a secular state, we're deeply religious about the religion of America. We rely on so many things on faith, without having to have any evidence. Like this belief about how anyone can make it in America if you're smart and you work hard. Well, for how many generations now has that been untrue? In some families, a lot. And in almost all families, my generation is not as well off as our parents, even though we worked just as hard, and more of us got more of an education than they did. It's staggering to me to read statistics of how many people in this country live in poverty: 20 percent of kids, right? Yet turn on the television and you still see rich people idolized. Popular culture reflects a population that still identifies with the ruling class.

You weave your scientific training into your writing, which is pretty unusual.

There's this whole realm of natural history metaphors and symbols you can use if you know about them that gives a kind of freshness to your writing, because most writers haven't studied science. People think it's sort of funny that I went to graduate school as a biologist and then became a novelist, but the process is so similar. What I learned is how to formulate or identify a new question that hasn't been asked before, and then to set about solving it, to do original research to find the way to an answer. And that's what I do when I write a book. It's very similar. I think I might be a lot more process-oriented than a lot of writers are. I've never talked with another writer about process who does it exactly the same way I do it. It used to make me certain I was doing it wrong. Now I just figure it's as good as any way. It works for me.

In the essays you let on that there have been days when you didn't think you could keep going, when you questioned your abilities as a writer.

I still have them. Beginning a book is really hard. I'm trying to begin one now and I just keep throwing stuff away and thinking, "Can I do this? I don't think I'm smart enough." But it has to be hard. You have to have a reverence for the undertaking. And I think reverence implies a certain lack of self-esteem, doesn't it?

If you're reverent towards something, you feel . . .

Lowly. You feel daunted and unworthy. But in this age of glorifying the individual and self-esteem, I think there's something healthy about being daunted. Cockiness doesn't lend itself to good writing. It really doesn't.

How was your recent book tour?

This book tour just took me from city to city to city, into hotel rooms out of whose windows I would look and see the same skyline. One of the things that was psychologically and emotionally tiring was that it was all city, and I was surrounded continually by people who took their city so seriously. I don't mean just their city, like, "Oh, this is Pittsburgh." But people who look around at the city and say, "This is what's real." For me, *this* is what's real. [As she said this, she gestured emphatically to the saguaro-studded canyon rising all around us.] We're just a blink in the eye of this. We haven't been around very long, and we're probably not going to persist. And it's sort of laughable that we take all of our stuff so seriously. We've had two hundred-year floods here in the last ten years, and both times the city was completely cut off, for days and days. You couldn't go anywhere. It was roaring water. And some things happened that were deeply reinforcing on the human level. For the first day you're still trying to get to work, or get to your appointments, and then slowly you give it up, and you realize that this whole schedule—all these things in our date book—are just little scratches on the surface of this old Earth, and she doesn't much care.

How do we build more awareness of that?

I think urban life is a big part of the problem. If people could just get out and look. And to just sit still and be. Ed Abbey, who was my neighbor, said something that continues to impress me in new ways. I told him I'd been to Zion, and I said, "It's enough to make you religious." And he said, "Those mountains don't inspire religion. They are religion."

In your new book, High Tide in Tucson, *in the essay, "The Spaces Between," you write, "I'm drawn like a kid to mud into the sticky terrain of cultural difference." You say, "I want to know, and to write, about the places where disparate points of view rub together—the spaces between. Not just between man and woman but also North and South; white and not-white; communal and individual; spiritual and carnal."*

The reason I'm attracted so much to those places and those moments is you can learn so much. You go through the world on some kind of search, and you take so much for granted. And when you run up against somebody else who's moving right beside you but looking for completely different stuff, it can stop you in your tracks, and you can start thinking, "Why am I looking for this?"

So few of us examine our motives and our mythology, the things that we believe in without question. Like humans are more important than any other species. Most people with your background and mine go through their whole lives without questioning that. I am more important than a Kirtland's warbler. Don't even think about it. And, so when you run up against somebody who says. "Of course the Kirtland's warbler is just as important as I am," that can throw you for a loop.

In *Pigs in Heaven* I wanted to choose a high-profile event in which a Native American has been adopted out of the tribe and in which that adoption is questioned and challenged. Because it brings into conflict two completely different ways of defining good, of defining value. The one is that the good is whatever is in the best interest of the child; the other is that the good is whatever is in the best interest of the tribe, the group, the community. What I really wanted to do in that book was not necessarily write about Indians. I wanted to introduce my readers to this completely different unit of good and have them believe in it by the end, have them accept in their hearts that that could be just as true as the other.

Your fiction, you've made clear, is not autobiographical, but the essays . . .

Are. It used to be people thought they knew all about me because they thought I was my characters. Now they do. I didn't really reveal anything that intimate in that book. I included a lot of details about where I live and so forth, only as kind of a springboard to issues or ideas. For example, I wrote about divorce. I didn't really write about my divorce. It seems like I did, but I didn't.

That it happened, yes.

That was sort of part of the public record already, anyway. Also, we moved right before the book came out, so people think they know all about my house, but they don't.

Including details about your life made the book more accessible?

That's the idea. It was so much like writing fiction. You use the same techniques. You create characters and you have a plot. All of the essays really are little stories that mean something, and what they end up being about is not the events but some larger ideas. It just happens that I used real people or real events or incidents in my life as the starting points. You can't just put the ideas there. You have to put clothes on them and make them walk around. I keep coming back to the term creative nonfiction to describe this book, because it really was more creative writing than journalism. You can look at the same event fifty different ways, so the story I chose to tell from a particular event was the creative part.

The choosing how to tell it?

And, I suppose before that, deciding what it means. What can you make of someone telling you, "Love it or leave it, b—h?" That can be at the starting point of a lot of different stories.

In that same essay you came back and said that that guy could think critically.

I speculate that if I asked him, "Do you think patriotism means turning your back on evidence that your country has done immoral acts?" I think he would say, "No." Then he'd say, "Prove it." I think "my country right or wrong" is not such a common slogan as "my country always right," and "by God I want to believe that, and so don't mess with me, don't confuse me with the facts."

But it's suspect to be a writer whose purpose in part is to change the world.

Oh, yeah. And it's funny that I still shock people when they say, "Why do you write?" and I say, "Well, to change the world." It's like heresy. It's like absolute heresy for an artist to say that. That's why I say it. Seven or eight years ago I couldn't.

You couldn't?

I thought it, but I couldn't admit it because I was afraid of not being taken seriously. Now I'm pretty confident of being taken seriously. Shocking but true. And so I feel I have an obligation to tell truths like that. You like what I write? Well, get this: I'm a pinko and I want to change the world.

Source: Robin Epstein, "An Interview with Barbara Kingsolver," in *Progressive,* Vol. 12, No. 9, February 1996, pp. 33–37.

Sources

Brown, Rosellen, Review, in *Massachusetts Review,* Spring 1991, p. 138.

Cooke, Carolyn, Review, in *Nation,* Vol. 251, No. 18, November 26, 1990, p. 653.

Gray, Paul, Review, in *Time,* Vol. 136, No. 13, September 24, 1990, p. 87.

Review, in *Antioch Review,* Fall 1990, p. 546.

See, Lisa, "Barbara Kingsolver: Her Fiction Features Ordinary People Heroically Committed to Political Issues," in *Publishers Weekly,* Vol. 237, No. 35, August 31, 1990, p. 46.

Smiley, Jane, Review, in *New York Times Book Review,* September 2, 1990, p. 2.

For Further Study

Andrews, Terry L., "Animal Dreams," in *Magill's Literary Annual,* Salem Press, 1991, pp. 38–42.

> This detailed and appreciative review brings out, among other things, the fairy tale aspects of the novel. Andrews writes that Codi is a "kind of unwitting Sleeping Beauty."

Barbara Kingsolver, in Signature Series' Contemporary Southern Writers, produced by the Annenberg/CPB Projects company, 1997.

> According to reviewer Jeannette E. Riley, this one-hour video presents "a comprehensive discussion of Kingsolver's influences, experiences, political beliefs, and dreams for the future." It also includes Kingsolver reading from her work, including *Animal Dreams.*

Beattie, L. Elisabeth, ed., "Barbara Kingsolver," in *Conversations with Kentucky Writers,* University of Kentucky Press, 1996, pp. 151–71.

> In a wide-ranging interview, Kingsolver says that she begins every novel with an important question that intrigues her and works her way toward the answer.

Berry, Donna, "An Interview with Barbara Kingsolver," in *Women Writers Speak Out,* Rutgers University Press, 1993, pp. 143–69.

> In this interview, Kingsolver talks about a wide range of topics and also reveals that of all her characters

Codi in *Animal Dreams* is the least like her: "she's so detached; she's so wounded and she's so cynical." Hallie, on the other hand, "is me."

De Marr, Mary Jean, *Barbara Kingsolver: A Critical Companion,* Greenwood Press, 1999.

> This comprehensive and clearly written analysis of Kingsolver's work, with a chapter on each of her four novels, is suitable for beginners as well as those with prior knowledge of Kingsolver.

Epstein, Robin, "An Interview with Barbara Kingsolver," in *Progressive,* Vol. 12, No. 9, February 1996, pp. 33–37.

> In this interview, Kingsolver talks about her background, her politics, the relationship between politics and art, her nonfiction work, and many other topics.

Fleischner, Jennifer, *A Reader's Guide to the Fiction of Barbara Kingsolver,* Harper, 1994.

> This is an informative and clearly written guide to Kingsolver's first three novels and her short stories.

Meadows, Bonnie J., "Serendipity and the Southwest: A Conversation with Barbara Kingsolver," in *Bloomsbury Review,* November–December, 1990, p. 3.

> Kingsolver explains that in *Animal Dreams* she "wanted to write about the way that loss of memory is the loss of self, both for a culture and an individual."

Newman, Vicky, "Compelling Ties: Landscape, Community, and Sense of Place," in *Peabody Journal of Education,* Vol. 70, No. 4, Summer 1995, pp. 105–18.

> Newman explores some of the main themes in *Animal Dreams,* including the idea of community and the role of autobiography in establishing personal identity.

Ryan, Maureen, "Barbara Kingsolver's Lowfat Fiction," in *Journal of America Culture,* Vol. 18, No. 4, Winter 1995, pp. 77–82.

> Examining Kingsolver's first three novels, Ryan finds much to praise, particularly the fact that Kingsolver writes traditional realistic fiction, but she also argues that Kingsolver's work is ultimately unsatisfying.

Bless Me, Ultima

Rudolfo Anaya
1972

First published in 1972, Rudolfo Anaya's *Bless Me, Ultima* has become the best-selling Chicano novel of all time. For twenty-two years, despite being available only through a small publisher, the novel sold 300,000 copies by word of mouth and was awarded the Premio Quinto Sol for excellence in Chicano literature. In 1994, the novel was finally printed by a major publisher in a mass-market edition to rave reviews.

Anaya drew from his experiences growing up in New Mexico during World War II to create the story of a young boy who must reconcile the many conflicting influences of his family, religion, and community. In the two years spanned by the novel, Antonio (Tony) Marez, who is six years old when the story begins, comes of age when he learns to recognize evil in the world and to navigate family expectations and religious ambiguity.

Critic Ray Gonzalez, in a review in *Nation,* states that "*Bless Me, Ultima* is our Latin American classic because of its dual impact—it clearly defines Chicano culture as founded on family, tradition and the power of myth. Through Antonio and Ultima, we learn how to identify these values in the midst of the dark clouds of change and maturity."

Author Biography

Rudolfo Alfonso Anaya was born on October 30, 1937 to Martin and Rafaelita Anaya in the rural vil-

Rudolfo A. Anaya

lage of Pastura, New Mexico, the fifth of seven children. Growing up in the small villages of Pastura and nearby Santa Rosa, Anaya was immersed in the oral culture of his Mexican-Indian ancestors and became familiar with the traditional farming and ranching practices that are depicted in his stories.

After moving to Albuquerque at age fifteen, Anaya graduated from Albuquerque High School in 1955. He attended Browning Business School from 1955 to 1958, then enrolled at the University of New Mexico where he earned both a B.A. (1963) and an M.A. (1968) in English. In 1972, shortly after finishing *Bless Me, Ultima,* Anaya also earned an M.A. in guidance and counseling from the University of New Mexico.

From 1963 to 1970, Anaya taught in public schools in Albuquerque. He then worked as a director of counseling at the University of Albuquerque. In 1974, he joined the faculty of the University of New Mexico's English department where he taught courses in creative writing and Chicano literature. He retired from teaching in 1994. He has been a guest lecturer at many universities, including Michigan State University, University of Indiana, Yale University, and University of Michigan.

In addition to being a teacher, Anaya is, of course, a writer. To date, he has published eight nov-

els and a collection of short stories, has edited many books on Chicano literature, and has experimented with scriptwriting. In 1971, he received the first of several literary awards, the Premio Quinto Sol award for *Bless Me, Ultima.* Some of his other awards include a National Chicano Council on Higher Education fellowship (1978–1979), National Endowment for the Arts fellowships (1979, 1980), the Before Columbus American Book Award (1980), the New Mexico Governor's Award for Excellence and Achievement in Literature (1980), a Kellogg Foundation fellowship (1983–1985) and the PEN Center USA West Award for Fiction for his novel *Alburquerque* (1994).

Plot Summary

Chapters Uno (One) through Cinco (Five): Before School Begins

Bless Me, Ultima opens with the *curandera* Ultima coming to live with Tony's family outside the village of Guadalupe. At this point, Tony is six years old: he has not yet begun school, and is innocent of the world. This innocence is shattered early on, however, when Tony's family learns that Lupito, a veteran returned from the war, has killed the town sheriff. Tony follows his father to the river, where the men of the village are gathering to confront Lupito, and watches as Lupito is shot and killed. This is the first of several deaths that Tony will witness.

The summer before Tony begins school, he spends a good deal of time with Ultima, who helps him to interpret his dreams and sort out his family's conflicting messages. At the end of summer, the Marez family, except for Tony's father, go to El Puerto to help his mother's family with the harvest.

Chapters Seis (Six) through Nueve (Nine): Tony's First Year of School

Tony goes to school in the fall, carrying the high hopes of his mother that he will become an educated man and ultimately a priest. Despite the fact that he is a quick learner and earns the respect of his teacher, Tony is an outcast because he is different—he is not a native English speaker, and rather than eating sandwiches for lunch like the other children, he eats tortillas, chiles, and beans. At school, he comes to understand "*la tristesa de la vida,*" or the sadness of life:

> I wanted to run away, to hide, to run and never come back, never see anyone again. But I knew that if I

did I would shame my family name, that my mother's dream would crumble. I knew I had to grow up and be a man, but oh it was so very hard.

However, Tony makes friends with some boys from other classes who come from Spanish-speaking families, and they are able to help each other through the ordeal of school.

Tony's three brothers return from World War II and start talking about opportunities outside of New Mexico, stirring up their father's inborn desire to wander and shattering their mother's dream of their becoming farmers and settling down. Two of the brothers, Leon and Eugene, soon leave town, telling Tony that he will have to be the one to fulfill his mother's dream. Andrew stays, saying that he will finish school.

At the end of the school year, because he has progressed so quickly and because he is a little older than the other children in his grade, Tony is promoted from the first to the third grade. On the way home from school on the last day, his friend Samuel tells him about a pagan god, the Golden Carp.

Chapters Diez (Ten) through Trece (Thirteen): The Summer After First Grade

The summer after Tony's first year of school is filled with events that cause him to see the world in a new light. One of these events occurs when Cico, a friend of Samuel's, befriends Tony and takes him to see the Golden Carp, forcing Tony to question his mother's Christian God.

That summer, a curse is laid on Tony's Uncle Lucas after he witnesses a meeting of three witches. The three witches are said to be the daughters of Tenorio Trementina, who owns a bar in El Puerto. The town priest being unable to lift the curse, Ultima agrees to cure Lucas. She brings Tony along to assist with the cure, and it is then that Tony first witnesses Ultima's powers.

Later in the summer, after Tony and Ultima have returned from El Puerto, Tenorio and some of his *compadres* arrive at the Marez home to take revenge on Ultima because one of Tenorio's daughters is dead, and he believes that Ultima is responsible. Ultima survives by passing through a door marked with holy needles in the shape of a cross, convincing Tenorio's men that she is not a witch. Tenorio is not through with Ultima, however, and his anger is fueled when the priest at El Puerto refuses to give his daughter a funeral mass and holy burial.

Chapters Catorce (Fourteen) through Diecinueve (Nineteen): The Next School Year

The new school year finds Tony in third grade along with his friends. The day before the Christmas holiday, the class is supposed to put on a Christmas play; however, there is a blizzard, and the only students to show up are Tony and his friends. Despite the fact that none of the girls or the main actors for the play are present, the teacher and the boys decide to put the play on anyway for the younger children who are at school. What follows is a comical farce.

Afterwards, making his way home from school through the blizzard, Tony comes upon a fight outside the local bar between Narciso and Tenorio. As the fight breaks up, Tenorio threatens to harm Ultima. Narciso decides to try to warn Ultima and goes to Rosie's house, the local whorehouse, to fetch Tony's brother Andrew. Tony, who follows Narciso at a distance, is shocked to see Andrew at Rosie's place, "the house of the sinful women." Andrew, believing Narciso to be drunk and making up stories, refuses to help him warn Ultima, so Narciso resolves to go by himself. On his way, with Tony still following, Tenorio confronts Narciso and kills him. Tony makes it home but comes down with a fever and has terrible hallucinations, and Ultima nurses him back to health. Later, Tony encounters Tenorio at the spot where he killed Narciso, and Tenorio threatens to kill Ultima.

Not long after the murder of Narciso, Tony's brothers Eugene and Leon return for a brief visit. When they leave, Andrew goes with them—it is clear that he feels responsible for Narciso's death.

In the spring, Tony starts catechism class. One of his classmates is the nonbeliever Florence, who attends class only because all of his friends are there. The questions Florence asks about God are ones to which Tony has few answers; this forces Tony to question his own faith. The day of their first confession, while playing with the other children, Tony is chosen to play the part of priest and listen to the others' confessions. When Florence says that he has not sinned, the children demand that Tony give him a tough penance. Tony refuses, and as a result, they beat him up. Afterwards, Florence tells Tony that he should have given him a penance, but Tony is glad that he stood his ground. Florence tells Tony, "You could never be their priest." On Easter, Tony receives his First Communion and is disappointed that he does not immediately have the answers from God that he had expected.

Chapters Veinte (Twenty) through Veintidos (Twenty-Two): The Next Summer

After school is out, a man named Tellez comes to the Marez family to get Ultima's help with a curse that has been laid on his house. Ultima, Tony, and Tony's father go to Tellez's house, and Ultima lifts the curse. It becomes clear that the curse occurred after Tellez defended Ultima's honor when he witnessed Tenorio insulting her.

Because of Florence's need for something to believe in and his disillusionment with the Christian God, Tony and Cico decide to tell him about the magic of the Golden Carp. However, when they go to find him, they find out that Florence has just drowned.

After such a tumultuous year, Tony's family decides that it would be good for him to live and work on the farm with his uncles for the summer. While he is there, Tenorio's second daughter dies, and Tenorio decides that the best way to get revenge would be to kill the owl that represents Ultima's spirit. Tenorio succeeds in killing the owl, and nearly kills Tony too before Tony's uncle kills Tenorio. Because the owl has been killed, Ultima dies soon after, and Tony buries the owl according to her directions. Tony describes the shot that killed Ultima's owl by saying, "That shot destroyed the quiet, moonlit peace of the hill, and it shattered my childhood into a thousand fragments that long ago stopped falling and are now dusty relics gathered in distant memories."

Characters

Cico

Cico is a friend of Samuel's who spends most of his time fishing along the river. He takes Antonio to see the Golden Carp.

Florence

Florence, another friend of Antonio's, attends catechism class at church with Antonio. Florence does not believe in God—he attends catechism because his friends are there—and his questions are troubling to Antonio, who does not have answers to all of them. Antonio and Cico decide to reveal the secret of the Golden Carp to Florence so that he will have something to believe in, but Florence drowns before they are able to show him the pagan god.

Horse

Horse is one of the boys from town whom Antonio befriends at church the summer before he begins school. They attend school and catechism class together. Horse is the bully of the group and is always described in terms related to horses: "I could hear the deep sounds a horse makes inside his chest when he is ready to buck"; "He chomped his teeth."

Le Grande

See Ultima

Andrew Marez

Andrew is one of Tony's older brothers. All the older brothers, Andrew, Eugene, and Leon, return from World War II feeling the wanderlust of the Marez blood. They soon leave again, telling Tony that he will have to be the son who fulfills their mother's dreams. Andrew decides to stay for a while and return to school. After refusing to help Narciso to warn Ultima, which results in Narciso's death at the hands of Tenorio, Andrew leaves home as well.

Antonio Marez

Antonio (also called "Tony" and "Anthony"), the main character and protagonist of the novel, is a six-year-old boy who lives with his family just outside Guadalupe, a small village in New Mexico. An intelligent, thoughtful boy, he finds himself pulled between the legacies of his mother's family, the Lunas, and his father's family, the Marez. He is not sure where he fits in, whether it is his destiny to be a farmer and perhaps a priest, which would please his mother, or to be a wanderer like the cowboys of his father's family. In addition, despite a strong belief in the Christian God, Tony begins to question the religion of his mother when he observes the powers of healing held by Ultima, an elderly woman who comes to live with his family and when he is introduced by a friend to a pagan god. Through the course of the novel, Tony witnesses several deaths, encounters grave danger, and gains knowledge of the world that will help him to determine where and how he fits into his family's conflicting expectations.

Eugene Marez

Eugene (Gene) is one of Tony's older brothers. Like Andrew and Leon, he returns from World War II feeling restless. Eugene, along with Leon, leaves Guadalupe while Andrew stays for a time to return to school.

Gabriel Marez

Gabriel, Tony's father, hopes for his sons to become like the *vaqueros,* or cowboys, of his family. He is haunted by lost opportunities of going west to California, where he believes one can still roam free. He sees his three older sons return from war and subsequently leave home, and feels despondent that, being tied down by family responsibilities and a steady job doing highway construction, he is unable to wander with them. Despite his disappointment, he is a loving and devoted father to his children.

Leon Marez

Leon is one of Tony's older brothers. He and Eugene both leave the town shortly after returning from World War II.

Maria Marez

Maria is a deeply religious woman who has high hopes for her youngest child, Tony. She is from the Luna family of El Puerto, which has a long tradition of farming, and she desires that her youngest son will not go the nomadic route of the Marez, as her three oldest sons have done, but that he will become a farmer like her father and brothers. In addition, her most precious hope for him is that he will become a priest.

Narciso

Narciso, seen as the town drunk by the community, warns the Marez family and Ultima when Tenorio is on his way to avenge his first daughter's death. When Tenorio's second daughter becomes ill, and Tenorio threatens to take revenge on Ultima, Narciso attempts to warn Ultima once again. However, he is killed by Tenorio on the path to the Marez home while Antonio looks on helplessly.

Samuel

Samuel is a friend of Antonio's from school. On the last day of school, Samuel tells Antonio about the Golden Carp, a pagan god, which makes Tony wonder, "If the golden carp was a god, who was the man on the cross? The Virgin? Was my mother praying to the wrong God?" Samuel tells Antonio that during the summer Cico will find him and take him to the Golden Carp.

Tellez

Tellez is a man from the Agua Negra ranch whose house is being attacked by ghosts that have been put under a curse by Tenorio's daughters. Ultima rids the house of the curse.

Media Adaptations

- In 1982, Rudolfo Anaya read sections of *Bless Me, Ultima* as well as his novel *La Tortuga* on a sound recording for American Audio Prose Library.

Tenorio Trementina

The owner of a tavern in the town of El Puerto, Tenorio has three daughters who are accused of witchcraft by Tony's mother's family. According to Tony's uncle, Tenorio's wife "made many people of the valley sick, some died from her curses. She paid for her sins, but not before she delivered three brujas [witches] to carry on her work." Ultima cures Tony's uncle of a curse evidently laid by the Trementina sisters, and shortly after this, Tenorio's daughters begin falling ill, and two of them die. Believing (perhaps justifiably) that their deaths are Ultima's work, Tenorio takes revenge.

Ultima

Ultima (also called "Le Grande") is a *curandera,* or healer, whose cures contain elements of Catholicism and Native American mysticism. She comes to live with the Marez family when she is very old and has no family of her own left in her village. Although Tony and his family see her as a benign healer, some in the community are afraid of Ultima because of her powers. She becomes a mentor to Tony, helping him to interpret his dreams and negotiate the dangerous terrain of his quest for self knowledge. After curing Tony's uncle of an evil spell, Ultima engages in a deadly interchange with Tenorio, whose three daughters are believed by the community to be *brujas,* or witches.

Vitamin Kid

Vitamin Kid is one of the boys from town whom Antonio befriends at church the summer before he begins school. They attend school and catechism class together. The Vitamin Kid, the fastest runner in town, is not known by any other name, even to the teachers at school.

Topics for Further Study

- Research the practice of *curandismo* (native healing) in the Southwestern United States, and evaluate Anaya's portrayal of the *curandera* Ultima.

- Discuss the ways in which Anaya uses paired ideas or dualities to develop the themes in *Bless Me, Ultima*.

- Contrast Anaya's depiction of the Catholic belief system with his portrayal of pagan beliefs (as represented by Ultima and the Golden Carp).

- *Bless Me, Ultima* is told from the point of view of the main character, Antonio, who is a six-year-old boy. In what ways does the use of the first-person narrator affect the impact of the story?

- Rudolfo Anaya, in an interview with Feroza Jussawalla, defined the "New World person" as one who "takes his perspective from indigenous history and spiritual thought and mythology and relationships. The New World person is a person of synthesis, a person who is able to draw, in our case, on our Spanish roots and our native indigenous roots and become a new person, become that Mestizo with a unique perspective." Explain how the character Tony fits into Anaya's definition of the New World person.

Themes

Loss of Innocence and Quest for Understanding

A major theme in *Bless Me, Ultima* is the transition from innocence to experience. As a six-year-old boy, Tony is innocent to the ways of the world; however, this quickly changes when he witnesses the killing of Lupito. Through the course of the novel, Tony undergoes many trials that move him from the state of innocence into the state of knowledge and experience.

With his new knowledge of the world, Tony wishes to comprehend *why* the evil things he witnesses happen—he yearns for understanding. He hopes that with his first Communion he will gain the knowledge of God; however, he is disappointed: "A thousand questions pushed through my mind, but the Voice within me did not answer. There was only silence. . . . The mass was ending, the fleeting mystery was already vanishing."

Disappointed with the Christian God's silence, Tony looks to the pagan god—the Golden Carp—and to Ultima's magic to find explanations for the evil he has found in the world.

Search for Identity

Another theme in the novel is Tony's search for identity among the conflicting expectations of his mother's and father's families. Tony's mother's family is the Luna family—Luna means "moon." The Lunas are farmers, and the founder of their family was a priest. Tony's father's family is the Marez family, meaning "sea." The Marez family is made up of *vaqueros* who appreciate the freedom to roam the land. Because her three older sons have gone the wandering ways of their father's family, Tony's mother wishes for Tony to settle down and become a farmer, or better yet a priest.

Tony feels all of his family's conflicting expectations weighing down upon him, and he wishes to find his own identity. Eventually, he discovers the possibility that he might be able to combine both of them when his father explains:

> We lived two different lives, your mother and I. I came from a people who held the wind as brother, because he is free, and the horse as companion, because he is the living, fleeting wind—and your mother, well, she came from men who hold the earth as brother. They are a steady, settled people. We have been at odds all of our lives, the wind and the earth. Perhaps it is time we gave up the old differences. . . . Every generation, every man is a part of his past. He cannot escape it, but he may reform the old materials, make something new.

Clash of Cultures

When Tony goes to school, he is confronted with a new culture: the English-speaking academic world. Although his mother encourages him to be respectful towards his teachers and to become a "man of learning," Tony does not find a mutual respect for his home culture when he goes to school. The other children taunt him because of his language and the food he brings for lunch.

Tony also finds that, despite what he has been taught at home and at church, there is the possibility of more than one source of divine knowledge: he is introduced to the existence of the Golden

Carp, a pagan god. This forces him to question his Christian beliefs. In addition, he witnesses Ultima as she removes curses that the Catholic priests have been unable to do anything about.

In the end, Tony finds that navigating among these divergent cultures is possible when he forges his own identity among them, taking pieces of each to suit his own purposes.

Style

Point of View

An integral aspect of the construction of *Bless Me, Ultima* is the point of view from which the story is told. The novel is narrated by the main character, Tony, who is six years old when the novel begins, and yet who is much more perceptive than a six-year-old—it is clear that the narrator is really an adult remembering and articulating the events of his childhood.

The use of the first-person narrator (who uses "I") means that the reader sees the action only through the eyes of one character, and this sometimes can lead to questions about the reliability of what the reader is told; however, in *Bless Me, Ultima,* Tony appears to be a reliable narrator whom the reader can trust to tell things the way they are and to give some important insights into what is happening.

In this case, the use of the first-person point of view adds to the depth of the novel and is integral to the novel's purpose: to portray Tony's quest for understanding and search for identity. By relating Tony's thoughts, dreams, and unspoken questions from his own point of view, the novel allows the reader to fully participate in his journey.

Language

Tony lives in a household and community where Spanish is the only language spoken, yet he goes to a school where only English is spoken, and the language of the novel reflects this duality. While the vast majority of the novel is written in English, certain aspects of the novel are always in Spanish: the chapter numbers, the cursing within dialogue, and words for which there is no good English translation (such as *curandera*). For readers who are not familiar with the Spanish language, most words can be deciphered within the context of the English words around them; however, a good Spanish-English dictionary might be helpful for literal translations (though many terms are in a re-gional dialect that will not be found in most dictionaries).

Anaya, in an interview with Feroza Jussawalla, states that writing in English came more naturally because he "was brought up and educated in this language"; however,

> Most of us Chicanos in the Southwest are surely bilingual. So it comes naturally sometimes to shift back and forth. But it is more important to use the rhythms of Spanish in our work, the rhythms of Spanish in the Southwest, which is a unique blend of Spanish.

The language used is integral to the novel's impact: it assists in characterization and in creating a realistic setting, where the world in which Tony moves is a heterogeneous mix of cultures.

Setting

In addition to the language of the novel, another way in which the divisions in Tony's life are portrayed is through the setting. On a literal level, the novel takes place in a village in New Mexico, in the Southwestern United States, in the mid-1940s. However, this setting can be seen to represent several divisions or borders.

First, the Marez home is on the outskirts of the village. Tony's mother wanted a house in the village proper, but his father won out, and they purchased some land across the river, on the border of the *llano*, or plains, where farming is hardscrabble but where Gabriel Marez feels close to the freedom of the *llano*. In addition, Las Pasturas and Puerto de Luna are towns in northern New Mexico; New Mexico's southern border abuts Mexico, and Tony's world is affected by the mixture of Hispanic and Indian cultures and Anglo influences. Finally, the time period of the novel reflects a border as well: early in the novel, World War II ends, and Tony's brothers return from the war. The war, though fought a world away from the small village in New Mexico, impacts the lives of the villagers in very real ways: when Lupito returns, he is said to have the "war sickness" and tragedy arises from this. Tony's three brothers return, but they have been introduced to the outside world and are not content to stay in their small village.

Historical Context

New Mexico

New Mexico was a Spanish colony from 1595 to 1821. When the Spanish explored the region, they found permanent communities (as opposed to

Compare & Contrast

- **1940s:** During World War II, the U.S. population, including the people living in New Mexico, is mostly located in small towns and rural settings. In 1940, thirty million Americans live on farms.

  1970s: Following World War II, the population begins moving toward the big cities, as farming becomes more centralized and therefore less practical and profitable for family operations. Others, including many Hispanic Americans, work on the factory-like farms owned by large landowners.

  Today: By the late 1980s, the rural farm population has dwindled to around five million. Today, the trend continues toward a small number of large-scale, corporate-owned farms.

- **1940s:** During World War II, there is strong support for the war effort among Americans. After the Great Depression of the late 1920s and 1930s, the war becomes an economic force that brings the country out of dire economic straits and under a cohesive cause. Thousands of Americans serve the war effort in both civilian and military roles, and those returning from the front receive heroes' welcomes.

  1970s: When Anaya publishes his first novel, the United States is well into its long military involvement in Vietnam. The Vietnam War changes many Americans' ideas about war: it is the first war to be shown on television, and the violence shocks many who are witnessing it from their homes. Additionally, there is widespread discontent, expressed to a large extent by students who are of age to be drafted, over American involvement.

  Today: More recently, the United States has been involved in several shorter military engagements, including the Gulf War in the early 1990s and the United Nations effort in Kosovo. Today, many people expect war to be "cleaner" than it was in World War II and Vietnam since advanced technology has created the possibility of precision-guided munitions. However, casualties are still the reality of war.

- **1940s:** According to the U.S. Census Bureau, in 1940 there are 1.6 million people in the United States under the category "persons of Spanish mother tongue."

  1960s: César Chávez organizes the primarily Hispanic farm workers in California, which leads to a cohesive movement and national awareness of many issues facing Hispanics. By 1970, the population of people with Spanish surnames is reported as 9.1 million.

  Today: The Hispanic population grows by 63 percent between 1970 and 1980 and by 53 percent between 1980 and 1990. Today, Hispanics make up about 10 percent of the U.S. population and 40 percent of the population of New Mexico. The Hispanic population is projected to reach almost 40 million by 2010. With these numbers comes increasing influence in the political arena.

---

nomadic tribes) along the Rio Grande; they called these pueblos after the small villages in southern Spain. They discovered that many of the plants and animals from their homeland could survive in the region—cattle, horses, sheep, goats, chickens, and pigs were among the animals they brought. They also introduced grains such as wheat and barley, fruit including apples, pears, peaches, and melons, as well as vegetables like lettuce, cucumbers, and chiles.

The Spanish found that there was little gold or other precious metals in the region, so the primary purpose of colonizing the area became the religious conversion of the native people. The Pueblo Indians were enlisted to build mission churches in each of the villages. However, the Indians resented the church's suppression of their native beliefs and thought they were being exploited by the Spanish labor policies. In 1680, the Indians revolted and drove the Spanish out of the area.

In 1692, Don Diego de Vargas reconquered New Mexico, but this time the colonizers managed to forge a sustainable relationship with the Pueblo Indians. During this time many communities were established, including the communities in which Rudolfo Anaya would be raised centuries later. These communities blended the culture of the Pueblo Indians with the Spanish-speaking Catholic tradition.

In 1821, Mexico won independence from Spain. In 1846, the region known as New Mexico was claimed by the U.S. during the Mexican War. The area was officially ceded to the U.S. by Mexico in 1848 in the Treaty of Guadalupe Hidalgo. The southern portion was added by a land purchase from Mexico in 1853. In 1863, the Territory of Arizona was created from the western part of the Territory of New Mexico, which created the boundaries of the current New Mexico.

It took 62 years for New Mexico to achieve statehood, most likely because of prejudice against the Catholic, Spanish-speaking culture within the region. However, New Mexico finally became the 47th state in 1910.

As can be seen in *Bless Me, Ultima,* throughout the first half of the twentieth century life remained largely the same in New Mexico's small villages—the descendants of the Pueblo Indians continued to farm the land and to maintain their unique blend of native religious beliefs and traditional Catholic doctrine. Additionally, they kept Spanish as their primary language. However, with the involvement of the United States in World War II, the lives of the inhabitants of the small villages changed irrevocably.

World War II

New Mexico contributed around 65,000 troops to World War II (1939–1945). In *Bless Me, Ultima,* Tony's brothers return from the war and find that, after seeing the world, they are not content to settle down in the small village. Another effect of the war can be seen in Lupito, who is afflicted by the "war sickness," probably post-traumatic stress disorder. Other soldiers, casualties of war, simply did not return. Though the war affected its soldiers differently, each one was affected in some way, and the communities were impacted in turn.

New Mexico also was the site of a unique aspect of the war. Because New Mexico's rugged terrain prevented people from populating large areas, the U.S. government determined that it would be a good location to conduct nuclear research. In 1943, the town of Los Alamos was created by the government to support a nuclear research laboratory. On July 16, 1945, the first atomic bomb was tested near Alamogordo at the Trinity Site. In *Bless Me, Ultima,* the villagers object to the bomb tests south of town, saying, "The atomic bomb, a ball of white heat beyond the imagination. . . . They seek to know more than God Himself. In the end, that knowledge they seek will destroy us all."

Critical Overview

When *Bless Me, Ultima* was first published in 1972, it barely received a blip on the radar screen of literary criticism, despite the fact that it won the Premio Quinto Sol for its literary merit. This critical oversight was most likely due to the fact that the book was published by a small publishing house and was written in a genre that had yet to be accepted by mainstream critics—that of the Chicano coming-of-age novel.

However, by the late 1970s, the novel had been noticed by a few critics. In 1976, Francisco Lomeli and Donaldo Urioste called *Bless Me, Ultima* "an unforgettable novel" and stated that it was "already becoming a classic for its uniqueness in story, narrative technique and structure." Daniel Testa, in the *Latin American Literary Review,* criticized the novel somewhat by calling it stereotypical:

> *Bless Me, Ultima* can be taken first of all as a good action novel, a work in which intense and dramatic happenings make up a considerable part. There are violent fights and deaths. The technique and calculated effects of certain scenes seem deliberately to have been drawn from popular literature and movies that reflect a legendary "wild" west, replete with stock situations and characters. . . . Some of the stereotyped elements used in the work are a Longhorn saloon, a poolroom, a bawdy house, a wise old Indian who lives in a cave, settlers and sheepherders, farmers and cowboys.

Testa went on to clarify that Anaya moves beyond stereotypes "by giving symbolic value to places and objects. . . . Anaya adds to the texture of his narrative by tapping other sources of folklore, legends, mythologies, and cosmologies." Testa was complimentary about Anaya's prose, saying that its intensity "is worthy of the dramatist or the short story writer."

In the 1990s, when *Bless Me, Ultima* was first published in a mass market edition, the novel received more intensive review—and it proved that it could withstand scrutiny and time. Charles Lar-

The first atomic bomb test, performed using the equipment shown here, took place on July 16, 1945, near Alamogordo, New Mexico.

son, reviewing the book for *World & I* in 1994, called the novel "one of the great works of Chicano literature." Larson further stated:

> What I admire most in Anaya's wonderful novel is the fusion of the two worlds out of which he writes. The folk traditions of his people (the holistic reverence for the earth; the healing powers of the curandera, Ultima; the belief that good can only be appreciated and understood when one has experienced evil) are melded into a novel that is stylistically fascinating because it incorporates dreams and visions, folktales, and oral history.

Like Larson, other critics have found much depth in the underlying mythology and traditions in *Bless Me, Ultima.* Some popular themes for critical analysis of the novel have included the Golden Carp, Ultima's blending of Catholic and native beliefs, Tony's dreams, and the religious quest. Acknowledging the caliber of the novel, critics have compared it to such accomplished works as *Moby Dick, The Adventures of Huckleberry Finn,* and *Portrait of the Artist as a Young Man.* Today, *Bless Me, Ultima* has the distinction of having spawned the most critical review of all contemporary Chicano novels.

Criticism

Emily Smith Riser

Riser has a master's degree in English literature and teaches high school English. In the following essay, she explores Tony's search for identity among conflicting forces in Anaya's story.

Rudolfo Anaya's *Bless Me, Ultima* tells the story of a young boy who is forced to grow up quickly amid violence and family turmoil. Six-year-old Antonio "Tony" Marez lives with his family in rural New Mexico, but the remoteness of the setting does not translate into an idyllic or pastoral life. By the second chapter, Tony has witnessed the killing of a man and has begun to question the ways of the world around him, including the way in which his own identity will be defined. In searching for his identity, Tony begins to realize that he must reconcile the many opposing expectations of his family and his community if he is to learn the answers for which he hungers.

Tony's life is fraught with opposing forces. One of the primary conflicts in the novel is the tension between his parents. Tony's father comes from a line of nomadic cowboys who ranged over the *llano,* the plains, never staying too long in any one place: "These were the people of my father, the vaqueros of the llano. They were an exuberant, restless people, wandering across the ocean of the plain." His mother, on the other hand, is a descendant of farmers who settled down and grew crops.

The house in which Tony's family lives represents these two conflicting ways of life: while they have settled onto a piece of land where they have a small farm, they are just on the border of the *llano.* Tony's parents' desires for their son stem from their relationship with the land. His mother wants Tony to be a farmer and maybe even a priest—she says, "I pray that he will take the vows, that a priest will return to guide the Lunas"—while Tony's father wishes that his sons will pull up roots and move west so that he can live vicariously through them: he complains, "Another day and more miles of that cursed highway to patch! And for whom? For me that I might travel west! Ay no, that highway is not for the poor man, it is for the tourist." Tony fears that no matter what he chooses to do in his life, and no matter how he chooses to live with the land, he will be denying some part of his blood.

Another issue encountered by Tony is that of religion. His mother is a devout Catholic, even

What Do I Read Next?

- Victor Martinez's *Parrot in the Oven: Mi Vida* won the 1996 National Book Award for Young People's Fiction. In powerful prose, it tells the story of Manuel Hernandez, a Mexican-American teenager living in a housing project in California, as he comes of age among a battling family and newly emerging passions.

- *The House on Mango Street*, by Sandra Cisneros, is made up of short vignettes about a young girl, Esperanza, growing up in a Latino section of Chicago, dreaming of the life she will have someday.

- Anaya wrote two more novels that, along with *Bless Me, Ultima*, make up his "New Mexican Trilogy": *Heart of Aztlan* (1976) and *Tortuga* (1979). In *Heart of Aztlan*, a man struggles to provide for his family in a barrio of Albuquerque, and goes on a mythic quest in order to help his community. In *Tortuga*, a teenaged boy is admitted to a hospital for crippled children, where he is initiated into a new way of looking at the world.

- *Pocho*, a novel by Jose Antonio Villarreal that was published in 1970, details the experiences of a young Mexican-American boy in California during the Depression who is torn between his parents' values and the ideas found in their new country.

- *And the Earth Did Not Devour Him*, by Tomas Rivera, is considered a Chicano classic. The book, which is not written in linear fashion but rather in layers of anecdotes, stories, and conversations, portrays images of a South Texas migrant worker community after World War II. The primary focus is on one boy's struggle for identity as he recalls being expelled from an Anglo school, the suffering of his family, and religious confusion.

- The 1998 book *Kaffir Boy: The True Story of a Black Youth's Coming of Age in Apartheid South Africa*, by Mark Mathabane, is a nonfiction account of one boy's struggle with racism as he comes of age in South Africa; he succeeds largely through hard work and a strong faith in advancing himself through education.

---

praying that Tony will one day become a priest. Tony himself appears to be devoted to the Catholic faith, attending catechism and taking the priest's words to heart. However, when a friend tells him about the golden carp, a pagan god, the possibility that there is another god besides the Christian one forces him to question his entire world view. He wonders, "if the golden carp was a god, who was the man on the cross, the Virgin? Was my mother praying to the wrong God?" Soon after, he sees the *curandera* Ultima succeed where the priest has failed: "The power of the doctors and the power of the church had failed to cure my uncle. Now everyone depended on Ultima's magic. Was it possible that there was more power in Ultima's magic than in the priest?" In the very next chapter, Tony first lays eyes on the golden carp. When he sees the pagan god, he thinks:

> The power of God failed where Ultima's worked; and then a sudden illumination of beauty and understanding flashed through my mind. This is what I had expected God to do at my first holy communion!

The character of Florence adds to Tony's confusion about religion. Florence, a friend of Tony's, does not believe in God and asks probing questions to which Tony has no answers. When Florence asks, "You mean I can . . . do a million bad things and then when I'm about to die I just go to confession and make communion, and I go to heaven," Tony answers "Yes," but thinks "No, it didn't seem fair, but it could happen. This was another question for which I wanted an answer." Tony prays that he will be given the answers when he takes his first communion, but again he is disappointed: "A thousand questions pushed through my mind, but the Voice within me did not answer. There was only

> It is in learning to combine the many seemingly irreconcilable elements of his life—family agendas, religious beliefs, and language—that Tony will learn his 'own truths.'"

silence." Faced with this silence, among his conflicting beliefs and doubts, Tony is forced to make his own way.

Tony is also caught between two cultural worlds: his Spanish-speaking family and friends, and the English-speaking circle he finds at school. Until Tony first goes to school at age six, he has heard and spoken only Spanish. Suddenly, he is inundated with a new language, new food, and new faces—and the other children are not friendly towards this child whom they perceive as different. Tony must learn to live in both of these worlds if he is to become the "man of learning" his mother envisions.

The structure of the novel helps to reveal the conflicts and ambiguities in Tony's life. For instance, the reader quickly notices that, while the novel is written for readers of English, it helps to have a grounding in Spanish as well: all of the chapter headings are in Spanish, and sometimes dialogue—especially curse words—also is in Spanish, with no translation. In addition, every few chapters the reader finds one of Tony's dreams, demarcated by italics. Again, this gives the sense that Tony is living in two separate worlds; this time, they are the worlds of dream and reality. Through his dreams, Tony sees a combination of the past and the future, and he seems to be working out his understanding of the events in his life. Another way in which the structure of the novel presents Tony's sense of ambiguity is the narrator's voice. Similar to Scout in *To Kill A Mockingbird,* Tony, as first-person narrator, sounds like an adult looking back on his childhood, even though during the events of the story he is a young child.

In the end, the divisive issues in Tony's life, which first seem to threaten his sense of a cohesive identity, actually prove to be his tool for coming of age: they are the catalyst for self-discovery. In the first part of the novel, Tony believes that he must choose between all of the opposing forces, but in the end he comes to realize that he can—and must—blend elements, combine opposites, to become his own person. Theresa M. Kanoza, in "The Golden Carp and Moby Dick: Rudolfo Anaya's Multi-Culturalism," notes that in the character of Ultima, Tony witnesses the merging of pagan and Christian beliefs. Kanoza states that "Recognizing that the disparate elements of creation work in concert, [Ultima] instructs Antonio to respect rather than to fear difference. . . . Her universe, in all its splendid diversity, is coherent, not chaotic."

With the help of Ultima, Tony learns that his mother's religion and a faith in the golden carp do not have to be mutually exclusive, and as an extension of this, he can also resolve his parents' expectations for him. Ultima tells Tony, "I cannot tell you what to believe. Your father and your mother can tell you, because you are their blood, but I cannot. As you grow into manhood you must find your own truths." However, in a dream, Ultima settles a dispute between Tony's mother and father by saying, "You both know . . . that the sweet water of the moon which falls as rain is the same water that gathers into rivers and flows to fill the seas." She is referring to the names of Tony's parents: his mother is a Luna, which means moon, and his father is a Marez, which means sea. Thus, she sums up her point by saying, "The waters are one." To Tony she says, "You have been seeing only parts . . . and not looking beyond into the great cycle that binds us all." It is in learning to combine the many seemingly irreconcilable elements of his life—family agendas, religious beliefs, and language—that Tony will learn his "own truths."

There are several points in the last few chapters of the novel where the merging of these opposites occurs. While traveling to the Tellez home with his father and Ultima, Tony has the realization that he has learned important values from both sides of his family:

> From my mother I had learned that man is of the earth, that his clay feet are part of the ground that nourishes him, and that it is this inextricable mixture that gives man his measure of safety and security. Because man plants in the earth he believes in the miracle of birth, and he provides a home for his family, and he builds a church to preserve his faith and the soul that is bound to his flesh, his clay. But from my father and Ultima I had learned that the greater immortality is in the freedom of man, and that freedom is best nourished by the noble expanse of land and air and pure, white sky.

Interestingly, Tony's father offers a way to reconcile his differences with Tony's mother when he says that "We have been at odds all of our lives, the wind and the earth. Perhaps it is time we gave up the old differences." Tony then realizes that "maybe I do not have to be just Marez, or Luna, perhaps I can be both," and he expands this understanding when he says, "Take the llano and the river valley, the moon and the sea, God and the golden carp—and make something new . . . can a new religion be made?" Tony takes inspiration from the priest who founded the Luna family by realizing that he, too, could change the old ways and create something new.

At the end of the novel, despite Ultima's death, imagery shows that Tony is learning to let the opposites coexist: "Around me the moonlight glittered on the pebbles of the llano, and in the night sky a million stars sparkled"; in other words, the moonlight of the Lunas and the *llano* of the Marez are joined in the cosmos. Tony says that "Sometime in the future I would have to build my own dream out of those things that were so much a part of my childhood." The reader is left with the impression that Tony will be successful in building his dream.

Source: Emily Smith Riser, Critical Essay on *Bless Me, Ultima,* in *Novels for Students,* The Gale Group, 2001.

Cordelia Candelaria

In the following essay excerpt, Candelaria offers an overview of Anaya's work and career, stating that the "evocative power" of Bless Me, Ultima *"lies in the crossweaving of cultural, social, and psychological levels of action to form a seamless, holistic unity."*

Principally because of his first novel, *Bless Me Ultima* (1972), Rudolfo Anaya is considered a major contemporary Mexican-American writer. The book, one of the few Chicano literary best-sellers, appears on high school and college curricula, holds an important place in the landscape of Chicano literary criticism, and (with some of his other novels) has been translated into German and Polish. The book's merit and market success have allowed Anaya to enjoy popularity simultaneously with relative critical acclaim. Since 1972 he has published four more novels and coedited several anthologies.

Anaya was born to Martin and Rafaelita Mares Anaya on 30 October 1937, in Pastura, a village lying south of Santa Rosa in eastern New Mexico. He attended public schools in Santa Rosa and Albuquerque despite an extended hospitalization for a spinal injury he suffered as a youth. He earned a

> **To read Anaya's work is to encounter a preoccupation with, as he describes it, 'instinct and the dark blood in which it dwells.'"**

B.A. (1963) and M.A. (1968) in English from the University of New Mexico, and he also has an M.A. (1972) in guidance and counseling from the same institution. In 1966 he married Patricia Lawless, who is also trained in guidance and counseling. From 1963 to 1970 Anaya taught in the Albuquerque public schools. He left to become director of counseling at the University of Albuquerque. His current appointment in the Department of English at the University of New Mexico began in 1974. He has received numerous awards and fellowships, including an honorary doctorate from the University of Albuquerque, the New Mexico Governor's Award for Excellence, and the President's National Salute to American Poets and Writers in 1980. Perhaps the most important of his honors is the Premio Quinto Sol awarded to *Bless Me, Ultima,* for it was his first national literary honor and a harbinger of later recognition, including grants from the National Endowment for the Arts and the National Chicano Council of Higher Education, and a Kellogg Fellowship.

To read Anaya's work is to encounter a preoccupation with, as he describes it, "instinct and the dark blood in which it dwells." The bringing of instinct to light is both an artistic and a moral imperative for Anaya, who perceives the writer's role in shamanistic terms. He points this out with painstaking care in his gloss to his *The Silence of the Llano: Short Stories* (*The Silence of the Plain: Short Stories,* 1982):

> The storyteller tells stories for the community as well as for himself. The story goes to the people to heal and reestablish balance and harmony, but the process of the story is also working the same magic on the storyteller . . . [who] must be free and honest, and . . . must remain independent of the whims of groups. Remember, the shaman, the *curandero* [folk healer], the mediator do their work for the people, but they live alone.

Anaya is also concerned with integrating into his work the Jungian ideas associated with intuition and feeling. Nowhere in his work is the integration of subjective insight as effective or inspired as in his first novel.

Bless Me, Ultima takes place in the cultural richness of its author's native soil (New Mexico), one of the continent's oldest communities, a point that bears stressing because primal antiquity girds Anaya's mythic worldview. The novel presents the maturation of Antonio Marez, a boy growing up in Guadalupe, a small New Mexico farm village. The book explores his relationship with his spiritual guide, Ultima, a *curandera*. Narrated in the first person by seven-year-old Antonio, the events in *Bless Me, Ultima* unfold as if in the present, but it is soon clear that temporal distance separates the narrator from the experiences he is describing. Anaya achieves this distance by opening the story with the boy's flashback to "the beginning that came with Ultima," a period of time that moves from the year he starts school to the end of the next year when he completes third grade after precociously skipping second. Anaya separates the narrative voice from the events narrated by endowing the narrator—not necessarily the boy in the thick of the plot—with a sensitivity and insight usually reserved for adult maturity. The distancing permits the maturity of the child's vision to work; otherwise the boy's sagacity would strain the reader's disbelief beyond suspension, a concern that has nonetheless bothered some readers.

The moment Antonio's parents welcome Ultima, the *curandera* they respectfully call "la Grande," into their household in bucolic Guadalupe marks the boy's first clear awareness of time and signals the start of his rite of passage from a state of timeless innocence to one of adolescent understanding of the weight of time. On the first page Antonio observes that "the magical time of childhood stood," while in the final chapter he muses, "sometimes when I look back on that summer I think that it was the last summer I was truly a child." Even the vast difference in ages between the boy and the elderly Ultima becomes an emblem of the temporal changes mirrored in the plot as he learns that "things wouldn't always be the same."

In the course of the novel Antonio enters public school where, despite the initial fear of leaving mother and hearth, he quickly excels academically and also successfully engages a social network outside his family. He is catechized into the Catholic church and struggles with his growing dismay at the artifice connected with its hierarchy and bureaucracy. Much of his struggle relates to his discovery of a genuine spirituality and legitimate morality outside the church—in nature, for example, and in the legends told by "Jason's Indian." More traumatically, he encounters four deaths, including two violent killings and the drowning of his special friend, Florence, a young "heretic." Anaya balances the traumas of the deaths with Antonio's participation in the life-affirming *curanderismo* practiced by Ultima. She provides him with the one stable certain part of his life, satisfying both his intellectual curiosity and emotional needs and, as a result, inspiring his spiritual growth as well.

Anaya textures his main story with a subplot focusing on Antonio's life within his family (parents, three brothers, and two sisters). He shares the family's agony over the fate of his three brothers who, in their youthful machismo, appear wayward and irresponsible to him, and he also serves as the central figure in his parents' bitter conflict over his destiny. Embodied in his father's aggressive Marez (i.e., turbulent seas) characteristics and his mother's more subdued Luna (i.e., gentle moon) traits—the wild vaquero versus the settled farmer—the family conflict divides him by tugging his natural loyalties and affections in opposite directions. Ultimately, the evocative power of the book lies in the crossweaving of cultural, social, and psychological levels of action to form a seamless, holistic unity.

Anaya expresses his preoccupation with instinct and blood in the dream sequences which filter and mediate for Antonio the conflicts, violence, and other traumas he encounters. Signaling his intuitive grasp of the importance of his dreams, Antonio continually thinks about them even though his youth prevents his full understanding. Each of his dreams has a noticeable effect on his outlook, conduct, and ultimately on (in Jungian terms) the individuation of his personality. For example, as early as the end of chapter 1, Antonio's recollection is that his "dream was good"; and the disturbing dream at the beginning of chapter 9 leads the story directly into an argument between Antonio's parents and his brothers. Antonio's dreams and their effect on him are an index to his development.

Chapter 14 effectively illustrates the efficacy of dreams to Antonio's self-insight. From the hilarity of a school play plagued by calamities to the horror of Narciso's cruel murder and the apocalyptic furor of the concluding *pesadilla* (nightmare), the chapter obtains its power from the wide range of subjects thrown together with unusually vivid force. By uniting the children's innocent bedlam with Tenorio's sinister mayhem, Anaya sets the stage for the *pesadilla,* the dream apocalypse that will hurl Antonio's entire life before him, "the whole town," the wicked and the good, the sacred and the profane. The nightmare drowns Antonio with "its awful power" as major and minor figures from his life swirl up in a fiery, bloody chaos of symbols. Besides cataloguing various tortures and rituals suffered by his friends and family members, the nightmare also portrays the boy's own "withering" death after which his "bleached bones [are] laid to rest . . . in front of the dark doors of Purgatory."

Important to the novel's ultimate affirmation, the end of the dream shifts the tumultuous horror of the *pesadilla* into a soothing tranquil scene and a healing experience:

> Evening settled over the land and the waters. The stars came out and glittered in the dark sky. In the lake the golden carp appeared. His beautiful body glittered in the moonlight. He had been witness to everything that happened, and he decided that everyone should survive, but in new form. He opened his huge mouth and swallowed everything, everything there was, good and evil. Then he swam into the blue velvet of the night, glittering as he rose towards the stars. The moon smiled on him . . . he became a new sun . . . to shine its good light upon a new earth.

Anaya transmutes the nightmare's chaos, pain, and violence into the surreal beauty of a nature pure and uncontaminated by human strife, a nature preserved in the indigenous mythology and *curanderismo* of Indo-Hispanic—in other words, mestizo—America. By suggesting that good and evil are meaningless abstractions within the timeless power of nature embodied in the night's beauty and the carp's power, the book offers a pantheistic resolution to the nightmare's New Testament-like apocalypse. The story's social realism vanishes into the private realms of dream, fantasy, and primordial legend.

Antonio's dream, like all the others steeped within his subconscious, expresses ideas that he will only fully comprehend in the future when he sets about reconstructing his (and Ultima's) story, and his mature reconstruction enables him to give form to the events which he experienced desultorily as a child. Yet, the boy Antonio intuits wisdom from his dreams. In chapter 15 he shows a more loving tolerance of his father and brothers, and he also exhibits a more realistic acceptance of "the

sons seeing the father suddenly old, and the father knowing his sons were men and going away." Throughout the novel dreams contribute to the individuation of Antonio's personality and the seasoning of his moral character.

Another central area of Antonio's life is his involvement with Jason, Samuel, and Cico, the boys who introduce him to the legend of the golden carp which holds that the fish was once a god who "chose to be turned into a carp and swim in the river where he could take care of his people." The legend at first confuses Antonio because "everything he had ever believed in seemed shaken. If the golden carp was a god, who was the man on the cross? The Virgin?" But he eventually fathoms the legend's message regarding the spiritual force of aboriginal nature: "I knew I had witnessed a miraculous thing," he thinks when the fish swims by Cico, "the appearance of a pagan god . . . ; a sudden illumination of beauty and understanding flashed through my mind. This is what I expected God to do at my first holy communion!" The dream he has that night makes explicit the holistic meaning of the legend which probes "beyond into the great cycle that binds us all." A significant part of Antonio's development apart from his family and Ultima relates to his network of school and friends. Through them he conquers many of the familiar fears common to boyhood, as well as those specific to rural Chicanitos (young Chicanos) like him who are teased for packing tortillas and beans instead of white bread sandwiches for school lunch. They "banded together" and in their "union found strength." Each boy has his special talent that adds to Antonio's expanding repertoire of worldly knowledge and experience, an expansion that edges him outside the family's orbit even as it helps him better to understand his family.

Bless Me, Ultima is essentially an extended flashback told in the first person by an involved narrator. Although it resembles a bildungsroman, the novel is technically not an apprenticeship novel because it is limited to only a couple of boyhood years and does not present Antonio's complete rite of passage to young manhood. Critic Daniel Testa notes that even though "the boy-hero of the story is only eight years old at the end . . . we are convinced that his character has been formed in a radically profound way." If analyzed alongside the main character in Anaya's novel *Tortuga* (1979), the main character of *Bless Me, Ultima* is part of a composite bildungsroman protagonist. Such an approach takes into account Anaya's perception of his first three novels as a "New Mexico trilogy" mak-

Vitamins, homeopathic medicines, and other products line the shelves at the shop of a Mexican curandero.

ing Clemente Chavez and his son, Jason, of *Heart of Aztlan* another resonating part of the character. Antonio's retrospection begins with Ultima's visit, but its depth of insight derives from the artistic process of recalling, ordering, and then sharing the story with others.

Bless Me, Ultima has sold over two hundred thousand copies. Critical analyses and assessments have been extensive and largely favorable. Antonio Marquez asserts that Anaya's work, "especially *Bless Me, Ultima,* has inspired the largest body of criticism in contemporary Chicano literature." Among the noteworthy extended studies are several which discuss the dream sequences in the book. For example, Roberto Cantu perceives the "structure and meaning" of the dream sequences as integral to both theme and plot, whereas Vernon E. Lattin places his analysis of the dreams within the context of the novel's violence and "horror of darkness." Especially illuminating of the work's narration and presentation of time is Daniel Testa's 1977 discussion of its "extensive/intensive dimensionality." Studies which examine *Bless Me, Ultima* within the context of Anaya's entire work are Antonio Marquez's overview in *The Magic of Words* and Cordelia Candelaria's in *Chicano Literature:*

A Reference Guide, which examines his use of Jungian themes. Of more recent interpretations of the novel, Jose Monleon's "Ilusion y realidad en la obra de Rudolfo Anaya" (Illusion and Reality in the Work of Rudolfo Anaya), while negative in its appraisal, is still very effective in its unified treatment of Anaya's three novels. Most of the criticism of this novel praises it for what Antonio Marquez calls "Anaya's imaginative mythopoesis and his careful and loving attention to the craft of fiction."

Source: Cordelia Candelaria, "Rudolfo A. Anaya: Criticism," in *Dictionary of Literary Biography,* Vol. 82: *Chicano Writers, First Series,* edited by Francisco A. Lomeli and Carl R. Shirley, Gale Research, 1989, pp. 24–35.

Carter Wilson

In the following essay, Wilson examines Bless Me, Ultima *outside of its usual characterization as "The Chicano Novel."*

Bless Me, Ultima deserves to be described outside of the implicit claims that it is The Chicano Novel, a category as fishy and as detrimental to any clear thinking about our expectations for fiction as The American Novel category has become. Among other things, the millions of chicanos in the U.S. may feel a unity of ancestry and a community in their oppression, but their experience of life is in no other way unified. . . . The people of the book themselves, small-scale farmers and cowboys, some possessing more than three centuries of history with their removed corner of the world, would not recognize themselves as "chicanos" at all. "Hispano" is what they were first called; "Mexican" is the name most of them call themselves to this day.

The place of *Bless Me, Ultima* is a vast place, and spectacular (which my dictionary coolly defines as "exciting wonder and admiration by unusual display"). At the present moment, most of us probably know it best through the good offices of Georgia O'Keeffe. What we sense in her New Mexico landscapes is that we have arrived at the painting at the very moment of climax in an epic struggle by an after-all puny human force with something we could call Bigness Itself.

A novelist has no recourse, as the painter does, to abstraction. . . . In *Bless Me, Ultima,* Rudolfo Anaya frames his huge landscape and the diverse possibilities for belief through the perceiving of a small boy.

From quite near the beginning of the book it is clear that, though the action will involve other characters, the primary conflict will be the struggle for possession of the boy narrator's soul and his destiny. It is a battle for control of his imagination. The "blessing" asked for in the title of the novel is really that singular benediction we all seek—the one which will give us surcease from endless attachment and disillusion with successive visions of how things are—or, more succinctly, the blessing called faith.

How well Anaya lets us participate in Antonio's conflict is a question we will have to deal with. But there is no doubting as the novelist lays them out one by one the great richness of the choices available to him. . . . Immensity of space seems to permit immense diversity in ways of viewing the world. Through history different peoples have come to live there, but their death, or loss of hegemony, has not caused their ideas of how things are to die. The place where Antonio grows up is like a flea market or back lot of beliefs.

His mother wants him to become a priest. Knowing the vocation planned for him, his school pals anoint him and say their confessions to him.

His maternal uncles hope he will follow them into farming. But if he goes along, ties himself to the land, Antonio almost inevitably will also have to yoke himself to the whole ancient Spanish/Mex-

> " Immensity of space seems to permit immense diversity in ways of viewing the world. Through history different peoples have come to live there, but their death, or loss of hegemony, has not caused their ideas of how things are to die. The place where Antonio grows up is like a flea market or back lot of beliefs."

ican tradition of endless clan feuding and murder, and of the intervention in human affairs through witchcraft. . . .

And then there is Ultima, the solitary old woman of the *llano,* no relation of blood, who is taken into Antonio's family out of respect for her past helpfulness to them and more simply for her generosity of spirit. Others think her a witch. The Marez people understand that all of Ultima's considerable knowledge is devoted only to good causes, to rectification. And of course, as the title of the book predicts, it is Ultima's blessing which takes hold of the boy's imagination. "And that," he says in the end, "was what Ultima tried to teach me, that the tragic consequences of life can be overcome by the magical strength that resides in the human heart."

Bless Me, Ultima is a novel of antecedents. Its fault is a certain impatience. Rudolfo Anaya seems not to have the time to render many things—scenes, feelings—which in patches he shows himself fully capable of doing. The narrator possesses the thinking vocabulary of an adult with its abstractions, but we are given no sense of who this rememberer has become, nothing of the interplay between the man and the boy occupying the same imagination at different levels of understanding. Anaya's second novel, *Heart of Aztlan* is more patiently wrought and, in that sense at least, a better piece of fiction. It is as though in the first book it was necessary for Anaya to establish lineage, lay specific claim to the heritage which would enable him to do what he was bound to do.

Source: Carter Wilson, "Magical Strength in the Human Heart," in *Ploughshares,* Vol. 4, No. 3, 1978, pp. 190–97.

Sources

Gonzalez, Ray, "Desert Songs," in *Nation,* Vol. 259, Issue 3, July 18, 1994, p. 98.

Jussawalla, Feroza, ed., Interview with Rudolfo Anaya, in *Interviews with Writers of the Post-Colonial World,* University Press of Mississippi, 1992, pp. 17–46.

Kanoza, Theresa M., "The Golden Carp and Moby Dick: Rudolfo Anaya's Multi-Culturalism," in *MELUS,* Vol. 24, No. 2, 1999, p. 159.

Larson, Charles R., "Summer of the Curandera," in *World & I,* Vol. 9, No. 8, 1994, pp. 324–30.

Lomeli, Francisco A., and Donaldo W. Urioste, *Chicano Perspectives in Literature: A Critical and Annotated Bibliography,* Pajarito Publications, 1976.

Testa, Daniel, "Extensive/Intensive Dimensionality in Anaya's *Bless Me, Ultima,*" in *Latin American Literary Review,* Vol. 5, No. 10, 1978, pp. 70–78.

For Further Study

Clark, William, "Rudolfo Anaya: 'The Chicano Worldview,'" in *Publisher's Weekly,* Vol. 242, No. 23, June 5, 1995, p. 412.

This overview of Anaya's life and works refers to an interview with Anaya in his New Mexico home.

Taylor, Paul Beekman, "Chicano Secrecy in the Fiction of Rudolfo A. Anaya," in *Journal of the Southwest,* Vol. 39, No. 2, Summer 1997, pp. 239–65.

Taylor discusses the ways in which Anaya uses aspects of two cultures, languages, and traditions to explore secrecy in his fiction. Secrecy is seen as a method of resistance to the dominant culture, an "effective weapon against the tyranny of Eurocentric political, technical, and cultural hegemony."

The Bride Price

Buchi Emecheta
1976

Buchi Emecheta in her novel *The Bride Price* (1976) tells the story of the clash between the traditional customs of a small Ibo village in Nigeria and the ever-encroaching influence of Africa's European colonizers, as seen through the eyes of a young girl. The bride price, a fee that is traditionally paid by the prospective husband's family for the prospective wife, is a theme that weaves its way throughout the novel. Emecheta uses this practice of bride price to literally, as well as symbolically, represent women's submission to men in African culture.

Male domination is not the only theme of this book. Emecheta also looks at the caste system in Nigerian culture that discriminates against descendents of slaves. Slavery in Africa consisted of one tribe kidnapping people from another tribe, then holding them captive and forcing them to work. Sometimes slaves were buried alive with their masters when their masters died. Descendents of slaves, although they were eventually freed under colonial rule, were never considered members of their adopted villages no matter how long they lived there, or how successful they became.

The Bride Price, although fictional, is somewhat autobiographical. The book draws on the events that Emecheta witnessed growing up in Nigeria. It is the third book that Emecheta has published, but it is the first one in which Emecheta offers a hint of hope that both the African woman as well as the descendents of slaves might overcome the potentially debilitating restrictions of their cul-

Buchi Emecheta

ture. Although Emecheta does not overtly criticize the traditional customs of her culture in *The Bride Price,* her writing has been criticized by male African writers for its negative portrayal of Nigerian customs. Despite this, Emecheta has become one of Africa's best-known women writers, and her books continue to investigate the themes of gender discrimination and the effects of caste that were initiated in *The Bride Price.*

Author Biography

Subjugation of women by men is a recurring topic that Buchi Emecheta confronts in her writing. It is a topic that she has experienced first hand not only in a general, cultural context but also in the realm of her personal life at home. At one point in her budding career, Emecheta's husband burned the manuscript of her novel *The Bride Price* in an attempt to stifle her desire for independence.

The road to independence was a long, torturous journey for Emecheta. She was born on July 21, 1944, to Ibo parents in the small village of Yaba near Lagos, Nigeria. Her parents both died when Emecheta was very young. Her adopted parents permitted her to attend the Methodist Girls' High

School until she was sixteen years old. At this point in her life, Emecheta married Sylvester Onwordi, the man to whom she had been engaged since the age of eleven. A year later, Emecheta gave birth to her first child. Shortly after, Emecheta gave birth to her second child and then departed for London to join her husband, who had gone there to study. Six years and five children from the day she was married, Emecheta found herself a divorced woman and a single mother who scrubbed floors to support herself, her children, and her drive to become a writer.

Emecheta had always wanted to be a writer. With this in mind, she used the story of her struggles, her failed marriage, and subsequent hardships of raising a family on her own to write her first book, *In the Ditch* (1972). The story was serialized in the *New Statesman* and was responsible for launching her writing career.

Emecheta's accomplishments (she has written eleven novels, five children's books, several plays, and an autobiography) have made her one of the most important female writers from Africa. Her books, which are published in several countries, have helped to enlighten readers about the role of women in Nigerian culture. This role had formerly been depicted only through the eyes and experience of male writers.

Although female writers are still in a minority among published African writers, traditionally, the art of storytelling was almost exclusively a female role. "In African oral tradition, women were very visible," says Obioma Nnaemeka in "From Orality to Writing: African Women Writers and the (Re)Inscription of Womanhood." Women were not only performers in the art of storytelling, they were also the "producers of knowledge, especially in view of . . . moral(izing) imperatives and pedagogical foundations." Women, through storytelling, recounted tribal histories and thus taught the younger generations how to live. But when the missionary schools were established in the villages, it was only the boys who were educated. Therefore, when it came time to putting stories down in print, it was the men who were first published.

Emecheta, despite the many road blocks in her life, was determined to become a writer. According to Nnaemeka, Emecheta has said that she had to write or else she "would have to be put in an asylum. Some people have to communicate, and I happen to be one of them." Her determination provided the stimulus to propel her through college, where she graduated with honors, and onto a career as a writer.

Plot Summary

Life and Death in Lagos

The Bride Price begins in Lagos, a port city in Nigeria, Africa. The opening scenes move quickly through the events that are about to drastically alter the lives of the Odia family: Ezekiel, the father; Ma Blackie, the mother; Nna-nndo, the son; and Aku-nna, the daughter and protagonist of this story. The setting of the story, a somewhat industrialized urban center, will later contrast with the family's move back to the traditional, agrarian society of the their ancestral village.

Unbeknownst to the mother and children of the Odia family, Ezekiel, the father, is dying. It is his farewell to his children (the mother, at this time, is visiting the country village of Ibuza) that sets the rest of the events in motion. In their culture, a woman without a husband is unable, the reader is told, to take care of herself or her children. The translation of Aku-nna's brother's name reminds Aku-nna of this fact. His name means, "father is the shelter." In Nigerian culture, "the mother is only a woman . . . boneless. A fatherless family is a family without a head . . . a non-existing family."

It is in the first three chapters of the novel that Emecheta covers the transition from Ezekiel's death and funeral to the eventual departure of his widow and children from the city. In the course of presenting this transition, Emecheta informs the reader of some of the major conflicts that she will explore in the remaining chapters of the book. She brings up the concept of the bride price, the woman's role in Nigerian society, the influence of the Ibo customs upon its members, and the clash between these customs and the effects of British colonization.

The name of the protagonist, Aku-nna, literally means "father's wealth." Her name refers to the bride price that her father will receive upon her marriage. "To him," the narrator says, "this was something to look forward to." Aku-nna, at the age of thirteen, is well aware of the meaning of her name as well as her role in her society. She would not let her father down. She would marry well to a man who could afford an expensive bride price. This is Aku-nna's role, as it is the role of every woman in her society. She would bring in wealth to her family in the form of a good bride price. Then she would bring wealth to her husband's family in the form of children, preferably all males.

Unfortunately Aku-nna's father, although he tells her that he needs only to visit the hospital for a short time, is overcome by an infirmity and dies. Aku-nna senses that something dreadful has happened to her father, but she neither is told directly by her relatives, who suddenly appear at her doorstep, nor does she ask direct questions. "Good children don't ask too many questions." Instead, she follows the dictates of her uncles and aunts as they come together to prepare for the funeral rites. She will eventually be told about the death of her father through the traditional art of storytelling.

It is through Ezekiel's funeral and burial that Emecheta first exposes some of the clashes between traditional society and the influences of British colonization. She tells the reader that Ezekiel was buried as he had lived "in a conflict of two cultures." She then relates the burial practices and beliefs of the traditional culture, which have been infiltrated by the belief in heaven and hell as preached by the Anglican ministers. Fearful of offending any of the gods, the Ibo people follow the ceremonial dictates of both cultures.

Return to Ibuza

Ma Blackie, Ezekiel's widow and Aku-nna's mother, returns to Lagos to discover that her husband has died. She had left Lagos to visit her homeland in hopes of regaining her fertility and giving Ezekiel another child. She knows that since she is without a husband, she cannot remain in Lagos and prepares her children for their return to Ibuza.

Ibuza is an agrarian village of Ibo people who "have a reputation for not minding what job they take on, so long as it brings money—a race who are particularly business-mad." It is in Ibuza that Ezekiel's older brother, Okonkwo, lives. Okonkwo already has several wives, but he, by virtue of his brother's death, inherits and eventually marries Ma Blackie. Okonkwo does this while looking forward to the bride price that Aku-nna will bring him. He is an ambitious man who covets the title of Obi, which he can claim if he has sufficient money.

It is in Ibuza, as she is walking toward the village on arrival, that Aku-nna meets Chike Ofulue, her future school teacher as well as her future husband. Chike is also a descendent of slaves, and, as such, friendship between Aku-nna and Chike, according to tribal custom, is strictly forbidden. Through a conversation between one of Okonkwo's wives and one of his children, the narrator states the serious nature of such a friendship. If it is true, as some of the villagers begin to suspect, that Aku-nna and Chike are developing a relationship,

> it was the greatest insult that could befall a family . . . which had never been tainted with the blood of a foreigner, to say nothing of that of the descendants of slaves.

As the reader already knows by this point in the story, the rumors concerning the relationship between Aku-nna and Chike are definitely true.

"Chike would have outgrown Aku-nna," the narrator states, "and maybe she would come to regard anything there might be between them as mere childish infatuation, if the adults had just left them alone." But the adults do not leave them alone. They tell their children what they can and cannot do without giving them much explanation. Aku-nna eventually learns to disregard their admonitions, relegating them to a substandard of "everyday trivia." Having lost her father to death and her mother to a complete immersion into the Ibo culture, Aku-nna feels isolated, alone. Chike is the only one she can turn to. Chike, for his part, is almost willing to forget about Aku-nna. However, he finds himself drawn to her, and when he witnesses the signs of her first menstruation, he is compelled to protect her. When a young woman experiences her first menstruation, it is the signal that she is available for marriage. Chike knows that young men will begin to gather in Aku-nna's house and their fathers will offer her father their bids on Aku-nna's bride price.

When Aku-nna fails to hide her second menstruation cycle from her cousins, it becomes publicly known that she is of marriageable age. Chike becomes aggressive in his protection of Aku-nna from other suitors and assaults Okoboshi, a boy from a neighboring village. Shortly afterward, Okoboshi's family steals into Aku-nna's village and kidnaps her. It is considered fair play for a man to kidnap a woman, thus forcing her to become his wife.

Escape

Using her wits, Aku-nna insults Okoboshi when he tries to rape her on their so-called wedding night. She tells him that she has already been "disvirgined" by Chike. Aku-nna is lying, but Okoboshi is so infuriated that he fails to test her story. Then, with the help of her brother and Chike, Aku-nna escapes from Okoboshi's family.

The last two chapters of the book find Aku-nna and Chike living outside of the village. They have a house, which they furnish, and then both of them secure rewarding jobs. In a short time, they are expecting a baby. This should signal a happy ending, but there is something wrong. Despite several generous attempts by Chike's father, Aku-nna's stepfather refuses to accept a bride price. Aku-nna is well aware of the tribal curse on young wives whose fathers do not accept a bride price: the expectant mother will die in childbirth. In the end, Aku-nna cannot completely step away from the traditions of her people. One of her last statements is that only in death will she win her freedom.

Characters

Okoboshi Obidi

Okoboshi is the young man with a limp who fights with Chike (Aku-nna's future husband) over Aku-nna. Later, Okoboshi's family kidnaps Aku-nna, an accepted village custom, in an attempt to make her Okoboshi's wife. After kidnapping her, Okoboshi tries to "devirgin" Aku-nna. When Aku-nna first sees him after she has been kidnapped, she notices that his smile "had a kind of crookedness about it; instead of gracing the centre [sic] of his face, the smile was drawn lopsidedly towards one of his ears. It was the smile of an embittered young man. He hated her, that much she could see."

Okoboshi attempts to force Aku-nna into having sex with him. He is stronger than she is, but she outsmarts him. She lashes out with verbal assaults to his pride. This scene between Okoboshi and Aku-nna is a pivotal point in the story. It is the first time that Aku-nna takes a very strong position in defending herself, using everything in her power to claim the life she desires, as opposed to the life that her culture has attempted to force on her. Okoboshi, in this respect, represents everything that Aku-nna finds repugnant about her traditionally male-dominated culture.

Aku-nna Odia

Aku-nna, the protagonist in this novel, is thirteen years old and living in the Nigerian city Lagos when the story opens. She is an intelligent young woman who knows, without being told directly, that she is "too insignificant" in the eyes of her parents. She is, after all, only a girl. She is also thin and at times very susceptible to disease. Her parents refer to her as an "ogbanje"—a living dead. Her mother often chides her by asking Aku-nna to make up her mind if she is going to live or die. It often appears that the only thing her parents look forward to, in respect to Aku-nna, is the bride price, the price her future husband will pay for her.

Aku-nna, right from the beginning of the story, has many questions about her family, her culture, and her role in society. She thinks about these questions, but she never voices them because in her culture it is considered worse than bad manners to ask them, especially coming from a girl. But it is these questions that drive Aku-nna throughout this story. She is on a quest for answers.

As if life in Lagos, which was still somewhat determined by traditional Ibo culture, is not troublesome enough, upon her father's death Aku-nna is forced to face even stricter interpretations of those traditions when she is taken back to the family's ancestral village, Ibuza. There Aku-nna is often criticized because of her modesty. She does not like bathing in the nude in public. She is also criticized because she is allowed to continue her schooling. But it is her friendship with Chike, a descendent of a slave, that is her final undoing.

It is with Chike that Aku-nna feels the most comfortable in asking those questions that have haunted her. She identifies with Chike's role, which is both part of the Ibo culture and yet strangely removed from it at the same time. Chike is her teacher in more ways than just at the missionary school that Aku-nna attends, and she falls in love with him. But to say that her relationship with Chike is her final undoing may be too simple. There are more complex factors involved.

By the time Aku-nna turns fifteen, she has grown accustomed to things in the Ibuza village. She learns about the European ways at school and goes home and faces the "unchanging traditions of [her] own people." Yet she is never able to make herself feel comfortable in either culture. Both Aku-nna and her brother are like "helpless fishes caught in a net: they could not . . . go back into the sea, for they were trapped . . . yet they were still alive because the fisherman was busy debating within himself whether it was worth killing them." In the end, it is Aku-nna's inability to free herself from the tangled net of her culture that, at least on a symbolic level, causes her death.

Ma Blackie Odia

Ma Blackie is a tall, dark-skinned woman. As is typical for an African woman, she is held responsible for not having given her husband, Ezekiel, more than two children, only one of which is a son. The novel begins with Ma Blackie, the mother of Aku-nna and Nna-nndo, leaving her family. She has gone back to her native village, Ibuza, to strengthen her fertility.

After her husband's death, Ma Blackie is adopted by her deceased husband's older brother and must take her children back to Ibuza. Ma Blackie is not the only wife of this brother, but she gratefully takes her place in his family, eventually becoming pregnant with the brother's child.

With life in Ibuza grounded in traditional customs, Ma Blackie does her best to comply with what is expected of her. She also tries to discipline her children so they, too, will be accepted and not become an embarrassment. If her children do not comply, it will appear to the villagers, Ma Blackie's relatives, that she has spoiled her children. When one of her children breaks any of the norms of village life, Ma Blackie is quick to publicly humiliate them. Ma Blackie often uses a harsh tone of voice with her daughter, as Aku-nna attempts to free herself from the subjugation imposed by the Ibuza tribe.

At first, Ma Blackie considers herself lucky that her children have turned out so well. She is a clever businesswoman, and with some of the money her husband has left her, she is able to save herself from the more physical chores required of other village women. She is also considered one of the elite of the village because she can afford to send her children to school.

In the end, Ma Blackie tries her best to save her daughter. Despite the fact that her new husband divorces her because of the shame Aku-nna has brought on his family, Ma Blackie attempts to counter the curse that this husband has placed on her daughter's life. She exits the story in a mix of cultural confusion, paying a witch doctor to counter her second husband's curse and then praying to the God of the Christians to help her through the delivery of her new child.

Ezekiel Odia

Aku-nna's father, Ezekiel Odia, is physically present only in the first few pages of the story. He has suffered from an ailing foot since serving the British troops in World War II. His death is the catalyst for all the dramatic changes in Aku-nna's life. Emecheta uses the father's funeral to introduce the culture clash between the Anglican rituals of the

Christian belief system and the native rituals of the Ibo tribe.

Although Ezekiel dies, his presence is felt throughout the story as Aku-nna constantly wonders how her life would have been different had her father lived. Had he lived, she would have grown up in Lagos, a city whose culture is more modern than the traditions of her country relatives. But Ezekiel, however citified, still maintained many traditional ways. He was caught in the middle of his African traditions and the ways of the Europeans. While he had his marriage blessed in the Anglican Church and served in a local Christian organization, he still sent his wife to the traditional gods of his people in order to increase her fertility, so she could give him another son. Ezekiel, after all, had paid a high bride price for his wife, and he believed he had a right to more sons. Had he lived, Aku-nna's life may have not differed as much as she imagines.

Aku-nna accepts the knowledge that her father favored sons. She knows that "she was too insignificant to be regarded as a blessing to this unfortunate marriage." Ezekiel pitied Aku-nna because she was small in build and light in color. But her name, which meant "father's wealth," he gave to her, "knowing that the only consolation he could count on from her would be her bride price." Ezekiel's final words to his daughter are: "Always remember that you are mine." This statement is later repeated by Chike, Aku-nna's future husband, symbolizing that an African woman always belongs to a man: her father at birth, her husband upon marriage.

Nna-nndo Odia

Nna-nndo Odia is Aku-nna's younger brother. His presence in this story serves as a reference point rather than as a character. Emecheta uses Nna-nndo in several instances to illustrate the differences between the roles of male and female children in traditional Ibuza society. Once their father has died, one of Aku-nna's aunts points out that it is a pity that Aku-nna's relatives will marry her off as soon as possible in order to pay for Nna-nndo's schooling. As the relatives are burying the father, they turn to Nna-nndo, the "man" whom his father (Ezekiel) has left behind, asking Nna-nndo to decide if Ezekiel is to go to heaven as a Christian or go down into the earth to the Ibuza god. Nna-nndo, younger than Aku-nna, seals his father's afterlife fate. In contrast, Aku-nna's only role at the funeral is to cry longer than her brother, because women were expected to show more emotion.

Later in the novel, Nna-nndo plays out the brief role of intermediary when Aku-nna is kidnapped. Nna-nndo brings a note to her from Chike (Aku-nna's future husband). Nna-nndo is the only person in the Ibuza village that understands and respects his sister's relationship with Chike. His loyalty is rewarded when Aku-nna and Chike, married and living away from the village, bring Nna-nndo to their home so that he might be better nourished, both physically and intellectually, than he would have been in the Ibuza village.

Nna-nndo is at Aku-nna's bedside as she is dying. She tells him not to worry. Her death has bought both of them freedom. And then, in a somewhat ironic twist, Chike tells Aku-nna that the infant she bore is a girl, and according to Ibuza lore, girls are "love babies." Aku-nna's last words are:

> 'Now, with our little girl, everybody will know. They will all know how passionately we love each other. Our love will never die.'

In some ways, this seems to negate the preference for male children, which Nna-nndo represented, that was held over Aku-nna's head for most of her life.

Okonkwo Odia

Okonkwo is the elder brother of Ezekiel Odia. Unlike his younger brother, Okonkwo has lived his entire life in the village of Ibuza. Okonkwo represents the embodiment of male domination and tradition in Emecheta's *The Bride Price*. It is Okonkwo who adopts Ma Blackie and her children when Ezekiel dies. But before his brother's death, Okonkwo displays his authority even over Ezekiel.

> 'If Ezekiel blames you for going back without finishing your treatment,' Okonkwo tells Ma Blackie, 'tell him I said you were to do so. Remind him, in case he has forgotten, that I am the eldest and first son of our father. It is for me to say the word, and for Ezekiel to obey.'

In the remaining story, Okonkwo does not change. He is the lord of his house and family, and he does not bend. Tradition and power are Okonkwo's masters.

The reader is told in the beginning of the story that the people of Ibuza have a "group mind." They come together to "help each other when in trouble or in need. . . . They are a people who think alike, whose ways are alike, so much so that it would not occur to any one of them to behave and act differently." Okonkwo is the epitome of this way of thinking. Coming from this state of mind, this long-held tradition, it is very difficult for Okonkwo to adjust to Aku-nna's rebellion.

But Okonkwo is not a simple man. He is clever and ambitious. He has his eyes on the red cap, the symbol of having achieved the high position of Obi, a place of honor among the Ibo people. In order to achieve that position, Okonkwo needs money, and Aku-nna's bride price would come at just the right moment. This money, though, would have to come from one of the well-to-do men in the village that Okonkwo chooses. With the title of Obi in sight, Okonkwo does make some small concessions. He does not force Ma Blackie into wearing rags for one year, the sign of a mourning widow. He allows Aku-nna to go to school, although it is Ma Blackie who pays Aku-nna's tuition. However, he is determined not to have Aku-nna go to college. He is also determined never to allow her to marry a descendent of a slave. In the end, he could not stop it.

When Aku-nna runs away and marries Chike, Okonkwo not only will not accept a bride price from Chike's father, he also divorces Ma Blackie by exposing his bare backside to her in public, a village custom. Still enraged by the disgrace that Aku-nna has caused, he forgets about the title of Obi and decides to vent his anger directly on Aku-nna. Okonkwo makes a small doll in the exact image of Aku-nna in an attempt to punish her through a slow and painful death. It is Okonkwo's power, or the power of her people's traditional beliefs, that Aku-nna feels pulling her toward her death.

Chike Ofulue

Chike Ofulue is the young man whom Aku-nna eventually marries. Chike is also the descendent of a slave. His grandmother, Obi Ofulue, had been a princess in one African tribe, then was kidnapped by another tribe and turned into a slave. When missionaries appeared in the village, slavery became illegal, and most slaves were turned over to the missionaries and educated. Thus, the former slaves, as well as their descendents, became the educated people of the village, taking on the roles of doctors, lawyers, and teachers. Despite their education and professional roles, the local villagers never accepted these descendents of slaves into their culture. And so it was for Chike and his family. They were tolerated, but there were strict taboos on how far relationships with these outsiders could go.

"You must be careful," one of Aku-nna's cousins tells her, referring to Chike, "that man . . . he's not one of us. No decent girl from a good Ibuza

family is allowed to associate with him. My father would rather see his daughter dead than allow such a friendship." And so Aku-nna is introduced to Chike. Chike's family does not fare much better. Chike's father warns him to stay away from Aku-nna, as his father does not want "a son of mine to bring shame on his [Aku-nna's step-father's] family."

"It is said," states the narrator, "that stolen water is sweet." This comment sums up the feelings inside Chike who defies both his father and the customs of his adopted village as he refuses to be told what to do in matters of the heart. Chike is drawn to Aku-nna's innocence and intelligence. He also is drawn to her dependence. He nurtures her through her school lessons, helps her understand her first menstruation, and protects her, as much as he can, from the traditional customs that offend her.

When Aku-nna is kidnapped, Chike realizes how much he loves her. He becomes determined to rescue her and, finally, make her his wife. Chike is a gentle man who provides Aku-nna with every comfort she needs. He is a gentle lover, who understands his wife's fears. He is an intelligent and sensitive young man who tries, in vain, to appease the customs of his former village by urging his father to pay the bride price. But he is helpless in his attempts to save his young, pregnant wife's life.

Themes

Gender Roles

One of the main themes in Emecheta's *The Bride Price* is the difference, in the Nigerian culture, between the roles of women and men. There are many incidents in this story concerning the gap between the privileges of men compared to those of women. It is taken for granted that if a boy wishes to go to school and his family can afford it, he will go. It is an exception, especially in the Ibuza village, for a girl to go to school. Even if she does attend, her education stops when she is married, usually around the age of fourteen.

The greatest difference between men and women, however, concerns the act of marriage. If a bride price, for instance, is accepted by the father of the girl, the young woman would have to go to the suitor's home and be married no matter whether she knew the suitor, liked the suitor, or had fallen in love with another man. Her father's decision is final. Also, a man who could not afford a bride price might "sneak out of the bush to cut a curl from a girl's head so that she would belong to him for life," and he would be able to "treat her as he liked, and no other man would ever touch her."

Sexuality is another area where the customs dictate different rules for both sexes. Young single men who have affairs with married women are tolerated through an intentional blindness on the part of an aging husband. If an old husband cannot satisfy the sexual needs of his many wives, "they knew better than to raise a scandal. In Ibuza, every young man was entitled to his fun." On the other hand, "A girl who had had adventures before marriage was never respected."

The most devastating inequality between men and women, however, is the lack of self-worth. "Aku-nna knew that she was too insignificant to be regarded as a blessing." She is a girl, and a marriage is not considered fortunate unless a man has sons. A woman's worth is measured only in the amount of money she might bring to her father in the form of a bride price.

Slavery and Oppression

Slavery is depicted straightforwardly in the character of Chike, who comes from an *oshu* family, a slave family. Although his grandmother had been a princess in a neighboring village, she was kidnapped and enslaved. After the Europeans came to Nigeria, slavery became illegal. The freed slaves were sent to missionary schools where they were educated. Although the freed slaves and their descendants eventually earned high professional salaries and owned big European-style homes, they were never accepted into the village. A father would rather kill his daughter than have her marry an *oshu*.

Emecheta uses the theme of slavery, however, not just in terms of the *oshu*. She also portrays women, in a sense, as slaves to men. A woman is bought and sold through the bride price. She is looked over, by her new owners, like a slave trader might look at his new slave. Her body becomes a commodity that will bring wealth to the family in the form of many children. After being kidnapped, Okoboshi's father "poured chalk, the symbol of fertility, on her breasts and prayed to his ancestors that Aku-nna would use it to feed the many children she was going to have for his son."

Defiance and Resistance

Defiance of the rigid rules of society rises slowly in this novel through the character of Aku-nna. It comes to her in small steps and bolts out of her in fits of fear or embarrassment. First, out of fear she speaks her mind and very decidedly re-

fuses to accept a ride on a bicycle. Next, out of embarrassment she refuses to take off her clothes and bathe in public. Little by little, she builds up her resistance until she finds herself involved in a relationship with Chike, the descendent of slaves, a relationship that is strictly forbidden. By encouraging this relationship, Aku-nna defies her mother and her stepfather, as well as the social laws of her entire culture. But even though she encourages the relationship, her defiance is passive, as if the relationship were growing on its own with Aku-nna tagging along behind it. She moves closer to Chike almost involuntarily. In one incidence, she wants to stop him from saying that their relationship is impossible, and she covers his mouth with her hand "not knowing where the boldness which was working inside her came from."

As the story builds to a climax, so does Aku-nna's courage build. Her courage, in turn, builds her defiance. After Aku-nna's menstruation has become public knowledge, she refuses "point-blank" to eat the chicken that has been slaughtered in her honor. At this point in the story, Aku-nna registers what very well might have been her first defiant thought. "She was beginning to feel that it was unjust that she was not to be allowed a say in her own life, and she was beginning to hate her mother for being so passive about it all." Her mother's passivity seems to awaken Aku-nna's defiance, and from this stage in the story, Aku-nna moves toward the climatic scene.

As she stands in front of Okoboshi, the young man who has kidnapped her as a potential bride, Aku-nna loudly and forcefully speaks out in an attempt to save herself. It is out of fear of not only being raped but also of being deprived of ever seeing Chike again that she finds her voice and creates a story so vile that Okoboshi leaves her alone. The vile story that she creates is a lie, but the lie represents the epitome of her defiance. She tells Okoboshi that she is not a virgin; and, furthermore, she lost her virginity to a descendant of a slave. In so doing, Aku-nna risks everything, possibly even her life.

> Her uncle would surely kill her on sight . . . but if she was forced to live with these people for long, she would soon die, for that was the intention behind all the taboos and customs. Anyone who contravened them was better dead . . . and when you were dead, people would ask: Did we not say so? Nobody goes against the laws of the land and survives.

That is how much courage it takes for Aku-nna to be defiant.

Topics For Further Study

- The beliefs of the Ibo people embraced both the traditional gods of their ancestors, as well as the Christian rituals of the European colonizers. Look over the passages that cover the death and burial of Ezekiel Odia. How do these belief systems work together? Where do they clash?

- Aku-nna and her brother, Nna-nndo, are raised according to their gender. What are the major differences in how their roles are defined? Although gender roles in America might not be as rigidly defined and the differences in raising boys and girls may be very subtle, do you think children in the United States grow up with any restrictions based on gender? List these restrictions, however slight, as they might appear, for instance, in the American home, or in teacher expectations in elementary school, or in relationships between young men and young women in high school.

- Ma Blackie is often caught up in her culture's traditions. However, she is an intelligent woman who has lived in the city and her thoughts differ slightly from the other woman in her village. In what ways does Ma Blackie break, or at least stretch, some of the boundaries imposed on her by her village traditions?

- Menstruation signals the emergence of a young girl into womanhood. In *The Bride Price* a traditional ceremony is performed to honor this transition. In American culture, there is little, if any, celebration of this passing from one stage to the other. If you could create such a ceremony, what elements would you include? Think about this transition as a rite of passage and write a description of such a ceremony. How could you use similar passages (like the metamorphosis of a butterfly) to symbolize change? Do you know of a poem that might be read to honor this transition? What role could men play? How might you use music, dance, and costumes?

- There is only slight, overt mention of Europeans and European culture in *The Bride Price*. However, despite the subtle references, European culture is definitely a strong and intrusive issue in this story of the Ibo people. Find passages that make references to the colonial powers. How are the Ibo people influenced by the European culture? Think in terms of the schools, the churches, and the European laws.

- Most of the world is ruled under a system of patriarchy—social organization marked by the supremacy of the male (or father) and the subsequent legal and economic dependency of women and children. The supremacy of the male is defined differently, according to various cultural standards, but the basic tenet remains the same: the male dominates the female. Compare the Ibo cultural standards to American standards. How do they differ? Are there any ways in which the patriarchal rules of the Ibo culture work to the advantage of the Ibo women? Are there any ways in which the Ibo women might have advantages over American women?

- The offering (the bride price) that an Ibo male must give the family of his intended bride could be looked at, as well as criticized, as an archaic form of purchasing a woman. However, the American (or European) tradition of buying an expensive diamond ring as a sign of engagement might similarly be looked at, as well as criticized, as another form of purchasing a woman. Are there any differences between the two traditions? What if you compared these traditions from a different point of reference such as Europe in the eighteenth or nineteenth century when arranged marriages were still prominent? What if you compared them in terms of European royalty where marriages were arranged to ensure peace between two countries?

Culture Clash

The clash of culture is first seen in the funeral scene in the opening chapters of the novel. Ezekiel, Aku-nna's father, lives somewhere between the two cultures, and, upon his death, his son must decide whether Ezekiel will go to the European (Christian) heaven or to the ancestral earth gods of the Ibo people. When his son chooses heaven, the narrator explains that the mourning women approve of the decision because "the heaven of the Christians was new, and foreign; anything imported was considered to be much better than their own old ways."

An even more significant, as well as more serious, clash in cultures is the infirmity that causes Ezekiel's death. Ezekiel was called to do his duty in the European war, during which he performed menial and dangerous tasks that the Europeans "could not bear." While standing for countless hours in the swampy fields of Burma, something happened to Ezekiel's foot. Although the cause is unknown, his foot never heals and eventually causes his death.

Europeans, at one time, encouraged slavery in Africa, but "suddenly stopped buying slaves and turned into missionaries instead." The missionaries, in turn, took in the former slaves and educated them. These slaves, much to the disdain of the traditional villagers, eventually went on to become the doctors, lawyers, and teachers in the community. They gained power, if not in the traditional hierarchy of the village, at least in the village's economy. Toward the end of the novel, Chike's father, a former slave whose wealth was based, in part, on a large plantation of cocoa beans and coconuts, wakes up one morning to find that all his plants have been cut down. With European law on his side, the courts find the guilty parties, who turn out to be the traditional villagers, retaliating against the marriage of Chike and Aku-nna. Despite the fact that "the whole of Ibuza came forward as witnesses against" Chike's father, the European law forces the village people to compensate the former slave. "The free men had to plant new cocoa for the slave." This does not improve relationships, the narrator states, and curses are "heaped on the family."

Style

Foreshadowing

Emecheta foreshadows many of the issues that she will eventually present in the body of the story. For instance, in the first chapter, Aku-nna's father,

in his farewell, tells Aku-nna to "always remember that you are mine." This statement foreshadows both the claim of Aku-nna's stepfather that will be held, literally, over Aku-nna's life, as well as the more sentimental version of this statement that Chike will voice in his attempts to express his love for Aku-nna.

In the second chapter, Emecheta discusses the group mind of the Ibuza people as they come together to take care of Aku-nna and her brother upon her father's death. This group mind, in this incident, is beneficial. However, it is the group mind that will eventually push Aku-nna toward her own death, as she is forced to leave the village. The group mind would rather see her dead than see her happily married to a former slave.

Aku-nna's father lived and died in what the narrator defines as "a conflict of two cultures." In the third chapter, Ezekiel is mourned and buried while the Ibo people, his relatives, try to decide whether to rely on their traditional beliefs or to take up and lean upon the newer, European customs. In this way, Emecheta foreshadows yet another conflict that is woven throughout the story: the clash between traditional and foreign definitions of law and custom.

Aku-nna's eventual defiance of her parents' traditional ways is foreshadowed by her refusal to take off her clothes and bathe in public upon her arrival in the village of Ibuza. Later, her defiance becomes more overt when she refuses to eat the ceremonial chicken that has been sacrificed in honor of her first menstruation. These actions foreshadow her climatic escape from her kidnappers and eventual denial of her culture when she marries a former slave.

Early in the story, Aku-nna is referred to as an *ogbanje,* or living dead. She is a child who picks up diseases so easily that her mother begs her "to decide once and for all whether she is going to live or die." Later in the story, Aku-nna's relatives also refer to her as an *ogbanje,* foreshadowing her untimely death.

Myths

The Bride Price is colored with stories of African mythology. The first is presented in the opening pages, as the reader is told that Ma Blackie, Aku-nna's mother, has returned to her ancestral village to "placate their Oboshi river goddess into giving her some babies." The river and goddess were a gift "to all Ibuza people from the greater gods. It was the right of all Ibuza's sons and daughters to come to have themselves cleansed by the river whenever they found themselves in difficulties." There is another story about the river goddess who had claimed the lives of hundreds of young Ibuza girls as they were crossing the swollen river on their way back from the market. The myth resolves the tragedy by conveying the thought that the young women "had been chosen to serve at the court of the beautiful goddess of the river." After mourning these young women, according to the myth, their mothers became pregnant. When most of these women gave birth to girls, it was believed that the river goddess had replaced "the ones she had taken."

There is also a god of the river that Aku-nna finds herself praying to when she crosses the river while in the midst of her second menstruation.

The myth of the *ogbanje,* or the living dead, is mentioned. Aku-nna is labeled with this name early in the story. One of Okonkwo's wives explains the fate of someone who is an *ogbanje.* "They are only in this world on contract, and when their time is up they have to go. They all die young, usually at the birth of their first baby. They must die young, because their friends in the other world call them back."

Metaphor

Emecheta uses extended metaphors in this story. The first exemplifies the conflict that Aku-nna and her brother feel, caught, as they were, between traditional culture and European customs. She creates an image of fish caught in a net, referring to Aku-nna and Nna-nndo as

> helpless fishes . . . [who] could not as it were go back into the sea, for they were trapped fast, and yet they were still alive because the fisherman was busy debating within himself whether it was worth killing them.

In another, longer metaphor, Emecheta has Aku-nna and Chike sitting under a tree, watching a group of brown ants.

> No single ant deviated from the main column, all followed the same route one after the other, as if at the command of a power invisible.

With this metaphor, Emecheta uses the ants and their willingness to follow that invisible power as an example of the people of Ibuza following the traditional ways without questioning the reasons behind them. When Aku-nna asks Chike why the ants are following one another, Chike responds: "Because each ant would be lost if it did not follow the footsteps of those in front, those who have gone on that very path before."

Aku-nna's death could be read as a metaphor. Why did she die? Was it because she was too young and malnourished as suggested by the doctor? Or was it because her stepfather, in vengefulness and voodoo-like practice, calls her spirit back home? If her death is looked at as metaphor, it plays out the main conflict of the story. Inside of Aku-nna, the clash between the European (scientific) world and the African (traditional) world ultimately lead to her death. Aku-nna's death acts as metaphor for all young African women who struggle with the new culture that cries out for independence and reliance on self, and the old culture that thinks with a male-dominated, group mind. Her death is symbolic of the psychological deaths that these women must pass through in an attempt to be reborn into a new role for themselves.

Emecheta, however, reminds the reader that contrary to this interpretation of the metaphor of Aku-nna's death, the villagers used it differently. Instead of freeing the women, the story of Chike and Aku-nna became a metaphor for death—a death with no heaven on the other side. "Every girl born in Ibuza after Aku-nna's death was told her story, to reinforce the old taboos of the land. If a girl wished to live long and see her children's children, she must accept the husband chosen for her by her people, and the bride price must be paid."

Historical Context

Politics

Lagos, the port city and at one time the capital of Nigeria, was given its name by the Portuguese who settled in Nigeria as early as the sixteenth century. It was out of Lagos that the Portuguese exported their flourishing slave trade. The Portuguese maintained control over the city until 1861 when the British took control and eventually abolished the trade. In the early 1950s, Nigeria was still under British control with a British governor ruling from Lagos.

Villages, especially among the Ibo people, usually consisted of scattered homesteads called compounds. Each compound housed a man, his immediate family and some relatives. A number of compounds made up a village that was usually populated by people all claiming a common ancestry. Each village had a chief who was, on the whole, left alone to rule his village in a traditional manner. There were, however, European officers, nearby, who guided the chiefs. Sometimes this guidance included influencing the choice of a chief based not on the qualifications of the candidate but rather on the ease with which the British could manipulate him. The British, in an attempt to prevent united opposition to its authority, kept Nigerian groups separated, using their chosen chiefs to help them in this effort.

Just prior to the 1950s, Nnamd Azikiwe, an Ibo man, joined Herbert Macaulay (called the father of modern Nigerian nationalism) to establish the National Council of Nigeria and the Cameroons. African men trained as soldiers in World War II, as well as restless youths, market women, educated villagers, and farmers, joined the National Council to protest the British tax laws and to demand political representation. Eventually succumbing to the pressure, the British gave up control, and Nigeria was granted independence on October 1, 1960.

Pre-Colonial Times

Before the colonization of Nigeria, traditional Ibo people were not united as a single tribe but rather lived in autonomous local communities. A typical village might include as many as five thousand people who could, in some way, trace their lineage back to the founder of the village. Linguists, who have studied the Ibo language, believe that some of these villages may have existed in the same location for as many as four thousand years.

Although the village was traditionally ruled by men, the people believed in common deities that included both gods and goddesses. Also, both men and women farmed, with women's work seen as complementary to the man's. Many women were, in fact, economically independent. Women were expected to give birth to many children, hopefully sons, to ensure the future of the group, but as she grew older, the woman received assistance from younger wives who took care of the children, so the older wife could farm and make crafts, thus allowing her the opportunity to achieve impressive economic status.

In the oral tradition, women were prominent storytellers. These stories were peopled with women characters as heroines and founders of great dynasties and civilizations. The women not only performed the stories, they also composed new stories or transformed old ones in order to incorporate a woman-centered perspective on village life. Women storytellers were also known to use political story-songs or abusive songs as forms of social control.

Colonial Times

European colonization influenced village life in many areas. There was the introduction of Western style education, the English language, and Christianity, as well as new forms of money, transportation, and communications. The Europeans also brought with them the Victorian concept that women belonged in the home, nurturing the family. With this concept came the emphasis on the man as the primary source for the economic stability of the family. It became the man's sole responsibility to grow cash crops like yams, while the woman was relegated to growing only subsistence crops that brought in less money. In addition, cheap goods from Japan and Europe were imported, thus diminishing the demand for local craft work that had, before colonization, been another source of income for the African women.

Victorian colonizers praised and encouraged the creation of a social and political hierarchy that privileged Nigerian men. One of these privileges was the encouragement that boys received to attend school. With males graduating from school in far greater numbers than females, it was not surprising that the first voices to be heard in Nigerian literature belonged to men. Stories, from that time, that concerned Nigerian women were always interpreted through the vision of the man. The first few women who emerged on the literary scene thus used male literary themes as their role models. Some Nigerian women were very active, during this time, in organizing protests against the colonial influences.

Independent Nigeria

Nigeria is marked by great differences not only in physical landscape and climate, but also in social organization. To the north, Moslem communities thrive. While the central area is sparsely settled and is the least developed part of Nigeria, the southern area, in contrast, is the most economically developed and is dominated by three distinct groups of people: the Yoruba to the west, the Edo in the center, and the Ibo people to the east.

After gaining independence from the British in 1960, these ethnic, as well as economical and educational, regional divisions caused very serious problems for Nigeria. Each region fought for power, fearful of domination by the others. Stress from ethnic competitiveness, educational inequality, and economic imbalance between the regions caused a breakdown in government, which ultimately led to the need of military control. Assassinations, ethnic

Compare & Contrast

- **Pre-Colonial Times:** Traditional rule is centered in the village with the chief as the head. Women affect decisions due to their strong economic status.

  Colonial Times: Due to the influence of European standards, women are subjugated to a domestic role and ruled by the male leader of the family. Although chiefs retain some autonomy in the village, they are overseen by local, European-based, government officials.

  1960: Nigeria is given full independence.

  1967–1970: Ibo people unite, secede from Nigeria, and form the country of Biafra until their surrender in 1970, when they are reintegrated into Nigeria.

- **Pre-Colonial Times:** Traditional religions based on multiple gods and goddesses prevail.

  Colonial Times: European influence brings Christianity to the Ibo people. During this time, a mixture of Christian and traditional Ibo religions prevails, although Europeans try to outlaw the traditional practices.

  1980: The majority of Ibo people are Christians, although some traditional beliefs still linger and are practiced openly. The practice of traditional religion is no longer illegal.

- **Pre-Colonial Times:** Children in the Ibo culture are trained to carry on their adult roles according to gender. Young boys learn about the agriculture of specific crops through apprenticeship training. Young girls learn their roles, which include agriculture and crafts from the women of the village. They also learn how to rear the younger children. There is no formal educational system.

  1843: The first missionary school is established in Nigeria. Girls are discouraged from attending.

  1914: There are fifty-nine government elementary schools, ninety-one missionary elementary schools, and eleven missionary secondary schools in all of Nigeria.

  1950: A three-tiered school system is established that includes: primary, secondary, and post-secondary schools. Over one million children attend elementary schools throughout Nigeria; thirty-six thousand attend secondary schools with 90 percent of this group coming from the southern portion of Nigeria (where the Ibo people live).

  1980: Forty-seven percent of all children attend school, and over one hundred thousand go on to college.

- **Pre-Colonial Times:** Women have the capability of gaining impressive economic status. Women's work is complementary to men's work. Through the help of younger co-wives, older women are free to work in the market, selling their produce and crafts. Women are blamed if they did not produce children; male children are the preferred gender. When a woman marries, she has less influence in her husband's family than his mother and his sisters. Single women (whether never married, divorced, or widowed) are looked down upon.

  Colonial Times: Male supremacy is encouraged. Economic status of women declines as they are not allowed to grow cash crops and are discouraged from working outside of the home.

  1980s: Although polygamy is still practiced, the support of co-wives has diminished. In 1982, a national feminist movement is inaugurated, and it calls for the abolishment of polygamy. However, the general population of Nigerian market women are against this decree. Although laws have been created to protect women's rights, women rarely receive any of their husbands' property upon their husbands' death. Single women are easily exploited economically with their property often being sold without their consent.

massacres, and a further breakdown in military rule eventually lead to an attempt of the Ibo people in the East to declare secession from the rest of Nigeria. On May 30, 1967, the Republic of Biafra was created. A war ensued over the next two years between Biafra and the ruling Nigerian government, leading not only to heavy casualties, but also to a plea by the Biafran government to the international community for food. The Ibo people were starving. On January 11, 1970, Biafra surrendered to government officials in Lagos.

Nigeria was subsequently divided into twelve different states to ease the ethnic tensions, but by 1976, the year that Emecheta published *The Bride Price,* civil rule had not returned to Nigeria.

Critical Overview

There is a great discrepancy between how Buchi Emecheta's book is received and reviewed inside her own country of Africa and outside of it. There is also a discrepancy between how African male and African female critics review her work. The discrepancy goes so far, in some instances, that the criticism becomes lost in a void of silence.

Female writer Professor Osayimwense Osa, for instance, in a 1996 essay published in *Research in African Literatures* declares that *The Bride Price* is a "masterpiece of African children's and youth literature that sophisticated younger readers will find as satisfying reading." Writing from a great distance from Africa, male critic Richard Cima in the *Library Journal,* says that Emecheta "in addition to presenting a fast-moving story with characters the readers can care about, the author gives a fascinating picture of pre-independent Nigeria."

The Bride Price is a "captivating Nigerian novel, lovingly but unsentimentally written," says Valentine Cunningham in the *New Statesman.* Emecheta creates "a world of ballad-like simplicity, enlivened by tenderly beautiful descriptions." Cunningham also states that Emecheta has proven herself, with the creation of this book, as a "considerable writer."

But Rosemary Bray in the *Voice Literary Supplement* (as quoted in *DISCovering Authors*) declares that "Emecheta is a prophet without honor." In other words, Emecheta is speaking out of the silence that male African writers have created in reference to the African woman. Emecheta is also speaking into a silence, in some regards, as the audience for whom she most wants to write—African women—often do not have access to her books.

Both the silence and the lack of honor multiply the closer Emecheta's work is examined, especially when it is examined under the microscope of feminism by male African critics. African literature has until recently been void of any female voice. Even today, African literature is dominated by male writers who have tended to depict female characters as being completely satisfied with their lives and their subjugation to African men. The emergence of female writers, such as Emecheta, challenges these male assumptions that include not only the female's submission to the male but also her approval and pleasurable response to that submission. Therefore, it is understandable that these African male writers do not like the image of the African women that Emecheta creates. Katherine Frank in *World Literature Written in English* claims that Emecheta's novels "compose the most exhaustive and moving portrayal extant of the African woman. She exposes and repudiates the feminine stereotypes of male writers and reveals the dark underside of their [male African writers] fictional celebrations of the African woman."

Emecheta's books, if not totally ignored or overlooked by African male critics—who dominate that country's writing—are criticized, in general, with a negatively charged tone. Cynthia Ward, in her article "Emerging Perspectives on Buchi Emecheta," puts it this way: Emecheta's "work has been and continues to be a catalyst for passionate debate over issues concerning the role of African women within their societies, cross-cultural experiences of gender and identity-formation, African 'patriarchy,' the responsibilities of the artist to her nation and culture and even what constitutes the canon of African literature: several African literary critics have pointedly excluded Emecheta from the list of African authors, claiming her viewpoint is not representative of African women." Ward goes on to say that much of Emecheta's literature is judged a "literary success or failure according to a notion of 'politically correct' behavior."

Obeonia Nnaemeka, writing in her essay "From Orality to Writing" states that male critics "often insist upon setting moral standards for these writers [Emecheta and a handful of other female African writers] with the result that any character who deviates from established expectations is heavily descended upon, condemned and disparaged." For instance, says Nnaemeka, one male critic, Taban Io Liyong, responds to Emecheta's hints of feminism in her writing with the comment: "I suspect that feminism may destroy that which up to now has enabled Africa to withstand all the buf-

Female members of the African Ibo tribe

feting from other cultures." Emecheta, by instilling a desire in her protagonist toward selfhood, in other words, is setting up the circumstances for a breakdown in African culture.

To male critics, feminism is a dangerous thing, but they forget, say Nnaemeka, that "historically, feminist activism has always been a part of the African women's experience. Although non-conformist characters continue to be marginalized," in novels like Emecheta's *The Bride Price,* the "inevitability of change is never in doubt." Emecheta belongs to the second generation of African female authors. Their (written) voices have been silenced for a long time. The first generation of female au-

thors did little more than mimic the writing of their male African predecessors. But storytelling that was told in a female voice has a long history in Africa. It is with Emecheta that the historical feminine voice is finally emerging in print.

Criticism

Joyce Hart

Hart is a freelance writer and former editor of a literary magazine. In the following essay, she looks at how feminist and postcolonial literary the-

> The Other refers to the concept of establishing a norm, then relegating everything that is not the norm to the sidelines where it becomes the Other."

ories define the Other, how Emecheta's novel demonstrates this categorization, and how her protagonist, Aku-nna, attempts to resist it.

Reference to the Other is used both in feminist and postcolonial literary theory. The Other refers to the concept of establishing a norm, then relegating everything that is not the norm to the sidelines where it becomes the Other. To make this a little clearer, in a patriarchal society, man is considered the norm. Everything is defined in terms of the masculine. In general, all who have masculinity as their biological trait are given power, priority, preference, and privilege. In other words, man is what is defined as important. Women, on the other hand, become the Other or the unimportant. They are categorized as the powerless and, thus, they are marginalized. Feminist literary theorists examine the marginalization of women that occurs in literature when man, or the patriarchy, is set up as the norm.

Postcolonial literary theorists examine the marginalization of groups of people who have been colonized by outside powers. In this case, it is the outside powers that have set themselves up as the norm. For example, when the Europeans descended on Nigeria, European law prevailed over traditional rules. European languages were used in schools. Schooling was based on the educational standards of Europe. European religious beliefs were ingrained in the minds of the indigenous people while the traditional practices were simultaneously outlawed. A postcolonial literary theorist looks at the ways in which the indigenous people, as well as their traditions, have become the Other.

In a colonized country like Nigeria, the setting of Buchi Emecheta's *The Bride Price,* this concept of the Other becomes even more complex. The indigenous people, as they prepare for independence (and, thus, enter a postcolonial era) have been changed. They have lived under colonial rule for many generations, and now they must decide what will become the new norm: what they have become under colonial rule or what they once were.

All these elements play themselves out in Aku-nna, the protagonist in *The Bride Price.* Relegated to the role of the Other by both the colonial powers and her patriarchal society, Aku-nna, once she becomes aware of her own marginalization, resists. Slowly she learns to vocalize her thoughts, which, in the beginning of the book, are heard only inside her head. It is through this development of her voice as she moves from daughter to wife, from city girl to country woman, from prepubescent teen to mother, that the reader gets a sense of how it feels to be the Other, and what it takes to resist and, hopefully, break down the confines of that role.

From the outset of this story, Aku-nna is still steeped in her traditional role. She wants to make her father proud of her and is determined to marry well so as to bring her father a good bride price. Once that issue is settled, she would first have her marriage "solemnised [sic] by the beautiful goddess of Ibuza, then the Christians would sing her a wedding march . . . then her father Nna would call up the spirits of his great, great-grandparents to guide her." This is Aku-nna's dream.

In the beginning, Aku-nna is very silent. Although concerned about her father's health and his aberrant behavior, she wants to question him, but she keeps her thoughts to herself because in "Nigeria you are not allowed to speak in that way to an adult, especially your father. That is against the dictates of culture." In the beginning, Aku-nna does not question those dictates.

There is a hint of tension building in Aku-nna, but that tension is not totally conscious. It is still quiet, like Aku-nna's voice. When questions build up inside of her, she reminds herself that "good children don't ask too many questions." When her father does not come home for supper as he had insinuated he would, she relaxes with the thought that in her culture her "neighbors would look after them . . . in that part of the world everyone is responsible for the next person." But Aku-nna feels betrayed by her father when she discovers, through her uncles, that he is not coming home, that he, in other words, has lied to her. It is the narrator's voice that must inform the reader about certain facts concerning the culture that Aku-nna herself has not yet learned. The narrator states that Aku-nna's people think with a "group mind." Not only do they think alike, but it "would not occur to any one of them to behave and act differently." Upon reflection,

Aku-nna forgives her father for lying to her. "He responded as much as their custom allowed—for was she not only a girl?"

It is during her father's funeral that the realization of being fatherless dawns on Aku-nna. "Nobody is going to buy you any more [clothes]," an aunt tells her. Then the aunt turns to another woman and says, "The pity of it all . . . is that they will marry her off very quickly in order to get enough money for Nna-nndo's [Aku-nna's brother] school fees." Then turning back to Aku-nna, the aunt continues, "This is the fate of us women. There is nothing we can do about it. We just have to learn to accept it."

With these thoughts stirring in her head, Aku-nna accepts her fate and leaves Lagos and her former life and returns to her parents' ancestral village. As she walks down the dusty road toward her village, a cousin tells her stories about village life, realizing that Aku-nna knew little about the customs of her people. Listening to the tales that her cousins relates, Aku-nna exclaims, "It's just like the stories you read in books." It is as if she has distanced herself from her own life, not yet realizing that she has become one of the characters in those books. It is also along this road that the first hint of rebellion expresses itself when Aku-nna stands her ground and refuses to take the bicycle ride that is offered her and then, later, refuses to undress to take a public bath. These are small discretions, but nonetheless they are Aku-nna's first steps toward asserting her opinions.

Once she reaches the village, Aku-nna watches as the women, who only minutes ago were laughing, immediately begin to cry. This abrupt change is Aku-nna's introduction into village life. At this point, although she thinks it strange that the women can change their emotions so quickly, she is resigned to join in. "After all, she was going to be one of them," she says. With this statement, it is apparent that Aku-nna is still trying to understand her role and accept the restrictions within it.

Two year pass between Aku-nna's arrival at the village and the next chapter in the story. Aku-nna is fifteen and attending school. Her education "by the Europeans," plus the fact that she has not yet had her first menstruation, set her apart from most of the other girls. In the meantime, Chike, the young man who is the descendent of slaves, falls in love with Aku-nna. He falls for her because "he had never seen a girl so dependent, so unsure of herself, so afraid of her own people." It is through Chike that Aku-nna learns to voice her thoughts

What Do I Read Next?

- *The Slave Girl* (1997), by Buchi Emecheta, as the title suggests, is about a young slave girl living in and dealing with Nigerian culture in the early part of the twentieth century. She is eventually freed when a man purchases her as a bride. Her freedom is in concept only, as she becomes her husband's property.

- Buchi Emecheta's *The Joys of Motherhood* (1979) takes place in Lagos, Nigeria. It is a story that continues along the same lines as Emecheta's *The Bride Price* (1976). It tells the story of the suffering of women in a male dominated culture caught in the clash of change as Nigeria works toward independence. Emecheta's own move toward unorthodox female characters intensifies in this novel.

- Jamaica Kincaid, who grew up in the Caribbean, writes a story about a 19 year old young woman who must leave her island homeland to work in the United States as an au pair. *Lucy* (1990) is the story of a young black woman struggling to find her own identity.

- In *Liliane: Resurrection of the Daughter* (1994), Ntozake Shange reveals the complexities of Liliane's life as she struggles against racism and bigotry in the United States. This story also deals with Liliane's angers and frustrations in dealing with the loss of her mother, as well as her relationships with her father and close friends.

- Zora Neale Hurston's *Their Eyes Were Watching God* (1937) is a tale about the challenges that face a young, black woman living in the American South. It is a coming-of-age story in which a young woman flees from a pre-arranged marriage and struggles to create an acceptable understanding of life.

- A young Haitian woman, Sophie, from Edwidge Danticat's *Breath, Eyes, Memory* (1994), is sent from Haiti to live with her mother in New York. Sophie's relationship with her mother is a key issue in this story, one that she does not fully comprehend until she finally returns to her homeland.

and gains the strength to resist the customs of her people. Her voice is still very quiet. She talks in secret to Chike. The reader is left to ponder whether she would have gained her voice at all had not a man been there to encourage her.

The first strong voice, although it is described as "faint and whispery," comes out of Aku-nna when Chike brings her things to help her through her first time of menstruation. They make slight sexual passes at one another, and when Chike asks what she thinks they should do about their forbidden relationship, Aku-nna responds: "Tell my people that you want to marry me." Chike is taken aback, but Aku-nna, gaining strength in both body and voice, covers his mouth with her hand "not knowing where the boldness which was working inside her came from." These actions and this voice are coming out of Aku-nna as if they did not belong to her. She seems to know neither the source nor the reason for them. "I always say the wrong thing, do the wrong thing. You are the only person I know who I am not afraid of." It is because of Chike that Aku-nna can speak. But her voice is still not strong enough. She is asking Chike to speak for her.

On her second cycle, the news of Aku-nna's menstruation goes public. Aku-nna realizes that from this point forward everything will be different. When the young girls around her begin to prepare her for the reaction to this news—the young men and their fathers bargaining a bride price with Aku-nna's stepfather—Aku-nna begins to understand more of the complexities of her newly embraced womanhood. She will soon be forced to marry, and her people will never consent to her marrying Chike.

> Little by little, the warm joy she had felt only minutes before seeped away. How could the world be so blind? Could not everyone see they [Aku-nna and Chike] belonged to each other? She had never felt so strongly about anything in her life.

It is through her love of Chike that Aku-nna discovers her hidden strength as well as her hidden self. Her wanting Chike is the first time that Aku-nna has admitted that she has a self. When she refers to the world being blind, it is her first awareness that this female self, in a patriarchal culture, has been defined as the one without power; in other words, she is the Other. It is not that the world is blind, but rather that the female self, in the male-dominated culture, has been made metaphorically invisible.

Despite her awareness of her position in her society and her impulse to resist her culture, on her way home from the fields, Aku-nna is afraid of dishonoring the god of the river by stepping into it while she is menstruating. This scene predicts the dilemma that will haunt Aku-nna until the end of the novel. Try as she must, she cannot rid herself of her culture.

When she returns home from the river, her stepfather (the "voice of authority, that authority which was a kind of legalised [sic] power") delineates Aku-nna's marginalized position, in case she had not yet figured it out for herself. She must marry according to his decision; and she must stop seeing Chike. "He was telling her, not in so many words, that she could never escape. She was trapped in the intricate web of Ibuza tradition. She must either obey or bring shame and destruction on her people."

Ironically, it is at this moment when she feels most trapped that Aku-nna also asserts her most independent and rebellious thought. "She was beginning to feel that it was unjust that she was not to be allowed a say in her own life, and she was beginning to hate her mother for being so passive about it all." Although Aku-nna is still not taking her life into her own hands, she is at least coming closer to doing so. First, she wanted Chike to stand up and speak for her. Now, she is berating her mother for not doing so. At this point, Aku-nna, at least, sees potential power in a female.

Aku-nna breaks with tradition by refusing to eat the chicken that has been slaughtered in her honor. However, she bows to tradition in the custom of allowing young suitors to fondle her breasts. She takes two pills that "deadened the pain," prays to God (possibly the Christian God, this time) to take her life if she should have to marry a man other than Chike, then goes out to meet the young men. Her protest against their groping and against the fear and anger that she experiences is a silent falling of tears. The masculine, in the form of Chike's fists, step in to rescue her. Once the tears are dry, Aku-nna again silently questions her role in her society. "What kind of savage custom was it that could be so heartless and make so many people unhappy?" When her mother, again, turns against her, Aku-nna reaches for Chike's hands.

Shortly after, when Aku-nna is kidnapped, it is not until she hears Chike's whistle, coming from the bushes, that "her numbed mind came alive." From that point on, she uses her own wits to save herself from being raped. An unrecognized voice rises up from somewhere deep inside of her.

> Maybe she was mad, because when later she re-membered all that she said to Okoboshi [her newly intended husband] . . . she knew that the line divid-ing sanity and madness in her was very thin. Out came the words, low, crude words, very hurtful and damaging even to herself.

This is the pivotal moment, the climax of the story. Aku-nna has figured a way to play the tra-ditions of her people against themselves. She makes up a story, telling Okoboshi that she is not a vir-gin. Not only has she taken away from Okoboshi the privilege of "devirgining" her, she has insulted him and his family by claiming that she lost her virginity to Chike. Since tradition has determined that this act with a descendent of a slave is taboo, Aku-nna has won a temporary victory. She has de-layed the rape by insulting Okoboshi. Although this sets up her ultimate escape to freedom, this is not the end of the story.

Chike, once again, rescues Aku-nna. And she, in the moment of victory, takes "refuge in passing out completely." The patriarchy may have changed faces, but, again, the masculine is the strength, and the feminine is the weakness. The two outcast char-acters, both marginalized into roles of the Other, leave the village and the traditions behind. Or do they?

At first it seems that joy has come into their lives. They live in a nice home, they buy nice fur-niture, they find jobs and are very happy. So happy are they that Aku-nna becomes fearful and again prays to the European God because too much hap-piness has come too quickly to them. And both of them pray to God every night to help them through Aku-nna's subsequent pregnancy. But it appears that the European God has been marginalized by the traditional deities. Aku-nna's stepfather, that voice of law, has called on the ancestral gods to curse Aku-nna because she has rebelled against his authority. She has disgraced him to such a degree that he refuses the bride price, multiplied many times over, offered by Chike's father.

Remembering that narrative passage from the beginning of the book, the one that describes what psychologists call the group mind—the mindset that demands all members of the tribe to think as one—brings this story full circle. "It would not oc-cur to any one of them to behave or act differently." The existence of the tribe depends on this. So when Aku-nna, more so than Chike who is even more marginalized than she, tries to think independently,

she finds that it is far more difficult than she imag-ined. She could run away. She could marry the man she loved. But she remains in bondage to the tra-ditional ways of her people. Her mind is connected to the group mind. And it is the group mind that sentences her to death.

It is interesting to see that the only hope of freedom in this story comes from being born so far out on the edge that tradition no longer cares about who you are or what you do. Aku-nna's baby girl is that hope of freedom. Aku-nna has paid for her child's freedom with her own life. That freedom, despite the high cost, is not, however, totally un-hindered. That child is still a female living in a pa-triarchal society whether or not she is accepted by her people. The independence comes to her at the price of not only losing her mother but of losing her grandmother, aunts, cousins, and all the men folk of the Ibuza village. To maintain that freedom, she must, as Emecheta herself must, remain an ex-patriate, possibly visiting her relatives but never living there. She lives so far out on the edge of the Other that she barely exists in terms of her own culture.

Source: Joyce Hart, Critical Essay on *The Bride Price,* in *Novels for Students,* The Gale Group, 2001.

Katherine Fishburn

In the following essay excerpt, Fishburn ex-amines narrative intention in The Bride Price *and how a Western reading of the text could result in an incomplete understanding of the novel.*

Narrative Intentions

Returning to the issue of narrative intention, the question raised by the ending of *The Bride Price* then becomes the following: toward what goal has this novel been oriented? Or, more specifically, what direction do *Western readers* expect this novel to take? Does this expectation help us un-derstand the novel, or does it interfere with under-standing? For those of us who were trained to find patterns in literature by Northrop Frye's *Anatomy of Criticism,* I would argue that the tacit assump-tions we bring to *The Bride Price* virtually ensure that we will (try to) read it as New Comedy. This mode, according to Frye, is commonly centered on "an erotic intrigue between a young man and a young woman which is blocked by some kind of opposition, usually paternal, and resolved by a twist in the plot." Although the blocking agents initially govern society, a new society emerges at the end "after a discovery in which the hero becomes

> " A Western reading would assume that tradition had somehow failed Aku-nna because it punished her for being herself. But the narrator's concluding remarks cast doubt on this interpretation. It will be recalled that the first time Emecheta wrote this book, the story ended with Aku-nna and Chike 'living happily ever after, disregarding their people.'"

wealthy or the heroine respectable." As we can see from the following outline, for most of Emecheta's novel this comic pattern holds true—just long enough for us to expect a happy ending. But, ultimately, the narrator disappoints our expectations: first by failing to redeem the hero, then by killing off the heroine and apparently agreeing that it is best that she die, and finally by reinstating the power of the old society.

When Aku-nna is thirteen years old, her father dies unexpectedly. Following tradition, Ma Blackie takes her two children back to Ibuza to live, where she marries her husband's older brother. Shortly after Ma Blackie's marriage, the community school teacher falls in love with Aku-nna and begins to court her. [Boy meets girl.] Their love is forbidden, however, because Chike is the descendant of slaves. [Outside interference tries to keep them apart.] Though Aku-nna is widely sought after by many suitors, she knows she will be happy only with Chike. Once she becomes eligible for marriage, one of her suitors arranges to kidnap her—which, according to custom, is a legitimate way of getting a wife. [Boy loses girl to outside interference.] To save her virginity after she is captured, Aku-nna tells Okoboshi the lie that she has already had sexual intercourse with Chike. She then finally escapes and runs off with the man she loves. [Boy regains girl.] Her uncle is so enraged by her scandalous behavior that he divorces her mother and re-

fuses to accept the bride price from Chike's father. [Here the comic plot begins to break down.] Aku-nna and Chike love one another deeply, but she never recovers from the fact that her village and family refuse to forgive her. The novel ends when Aku-nna dies giving birth to a daughter whom Chike names Joy. Following Aku-nna's death, the narrator concludes the novel with an extraordinary paragraph, in which she explains that ultimately Chike and Aku-nna reinforced "the traditional superstition" they had been unwittingly challenging. Moreover, she tells us that Aku-nna's death is used by her people as an object lesson to young girls, who are warned not to pick husbands on their own and to make sure their bride price is paid. If it is not paid, they will surely die, like Aku-nna, in childbirth. This cautionary tale, according to the narrator, still carries "psychological" weight today, but why it does is "anybody's guess."

If we have been reading the novel expecting a comic resolution, not only are we astounded by Aku-nna's untimely death, but we are at a loss as to what to make of the narrator's attitude toward it. Are we to mourn Aku-nna and pity her for her foolishness? Is her death tragic? Or is it a necessary punishment for her sins? Should we be glad for her society that its values were upheld? But if, indeed, Aku-nna must die, we expect at least the narrator to be sorrowful over this necessity. When she expresses no sorrow, she challenges us to rethink the genre we have been using to understand the novel. Clearly, the conflict between an individual and her society is more complicated here than we had originally been led (by our own cultural expectations) to believe. A Western reading would assume that tradition had somehow failed Aku-nna because it punished her for being herself. But the narrator's concluding remarks cast doubt on this interpretation. It will be recalled that the first time Emecheta wrote this book, the story ended with Aku-nna and Chike "living happily ever after, disregarding their people." But Emecheta finally concluded that the community's values were more important than a (Western-style) happy ending. So when she rewrote the story, she created a girl who purposely picked "her own husband because she was 'modern' but was not quite strong enough to shake off all the tradition and taboos." Aku-nna is thus destroyed by the guilt she feels for having disobeyed her mother and uncle. This outcome, justifiable as it might appear to Emecheta, troubles most Western readers, however, because of our predisposition to side with these two lovers, who have become social outcasts. It troubles us, in other words, because the beliefs it is based on are embedded in a tradition alien to our own.

At the same time, an obverse reading to the one just proposed—that Akunna fails her people by violating tradition—seems equally questionable since for most of the novel the narrator is extremely sympathetic to this rebellious heroine. Emecheta achieves this sympathy, in part, by narrating the novel from Aku-nna's point of view. The opening scenes, for example, seem calculated to pull on our heartstrings, as we witness first the unusually close relationship between father and daughter—and then see this bond torn apart by the father's unexpected death. In fact, Emecheta's heroines are usually closer to their fathers than to their mothers. Aku-nna's relationship, in particular, seems to symbolize that she would like to take over the role of the father by deciding for herself what she will do. After her father dies, it seems significant that Akunna temporarily loses her voice during the mourning rituals. This double loss (father/voice) suggests that in losing her father she has lost an advocate. At the same time, the death of her father can be seen symbolically as the Death of the Fathers; for once she has regained her voice, she "speaks out" against the Will of the Fathers by going against tradition. But hers is an ill-fated rebellion, soon silenced by the Voice of Tradition. What happens here is similar to what Peter Brooks describes as happening in Balzac's *La Peau de chagrin* (suggesting that some European fiction can, indeed, help us understand Emecheta's novels). When the father dies, Brooks argues, "the Name-of-the-Father—the father as prohibition, law, 'morality'—emerges only the stronger, to be submitted to in full abnegation, or else rejected in a total revolt." Aku-nna's rebellion fails, as we see later, because she is incapable of marshalling the resources needed for the total rebellion Brooks identifies. But before the failure becomes manifest, Aku-nna does seem to be assuming her father's protective mantle.

Once Aku-nna moves to Ibuza, for example, she becomes convinced that she will have to help take care of her mother and thinks she might be able to do so by becoming a teacher. She recalls sadly at this point that her father had wanted her to have more education. But this same loving father has named his daughter "Aku-nna, meaning literally 'father's wealth,' knowing that the only consolation he could count on from her would be her bride price." What the narrator means by "consolation" is not entirely clear, however. Does Ezekiel need consolation because he is disappointed that

Aku-nna is not a son? Or does he need it because he will lose Aku-nna to another man? Or both? Whatever the meaning, Aku-nna herself is not upset by the arrangement. In fact, she only hopes she will not be a disappointment to him. Our sympathy for Aku-nna deepens after her father's death, when we see how ill at ease she is in her new surroundings. Though Ibuza is the village of her ancestors, Aku-nna is so unfamiliar with the customs of her people that one of her young relatives chastises her for her ignorance. Her mother is not much help either. It is not only ignorance but also shyness that makes the transition hard for Aku-nna. Not having been raised in Ibuza, for example, she cannot understand why it is acceptable for men to see her bathing naked in the stream or for her suitors to play roughly with her breasts. These customs are also alien to Western readers, who probably have much the same reaction to them as Aku-nna. Perhaps we sympathize with her as much as we do because she is like us in being unfamiliar—and uncomfortable—with Ibuza customs.

For his part, Chike makes a perfect Western hero. He is a handsome, charming, reformed rake who is absolutely devoted to his new love—treating her with kindness and compassion when everyone else ignores her. Perhaps the most touching scene in the novel occurs when Aku-nna gets her menarche during school. She is in pain and embarrassed, but Chike is so gentle and tactful that she lets him take care of her. After giving her an aspirin, he loans her his jacket so no one can see the blood on her dress; later he brings her a supply of sanitary napkins with a little booklet explaining what to do—all this from a man whose culture still teaches that a menstruating woman is unclean. It is no wonder Aku-nna falls in love with Chike. We practically do ourselves. Our sympathy only intensifies when it becomes clear that Chike and Aku-nna will not be allowed to marry because his ancestors were slaves. To us, this is a prohibition that makes very little sense. But the villagers and the narrator insist that for her "to marry the descendant of a slave would be an abomination." Class differences we might be able to accept (especially if we were British), but this goes beyond class. Chike, in fact, comes from a wealthier (and better-educated) family than Aku-nna. Nor would we regard marriage to the descendants of slaves as an abomination. Such events occur without censure—or comment—all the time in our culture. In sum, Western readers have trouble anticipating—and accepting—the ending of *The Bride Price* because the narrator focuses so much attention on Aku-nna and Chike's courtship ritual. In watching them meet and gradually fall in love, we ourselves become emotionally involved in their relationship—especially as they have to contend with the older generation's prohibitions. Illustrative of the difference between African and Western readings is Chikwenye Okonjo Ogunyemi's description of Aku-nna and Chike's relationship. Where I as a Western reader enjoy the emotions evoked by their touching love story, Ogunyemi dismisses the "sentimentality evoked by the lovesick couple." How, then, are we to read this novel? Since our Western comedic genre is not particularly useful, we need to ask if we have any other genres that might do a better job of helping us understand Emecheta's novels.

Epic or Novel?

Bakhtin makes several distinctions between the epic and the novel that are useful to Western readers trying to understand Emecheta's fiction. The epic he associates with the "absolute past" and the power of tradition because it speaks in the monologic voice of unquestioned authority. The novel, on the other hand, "is determined by experience, knowledge and practice (the future)." Its dialogic (competing) voices speak in "unofficial language and unofficial thought." In short, where the epic is a closed genre reflective of what has already occurred, the novel is open—to the present and the future. As such, the novel is almost by definition a progressive genre. Since we in the West believe that Chike and Aku-nna would do no lasting harm to society by falling in love and marrying, at first glance "epic" seems a more suitable term to describe *The Bride Price* than "novel," as it certainly appears to valorize the past and to reaffirm tradition. Because we value individual rights over community rights and because we cannot take seriously the taboos surrounding the descendants of former slaves, we think Chike and Aku-nna should be free to marry. From our perspective Aku-nna's punishment by death is unwarranted, unmotivated, and implausible. To us, this ending is reactionary, invoking the archetypal endings of an absolute past when heroines were not free to do and become what they wanted.

But if we read the novel from more of an Africanized perspective, the ending, while perhaps not very progressive, does not seem to be particularly reactionary. It is conservative in that it does reestablish the old society, but Aku-nna and Chike's transgressions apparently threaten the very fabric of village life—as is evident in the villagers' response. In revenge for Aku-nna's behavior, for example, the Ofulues destroy all the vegetation on the plantation owned by Chike's father, and Ma Blackie's new husband divorces her. Though we in the West are horrified that Aku-nna must die to reaffirm her people's tradition, the narrative suggests that the sacrifice of this individual rebel is necessary for the well-being of the community. In her death, moreover, Aku-nna signals that she has accepted the importance of tradition. Because these traditions can be quite flexible, Ward argues that it is not necessary for Aku-nna to accept them blindly. But Alasdair MacIntyre, another student of tradition, sheds a different light on the situation when he argues that because an individual is part of an ongoing (narrative) history, she becomes, consciously or not, "one of the bearers of a tradition"—an assertion the novel seems to support. For even though Aku-nna might have felt initially that her actions were her own and thus of little interest to the community, she soon comes to realize that she herself is the community, that what she and Chike do affects everyone, not just themselves. After trying to make a life for herself, she realizes that she can live only within the community that raised her. Her death therefore becomes a symbol for the fact that she has finally accepted her role as a bearer of her people's African traditions.

But for us in the West to see that the ending of *The Bride Price* is not necessarily so tragic, we have to be able to foreground our own prejudices—and listen to the competing voices that, in Bakhtin's terms, make this more a novel than an epic. Whereas the monologic epic has a "singular belief system," the dialogic heteroglossia of a novel makes for multiple competing belief systems. Bakhtin finds, moreover, a correlation between what a character does and says—with the one informing the other ideologically. In the dialogic or competitive environs of a novel, unlike the monologic world of epic, the hero's discourse is constantly being challenged, leading Bakhtin to argue that the "idea of testing the hero" may be the single most important "organizing idea in the novel." Here Bakhtin distinguishes between "authoritative discourse" and "internally persuasive discourse"—which I invoked in my discussion of Adah Obi. Authoritative discourse originates externally in religion, politics, and morality. It is, therefore, associated, like the epic, with the authority of the past and treated like "the word of the fathers. . . . It is akin to taboo." Internally persuasive discourse reflects the ideology of the individual character, but, in direct contrast to authoritative discourse, it carries no status in society. Within a novel (but never an epic), these two kinds of discourses engage one another dialogically in the consciousness of a single character, helping to form his or her belief system. In what I will then call Emecheta's *novel,* the struggle between Aku-nna's internal discourse and the authoritative discourse of her African fathers can be seen most readily in how the hero/heroine copes with the pressures of tradition. Though Aku-nna listens to her own internal discourse and finds the courage to reject certain traditions, others she dutifully accepts.

Let us first look at the customs Aku-nna accepts, those that have to do with menstruation—the symbol of her womanhood that signifies her marriageability. She begins with a minor rebellion that she is unable to sustain. Because she does not want her family to arrange a marriage for her, she keeps the fact of her menarche secret for two months. She reveals her secret to her friends only when she needs to consult with them whether it will be permissible for her to cross a stream in her "unclean" condition. Far better to tell her friends, she thinks, than to risk being treated forever "as an outcast leper." When Aku-nna finally does cross the stream, she prays "that the god of the stream would be lenient with her for this terrible sin she was committing." This scene at the river suggests the differences between Emecheta's African and our Western attitudes toward nature, a difference that would certainly seem to favor Africa. Though it would never occur to most Westerners that they could sin against a river no matter what the act involved, we might all be better off if we were able to conceive of this possibility, as much of the world continues to use its fresh waterways (and its oceans) as repositories of untreated sewage. But Aku-nna is a traditional African woman who has been taught by her people the necessity of maintaining the purity of the village water supply. This teaching has been reinforced through myth and taboos to such an extent that it constitutes the very fabric of Aku-nna's being. Rather than reading these taboos as evidence of the sexism in Aku-nna's culture, Western feminists might better ask what is served by such customs. Philomina Chioma Steady argues, for example, that the taboos surrounding menstruation are not as misogynistic as they might seem to Westerners, since semen also "can be seen as polluting."

Though it simply does not occur to Aku-nna to question her unclean status as a menstruating woman, she does question other taboos—if only implicitly. In Bakhtin's terms, Aku-nna represents a "potential discourse," which is largely unspoken but

nonetheless quite evident from her actions. In this novel, the authoritarian, closed language of the fathers (custom, tradition, taboo) is continually being challenged by the unofficial, open language of the daughters—a challenge seen in most of Emecheta's other novels. Though the language spoken by the daughters is not the revolutionary woman's language called for by French feminists, the terms of the battle are quite similar. Emecheta herself clearly establishes the primacy of the fathers' language. As soon as Aku-nna's stepfather, Okonkwo, learns that she has begun menstruating, he tells her she must give up her friendship with Chike, speaking to her in "the voice of authority . . . which was a kind of legalised power. He was telling her, not in so many words, that she could never escape." The discourse of the fathers is so powerful that Okonkwo needs no words to tell Aku-nna she is trapped by tradition. She knows it, and the knowledge destroys her. Because the men hold the women enthralled by the power of the authoritative discourse of the fathers, the daughters must speak another language (an internally persuasive unofficial discourse) if they are ever to liberate themselves. When Aku-nna is kidnapped, it looks for a while as if she just might have the will to speak such a language. She is so sickened by the prospects of being married to Okoboshi that she achieves a mysterious strength that gives her courage to defend herself and "fight . . . for her honour." Significantly, she saves herself by what she says—and what she says is a lie. It is a lie that overturns reality by challenging the legitimacy of the fathers' discourse. Furthermore, it is a lie that insults Okoboshi's manhood. Aku-nna says scornfully that his father is merely a "dog chief," since all he has been capable of stealing is "a girl who has been taught what men taste like by a slave." But hers is a doomed rebellion. Though she successfully defends herself against her kidnapper's sexual advances, she is soon discouraged by the realization that she has nowhere to run. Because she has brought shame on her family, her uncle prevents her mother from intervening and would kill her himself if he caught her. But Aku-nna knows that if she has to stay with her kidnappers, she will not live long since no one violates "the laws of the land and survives." Even after betraying her people, Aku-nna remains a believer, begging Chike, for example, to pay her bride price so she will not die in childbirth. Though Chike's father offers her uncle a large sum of money, Okonkwo refuses to accept it. Determined to kill this girl who has brought such shame on his household, Okonkwo makes a fetish in Akunna's image, the purpose of which is to force her to come home. Soon Aku-nna tells Chike's father that her stepfather "calls me back in the wind." Though she vows to stay, inevitably she surrenders to the authority of the fathers' discourse—the "voice" that tells her to return to her family.

Heteroglossia and Textual Plurality

Although Aku-nna's internal discourse is no match for the authoritative discourse of her African fathers and she herself is ultimately silenced by death, the novel itself is a veritable forum of competing discourses. Additional heteroglossia is evident, for example, in statements such as the following one, which describes Ma Blackie's attempts to have a third child by Ezekiel; desperate, she returns to her village in hopes that she can "placate their Oboshi river goddess into giving her some babies." There is no way that this statement can have the same meaning for Westerners as it would for Africans. It is not even clear that it would have any meaning for Westerners, if by this we mean to imply we actually think we understand what has been said. For, at best, we would probably consider it a quaint notion that a river goddess would have anything at all to do with fertility. We certainly would never believe it. What is a river goddess anyway? More particularly, what is an *Oboshi* river goddess? This passage and our questions about it suggest that Emecheta has not forsworn her African point of view, for the narrator never questions the premise behind Ma Blackie's attempts to placate the river goddess. There is absolutely no suggestion that the narrator thinks it is either a quaint or irrational approach to what (most) Westerners would regard as a straightforward medical problem. The question arises, therefore, of how we Westerners are to read Ma Blackie's behavior and informing beliefs. Do we accept her behavior on its own terms and regard it as rational, or do we judge it on our terms and regard it as irrational? At the very least, if we are sincere about trying to make sense out of an alien practice, we might do well to return once more to Peter Winch's advice about understanding Azande magic. It will be recalled from my discussion of his ideas in previous chapters that Winch believes it is wrong for us to try to force the Zande category into our own familiar distinction between science and non-science. Instead, because it is, after all, we who want to understand them, we have the far more difficult challenge of trying "to extend our understanding" of their categories. As we have already seen in our discussion of genres, Bernstein argues that the "primary issue [for Winch] is not whether the Azande make logical inferences according to the same rules

that we use." Rather, what is at issue is "how we *classify* what they are doing."

To return, then, to the practice in question, Ma Blackie's visit to a river goddess. In describing the place of river goddesses in African culture, Elaine Savory Fido reports that such a "deity is usually beautiful, seductive, powerful," whose actions "can vary between malevolence and protective good nature." This description, however, does not offer much help to us Western readers who are still not quite sure how to categorize the concept of a river goddess. What we want to know is, how does placating a river goddess compare, for example, with our Western notion of prayer? How does it compare with soliciting advice from a medical doctor? Or are both these categories insufficient for understanding what is going on here? Is there a genre somewhere between faith and medical science that might be more useful to us in coming to terms with Ma Blackie's pilgrimage? Moreover, have the attitudes of Igbos themselves toward their own river goddesses changed significantly over the years? How would these or other African readers today interpret Ma Blackie's behavior? Would they find the behavior quaint and outdated? Or would they find real value in what she is doing? Unfortunately, Emecheta's novel remains silent on these questions—and in so doing reminds us of the differences that separate us.

Other examples of heteroglossia (which lead to similar problems of classification and interpretation) can be found in the African terminology that Emecheta includes—terms that also reflect a worldview alien to that of the West. As a child, Aku-nna gets sick every time an illness goes around; she is sick so often that Ma Blackie often implores her daughter to make up her mind if "she was going to live or die." This seems relatively clear. Any distraught Western parent might say the same thing. But then the text continues with the information that Ma Blackie could not tolerate "a 'living dead', an *ogbanje*". Emecheta does not stop to explain just what the term "living dead" means to these people. It does not mean what Westerners mean by it. It is not the same as a zombie. An ogbanje is a baby or small child who refuses to stay alive or dead: to torment its parents, it keeps getting born and then dies soon thereafter. In other words, if a family has three or four young babies die, it is the same ogbanje being born over and over again.

Ezekiel's response to his wife's infertility is another classic example of the heteroglossia in this novel, as it moves from one worldview to another in a single sentence. Keenly disappointed by the fact that he has only one son, he reminds Ma Blackie how unfair it is since once he had "paid this heavy *bride price*[,] he had had their marriage *sanctified by Anglicanism*" (emphases added). Ezekiel's funeral is a more extensive example of heteroglossia, as its components are created out of a melange of the old and the new. When it comes time to decide who gets to stay beside the body, Ezekiel's friends are faced with a real problem since the choice of mourners will determine where he goes after death. The men want him to join his father in the earth, but the more rebellious Lagos women "preferred Nna to go to heaven," attracted as they are to the exotic "imported" religion. In making the distinction between the old and the new, the narrator unexpectedly describes the old way as "pagan"—thus raising the question of whether she shares the Christians' negative perception of indigenous African religions. This question is raised in another passage when the narrator, having been a kind of advocate for her culture, suddenly takes the viewpoint of an outsider (who seems to have her own problems with classification). It is relatively easy, the narrator notes, for a visitor to see that Ibuza is an Igbo village. It is harder, however, to decide "whether to classify the people as Christians or pagans." As much as the term "pagan" sticks out here, it is also not clear what the term "Christian" means to people who believe in river goddesses, bride prices, and ogbanjes. Certainly, it does not quite mean what it would to a Western Christian. Other terms that are familiar to Westerners also have a different meaning in this African novel. The concept of "father" is extended to those male relatives who take care of children; "and in Ibuza one's brother-in-law was also given the title of husband." Some children might have such an abundance of "mothers" and "fathers" that they "may not see much of [their] true parents." The fact that the narrator explains these customs at all, of course, suggests a Western influence—for African readers (or at least most Nigerian readers) would already know about them and not need to have them explained.

In sum, in *The Bride Price* there is, indeed, a rich and complex dialogic relationship between the voices of tradition and those in rebellion against tradition—the very dialogic heteroglossia that helps qualify this text as a novel. But even though Aku-nna's unofficial challenge to authoritative discourse helps open the text to many interpretations, Aku-nna herself eventually does allow the Voice of the Fathers to overwhelm her internal voice, graphically

reminding us of how dependent we are on others for our sense of self and our sense of reality.

Competing Discourses and the Construction of Reality

In *The Social Construction of Reality,* Berger and Luckmann describe a dialogic relationship between the individual and society that is similar to the one Bakhtin describes. Though objective and subjective reality can be characterized as basically "symmetrical," on Berger and Luckmann's view, there is always more objective reality than an individual can internalize. Because we simultaneously experience ourselves as a part of, and apart from, society, the status of the relationship between external and internal reality, then, is always being negotiated; in short, it is dialogic and dialectical. The "instrument" of our socialization, moreover, is language itself as it has been incorporated in "moral instruction, inspirational poetry, religious allegory and whatnot." At the same time that the maintenance of external reality is dependent on our conversation with others, the maintenance of an individual's subjective reality is also dependent on our various language systems. In sum, language defines us as human and saves us from the terrors of isolation. As Emecheta's novel convincingly illustrates, because of our (discursive) interdependence, even the simplest challenges to everyday reality are hard to maintain without some sort of group support. In most cases of individual rebellion, according to Berger and Luckmann, the heretic surrenders to the superior strength of the community with very little fanfare. In extreme cases, however, when someone seriously threatens everyday reality, society takes more active measures to protect itself by trying to re-educate the rebel. In effect, the rebel is talked out of her heresy through the therapeutic maneuvers of the analyst's couch or the confessional. If this relatively benign persuasive route fails, society labels the heretic insane or criminal and, if necessary, incarcerates her for either her own or society's good. African societies may be less threatened by heretics, may try to call them back to the fold by the informal intervention of relatives or friends, but the principle remains intact: individuals must fit into their social roles. The person who fails to be socialized, according to Berger and Luckmann, "is socially predefined as a profiled type—the cripple, the bastard, the idiot, and so on." Such predefining has the socially desirable consequence of denying both plausibility and permanency to any heretical self definitions that the individual might dream up.

So it is in *The Bride Price.* For whatever reason, Aku-nna does not accept all teachings of her people's authoritative discourse as her own. But in rejecting one of her people's most fundamental tenets, she fails to find enough external support to sustain her rebellion. Though Chike clearly adores her, his love is not enough to counter the overwhelming influence of what Bakhtin calls tradition "sacred and sacrosanct." Though the discourse of *The Bride Price* is not to be *equated* with that of an epic, therefore, the ideals of the past are justified and reconfirmed here in a process that is *similar* to what occurs in an epic. Tradition is not only how things were done but how they are still done. When Aku-nna's father dies, for example, even though Ma Blackie is still alive, her people treat Aku-nna like an orphan. Even in modern-day Nigeria, the narrator observes, a family without a father is "in fact a non-existing family. Such traditions do not change very much." In Berger and Luckmann's terms, therefore, we might say that Aku-nna has been socially predefined as an "orphan"—or, at the very least, she has been allowed to forget that she is a child of the community and must abide by its conventions. Chike is by birth socially predefined as an outcast. When they fall in love and break a taboo, therefore, they are simply acting out the outsider status they seem already to have. Because they are outsiders, their actions can have no validity or merit. Chike is doomed to social approbation and isolation because of his ancestry, but Aku-nna must be reunited with her people, if only in death—for tradition must be honored. Because this is a novel and not an epic, however, the ideals of the past are also shown to be vulnerable to challenge—a vulnerability that we have already seen in the text's abundant dialogic heteroglossia.

Though, indeed, Aku-nna herself fails the heroine's test and is ultimately silenced by death, neither side achieves narrative hegemony. The fathers fail to silence the heroine's internal discourse (Aku-nna never does go home), and the heroine fails to overthrow the fathers. Complicating the issue for Western feminist readers, however, is the fact that the fathers' language represents traditional African values, whereas the daughter's language, in some respects, represents almost a Western alternative to these old ways. Lest we think that the novel's meaning lies only with the daughter's voice, however, it is important to remember that the narrator speaks in yet another voice—one that is richly complex and full of contradictions.

In *The Bride Price,* as in all of Emecheta's fiction, the narrator functions as a kind of mediating voice between the fathers' and daughters' discourse—and between an African and Western discourse. Because Emecheta's narrator mediates between cultures, we might even suggest, adapting an idea from Marcus and Fischer, that she is functioning as an ethnographer. Envisioning the ethnographer as positioned *outside* the alien culture, however, they suggest—borrowing themselves from Clifford Geertz—that an ethnographer juxtaposes the alien culture's "experience-near or local concepts" with those "experience-far concepts that the writer shares with his readership." For my purposes I want to reverse the stance and suggest that the writer (narrator) in Emecheta's case is more likely to share the experience-near or local concepts with her subjects and, as a consequence, is frequently not speaking in terms familiar to her readers. Though we, as Western readers, may be tempted to see the narrator as speaking primarily in experience-distant concepts (our own), I think it is a temptation we must work to overcome. This shift cannot help but remind us that much of what we read is truly alien to our Western experience and not easily accommodated within our own horizons. Only by accepting these differences, after all, do we have any hope of seeing ourselves anew. This is not to say that we are so locked into our own language game that we cannot understand anything in the alien culture; it is to say that it is more difficult to understand than we might wish—or think. For Marcus and Fischer, when we attempt to understand across cultures, the ethnographer functions for us "as mediator between distinct sets of categories and cultural conceptions that interact in different ways at different points." From this I infer that we can expect some interactions to be relatively painless while others will be almost unbearably difficult. Clearly, there is much in Emecheta's fiction I feel confident I understand. But I am equally confident that much of this confidence is misplaced.

Following the passage cited previously in which Okonkwo has told Aku-nna to break off relations with Chike, for example, is this statement: "He walked away, leaving her standing there by the egbo trees, *for he must not come near or touch her now when she was unclean*" (emphasis added). What is unclear in this sentence is whose point of view the italicized part represents. It immediately follows Okonkwo's authoritative statements and could represent his thinking. Yet it is contained in a paragraph that expresses Aku-nna's point of view and internal thinking. We can be certain that Okonkwo, the Voice of the village Fathers, would

A woman from the East African Dorze tribe is ceremonially kidnapped on the way to her wedding

share the perception that she is unclean. We can also be pretty certain from what occurred at the stream that Aku-nna shares the same perception. But we cannot tell whether the narrator joins them. In short, though we know who *could* be speaking, we are not sure who *is* speaking. According to Barthes, a text's plurality reveals itself in our inability to decide who is speaking—in fact, the "more indeterminate the origin of the statement, the more plural the text." The more plural the text, we might add, the more difficult our interpretive task of understanding. While we might simply be content, in this postmodern age, to enjoy the novel's plurality and let it go at that, if we accept Emecheta's texts as ethnographic documents (as they perforce must be accepted, at least to a certain degree), unthinkingly embracing their plurality seems a facile solution to a problem of "translation" that deserves more careful attention. At other times, however, submitting to the plurality of Emecheta's texts seems the "right" thing to do. Since the people who inhabit Emecheta's novel are, for the most part, not plagued by what Bernstein calls Cartesian anxiety, submitting to the plurality of her texts certainly seems an African thing to do.

Source: Katherine Fishburn, "The Sense of an Ending," in *Reading Buchi Emecheta,* Greenwood Press, 1995, pp. 80–92.

Kirsten Holst Petersen

In the following essay excerpt, Holst Petersen examines The Bride Price *as "a logical development" of Emecheta's autobiographical writing.*

It comes as no surprise that the manuscript Francis burned in *Second Class Citizen* surfaces as Emecheta's 1976 book, *The Bride Price.* With this book, set in the early 1950s in Lagos and Ibuza, she departs from her own life story. Despite this radical shift in subject matter, *The Bride Price* is a logical development of her writing. She continues to explore the injustices of caste, one of her main concerns in the first two books, but the emphasis is somewhat different. Whereas in her autobiographical books Emecheta stresses the possibility of overcoming the restrictions of caste or castelike conditions through personal initiative, in *The Bride Price* and the following novels set in Nigeria she stresses the destructive potential of rigid caste structures, which persist in the otherwise rapidly changing Igbo society. Her main pre-occupation continues to be the role of women. Aku-nna, her name significantly meaning "father's wealth," is a young girl of thirteen when her father dies, and she is forced to move from Lagos with her mother and brother back to their village. Her desire to continue school is frowned upon but accepted, as educated girls fetch higher bride prices. Aku-nna is alienated from the village youth and falls in love with the school-teacher. He, however, is the victim of another caste structure: he is a descendant of slaves and thus not allowed to marry a freeborn. True love runs its course—they elope under dramatic circumstances, get married, and settle down to a good life, supported by the oil boom, education, and Western values, but tradition takes its revenge. The bride price is not paid, and according to tradition the bride must die in childbirth, which is what Aku-nna does. Emecheta's explanation for this hovers uneasily between either presenting it as a psychological effect of a strongly held belief—resulting in fear and fatalistic surrender—or using modern medical terminology. The book thus ends with the defeat of what is clearly portrayed as progressive forces, but this somewhat surprising defeat only helps to highlight the injustice of the situation.

Source: Kirsten Holst Petersen, "Buchi Emecheta," in *Dictionary of Literary Biography,* Vol. 117: *Twentieth-Century Caribbean and Black African Writers,* edited by Bernth Lindfors and Reinhard Sander, Gale Research, 1992, pp. 161–62.

Sources

Cima, Richard, Review, in *Library Journal,* April 1, 1976, pp. 922–923.

Cunningham, Valentine, Review, in *New Statesman,* June 25, 1976, p. 856.

"(Florence Onye) Buchi Emecheta: Criticism," in *DISCovering Authors,* Gale Research, Inc., 1996.

Frank, Katherine, "The Death of the Slave Girl: African Womanhood in the Novels of Buchi Emecheta," in *World Literature Written in English,* Vol. 21, No. 3, Autumn 1982, pp. 476–497.

Nnaemeka, Obioma, "From Orality to Writing: African Women Writers and the (Re)Inscription of Womanhood," in *Research in African Literatures,* Vol. 25, December 22, 1994, pp. 137–158.

Osa, Osayimwense, "Africa in Literature for Children and Young Adults: An Annotated Bibliography of English-Language Books," in *Research in African Literatures,* Vol. 27, March 1, 1996, pp. 221–226.

Porter, Abioseh Michael, "'Second Class Citizen': The Point of Departure for Understanding Buchi Emecheta's Major Fiction," in *International Fiction Review,* Vol. 15, No. 2, Summer 1988, pp. 123–129.

Ward, Cynthia, "Emerging Perspectives on Buchi Emecheta," in *Research in African Literatures,* Vol. 28, June 22, 1997, pp. 182–186.

For Further Study

Achebe, Chinua, *Things Fall Apart,* Heinemann, 1958.
Read Achebe to get a male's perspective on some of the same issues that Emecheta writes about in reference to the African experience. This is Achebe's first novel about Nigerian tribal life, and it takes place during Nigeria's fight for independence. It tells of the downfall of one Nigerian man as his traditional African culture crumbles around him.

Comparative Literature and Culture: A WWWeb Journal, http://www.arts.ualberta.ca/clcwebjournal/clcweb00-1/asante-darko00.html (March 2000).
Professor Kwaku Asante-Darko from Lesotho, Africa, discusses postcolonial literature written in Africa. He examines the differences between aspects of African literature and European and colonial literary tradition.

Fraser, Gerald, "Writer, Her Dream Fulfilled, Seeks to Link Two Worlds," in *New York Times,* June 2, 1990, p. 15.
Fraser gives a brief literary biography of Buchi Emecheta. This article has several long quotes from Emecheta, as well as some background information on her struggles to become a published writer.

Hooks, Bell, *Feminism Is for Everybody: Passionate Politics,* South End Press, 2000.
Writing from an African-American perspective, hooks offers a clear and inspired overview of what feminism is and how it affects everyone.

Lagos Online, http://www.lagos-online.com (May 8, 2000).
For an interesting and personal perspective on life in Lagos today, visit this web site to read postings written by Nigerian students and community leaders. One particular posting written by Reverend Felix Ajakaye, "Yesterday, Today and Tomorrow," discusses the problems Nigeria faces concerning the vast diversity in cultures between multiple Nigerian ethnicities.

Maier, Karl, *This House Has Fallen: Midnight in Nigeria,* Public Affairs, 2000.
This interesting book is about the history of Nigeria, told with a sense of humor despite many horrifying details. Although, according to Maier, the outlook for Nigeria's future is grim, he tells inspiring stories about the people's resilience and sense of humanity in their struggle for independence.

Marriage and Slavery in Buchi Emecheta, http://landow.stg.brown.edu/post/nigeria/emecheta/marriage.html (June 25, 2000).
This web site, dedicated to postcolonial literature in Nigeria, discusses one of Emecheta's main themes: Nigerian women's enslavement to men.

Postimperial and Postcolonial Literature in English, http://landow.stg.brown.edu/post/nigeria/ (June 2000).
At this web site, students from Brown University English classes have researched the role of women in Nigeria during pre-colonial, colonial, and postcolonial times. This site also offers information on Buchi Emecheta and other Nigerian writers.

Soyinka, Wole, *The Open Sore of a Continent: A Personal Narrative of the Nigerian Crisis,* The W. E. B. DuBois Institute Series, Oxford University Press, 1997.

Wole Soyinka, a Nobel laureate, tells the story of Nigeria's struggle for independence and the consequences of the brutal dictatorship of General Abacha. Soyinka states that Nigeria might experience a series of acts of civil disobedience, and his book tries to offer suggestions on how to carry this off successfully.

Ward, Cynthia, "Reading African Women Readers," in *Research in African Literatures,* Vol. 27, September 1, 1996, pp. 78–79.

In this interesting article on the difficulties presented to the European mind when trying to read and understand literature written by non-Europeans, Ward discusses the different ways that various cultures pass down stories from one generation to the next, both in oral and written traditions.

The Edible Woman

Margaret Atwood

1965

Margaret Atwood's *The Edible Woman* is about women and their relationships to men, to society, and to food and eating. It is through food and eating that Atwood discusses a young woman's rebellion against a modern, male-dominated world. The female protagonist, Marian McAlpin, struggles between the role that society has imposed upon her and her personal definition of self; and food becomes the symbol of that struggle and her eventual rebellion. In the essay, "Reconstructing Margaret Atwood's Protagonists," Patricia Goldblatt states that "Atwood creates situations in which women, burdened by the rules and inequalities of their societies, discover that they must reconstruct braver, self-reliant personae in order to survive." At the end of *The Edible Woman,* Marian partially reconstructs that new persona, or concept of self, through a renewed relationship to food.

The Edible Woman was published at the same time that feminism was experiencing a renewed popularity among political movements. But as Darlene Kelly notes in "Either Way, I Stand Condemned," the rhetoric of political movements "is often at odds with reality." In other words, the concepts of women's liberation were in contrast with the actual experience in women's day-to-day lives. Also, anorexia, although known in the medical profession, was not a popular topic of conversation in the lay community. Eating disorders were diagnosed in a doctor's office but were not being widely discussed in women's magazines. Having been published in this era prior to full-blown discussions

of women's rights and women's health issues, *The Edible Woman* received many reviews that mainly emphasized the book's literary techniques.

Author Biography

Margaret E. Atwood, born in Ottawa, Canada, in 1939, spent most of her early years in the wilderness areas of Northern Quebec. She lived with her family in a log cabin that had no electricity, no running water, and no television or radio. It was in this isolated setting that she learned to entertain herself by reading books like those by the Brothers Grimm and Edgar Allan Poe.

Not until she was eleven years old, when her family moved to Toronto, did she attend school full-time. In Geraldine Bedell's "Nothing but the Truth Writing between the Lines," Atwood reportedly said that upon her introduction to city life, as contrasted with her own unconventional childhood, all social groups seemed to her "equally bizarre, all artifacts and habits peculiar and strange." This outsider view plus her early and intense fascination with literature may have been responsible for pulling her toward writing, for by the time she graduated from high school, her graduation yearbook declared that Atwood's intentions were to write the great Canadian novel.

In 1961, the same year Atwood graduated from the University of Toronto, she was awarded the E. J. Pratt Medal for her collection of self-published poems titled *Double Persephone*. Five years later, while she was enrolled as a graduate fellow at Harvard University, she won the Canadian Governor General's Award for another early collection of her poems, *The Circle Game*.

Atwood described this time of her life in a speech she delivered at Hay on Wye, Wales, in 1995:

> After two years at graduate school at the dreaded Harvard University, two broken engagements, a year of living in a tiny rooming-house room and working at a market research company which was more fun than a barrel of drugged monkeys and a tin of orange-flavoured rice pudding, and after the massive rejection of my first novel, and of several other poetry collections as well, I ended up in British Columbia, teaching grammar to Engineering students at eight-thirty in the morning in a Quonset hut. It was all right, as none of us were awake.

Atwood sent her first novel, *The Edible Woman,* to a publisher who subsequently lost it.

Margaret Atwood

Four years later, after Atwood won her awards for poetry, this same publisher took her out to lunch and promised to publish her novel. When Atwood asked him if he had read it, he answered no. As fate would have it, the timing of the book's publication (1969) matched a resurgent interest in women's rights and feminism, thus promoting a concurrent interest in *The Edible Woman.*

Over the years, Atwood has written, among other things, several books of poetry, novels, short stories, children's stories, a radio play, and a play for television. She is known internationally as a champion of Canadian literature.

Plot Summary

Part One

The Edible Woman begins with a first-person narrator in the voice of the female protagonist, Marian McAlpin. For the first several chapters Marian describes her relationships to her roommate, Ainsley; her boyfriend, Peter; and her pregnant friend, Clara. Marian also describes her job, which requires her to take the technical language of survey questions and translate it into a language that the layperson will understand. When asked to substitute for one of the company's surveyors, Marian reluctantly goes from house to house asking people their opinions about a beer ad that will soon be broadcast on the radio. It is during this survey that Marian meets Duncan, an unconventional young man who throws Marian off guard with his lies and almost immediate admittance of his dishonesty.

After watching Clara interact with her children, Marian's roommate, Ainsley, announces that she wants to get pregnant. When Marian asks if this means that Ainsley wants to get married, Ainsley says no. She wants to raise the child by herself. She also wants to choose a man who will not make a fuss about getting married. Ainsley then proceeds to make inquiries about a friend of Marian's whose name was mentioned while they were dining at Clara's house. The old friend is Len Shank, and he has the reputation of a being a womanizer.

Peter is introduced in a phone conversation with Marian, in which he tells her about the engagement of his last remaining bachelor friend. A day later, in an attempt to wear off his depression, Peter and Marian have sex in the bathtub, a setting that Marian describes as Peter's attempt at being spontaneous. Marian is disturbed with the incident, and for a variety of other reasons from that point until the end of the story her discomfort intensifies.

In a restaurant Marian introduces Peter to Len. Marian is surprised when Ainsley appears at their table. At this point Marian realizes that Ainsley has targeted Len as the proposed father of her child. Through the rest of the evening, Marian is caught up in emotions that she does not understand. She finds herself crying without knowing the reason, and, later, she runs away. When the group reunites at Len's apartment, Marian hides under a bed. Eventually she is confronted by Peter, and she tells him she didn't know what she was doing. But before saying good night, Peter proposes marriage by telling her that it is time for him to settle down. Marian accepts and relinquishes to Peter all responsibility for making decisions.

Shortly after her engagement, Marian bumps into Duncan at a laundromat. It is the first time they have seen one another since the survey. They share an abbreviated conversation, then kiss, stare at one another, and depart.

Part One ends with Marian commenting on her engagement, concluding that although her actions have recently been inconsistent with her true personality, life is run on adjustments. She then sees one of her childhood dolls and remembers how she used to leave food with this doll overnight but was always disappointed in the morning when the food had not been eaten. With this image, Atwood leads into the next section, which deals with Marian's eating problems.

Part Two

Part Two begins with a third-person narrator. Instead of being inside Marian's head, the narrator now looks at Marian from a distance. There are other shifts as well. Clara has given birth to her third child and is once again in "possession of her own frail body." Peter has begun to stare at Marian as if he were trying to read her as he would read a manual of how to work a camera. Also in this section, Marian and Duncan's relationship intensifies. The more fascinated she becomes with Duncan, the less suited she is for coping with her life with Peter.

It is at this point of the story that Marian has her first troubled encounter with food. At dinner with Peter, she looks down at her plate, and instead of seeing a steak, she sees the live animal from which it was taken. She watches Peter cutting his steak and refers to it as if he were operating on a cow. Along with Marian's increasing inability to eat food, she also imagines that her body is beginning to disappear. The first images come to her in a dream in which her feet and hands are disappearing.

Marian meets with Duncan again, finding his "lack of interest [in her] comforting." She also tries to convince herself that her relationship with Duncan has nothing to do with Peter although she fears that if the men were ever to meet one another, they might end up destroying one another.

In contradiction to his lack of interest, Duncan tells Marian that he needs something real in his life. He's hoping it is Marian. He then adds that to find out if she is real, he wants her to peel herself out of all the woolen layers that she is wearing and go to bed with him. Marian agrees, but they do not know where to go, except to a hotel where Marian would be looked at as a prostitute. They do not go to the hotel this time, but this scene is a foreshadowing, or preview, of a later scene in which Marian is wearing a sequined red dress and has her face made up. She realizes, in this later scene, that she does look like a prostitute and even encourages that impression by flirting with the hotel clerk.

The last section of Part Two tells of Peter's party and its aftermath. Marian's eating patterns have eliminated all natural foods. She is down to "eating" only vitamin pills. Peter remains unaware of her problems and suggests that for the party she should buy a new dress, something less "mousy" than her normal wardrobe. He also hints that she should do something with her hair. Although Marian feels uncomfortable in the new red dress and new hairdo, she succumbs to Peter's wishes.

Before the party, Marian takes a bath, during which she sees three separate versions of herself reflected in the hot and cold water taps and the faucet. Later, in her bedroom, she again sees three images. This time it is two of her dolls on either side of a mirror, with her own reflection in the middle. When she stares at the three images, she feels that the dolls are pulling her apart.

After Marian puts on her new red dress, Ainsley makes up Marian's face, attaching false eyelashes to her lids, and teaching Marian how to create an alluring but false smile. Later, at the party, Marian explores her new image in a mirror and wonders what is beneath the surface, holding her together. Everything that she sees of herself is false.

Despite her assumption that she is coping at the beginning of the party, in the end Marian runs away. She searches for Duncan, who has refused to enter Peter's apartment once he sees how Marian is dressed. She finds him, and they finally have sex. Later Duncan takes her for a long walk and literally and symbolically points out her way back home.

The next day, Marian bakes a cake-woman, clothing her as if the cake-woman were wearing a red dress. She makes this cake-woman as a test for Peter. Peter fails the test, refusing to take part in the parody. So Marian eats the cake herself.

Part Three

Marian cleans up the apartment and plans to move on. In the last few sentences, she tells Duncan that she is eating again, and he welcomes her back to reality. Then she watches Duncan finish off the cake.

Characters

Clara Bates

Clara is a somewhat neglected and very pregnant friend of Marian McAlpin, the protagonist. Marian has difficulties talking to Clara. Marian states that "more and more, Clara's life seemed cut off from her, set apart, something she could only

gaze at through a window." Clara is pregnant with her third child at the beginning of the story. She dropped out of college with her first pregnancy and has been having children ever since. She describes her children as "barnacles encrusting a ship and limpets clinging to a rock." In *The Edible Woman,* the image of marriage and motherhood are pitted against the image of the single, professional woman. Clara is a symbol of traditional motherhood as well as an extreme example of someone who has made a very literal self-sacrifice by giving up her studies to have her children. Clara is also used as a contrast to Ainsley's more radical approach to motherhood. Marian describes Clara in terms such as weary, isolated, bored, and needing rescue.

Joe Bates

Joe is Clara's husband. He is a philosophy instructor, and the parent most responsible for keeping his children fed and diapered. He cleans house and cooks, and tends to think of "all unmarried girls as easily victimized and needing protection." Joe is very protective of Clara to the point of believing that she (and all women) "shouldn't be allowed to go to university at all; then they wouldn't always be feeling later that they've missed out on the life of the mind." Marian describes Joe as a "shaggy man with a slight stoop." Joe stands in contrast to Len Shank who "is horrible with women, sort of a seducer of young girls." When Joe is asked what he thinks of Len Shank, Joe says, "He's not ethical."

Mrs. Bogue

Mrs. Bogue is Marian's department head at Seymour Surveys. She symbolizes the professional woman. Marian looks at Mrs. Bogue as a possible future self. Marian sees Mrs. Bogue as attempting to preserve a sense of humanity in a mechanized world, as when Mrs. Bogue shouts to the male executives: "We're working with humans, not with machines."

Duncan

Duncan is the moody, manipulative graduate student with whom Marian has an affair. He appears to be incapable of loving anyone, as he is so totally wrapped up in his own needs. However, it is through Duncan that Marian is able to grope her way through a challenging journey of lost identity and eventually grasp a better image of herself. Marian describes Duncan as being "cadaverously thin" and his eyes are "obstinately melancholy, as though

Media Adaptations

- Margaret Atwood wrote two screenplay versions of *The Edible Woman* for Minotaur Films in 1970 and for Windfall Ltd. in 1971.

- Dave Carley wrote a play adapted from Margaret Atwood's novel *The Edible Woman.* The play premiered with the 2000 summer season in both Canada and the United States.

he was assuming the expression on purpose." When he smokes a cigarette, she says that he is like "a starved Buddha burning incense to itself."

Duncan is the antithesis of Peter, Marian's fiancé. Duncan is not very attractive and appears to have little sense of direction in regard to his future. Duncan pulls Marian into his life through pity, but just as Marian starts to lean toward him, he pushes her away by exposing his own manipulative techniques. Despite the layer of lies in which Duncan hides, he convinces Marian that he needs something real in his life. Marian has trouble resisting him. Duncan represents adventure. He is spontaneous and unconventional. He hopes that Marian is real and proposes that she go to bed with him so he can find out for sure. "God knows you're unreal enough now, all I can think of is those layers and layers of woolly clothes you wear." Duncan encourages Marian to get rid of all the outer layers and expose herself to him. Later at Peter's party, when Duncan sees Marian in her red dress and makeup, he says, "You didn't tell me it was a masquerade. Who the hell are you supposed to be?"

It is through Duncan that Marian finds her path back to herself. In the last passages of the book, Duncan tries to sum up the journey but then decides that all that really matters is that Marian is "back to so-called reality."

Fish

See Fischer Smythe

Marian McAlpin

Marian McAlpin is the protagonist. Toward the end of the book, Marian says, "I'm coping, I'm cop-

ing." These words sum up Marian's character. Darlene Kelly in her essay "Either Way, I Stand Condemned" says that "Marian is a pawn, not of fate . . . but of other people. In the hands of her fiancé, of her roommate, of her colleagues, of her friends, and of her acquaintances, she is completely passive and suggestible." And in Marian's own words, when presented with ideas that contradict her own beliefs, she says, "I would simply have to adjust to the situation." Kelly continues, "Marian is like fresh putty on whose receptive form one imprint rapidly succeeds another."

Marian copes with her roommate Ainsley's radical ideas about getting pregnant without first getting married. Marian copes with Peter's moods, adjusting her emotions around his. Marian copes with Duncan's manipulation of her sentiments. She copes with his lies and his self-absorption. She copes with a boring job, a snoopy landlady, a sloppy apartment. She even copes with her slowly diminishing appetite and inability to eat.

As Patricia F. Goldblatt sees it in "Reconstructing Margaret Atwood's Protagonists," Marian is an "exiled little girl" who clings to the notion that her life "will be improved by the arrival of a kind stranger, most likely a handsome suitor." Marian finds a man. Actually she finds two. Then she stops eating. She also loses contact with herself. "After a while I noticed . . . that a large drop of something wet had materialized on the table . . . I poked it with my finger . . . before I realized with horror that it was a tear." Marian was losing contact with her body. Reinforcing this concept Goldblatt adds that Marian's "mind and body have split away from each other." Deeper into the story, Marian dreams that she is dissolving. And when she takes a bath, she refers to herself as "the body that was . . . somehow no longer quite her own."

But once again, Marian copes. She bakes a cake. Although she smiles in the last passages, she must endure as Duncan eats her cake "without exclamations of pleasure, even without noticeable expression." Despite this, Goldblatt believes that "women trust methods that have helped them cope in the past in order to alter the future. . . . The womanly art of baking provides Marian with a way to free herself."

Office Virgins

Millie, Lucy, and Emmy are three single women who are known collectively as the Office Virgins. They work with Marian at Seymour Surveys. They are, as Marian states, "all artificial blondes" and all "virgins." Their thoughts about virginity/sexuality are representative of the standard societal views of the early 1960s. Millie believes that it is easier to wait until you are married. Lucy wonders what people would say, and Emmy, "the office hypochondriac," believes it would make her sick. Lucy is singled out toward the end of the novel at Peter's party where Marian finds Lucy flirting with Peter. Then Marian catches Peter "grinning boyishly" back at Lucy. Lucy symbolizes the artificial woman that Marian feels she has become for Peter's sake.

Leonard Shank

Len is an old college friend of Marian and Clara. He is described as a womanizer of very young women, and he and Ainsley become involved in a twisted game of one player trying to outsmart the other. His goal leans toward "corrupting, as he called it, greenish girls." Ainsley's goal is to trick him into getting her pregnant. Len stands in opposition to the fatherly role of Joe Bates. Marion describes Len in this way: "He was a self-consciously-lecherous skirt-chaser; but it wasn't true as Joe had said, that he had no ethical sense. In his own warped way he was a kind of inverted moralist . . . he was constantly accused by women of being a misogynist and by men of being a misanthropist, and perhaps he was both."

Fischer Smythe

Fish is a graduate student and roommate of Duncan. His most prominent scene is at what David L. Harkness, in his essay "Alice in Toronto: The Carrollian Intertext in *The Edible Woman,*" refers to as the Mad Tea Party. It is Fish who recites the interpretation of *Alice in Wonderland* that Harkness says various critics have used as an "inroad to understanding the novel, taking Marian as a type of 'Alice' and Duncan as a type of 'Mock Turtle.'" Fish uses a Freudian interpretation of *Alice In Wonderland,* stating that the story consists of these points:

> Of course everybody knows Alice is a sexual-identity-crisis book . . . this is the little girl . . . trying to find her role . . . as a Woman. One sexual role after another is presented to her but she seems unable to accept any of them . . . she rejects maternity . . . nor does she respond positively to the dominating-female role . . . you can't say that by the end of the book she has reached anything that can be definitely called maturity.

By the end of *The Edible Woman,* Fish steps into Ainsley's life as a substitute father figure for her unborn child.

Ainsley Tewce

Ainsley is Marian's roommate. Ainsley represents the progressive, alternative woman. She is aggressive and determined. She shuns the role that society tries to impose on her. She is also manipulative, and by the end of the story, several contradictions in her personality are exposed.

In the beginning, Marian defines herself in contrast to Ainsley, who "had a hangover, which put me in a cheerful mood—it made me feel so healthy." Minutes later, Marian compliments herself on her "moral superiority" over Ainsley. Marian also states that she and Ainsley "don't have much in common."

Ainsley looks at men differently than Marian does. Ainsley plays with men "pretending to be terribly interested" in them. She says that she does not want a man to take care of her, treating her as if she were a "thing." She also claims that she is anti-marriage. When she announces that she wants to get pregnant, she responds to Marian's questions by saying, "No, I'm not going to get married. . . . The thing that ruins families these days is the husbands." At Ainsley's strongest point in the story, she declares, "How is the society ever going to change if some individuals in it don't lead the way?"

However, halfway through the story, Marian makes a statement that signals her and Ainsley's reversing roles: "Our positions have shifted in some way I haven't yet assessed." After that point, Ainsley's character becomes contradictive to her initial stance as the new, independent woman.

By the end of the story, Ainsley is convinced that it is psychologically unhealthy to raise a child alone, and she basically takes the first man who comes along to become her husband. She is also horrified to see Marian eating the cake-lady. In turn, by the end of *The Edible Woman,* Marian suggests that there is a connection between Ainsley and their landlady, a connection that Marian had never seen before. "How did she manage it, that stricken attitude, that high seriousness? She was almost as morally earnest as the lady down below."

Trevor

Trevor is Duncan's second roommate, also a graduate student. Duncan says that Trevor "subconsciously thinks he's my mother."

Trigger

Trigger is the last of Peter's friends to get married. As his name implies, Trigger's marriage triggers Peter to make a marriage proposal as well.

Peter Wollander

Peter is Marian's fiancé. Marian considers Peter a good catch: "He was ordinariness raised to perfection." He is a lawyer whose status is "rising . . . like a balloon." His living quarters give a hint about his personality. He lives in an apartment building that is still under construction for which he receives a discount on his rent in exchange for allowing his residence to be used as a model apartment. The one room that is most completely furnished in his apartment is his bedroom, in which hangs a collection of weapons: "two rifles, a pistol, and several wicked-looking knives."

Peter thinks of most women as "designing siren[s]" who carry men off. After one of his friends gets married, Peter attacks his bride, "accusing her of being predatory and malicious and of sucking poor Trigger into the domestic void." Shortly after Peter loses his last bachelor friend to marriage, he proposes marriage to Marian, relenting with the sentiment that "it'll be a lot better in the long run for my [law] practice." Peter views Marian as a "sensible girl" and confesses that sensibility is "the first thing to look for when it comes to choosing a wife."

Peter is confident, but Marian believes that most of this confidence comes straight out of the popular fiction and men's magazines that he reads. For instance, he and Marian have sex in his bathtub. Marian is not comfortable in this scene, thinking that Peter's choice of setting may have come to him from a murder mystery that he's recently read.

Throughout the story, Peter tries to change Marian to match his image of the perfect woman. It is Peter's version of femininity that pushes Marian into buying the red, sequined dress for the party at the end of the story. And it is at the party that Marian asks Peter if he loves her. "Of course I love you . . . I'm going to marry you, aren't I? And I love you especially in that red dress." Then as Peter tries to take a photograph of her, he tells her to "stick out your chest, and don't look so worried darling, look natural." In the end, Peter fails Marian's test.

Woman Down Below

This is Marian's landlady who lives on the first floor of the rooming house. She and her pubescent daughter are known respectively as The Woman Down Below and Child. Marian describes the child as looking cretinous or stupid. The woman down below enforces rules, checks on visitors, and in other ways tries to control Marian's and Ainsley's actions, always for the sake of protecting the innocence of this child. For "whatever happened the child's innocence must not be corrupted." The Woman Down Below symbolizes a kind of strict mother figure, or generalized, conservative voice of society, who does not approve of male visitors, drinking alcohol, or leaving a ring of soap scum around the bathtub.

Themes

Search for Self

Marian McAlpin, the protagonist in *The Edible Woman,* begins her story by relating in the first few lines that she is "all right . . . if anything I was feeling more stolid than usual." The use of the word "stolid" is interesting for at first glance it might be misread as "solid," which is exactly the opposite of what Marian soon will feel. On top of this, the actual definition of "stolid" is to be "impassive and unemotional," which also is in opposition to what Marian will soon experience as she searches for a definition of self, one of the two main themes in *The Edible Woman.* Another curious observation is Marian's supposition that feeling "stolid" (another definition of this word is "slow witted") is, in her words, "all right." The fact that Atwood imposes this word on Marian at the very beginning of the story suggests that the young female protagonist, in terms of her concept of self, is, at best, a bit confused.

Later when she goes to work, Marian is asked to sign a pension plan document. This not only depresses her, it throws her into a "superstitious panic." In Marian's mind, she has now become committed to a future "pre-formed self" who has been put, in the form of the signed document, into a file in a cabinet and "shut away in a vault somewhere and locked." Marian does not fully understand her uneasiness concerning this document, and she has trouble ridding herself of her fears that someone has taken something away from her. She feels locked into a future self from which she cannot escape.

Topics For Further Study

- Americans are constantly exposed to ads each day via television, radio, billboard signs, and printed material. But even more interesting is the general acceptance of consumers to wear apparel with company names stamped in large letters across their heads, backs, and feet. Take a class survey of how many people object to wearing company logos on their clothes. Then debate the pros and cons of such a practice, keeping in mind topics such as consumer rights and possible actions that consumers might take to ban this type of free advertising.

- Today, even though women have gained more rights and recognition, the industrial world is still very much a patriarchal society. Think about what a matriarchal society might be like, then discuss what you think the differences between the two societies would be in terms of employment and marriage.

- A woman often has to choose between motherhood and a profession. If she wants both, she finds herself in a constant battle to meet the responsibilities of both. If she chooses to work full time, her children are often left in day-care centers for long periods of time. What do you see as the future solution for this problem? Should one of the parents stay at home to raise the children until they are at least of school age? Which one? And should there be monetary compensation for the stay-at-home parent? If so, where do the funds come from? Or should the government and businesscommunities work together to establish more accessible day-care centers? And how do you propose day-care centers could be improved?

- For Peter's party, Ainsley applies lipstick, eyeliner, and false eyelashes to Marian's face. This application of cosmetics is an accepted practice for women. Discuss how you think this practice came to be accepted. What are the psychological implications of women being encouraged to wear makeup? And why do you think societydiscourages men from wearing makeup?

- The concept of femininity can be so broadly defined that it includes images that range from being seductive to being submissive. How would you define femininity today, and how do you think that term has changed since your parents' generation, and since your grandparents' time?

Without consciously knowing what she is doing, Marian searches for clues to her identity by observing the women around her. She has little in common with her roommate, Ainsley, whom she describes as a "quick-change artist" who likes to wear clothes that are neon pink and too tight across her hips. When Marian considers talking about her own concerns about her future to Ainsley, Marian hesitates, knowing that Ainsley might mock her.

Neither does Marian identify with her friend Clara, whom she has neglected because she feels Clara needs her only as an entertainer, "someone who would listen to a recital of [her] problems." Marian feels Clara is pulling on her in an attempt to be rescued from boredom. Clara is pregnant, and Marian describes her as looking like a "strange vegetable growth, a bulbous tuber." Clara, Marian

says, represented in her youth "everyone's ideal of translucent perfume-advertisement femininity." However, in Marian's mind, Clara is fragile, passive, and impractical. Marian pities Clara. Every time she encounters Clara, Marian stares at the wall or the ceiling, struggling to find something to say. Clara is motherhood personified, an identity that Marian would like to put off for some time, possibly store somewhere behind a glass wall where she could gaze at it from time to time without taking part. When she leaves Clara in the hospital after the birth of Clara's third baby, Marian feels as if she has "escaped, as if from a culvert or cave. She was glad she wasn't Clara."

Marian fares no better in trying to identify herself with the image that men have of women. Her fiancé, Peter, thinks of most women as "predators," while her friend Duncan thinks of women as nurse-maids for men; and Len, an old college friend of Marian's, either uses women for sex or puts them on pedestals and adores them. Clara's husband, Joe, sees women as vulnerable victims, easily preyed upon.

Unable to find a suitable definition of her identity outside of herself, Marian turns inward. But when she looks in a mirror, a symbol of turning in, she sees only "a vague damp form . . . not quite fo-cussed . . . something she could not quite see . . . whatever it was in the glass . . . would soon be quite empty."

By the end of the story, although Marian has not completely defined her identity, she is at least aware of her need to do so. In creating the sym-bolic cake-woman, she attempts to rid herself from the false and empty identities that have prevailed throughout the story. She describes the cake-woman as "an elegant antique china figurine . . . its face doll-like and vacant."

A final breakthrough occurs when Marian re-gains her hunger and starts devouring the cake-woman. When confronted by Ainsley's remarks that Marian is rejecting her femininity by eating the cake-woman, Marian responds: "Nonsense, it is only a cake."

Gender Roles

Closely related to her search for identity is Marian's attempt to define her role as a woman. Initially she gets lost in other people's definitions. Early in their relationship, Peter defines Marian's role as "the kind of girl who wouldn't try to take over his life." In response, Marian says that Peter's definition suits her. Their roles, she says, were de-fined at face value and as long as they saw each other infrequently, the "veneer," or thin coating, wouldn't have a chance to rub off.

But who decides what roles are to be played? Are people, especially women, always going to be told from some external source that they have a role in life to play? Does a woman have a life or is she only an actor in a play? These are some of the ques-tions that Atwood seems to be asking. It is the roles that begin to disintegrate as Marian and Peter's re-lationship becomes more involved and as Marian tries to step out of the play that she and Peter have written.

Marian first notices a slight distortion in their preconceived roles when Peter talks about things that Marian finds offensive. She rationalizes that Peter is not acting like himself. She wants him to slip back into his role and talk in his "normal voice." Conversely, when Marian acts in a way contrary to the role Peter has created for her, Mar-ian says that he gives her "a peculiar look, as though he was disappointed with me."

One night Marian lets go of Peter and begins to run. She says, "I had broken out; from what or into what, I didn't know." After breaking away from him, Peter scolds Marian: "Ainsley behaved herself properly, why couldn't you? The trouble with you is . . . you're just rejecting your feminin-ity." Since Marian knows that Ainsley is playing a game to seduce a man into getting her pregnant, this statement of Peter's is rather ironic. However, despite the irony, Marian does a complete turn-around and slips back into her role, succumbing to Peter's proposal of marriage for reasons that may have been "a little inconsistent with [her] true per-sonality," she says. Marian likes the security of having a man make the major decisions in her life, of having a man play the role of the provider. She has sensed the confines of their role-playing, but she cannot, at this point, see beyond them. The struggle against those roles consumes her for the rest of the story, ending in an eventual, though somewhat passive, breakthrough.

Marian tests Peter, in the end, with the cake-woman. At the same time, she is also testing the role that she has been playing. "If Peter found her silly [for making the cake and asking him to eat it] she would believe it, she would accept his version of herself." As she watches him, waiting for him to react to the cake-woman, she thinks about how easy it is to see Peter (as well as her role-playing) as normal and safe, but the "price of this version of reality was testing the other one." In other words, the roles she and Peter had created were at odds with a deeper sense of herself. When she puts the cake-woman in front of Peter, she accuses him of trying to destroy her. "This is what you really want," she tells him, referring to the cake-woman, the false image or the role that he has encouraged her to play. She wants him to eat the cake-woman and laugh at the play. But instead, Peter doesn't seem able to break out of his role and seems inca-pable of seeing Marian outside of hers. She has changed, and he no longer recognizes her. After he leaves, Marian thinks of Peter as "a style that had gone out of fashion."

Style

Point of View

One of the most obvious style techniques that Atwood uses in *The Edible Woman* is her unusual use of point of view, or the perspective from which the story is told. Atwood begins the story with a first-person narrator, Marian McAlpin, telling the story from her own perspective, almost sounding as if she were talking to herself.

However, immediately following Marian's engagement to Peter, Atwood changes the narrator, and for the entire second part of the book, the story is told from a third-person point of view. This distances the reader from Marian, just as Marian begins distancing her mind from her body. Darlene Kelly says in "Either Way, I Stand Condemned" that Marian "seems always out of touch with reality, even with who she is . . . this estrangement from herself corresponds perfectly to her use of a detached, third-person voice." In the last two chapters of the book, Marian comes back to herself with the statement, "Now that I was thinking of myself in the first person singular again, I found my own situation much more interesting." Correspondingly, Atwood switches back to a first-person narration.

Cultural Attitude

Prevalent in *The Edible Woman* is the cultural attitude of the early 1960s toward women and the institution of marriage. This was a time prior to the revitalization of the women's movement, a time when women were expected to marry and upon that marriage to quit their jobs, if they had them, and stay home and have children. "Atwood's pragmatic women," says Patricia Goldblatt in "Reconstructing Margaret Atwood's Protagonists," were "young women blissfully building their trousseaus and imagining a paradise of silver bells and picket fences." Goldblatt continues, "these women . . . search for a male figure, imagining a refuge. Caught up in the romantic stereotypes that assign and perpetuate gender roles, each girl does not doubt that a man is the solution to her problems." Struggling against the patriarchy, or male-dominated society, and the roles that society imposes on women, the female characters in *The Edible Woman* each deal with the cultural attitude in their own way, each coming to different conclusions, each taking different paths.

Figurative Language

Food and eating are the prominent metaphors, or images, in *The Edible Woman*. Beginning with the title of the book and journeying through the final chapters, someone or something is either being described in terms of food, or is being eaten. Besides the obvious and plentiful breakfasts, lunches, and dinners that prevail throughout the book, Marian uses food to describe herself and her environment. For instance, her office is "layered like an ice-cream sandwich" with her department being the "gooey layer in the middle." And in one of Marian's dreams she says that her feet were dissolving like "melting jelly."

Emma Parker in "You Are What You Eat: The Politics of Eating in the Novels of Margaret Atwood" says that "eating is employed as a metaphor for power." Those who eat are the powerful, Parker says, and those who don't are the powerless. As Marian's wedding approaches, she begins to feel that Peter is consuming her. This is when Marian stops eating. There are several scenes where Marian cannot eat, but she sits watching Peter eat without restraint. At the end of the book, Marian offers herself as food to Peter in the form of a cake. It is at this point, when Marian has reestablished her power within herself, that Peter is unable to eat the cake, and Marian eats it for him. "Food is one of the few resources available to women," says Parker. Females, in the cultural context of this story, control food. It is their major responsibility to buy and cook food. Parker says that in Atwood's works, "food functions as a muted form of female self-expression."

Historical Context

Historical and Cultural Context

Patricia Goldblatt in "Reconstructing Margaret Atwood's Protagonists" begins her essay by describing the historical and cultural context within which Margaret Atwood lives and works:

> Margaret Atwood weaves stories from her own life in the bush and cities of Canada. Intensely conscious of her political and social context, Atwood dispels the notion that caribou-clad Canadians remain perpetually locked in blizzards while simultaneously seeming to be a polite mass of gray faces, often indistinguishable from their American neighbors. Atwood has continually pondered the lack of an identifiable Canadian culture. . . . In an attempt to focus on Canadian experiences, Atwood has populated her stories with Canadian cities, conflicts, and contemporary people.

Atwood and a handful of other women writers in Canada are considered to have marked a turning

Compare & Contrast

- **1965–1969:** Forty women in Canada are reported to have died because of illegal attempts to end their pregnancies.

  1968: The McGill Student Society publishes "The Birth Control Handbook" although the distribution of information on birth control is illegal in Canada. It becomes an underground bestseller.

  1969: The House of Commons in Canada passes an Omnibus Bill covering birth control. The dissemination of birth control information is decriminalized.

  1991: A federal law that would legalize abortions in Canada is defeated although it is legal in some provinces.

  1992: The number of abortions in Canada exceeds 100,000.

- **1969:** The Montreal Women's Liberation Movement is founded.

  1990: A young man shoots and kills fourteen young women in Montreal, stating "You are all feminists."

  1993: The Canadian federal government sets up a panel on violence against women.

- **1973:** A farm wife is denied half-interest in the farm that she and her husband built together. Her work is seen simply as the fulfillment of her wifely duties.

  1984: The Canadian Royal Commission on Equality in Employment makes recommendations for sweeping changes in this area but later tables its report.

  1970: In Canada, almost 52 percent of families with children headed by single mothers are poor.

  1984: The percentage of poor, single-mother families rises to 62 percent.

  Today: The percentage of poor, single-mother families stands at 50 percent.

- **1970:** Women make up 37 percent of full-time undergraduate students in Canadian universities.

  1983: Women make up 56 percent of full-time undergraduate students in Canadian universities.

  1989: Twenty-five Canadian universities have women's studies programs.

  1991: York University in Canada admits its first students into a Ph.D. program in women's studies.

---

point in Canadian literature. Her first novel, *The Edible Woman,* was written before the resurgence of the women's movement, but the ideas in her novel helped to spark the need for change.

Atwood attended college during the 1960s, both in Canada and in the United States. It was during this time that the feminist movement, also referred to as the Women's Liberation Movement, experienced a renaissance in both countries. Intrinsically involved in this rebirth were two books that Atwood has admitted reading. Darlene Kelly, in the essay "Either Way, I Stand Condemned," states that "Margaret Atwood recalls that when

she composed the book [*The Edible Woman*] in 1965 there was no women's movement in sight, 'though like many at the time I'd read Betty Friedan and Simone de Beauvoir behind locked doors.'"

Friedan's book was called *The Feminine Mystique,* and it raised awareness of the suppression of women's rights to work outside of the home. Women should be allowed, Friedan observed, to have the same freedom as men. Friedan also attacked the conditioning of women to accept passive roles and depend on male dominance. Two years after Friedan's book was published, Friedan helped start the National Organization of Women (NOW).

Simone de Beauvoir's book, *The Second Sex,* discusses how women always define themselves in relation to men. One of her basic concepts is that of the "other," as in how men see women not as a being like them, a peer or collaborator, but rather that they see women in the same way that they see a stranger or someone foreign to their country. Women, de Beauvoir suggests, have submissively accepted this role, which has been imposed on them by men.

These books raised women's awareness about their role in society. This awareness led to the organization of women's liberation groups in Canada. These groups began to form in the late 1960s, most of them as consciousness-raising groups. In other words, women gathered together to discuss common problems and to help make one another aware of issues of oppression. The issues focused on economic and social equality.

According to the article "A Battle Not Yet Won" by Rupert Taylor,

> feminists of the 1960s concluded that the whole of society is pervaded by a sexism that relegates all women to a subservient role. Sexism is a deep-rooted, often unconscious, system of beliefs, attitudes, and institutions in which distinctions between people's worth are made on the grounds of their sex and sexual roles.

Taylor continues by pointing out that a man who is a sexist sees women as inferior. Having had these issues brought into women's awareness, one of the major issues of feminism during the 1960s was for women to gain control over their bodies. As these groups progressed, they joined together into larger groups, giving them a stronger voice and helping them influence their government and judicial systems, changing laws which would eventually lead to great equality.

Canada's federal government set up the Royal Commission on the Status of Women in 1967 to examine women's role in society; three years later, the commission made 167 recommendations for greater equality for women.

Critical Overview

In 1961, at the age of nineteen, Margaret Atwood wrote a collection of poems that she self-published. The collection was called *Double Persephone* and it won her the prestigious E. J. Pratt Medal. In 1966, another Atwood poetry collection,

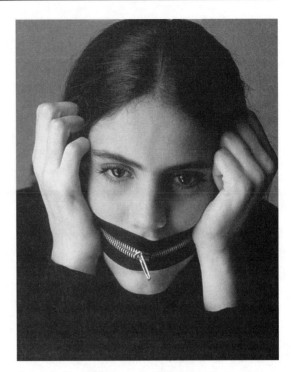

A symbolic representation of anorexia

The Circle Game, won her the Canadian Governor General's Award. This was how she launched her career as a writer.

The Edible Woman was the first novel that Atwood wrote. At the time of its publication, Atwood was considered a poet. This may have played a part in the somewhat discouraging reviews of her first published attempts at prose. The book is described as being thin and tedious by several reviewers. Many of these reviewers do, however, see the potential in Atwood's writing and hold out hope that her next attempt at writing prose will be much better.

For example, in 1969 in a review in the *Times Literary Supplement,* Andre Deutsch writes that "at its best the novel exactly catches [Marian McAlpin's] compulsive behaviour and her unspoken difficulties . . . but the author's tendency to shy away from her own interests and her failure of nerve quite spoil these moments." In a 1970 review in the *Saturday Review,* Elizabeth Easton says, "Margaret Atwood, a Canadian poet, tries hard to be whimsical about all this [the plight of Marian McAlpin] but what might be briefly amusing becomes tedious when presented lengthily in rambling fashion. . . . Sharp imagery cannot make up for trite characterization and lack of plot."

John Stedmond in the *Canadian Forum* in 1970 states that

the novel as a whole does not live up to the promise of its parts. The characters, though clearly sketched, do not quite jell and the narrative techniques creak a little. . . . The novel's approach to the 'position of woman' question is fresh and the method of dealing with it is full of possibilities. But the potentialities are disappointingly unrealized. The author's second book should be better.

In the *Library Journal* in 1970, John Alfred Avant says,

Atwood, a young Canadian poet, can do nice things with a prose style; some of her phrases work themselves out in perverse little ways . . . but the material here is terribly thin. The characters are essentially uninteresting; and the situation . . . might do for a short story but just isn't enough for a novel. I can't recall a book more padded with tedious, irrelevant detail. There's no reason to purchase *The Edible Woman;* but Atwood . . . might some day write a novel worth reading.

T. D. MacLulich more specifically calls *The Edible Woman* a work of art. In his essay "Atwood's Adult Fairy Tale," he finds it a perplexing book: "My reaction to *The Edible Woman* does not seem to match the prevalent opinion." He contends that many critics view this book as a novel about external events only and that is the reason for the critical disinterest in this novel. "Today a novel about events in the external world is thought of as somehow more superficial than a novel which seeks to portray inner psychological events." MacLulich goes on to describe *The Edible Woman* as a "parable illustrating the complex nature of society." In conclusion MacLulich says,

The unresolved ending of *The Edible Woman* forces the reader to attempt his own interpretation of the novel's meaning. Atwood does not serve her message up on a platter, but lets the symbols and incidents reverberate within the reader's mind, in the manner in which . . . art has always worked within the human mind.

Since the publication of *The Edible Woman,* Atwood has written many more books. She has sold millions of copies of her books, which have been translated into twenty different languages. Her works are taught in 78 percent of all British universities.

Criticism

Joyce Hart

Hart, a former college professor, is a freelance writer and editor who has written books for the study of English as well as nonfiction articles for national magazines. In the following essay, she discusses the themes of the search for self and gender roles in Atwood's novel.

Reading Margaret Atwood's *The Edible Woman* is similar to eating a tofu sandwich. Both the book and the sandwich begin and end in the same way, and the flavor of the book and the tofu sandwich depend on the spices that are added to it.

Tofu is a nutritious, but pallid, bean curd. If no spices are brought to it, the satisfaction of eating a tofu sandwich is minimal. In comparison, if no understanding of the complex social issues surrounding *The Edible Woman* is brought to the reading of this book, the story might be simplistically summed up as follows: nice, refined, middle-class young woman has no clue what to do with her life. She has a dull, egocentric boyfriend and a dull, going-nowhere job. She meets an eccentric, self-absorbed second young man and has an affair. First boyfriend proposes marriage. Nice refined young woman accepts the proposal, then rejects it. In the end, nice, refined, middle-class young woman has no clue what to do with her life.

If, however, a little time is taken to investigate the spices that might compliment tofu and add flavor to this sandwich, and the sandwich is eaten a little more slowly, a little more consciously, the satisfaction rating increases. Correlating the story to this second version of the sandwich, the novel becomes a little more interesting: college-educated 1960s woman is dissatisfied with her role in a patriarchal society. Although she is somewhat intrigued with her job and her independence, she jumps at the chance to marry as a means of retiring from the job and the responsibility for having to make her own decisions. She thinks she loves her fiancé and that he loves her. She believes that, at least, she and her fiancé will create an organized home and a rational relationship. These assumptions are somewhat altered when she meets an eccentric male graduate student who challenges her beliefs. Eventually she realizes that she does not fit into the role that her fiancé and her society want her to play out, and she loses her appetite. In the end, college-educated 1960s woman is dissatisfied with her role in a patriarchal society, and her new awareness is at least the first step in resolving her conflicts.

The third possible sandwich recipe involves a little more time, a little more background information in the culinary arts, and a little better understanding of nutrition. The ultimate eating experience is comparable, now, to dining in one of the finest gourmet restaurants. In these terms, the synopsis of the story would read as follows: college-educated, intelligent, 1960s woman struggles with the complexities of feminism and sexuality in a patriarchal, or male-defined, society. She attempts to come to terms with the classic challenges of most females living in a male-dominated world: the body versus mind dichotomy; the profession versus motherhood conflict; and the sanity versus insanity definitions imposed on her by roles that were constructed by men and no longer fit the times, or more significantly, her needs. She lashes out, and tries to run away from her fiancé and her proposed marriage. She also tries to run away from herself, which results in a breakdown and eventual breakthrough in identifying her own basic elements. In the end she bakes a cake-woman in her own image, tests her assumptions by testing her fiancé who fails, and with her appetite returned she proceeds to eat the cake herself. However, when the cake is finally consumed, this college-educated, intelligent, 1960s woman must still struggle with the complexities of feminism and sexuality in a patriarchal, male-dominated society.

To describe Atwood's *The Edible Woman* as a tofu sandwich is not a criticism. Or at least it is not a criticism of Atwood's writing. After all, tofu is made from soybeans, one of the most completely nutritious vegetables that humanity has cultivated. The allusion to a tofu sandwich is more of a critique of the role of the reader. Read the book quickly, and *The Edible Woman* is entertaining. Read the book more carefully, looking at Atwood's use of food as metaphor, understanding the psychological implications of eating disorders, and fully realizing feminist concerns, and *The Edible Woman* deepens with issues that are still relevant today.

First, there is the bread of the sandwich. This idea of a sandwich, in some ways, comes from Atwood herself. As Darlene Kelly states in her essay "Either Way, I Stand Condemned," Atwood describes *The Edible Woman* as a circle in which the heroine ends where she began. The search for one's place, a recurring theme in all of Atwood's fictional writing, begins with this book, her first novel. But

> " Although she is somewhat intrigued with her job and her independence, she jumps at the chance to marry as a means of retiring from the job and the responsibility for having to make her own decisions."

Marian McAlpin, the main character in *The Edible Woman,* fails, according to Kelly, to "clearly and unambiguously carve out such an abode." A possible reason for this failure, Kelly adds, may be that the book was "written at a time when what was wrong with the old order had been spelled out but the alternatives had not." So the reader is left without answers, like the protagonist, at the end.

But the bread acts only as the cover of the sandwich, and everyone knows not to judge a book by its cover. There is still the "meat" of the sandwich that must be examined. During the 1960s, with its renewed interest in the feminist movement thanks to books like Simone de Beauvoir's *The Second Sex,* women were focusing on what was missing in their lives. They questioned the roles of their mothers who, for the most part, had not gone to college, who had not, except possibly during World War II, held jobs, and who, in their early twenties, were married and already had children.

Kelly states that by the time Atwood wrote *The Edible Woman,* marriage had been critically examined and found wanting by feminist writers like Simone de Beauvoir. Although it was popular jargon to accuse women of "trapping" men into marrying them, or to define a man as a "good catch," women of the 1960s were beginning to see that it was they who were being caught and trapped in the confinement of marriage. Kelly says, "By restricting a woman to what de Beauvoir called 'immanence,' that is, the confinement of her activity to home and family, marriage was said to inhibit the full deployment of a woman's talents in the social, political, and professional realms."

But what are the alternatives? This is the question that Atwood attempts, but fails, to answer, not because she falls short of her goal, but rather because in that historical timeframe, there were no

What Do I Read Next?

- Margaret Atwood's prizewinning 1996 novel *Alias Grace* is about a young woman who is accused of murder. Atwood provides a vivid portrait of the status of women in nineteenth-century Canada.

- Margaret Atwood's *Dancing Girls and Other Stories* (1982) is a collection of short stories about women, relationships, and life.

- Betty Friedan's *The Feminine Mystique,* published in 1963, explores the causes of women's frustrations with their traditional roles in late 1950s and early 1960s America. It describes the sense of personal worthlessness that women were feeling during those decades, as their roles demanded that they seek their identities only as wives and mothers.

- Kate Millett's *Sexual Politics,* published in 1970, was one of the first major theoretical works in the renaissance of feminism. It helped to define the ideas and goals of the women's movement.

- Virginia Woolf is often called the mother of twentieth-century feminist literary criticism. Her book *Orlando* (1928) analyzes the way gender determines the individual's relationship to property and art at different moments in history.

- Alice Munro, another Canadian writer, has a collection of short stories called *Open Secrets: Stories* which was written in 1994. The stories focus on the struggles of women to find their identity as well as to discover their roles in society.

- Alice Walker's *You Can't Keep a Good Woman Down* (1981) is a collection of short stories that explores the lives of modern African-American women who are searching for empowerment, love, and friendship.

- Germaine Greer, author of *The Female Eunuch,* which helped popularize feminism, has written a new book titled *The Whole Woman* (1999). In it she modernizes her views about the women's movement, highlighting her concerns about love and power.

- Fannie Flagg's *Fried Green Tomatoes at the Whistle-Stop Cafe* (1987) is a book that is both humorous and poignant. It tells a story on two separate levels of time, following key moments in the lives of three women in their search for love and friendship.

---

answers. It is this open-ended finale in *The Edible Woman* that becomes one of the book's most fascinating elements. It is this unanswered question that Atwood was smart enough and brave enough to leave unanswered. It is this unanswered question that not only allows, but also invites her readers and literary critics to add their own flavors and spices to the sandwich.

To see Atwood's book as a sandwich is not too far flung an idea, as food is a very central part of *The Edible Woman.* Emma Parker states in her essay "You Are What You Eat: The Politics of Eating in the Novels of Margaret Atwood" that in Atwood's writing, "food imagery saturates [her] novels and becomes the dominant metaphor the heroines use to describe people, landscape, and emotion." The first chapter of *The Edible Woman,* for instance, opens in the kitchen with Marian making breakfast. Before the end of this chapter Marian is hungry and eating again. At the beginning of the second chapter, Marian is at work, where she is being asked to sample more food. She also describes the company where she works in terms of food, such as it is layered "like an ice cream sandwich." Before the second chapter ends, Marian goes to lunch, where she talks to her friends about people who live in Quebec and eats too many potatoes. And not to belabor the point, but just to demonstrate the saturation level of food and consumption in *The Edible Woman,* in the third chapter Marian is assigned the task of taking a survey about beer, is asked to write a letter to a woman who found a fly in her cereal, is turned down for a dinner date by her soon-to-be fiancé, Peter, then as she is thinking about what food she has in the freezer at home, she is interrupted by a phone call from a friend who invites her to dinner. And all of this food talk occurs in just the first twenty-five pages of the novel.

Not until Part Two of the novel, after Peter and Marian become engaged, does Marian have her first real difficulty with food. She realizes, of course, that if the problem persists, it could lead to her death, but she feels powerless in finding a solution. Her body acts on its own volition, as if Marian's mind has lost control over it. It is also at this point in the story that Atwood changes the voice of the narrator. She switches from first person (Marian's voice) to a third-person observer. With this structural change, Atwood distances the reader from Marian, just as Marian's body distances itself from her mind, just as Marian distances herself from food.

While Marian and Peter are sitting in a restaurant, Marian looks at the steak on her plate not as a meal, but rather as a part of a living mammal "that once moved and ate and was killed, knocked on the head as it stood in a queue like someone waiting for a streetcar." Not only does Marian see it as a once-live animal, she takes it one step further. She personifies the steak, making its history include the human action of waiting for a bus, something that Marian does almost every day. This is the first hint that Marian is beginning to feel like food; beginning to feel that she, too, is being consumed. In this same scene, just as Marian pushes away from the steak, she also senses her own helplessness and supposed inferiority to Peter. "She meant to indicate by her tone of voice that her stomach was too tiny and helpless to cope with that vast quantity of food. Peter smiled and chewed, pleasantly conscious of his own superior capacity."

At the time Atwood wrote *The Edible Woman,* public awareness of eating disorders like anorexia was negligible. Despite this lack of information, Atwood seems to have intuitively made her own conclusions about the significance of women and their relationship to food. Parker states that Atwood uses eating "as a metaphor for power and [it] is used as an extremely subtle means of examining the relationship between women and men. The powerful are characterized by their eating and the powerless by their non-eating."

In the essay "No Bread Will Feed My Hungry Soul: Anorexic Heroines in Female Fiction," Dr. Giuliana Giobbi states that "anorexic girls are actually uncertain, asocial, fundamentally shy persons who lack any power of initiative." Dr. Giobbi continues that anorexia is an attempt "to escape from the hardships of adult life." This turning away from the adult world can be seen in Marian when Peter proposes marriage and later asks her to choose a date for the wedding. Marian's response comes out impassively: "I heard a soft flannelly voice I barely recognized, saying, 'I'd rather have you decide that. I'd rather leave the big decisions up to you.' I was astounded at myself. I'd never said anything remotely like that to him before. The funny thing was I really meant it."

David L. Harkness also postulates that Marian's loss of appetite is a symbolic turning away from the responsibilities of adult life. Harkness, in his essay "Alice in Toronto: The Carrollian Intertext in *The Edible Woman,*" compares Marian to Alice in their dual descent into a fantasy world where they both try to evade the issues surrounding growing up and having to make decisions. Harkness compares Marian to Alice but states that whereas Alice is "eternally young and can return to Wonderland without risk, Marian . . . is not a character in an engaging children's book. She does grow older, and . . . though she may not necessarily live happily ever after, she does manage to achieve some measure of personal growth and psychic integrity and thus go on to a happy ending."

While Harkness believes Marian eventually finds a happy ending that ending is not evident in Atwood's book. There is hope, however. She is, after all, eating again. Not only is she eating, she is consuming the image of femininity that she found, at last, so artificial. "'I'll start with the feet,' she decided." Then "she plunged her fork into the carcass, neatly severing the body from the head." So ends the artificial cake-woman, and so ends the book.

Source: Joyce Hart, Critical Essay on *The Edible Woman,* in *Novels for Students,* The Gale Group, 2001.

Coral Ann Howells

In the following essay excerpt, Howells examines The Edible Woman *within the context of Betty Friedan's* The Feminine Mystique, *finding many thematic similarities between the works but arguing that Atwood's novel greatly differs in its "dimensions of fantasy and metaphorical thinking."*

> *The Edible Woman* goes beyond women's anger and bewilderment in its exploitation of the power of laughter to reveal the absurdities within social conventions."

In this chapter I shall trace Atwood's exploration of sexual power politics through social myths of femininity and representations of the female body in two texts which mark very different stages in her writing career and in the history of feminism. *The Edible Woman,* her first novel, appeared in 1969 at the beginning of 'second wave' feminism, whereas the savage little fable 'The Female Body' written 20 years later (after *Bodily Harm, The Handmaid's Tale,* and a woman artist's paintings of the female body in *Cat's Eye*) belongs to the explicitly political context of feminism in the early 1990s, laying out the implications of patriarchal myths and fantasies about women with diagrammatic simplicity. The differences between these texts also explain why my chapter title reverses the terms of Toril Moi's influential essay of the mid-1980s, 'Feminist, Female, Feminine', in order to indicate the direction in which Atwood's work has shifted.

The Edible Woman belongs to a specific moment in the history of North American postwar feminism, which registered the first signs of the contemporary women's movement in its resistance to social myths of femininity. This is the territory charted by Betty Friedan in *The Feminine Mystique* (1963), a study that Atwood herself read 'behind closed doors' like many other young women at the time, and I propose to read *The Edible Woman* in that context. Atwood and Friedan highlight the same new area of gendered social concern, and the thematic issues in *The Edible Woman* could even be classified under the chapter headings in Friedan's book. However, the very title of Atwood's novel signals significant differences with its dimensions of fantasy and metaphorical thinking which are absent from Friedan's sociological treatise, for *The Edible Woman* is an imaginative transformation of a social problem into comic satire

as one young woman rebels against her feminine destiny. Whereas *The Feminine Mystique* documents the anxieties and frustrations felt by a whole generation of young women in America in the 1950s and early 1960s, *The Edible Woman* goes beyond women's anger and bewilderment in its exploitation of the power of laughter to reveal the absurdities within social conventions. This is a subversive rather than a confrontational novel which engages obliquely with social problems, adopting the form of a parodic revision of a traditional comedy of manners with its fixation on the marriage theme. Here Atwood mixes those earlier conventions with the language of 1960s advertising and cookery books, adding a dash of popular Freudianism and a few of the Jungian archetypes so fashionable in literary criticism of the 1950s and 1960s, to produce a satirical exposure of women's continuing conditions of entrapment within their own bodies and within social myths. The novel mounts its attack on social and gender ideology very wittily, though it bears the mark of its historical period with its deprecatingly feminine glance back over the shoulder when one of the characters comments, 'I don't want you to think that all this means anything'. It is part of Atwood's playful ambiguity that the speaker here is male. That same speaker, a young graduate student in English literature, happens to be the novel's most vigorous critic of gender stereotypes, of advertising and of the consumerist ethic. Under a series of comic masks Atwood's novel explores the relation between consumerism and the feminine mystique, where one young woman's resistance to consuming and to being consumed hints at a wider condition of social malaise which the new feminist movement was just beginning to address. . . .

The role of Margaret Mead as the professional *spokesman* [my Italics] for femininity would have been less important if American women had taken the example of her own life, instead of listening to what she said in her books. Margaret Mead has lived a life of open challenge.

Atwood's dramatisation of the contradictions within the concept of femininity according to the 'functional freeze' doctrine provides some of the best comedy in *The Edible Woman* in her two parodic versions of earth-mothers, one a passive victim of the feminine mystique and one (a former psychology student and evidently a devotee of Margaret Mead) whose relentless pursuit of a father for her child 'bore a chilling resemblance to a general plotting a major campaign'.

In North American society of the late 1950s and 1960s where 'adjustment' for a woman meant accepting a dependent 'feminine' role, it was as Friedan says, 'very hard for a human being to sustain such an inner split—conforming outwardly to one reality, while trying to maintain inwardly the values it denies'. In a chapter whose full title is 'Progressive Dehumanization: the Comfortable Concentration Camp', Friedan glances at the territory of female neurosis which Atwood's novel explores with such imaginative insight:

> If the human organism has an innate urge to grow, to expand and become all it can be, it is not surprising that the bodies and the minds of healthy women begin to rebel as they try to adjust to a role that does not permit this growth.

Friedan cites case histories of women suffering from fatigue, heart attacks and psychotic breakdowns, a catalogue of female hysterical illness induced by women's attempts to conform to the (impossible and undesirable) codes of the feminine mystique. It is precisely in that speculative area of pathology so 'puzzling to doctors and analysts' that the nervous eating disorder of Atwood's heroine is located, where the female body becomes the site of victimisation, internal conflict and rebellion.

I think I have said sufficient to establish that *The Feminine Mystique* may be an appropriate lens through which to read *The Edible Woman* as social critique, for it is a 1960s story of a woman's identity crisis provoked by pressures against which she finds herself seriously at odds. Marian MacAlpin is a young graduate in her twenties with an independent income, living in Toronto and sharing an apartment with another young woman, Ainsley Tewce. She also has a boyfriend to whom she becomes engaged, Peter Wollander, an ambitious young lawyer with a passionate interest in guns and cameras. The narrative traces the stages of Marian's rebellion against social conformity as she becomes increasingly disillusioned with her job and her fiancé to the point where her inner conflict finds its outward expression in an eating disorder whose symptoms resemble anorexia nervosa. While the novel hints at the connection between social institutions and personal relations which would become the central theme in Atwood's collection of poems *Power Politics* (1971), it cannot easily be classified as a realist text for it insistently challenges the conventions of realism by its excursions into fantasy and its flights of metaphorical inventiveness. *The Edible Woman* is a comedy of resistance and survival which subverts social definitions from within, shown by the way Marian finally wins her

independence from the feminine mystique through her traditionally feminine gesture of making a cake, which she offers to the two men in her life. Her fiancé refuses it; her strange changeling mentor and guide, Duncan the graduate student in English, helps her to eat it all up. Clearly, an iced cake in the shape of a woman is the central metaphor for Marian's perception of woman's condition and fate as decreed by the feminine mystique so that her cake-baking is both a gesture of complicity in the domestic myth and also a critique of it. Atwood described the tea ritual as 'symbolic cannibalism', with the cake as simulacrum of the socialised feminine image which Marian rejects; but it is also of course a party game with Duncan as the 'child' and Marian as the 'mother' once again in control. Eating the cake is an act of celebration which marks the decisive moment of Marian's recovery from an hysterical illness and her return to the social order. Once again she becomes a 'consumer', for it is difficult if not impossible to reconstruct one's identity outside the symbolic and social order, and individual survival is likely to mean compromises with society. This is a conclusion similar to the one in *Surfacing* (1972), and Atwood's comment on the similarities between the two books draws attention to what her female protagonists have accomplished in finding new subject positions for themselves more in harmony with the world they live in.

As a woman writer Atwood has always been intensely aware of the significance of representations of the female body, both in terms of a woman's self-definition and as a fantasy object:

> The body as a concept has always been a concern of mine. It's there in *Surfacing* as well. I think that people very much experience themselves through their bodies and through concepts of the body which get applied to their own bodies. Which they pick up from their culture and apply to their own. It's also my concern in *Lady Oracle* and it's even there in *The Edible Woman*.

The originality of *The Edible Woman* lies in its exposure of the 'sexual sell' promoted by the feminine mystique, for the narrative reveals how social paradigms of femininity may distort women's perceptions of their sexuality in the interests of creating childlike or doll-like fantasy figures. A young woman like Marian, sensitised as she is to the social script of gender relations and feminine expectations, seems to have little consciousness of her own body either in terms of its maternal urges or its erotic pleasures. Female bodies and biological processes like pregnancy, childbirth and menstruation figure in the novel, but they are treated with a measure of comic detachment. When viewed through Marian's eyes, sexually mature female bodies become grotesque and rather disgusting, whether it is her friend Clara's pregnant body or the fat ageing bodies of her fellow office workers at the Christmas party or the fiasco of the coast-to-coast market research survey on sanitary napkins, where some of the questionnaires 'obviously went out to men' ('Here's one with "Tee Hee" written on it, from a Mr Leslie Andrewes').

In contrast to Marian, her friends Clara and Ainsley celebrate women's biological destiny, though their different approaches to motherhood turn them into parodic images of the maternal principle. Clara, who enters the narrative heavily pregnant with her third child, looks to Marian 'like a boa-constrictor that has swallowed a water melon'. Marian sees her as one of the casualties of the female life, a representation of the duplicities of the feminine mystique which could transform a girl who was 'everyone's idea of translucent perfume-advertisement femininity' into a kind of female monster, the helpless victim of her own biology:

> She simply stood helpless while the tide of dirt rose round her, unable to stop it or evade it. The babies were like that too; her own body seemed somehow beyond her, going its own way without reference to any directions of hers.

There are several ironies here, not least a foreshadowing of Marian's own bodily insurrection, but the most obvious is that Clara's own attitude to motherhood is quite savagely unmaternal: 'Her metaphors for her children included barnacles encrusting a ship and limpets clinging to a rock'. Yet when Clara's baby is born, she describes the process to Marian with a kind of rapture: 'Oh marvellous; really marvellous. I watched the whole thing, it's messy, all that blood and junk, but I've got to admit it's sort of fascinating'. Marian's response is not one of sympathy but of alarm at possibly being implicated by her age and her gender, and she escapes from the maternity hospital 'as if from a culvert or cave. She was glad she wasn't Clara'.

If Clara represents woman's passive fulfilment of her biological destiny, then Ainsley represents a more intellectualised approach to maternity as she embarks on it as a social project with the aim of becoming a single parent. (Ainsley's derogatory remarks about men and fatherhood are amusingly similar to those of Offred's mother in *The Handmaid's Tale* written 20 years later). Her programme is entirely ideological and in a curious way academic and theoretical:

'Every woman should have at least one baby.' She sounded like a voice on the radio saying that every woman should have at least one electric hair-dryer. 'It's even more important than sex. It fulfils your deepest femininity.'

Ainsley's pursuit of Marian's friend Leonard Slank, a notorious womaniser with a penchant for inexperienced young girls, works as a comic reversal of the traditional seduction plot exposing the dynamics of the sexual game in all its duplicity. Ainsley's artful imitation of youthful innocence ('It was necessary for her mind to appear as vacant as her face'), and Leonard's pose of world-weary drunken lecher are equally false, as is revealed when she triumphantly announces to him that she is pregnant. He collapses in a crisis of Freudian horror:

> Now I'm going to be all mentally tangled up in Birth. Fecundity. Gestation. Don't you realize what that will do to me? It's obscene, that horrible oozy . . .

'Don't be idiotic,' Ainsley said '. . . You're displaying the classic symptoms of uterus envy.'

It is Leonard who is the casualty in this battle between the sexes. However, as part of the comic deconstruction of stereotypes here, the most passionate advocate for the maternal principle is a male Jungian literary critic, the graduate student Fischer Smythe, who is obsessed with archetypal womb symbols and who in turn becomes fascinated with the pregnant Ainsley as an Earth Mother figure just as Leonard Slank recoils from her 'goddam fertility-worship'. Indeed, it is the male characters who display far more interest in female biology than the women and whose language rises to heights of eloquence or abuse in their fantasy representations of the female body. By contrast, Marian refuses to get involved either with Ainsley's 'fraud' or Clara's domestic chaos.

Not only does Marian feel threatened by childbearing but she also feels alienated from her body in other ways as well. At the office Christmas party, surrounded by the fat and ageing bodies of her colleagues, Marian's perspective shifts from a kind of anthropological detachment to a sudden shocked recognition that she too shares this mysterious female condition:

> What peculiar creatures they were; and the continual flux between the outside and the inside, taking things in, giving them out, chewing, words, potato-chips, burps, grease, hair, babies, milk, excrement, cookies, vomit, coffee, tomato-juice, blood, tea, sweat, liquor, tears, and garbage . . . At some time she would be— or no, already she was like that too; she was one of them, her body the same, identical, merged with that other flesh that choked the air in the flowered room

with its sweet organic scent; she felt suffocated by this thick sargasso-sea of femininity.

We begin to understand that Marian does not wish to turn into any of the models of adult women offered by society, and that behind her conventional femininity lies a horror of the body which relates to her fear of growing up signalled either by marriage, maternity or the office pension plan. She wants none of these futures, and it is in this context of challenge to the discourses of both femininity and adulthood that her hysterical eating disorder needs to be interpreted.

The design of the narrative with its radical shift from the first person narration in Part 1 to the third person in Part 2 underlines Marian's loss of an independent sense of self; it is also Part 2 which signals the onset and crisis of her nervous disease. As the bride to be, she has already opted out of the professional world and has nothing to do but wait passively for her wedding: 'It was all being taken care of, there was nothing for her to do. She was floating, letting the current hold her up.' Under the spell of the feminine mystique, she is merely biding her time, yet there are signals that this is for Marian what Friedan would call 'The Mistaken Choice'. Though an apparently willing victim, Marian is troubled by her strange eating disorder and by inexplicable intimations of 'sodden formless unhappiness'. Perhaps the best gloss on her state is provided by another victim of the feminine mystique in the late 1950s, the American poet Adrienne Rich, who writes about her own condition using similar imagery of drifting and self division: 'What frightened me most was the sense of drift, of being pulled along on a current which called itself my destiny, but in which I seemed to be losing touch with whoever I had been, with the girl who had experienced her own will and energy almost ecstatically at times, walking around a city or riding a train or typing in a student room'. It is the concept of freedom which Duncan represents, enhanced in his case by a Peter Pan pose of childlike irresponsibility as he refashions the world according to his own wishes and so fantasises an alternative reality. He challenges all Marian's traditional ideas of masculinity, romantic love and parent-child relations, while his 'family' of two other male graduate students, Trevor and Fish, forms a gaily subversive trio who transgress traditional gender roles, dedicated as they are to the domestic arts of washing and ironing, cooking and parenting. Caught between this playful student world and the world of social conformity, Marian loses any sense of herself as a unified subject, beginning to hallu-

cinate her emotional conflict in images of bodily dissolution and haunted by hallucinations of fragmentation. Lying in the bath on the evening of the first party which she and Peter are giving as an engaged couple, she begins to believe that her body is 'coming apart layer by layer like a piece of cardboard in a gutter puddle.'

That party, to which all the main characters in the novel are invited, represents the climax of Atwood's 'anti-comedy':

> I think in your standard 18th-century comedy you have a young couple who is faced with difficulty in the form of somebody who embodies the restrictive forces of society and they trick or overcome this difficulty and end up getting married. The same thing happens in *The Edible Woman* except the wrong person gets married . . . The comedy solution would be a tragic solution for Marian.

Atwood's fictional method is what is now recognised as a feminist revision of a traditional genre highlighting the artifice of literary conventions and the social myths they inscribe. There are other divergences from traditional comic patterns here as well. Not only is the artifice of femininity exposed ('You didn't tell me it was a masquerade', says Duncan, looking at Marian's lacquered hair and her slinky red dress) but the party provides the first occasion when the male protagonists speak about femininity from their own perspective, revealing a surprisingly high level of masculine anxiety about this topic. The most devastating attack on the feminine mystique comes from Clara's husband Joe, the philosophy lecturer, who earnestly challenges such mythologising, making a political statement from his personal point of view as a husband and a teacher:

> She's hollow, she doesn't know who she is any more; her core has been destroyed . . . I can see it happening with my own female students. But it would be futile to warn them.

At last Marian knows what she does not want, and so she escapes from the social script to her unscripted meeting in the laundromat with Duncan and into their brief liaison in a sleazy hotel. Though it begins as a parody of lovemaking with Duncan's complaint that there is 'altogether too much flesh around here' (an echo of Marian's own disgust with female bodies), it ends rather differently with him gently stroking her 'almost as though he was ironing her'. There is also a suggestion of their wilderness affinity as Duncan's face nudges into her flesh, 'like the muzzle of an animal, curious, and only slightly friendly', and it is in the wilderness of a Toronto ravine to which he guides her that Mar-

*A women's rights rally in Farragut Square in
downtown Washington, D.C., in 1970*

ian's undramatised clarification of mind occurs.
Duncan's action in leaving her alone there is exactly what Friedan might have prescribed for be-
wildered dissenters from the feminine mystique,
'for that last and most important battle *can* be
fought in the mind and spirit of woman herself.'

By following her own line of metaphorical
thinking, Marian discovers a way to solve what for
her is an ontological problem, 'some way she could
know what was real: a test, simple and direct as lit-
mus-paper.' The test is of course the cake which
she bakes and then ices in the shape of a woman,
a transformation of science into domestic ritual.
Gazing at the cake lady and thinking of her destiny
she says, 'You look delicious . . . And that's what
will happen to you; that's what you get for being
food.' However, when offered the cake Peter flees,
either from Marian's literalised metaphor or from
her undisguised hostility, probably into the arms of
Lucy, one of Marian's office friends with 'her delicious dresses and confectionery eyes.' Maybe
Marian was right and an 'edible woman' was what
Peter had really wanted all along. It is as if a spell
has been broken: Marian's confusion falls away,
and recognising that 'the cake after all was only a
cake' she starts to eat it. Only Ainsley, ever alive
to symbolic implications, bothers to translate the

significance of Marian's cake eating, ironically
echoing Peter's earlier accusations. 'Marian!' she
exclaimed at last, with horror. 'You're rejecting
your femininity!' This interpretation is confirmed
by Marian's 'plunging her fork into the carcase,
neatly severing the body from the head.' That violent gesture with its parody of vampire slaying carries a further implication that the feminine image
has been draining Marian's life blood but will have
the power to do so no more.

The third section with its energetic return to a
first person narrative, 'I was cleaning up the apartment', is devoted to tidying up the plot in a comic
dénouement where it is significant that the three
women protagonists survive better than the men:
Peter has left and Marian is once again independent; Leonard Slank has had a nervous breakdown
and is being cared for by Clara like another of her
numerous children, while Ainsley has fulfilled her
biological mission while managing to conform
neatly to social convention by marrying Fischer
Smythe and going off to Niagara Falls for their hon-
eymoon. Marian's house-cleaning works as another
domestic analogy for her own rehabilitation, as her
response to Duncan's phone call suggests: 'Now
that I was thinking of myself in the first person singular again I found my own situation much more
interesting than his.' Their tea is a replay of Peter's
visit, though with the important differences that
Duncan eats the cake (described by Marian as 'the
remains of the cadaver') and that they talk together
in a way that she and Peter did not manage to do.
It is a curious conversation in which Duncan casually offers five possible interpretations of the preceding narrative action as if he were commenting
on a literary text in a graduate seminar. The one
reading he categorically rejects is Marian's assertion that Peter was trying to destroy her:

'That's just something you made up'. Instead,
he multiplies the possibilities around the question:
Who has been trying to destroy whom? Duncan's
ironising (like his passion for ironing things out flat)
represents a deliberate distancing from Marian's
personal crisis in a general comment on human behaviour. Such a device with its opening up of multiple perspectives shifts any reading of this novel
beyond a single feminist focus, implying that the
politics of gender is only one example of the power
struggles in any relationship. It is Duncan who has
the last word, transforming this into a comedy of
good manners as he finishes cleaning up the cake:
'"Thank you," he said, licking his lips. "It was delicious".' He is the good child who says thank you
as Marian the mother regards him with a smile. Yet

the ending is not quite the sentimental resolution it may look at first glance, for Duncan remains an enigma, and on a psychological level his eating of the cake resembles nothing so much as the activity of the Sin Eater, a role assigned to the therapist in one of Atwood's later stories.

The domestic scenario raises one last point which relates to the important question of female creativity. It is significant that Marian has chosen to make her protest through a traditionally feminine mode which bypasses language: 'What she needed was something that avoided words, she didn't want to get tangled up in a discussion.' She thinks that she has accomplished her purpose, though as any reader in the 1990s would note, none of the three young women—Marian, Ainsley nor Clara—has escaped from their culturally defined gender roles; they are still producing cakes and babies. This leaves unresolved the issue of women's attempts to establish themselves as independent speaking subjects working creatively through writing or painting, a topic to which Atwood will return in *Surfacing, Lady Oracle* and *Cat's Eye.*

Twenty years later Atwood is still preoccupied with 'writing woman', both in the sense of woman as writer and woman as written about, though we might expect that a fable belonging to the 1990s like 'The Female Body' would show a more explicitly feminist awareness of the political and theoretical dimensions within representations of the feminine than a novel written at the end of the 1960s. In both texts the focus is on woman as spectacle or fantasy object of desire and violence, and representations of the female bodies in the later text double back to take in the same images of fashionable femininity or women's captivity as in *The Edible Woman.* In both, women are represented as victims: a woman being eaten alive (playfully figured as a sponge cake) and woman as murder victim.

Source: Coral Ann Howells, "'Feminine, Female, Feminist': From *The Edible Woman* to 'The Female Body,'" in *Margaret Atwood,* Macmillan, 1996, pp. 38–54.

Sources

Atwood, Margaret, "Margaret Atwood, Writing Philosophy," Waterstone's Poetry Lecture Series delivered at Hay On Wye, Wales, June 1995, taken from "Canadian Poets" on the Canadian Poetry website, University of Toronto, 2000, www.library.utoronto.ca/canpoetry (last accessed March, 2001).

Avant, John Alfred, Review, in *Library Journal,* Vol. 95, No. 16, September 15, 1970, p. 2934.

Bedell, Geraldine, "Nothing but the Truth Writing between the Lines," in *Independent on Sunday,* September 1, 1996, p. 17.

Deutsch, Andre, Review, in *Times Literary Supplement,* No. 3527, October 2, 1969, p. 1122.

Easton, Elizabeth, Review, in *Saturday Review,* Vol. 53, October 3, 1970, p. 40.

Giobbi, Giuliana, "No Bread Will Feed My Hungry Soul: Anorexic Heroines in Female Fiction—from Examples of Emily Brönte as Mirrored by Anita Brookner, Gianna Schelotto and Alessandra Arachi," in *Journal of European Studies,* Vol. 27, No. 105, March, 1997, pp. 73–92.

Goldblatt, Patricia F., "Reconstructing Margaret Atwood's Protagonists," in *World Literature Today,* Vol. 73, Spring 1999, p. 275.

Harkness, David L., "Alice in Toronto: The Carrollian Intertext in *The Edible Woman,*" in *Essays on Canadian Writing,* No. 37, Spring 1989, pp. 103–11.

Kelly, Darlene, "Either Way, I Stand Condemned," in *English Studies in Canada,* Vol. 21, No. 3, Sept. 1995, pp. 320–32.

MacLulich, T. D., "Atwood's Adult Fairy Tale: Levi Strauss, Bettelheim, and *The Edible Woman,*" in *Essays on Canadian Writing,* No. 11, Summer 1978, pp. 111–29.

Marshall, Tom, "Atwood Under and Above Water," in *Harsh and Lovely Land: The Major Canadian Poets and the Making of a Canadian Tradition,* University of British Columbia Press, 1979, pp. 154–61.

Parker, Emma, "You Are What You Eat: The Politics of Eating in the Novels of Margaret Atwood," in *Information Access Company,* Hofstra University, 1995.

Stedmond, John, Review, in *Canadian Forum,* Vol. 49, February 1970, p. 267.

Taylor, Rupert J., "A Battle Not Yet Won (Women's Rights Past and Present)," in *Canada and the World Backgrounds,* Vol. 60, January 1, 1995, p. 4.

For Further Study

Dodson, Danita J., "An Interview with Margaret Atwood," in *Critique: Studies in Contemporary Fiction,* Vol. 38, No. 2, Winter 1997, p. 96.

> This discussion of Atwood's novel *The Handmaid's Tale* explores her views on feminism, postcolonialism, and utopianism.

Patton, Marilyn, "Lady Oracle: The Politics of the Body," in *Ariel: A Review of International English Literature,* Vol. 22, No. 4, October, 1991, pp. 29–48.

> Patton claims that Atwood's work is often analyzed primarily with psychological interpretations. Patton prefers to look at Atwood's stories in terms of politics.

Little Women

Louisa May Alcott
1868

Without a doubt, *Little Women* remains Louisa May Alcott's best-known work. Its charm and innocence continue to engage readers, despite the fact that the social and familial reality depicted is very different from contemporary domestic life. Jo March is regarded as one of the most complete, self-possessed, and best-loved characters in children's literature. In fact, many boys find that they can relate to her almost as easily as girls can. While some present-day readers find Jo and her sisters too good to be realistic, according to the standards of Alcott's society, the March girls are flawed and vulnerable. The author dared to give her characters faults such as selfishness, vanity, temper, and bashfulness—qualities never seen before in such young characters.

Alcott wrote the book for girls with the sole aim of making money with its publication. After part one was published as a complete work, readers demanded to know more about the fates of the Marches. Alcott wrote *Good Wives* which is now published with part one as a complete work. Although the author wrote the books reluctantly, she earned the money she sought and found that her subsequent titles of all kinds were widely read. She never imagined, however, that *Little Women* would enchant generations of readers and become a classic of children's fiction. Critics often note that the book's particular appeal lies in its illustration of a uniquely American household and its individual members. Almost any reader can identify with at least one of the four girls. Readers are also drawn

into the story by the colorful minor characters, the development of the March girls, and the attention to detail. The intricacies of education, housework, speech patterns, and manners are depicted with remarkable clarity, which better enables modern readers to envision and understand the world of the Marches.

Author Biography

Born on November 29, 1832, in Germantown, Pennsylvania, Louisa May Alcott is best remembered for her books about the March family, especially her children's masterpiece, *Little Women.* From the 1840s into the late 1860s, Alcott (under the pseudonyms A. M. Barnard and Flora Fairchild) also wrote sensational novels and thrillers for adults, most of which are no longer in print. Ironically, Alcott preferred her adult novels to the children's novels that account for her lasting fame.

The Alcotts lived in Concord, Massachusetts, with friends and neighbors such as Ralph Waldo Emerson, Henry David Thoreau, and Nathaniel Hawthorne. Alcott's youth was shaped by both the philosophical climate and the poverty in which she lived. Bronson Alcott, Louisa's father, was a transcendentalist thinker and writer who refused to take work that was not related to education or philosophy. (Transcendentalism is a philosophy that holds that there is an ideal spiritual reality beyond material reality.) Unemployed, he committed to educating his four daughters, Anna (Meg in *Little Women*), Louisa (Jo), Elizabeth (Beth), and May (Amy). A radical pioneer in education, his experiments yielded an erratic but thorough education for his daughters. In 1843, he initiated a large-scale experiment known as Fruitlands, an effort to create a utopian society. Within a year, it failed, and while Alcott seemed flippant about the failure, this experience showed that Bronson could not be relied upon to support the family. Responsibility fell on Alcott's mother, Abba, who came from a respected Boston family. For thirty years, she did the housework and supported the family as a social worker.

Recognizing their daughter's talent, Bronson and Abba placed heavy expectations on her. She was a creative, difficult, and willful girl who was both moody and loyal. As a child, Alcott doted on Emerson and accompanied Thoreau on nature walks in the area of Walden Pond. Although surrounded by transcendentalists, she eventually rejected the philosophy as too abstract, using fiction

Louisa May Alcott

to give voice to her objections. Still, Alcott's writing demonstrates her acceptance of the transcendentalist emphasis on self-reliance and independence.

Little Women contains many autobiographical elements, and critics are quick to note that the stormy character Jo is modeled after Alcott herself. This novel, along with the seven others featuring the March family, is cherished for its cheerful depiction of domestic life, its wholesomeness, and its ability to teach life lessons without the preachy quality found in other children's novels.

Alcott began *Little Women* in 1868, after the Civil War, in which she had served as a nurse during the winter of 1862–1863. She completed part one in only six weeks, and did not revise it as she was in the habit of doing for her adult fiction. It was published as a complete novel. When her public demanded to know more about the Marches, she wrote part two the following year. The novel alludes to the war, but does not include lengthy passages about its disastrous effects on American families and the country as a whole. Her contemporaries, after all, did not need such explanations. In her introduction to the novel, Ann Douglas observes, "*Little Women,* like its avowed model, *Pilgrim's Progress,* is in part an allegory. Alcott was writing about a house in conflict but not divided, a family that offered an analogy and possibly a corrective to America."

By the time *Little Women* was published, Alcott had already become fiercely private. She dreaded interacting with her readers, preferring instead to stay home with her family. Her brief stint as a nurse left her health permanently weakened, a condition that got worse with age. She never married, and, as she grew older, she took very seriously her role as the provider and caretaker of her family. In the end, she was unhappy and unsatisfied with her life. She believed, as do many critics, that her talent was greater than the children's books for which she is so fondly remembered. Alcott died on March 6, 1888, in Boston.

Plot Summary

Part One, Chapters 1–12

The March girls—Meg, 17, Jo, 16, Beth, 14, and Amy, 12—bemoan the fact that Christmas will be lacking because their poverty prevents them from having gifts and their father is away in the Civil War. Resolving to be better people, they decide to play Pilgrim's Progress, an ongoing make-believe in which they follow the allegorical travels of Christian in John Bunyan's *Pilgrim's Progress*. On Christmas day, the girls take their breakfast to the Hummels, a needy family nearby. Later, they discover that their wealthy neighbor Mr. Laurence has rewarded their kindness with flowers and treats.

Jo and Meg attend a dance at a neighbor's house, and while Meg dances, Jo hides behind a curtain. She finds Mr. Laurence's grandson, Theodore ("Laurie"), also hiding. They become quick friends, and when Meg twists her ankle, Laurie gives the girls a ride home.

With the holidays over, the girls resume their routines. Meg is a governess, Jo is the companion of feisty Aunt March (Mr. March's aunt), Beth studies at home, and Amy goes to school. Each girl has an artistic talent: Beth loves music, Jo writes stories and plays, Meg acts in Jo's plays, and Amy draws and sculpts clay.

The girls readily befriend Laurie and his grandfather and visit their luxurious house, enjoying the conservatory, the library, and the piano. The March girls even allow Laurie into their secret club. They set up a post office between the houses in which they can exchange letters, books, flowers, and packages.

Amy buys pickled limes for her friends at school, as this is the fashionable thing to do. When the teacher, who has forbidden students to bring limes to school, catches her with them, she is scolded, her hands are swatted, and she is made to stand in front of the class until recess. Humiliated, she goes home, where Mrs. March tells her she can study at home with Beth rather than return to school.

In a tantrum because Jo and Meg will not let her accompany them to the theater with Laurie, Amy burns the book Jo has been writing. Jo is furious and unforgiving until Amy follows her to ice skate with Laurie and falls through the ice because Jo did not caution her. Jo is ashamed and forgives her sister while resolving to control her anger.

Meg visits her wealthy friend, Annie Moffat, and feels uncomfortable in her shabby clothes. Her friends dress her up for a dance and she soon feels foolish for being treated like a doll.

While Aunt March and Meg's employers are away, the girls say how much they would like to do nothing but play. To teach them a lesson, Marmee agrees to free them of all chores for one week. One disaster after another ensues, and the girls learn the value of work.

Laurie hosts a picnic across the river and invites the girls to join him and his friends. They eat, talk, and play games, and it becomes apparent that Mr. Brooke, Laurie's tutor, has eyes for Meg.

Part One, Chapters 13–23

Jo submits stories to a local newspaper, and the family is ecstatic when they are published. Marmee receives a telegram with the news that her husband is ill and she should come right away. Mr. Laurence sends Mr. Brooke to accompany her on the trip, and the girls worry and promise to write often. Because Marmee is faced with borrowing money, Jo sells her beautiful hair for twenty-five dollars. While Marmee is away, Beth tries to get the other girls to visit the Hummels. When Beth contracts scarlet fever from the sick Hummel baby, the other March girls are ashamed of their selfishness. To protect her from the disease, Amy is sent to live with Aunt March until Beth recovers, and the old woman is quite taken with the young girl. When Beth's condition worsens, they send for Marmee, but the fever breaks just before she arrives. All are relieved and happy to be reunited.

Jo tells Marmee that Mr. Brooke is in love with Meg. Marmee explains that on the trip, Mr. Brooke told her and Mr. March that he loved Meg and hoped to marry her. They said he could make plans, but that Meg was too young to be engaged. When Laurie suspects that Jo knows something about the couple that she will not tell, he plays a cruel joke. He sends Meg letters signed with Mr. Brooke's name. When he is caught, he is regretful and Meg is embarrassed.

Christmas arrives again and Laurie surprises the Marches by bringing Mr. March home.

Mr. Brooke visits Meg and tells her that he loves her and hopes she can learn to feel the same way. Playing games, she acts very cruelly toward him until Aunt March interrupts and Mr. Brooke leaves. Aunt March tells Meg that Meg can do better than Mr. Brooke, and that if she marries him, she will be out of her aunt's will. Indignant, Meg says she can marry whomever she pleases and that Mr. Brooke is a fine man. Aunt March leaves, and Mr. Brooke returns, having overheard everything. The couple agrees to marry, although they will have to wait three years for Meg to grow older and Mr. Brooke to make living arrangements.

Part Two, Chapters 24–35

Three years have passed, and Meg prepares for her wedding. The war is over, and Mr. March is a minister. Aunt March has released Jo from her duty and instead employs Amy to be her companion, paying her with expensive art lessons. Beth is still a homebody, and her health is frail since her fever. Jo sells stories and enjoys life as a writer, feeling quite independent. She enters a contest and wins $100, and the family is very impressed with the sensational story. Papa commends his daughter, adding that he thinks she can do even better. When Jo finishes her novel, she submits it for publication but is advised that it requires major revisions. Torn between her commitment to the novel as it is and wanting to get it published, she decides to go ahead and "chop it up." Reviews are mixed, and Jo regrets her compromise, but she learns about the rigors and trials of being a novelist.

Resigned to the upcoming marriage, Aunt March's stance has softened, and she purchases beautiful linens for the couple's new home. Laurie tells Jo she will be the next to marry, but she responds that she has no interest in such things. On the day of the wedding, family and a few friends gather at the March home for a lovely, simple wedding.

Meg soon finds that married life is satisfying, if not a fairy tale. She has twins, a boy and a girl named Demi and Daisy.

Aunt Carrol plans a trip to Europe, and Aunt March pays for Amy to go along so she can study art. Jo decides to go to New York, where she will teach at a boarding house. There, she meets Professor Bhaer, a charming, poor, German man. When Jo returns home in the summer, Laurie tells her he loves her and wants to marry her. She turns down his proposal, which devastates him. A few weeks later, Mr. Laurence leaves for Europe and Laurie decides to accompany him.

Part Two, Chapters 36–47

Beth's health has been declining steadily over the years, and now she dies peacefully.

In Europe, Laurie makes a last effort to change Jo's mind by correspondence. When she again declines, he begins to correspond with Amy, whom he has seen in his travels. The news of Beth's death sends Laurie to find Amy at once, and romance blooms.

Amy and Laurie return from Europe married, and Jo is surprised but delighted for the union of her little sister and best friend. Professor Bhaer becomes a regular visitor to the March home. One day, he tells Jo he loves her and she kisses him. Aunt March has died and left a country home, Plumfield, to Jo. When she and Bhaer marry, they open a boys' school there.

The family has expanded with husbands and children, but the girls find it as happy as when it was just the four of them, Marmee, and Papa.

Characters

Professor Friedrich ("Fritz") Bhaer

On her trip to New York, Jo meets Professor Bhaer, a German man with a thick accent. He is a stout, educated, older man who takes care of his two orphaned nephews, Franz and Emil. Because he is a bachelor, he undertakes such domestic tasks as cleaning and darning his own socks.

When Jo returns home, Bhaer makes frequent visits, and he and Jo eventually marry. He encourages her to keep writing, but to challenge her talent by writing good fiction rather than the sensationalistic pieces she usually writes. He and Jo open a boys' school at Plumfield.

Mr. John Brooke

Mr. Brooke is Laurie's tutor. As he gets to know Meg, he falls in love with her. In accordance

Media Adaptations

- *Little Women* has been adapted for the screen on numerous occasions. The first was a silent movie produced by G. B. Samuelson in 1917. In 1918, William A. Brady Picture Plays produced another silent version, adapted by Anne Maxwell. One of the best-known adaptations was produced in 1933 by RKO Radio Pictures, adapted for film by Sarah Y. Mason and Victor Heerman, starring Katharine Hepburn as Jo. In 1949, an adaptation by Mason, Heerman, and Andrew Solt was produced by MGM, starring June Allyson as Jo, Elizabeth Taylor as Amy, Janet Leigh as Meg, and Peter Lawford as Laurie. In 1994, Columbia Pictures produced a film adaptation by Robin Swicord, starring Winona Ryder as Jo, Kirsten Dunst as Amy, Claire Danes as Beth, Eric Stoltz as Mr. Brooke, and Susan Sarandon as Marmee.

- *Little Women* was adapted for television in 1958 in a production by CBS Television. Another television production was released in 1970, directed by Paddy Russell. In 1978, an adaptation for television by Susan Clauser was produced by Universal TV, starring Meredith Baxter as Meg, Susan Dey as Jo, Eve Plumb as Beth, Greer Garson as Aunt March, and William Shatner as Professor Bhaer.

- Numerous audio adaptations have been made for listeners to enjoy the story on tape. These include releases by Books in Motion, 1982; Audio Book Contractors, 1987; Harper Audio, 1991; DH Audio, 1992; Dove Entertainment, 1995; Soundelux Audio Publishing, 1995; Sterling Audio Books, 1995; Penguin, 1996; Blackstone Audio Books, 1997; Random House Audio Books, 1997; Trafalgar Square, 1997; Bantam Books, 1998; Books on Tape, 1998; Brilliance Audio, 1998; Monterey Soundworks, 1998; and Naxos Audio Books, 2000.

with her parents' request, he waits to marry Meg until she turns twenty. This period gives him an opportunity to establish himself and buy a house. Although Mr. Laurence offers to help Mr. Brooke, the young man refuses, preferring to make his own way without incurring any debt.

Mr. Brooke takes a job as a clerk and earns a modest living for himself and his new bride.

Hannah

Hannah is the March family's housekeeper. She is colorful and energetic, and she loves the family dearly. She has been with the family since Mr. and Mrs. March married, and she gave Mrs. March her first cooking lessons.

Mr. Laurence

Mr. Laurence is Laurie's grandfather. Until the March sisters meet him, they imagine him to be a daunting man who is distant and stern. Once they get to know him, however, they find him to be generous and warm. He takes a special liking to Jo for her audacity, and he feels special warmth toward Beth.

Theodore Laurence

See Laurie

Laurie

Laurie is the next-door neighbor and is the same age as Jo, his best friend. Although Laurie is wealthy, the economic difference between himself and the Marches does not factor into their relationships. Laurie is instructed at home by a tutor, Mr. Brooke, and later attends college. Laurie is a handsome, friendly, intelligent, witty, and dashing young man who delights in the capers of his neighbors.

Laurie lives with his grandfather, Mr. Laurence, because both of his parents have died. Mr. Laurence was very displeased when his son married Laurie's mother, an Italian woman who was accomplished in music. Living with only his grandfather, Laurie is lonely and therefore treasures his friendships with the March girls and Marmee.

After graduating from college, Laurie proposes to Jo, who rejects him. Devastated, he accompanies his grandfather to Europe, where he and Amy fall in love and marry.

Amy March

Amy is the youngest of the March girls and is twelve at the beginning of the novel. She is spoiled and throws tantrums, and her family strives to correct her behavior before she gets older. Like Meg, Amy loves luxuries and takes an interest in her appearance that is unusual for someone so young. She is also concerned with behaving properly and being popular among her peers. Her pride is her beautiful hair, which falls into golden ringlets. Amy is the artist of the family and spends time drawing and sculpting animals out of clay.

When Beth becomes ill, Amy is sent to stay with Aunt March, who likes the little girl very much. Aunt March releases Jo from her duty as a companion and instead employs Amy, for whom she provides expensive art lessons. Amy travels with another family member to Europe (at Aunt March's expense). While Amy is in Europe, Beth dies and Laurie (also traveling in Europe) finds Amy to comfort her. The two fall in love and marry.

Amy's marriage is comfortable because she marries a man she cares for who happens to be wealthy. Unlike the other sisters, Amy never has to worry about work and has all the fine things she always desired.

Aunt March

Mr. March's aunt, Aunt March is a wealthy widow whose views represent the typical opinions of the time. She believes that Meg, with her beauty, should set her sights on marrying a rich man to provide for her and her family. When Meg considers Mr. Brooke's offer of marriage, Aunt March threatens Meg, saying that if she marries him, she will never get any of Aunt March's money. However, she eventually softens and makes a lovely gift of linens for the couple.

In the beginning of the story, Aunt March pays Jo to be her companion but later hires Amy instead. She is taken with Amy's lively, yet prim nature and hopes to mold her.

When Aunt March dies, she leaves her country home, called Plumfield, to Jo.

Beth March

Beth is the second youngest of the March girls. She is fourteen as the story opens, and she is painfully shy and withdrawn. Although she loves her family and is comfortable with them, she is fearful of strangers and relies on Jo to watch over her. Too shy to attend public school, she studies at home. Beth never makes plans for the future and never talks about having any dreams; she seems perfectly content with her life as it is and expects it to stay the same.

Beth's disposition is sweet, selfless, and warm. She never asks for anything for herself and seeks only to make those around her happy. Her talent is for music, and she makes do on an old worn-out keyboard until Mr. Laurence allows her to play the beautiful piano at his house. She and Mr. Laurence develop a grandfather-granddaughter relationship that fulfills them both.

While caring for a poor family, Beth contracts scarlet fever and becomes extremely ill. Her fever breaks before it claims her life, but her health is permanently compromised by the ordeal. Years later, her health finally gives out, and Beth dies as a young woman.

Josephine March

The second eldest of the four March sisters, Jo is independent, tempestuous, vivacious, clever, and self-confident. She struggles throughout the story to learn to control her temper and her tendency to hold a grudge. She is a tomboy who is more interested in reading and playing games than in primping or gossiping with girls her age. She is sixteen when the story opens, and she has no desire to get married, preferring the happy and satisfying life she enjoys with her family. In fact, when Meg prepares for marriage, Jo is very upset at the prospect of the family breaking up. No longer in school, Jo is the paid companion of Aunt March, a duty she fulfills out of obligation.

Jo has a special relationship with Beth, the next youngest sister. While all of the girls look to Marmee for guidance and advice, Jo watches over Beth and provides additional sisterly support. Jo's relationship with Beth reveals a soft, maternal side of Jo that is rarely seen.

Besides reading, Jo loves to write plays and short stories. The girls enjoy performing Jo's plays, in which she always plays the men's roles. After having two of her stories accepted for publication by a local newspaper, Jo takes her writing more seriously, falling into whirlwind "fits" of writing. Writing brings her success and allows her to earn money doing something she loves. As she observes other young women, Jo is proud of herself because she is able to earn her own money and feel independent. Jo writes a novel, which is accepted for publication only after substantial revision. Jo agrees to the overhaul because she is anxious to get the book published.

Jo's best friend is the wealthy young man next door, Laurie. Jo appeals to him because he can relate to her almost as if she were a boy. Their friendship is characterized by equality, love of books, and a sense of adventure. After graduating from college, Laurie proposes to Jo, but she rejects his proposal, despite knowing that their friendship will be forever changed. Most critics agree that she turns him down because he will never take seriously her career as a writer and because she loves him in a sisterly way, not as a lover. When Laurie marries Amy, Jo is genuinely happy for them. Eventually, Jo marries Professor Bhaer, an older man who is poor, educated, and supportive of her career. Together, they start a school for boys at Plumfield and later have two boys of their own.

Marmee March

Marmee is the girls' mother. She is a strong, confident, reliable woman who provides moral instruction, guidance, and support for her daughters at every stage of their lives. While her husband is away at war, Marmee must care for the house and the four girls on her own. She never appears to struggle, however. She makes certain demands on the girls so that they will learn valuable lessons about life.

Marmee encourages her girls to think for themselves and to pursue true happiness, which, she believes, does not necessarily come from having money. If her daughters never marry, Marmee will be satisfied as long as they are wise, respectable, and accomplished women. She tells Meg that the secret to a good marriage is mutual understanding. She and Mr. March each have their gender-specific duties, but they cooperate with each other and have their own identities.

Meg March

Meg is the eldest of the four girls. Seventeen as the book opens, she is drawn to domestic affairs and feels rewarded when she is able to please those around her. Being old enough to remember times before her family lost its money, she longs for many of the luxuries she can no longer enjoy. She works as a governess for the Kings, who have two children.

Meg has a special relationship with Amy, and acts as her advisor and protector. Meg and Amy have some superficial qualities in common, such as vanity and love of finery, but Meg's temperament is much gentler than Amy's is.

Meg is regarded as beautiful and, as a result, she struggles with her own vanity. She adores wearing fine dresses and having nice things, but such items remain out of reach. When Laurie's tutor, Mr. Brooke, proposes to her, she accepts despite the fact that he is a poor clerk. She sees that he is a good and honest man, and overcomes her disappointment that they are not a well-to-do couple.

Meg delights in domestic activities such as cooking, sewing, and keeping the house in order. Her marriage to Mr. Brooke is happy, but she has difficulty with the initial transition because she wants so badly to be the perfect wife to him. They have twins, a boy named Demi and a girl named Daisy. Meg and Mr. Brooke's gender roles are traditional—he works and disciplines the children, and she does all household work.

Mr. March

The March girls' father, "Papa" (or "Father"), is away serving as a chaplain in the Civil War. He writes loving letters home to his family, and when he is stricken with illness, Marmee leaves the girls to take care of him.

After the war, Mr. March returns and takes a position as a minister in a local church. His days are filled with ministering to his parishioners and interacting with an interesting and diverse group of people. Just as the sisters are based on Alcott's own sisters, Mr. March is based on Alcott's father. Although Mr. March is an important figure in the family's life, he is seen very little in the action of the novel.

Annie Moffat

A wealthy friend of Meg's, Annie invites Meg to stay with her for two weeks, and they dress up for a dance.

Teddy

See Laurie

Themes

Gender Roles

Little Women challenged assumptions about women in nineteenth-century America. Marmee tells her daughters that they should not feel obligated to find husbands, but should seek fulfillment on their own. In chapter 9, she tells Meg and Jo:

> My dear girls, I *am* ambitious for you, but not to have you make a dash in the world—marry rich men merely because they are rich, or have splendid houses, which are not homes because love is wanting. . . . [B]etter be happy old maids than unhappy wives, or unmaidenly girls, running about to have husbands. . . . Leave these things to time; make this home happy, so that you may be fit for homes of your

own, if they are offered you, and contented here if they are not.

Through her example, Marmee shows that a home can be run successfully without a man supporting it, as hers is while Mr. March is away at war. While many women, like Aunt March, expected young women to pursue wealthy men, Marmee sees the value of marriage differently.

Jo is fascinating as a study of female independence in early American society. She is a tomboy who is scolded by her sisters for whistling, using slang, and behaving in "unmaidenly" ways. In chapter 1, Jo tells Meg:

> I hate to think I've got to grow up, and be Miss March, and wear long gowns, and look as prim as a China aster! It's bad enough to be a girl, anyway, when I like boys' games and work and manners! I can't get over my disappointment in not being a boy; and it's worse than ever now, for I'm dying to go and fight with Papa, and I can only stay at home and knit, like a poky old woman!

Jo is brash, outspoken, lively, and clever. She proclaims, "I am not afraid of anything," voicing an attitude altogether different from that of the stereotypical prim and proper young lady. As she matures, she takes more care with her appearance and adopts more ladylike mannerisms, but she does not sacrifice the sense that she is equal to any man.

Adolescence and Identity

Although Meg, Jo, Beth, and Amy grow up in the same household, they develop very distinct identities. Marmee encourages them to be confident in themselves and to mature in wisdom and self-knowledge. Adolescence is a difficult period for anyone, so the girls' struggles are universal. Throughout the novel, the girls' basic identities remain consistent, but as they grow up, they come to understand their faults and work to improve themselves.

Meg's identity is anchored in pleasing her family, be it her mother and sisters or her husband. She is domestic and thrives on homemaking. Jo is stormy and independent, but eventually learns to control her temper. Even as an adult, the self-reliance she values is important in her decision-making. Jo is an unconventional person, so it is no surprise that she ultimately lives an unconventional life. Beth is harmonious and selfless. Were it not for her untimely death, she would likely have continued to grow as a warm and giving person who stays close to home. As the youngest, Amy is somewhat spoiled and acquires a taste for the finer things. This identity is fed by her marriage to Lau-

Topics for Further Study

- Imagine you are assigned to create a soundtrack for *Little Women*. Think about each of the four March girls, Laurie, and Marmee. Choose a song or musical composition that best reflects each character's personality, dreams, and emotional landscape. What are the songs that you choose?

- Research birth-order theories and consider how the dynamics among the sisters support or refute such theories. Report on your findings.

- Although modern wars have important roles for women, the Civil War was much more of a man's war. See what you can learn about women during the time of the Civil War. In what ways did they contribute to the war effort both on the front (in hospitals, for example) and at home?

- Examine the lives of other prominent American women writers to see if there are parallels between their life experiences and Louisa May Alcott's. Do you find that they are vastly different, or that there are significant similarities? Also, did most women use their given names, or did they take pseudonyms, perhaps even male pseudonyms (such as British author George Eliot)? How do you account for the decision to reveal female gender (or not) as a writer in the nineteenth century?

rie, a wealthy husband who will dote on her and give her everything she desires.

Wealth and Poverty

The Marches are poor, although not so poor that they cannot help others. There is never any danger of the March family starving or losing their home, but they all know that they have little money to spare and must economize. Alcott teaches that everyone, even those who have little, has something to offer the world. Marmee and Beth's dedication to the poor German family, the Hummels, is evidence that for all their complaints, the Marches are quite fortunate. Laurie, who comes from a wealthy family, lives right next door to the Marches, and the contrast between the two houses is striking. In chapter 5, Alcott writes, "A low hedge parted the two estates. On one side was an old, brown house, looking rather bare and shabby. . . . On the other side was a stately stone mansion, plainly betokening every sort of comfort and luxury."

The economic inequality between the families, however, has no effect on their relationships. The girls enjoy visiting the Laurences' home to browse the library, admire the art, or stroll among the flowers in the conservatory. Yet there is no bitterness or deep envy. In fact, when the Laurences offer gifts, the Marches feel compelled to return the kindness, and do so without feeling that their offerings are any less valued. The affection between the families neutralizes economic differences that would taint weaker relationships.

Alcott shows, too, that the Marches are rich in ways that the Laurences are not. The Marches, after all, have a house full of lively girls who love one another and have fun together. There is a mother and a father, neither of which Laurie has, and a strong family foundation. Laurie admits to Jo that he watches the activities of the March house, and she understands his loneliness. Once they are friends, the girls make an effort to include Laurie in their fun, including initiating him into their secret club. By presenting the disparities between the two families as she does, Alcott clearly shows her young readers that there are many kinds of wealth and poverty.

The "Good Match"

Although Aunt March attempts to exert her influence to see that Meg is married to an appropriately rich young man, Marmee knows better. Mr. Brooke accompanies Marmee to visit her sick husband and is forthright about his feelings for Meg. Marmee and Mr. March see that he is an honorable man who is a good match for their daughter. Still, the decision is Meg's—if she could not love Mr. Brooke, her parents would in no way force the union. This difference of opinion about what constitutes a "good match" shows the social views of the time, as expressed by Aunt March, in contrast to Alcott's own views, as expressed by Marmee.

Readers are often surprised and disappointed that Jo rejects Laurie's proposal of marriage. They are great friends, and he is charming, handsome, and passionate. Jo knows, however, that Laurie regards her writing as just another "lark" and would never fully support her efforts to make a career of writ-

ing. Further, it is clear that Jo's feelings for Laurie are friendly, even sisterly, and she cannot love him romantically. Her decision not to marry him is respectful of herself and of Laurie, as she wants him to have a wife who will love him as a wife should. By marrying Professor Bhaer, Jo can be herself, an independent woman who enjoys writing and teaching. Bhaer does not discourage her writing, but encourages her to try to do better than the sensational stories that come so easily to her. Sarah Elbert in *A Hunger for Home: Louisa May Alcott and "Little Women,"* concluded, "Jo's journey is the only fully complete one in *Little Women* and it involves her learning to tell true love from romantic fancy." Elbert added that while the girls are ultimately paired up with men they truly love, Jo's marriage comes closest to Alcott's ideal, largely because Jo is closest to Alcott's ideal woman.

At first, the marriage of Laurie to Amy seems odd, but Alcott shows how well-matched they are for each other. They both have fine tastes and prefer a lifestyle of luxury to hard work. Further, Amy likes to be taken care of, something Jo would never allow Laurie to do for her.

Style

Point of View

Little Women is written from a third-person omniscient perspective. The narrator knows the girls' personalities, thoughts, and feelings intimately. This allows the reader to see happenings that the family often does not, such as when Jo cries because she is secretly disappointed that Amy is the one going to Europe.

The narrator also knows the girls' futures, as there are occasional references to what will happen at a future time. Alcott uses both subtle foreshadowing and explicit references to future events. When the Marches and the Laurences set up their makeshift post office, the Laurence's gardener sends a secret love letter to Hannah, the March's housekeeper. Alcott comments, "How they laughed when the secret came out, never dreaming how many love letters that little post office would hold in the years to come!" This statement not only intrigues adolescent readers, but also foreshadows future pleasant letters as well as the cruel joke Laurie plays on Meg by sending forged love letters.

The omniscient narrator does not abuse her power by censoring the characters' faults and mishaps. On the contrary, flaws and bad judgment are included in the story to add a dimension of realism and make the characters believable. Laurie's cruel joke on Meg, Meg's silly domestic dramas as a wife, Jo's intentionally not telling Amy to be careful on the ice—all of these show the characters as human beings with faults.

Structure

The structure of *Little Women* is episodic, alternating stories of each of the sisters. Each chapter focuses primarily on an incident in one of the girls' lives. This structure accomplishes two things. First, it requires a relatively short attention span that is appropriate for Alcott's young audience. Second, this structure makes it easier to see the girls' growth as young women. Rather than charting subtle cues, as an author might in an adult novel, Alcott allows the reader to see changes in the characters each time they are revisited. For example, at the beginning of the novel, Jo is unconcerned with her appearance and keeps her hair down, her clothes crumpled, and her boots untied. In subsequent scenes, Jo is seen tying her boots and putting her hair up, so that the reader notices the changes easily. Readers become aware that while they were watching Meg, Beth, and Amy, Jo grew up a little. The same is true for the other sisters, too.

Domestic-Centered Settings

Given the novel's time period and cast of characters, it is no surprise that the book is filled with domestic concerns and activities. Alcott takes this focus further, however, with her attention to detail and her settings. She is frequently commended for the amount of detail in the story with regard to clothing, manners, appearance, sewing, and entertaining. The critic Madeleine B. Stern commented that Alcott's accomplishment is in presenting universal themes brought to life by domestic details and "local flavor." She adds, "By its documentary value alone, *Little Women,* as an index of New England manners in the mid-century, would be accorded a place in literary history."

Most of the action in the story takes place in the March home. When family members travel, as when Amy goes to Europe, news of the trip is related through letters sent home. When scenes unfold somewhere other than the March home, they are generally in a nearby house (such as Laurie's or Annie Moffat's) or some other domestic setting like the outdoor picnic Laurie hosts. Confining the settings in this way serves to keep the reader's attention on the household as the girls' lives unfold in familiar surroundings.

Foreshadowing

Throughout the novel, Alcott uses foreshadowing to suggest to her readers what lies ahead. Foreshadowing is a technique that establishes the narrator's credibility and creates an air of suspense that compels the reader to keep reading. At the end of part one, Jo bemoans the fact that Meg will marry Mr. Brooke and leave home. Laurie tries to console her by saying that they will have great fun after Meg is gone, and that they will go on a trip abroad to lift Jo's spirits. Jo only responds that Laurie's plan is nice, but "there's no knowing what may happen in three years." Three years later, Meg marries, and, shortly after, Laurie graduates from college and proposes to Jo. When she rejects him, he is devastated and goes abroad without her.

Beth's death is foreshadowed on at least three occasions. Early in the novel, in chapter 4, Alcott writes:

> There are many Beths in the world, shy and quiet, sitting in corners till needed, and living for others so cheerfully that no one sees the sacrifices till the little cricket on the hearth stops chirping, and the sweet, sunshiny presence vanishes, leaving silence and shadow behind.

This passage foreshadows Beth's untimely death and the deep grief felt by her family at her passing. Later, as Jo considers whether or not to overhaul her novel manuscript for publication, Beth says only that she wants to see the book printed soon, and there is something in the way Beth says "soon" that propels Jo into action. Finally, as Amy prepares to leave for Europe, she tearfully hugs Laurie good-bye as she asks him to look after the family. He promises to do so and says that if anything should happen, he will come and comfort her. Alcott adds that he promises this "little dreaming that he would be called upon to keep his word." In fact, Beth dies shortly thereafter. She is able to see Jo's book in print, and her death comes while both Laurie and Amy are in Europe. He finds her and comforts her, after which they fall in love and marry.

Historical Context

The Role of Women in Nineteenth-Century America

In the nineteenth century, women were responsible for creating warm, happy homes for their husbands and children. While some families hired servants, most could not afford to hire help. The duties of running a household were staggering. A woman prepared three rather elaborate meals every

Compare & Contrast

- **1860s:** Children's books generally depict innocent, flawless children in innocent stories. Characters are one-dimensional and stories are strongly oriented toward teaching virtue.

  Today: The Newbery Medal is awarded to Christopher Paul Curtis' *Bud, Not Buddy,* a story about a ten-year-old boy who runs away from his foster home in search of his father. One of the Caldecott Honor Books is Audrey Couloumbis' *Getting Near to Baby,* which tells the story of two sisters dealing with the death of their baby sister. Another Caldecott Honor Book is Molly Bang's *When Sophie Gets Angry—Really, Really Angry,* a story about a little girl's temper tantrum.

- **1860s:** Scarlet fever, which typically afflicts children between the ages of two and ten, is often fatal, as treatments are terribly inadequate. Even when children survive, they often suffer poor health for years.

  Today: Since the discovery of penicillin, scarlet fever rarely claims lives. In fact, patients treated for the disease rarely even suffer lingering problems. In addition, scarlet fever is not as severe as it once was, either because the strain has weakened or because people have become more resistant to the disease.

- **Early 1860s:** The best-selling fiction books are Charles Dickens' *Great Expectations* and *Little Dorrit,* Wilkie Collins' *The Woman in White,* Mrs. Henry Woods' *East Lynne,* and Mary E. Braddon's *Lady Audley's Secret.* They are stories of crime with plots featuring bigamy, incest, and apparitions.

  Today: The best-selling fiction books include J. K. Rowling's Harry Potter series, John Grisham's *The Testament* and *The Brethren,* Seamus Heaney's translation of the classic *Beowulf,* Isabel Allende's *Daughter of Fortune,* and Arthur S. Golden's *Memoirs of a Geisha.* These wide-ranging stories feature wizard apprenticeship, deception in a federal prison, adventure and romance, and coming of age in pre-World War II Japan.

- **1860s:** Young women are expected to learn cooking, sewing, laundering, and parenting. In addition, proper young ladies are well-mannered, graceful, polite, and soft-spoken. Although many women work in "men's" jobs during the Civil War, they return to their places at home once the men return from war.

  Today: Women occupy virtually every career field available. They are doctors, judges, astronauts, scientists, writers, legislators, engineers, and more. At the same time, they have the option of choosing to stay home and take care of the home and rear children. Although there are lingering social norms about what constitutes ladylike behavior, millions of women have little regard for such social restrictions.

---

day. Housecleaning, laundry, mending, and ironing were all done with painstaking care. Daughters were expected to help with housework to expedite chores and also to learn skills for their own future households.

Women were also accountable for the actions of the family outside the home. If a man took up excessive drinking or gambling, for example, his wife was blamed for not creating a suitable home environment. To create an ideal home, the wife handled all housework in addition to being polite, selfless, virtuous, and loving.

Despite the heavy domestic demands placed on a woman, it was sometimes necessary for her to seek additional work for economic reasons. While many tried to take work they could perform at home, such as laundry or sewing, others worked as governesses, teachers, or companions to the elderly. In some cases, women were able to make a living in the creative arts, such as writing. This was quite challenging because women were assumed to be inferior to men, and proper women were not expected to know very much about the outside world.

Philosophical and Social Reforms

Little Women opens during the Civil War, which took place from 1861 to 1865. Prior to that event, New England experienced a rise in philosophical interest and the spread of reform-mindedness. The Transcendental Movement was underway, especially in Massachusetts, where Ralph Waldo Emerson and Henry David Thoreau lived. Transcendentalism rejected Puritanism, religious dogma, and strict adherence to rituals. Instead, it embraced individualism and naturalism, maintaining that there is a deep connection between the universe and the human soul. American transcendentalism officially began in 1836 in Boston, with the formation of the Transcendental Club, whose members included Emerson, Thoreau, Margaret Fuller, and Bronson Alcott.

Early in the nineteenth century, middle-class women began joining evangelical societies that promoted social and moral reform. As conflict mounted over the issue of slavery, women became involved, and by 1850 most members of abolitionist groups were women. From these beginnings sprang the women's rights movement, which would steadily gain momentum well into the twentieth century.

Education

Nineteenth-century formal education in America was limited, as evidenced by the fact that in 1860 there were only a hundred public high schools. Although there were more elementary schools, only about half of all children attended, and then only for forty-five days per year. Children were taught reading, writing, spelling, and arithmetic, and sometimes history, geography, and grammar. Learning took the form of memorization and recitation, as opposed to critical thinking or creativity. This approach contrasts to Bronson Alcott's teaching methods, which were designed to encourage his daughters to think for themselves and learn facts instead of memorizing them for the short term.

Louisa certainly understood the distinction between her educational experience and that of many of her peers. Many families who were dissatisfied with public schooling opted to teach their children at home. Those who could afford it hired tutors for their children, as represented in the novel by Laurie's tutor, John Brooke. Formal education gener-

ally ended when a student turned fourteen or fifteen, especially when the student was female.

Discipline in public school was often harsh and humiliating. Corporal punishment, such as spanking or swatting, was common, although not all parents agreed with these methods. In *Little Women*, Amy is subjected to this sort of treatment by her teacher when she is caught with limes at school. Her teacher swats her hands and forces her to stand in front of the class until recess. Mrs. March agrees not to send Amy back to school, so she pursues her studies at home with Beth.

The Civil War

When the Civil War ended, more than 600,000 men had lost their lives and others were disabled. More Americans died in the Civil War than in all other American wars combined from the colonial period through the Vietnam War. It is unknown how many civilians were killed by guerrillas, deserters, and soldiers.

Because so many men were killed or seriously wounded in the war, American families were faced with the difficult task of supporting themselves without the help of the man of the house. Meager pensions to widows and veterans were not enough to restore financial stability. To make matters worse, most men were forever changed by the experience. Most had never traveled beyond their home towns, and serving in the military took them far away where they faced loneliness, fear, and daily confrontation with death and suffering. As veterans, they assembled in organizations and fostered a sense of patriotism for their sacrifices. For African Americans, serving in the military was beneficial in its own way because they could then make strong cases for citizenship.

During the war, women assumed larger roles in the social structure. They became temporary nurses, clerks, and factory workers. A few hundred women even disguised themselves as soldiers and fought on the battlefields. Once the war was over, however, traditional roles were resumed.

The economic consequences of the war were formidable. Consider that in 1860, the federal budget was $63 million, and by 1879, the total expenditures for the war were calculated at over $6 billion. This created extreme debt and limited the government's ability to function as it had prior to the war. In the South, economic hardship became the norm. Railroads, industrial operations, mechanical equipment, and livestock had been spent or destroyed. In contrast, the economy in the North

(From left) Winona Ryder as Jo, Trini Alvarado as Meg, Kirsten Dunst as Amy, Susan Sarandon as Marmee, and Clare Danes as Beth in the 1994 film version of the novel

thrived during and after the war. Statistics show that between 1860 and 1870, Northern wealth increased by 50 percent, while Southern wealth decreased by 60 percent. The Reconstruction Period, which represented efforts to reunite the country in political, economic, and social terms, would last twelve years—triple the length of the war.

Critical Overview

Although Louisa May Alcott wrote *Little Women* in 1868 for the sole purpose of making money, the novel is without question her most notable and enduring work. In fact, the book as it is read today contains the original text and its sequel, *Good Wives,* which was written a year after the first part. The second part was written in response to the demands of Alcott's young female readers, who were drawn to the individuality displayed by the novel's characters and wanted to know what would become of them. Upon the April 14 release of part two, Alcott's publisher was shocked by its sales. By the end of May, more than 13,000 copies had sold—an incredible number at the time, and especially surprising because the book was written for young

girls, not the general public. Critical response in 1868 and 1869 was as favorable as the readers' response, and Alcott was among the first children's authors to be taken seriously by literary critics. A review in *Nation* declared *Little Women* an "agreeable" story that appeals to juvenile and adult readers alike. The critic wrote that the March girls were "drawn with a certain cleverness."

When the second part of the novel was published, a critic wrote in *Harper's New Monthly Magazine* that it was perhaps too mature for adolescent girls, but that it rings true by not resorting to the "false sentiment" so common in children's literature. In fact, Alcott's contemporaries as well as modern-day critics agree that the novel is remarkable for its reality and depth, standing in stark contrast to the too-sweet, overly didactic stories available to children at the time. Children were generally depicted as perfect and innocent, but Alcott gave her characters flaws and made no effort to conceal them. They remain virtuous, however, because they are aware of their weaknesses and strive to correct them. In modern terms, the characters in *Little Women* seem a bit too perfect, as many critics argue, but in the context of the mid-nineteenth century, they were characters whose likeness had never been seen. Not all critics praise the novel, however. Biographer Martha Saxton viewed *Little Women* as a sell-out for Alcott, who, according to Saxton, had great talent, yet squandered it on a book that was preachy and sentimental. Jane Gabin in *Reference Guide to American Literature,* on the other hand, deemed *Little Women* "markedly superior to other books of its genre" because of its unobtrusive "sermonizing" and its well-rounded characters. She added that in other books of the time, the villains and the heroes were clearly identified, but in Alcott's book, even the heroes have flaws and make mistakes. Lavinia Russ of *Horn Book* had a different view on the appeal of the book, arguing that the story teaches that life does not always provide neatly bundled happy endings, but that girls should still strive to be good people.

Alcott's sense of the challenges and joys of adolescence continues to impress readers. Since its publication, *Little Women* has never gone out of print, and some scholars attribute its staggering success to the universal themes of growing up and to Alcott's honest portrayal of the feelings, thoughts, worries, and delights that accompany it. In *New England Quarterly,* Madeleine Stern observed:

> The author's knowledge of adolescent psychology reveals itself in twofold form throughout the work, for it consisted first of an appeal to adolescents, the skill of making them laugh or cry, and secondly of an ability to describe adolescents, to catch and transfix the varied emotions and thoughts of the young.

Feminist critics are divided about the portrayal of females in *Little Women.* While some criticize the heavily domestic depiction of womanhood, others praise Jo as a breakout figure who blazes her own path and is able to have both love and a career. The fact that, in part two, Jo marries a man who is older and lacks passion seems too great a compromise to some critics who admired Jo's steadfast adherence to her principles in part one. Further, they interpret her working at Plumfield with her husband as sacrificing her writing after marriage.

Although the book is filled with submissive women who are content with domestic life (such as Meg), a great deal of feminist attention concentrates on Jo. Brigid Brophy of *New York Times Book Review* agreed that while the book is heavily sentimental, it still works because of the extraordinary character of Jo. Less taken with the novel, Elizabeth Janeway in *Only Connect: Readings on Children's Literature,* described it as "dated and sentimental and full of preaching and moralizing," but admitted that Jo makes the book worth reading nonetheless. She wrote that "Jo is . . . the one young

woman in nineteenth-century fiction who maintains her individual independence, who gives up no part of her autonomy as payment for being a woman." Alison Lurie of *New York Review of Books* seems to agree with this notion, as she commented:

> From a mid-nineteenth century perspective, *Little Women* is both a conservative and a radical novel. . . . In contemporary terms, [Jo] has it all: Not only a household and children but two careers and she doesn't have to do her own housework and cooking.

Critics continue to debate the lasting qualities of *Little Women.* Whether it is the novel's touching presentation of growing pains, the triumphant female figure Jo, or the overall "human truth," as British author and critic G. K. Chesterton claims, there is no doubt that the novel as a whole has an enduring appeal. Despite its setting in a time and place unfamiliar to modern readers, the novel continues to speak to children and adults in a way that transcends mere nostalgia.

Criticism

Jennifer Bussey

Bussey holds a master's degree in interdisciplinary studies and a bachelor's degree in English literature. She is an independent writer specializing in literature. In the following essay, she discusses autobiographical elements in Alcott's novel in contrast to the fictional decisions the author made. Factors such as Alcott's duty to her readership and wish fulfillment are considered.

That Louisa May Alcott's classic *Little Women* is heavily autobiographical is well known among literary scholars. Perhaps because she wrote the book merely for money, she found it economical to lift people and events out of her own life to create the story. Part one was written in 1868 and was intended to be the only story about the March family. Readers, however, were captivated by the girls and demanded to know more about their lives. The following year, Alcott wrote *Good Wives,* which now appears as part two in *Little Women.* Readers were thrilled with the continuing story of the Marches, although Alcott's intentions were not merely to appease her readers by writing a naive and romantic story. In part two, fiction overshadows fact, which leaves readers and scholars to wonder how Alcott made decisions about the fates of the sisters. While it is clear that certain aspects of part two are designed to satisfy her readership, oth-

> After the failure of Fruitlands (Alcott's father's attempt to establish a utopian society), Alcott realized that her father could not be relied upon to support his wife and daughters."

ers clearly are not. Was Alcott compromising with her readers (between what she knew they would want and what she thought was realistic), or was she exercising a bit of wish fulfillment in her novel?

Part one of *Little Women* is brimming with autobiographical elements, from important plot developments to minor details. Some scholars suggest that Alcott's initial reluctance to write the book, her quick completion of the manuscript in six weeks, and her minimal editing all indicate that she undertook writing the novel as a task to finish as quickly as possible. Using her life as a template allowed her to make shortcuts without sacrificing realism, characterization, or interesting story developments.

Each of the four sisters was modeled after one of Alcott's own sisters. Meg is the literary counterpart to Anna, Jo is Alcott's alter ego, Beth is the book's version of Elizabeth, and the letters of Amy's name can be rearranged to spell out her real-life inspiration, May. Most of the events in part one are based on actual events in Alcott's life, such as Meg's marriage and Jo's profound disappointment at having the family separated. Also, the Alcott girls donated their Christmas breakfast to a needy family one year, Alcott won a hundred dollars in a writing contest, and the girls often performed plays for neighborhood girls. Growing up, Alcott loved spending time with her sisters as much as Jo does, and she resolved early in life to be responsible for taking care of the family. After the failure of Fruitlands (Alcott's father's attempt to establish a utopian society), Alcott realized that her father could not be relied upon to support his wife and daughters. Alcott's mother realized this, too, and, like Marmee, worked diligently to be sure the family's needs were met. Mr. March is physically or emotionally absent throughout *Little Women,* and Alcott's father was not a reliable breadwinner or confidant.

Part one is more character driven than part two, presumably because Alcott is simply telling about the people in her life. It is unsatisfying as a self-contained story, as it only introduces the girls, describes some of their scrapes, and tells how Meg comes to be engaged. Many scholars regard it as plotless, concluding that its success came from its detailed setting, quick pace, and delightful characters with whom young readers could readily identify. Because most characters in children's books at the time were too perfect, readers were less interested in what eventually became of them. In *Little Women,* however, readers saw themselves in the pages of the story and longed to know how things turned out for the March girls. Thus, being character driven is part one's strength.

In addition, part one reveals a great deal about Alcott's perceptions of her family life. Mr. March's absence reflects Alcott's inability to create a believable, involved father in an autobiographical work. Because her father was not an ideal paternal figure, she would have had difficulty imagining the familiar setting with a wonderful, warm, and connected father. Alcott's solution is to have Mr. March away at war, and then busy with his own affairs when he returns. Unlike the father, the sisters are all drawn with loving detail. Each sister has a unique personality, rather than a generic childlike temperament. Alcott's presentation of young girls who are flawed and struggling with growing up was revolutionary at the time. Her multidimensional characters reveal her closeness to her sisters and perhaps her belief that readers would love them even with their flaws, as she did.

In the character of Jo, Alcott reveals much about her perception of herself. Jo, like Alcott, is more interested in writing and in seeing her family happy than in finding a husband or in being proper. Jo is a coltish young woman who has far to go before she matures into her own brand of womanhood. Alcott never quite fit into the social circles around her, and she was never much interested in making friends or marrying. In fact, by the time *Little Women* was released, Alcott had become rather private and withdrawn. While her adoring readers wanted to know all about the woman who wrote such a lovely book, she preferred to keep to herself. Neither Jo nor Alcott can be described as a misfit, but their priorities are themselves and their families.

The novel's Laurie does not have a direct counterpart in real life, as Alcott never had such a friend as Laurie. He is a composite of many young men Alcott knew, and her inclusion of him in Jo's small circle indicates that Alcott felt more at ease with young men her age than with young women. The things Jo and Laurie have in common are the things that interested Alcott, and things she did not observe as being important to women in her peer group.

Not having planned a part two, Alcott had a difficult task before her as she set about writing it. In part one, she relied on her own immediate surroundings for material and inspiration, but with part two, she created characters and events. Alcott had important decisions to make about the paths her characters' lives would take. She was writing in response to her readership, so she made some effort to appease them, but some of the plot developments are unexpected and disappointing to readers. Despite her desire for luxurious things, Meg marries a poor clerk and learns to be happy with a simple lifestyle. (Alcott's sister Anna also hoped for wealth yet married a poor man, so, here again, the author draws from her own life for material.) Most readers want Jo and Laurie to marry, but Jo rejects Laurie's proposal, only to marry an unlikely husband. Students of Alcott are curious about her reasons for these plot developments.

While it is tempting to imagine that Alcott wrote for Jo a fate she had hoped for herself, the author's correspondence proves otherwise. She knew that readers desperately wanted to see Jo marry, but Alcott was unwilling to make the obvious choice of Laurie as a husband. Alcott understands Jo so completely that she cannot allow her to marry Laurie, even though it disappoints most readers. Jo loves Laurie as a brother, not as a husband, and she knows that he does not fully appreciate how important her writing is to her. As his wife, she would be expected to socialize in high society and behave like a lady. Knowing herself well enough to know that the marriage would not be fulfilling, Jo refuses his proposal. When Laurie eventually meets up with Amy in Europe and they fall in love, Jo is truly happy for them both. She understands that her sister will love Laurie as he deserves to be loved and that she will be able to enjoy the wealthy life she so desires. Amy will let Laurie take care of her, something with which Jo would never be comfortable, even though it makes Laurie feel manly and needed. For Laurie, the union is ideal because he can be loved and he has someone interested in fashion, society, and entertaining.

What Do I Read Next?

- *Little Men* (1871) is the sequel to *Little Women*, and tells of Jo's life at Plumfield, where she runs a school for boys. Although the boys are often rowdy, Jo and her husband enjoy teaching them, along with their own two sons.

- In *Jo's Boys* (1886), Alcott continues the adventures of the boys from Jo's school at Plumfield. Now that the boys have grown into men, they follow very different paths in life.

- Nina Baym's *Women's Fiction: A Guide to Novels by and about Women in America, 1820–1870* (1978) provides a useful overview of trends in women's literature in the mid-nineteenth century. Baym considers 130 novels by forty-eight authors.

- Frances Hodgson Burnett's classic *The Secret Garden* (1911) is the story of Mary, Colin, and Dickon, whose moody dispositions are lightened by the discovery of a secret garden that inspires their imaginations. As they restore the little paradise, they learn about life and personal growth.

- Lucy Maud Montgomery's *Anne of Green Gables* (1908) is the story of a lively, mischievous orphan sent to a family who was expecting a boy. As she and her new parents learn about each other, they learn that their finding each other was lucky after all.

- *Louisa May Alcott: A Reference Guide* is Alma J. Payne's 1980 guide to the work of one of America's most beloved children's authors. It is a handy reference for any serious student of Alcott's work.

- *Critical Essays on Louisa May Alcott* is Madeleine B. Stern's 1984 collection of original criticism on Alcott's work. Stern is regarded as an expert on Alcott, and these essays cover a wide range of issues and considerations of the author's work.

In other words, Amy thrives in the lifestyle that Laurie loves. (The union between Amy and Laurie is completely the product of Alcott's imagination, as May never married in real life.)

To provide a fitting husband for Jo, Alcott created Professor Bhaer, not because he is the type of man Alcott herself dreamed of meeting, but because he is almost comical as a romantic figure. While unusual, he is a good match for Jo, but Alcott's decision to direct Jo's life in this way was, in a sense, her way of snubbing her nose at traditional, predictable, sentimental romance. Professor Bhaer, then, seems to be a literary compromise between readers' desires and writer's attitudes. It is reasonable to believe that Alcott hoped to demonstrate to her readers the importance of keeping one's mind open in matters of love. After all, other passages in the book advise against marrying for any other reason than true love and happiness, a view that was not widespread at the time.

Professor Bhaer is not the dashing romantic figure Laurie is. Like Laurie, Bhaer is also a composite, but seems to be largely modeled after the Alcotts' friend, Ralph Waldo Emerson, whom the author admired very much. Jo respects Bhaer because he is poor but happy, thoughtful, self-sufficient, and good-hearted. Further, he takes her writing seriously, encouraging her to give up working on the sensational stories she is accustomed to writing and instead to concentrate on writing quality fiction. He supports her talent and admires her lively independence. Jo's marriage to him allows her to be herself and to have both a career and love.

Alcott never married, but instead fulfilled her commitment to care for her family. She lived at home her entire life, writing and earning a considerable income for the household. Scholars speculate that in the novel, if Beth had not died, Jo would probably never have married. Beth's passing, however, left Jo free of family obligations. Yet in Alcott's life, Elizabeth died and the author still stayed home. Perhaps this was because her father did not contribute to the family's finances much, or perhaps it was because Alcott never met her unusual-but-fitting match, as Jo did. She once commented that writing seemed to be her destined lifelong companion.

Perhaps the most disappointing event in the book is Beth's passing. Alcott's sister Elizabeth died at the age of twenty-three, so writing about Beth's death in the novel was undoubtedly very painful for Alcott. Here there is neither compromise nor wish fulfillment. Like Jo, Alcott was up-

set by the loss of her older sister to marriage and then devastated by the loss of her younger sister to illness. In Alcott's characterization of Beth as a saintly and frail child, the reader has a sense of Alcott's feelings about her own sister. It is common for people to exalt those who have died, especially those who have died young. Throughout the novel, Beth is regarded as a dear and selfless child whose example the sisters try to follow.

Undoubtedly, the life of Alcott's fictional counterpart Jo turned out happier than the author's did. Jo's life with Professor Bhaer was one Alcott did not want for herself, but one that did please her readers. While Jo had a devoted husband and a school for boys, and maintained her zest for life, Alcott had only her writing. She did not even particularly care for the children's books that brought her such fame and success; she preferred her adult thrillers, which garnered little attention. Unfortunately, Alcott could not foresee that, regardless of her own opinions of her work and her solitary life, she would be remembered fondly for generations and regarded as an American literary treasure.

Source: Jennifer Bussey, Critical Essay on *Little Women,* in *Novels for Students,* The Gale Group, 2001.

Ann B. Murphy

In the following essay excerpt, Murphy surveys critical approaches to Little Women, *finding "the novel does not permit rigid answers" to attempts to analyze its meaning and significance. Comparison is made with Mark Twain's* Adventures of Huckleberry Finn.

Twenty years of scholarship about Louisa May Alcott's most famous and enduring work, *Little Women,* testifies to the complicated process of reexamining a novel widely recognized as a classic in American children's literature. This critical reevaluation of Alcott has been complicated by the publication of her previously uncollected and largely unavailable gothic thrillers, which reveal a new dimension to the familiar author, both enriching our reactions to *Little Women* (especially to the silencing of Jo March's own anxious authorship of pseudonymous thrillers) and confirming our sense of the subversion in that sentimental text.

Biographies exploring the darker side of Alcott and reinterpreting her complicated family, as well as ongoing feminist work retrieving, recuperating, and reenvisioning American literature and cultural history, have all contributed to the scholarship on Alcott during the past two decades. Yet the text of *Little Women* remains something of a tarbaby, a sticky, sentimental, entrapping experience or place rather than a knowable object—and thus a fitting emblem of its own subversive content, which resists women's objectification and seeks a new vision of women's subjectivity and space. Some critics begin by directly recognizing the extraordinary power this work had for them and others in childhood. Others approach the novel with more apparent detachment, focusing on its repressive domesticity. For most of us, however, *Little Women* is a troubling text, a childhood icon that still resonates with images of positive female community, ideal and loving motherhood, and girlhood dreams of artistic achievement. Our reactions to the incarceration of Meg in claustrophobic domesticity, the mysterious, sacrificial death of good little Beth, the trivialization of Amy in objectifying narcissism, and the foreclosure of Jo's erotic and literary expression, are inextricably connected to our memories of our own struggles against these fates.

Not surprisingly, then, there is remarkable disunity in the contemporary reappraisals of the meaning and significance of Alcott's novel. Indeed, the disagreement is so pervasive and individual opinions so frequently contradictory, within and between essays, as to suggest both the abiding and seductive power of this text for many female readers, and the rich plenitude of its still unexplored critical possibilities Is *Little Women* adolescent, sentimental, and repressive, an instrument for teaching girls how to become "little," domesticated, and silent? Is the novel subversive, matriarchal, and implicitly revolutionary, fostering discontent with the very model of female domesticity it purports to admire?

The novel does not permit rigid answers to these questions. To account for its enduring power, *Little Women* must instead be seen as a multifaceted novel, a children's book regarded (or at least defined) as "moral pap" by its author. It preaches domestic containment and Bunyanesque self-denial while it explores the infinity of inward female space and suggests unending rage against the cultural limitations imposed on female development. Like the patchwork quilts of her predecessors and contemporaries, Alcott's novel assembles "fragments into an intricate and ingenious design" containing both messages of "female patience, perseverance, good nature and industry" and "an alternative model of female power and creativity." Its power derives from its contradictions rather than prevailing despite them.

> " Yet the text of *Little Women* remains something of a tarbaby, a sticky, sentimental, entrapping experience or place rather than a knowable object—and thus a fitting emblem of its own subversive content. . . ."

At the same time, the terms of critical debate over *Little Women* are themselves instructive because they point obsessively to crucial episodes and characters, and to the book's uneasy closure. Thus Carolyn Heilbrun finds in Jo March "the single female model continuously available after 1868 to girls dreaming beyond the confines of a constricted family destiny to the possibility of autonomy and experience initiated by one's self," but she concludes that "Alcott betrayed Jo" and suggests that Jo is a positive model only if we overlook her marriage. Patricia Spacks places the emphasis differently, finding that *Little Women* enforces repressive lessons in female docility, passivity, and silence, while its "glorification of altruism as feminine activity . . . reaches extraordinary heights." For Spacks, Jo's marriage is not ambiguous but punitive, not a betrayal but the logical culmination of the novel's didactic and regressive intent.

By contrast, Nina Auerbach concludes that the novel's portrayal of female materiality and self-sufficiency subverts ideals of domesticated womanhood, and that the matriarch, Mrs. March, allows her daughters "the freedom to remain children and, for a woman, the more precious freedom *not* to fall in love." Including the entire March trilogy in her appraisal, rather than the single novel, Auerbach claims that by the end Jo "has attained the position of Marmee, but her title is more formidable than that comfortable, clinging name." Rather than a betrayal or punishment, then, Alcott's treatment of Jo, and the implications of her marriage, are eventually affirmative, even triumphant.

Elizabeth Langland and Madelon Bedell both incorporate these tensions within their analyses, positing a multilayered text with ambivalent, even contradictory messages. "The narrative surface of *Little Women* asserts that marriage is woman's ful-

fillment. Underneath this principal narrative, however, lies a possibility closer to Alcott's experience," Langland claims, finding that covert text primarily embodied in Jo, who resists the book's
lessons in "disengagement from the active world
and its strife and a retreat from self-assertion into
marriage." Similarly, Bedell finds that beneath the
surface narrative lies "the legend, which the story
masks. The theme of the legend is also concerned
with the sisters' struggles against the inevitability
of growing up, of leaving the delightful state of
childhood for the restricted, narrow, and burdened
condition of womanhood."

Again and again, as this brief review suggests,
feminist critics collide against the sticky, protean
implications of this ostensibly childish text: the absent, passive, feminized father who yet ruthlessly
diminishes his "little" women; the radically present, loving, self-sacrificing—and perpetually angry—mother who makes girlhood so literally seductive and adulthood so utterly deadly; the erotic,
rich, musical, half-Italian brother-lover, Laurie,
whom Jo eventually rejects for the elderly, patriarchal German professor; and above all Jo March,
with whom we all so passionately identified:
gawky, loving, intense, funny, furious, creative,
and incredibly active. It is through Jo that we are
compelled to question the painfully limited choices
available to women artists. It is through Jo that we
are forced to acknowledge acute discontent with
Bunyan's model of Pilgrim's Progress—and the
nineteenth-century model of active girls dwindling
into docile little women. It is through Jo that we
experience the complicated intersections and over-
lappings of eroticism, anger, and creativity—and
mourn the apparent effacing of all three by the
novel's end, without truly believing they are indeed
gone.

Whether we see *Little Women* as "a perfectly
disgusting, banal, and craven service to male supremacy" or "a gratifying taste of [Alcott's] simple, stable vision of feminine completeness," we
cannot evade the textured ambiguity and quiltlike
complexity of its image of female development, the
deep uncertainty with which Alcott struggles to
portray female loss of freedom through accultura-
tion and adolescence as somehow enhancing and
morally sustaining. In fact, these tensions and am-
bivalences contribute to the power of *Little Women*,
focusing attention on the insidious as well as sustaining elements of the myth of female moral superiority and on the disjunctions between male and
female stories of maturation. . . .

An initial focus on caring for the self in order to ensure survival is followed by a transitional phase in
which this judgment is criticized as selfish. The criticism signals a new understanding of the connection
between self and others . . . the concept of responsibility. . . . This concept . . . and its fusion with a maternal morality . . . characterizes the second perspective. . . . However . . . the exclusion of herself
gives rise to problems in relationships, creating a disequilibrium that initiates the second transition . . . a
reconsideration of relationships . . . to sort out the
confusion between self-sacrifice and care. . . . The
third perspective focuses on the dynamics of relationships and dissipates the tension between selfishness and responsibility through a new understanding
of the interconnection between other and self.

While the surface narrative or pattern of *Little
Women* may well be the standard sentimental
"moral pap" produced in the nineteenth century to
show girls their proper sphere, at least one of its
many subtexts or pieces follows quite closely the
outline of female ethical development suggested by
Carol Gilligan. It does so, too, with the clearly subversive suggestion that such an alternative model
of maturation is morally superior to (warring,
money-hungry) male development. The novel
opens on Christmas Eve, and the first words we
hear are complaints about a lack of presents—of
material presence. Quickly, however, the March
sisters come to see their complaints as selfish: "I
am a selfish girl!" Amy exclaims, "but I'll truly try
to be better." During the course of book 1, the sisters struggle heroically against such selfishness,
moving toward understanding themselves in relation to others.

During these pilgrimages, Meg learns about
the venality of high society, and by implication
American capitalism, accepting in its place the alternate model of female adulthood Marmee offers:
"I want my daughters to be beautiful, accomplished, and good; to be admired, loved, and respected; to have a happy youth, to be well and
wisely married, and to lead useful, pleasant lives."
Amy, the least likeable and most narcissistic and
ambitious of the four, learns—with Marmee's
help—that "there is not much danger that real talent or goodness will be overlooked long; even if it
is, the consciousness of possessing and using it well
should satisfy one." Beth, whose selfishness is less
immediately obvious, learns—without help from
Marmee—that her debilitating shyness may in fact
be an unkindness to others. Jo, of course, battles
the ferocity of her selfish anger. In the process of
her arduous journey, Jo learns "not only the bitterness of remorse and despair, but the sweetness of

self-denial and self-control"—again instructed by Marmee.

By the end of book 1, these struggles produce significant changes that are named and approved by their father upon his return. The initial sacrifice of material goods—Christmas breakfast—has been so internalized that Meg abandons her vanity and materialism and becomes submissive to her comparatively impoverished future husband. Amy makes a will renouncing all her worldly goods. Beth nearly dies in sacrificial service to others, and Jo renounces not only her beautiful hair but her beloved sister, Meg, and the illusions of safety and childhood as well.

Book 2 marks their more painful attempts to negotiate a reconciliation between a notion of goodness equated with extreme self-sacrifice and the needs of their own authentic characters. Meg struggles to be both a nurturing mother and a fully sexual adult woman in her marriage, and she seems to achieve some kind of balance, moving beyond her initial self-immersion in the nursery and learning to share child care responsibilities with her husband. Amy devises a socially appropriate balance between narcissism and selfishness, becoming her own most triumphant art object: "Everything about her mutely suggested love and sorrow—the blotted letters in her lap, the black ribbon that tied up her hair, the womanly pain and patience in her face; even the little ebony cross at her throat seemed pathetic to Laurie."

Beth, of course, dies from a mysterious disease arising from terminal goodness—from her inability to distinguish between nurturing others and the radical self-denial expected of femininity. Jo, after rejecting erotic love and renouncing a literary career, acknowledges her own vulnerability and need: "A sudden sense of loneliness came over her so strongly that she looked about her with dim eyes, as if to find something to lean upon." Her marriage to Professor Bhaer offers her a way to balance personal need and cultural expectations: "I may be strong-minded, but no one can say I'm out of my sphere now," she tells her fiance, "for woman's special mission is supposed to be drying tears and bearing burdens. I'm to carry my share, Friedrich, and help to earn the home. Make up your mind to that."

Yet while this heroic pattern certainly exists and provides some of the book's insidious power— a message of consolation to young girls for the loss of childhood freedom—it is mitigated and contradicted by its own terms, as well as by other, seriously conflicting, messages. Most notably, the journeys toward selflessness in book 1 and interconnection in book 2 are undercut both by an obsessive diminution of their context and by the incessant imagery of patriarchal observation that renders nearly every ethical achievement artificial, theatrical—an objectivized scene. Meg's domestic battles in book 2, for example, take place in a home so minuscule it is hard to imagine adult human beings living in it: "The little brown house . . . was a tiny house, with a little garden behind and a lawn about as big as a pocket handkerchief." The last vision we have of Meg, before she disappears completely from sight in the text, describes her as "on the shelf": "Safe from the restless fret and fever of the world . . . learning . . . that a woman's happiest kingdom is her home, her highest honor the art of ruling it not as a queen, but as a wise wife and mother."

More ambiguously, Amy's artistic efforts are consistently described as comical or insignificant, their only permanent memorial being a suggestively oedipal gouged foot. Her work is either trivial (mudpies) or dangerous (burning, cutting, immobilizing). Although she apparently continues her lethal artistic activity after her marriage—turning her frail daughter into yet another aesthetic object—she decides after only one trip to Rome that "talent isn't genius" and gives up all her "foolish hopes," as if possessing the genius of Michelangelo were a woman's only excuse for pursuing artistic activity, as if she had no responsibility to nurture mere talent. Beth, of course, is rendered literally angelic and eventually nonexistent rather than simply tiny: like Meg she is safely removed from the trials of life, and her death is the clearest message in the novel about the ominous dangers of selflessness.

Still, it is Jo's struggle that most directly reveals Alcott's ambivalence about female morality and betrays the rage beneath the obsessive diminution. When Amy burns Jo's much-cherished manuscript, Jo is quite naturally furious—and thus guilty of being quick-tempered. Yet even Jo refers to the manuscript as her "little book," while the narrator explains that "it was only half a dozen little fairy tales . . . [and] it seemed a small loss to others." Later, Meg advises Amy on how to make up with Jo, telling her "You *were* very naughty, and it *is* hard to forgive the loss of her precious little book," suggesting by her emphasis that Amy was not very naughty and that the little book was not so precious. While the cause of Jo's impermissable anger is ruthlessly minimized, the consequences are nonetheless enormous—and deadly: Amy falls through the ice and nearly drowns.

The narrative emphasis on the triviality of these tribulations (especially in bk. 1), so ominously shadowed by images of death, suggests Alcott's own ambivalence about the cult of feminine altruism and its domestic context. Furthermore, she portrays the entire pilgrimage itself as an act, a game; the progression of the girls' roles is objectivized, viewed, and judged by a benevolent, absent patriarch. The sisters are learning not simply to be selfless, but to be objects, viewed by patriarchal subjects. Amy's original sense of selfishness, for example, originates in a desire to be seen differently by her father, while Marmee's image of ideal womanhood is explicitly of an Other, a third-person object: "beautiful, accomplished, good, admired, loved, respected." Her sermon on anger reinforces this objectification, for she conveys her own laborious process of learning to control her anger specifically as an experience of being watched, observed, and judged by her passionless husband.

Alcott's penchant for the theatrical is well known, and numerous critics have noticed the degree to which the role of the little woman is a (painfully) learned one: "Indeed, discovering the real self of the woman playing the little woman is an impossible task, in part because the essence of the role is that it appears to be the 'real' self." The March sisters' pilgrimage is a game in a way that Huck's river voyage most emphatically is not. Yet the game is as life-threatening and dangerous as anything Huck experiences, precisely because it excludes as hostile the entire outside world (defined by distant, deadly warfare, diseased and demanding poor families, and venal, trivial society) while imposing an ostensibly empowering role of female altruism which offers moral superiority as compensation for domestic bondage, gouged artistic aspirations, deadly self-sacrifice, and the immolation of voice.

The terms in which Alcott depicts this voyage of female ethical development suggest the impossibility of either freely choosing or fully rendering in fiction a new understanding of the woman-self in relation to others, if that understanding must be achieved within a culture that defines women as powerless and marginal, and confines all new understandings to the old, safe, and imprisoning domestic sphere. Yet the female pilgrimage Alcott traces is strikingly close to the shape of female ethical development Gilligan has described, and however impossible Alcott found it to move this pilgrimage fully beyond the confines of her own culture, the radically assertive image of female self-worth, struggle, and heroism she portrays in *Little Women* surely accounts for some of the book's insidious hold over its readers.

Carol Gilligan's theories of female ethical development begin to explain the power of *Little Women* by suggesting an underlying shape and direction for a reading of its characters' pilgrimage and an interpretation of its narrative failure, as located in its collapse against the borders of patriarchal culture. The feminist psychoanalytical theories of Nancy Chodorow, Jessica Benjamin, and Jane Flax—among many others—offer insights in their explorations of the site of collapse, the precise place where female narrative collides against patriarchal boundaries—the problem of desire. Indeed, the pattern of the female infant's differentiation, as traced by these theorists, strikingly prefigures the pattern of conflict, and apparent impossibility of resolution, that the adult female experiences and that Alcott's novel so vividly demonstrates in Jo's struggle for love and voice.

Feminist theorists have begun to deconstruct and problematize the classical Freudian model of infant development, with its patriarchal assumptions about the nature of individuality, eroticism, and female otherness, and to reveal its implicit contradictions, while suggesting an alternative, less oppressive model of subjectivity, according to which "differentiation happens *in relation to* the mother. . . . Separateness is defined relationally; . . . adequate separation, or differentiation, involves not merely perceiving the separateness, or otherness, of the other. It involves perceiving the person's subjectivity and selfhood as well." Central to much feminist theory is the return of the mother, not as scapegoat or savior, but as the primary, if inadvertent, enforcer of patriarchal values as well as their victim, and thus as fulcrum of the private and public. Such a perspective leads to a radically new understanding of the way a child's development is culturally determined, especially by the effect on the individuation of female—and male—infants. The institution of motherhood in a patriarchal culture achieves not only the reproduction of mothering but the perpetuation of patriarchy. . . .

Much of *Little Women's* power derives from its exploration of the previously repressed, complex mother-daughter relationship, without portraying that bond as either idealized perfection or pernicious destruction. Marmee loves and socializes, nurtures and stifles her daughters, offering them a vision of perfect love and oneness that heterosexuality cannot hope to duplicate, and an alternate model of identity through community, domesticity, and altruism that their culture can only tolerate by subsuming it in the archetype of female goodness that kills Beth. Thus the dream of reconciliation—of expressing subjectivity in/through community—is, like the quest for ethical development, subverted by the limitations of a patriarchal culture that consistently trivializes the female's narrative and objectivizes her subjectivity. The vision of community, altruism, and caring for others that Marmee expresses is either ambiguous (as in her request that they give their Christmas breakfast for the poor), or destructive (as in the painful, diseased effect of Beth's extreme selflessness), or trivialized (as in the girls' foolish, domesticated experiences spending one week pleasing only themselves).

Even more profoundly, however, Marmee's active presence in this text raises the dangerous possibility of nonphallic eroticism, a different focus of desire. Once again, the contrast with Huck Finn is instructive. Huck's journey downriver, away from the Widow Brown and civilization, conforms with remarkable precision to the young boy's patriarchally enforced and approved development:

"The salient feature of male individuality is that it grows out of the repudiation of the primary identification with and dependency on the mother . . . [leading] to an individuality that stresses . . . difference as denial of commonality, separation as denial of connection; . . . where independence seems to exclude all dependency rather than be characterized by a balance of separation and connection." In moving downriver, Huck moves consistently away from dependency and connection, separating completely from the trappings of civilization in his quest for absolute independence. Jo March, of course, neither seeks nor achieves such a selfhood. Rather, her intensely loving connection with her mother has fostered "a balance of separation and connectedness, of the capacities for agency and relatedness." Her crisis occurs not so much from a need to resist dependency or assert autonomy as from a need to express desire. However, this quest is deeply complicated by the same powerful maternal figure who offers hope of a more balanced vision of identity.

For Marmee's seductive, loving presence, which creates a profound and inescapable homoerotic undercurrent throughout the novel, eventually subverts the appeal of heterosexual eroticism

entirely, while the text utterly refuses to imagine or tolerate any other kind of desire. Thus while homoeroticism is never permitted direct expression, it dominates the actions and feelings of the female characters. Even Meg's first thought, after being married, is of her mother: "The minute she was fairly married, Meg cried, 'The first kiss for Marmee!' and turning, gave it with her heart on her lips." More significantly, when Jo confesses her loneliness and desire for love after Beth's death, she rejects her mother's characterization of heterosexual love as "the best love of all," claiming "Mothers are the *best* lovers in the world, but I don't mind whispering to Marmee that I'd like to try all kinds."

Yet the distorting compromises enforced by patriarchal culture require that a girl repress her primal, homoerotic love for her mother, shifting instead to a learned, differentiating heteroerotic love for her father. Just as the patriarchal context of their pilgrimage prevents the sisters from fully exploring the potential of a new understanding of the self in relation to others, or a new vision of separateness defined relationally, the imperatives of phallocentric culture demand that women resist "our earliest carnal interaction" with mothers, thus producing "women [who] are encouraged to behave narcissistically as sex objects or masochistically as mothers, either position being a defense against the female body's resonance with primitive fears and needs." Both reactions are distinctly evident in *Little Women,* from Amy's narcissistic objectification of herself to Meg's domestic retreat into invisibility and Beth's deadly masochism.

Jo most vividly acts out the painful implications of this culturally distorted psychic and erotic development. Jo is the most passionate in her resistance to adulthood, and especially to heterosexuality, wanting to marry Meg herself to keep the childhood family intact and wishing that "wearing flat-irons on our heads would keep us from growing up." Jo is also the most tormented about her own gender, presenting herself constantly in masculine images. Her cross-dressing language and behavior reflect very real conflict: as a boy, Jo would be socially independent, able to go off to war with her father, or to "run away [with Laurie] and have a capital time." More importantly, she would also be compensated for the price of that independence— the loss of her pre-oedipal oneness with Marmee— by the "promise of another mommy as a reward for the renunciation" of her maternally directed desires. Thus her desire to be a boy reveals her erotic attachment toward her mother, while her culture denies Jo both the possibility of independence and the promise of sexual gratification that patriarchy offers boys. At the same time, the nurturing female community of her family, rather than providing an alternative world, is eroded by death and marriage and shadowed by suggestions of triviality and patriarchal observation and objectification.

Jo's terror of heterosexuality is the most obvious result of her passionate attachment to Marmee, while her sense of her own "sexuality is muted by the fact that the woman she must identify with, her mother, is so profoundly desexualized." Numerous critics have noted, for example, how foolish and unconvincing are the stated terms of her rejection of Laurie. "Our quick tempers and strong wills would probably make us very miserable. . . . I'm homely and awkward and odd and old, and you'd be ashamed of me . . . and I shouldn't like elegant society and you would, and you'd hate my scribbling." Jo and Laurie get along so well precisely because of their passions (quick tempers and strong wills), while Laurie has always been the most devoted advocate of Jo's literary endeavors (unlike her eventual husband, Professor Bhaer, who oversees the burning of all her writing). Furthermore, our initial image of Laurie is of a moody, passionate Italian musician, and hence of someone equally bored by the triviality of elegant society, the Romantic ideal brother-lover, not the wealthy Indian tea merchant he somewhat implausibly becomes.

Beneath the superficial absurdity of these claims is Jo's bitterly negative self-image, a wounded self-esteem entirely consistent with her vehement maternal identification in a patriarchal culture. However, Jo's refusal of Laurie is essentially and explicitly an absolute rejection of heterosexual passion: "I don't see why I can't love you as you want me to. I've tried, but I can't change the feeling, and it would be a lie to say I do when I don't." Her most intense attachment is to Marmee; she wants to mother Laurie, not marry him. The ambiguity of Jo's rejection of him derives not from her repudiation of romantic love and the conventional "happy ending" but from the fact that she cannot, within the confines of this text and of heterosexuality, find any way to act out her own desires.

When Jo does finally marry, she turns to the elderly and impoverished scholar, Professor Bhaer, and she does so not in passion but in need, companionability, and loss. Moreover, she turns finally to a man identical to her own father, a weak yet punitive figure who reinforces that cruelly negative self-image which Laurie so consistently challenged. Jo's husband is both suggestively feminine (poor, alien, and powerless) and explicitly patriarchal (scholarly, repressive, and authoritarian). Her marriage suggests a capitulation to the conventional Freudian narrative of female development in which a woman marries her father. If she cannot marry Marmee, or love another woman erotically, she can follow the dictates of her culture by becoming her mother and marrying her father. In doing so, she confirms the elusive authority of Mr. March, who, despite his physical absence from the text, is the primary agent of trivialization and objectification. Moreover, Jo confirms the inadvertent authority of her mother as a socializing force, a woman who produces daughters adept in sacrifice and suffering but unequipped to express desire of any kind.

In portraying the maternal figure as radically present and vocal, Alcott reveals the enormous difficulties daughters experience in finding their own identity under such a powerful shadow—especially in a patriarchal context that refuses to tolerate a vision of active, communal subjectivity and that cannot tolerate any challenge to phallocentric eroticism. Yet Marmee's subversive presence also violates the usual narrative of female development. Jo remains inescapably the subject of her own story, and her eventual marriage is enormously complicated, rejecting conventional heterosexual romantic models of erotic love, while reconciling her with her father (or with patriarchy) and offering her a place of her own. As comrade, teacher, and mother in the school she inherits from her aunt and manages with her husband, she creates a life that combines intimacy and community with agency and independence. The conclusion of her oedipal narrative moves tentatively, ambiguously, toward a new statement of desire, "a relationship to desire in the *freedom to:* freedom to be both with and distinct from the other."

The power of *Little Women* derives in large measure from the contradictions and tensions it exposes and from the pattern it establishes of subversive, feminist exploration colliding repeatedly against patriarchal repression. Like the log cabin quilt pattern Elaine Showalter uses to explore the underlying structure of *Uncle Tom's Cabin, Little Women,* too, is constructed on a "compositional principle . . . [of] contrast between light and dark," between exploration and entrapment, desire and denial, expression and repression. What Showalter terms the "symbolic relationship to boundaries" in the quilting pattern perfectly expresses the narrative pattern in *Little Women,* which consistently moves us to the outer boundaries of representational fiction in its effort to depict a resolution beyond the either/or constraints of the author's culture.

The text is constructed of contrasting pieces that depict both the female narrative of ethical development and its dark, insidious alternative of static female saintliness; both the passionate quest for a reconciliation of desire with separation and its darker suggestions about maternal eroticism, coercion, and socialization, both the artist's search for authentic female voice and its painful shadowing image of the failure of existing forms to express that voice. In each voyage or pilgrimage—each pattern of female quest—Alcott moves the narrative simultaneously to the borders of possibility in patriarchal culture and to the deep core of yearning for maternal oneness. This book is passionately memorable for young girls because it warns of the dangers that lie ahead—domestic incarceration, narcissistic objectification, sacrificial goodness, and the enforced silencing of voice, eroticism, and anger—and partly because it offers an alternative vision of adulthood-in-community, of female subjectivity, and above all of female oedipal narrative, restoring the lost, maternal presence in our lives.

The sites where Alcott's narrative flounders, where the shape of her textual pattern crashes against the absolute nature of her culture's borders, are the sites we are still exploring today. If her novel fails fully to sustain an image of resolution that transcends either/or choices, her failure suggests much that remains real and enduring in our own experience.

Source: Ann B. Murphy, "The Borders of Ethical, Erotic, and Artistic Possibilities in *Little Women*," in *Signs: Journal of Women in Culture and Society,* Vol. 15, No. 3, Spring 1990, pp. 562–85.

Sarah Elbert

In the following essay excerpt, Elbert discusses the major themes in Little Women: *"domesticity, the achievement of individual identity through work, and true love."*

> I may be strong minded, but no one can say I'm out of my sphere now, for woman's special mission is supposed to be drying tears and bearing burdens. I'm to carry my share, Friedrich, and help to earn the home. Make up your mind to that, or I'll never go.

"Jo March," *Little Women,* Chapter 46

The title of Louisa May Alcott's most famous book is taken from a commonplace nineteenth-century term. In the opening chapter, Marmee reads a Christmas letter from her absent husband to his daughters, which tenderly admonishes them to

The Alcott home in Concord, Massachusetts

"conquer themselves so beautifully that when I come back to them I may be fonder and prouder of my little women." This sentimental diminutive is puzzling in a feminist who was concerned with augmenting, rather than diminishing, woman's status. Such belittlement was part of the woman problem, as Alcott knew. The title appears even more puzzling when we consider that *Little Women* deals with the problems common to girls growing into womanhood.

Alcott had no intention of sentimentalizing the struggles of young women, so we must look elsewhere for an explanation of the title. We find one in the works of Charles Dickens, which Alcott read and took with her to the Union Hotel during the Civil War. For several decades Dickens had moved English and American readers to tears with his tender depictions, imitated but never equalled, of childhood woe. Dickens cared most deeply for the misery of exploited children, abused strangers in a venal adult world, but often remarkably capable of fending for themselves. Dickensian girls are particularly self-reliant, able to care for their siblings by the time they are "over thirteen, sir," as the girl "Charley" says to Mr. Jarndyce in *Bleak House.* In *Bleak House,* in fact, the term "little women" makes a prominent appearance. Esther, ward of the generous, sweethearted Mr. Jarndyce, has the distinc-

> " The virtues of mutual self-sacrifice and domestic cooperation, however, must be proven to the March girls before they can recognize how important such virtues are to their self-realization. Independent-minded and childishly selfish, the girls must learn how to shape their individualities in harmony with the interests of the family."

tion of becoming the first well-known "little woman" in literature. Her guardian says to her, "You have wrought changes in me, little woman," indicating that she has widened and deepened his sensibilities and hence his philanthropy.

Esther saves many people during the course of the novel, including the girl "Charley" whom she takes in and nurses through a bout of smallpox. Charley herself had contracted the disease from Jo, another pathetic Dickensian orphan. Inevitably, Esther comes down with smallpox, which leaves her face scarred and sets her musing about the meaning of "little woman."

Although only twenty-one years old, Esther has been close to death and realizes how short time is for "little women." No longer a child, yet not an adult, she finds life fleeting and precious. Dreadfully confused, she talks about the stages of her life, feeling herself at once "a child, an elder girl, and the little woman I had been so happy as." The problem, she thinks, is that the stages are not so distinct as she had once innocently supposed. Rather, they seem joined together and weighted down by similar "cares and difficulties," which are hard to reconcile or understand.

When Louisa May Alcott employed the term "little women," she infused it with this Dickensian meaning. *Little Women* portrays just such a complex overlapping of stages from childhood to elder child, little woman to young woman, that appears in *Bleak House.* Like Esther in that novel, each of

Alcott's heroines has a scarring experience that jars her into painful awareness of vanished childhood innocence and the woman problem.

Esther's job as part-time narrator in *Bleak House* is given to Jo in *Little Women,* but there the resemblance between the two characters ends. Jo comes close to bounding off the pages of her book; an American heroine, she has fits of exuberance alternating with sighs of half-chastened humility. Unlike Esther, and very much like her creator, Jo writes a story that succeeds miraculously even though she "never knew how it happened." "Something," Jo declares, "got into that story that went straight to the hearts of those who read it." She put "humor and pathos into it," says saintly Mr. March, sure that his daughter had "no thought of fame or money in writing" her story.

In fact, of course, Louisa May Alcott, unlike Jo, produced the story of *Little Women* in record time for money. As she reviewed the first page proofs, she found that "it reads better than I expected; we really lived most of it and if it succeeds that will be the reason of it." Five succeeding generations have laughed and cried over *Little Women.* It may well be that each generation has its own favorite incidents and lessons. What remains indisputable is that every generation's critics and fans love Jo. What appeals to readers across time may therefore be Alcott's depiction of the woman problem, the conflict between domesticity and individuality that first presents itself at just the moment when little women move from girlhood to womanhood.

Themes in *Little Women: Domesticity*

The novel develops three major themes: domesticity, the achievement of individual identity through work, and true love. The same motifs appear in *Little Men, Jo's Boys, Eight Cousins, Rose in Bloom* and *An Old Fashioned Girl.* None has been out of print since first written. Together they comprise a fictional record of liberal feminist ideology, process, and programs from 1867 through 1886 in America.

From the outset Alcott established the centrality of household democracy, underscoring the importance of "natural" cooperation and mutual self-sacrifice within family life. The March cottage shelters the four sisters and their parents, all of whom love and depend upon one another. Even the family poverty, so reminiscent of Louisa's own, serves to reinforce democratic practice in the family. With the help of Hannah, who worked as a maid for Mrs. March in better days and now considers herself a "member of the family," all the women work together to accomplish household chores, making the most of meager means by sharing everything.

The virtues of mutual self-sacrifice and domestic cooperation, however, must be proven to the March girls before they can recognize how important such virtues are to their self-realization. Independent-minded and childishly selfish, the girls must learn how to shape their individualities in harmony with the interests of the family. In an important episode Alcott describes the tactics used by Mrs. March to win her daughters to a higher social standard.

After listening to Jo, Meg, Beth, and Amy pine for the "vacations" enjoyed by wealthier friends, Marmee agrees to release them from domestic duties for one week. She allows them to structure their time in any way they please. On the first morning, the neat inviting cottage is suddenly a different place. Meg, coming down to a solitary breakfast, finds the parlor "lonely and untidy," because "Jo had not filled the vases, Beth had not dusted, and Amy's books lay about scattered." Before long, selfishness produces more domestic disasters, which increase alarmingly as the week progresses. Jo gets sunburnt boating too long with Laurie, and headachy from spending hours devouring her cherished novels. "Giving out" her ordinary sewing chores, Meg falls to "snipping and spoiling" her clothes in an attempt to be fashionable. Amy sketches lazily under a hedge and getting drenched by a summer rain, ruins her best white frock. Beth makes a mess out of her doll's closet, leaves the mess, and goes off to practice some new music. By the end of the day, she is left with "the confusion of her closet" and, "the difficulty of learning three of four songs at once." All these small troubles make the girls grumpy and ill-tempered.

The experiment, however, is far from over. Excessive attention to self-pleasure produces a scarcity of necessities, including food. Emulating the little red hen, Mrs. March decides that those who do not work shall not eat. She gives Hannah a holiday, and the maid leaves with these parting words: "Housekeeping ain't no joke." Unable to rely on the experience and counsel of Hannah and their mother, the girls produce a breakfast featuring "boiled tea, very bitter, scorched omelette, and biscuits speckled with saleratus." Jo caters a luncheon for friends, only to discover that she can't make anything "fit to eat" except "gingerbread and

molasses candy." So she sails off to purchase "a very young lobster, some very old asparagus, and two boxes of acid strawberries." She boils the asparagus for an hour until the heads are "cooked off" and the stalks "harder than ever." She undercooks the lobster and the potatoes, and sprinkles salt instead of sugar on the strawberries. . . .

Returning home to find her daughters miserable over the death of Pip and their failures as homekeepers, Mrs. March easily persuades them to admit that "it is better to have a few duties, and live for others." This experiment, she says, was designed to show you "what happens when everyone thinks only for herself. Now you know that in order to make a home comfortable and happy," everyone in it must contribute to the family welfare. Marmee has also proven to the girls that domestic work is real work, giving women a "sense of power and independence better than money or fashion." She has shown them that home life becomes a "beautiful success" only if work alternates with leisure, independence with cooperation and mutual concern.

Although this episode deals almost exclusively with girls, Alcott integrated men into her vision of cooperative family life. Men too should benefit from and participate in this family experience, but only on the grounds that they respect the independence and equal authority of women within the home.

Accepting, even glorifying the importance of women's domestic work, Alcott emphasizes that men are homeless without women. Since the ability to create a home and sustain a family supercedes fame and money as evidence of success and civilization, it follows that women have already proved themselves in the world; thus their ability to extend their sphere is unquestioned in *Little Women*. Homeless men, despite wealth, wages and worldly experience, are motherless children. Meg's suitor, John Brooke, is attracted to the March cottage in large part because he is a lonely young man who has recently lost his mother. Laurie is motherless, which excuses most of his faults, and Mr. Laurence, his grandfather, has neither wife, daughter, or granddaughter. Mr. March alone has a proper home and knows his place in it, returning from the war to augment, but not supercede, Marmee's authority. He wholly accepts the female abundance around him, tending the flock of his tiny parish and leaving domestic arrangements to his womenfolk. . . .

Alcott advances ideas about the place of men in the family that emerged out of her domestic experiences with her parents, despite her belief in universal laws of progress and democracy. On the whole, she does not paint a compelling picture of marital equality in *Little Women.* Instead she presents the possibility of educating and parenting a new generation of little men and little women. In the second part of *Little Women* Alcott describes the married life of John and Meg Brooke. Theirs is no ideal egalitarian marriage, but then John Brooke was not raised by Marmee. The single wage-earner for his family, John provides a domestic servant but does not share domestic chores himself, except for disciplining his son in the evening. Meg is totally dependent upon his income both for household and personal expenses. Careful of her household accounting, she nevertheless often behaves like an impulsive child. On one occasion, she is tempted by a length of lovely violet silk while shopping with an old friend, Sallie Moffet. The silk costs fifty dollars, an enormous sum to the young couple. When Meg tells John that she has bought the silk, he responds only that "twenty-five yards of silk seems a good deal to cover one small woman, but I've no doubt my wife will look as fine as Ned Moffet's when she gets it on." Meg is overwhelmed with remorse at her own selfishness. Sallie generously buys the silk, whereupon Meg uses the fifty dollars to buy a new overcoat for her husband.

In a chapter called "On the Shelf," Meg's docility appears as her greatest virtue and her most serious domestic flaw. Docility is a fine quality in a daughter, even a sister, Alcott admits, but dangerous in a wife. Meg becomes dowdy and dependent, isolated in her little cottage with two small children. John spends more time away from home, provoking Marmee to confront Meg, but not her son-in-law, reminding her that "it's mother who blames as well as mother who sympathizes."

Mother shares her domestic secret: a good marriage is based on mutuality of interests and responsibilities. Marmee herself learned this as a young wife, when after a hard time caring for her children, she welcomed father's help. Now, she says, he does not let business distract him from domestic details, and she remembers to interest herself in his pursuits. "We each do our part alone in many things, but at home we work together, always." Marmee's advice is heeded; Meg pays more attention to the niceties of her dress, tries to talk about current affairs, and cedes to her husband some measure of child management.

According to Alcott, the reform of domestic life required restoration of a mutuality that had vanished with the separation of home and work. Yet of all the domestic advice presented in *Little Women,* this lesson carries the least conviction. Mr. March is the minister of a small parish and presumably home a great deal. John Brooke, on the other hand, is a clerk, far removed from his home and children. As we shall see, Alcott can only offer model domesticity in utopian settings where cooperative communities reappear in feminist forms.

Flying Up: Little Women Grow Up to Be Themselves

When Louisa finished writing part two of *Little Women,* she suggested "Wedding marches" as a possible title. She changed it, however go "Birds Leaving the Nest," or "Little Women Grow Up," because she did not wish to suggest that marriage should be the focal event for growing girls. Instead she argues that girls who take trial flights from secure homes will find their own paths to domestic happiness. They might choose independent spinsterhood or some form of marital bonds that range from partial to complete "household democracy." For Alcott, sisterhood and marriage, though often contradictory, are equally valuable possibilities for women. Fully realized sisterhood becomes a model for marriage, not simply an alternative to it. Together, marriage and sisterhood guarantee that individual identity and domesticity will be harmonious.

Meg, the eldest and most "docile daughter," does not attain Alcott's ideal womanhood. Democratic domesticity requires maturity, strength, and above all a secure identity that Meg lacks. Her identity consists of being Marmee's daughter and then John's wife. Yet she and John are well matched. Neither really wants sexual equality in the dovecote. When Meg leaves home to work as a governess she accepts a three-year engagement period, dreaming that she will have much to learn while she waits. But John says, "You have only to wait; I am to do the work." Alcott accepts the limitations of temperament and circumstance in Meg, as she does in all her characters. In *Little Men,* however, Meg's widowhood grants her the circumstances to develop a stronger side of her character.

Fashion provides a counterpoint to feminism in *Little Women.* Jo's strong sense of self is established in part by her rejection of fashion, which she perceives as a sign of dependency and sexual stereotyping. Amy, on the other hand, struggles against her burden of vanity, which has its positive side in her "nice manners and refined way of speaking." Amy must learn that appearances can be deceiving, whereas Jo must learn that appearances do count in the larger world. Meg's vanity may be one reason she is linked to Amy in the game of "playing mother," wherein Meg and Jo watch over their sisters "in the places of discarded dolls." Jo obviously rejects Amy early in their lives. Amy's flat nose, her chief "trial," as she says, is supposedly the result of careless Jo's dropping her baby sister onto a coal-hod.

Jo's lack of vanity about clothes at first conceals her pride both in her writing talent and in her exclusive relationship to Laurie. Laurie enjoys Jo's vivid imagination; it gives color and vivacity to his own lonely childhood. Keeping Amy out of pleasurable excursions with Laurie is one of Jo's main "faults." Left at home once too often, Amy burns a collection of Jo's painstakingly written fairy tales as revenge. Furious, Jo leaves her behind again when she and Laurie go skating. Amy follows behind and is almost killed by falling through the thin ice. Penitent, Jo vows to curb her temper and cherish Amy. Accepting the fact that she is not the only independent and talented member of the family is part of Jo's growing up.

Her notion that she is "the man of the family" is a more serious problem in the story. In a strange way this too plays itself out around fashion. Jo has her first serious encounter with Laurie at a neighborhood dance, where she is uncomfortably dressed up to accompany Meg on their first "grown up" social expedition. Meg's woes arise from her desire for fashionable frippery; she dances in overly tight high-heeled slippers that cripple her before the dance is over. Jo wears sensible shoes, but cannot dance because "in maroon, with a stiff gentlemanly linen collar and a white chrysanthemeum or two for her only ornament," she is pledged to hide the scorched back of her "poplin" gown. Therefore she must stand quietly or hide in a corner in penance for her habit of standing too near the fire. The Laurence boy is shy, a stranger to the neighborhood who has spent much of his childhood in a Swiss boarding school. He wears two "nice pearl colored gloves" and dances well, volunteering to polka with Jo in the privacy of a hall. Jo is suddenly aware that the gentility she rejects as too "lady-like" can be quite acceptable when it is "gentlemanly," or in other words, gender-free. Her regret at having only one good glove (the other is stained with lemonade) signals her growth from tomboyhood to womanhood in the feminist sense of the term. Jo is somewhat confused, having made a cause celebré out of being a sloppy, rough boy who clumps about in un-

laced boots. Now she finds herself attracted by Laurie's "curly black hair, brown skin, big black eyes, handsome nose, fine teeth, small hands and feet." She observes her new model closely: "Taller than I am," says Jo, and "very polite for a boy, altogether jolly." Finding her sartorial model in the opposite sex, Jo decides she can grow up to be a splendid woman with neatly laced boots and clean linen. She does not want Laurie as a sweetheart; she wants to adopt both him and his air of freedom and elegant comfort.

Meg can easily sympathize with Amy. Both love pretty things and are well regarded by wealthy relatives who appreciate their social graces and attention to niceties of dress. Mr. Laurence buys Meg her first silvery silk dress, a seemingly harmless and generous act. But because she is always dependent upon someone else's generosity, poor Meg must forego her next silk gown five years later. Meg elicits the reader's sympathy, however, while Amy's tastes seem symptoms of a selfish, superficial character.

First of all, Amy is too young to care about jewelry or fashionable frocks in the first half of *Little Women*. Nevertheless, she cares a great deal for them; she covets a schoolmate's carnelian ring, and preens and postures in front of her friends while exaggerating her family's lost wealth and status. Amy's pretensions lead her into trouble in the famous incident of the "Pickled limes." Fashionable little school-girls have allowances, but Amy has none. As a result she has gone in debt to chums who treat her to the current delicacy—pickled limes. Meg then gives Amy a quarter, and the delighted girl purchases a bag of limes.

Mr. Davis, the school master, has forbidden treats in his classroom. Discovering that Amy has hidden limes in her desk, he calls her to the front of the room and humiliates her with "several tingling blows on her little palm." The author suggests that this incident might mark the beginning of Amy's maturation. Instead, Marmee and Jo rescue Amy by giving her a vacation from school. A small lecture by Marmee on the "power of modesty" does not alter the fact that Amy has had her burden lightened.

Later, at a charity fair, Amy is unfairly treated by rich and envious girls. This time she tries to "love her neighbor" and modestly allows her trinkets to be sold by a rival. Once again, this time augmented by Laurie and his friends (who have been commandeered by Jo) the family sails to Amy's rescue. They buy back Amy's trinkets and all the bouquets (provided by the Laurences' gardener) on sale at Amy's unfashionable booth. If this were not enough, Amy's Aunt Carrol, hearing of her niece's delicate manners, talented fancy work, and Christian forbearance at the charity fair, rewards her with a trip to Europe as her companion. Poor Jo, who engineered the rescue, is left behind, too unfashionable and forth-right to be patronized. On one occasion Jo tells Amy, "Its easier for me to risk my life for a person than to be pleasant to him when I don't feel like it." Amy replies that "women should learn to be agreeable, particularly poor ones; for they have no other way of repaying kindnesses they receive. If you'd remember that, and practice it, you'd be better liked than I am because there is more of you." It is precisely because Jo is indeed more substantial that the author grants Amy a free holiday in Europe and eventually a wealthy indulgent husband.

Amy and Laurie grow up together in Europe. Both are fashionable, inclined to indolence and coquetry. Both have talent, Amy for painting and Laurie for music, but only enough to please friends in polite salons. Neither is put to the test of earning a living. Both are also inclined toward "illusion" in dressing themselves and appreciating each other's refined taste. Their growing up, however, does require a degree of honesty: they admit that "talent isn't genius and you can't make it so."

Despite the sniping and competition for parental love, social approval, and material rewards, Amy and Jo share one great loss that matures them both. The central tragedy of *Little Women,* one that generations of readers remember, is Beth's death in the final part of the book. Loving home the best, gentle Beth never wants to leave it; perhaps she would never have done so. She grows more fragile each year, and in her last months confides to Jo feeling that she was never intended to live long. Her short speech is also her longest in the novel:

> 'I'm not like the rest of you; I never made any plans about what I'd do when I grew up; I never thought of being married, as you all did. I couldn't seem to imagine myself anything but stupid little Beth, trotting about at home, of no use anywhere but there. I never wanted to go away and the hard part now is the leaving you all. I'm not afraid, but it seems as if I should be homesick for you even in heaven.'

Jo's maturation is sealed by her grief over Beth's decline. The chapter entitled "Valley of the Shadow" sketches a household that revolves around Beth's room for one year. Everyone, including Beth, knows she is dying. Jo writes a long poem to her sister in which she acknowledges that true sisterhood is born in shared domestic experiences, and that such loving ties cannot be severed:

> Henceforth, safe across the river,
> I shall see forevermore
> Waiting for me on the shore.
> Hope and faith, born of my sorrow,
> Guardian angels shall become,
> And the sister gone before me
> By their hands shall lead me home.

Wasted away, suffering with "pathetic patience," Beth's death releases her parents and sisters to "thank God that Beth was well at last." Beth's self-sacrifice is ultimately the greatest in the novel. She gives up her life knowing that it has had only private, domestic meaning. Only the March family knows and loves her sweet "household spirit."

Nobody mourns Beth more than Jo, her opposite in temperament as well as her partner in the bonds of sisterhood. Beth is shy and Jo is as frank and fearless as her fictional heroes. Beth never has any plans, and Jo is full of plots and dreams. Their commonality lies in the simple fact that both of them value their sororal relationship above any other unions.

When Meg becomes engaged and Jo feels she is about to lose her "best friend," Laurie declares that he will stand by Jo forever. Jo gratefully shakes his hand, saying "I know you will, and I'm ever so much obliged; you are always a great comfort to me, Teddy." But Laurie turns out to be a boy, not Jo's sister after all. Jo's rejection of Laurie's suit is her first grown-up act, and her trip to New York to become a writer is her first flight into the world. Beth's death, through which she escapes the awful problem of growing up, triggers Jo's maturation. She does leave home to go "across the river." Jo's journey is the only fully complete one in *Little Women* and it revolves her learning to tell true love from romantic fancy. She must do so in order to reproduce her lost sisterhood in a new, feminist domestic union.

True Love Found

The ability to distinguish true love from romantic fancy is a prerequisite for a woman's growing up in *Little Women.* True love involves mutual self-sacrifice and self-control, and requires the kind of man who can make the household the center of his life and work. Romance, on the other hand, is inherently selfish, passionate, and unequal.

Ultimately all the surviving heroines are paired off in true love. Jo, however, proves closest to Alcott's ideal because she rejects Laurie Laurence. At one point Jo tells Laurie that they are unsuited to one another because both have strong wills and quick tempers. Unpersuaded and unreasonable, the spoiled young man presses his suit, forcing her to tell him a harder truth: she does not love him as a woman loves a man, and never did, but simply feels motherly toward him.

Jo does not want to be an adoring adornment to a fashionable man's home. Nor will she give up her "scribbling" to satisfy Laurie. She knows he would hate her writing, and that she "couldn't get on without it." Laurie shared the secret of Jo's pseudononymous stories in the past, but he really views her writing as just another glorious lark. Laurie's proposal reveals just how much "scribbling" really means to Jo. If merely saving her "pathetic family" from poverty were her only motivation, she might marry Laurie and enrich them all. She might even produce leisured, graceful literature under his partronage. But she won't be patronized and she won't concede. "I don't believe I shall every marry," she declares. "I am happy as I am, and love my liberty too well to be in any hurry to give it up for any mortal man."

Laurie stubbornly refuses to believe her, even though she has made perfectly clear that, like Louisa Alcott, she prefers "paddling her own canoe." Laurie insists that Jo has some unknown romantic rival in mind who will induce her to give up her foolish notions of independence and "live and die for him." Exasperated, her limited patience turns to defiance. "Yes, I will live and die for him," she declared, "if he ever comes and makes me love him in spite of myself, and you must do the best you can." We do not know if Jo really means that she would yield to a "great romance," or is merely angry enough to tell Laurie that his worst "envious" fantasy is what he deserves. Possibly, Jo also recognizes passions in herself, however hard she struggles to keep them under control. She certainly experiences more than "moods;" she has genuine emotional depth and active fantasies, which she usually transforms into tragi-comic family operas or melodramatic stories.

In the nineteenth-century world of *Little Women,* there are only two alternatives following the sexual equality of childhood: romantic love or rational affection. With considerable regret Jo chooses the latter, because she must forego forever the equality she once knew with Laurie, her exu-

berant companion in childhood. Jo's decision, as Alcott knew, presents the reader with a bitter pill, for nearly everyone wants Laurie to win Jo. Yet the author has her heroine firmly reject any "silliness" from the start. She enjoys being Laurie's chum, plays at being his mother, but is never tempted to be his domestic companion.

It is precisely because Alcott makes Laurie such an irresistable boy-man that the reader must take Jo's refusal seriously. The youthful sweet surrogate sister develops into a handsome, passionate suitor. Moreover, Jo is physically attracted to Laurie, and frequently observes his handsome face, curly hair, and fine eyes. She hates it when he briefly ruins his romantic looks with a collegiate pose. The reader as well as Jo feels the power of Laurie's sexuality and the power he tries to exert over her. Yet if he calls her "my girl," meaning his sweetheart, she calls him "my boy," meaning her son.

Jo's refusal is not prompted by love for a rival suitor. In New York she works as a governess to children in her boardinghouse and scribbles away for the penny-dreadful newspapers. Soon she encounters Friedrick Bhaer helping a serving maid. Bhaer's life, unlike Laurie's, is not the stuff of romance. Forty-years old, "learned and good," he is domestic by nature and darns his own socks. He loves flowers and children and reads good literature. Moreover, he insists that Jo give up writing blood-and-thunder tales and learn to write good fiction. He gives her his own copy of Shakespeare as a Christmas present. "A regular German," Jo says,

> rather stout with brown hair tumbled all over his head, a bushy beard, good nose, the kindest eyes I ever saw, and a splendid big voice that does one's ears good, after our rusty, or slipshod American gabble. His clothes were rusty, his hands were large, and he hadn't a really handsome feature in his face, except his beautiful teeth; yet I liked him, for he had a fine head, his linen was very nice, and he looked like a gentleman, though two buttons were off his coat, and there was a patch on one shoe.

Bhaer is a man Jo can love and marry.

A mature adult capable of raising his two orphaned nephews, he does not need Jo to mother him, although she is drawn to do so. Bhaer is more attracted to her youth and independent spirit. Nevertheless, he bestows his affection upon her by appreciating both her Old World "gemutlichkeit" and her American self-reliance. In a way he is Santa Claus, giving gifts despite his poverty to friends and servants alike. In one scene Bhaer buys oranges and figs for small children while holding a dilapidated blue umbrella aloft for Jo in the rain. Unlike

Father March, who is a fragile invalid, Father Bhaer is a strapping, generous man.

There is no end to his domesticity or his capacity for cooperative self-sacrifice. Matching his paternal benevolence to Jo's maternal abundance, Bhaer does the shopping for both himself and Jo. As Alcott describes him, he "finished the marketing by buying several pounds of grapes, a pot of rosy daisies, and a pretty jar of honey, to be regarded in the light of a demijohn. Then, distorting his pockets with the knobby bundles, and giving her the flowers to hold, he put up the old umbrella and they travelled on again." Contrast this fulgent account of a man who understands the "household spirit" with Laurie, who cannot even direct the maids to plump his pillows properly, or with John Brooke, who magisterially sends the meat and vegetables home to Meg (no knobby bundles in his pockets!).

Meanwhile, Laurie has returned from Europe with Amy, and they tell the story of their Swiss romance. Laurie has found a perfect mate in Amy, who will be very good at giving orders to their servants, having practised in her imagination for years. Theirs will also be an equal marital partnership, though somewhat different from that of Jo and Fritz, and very different from the frugal conventions of Meg and John.

Jo, the last sister to leave home, might never have accepted Professor Bhaer's proposal were it not for Beth's death. Fritz has found a poem of Jo's expressing the deep love and devotion she feels for Meg, Amy, and Beth. We are "parted only for an hour, none lost," she writes, "one only gone before." Tenderly Bhaer declares: "I read that, and I think to myself, she has a sorrow, she is lonely, she would find comfort in true love. I haf a heart full for her."

Bhaer has all the qualities Bronson Alcott lacked: warmth, intimacy, and a tender capacity for expressing his affection—the feminine attributes Louisa admired and hoped men could acquire in a rational, feminist world. As Marmee says, he is "a dear man." He touches everyone, hugs and carries children about on his back. Bronson, despite all his genuine idealism and devotion to humanity, was emotionally reserved and distant. Fritz Bhaer loves material reality, is eminently approachable, and values all the things that Bronson Alcott rejects, such as good food, warm rooms, and appealing domestic disorder, even though he is a "bacheldore" when Jo meets him.

Bhaer's love for Jo gives him courage to conquer the barriers between them, including his poverty and age, his foreignness and his babbling, unromantic self. They decide to share life's burdens just as they shared the load of bundles on their shopping expedition. Jo hopes to fulfill "woman's special mission" of which is "drying tears and bearing burdens," so that nobody will ever again call her unwomanly. She resolutely adds the feminist postscript: "I'm to carry my share Friedrich and help to earn the home. Make up your mind to that, or I'll never go." She has her family duty and her work to keep her busy, while Fritz goes west to support his nephews before he can marry. The marriage contract they arrange is very different from that of Meg and John at the end of *Little Women,* part one.

Source: Sarah Elbert, "Reading *Little Women,*" in *A Hunger for Home: Louisa May Alcott and "Little Women,"* Temple University Press, 1984, pp. 151–65.

Sources

Brophy, Brigid, "A Masterpiece, and Dreadful," in *New York Times Book Review,* January 17, 1965, pp. 1, 44.

Chesterton, G. K., "Louisa Alcott," in *A Handful of Authors: Essays on Books and Writers,* Sheed and Ward, 1953, pp. 163–67.

Elbert, Sarah, *A Hunger for Home: Louisa May Alcott and "Little Women,"* Temple University Press, 1984.

Gabin, Jane S., "*Little Women:* Overview," in *Reference Guide to American Literature,* 3rd edition, St. James Press, 1994.

Janeway, Elizabeth, "Meg, Jo, Beth, Amy, and Louisa," in *Only Connect: Readings on Children's Literature,* edited by Sheila Egoff, G. T. Stubbs, and L. F. Ashley, Oxford University Press, 1969, pp. 286, 288, 290.

Lurie, Alison, "She Had It All," in *New York Review of Books,* March 2, 1995, pp. 3–5.

Moss, Joyce, and George Wilson, eds., *Literature and Its Times: Profiles of 300 Notable Literary Works and the Historical Events That Influenced Them,* Vol. 2: *Civil Wars to Frontier Societies (1800–1880s),* The Gale Group, 1997.

Review of *Little Women,* in *Harper's New Monthly Magazine,* Vol. 39, August 1869, pp. 455–56.

Review of *Little Women,* in *Nation,* Vol. 7, No. 173, October 22, 1868, p. 335.

Russ, Lavinia, "Not To Be Read on Sunday," in *Horn Book,* October 1968, pp. 524, 526.

Saxton, Martha, *Louisa May: A Modern Biography of Louisa May Alcott,* Houghton Mifflin, 1977.

Showalter, Elaine, *Sister's Choice: Tradition and Change in American Women's Writing,* Clarendon Press (Oxford), 1991, pp. 42–64.

Stern, Madeleine B., "Louisa May Alcott: An Appraisal," in *New England Quarterly,* Vol. 22, No. 4, December 1949, pp. 475–98.

For Further Study

Cogan, Frances B., *All American Girls: The Ideal of Real Womanhood in Mid-Nineteenth Century America,* University of Georgia Press, 1989.
   Cogan presents a historical perspective on women's roles in mid-nineteenth century America, including their expected educational levels, skills, aspirations, and manners. She suggests that in addition to the traditional view of womanhood, there was a competing view of a more dynamic, independent type of woman emerging in literature.

Fetterley, Judith, "*Little Women:* Alcott's Civil War," in *Feminist Studies,* Vol. 5, No. 2, Summer 1979, pp. 369–83.
   Fetterley proposes that Alcott's text reflects compromises in style and content that came about as the result of the demands placed on the author by her publisher and her public.

Jefferson, Margo, "Books of the Times: *Little Women, Growing Up Then and Now,*" in *New York Times,* December 21, 1994.
   Jefferson describes the March household as being as divided as its author, and relates the classic novel to Gerald Earley's *Daughters: On Family and Fatherhood.*

Meyerson, Joel, and Madeleine B. Stern, eds., *The Selected Letters of Louisa May Alcott: A Life of the Creator of "Little Women,"* University of Georgia Press, 1995.
   This collection of Alcott's correspondence gives insight into her domestic life, her thoughts, and her personality apart from her success as a children's writer.

Stern, Madeleine B., ed., *Behind a Mask: The Unknown Thrillers of Louisa May Alcott,* William Morrow, 1997.
   These frightening, passionate, and suspenseful tales reveal the other side of Alcott's writing, which she preferred to her better-known children's stories.

Mrs. Dalloway

Virginia Woolf
1925

Virginia Woolf's *Mrs. Dalloway,* published in 1925, was a bestseller both in Britain and the United States despite its departure from typical novelistic style. *Mrs. Dalloway* and Woolf's subsequent book, *To the Lighthouse,* have generated the most critical attention and are the most widely studied of Woolf's novels.

The action of *Mrs. Dalloway* takes place during a single day in June 1923 in London, England. This unusual organizational strategy creates a special problem for the novelist: how to craft characters deep enough to be realistic while treating only one day in their lives. Woolf solved this problem with what she called a "tunneling" technique, referring to the way her characters remember their pasts. In experiencing these characters' recollections, readers derive for themselves a sense of background and history to characters that, otherwise, a narrator would have had to provide.

In a sense, *Mrs. Dalloway* is a novel without a plot. Instead of creating major situations between characters to push the story forward, Woolf moved her narrative by following the passing hours of a day. The book is composed of movements from one character to another, or of movements from the internal thoughts of one character to the internal thoughts of another.

Mrs. Dalloway has been called a *flâneur* novel, which means it depicts people walking about a city. (*Flâneur* is the French word for a person who enjoys walking around a city often with no other purpose than to see the sights.) The book, as is typi-

cal of the *flâneur* novel, makes the city, its parks, and its streets as interesting as the characters who inhabit them.

Clarissa Dalloway's party, which is the culminating event of the book, ties the narrative together by gathering the group of friends Clarissa thinks about throughout her day. It also concludes the secondary story of the book, the story of Septimus Warren Smith, by having Dr. Bradshaw arrive at the party and mention that one of his patients committed suicide that day.

The book's major competing themes are isolation and community, or the possibilities and limits of communicativeness, as evidenced by Clarissa's abiding sense of being alone and by her social skills, which bring people together at her parties.

Author Biography

Virginia Woolf was born in 1882 in London, England. She was the daughter of Leslie Stephen, an eminent man of letters, and Julia Prinsep Jackson Duckworth. The Stephen-Duckworth household had many children and was financially secure. Woolf had free rein of her father's extensive library, and was able to educate herself thoroughly.

Woolf was brought up in a scholarly and creative environment. Following her father's death in 1904, Woolf and three of her siblings moved to a house in Bloomsbury (a neighborhood of London) where they cultivated a similar atmosphere. Woolf began writing and publishing at this time, mostly literary criticism, and not yet fiction. In 1907, when her sister Vanessa (a painter) married art critic Clive Bell, Woolf and a brother moved to another house. The writers, intellectuals, and artists who met at this house played central and pivotal roles in British early twentieth-century intellectual and cultural history. They were known as the Bloomsbury group, and they espoused a number of common views; for example, most were pacifists. To Woolf, questions of gender, gender difference, and sexuality became extremely important. She was interested in the commonalties of men and women as well as their differences, and she argued that artists had androgynous minds.

Woolf began publishing fiction in 1915, and it was with her third novel (*Jacob's Room*, 1922) that she began to show maturity as a writer. *Mrs. Dalloway,* her fourth novel, is evidence of the consol-

Virginia Woolf

idation of a major and rare fictional talent. Woolf went on to publish more novels, and these, together with her extensive non-fiction publications, amount to one of the most distinguished bodies of literature in the English language.

Virginia Woolf (then Virginia Stephen) married Leonard Woolf, a politician and writer, in 1912. Despite the success of her marriage and publishing career, she suffered bouts of mental disequilibrium throughout her life, periods of madness or near-madness that terrified her. After each recovery she was haunted by the thought that the next time she might not return to sanity. This fear, along with the depressing events of WWII, finally proved too much for her to bear. Convinced that Hitler's forces would prevail, and mired in a period of depression, Woolf committed suicide by drowning in Lewes, Sussex, England on March 28, 1941.

Plot Summary

Section 1

Mrs. Dalloway begins with a sentence that is also its first paragraph: "Mrs. Dalloway said she would buy the flowers herself." The second paragraph mentions that "doors would be taken off their hinges," so it is possible to determine that there will be an event at Mrs. Dalloway's house that day, and that Clarissa is going out to buy flowers for the affair.

Setting out for her purchases reminds Clarissa of how she used to "burst open the French doors" at Bourton, the country house of her youth. She also remembers, in connection with Bourton, a close friend of her youth, Peter Walsh. On the way to the flower shop, Clarissa runs into another old friend, Hugh Whitbread. Section 1 ends when, from within the flower shop, Clarissa hears the loud sound of a car backfiring.

Section 2

The sound of the car backfiring facilitates a shift in which character's point of view dominates the narrative. Septimus Warren Smith, a major character, is introduced in this way. Septimus and his wife, Lucrezia, are walking along the street where the flower shop and back-firing car are located, on their way to Regent's Park. Septimus is mentally disturbed, a young man who has come back from the First World War (WWI) suffering from shell shock. The public sounds of the car backfiring and an "aeroplane" roaring overhead allowed Woolf to register, besides the points of view of Septimus and Lucrezia, the points of view of a number of passersby who are not major characters in the book.

Section 3

Clarissa arrives home, having ordered the flowers. She finds that her husband has been invited to lunch at Lady Bruton's. She decides to mend the dress that she will be wearing that evening at her party. Once again, she thinks about various people, things, and her past, and so the novel builds a sense of her character and what issues are pertinent to her. One significant person she thinks about is Sally Seton, a close friend of her youth, with whom she had been in love.

Peter Walsh drops by unexpectedly; Clarissa is not aware that he has returned to London from India. With this visit, the past enters the present forcibly, as the man who preoccupied Clarissa's thoughts that morning appears in person. She invites him to her party.

Section 4

Section 4 follows Peter Walsh on an amble about town after he leaves Clarissa's house. He also thinks about their past, how he loved Clarissa, and how he found fault with her. He thinks about her party that evening and her parties in general. He ends up in Regent's Park (where the book left Septimus and Lucrezia), where he falls into a slumber on a bench.

Section 5

This section is very brief and appears to record Peter's sleeping dream in which a figure referred to as the "solitary traveller" is the principal protagonist.

Section 6

Peter awakes and ruminates over Clarissa, Bourton, Sally Seton and Richard Dalloway: how he loved Clarissa, had been jealous of Richard, had been close to Sally, and had criticized Clarissa.

Section 7

Section 7 is the lengthiest of the eight sections of the U.S. edition of the novel (the first published British edition had twelve sections). The location of Regent's Park, where Peter has been snoozing, and where Septimus and his wife have been sitting on a bench, facilitates a shift from Peter Walsh back to the troubled young couple. They are waiting for their noon appointment with Dr. Bradshaw. Much of this section is Septimus' point of view, and so the reader gets a glimpse into the workings of his distressed and strained mind. Lucrezia agonizes about her husband's condition and how people must see that all is not well with them.

Moving back to Peter, the reader finds that he is still musing about the past, how Clarissa is a snob who loves high society, and how her snobbery and love of comfort led her to choose Richard Dalloway over himself for a husband.

As Peter leaves the park, he walks by an old vagrant woman singing a song; Septimus and Lucrezia pass the same woman at the same time, and so the narrative shifts to the couple again. At this point, Septimus's history is presented: how he came to London showing great promise, but returned from the war traumatized. From Lucrezia's thoughts, the reader learns that Septimus has threatened to kill himself.

At noon, Big Ben strikes. Clarissa hears it at home while she is mending her dress, and Septimus and his wife arrive for their appointment at the establishment of Sir William Bradshaw. Bradshaw promises to arrange for Septimus to go to a rest home because he sees that the young man's condition is grave and advanced. The narrative then discusses doctors such as Bradshaw, questioning the methods and assumptions by which they diagnose and practice.

The scene now shifts to Richard Dalloway, at his lunch with Lady Bruton. Hugh Whitbread has also been invited. Lady Bruton wants their help revising a letter she has composed to the *Times* about the need for emigration; Hugh quickly edits it after lunch.

The two men leave Lady Bruton's. Hugh stops to buy a gift for his wife and Richard decides to buy and deliver flowers to Clarissa. Clarissa is pleased and informs Richard that their daughter, Elizabeth, is with Miss Kilman, her history tutor.

The narrative now shifts to Elizabeth and Miss Kilman. They go to tea in a department store, and Elizabeth sets out on her own for a bus ride and a short walk before she returns home to ready for the party that evening.

Septimus and Lucrezia, by this time, have returned home to pass the afternoon in their apartment. Dr. Holmes, a doctor Septimus dreads, forces his way inside. Septimus's madness and his horror of doctors' control over him leads him to jump from the apartment window to his death.

The sound of Septimus's ambulance is heard by Peter Walsh, who is on his way back to his hotel.

Section 8

Clarissa's party is beginning; guests are arriving. Clarissa is experiencing anxiety, convinced that her party will be a failure. But it seems to be a success, and she makes the rounds of her guests. Sally Seton arrives, surprising Clarissa because Clarissa is not aware that Sally is in London from the country. The Prime Minister shows up, making everybody feel very satisfied that they are such distinguished company. Sally and Peter chat and wait for Clarissa to mingle with others before she can visit with them. Finally, guests begin to leave. Richard goes to join his daughter, and Clarissa goes to talk to her old friends. Upon seeing Clarissa move toward him, Peter feels great pleasure that this event has ended his day.

Characters

Dr. Bradshaw

See Sir William Bradshaw

Sir William Bradshaw

While Dr. Bradshaw, unlike Dr. Holmes, immediately grasps the gravity and nature of Septimus's condition, he is still not a likable character. He seems very similar to Dr. Holmes. The book's argument against these doctors is that they are primarily concerned with managing individual cases of social and psychological distress without being interested in the causes of such problems. Thus, these doctors are still a part of the problem. They help to maintain the status quo by smoothing over difficulties instead of approaching psychological disturbance as evidence of deep social problems that must be addressed.

Lady Bruton

Lady Bruton is the character with whom Richard Dalloway and Hugh Whitbread have lunch. She is a woman of strong character and active in public and political life. She always uses her influence in matters about which she feels strongly. Her new interest is in emigration, that is, encouraging young British couples to emigrate to Canada, one of the British Commonwealth countries. She asks Richard and Hugh to revise her letter to the editorial section of the major London newspaper, the *Times,* the forum in which she plans to air her views.

Daisy

Daisy is referred to in passing as the woman whom Peter Walsh is to marry. Peter is in London arranging matters for her divorce, among other business, as she is presently married.

Clarissa Dalloway

Clarissa Dalloway is the principal character of *Mrs. Dalloway,* since it is her party that gives definition to the narrative and her point of view dominates the book. She was born Clarissa Parry, and the day the novel takes place, she is approximately fifty years old. Her husband is Richard Dalloway, and they have one child, Elizabeth. The overwhelming impression Clarissa gives is that she is a solitary, even isolated, being, and that she is often consumed with thoughts or feelings of death and mortality. This is not only because her thoughts of friends are for those of her youth and not present ones, but also because she seems to desire isolation. She chooses Richard Dalloway over Peter Walsh as a husband not because she loves him more, but because she believes Richard will not consume all of her personality and time, or all of her emotional and intellectual reserves. Clarissa

Media Adaptations

- *Mrs. Dalloway* was adapted into a film of the same name in 1997, directed by Marleen Gorris. It stars the venerated British actor Vanessa Redgrave as Clarissa Dalloway.

sleeps in her own room, in a small single bed that is likened to a coffin, and such suggestions and imagery of isolation and death surround her throughout the book.

The reader gains a sense of Clarissa's character both from her own thoughts and from what other characters, especially Peter, think about her. Besides the fact that she has inspired love, which speaks well of her, she is also someone whom others, and herself, think flawed. Peter's notion that she is the "perfect hostess" sums up this suspicion of her weakness. Clarissa is well-off and does not work, putting her in a position to cultivate her preferences, which are the pursuits of beauty and social harmony. While she knows that these are worthy pursuits, she and her friends nevertheless wonder whether this is a wholly ethical way to live. The question she and they ask is whether or not she should be more like her husband or Lady Bruton and take a more obviously practical role in public and political life.

Elizabeth Dalloway

Elizabeth Dalloway is Clarissa's daughter. She is just coming of age, and she is somewhat in the thrall of her history tutor, Doris Kilman. However, Elizabeth is also her own person. When she goes out on a shopping trip with Miss Kilman, she soon parts from her tutor and steals a few hours to be by herself before she must return home to get ready for her mother's party.

Richard Dalloway

Richard Dalloway, despite being Clarissa's husband, does not play a large role in the novel. He was not as close to Clarissa as Peter and Sally were during their youthful days. Rather, in the various characters' memories of their mutual past, Richard

is a late arrival on the youthful scene. He arrives around the time Clarissa is thinking about marriage and presents himself as the perfect husband for her, in contrast to Peter. He is a politician and member of Parliament and the Conservative Party, demonstrating Clarissa's and his relative social and political conservatism, especially compared to Peter and Sally.

Ellie Henderson

Ellie is Clarissa's cousin, whom Clarissa invites to her party at the last minute at the request of a mutual acquaintance. Ellie is not well-off and gets out very seldom, so she is grateful to have the opportunity to attend such an exciting affair.

Dr. Holmes

Dr. Holmes is an overbearing and controlling doctor who does not understand Septimus's condition and whose ignorance and arrogance do Septimus more harm than good. His arrival at Septimus's apartment is the last straw for the young man. Rather than fall under Holmes's control, Septimus throws himself out of a window, killing himself.

Miss Doris Kilman

Doris Kilman is a single, educated woman to whom life has not been particularly kind or just. While she possessed employment of some security before the war, her refusal to jump on the war bandwagon and call all Germans enemies made her unpopular and caused her to be dismissed from her post. Left to fend for herself during the lean war years, she scrapes together a living from incidental tutoring and lecturing. She feels great bitterness about her misfortunes and develops a religious fanaticism that makes her extremely unpopular with Clarissa, who fears and resents the woman's influence on Elizabeth.

Lucy

Lucy is the principal housemaid in the Dalloway home, and she and the cook are primarily responsible for readying the house for the party.

Aunt Parry

See Miss Helena Parry

Miss Helena Parry

Clarissa's aunt is a minor character in the book. She figures early on as the relative at Bourton whom the younger people seem to enjoy shocking. She surprises Peter at the end of the book by still being alive and by being present at the party.

Sylvia Parry

Sylvia, Clarissa's sister, is only mentioned in passing, but is significant nevertheless. She was killed by a falling tree at Bourton. The name "Sylvia" is Latinate, meaning "wild" or "woods." Her death signifies the death of youth and freedom, as Clarissa's freedom and youth ended at Bourton when she decided to marry. That is, her life since Bourton has been one in which she is not so much her own person as Richard's wife.

Rezia

See Lucrezia Warren Smith

Lady Rosseter

See Sally Seton

Sally Seton

Sally, with Peter and Clarissa, was a member of the close triangle of friends who often spent time together at Bourton. Sally delighted her friends with her vibrant personality and her legendary exploits. Clarissa was so taken by Sally that she fell in love with her, as she realizes years later. Sally, like Clarissa, went on to marry, marrying a self-made man whose success eventually earns him high social distinction, giving Sally the title "Lady Rosseter."

Lucrezia Warren Smith

Lucrezia, or Rezia, is Septimus's wife. He met her in Italy where he was stationed for part of WWI, as Italy was one of Britain's allies during the war. While she was happy to marry Septimus and set out to a foreign country, now in London she is in despair because Septimus is no longer the same man she married. His war trauma is now deep-seated and advanced and she finds herself alone and confused about what is happening to her husband.

Septimus Warren Smith

After Clarissa, Septimus is the character of most importance. His story parallels Clarissa's to a certain extent, as both characters are radically isolated and seem at odds with prevailing forces in the world. Septimus came to London as a young man in search of a career, and he showed early promise. He was an excellent worker interested in furthering his education, but then he went off to war. He returned from the war having fought bravely, but also with shell shock, a condition little understood at the time. He and his wife first seek help from a general practitioner, instead of immediately consulting the psychological specialist, Dr. Bradshaw,

demonstrating people's unfamiliarity with mental disease and how to manage it at the time. Septimus is a portrait of a distressed mind, going through the hours of his last day, entertaining delusional thoughts and experiencing hallucinations, and ultimately, killing himself.

Peter Walsh

Peter Walsh is an Anglo-Indian, that is, a British citizen who worked in India during Britain's administrative colonial control of that country. At the time of the book's events, he is visiting London. Peter is defined mostly by his having been deeply in love with Clarissa Dalloway and by his intention, during his youth, to marrying her. In fact, he still seems to be in love with her, despite having married after she rejected him, and despite the fact that he is planning to marry for a second time. Of the group of close, youthful friends, Sally, Clarissa and himself, he seems more like Sally than like Clarissa. Sally and Peter were very lively; they took chances and espoused forward-looking political and social views.

Hugh Whitbread

Hugh Whitbread is deemed by most characters in the book (Peter, Sally, Richard) to be dull and uninteresting. There is the sense that he is a little ridiculous and quite conventional. Clarissa has the most sympathy for him as she appreciates his good qualities. Foremost amongst his good points are his loyalty and obedience. He always tried to please his mother and he looks after his ailing and fragile wife, Evelyn, dutifully.

Themes

Consciousness

Although it is difficult to imagine, the novel is a relatively new literary form. Poetry and drama (plays), for example, have a much longer history. The novel, however, did not arise as a unique genre until the late eighteenth century. According to literary historians, it arose along with, or partly because of, the rise of the individual.

It is said that Woolf's style, and that of other early-twentieth-century novelists, represents a culmination of this connection between the novel and the individual. Before there were "individuals," so to speak, a person lived his or her life according to what was determined from the outside or according to what society decreed was correct. A person did not go through life assuming that he or she

Topics for Further Study

- Research shell shock in relation to WWI. How do treatments for war trauma today differ from those used then?

- What was the role of women during WWI? How did women contribute to the war effort in Britain?

could make personal, or individual, decisions and choices. The literary historians argue, then, that when this new type of person, this "individual," began to exist, it needed new literary forms to express itself. The novel was one of these forms.

What comes with being an individual is a sense of separateness and uniqueness, a sense of being apart. One way this sense of being separate is cultivated is by each person focusing on, or developing a sense of, his or her own mind or consciousness. The novel is a literary form of the individual, literary historians argue, because novelists present and explore characters who have significant interior lives.

In novels such as *Mrs. Dalloway,* consciousness and an internal life are central preoccupations. *Mrs. Dalloway* is largely made up of the internal thoughts of its various characters. It is for this reason that novels like *Mrs. Dalloway* represent a culmination of an historical process of individuation. Preceding novels had not so intensively focused on the interior life of characters, or on what characters thought to themselves. That is, the characters in *Mrs. Dalloway* and similar novels are featured as individual thinkers even more than they are presented as persons interacting socially with others. It is the characters' individual qualities that are highlighted.

In a sense, the character of Clarissa Dalloway is a representation of extreme, problematic individualism, in that she recognizes her absolute isolation. She is distant from her husband, she appears to have few current friends, and she secludes herself in her own small room as if she were a quiet nun in a convent or a solitary prisoner in a cell. The reader derives this

sense of an absolutely isolated consciousness when, for instance, Clarissa watches the old woman across the way. Unseen, looking out from the window of her solitary chamber, separated from the woman by walls and distance, Clarissa seems trapped within the confines of her own consciousness.

The novel seems to ask if people can truly communicate and connect if each is enclosed within his or her own consciousness. Whether the novel resolves this issue, or merely explores it, is for each reader to decide. Is Clarissa's party evidence of true communion between people despite separateness? Does the imagery of waves and connecting threads and webs complicate the imagery of isolation? Do the depictions of shared public sights and sounds indicate fully shared experience, or simply common experience differently understood?

Social Change

Some critics believe that *Mrs. Dalloway* is an apolitical and an asocial novel about individual internal life as opposed to social life. Others insist that the political and social context of the time is included in the book and important to its events. Critics who believe the novel is concerned with social and political events and developments of the time, consider it a novel of suggestion, not argumentation. Woolf dropped hints and touched lightly on social and political developments, they say, and a discerning reader is able to make out intended meanings from the author's allusions.

For example, WWI is obviously important to the sense of the novel. It is what ruins Septimus's life and career and what hounds him to his death.

Additionally, the histories of Septimus and Dr. Bradshaw indicate that classism is on the wane in the Britain of *Mrs. Dalloway.* Whereas a person's social class determined his or her possibilities in earlier days, now Bradshaw has risen from humble circumstances to greatness, having earned a title (he is *Sir* William Bradshaw). Similarly, the lower-middle-class Septimus, before the war, was on his way to a brilliant career and upward social mobility.

The reader also learns that the political and social scene of Britain is changing significantly, as details of the rise of the Labour Party and of unrest in India are revealed. These details indicate the shifting of political power to the party that represents the interests of the broadest population, instead of remaining faithful to the interests of the old, aristocratic ruling classes. It also shows non-European nations beginning to agitate for freedom from foreign intervention and control.

Also significantly, Elizabeth Dalloway's rumination over a career indicates how the education of young women and their social positions are changing. As opposed to only having indirect influence through their husbands, like Lady Bruton, young women like Elizabeth can have public careers in their own right. Thus, *Mrs. Dalloway* stays true to Woolf's assertion, expressed in her essay "Mr. Bennett and Mrs. Brown," that, around 1910, human character and society changed: "All human relations have shifted—those between masters and servants, husbands and wives, parents and children. And when human relations change there is at the same time a change in religion, conduct, politics, and literature." In short, those persons and classes traditionally without social or cultural power appear in *Mrs. Dalloway* as coming into a position to exercise their rights, to have appreciable social influence, and to achieve upward social mobility.

Style

Narration and Point of View

From the very first sentence, *Mrs. Dalloway* shows the secure meshing of a third person (external) narrator's point of view with a first person, character's point of view, such that it is not possible to separate or distinguish the two: "Mrs. Dalloway said she would buy the flowers herself." If the two had been clearly separated the sentence would read: "Mrs. Dalloway said, 'I will buy the flowers myself'," or would have included the word "that": "Mrs. Dalloway said *that* she would buy the flowers herself." In this second case, the reader would assume that the words following the word "that" were not necessarily faithful to Mrs. Dalloway's thought or speech, but rather that they are a narrator's interpretation or summary. Instead, what Woolf perfected in this novel is a style of narration that literary critics have called "represented thought and speech," capturing the motions of a mind thinking in the past tense, third person. A narrator presents character thought and speech, but the narrator's words are wholly and immediately imbued by the voice and style of the particular character in question; there is no way to separate narrator and character. Woolf invented an elegant and efficient way of moving between and representing multiple characters' speech and thought; the clumsiness of excessive dialogue or of switching between sequences of different characters' thoughts presented in the first person is avoided. Related terms in literary criticism are re-ported thought and speech, free indirect discourse, and stream-of-consciousness.

Time

Mrs. Dalloway is striking for the way that its events occur within a single day. This unusual strategy announces the novel's complication of time in general. For example, while most people tend to think of time in terms of the regular clicking away of the clock—of seconds, minutes, hours, and days—this book shows how people can relive, through the operations of memory, whole years within the space of minutes. Peter and Clarissa walk a few paces in London and remember major periods of their youth, how these years affected them, and how they shaped their lives.

On a related theme, the novel multiplies time by presenting the thoughts of myriad characters, each of whom remember and experience time, the past and the present, in different ways. In this novel, chronological time is only one sense of time, as the characters bring the past into the present, allow the meaning and remembrance of the present to be shaped by the past, and shape memories of and feelings about the past with experience in the present.

Character Double

Septimus Warren Smith can be seen as Clarissa's double in the novel. As a character double, he is a character whose attributes and story fill out the character and story of Clarissa. According to the literary critic Alex Page, in "A Dangerous Day: Mrs. Dalloway and Her Double," "Septimus's character is in all essentials Clarissa's, but taken to a deadly extreme." Where Clarissa is isolated, Septimus is disassociated from reality; where Clarissa manages the disappointments and strictures society imposes upon her, Septimus buckles under greater pressures. The close connections of these characters is made clear by Clarissa's deep upset when Dr. Bradshaw informs her, at her party, that one of his patients committed suicide that day. She retreats from her guests in shock when Bradshaw mentions Septimus's death, as if she herself were susceptible to the same degree of despair that destroys the young man.

Historical Context

The New Modern Era

The nineteenth century ushered in developments that profoundly changed European society. Mercantilism and industrialism created a powerful

Compare & Contrast

- **1920s:** In Britain, the Labour Party rises to power, women get the right to vote, and the first major wave of communication and travel technologies are incipient or, in some cases, widely established (radio, telephone, telegraph communications; automobile and airplane travel).

   Today: International communications and connections have progressed to such an extent, due to computer technology and the Internet, that the term "globalization" is in common use. The modern world foreseen in the 1920s has definitively arrived.

- **1920s:** Modernism, the set of artistic movements that try to express, through form and style, the cultural and social changes of a brand new century, is flourishing. The modernists profess internationalism.

   Today: Art at the close of the twentieth century is defined by postmodernism. The name of this new set of movements suggests how its forms are both tied to modernism (post*modernism*), and in some ways defined against modernism (*post*modernism). Postmodernists examine and question globalization and transnationalism.

- **1920s:** While the American colonies of Europe (i.e., the United States and the nations of South and Central America) have long since established themselves as independent nations, the twentieth century is characterized by nationalist and independence movements in Europe's remaining colonies (in Asia and Africa). These movements are not brought to a close until the 1960s.

   Today: Colonies no longer exist; rather, a group of independent nations cover the globe.

---

new class. The cultural, political and economic might of this new class, the bourgeoisie or middle-class, soon overtook that of the aristocratic classes that had controlled nations and empires before. The spread of democracy and workers' rights movements also characterized the nineteenth century. It was not until after World War I (1914–1918), however, that a deep sense of how extremely and permanently European society had changed prevailed.

Mrs. Dalloway registers this sense of the end of an era. Clarissa's Aunt Parry, the aged relic who makes an appearance at Clarissa's party, represents this decline and this ending of an old way of life. The old woman likes to remember her days in Burma, a time and place suggestive of the height of British imperialism and colonialism. But, as Lady Bruton's distressed comment about the situation in India makes clear, the old days of paternalistic European colonialism are over. India and other colonies that used to be comfortable homes for colonials like Clarissa's aunt are now uncomfortable places where the beginnings of serious battles for independence are occurring.

Lady Bruton also mentions the Labour Party's ascendancy. (This new party gained a parliamentary majority in England in 1924, the year before *Mrs. Dalloway* was published.) This detail indicates how the England of this time had become radically modern in its move to a fuller social democracy, the political system that still characterizes most modern nations today, including the United States. The Labour Party's name indicates its representation of rule by the people, for the people, as opposed to rule by an aristocracy or an oligarchic class.

Elizabeth Dalloway, a young woman considering a career, is also an indicator of change, as entering the working world was a social possibility not available to women before this time.

WWI

WWI bears comparison with the Vietnam War. Like this more recent war, it is remembered as a war that many thought should have been avoided and that traumatized its soldiers. It was an imperial war in two senses. First, it was an attempt to limit the European encroachments of Prussian imperial rule and power. Second, it was partially provoked by border skirmishes among European nations on the African continent (European nations had begun colonizing African territories in the late nineteenth century). It was a power struggle pertaining to traditional European ruling classes and had very little to do with the everyday concerns and struggles of most European citizens.

What was shocking about the war was how long it dragged on and how many casualties it produced. (It lasted four years and millions of young men died or were terribly wounded.) The style of fighting developed in this war was trench warfare. In trench warfare, soldiers dig deep ditches from which they shoot at the enemy. When given the order to charge, they climb out of these trenches and meet the enemy head-on. These cramped, claustrophobic trenches were breeding grounds for disease, as they were muddy and wet from frequent rainfall. Soldiers felt that the trenches were as much ready-made earthly graves as they were protection from enemy fire. Also, poison gas (mustard gas) was used during WWI, and soldiers caught by the fumes without gas masks died or suffered horribly.

Enemy soldiers often formed friendships during cease-fire periods in the space of no man's land between opposing trench lines. Soldiers on both sides felt strongly that their real enemies were not each other, but the officers, politicians and generals who were running the war. The carnage, mutilation, and terror of this badly managed war resulted in a host of traumatized war veterans. This trauma was given the name "shell shock" in the years following the war. Septimus Warren Smith, who was a brave soldier, but who ends up a suicidal, ruined man, indicates Woolf's condemnation of this unfortunate war.

Critical Overview

All of Woolf's publications, fictional and non-fictional alike, have received a great deal of critical attention. A bibliography of criticism on Woolf would be a very hefty book in its own right, as her work has been the subject of intense study since she began writing, and it is still a major topic today. Considered equal to the likes of Shakespeare, James Joyce, and Charlotte Brontë, Virginia Woolf is indisputably one of the English language's greatest literary voices.

Major topics in the criticism on *Mrs. Dalloway* are the significance of Clarissa's party as the culminating event of the book, and Peter Walsh's and others' criticism of her parties. At one point in the novel, Clarissa is plagued by a bad feeling. With some thought, she arrives at the source of her anxiety: "Her parties! That was it! Her parties! Both of them [Peter and Richard] criticised her very unfairly, laughed at her unjustly for her parties. That was it! That was it!" She goes on to think: "Well, how was she going to defend herself?"

Critics have defended Clarissa amply by theorizing the significance of the opposition of Richard, parliamentarian and politician, and the seemingly apolitical, spoilt Clarissa, giver of parties and lover of beauty. For Suzette A. Henke, in "*Mrs. Dalloway:* the Communion of Saints," Clarissa's party is akin to a sacred mass, "a ritual culminating in sacred communion." In the opinion of Jeremy Hawthorn, in *Virginia Woolf's "Mrs. Dalloway": A Study in Alienation,* the party "is not just Clarissa's gift, it is the occasion for communal giving . . . which will recharge the participants' social sense and . . . allow them temporarily to escape from their alienated selves."

Other critics, along these lines, suggest Woolf's book argues that politicians like Richard would not be so busy cleaning up the messes of the world if people were brought up to love harmony, communication, community, and beauty before all other things. It is not, then, that *Mrs. Dalloway* is an apolitical or anti-political novel, these critics argue, but rather that its politics are radically different from the norm—the book advances a politic of beauty and community, as it were.

Many feminist critics suggest that this opposition of political styles is a gender issue. To these critics, it seems that Woolf understands that traditional women's work (mothering children, maintaining family bonds) emphasizes social bonding over competition. Women, therefore, and books like *Mrs. Dalloway,* have important lessons for society at large, and suggest how it might function more smoothly.

Related to considerations about the significance of Clarissa's parties are estimations about the novel's connection to contemporaneous social and political events. Until perhaps the last twenty years of Woolf criticism, a prevailing view was that Woolf was not at all interested in the "real world." The novelist E. M. Forster, Woolf's famous contemporary, stated in his book *Virginia Woolf* that "improving the world she [Woolf] would not consider" was not her intention. Yet, as other critics point out, such an opinion does not hold up when the author's own diary records that the novel's purpose was "to criticise the social system, & show it

John Standing as Richard and Vanessa Redgrave as Clarissa in the 1997 film version of the novel.

at work, at its most intense." (This entry concerning *Mrs. Dalloway* can be found in Vol. II of *The Diary of Virginia Woolf.*)

Critics who examine this aspect of the novel discuss Woolf's subtle, if not wholesale, indictment of the outdated and overly conservative attitudes of Richard, Lady Bruton, and Hugh, and argue that the suffering of Septimus is to be understood as the result of such problematic views and policies. The prevailing attitude today concerning the book's politics, and Woolf's social views in general, is expressed succinctly by Suzette A. Henke (in the article previously cited): "All of Virginia Woolf's major novels suggest an intellectual commitment to feminist, pacifist, and socialist principles."

Another topic in the criticism of *Mrs. Dalloway* is an examination of Septimus and Clarissa as problems in psychology and mental health. Knowing that Woolf herself suffered bouts of mental disease, they find these characters' portraits a wealth of information. Another significant body of criticism focuses on questions of sexuality in the novel, considering, for example, Clarissa's love for Sally Seton. Some critics suggest that Clarissa's extreme feelings of isolation are to be understood partly as the result of a deleteriously suppressed homosexuality. In "Clarissa Dalloway's Respectable

Suicide," Emily Jensen expresses this view: "No simple girlhood crush, Clarissa's love for Sally Seton is a profound reality that permeates her adult life." This critic goes on to say that Clarissa's suppression of this love is a sort of suicide, a death in life, "on a par with Septimus Smith's more obvious suicide." Jensen approaches Septimus as Clarissa's double, that is, as a character who aids the reader in arriving at a fuller understanding of Clarissa. Jensen's essay, in this way, intersects with yet another significant set of inquiries into the novel, which considers the book's clusters of characters, especially the clustering or doubling of Septimus and Clarissa.

Criticism

Carol Dell'Amico

Dell'Amico teaches English at Rutgers, the State University of New Jersey. In this essay, she examines the question of plot in Virginia Woolf's novel.

Mrs. Dalloway is a work of literature that can be classified as narrative fiction. That is, it tells a story, or a narrative, that is fictional, or made-up. Novels and short stories are narrative fictions usually structured by a plot. But *Mrs. Dalloway* is a novel without a plot. This essay examines what this means and why the author might have chosen to eschew this typical narrative convention.

In *Aspects of the Novel,* Woolf's contemporary, E. M. Forster, explains the difference between story and plot in the following way:

> A plot [like a story] is also a narrative of events, the emphasis falling on causality. "The king dies and then the queen died," is a story. "The king died, and then the queen died of grief" is a plot. The time-sequence is preserved, but the sense of causality overshadows it.

A plot, then, establishes causal relationships between characters, or between characters and events. Moreover, for a novel to be said to have a plot, this series of interconnected events must unify the entire story or determine most of its major happenings. To relate the story of a novel is simply to relate events and situations as they happen, page by page, in a book; to relate the plot involves capturing the reasons why the things that happen happen. While *Mrs. Dalloway* certainly establishes causal relationships between characters and events, the novel cannot be said to have a plot because a network of causality does not unify the entire book.

On the contrary, the book takes great trouble to establish how it is different, in this respect, from most novels. Chance and coincidence, instead of purposeful interconnection, structure the book. Peter Walsh, a very important character, arrives by chance at Clarissa's on the day of her party. Sally Seton, another important character, arrives at Clarissa's party unexpectedly and also by chance. Septimus Warren Smith is also a major character in the book who is only tangentially related to the other major characters. The connection of Septimus to the other characters is determined by chance and locale, not by any social connections these characters have in common. Septimus and Clarissa pass each other by chance, as both are on Bond Street at the same time. Septimus and Peter Walsh also pass each other by chance, just outside Regent's Park, neither knowing that the other exists. Indeed, it is the single day, the Wednesday in June 1923, that unifies the book, and nothing else.

Plots make what happen in a novel seem natural and inevitable. But plots are really just constructed by authors, and so the events depicted in novels are not inevitable at all. Woolf's plotless book of chance and coincidence plays on the way

> " While *Mrs. Dalloway* certainly establishes causal relationships between characters and events, the novel cannot be said to have a plot because a network of causality does not unify the entire book."

that plot is a series of "coincidences" made to look like naturally or casually connected events by the careful work of a controlling author.

Most stories that are written and read have plots. The writer makes certain decisions about characters (their personalities and qualities), and about characters' relations to other characters or to social forces and events. The author then comes up with a plot built upon the likely responses and actions of character types in relation to other character types or in relation to social happenings. The author, in this way, feels that it is possible and desirable to predict how certain types of people will think and behave. The author also feels that certain social forces are describable and likely to have certain predictable effects on certain types of persons. The author who settles on a plot, then, is confident that he or she knows a great deal about human nature and about how the world works.

This confidence about personality type, social type, and how the world works was never more developed than in the novels of the nineteenth and very early twentieth centuries. Typical to these novels is a narrator who tells the reader all about the particular character—his or her thoughts and desires, his or weaknesses and strengths. These narrators also explain why a character acts the way he or she does. Authors, through their narrators, showed themselves to be experts—experts in psychology and sociology. In fact, it is no surprise that the academic sciences of sociology and psychology arose around the turn of the century; people and their lives were, quite literally, becoming sciences. Woolf discusses this science of writing, or this novelistic science of psychological and social knowledge in her essay "Mr. Bennett and Mrs. Brown."

What Do I Read Next?

- *To the Lighthouse* (1927) was Woolf's next novel, after the success of *Mrs. Dalloway*. It concerns a large family spending a summer at the seaside, much like Woolf's own family did during her childhood.

- *Ulysses* (1922), by James Joyce, is a challenging book. The title refers to the famous classical Greek story of a man's epic travels (those of Odysseus, also called Ulysses). The epic journey, it has been said, refers less to the main character's (Ulysses'/Leopold Bloom's) perambulations through Dublin and more to the journey the reader experiences as he or she reads through the extraordinary stylistic shifts that make up this modernist novel. Like *Mrs. Dalloway, Ulysses* takes place within a single day and characterizes a city as well as its characters.

- *The Hours* (1998), by Michael Cunningham, is a recently published novel based on Woolf's *Mrs. Dalloway*. It interweaves the lives of three women in three times: Virginia Woolf in 1923, a 1949 Woolf fan in Los Angeles, and a present day Clarissa, planning a party.

- *The Sound and the Fury* (1929), by William Faulkner, is a novel whose stylistic beauty and experimentation represent an American modernism contemporaneous to the experiments of Virginia Woolf and James Joyce abroad.

"Mr. Bennett and Mrs. Brown" introduces a fictional character, a Mrs. Brown (who is riding in a railway carriage), and then shows how the various well-known and popular writers who immediately preceded Woolf would have presented her in their fiction. These major novelists she terms Edwardians, as King Edward was then the king of England. The writers in question are H. G. Wells, Arnold Bennett, and John Galsworthy.

Since Mrs. Brown is a character who appears to be in straightened circumstances and is most likely not particularly well-educated, Woolf parodies Wells' style in the following way:

> Seizing upon . . . the unsatisfactory condition of our primary schools with a rapidity to which I can do no justice, Mr. Wells would instantly project . . . a vision of a better, breezier, jollier, happier, more adventurous and gallant world where . . . these fusty old women do not exist.

Her criticism of Wells, then, is that he is a utopian, a writer not so much interested in presenting the intricacies and mysteries of character and personality, but rather more interested in expounding his theories and views about how society can be perfected. Galsworthy, Woolf asserts, would no sooner introduce such a character than launch into an authorial tirade "[b]urning with indignation, stuffed with information, [and] arraigning civilization." Again, the intricacies and instabilities of individual characters are left behind, and the author's views about the world and about certain typical character types are expounded at length instead. What Bennett would do, says Woolf, is bury this character under a mountain of descriptive details—what she is wearing, where she comes from, what the railway carriage she is riding in looks like, and so forth. Once again, left behind would be any understanding of the character's complexities.

Only the new Georgian writers such as herself, says Woolf, or such as James Joyce or D. H. Lawrence, have returned literature to its proper domain, where inquiry and delicacy are as important as the author's views about what can and should be done to ameliorate the condition of society. (She terms herself and her contemporaries Georgians because King George succeeded King Edward in 1910.)

Given Woolf's sense of the overweening confidence and all-knowing attitude of the writers that preceded her, her decision to write a novel without a plot can be understood. To eschew or avoid plot, within this historical and intellectual context, means to suggest that an all-knowing stance is not always productive. Since deciding on a plot means having definitive views about social types and social forces, writing a plotless novel suggests that perhaps it is better, at times, to be a person who approaches the world as a questioner, as one seeking knowledge and enlightenment, as opposed to one who already knows everything or who has answers to solve every social problem.

Since the reader of a novel tends to intellectually identify with the stance of the narrator, the reader of one of Bennett's novels, for example, is made into an all-knowing, god-like figure. The reader, like the narrator, is in a position of knowing more than any character and of having full understanding of how the world works. The reader of a novel without a plot, in contrast, is put into the position of one who must explore and question the relationship between things. Not everything is answered for this other reader; not everything is known. The reader of a more experimental, plotless novel is a reader who is encouraged to question reality, to not assume full knowledge. This other reader is one who is asked to think and explore, as opposed to simply receive knowledge and apply it; this reader is encouraged to ask why things are the way they are and how they might be changed, as opposed to simply having answers and ideas presented to him or her on a platter.

Writers such as Woolf believed that psychological and social knowledge in novels was becoming too pat, that character and plot were becoming predictable, mimicking the latest treatise written by a politician, a sociologist, or a psychologist. There are deeper reasons, however, to turn away from an all-knowing, scientific approach to character and plot. At issue was not simply remembering to be a thinker and explorer, but also the question of whether humankind was in control to the extent it was convinced it was. To know social types and how the world works means to be in control of the world. But was humankind in such full control?

If humankind wasn't in such full control, then the need to think hard about social problems was still a priority, and feelings of over-confidence about the state of knowledge were a danger. For instance, Europeans of the nineteenth century believed in progress: humankind was inventing machines and building institutions and cities that were making life on earth better for all. But, asked writers like Woolf, was humankind really progressing? Was the story or plot of progress true to reality? Was scientific knowledge really explaining and controlling the world in beneficial and predictable ways? Things changed, to be sure, but was humankind progressing morally, in the way that really mattered? Were more people truly better off than before? In fact, the industrial revolution, with all of its machines, may have made work easier and faster, but a new class of impoverished factory workers merely had replaced a propertyless agricultural peasantry. Technology brought airplanes and railroads, but it also made war that much more efficiently destructive.

Not all writers or artists contemporaneous to Woolf who were making interventions into typical artistic forms thought the same way. Many of them celebrated technological advances. What most agreed upon, however, was the need to pause and take stock of science's progress, to make sure that it produced the benefits promised, and not a new type of misery. Thus, to refuse plot is to refuse the typical stories of the time, the typical stories people were telling themselves about the world and progress. Since people make sense of the world by telling stories about the past and the present and about how things work, to refuse plot is to intervene into social narrative and insist that the old stories or the old ways of explaining social life need adjustment or examination.

By not constructing a plot, Woolf offers her readers the opportunity to make up a new story about social life. Readers surprised at such a startling departure from typical novelistic form are invited to ask why there is no plot, what it means when an author decides to be different. If a reader is not told how everything in a novel is tied together, it is up to him or her to do the work. In this way, the reader of *Mrs. Dalloway* can figure out for him- or herself why things are the way they are, or how things might have been, or could be, different.

Source: Carol Dell'Amico, Critical Essay on *Mrs. Dalloway,* in *Novels for Students,* The Gale Group, 2001.

Arnold Bennett

In the following early negative review of Mrs. Dalloway, *Bennett identifies Woolf as the leader of a new school in writing and criticizes her work for lacking vitality.*

My remarks last week about the younger novelists have aroused some complaint, and it has been said to be odd that I, for years the champion of the young, should turn and rend them. I will therefore proceed further. What I have already written is nothing compared to what I will now write.

The real champion of the younger school is Mrs Virginia Woolf. She is almost a senior; but she was the inventor, years ago, of a half-new technique, and she alone, so far as I know, came forward and attacked the old. She has written a small book about me, which through a culpable neglect I have not read. I do, however, remember an article of hers in which she asserted that I and my kind could not create character. This was in answer to an article of mine in which I said that the sound drawing of character was the foundation of good fiction, and in which incidentally I gave my opin-

A 1913 suffragette parade in London's Victoria Park. The park is near the route Clarissa takes on her walk

ion that Mrs Woolf and her kind could not create character.

I have read two and a half of Mrs Woolf's books. First, *The Common Reader,* which is an agreeable collection of elegant essays on literary subjects. Second, *Jacob's Room,* which I achieved with great difficulty. Third, *Mrs Dalloway,* which beat me. I could not finish it, because I could not discover what it was really about, what was its direction, and what Mrs Woolf intended to demonstrate by it.

To express myself differently, I failed to discern what was its moral basis. As regards character-drawing, Mrs Woolf (in my opinion) told us ten thousand things about Mrs Dalloway, but did not show us Mrs Dalloway. I got from the novel no coherent picture of Mrs Dalloway. Nor could I see much trace of construction, or ordered movement towards a climax, in either *Jacob's Room* or *Mrs Dalloway.* Further, I thought that both books seriously lacked vitality.

These three defects, I maintain, are the characteristic defects of the new school of which Mrs Woolf is the leader. The people in them do not sufficiently live, and hence they cannot claim our sympathy or even our hatred: they leave us indifferent.

Logical construction is absent; concentration on the theme (if any) is absent; the interest is dissipated; material is wantonly or clumsily wasted, instead of being employed economically as in the great masterpieces. Problems are neither clearly stated nor clearly solved.

The new practitioners have simply returned to the facile go-as-you-please methods of the eighteenth century, ignoring the important discoveries and innovations of Balzac and later novelists. How different is the new school of fiction from the new school of painting, with its intense regard for logical design!

Lastly, there is absence of vital inspiration. Some novelists appear to have no zest; they loll through their work as though the were taking a stroll in the Park. I admit that I may be wrong on the second count; I may be blind to evidences of a design which is too subtle for my perception. But I do not think that I can be wrong on the first and third counts.

And I admit that some of the younger school write very well. In the novels of Mrs Woolf some brief passages are so exquisitely done that nothing could be done better. But to be fine for a few minutes is not enough. The chief proof of first-rateness is sustained power.

Source: Arnold Bennett, "Another Criticism of the New School," 1925, reprint, in *Virginia Woolf: The Critical Heritage,* edited by Robin Majumdar and Allen McLaurin, Routledge & Kegan Paul, 1975, pp. 189–90.

Manly Johnson

In the following essay, Johnson offers an overview of Mrs. Dalloway, *focusing on its theme of insanity.*

In her . . . novel, *Mrs. Dalloway,* [Woolf] continues to work out her problems of theme and form along the lines laid out first in the short stories and *Jacob's Room.* Thus most of the "ideas" in *Mrs. Dalloway* are carried over from *Jacob's Room,* though she adds the major theme of insanity. But that is also simply a development of two ideas in the preceding novel: (1) that there must be a positive (loving) connection between the inner and outer life; and (2) that institutional power is the expression of a negative (unloving) connection, Jacob's death being attributed to war, a manifestation of institutional mania for power over individuals.

Millions of Jacobs died in 1914–18, Woolf insists, because of this mania in high places. Now, in *Mrs. Dalloway,* Virginia Woolf shows us another victim—Septimus Warren Smith, who is clinically insane as a result of four years in combat. Smith falls into the hands of two medical practitioners whose energies are directed toward dominating their patient instead of healing him.

Clarissa Dalloway, too, is passing through a mental crisis, precipitated partly by a recent severe illness. During the single day in which the events of *Mrs. Dalloway* take place, the stories of these two—Clarissa and Septimus—are intertwined, though they never meet. Clarissa moves away from isolation toward an acceptance of life in all its puzzling complexity; Septimus moves ever deeper into isolation and finally suicide.

The narrative present of *Mrs. Dalloway* spans most of a bright, warm June day in London some five years after the war of 1914–18. But the tunneling into the past (Virginia Woolf's expression) goes back for thirty years. Readers familiar with *The Voyage Out,* in which the Dalloways appear briefly, will find no mention of that part of their past in this novel. All events, both past and present, build toward Clarissa's dinner party, when they are brought together in new relationships. The following summarizes briefly the major characters and action leading up to the party.

> " But memory is inferior to present experience. What Clarissa loves now, she is certain, is before her eyes in the bright June morning: trees, and mothers with babies, the activity in nearby streets, the park itself appearing to lift its leaves 'brilliantly, on waves of divine vitality.'"

Mrs. Dalloway leaves her house in Westminster to buy flowers. On the way, she meets an old acquaintance, Hugh Whitbread, a functionary in the royal household. Later she observes a royal car passing through the streets and an airplane skywriting. Septimus Smith, a man in his early twenties, is seated on a bench in Regent's Park with his Italian wife Lucrezia (Rezia). He has spent four years in the war and is now mentally ill. He sees the skywriting and thinks that "they" are trying to get messages to him from the dead. Dr. Holmes, a general practitioner, has advised Mrs. Smith to get her husband interested in "real" things. But they are now on their way to see a specialist, Sir William Bradshaw.

Peter Walsh, in love with Clarissa thirty years ago, leaves the Dalloway house, where he has talked to Clarissa for the first time in many years, and walks toward Regent's Park. He follows a woman, out of sexual fantasy, until she disappears into a house. In the park, he naps, sitting on a bench. Leaving the park, he passes Septimus and Rezia and outside encounters a street singer, an old woman, singing a love song.

Richard Dalloway, Clarissa's husband, Member of Parliament, is at Lady Bruton's for lunch. She is a prominent society hostess who likes being involved with government affairs and moving masses of people around in various projects of her invention. Hugh Whitbread, Clarissa's old friend, is also a guest. Lady Bruton wants these two men, both involved in government, to help her with one of her projects.

Septimus and Lucrezia keep their appointment with Sir William, who sees that the case is serious and advises Lucrezia to place her husband in a sanatorium. By now, Septimus identifies both doctors as his special persecutors. Both are, in fact, more interested in exercising power than in treating individuals.

Elizabeth Dalloway, Clarissa's daughter, about eighteen, leaves the Dalloway house for an afternoon with Miss Kilman, a woman of extraordinary unattractiveness. She is a religious zealot and has been proselytizing Elizabeth. Clarissa also fears that there is an unhealthy sexual relationship developing between the two. But as they take tea, Miss Kilman loses her hold on the girl. Elizabeth leaves the tea shop alone, boards a bus, and rides through London on a kind of voyage of independence, from which she returns "calm and competent."

Septimus and Rezia are in their sitting room. She is making hats, he going through the notes he has made of messages from the dead: "do not cut down trees; Universal love; the meaning of the world." Dr. Holmes chooses this moment to call— Dr. Holmes who "seemed to stand for something horrible to him. 'Human nature' he called him." As Holmes forces his way past Rezia into the room, Septimus leaps to his death. The novel concludes with the long section about the Dalloway party that evening, with the horror of Septimus's death offset by Clarissa's renewed vitality.

As Clarissa goes through the hours before her dinner party, she is besieged by memories of the past—stirring up doubts about her marriage to a man caught up in the endless round of politics; doubts about her daughter; and, most of all, doubts about herself. For she has just recovered from an illness, and to walk out into the bright June day is for her like the beginning of a new life—except for memories and the demands of the future that lie heavy upon her.

What she remembers is "scene after scene at Bourton," the country house where she grew to womanhood. Thirty years ago at Bourton, Clarissa and Peter Walsh had been much together. Clarissa came to feel that Peter's insistence on sharing everything, and his critical assessments, were finally intolerable, and she broke off their relationship. Yet there had been something vital between them, and in the years afterward Clarissa would never be certain she did not still love him.

Clarissa was also drawn to the energetic, attractive Sally Seton, who had shocked old Mrs. Parry at Bourton by running naked down the hall to the bathroom. Clarissa's memories of Sally are still, after thirty years, full and rich—how Sally had given her a flower and kissed her on the mouth just before Peter came upon them at the fountain one evening. The emotionally charged involvements with Peter and Sally were factors in Clarissa's decision to marry the steadier Richard Dalloway. And this decision, too, she believes thirty years later, had been a wise one. Peter would have destroyed her with his constant intrusions and critical remarks; and Sally would have dominated her.

These were Clarissa's memories as she went about preparing for her party that night, not just of events and relationships, but also a recollection of the atmosphere in which they occurred: the excited conversations, the laughter, the intuitive awareness of cross-purposes. These had been signs of life intensely felt, and she remembers how intense they had been.

But memory is inferior to present experience. What Clarissa loves now, she is certain, is before her eyes in the bright June morning: trees, and mothers with babies, the activity in nearby streets, the park itself appearing to lift its leaves "brilliantly, on waves of divine vitality." Clarissa sees this creative energy flowing from nature and shaping the present moment, the vital force of which is frequently symbolized by trees.

But the most attractive aspect of vitality appears in humans going about their business and their play—the "conduct of daily life" described in *Jacob's Room* as better than "the pageant of armies drawn out in battle array." A vision similar to that observed by Jacob, and identical in meaning, is experienced by Elizabeth when she cuts loose from Miss Kilman and in her excitement sets out to explore the city. She likes the uproar of the streets; she seems to hear the blare of trumpets, as if the crowds are marching to military music. The noise of the people in the streets is a "voice, pouring endlessly." This would carry them along. There is a Dickensian delight in movement and sounds in the description of Elizabeth's recommitment to life on her own, echoed by what Peter Walsh encounters on the warm June evening as he walks toward Clarissa's house—people opening doors, entering motor cars, rushing along the streets.

Despite these manifestations of human energy in masses, Woolf establishes the vital quality of life most strikingly in two solitary old women—one the street singer heard by Peter Walsh, the other the occupant of a room across the way from Clarissa's house. The old street singer's song at first is hardly intelligible; certainly she is no picture of vitality—nearly blind, and in rags. Her song, however, celebrates the invincible power of love, how love had lasted a million years, bubbling up like an ancient spring spouting from the earth, greening things, fertilizing.

> Still remembering how once in some primeval May she had walked with her lover, this rusty pump, this battered old woman . . . would still be there in ten million years . . . the passing generations—the pavement was crowded with bustling middle class people—vanished like leaves, to be trodden under, to be soaked and steeped and made mould of by that eternal spring.

The whole passage about the street singer is one of those Woolf developed more through the devices of poetry than of prose. Its effect depends on the persuasiveness of the imagery to transform the reader's feeling for the old woman, whether pity or revulsion, into wonder and admiration. A tree without leaves, she is still an instrument from which the wind of creative energy elicits a song: "Cheerfully, almost gaily, the invincible thread of sound wound up into the air, like the smoke from a cottage chimney." It is an evocative piece of writing, persuasive indeed—but not convincing. The metaphors of the rusty pump and the cottage are obtrusive. The reader sees what they are meant to do and feels the poetry of them, but with reservation.

The second incident involving an old woman occurs in the course of the party at Dalloway's house. In developing the significance of this scene, Woolf employs a more successful technique. She does not attempt to move the reader by poetic statement to believe that the old woman represents life without despair. The scene is depicted in a matter-of-fact way. As Clarissa watches an old woman in her room across the street preparing for bed, there are none of the verbal associations with love, as in the street singer's song, to make their frank appeal to the reader's emotions. Yet the significance of what Clarissa sees, though tentative even in her mind, is sufficient to offset the despair that has been rising in her.

This episode occurs after Clarissa hears at the party about the young man (Septimus) who has killed himself. Thinking about his suicide, Clarissa feels that the disaster, the disgrace of Septimus, is hers. Guilt floods her: "She had schemed; she had pilfered." But, thinking that she doesn't deserve to be happy, nevertheless she is. Now she rejects the triumphs of youth, and has committed herself wholly to the process of living—"creating it every moment afresh."

On a previous occasion, when Clarissa had been sorting out her thoughts about the religious zealot Miss Kilman, she had seen the old woman climb the stairs to her room, alone, as if self-contained in her life. To Clarissa there had been something solemn in it. But with Miss Kilman and Peter Walsh on her mind—those two proselytizers of religion and "love"—she had thought of the old woman in connection with that kind of love and religion that can destroy the privacy of the soul the old woman seemed to have. The "supreme mystery" was this: "here was one room; there was another. Did religion solve that, or love?"

Now at the party, as she watches the old woman again, seeing her move around, Clarissa is fascinated. Several things are coming together in Clarissa's mind—the idea of the privacy of the soul, and the mystery of the separation of human lives; these things joining with her awareness of the activities, the laughing and shouting, going on all around her at the party. Suddenly no longer in despair, she no longer pities herself, nor the young man who had killed himself. As the old lady's light goes out, Clarissa thinks of that whole house, dark now, with all this activity going on around it. Putting out the light was like dying. It did not stop the activity of living; the pageant of life went on.

Clarissa takes comfort in this train of thoughts because of her "theory," confided to Peter Walsh in the old days. They had been riding up Shaftesbury Avenue in a bus when she felt herself everywhere—not "here, here, here," she said, tapping the back of the seat, "but everywhere." Her comfort in the relationship that she felt between the old woman across the way and the young man who killed himself derives from that part of her theory about the affinities between people and how one must seek out those who complete one: the "unseen part of us" might survive, "be recovered somehow attached to this person or that."

The line from Shakespeare, "Fear no more the heat of the sun," appearing several times, explains Clarissa's cryptic remark about the young man's suicide: "She felt glad that he had done it; thrown it away." One need not fear the disasters of the physical life. Clarissa feels that if the young man had thrown his life away, she has caught it in hers. If the young man could complete his life in hers, then Clarissa could complete her life in others. It was a mystery—"here was one room; there was another"—but no longer a despairing mystery. This quality of excitement bubbling up from new-born vitality is what Peter Walsh recognizes in Clarissa at the book's conclusion: "What is it that fills me with extraordinary excitement? It is Clarissa, he said."

Virginia Woolf celebrated this ongoing vitality in many ways in her novels—welling up in love, at parties, and in the ordinary business of everyday life. She placed it in opposition to the mania of those in positions of power to control the course of events. In *Jacob's Room,* these were the men in clubs and cabinets. In *Mrs. Dalloway,* signs of power are everywhere: the royal coat of arms emblazoned on Hugh Whitbread's dispatch case; the automobile and a face "of the very greatest importance" glimpsed against its dove-gray interior; the ceremonial marching of troops; and the prime minister himself at the Dalloways' party.

Accompanying these symbols and panoply of institutional power, there is the pervasive sense of the damage done to human lives by the individual wielders of power: the waste of Hugh Whitbread's genuine qualities in the servilities of his position as a court functionary; the persistent meddling of Lady Bruton, utilizing her position in society to move people around as if they were pieces in a little game of her own. When Lady Bruton naps, we are informed, her arm assumes the position of a field marshal's holding his baton.

This malicious observation springs out of Woolf's indignation, but one of the measures of her skill as a novelist is the ability to discipline strong feelings into the lasting instrument of art: for instance, the subtle paralleling of the dove-gray car of Sir William Bradshaw to the royal car. Sir William, the psychiatrist who takes over Septimus Smith from Dr. Holmes, is another manifestation of the established order as malevolent. His sinister compulsion to dominate those who come within his control is linked through the case of Septimus to the political powers in Whitehall: it is "they" who provided the shambles of war in which his sanity was damaged, and it is Sir William who completes the job.

We are never allowed to forget the war: the painful picture of Lady Bexborough opening a bazaar with the message in hand of her son's death in combat; the company of soldiers marching to a cenotaph; and through it all the presence of Septimus Smith, a shambling, broken figure, who signals institutional guilt whenever he appears.

Virginia Woolf exposes relentlessly the mania to dominate of people like Lady Bruton, Sir William, and Dr. Holmes. The clinical madness of Septimus is represented as a consequence in their manipulations—indirectly, as in the case of Lady Bruton's political and social schemes, and directly in the perverted "healing" of Bradshaw and Holmes.

Septimus is the victim of a war-induced neurosis. Having volunteered early in the war of 1914–18, he suffered for four years the frustration of his idealistic impulse to "save England for Shakespeare." Withstanding the successive traumas of combat, he is stricken by the survivor's guilt after his friend Evans is killed. Crippled within, he seeks out Lucrezia to marry her, with the instinctive knowledge that her health is what his sickness needs. She appears to him as the tree of life,

> as if all her petals were about her. She was a flowering tree; and through her branches looked out the face of a lawgiver, who had reached a sanctuary where she feared no one.

His instinct was right and she is good for him, but because she is inexperienced and a foreigner, she is not capable of protecting him against the malpractices, condoned by society, of such "healers" as Holmes and Sir William.

Sir William, a large distinguished-looking man, would not appear to be insane in any clinical sense. But he makes everyone profoundly uneasy in his presence. He is a self-made man, we discover, who has permitted himself to be shaped by the materialistic values that reward domination. In treating his patients he invoked all the forces of society to gain their submission. "Naked, defenceless, the exhausted, the friendless received the impress of Sir William's will. He swooped; he devoured. He shut people up." In his compulsion to put people away, Woolf casts Sir William as an agent of death. For insanity, as she describes it, is isolation from people, from things, from all the stuff of life—death, in short.

Sanity she identifies with life—the physical substance of it—women nursing babies, the blare of trumpets, legs moving energetically down the street. Even Richard Dalloway holding Clarissa's hand, though not the passionate moment of the kind he had imagined when he resolved to say I love you, is a moment of shared physical intimacy—it lives.

Peter Walsh, on the contrary, creating lurid fantasies around the woman he follows through the streets, is to a degree insane, to a degree dead, in that what he submits himself to is isolation: "All this one could never share—it smashed to atoms." The emptiness of Walsh's fantasy is like that of Katharine Hilbery's dream in *Night and Day*—her "magnanimous hero" riding his horse by the sea— a waste of imaginative power.

Walsh is torn between wanting to share and wanting to isolate himself. His life had been a constant vacillation, chasing one woman, then another, interspersed with "work, work, work." So that when in the end he is strongly moved by the vitality of Clarissa, it is not certain that this commitment is anything more than physical attraction or more than momentary. What is certain is that Clarissa has come through her own struggle against self-isolation and confirmed her rebirth into the health of shared existence.

In giving the "world of the sane and the insane side by side" (her primary objective in this novel), Virginia Woolf shows the sane reaching out to life—like Clarissa, recognizing in the old woman across the street someone whose life touches hers. Though her treatment of this idea is lyric, she does not attempt to screen the unpleasant or tragic with lyricism. Death is the dissonance that keeps her song complex and intriguing. In Clarissa, for instance, there is double awareness of mortality—through her recent serious illness and through having witnessed in girlhood the death of her gifted sister, crushed by a falling tree. The tree, so often in Woolf's writing the image of persistent life, by this accident reinforces the ambiguity of existence—like the light of *Night and Day,* it contains a portion of its opposite.

Many circumstances in *Mrs. Dalloway,* including the terrifying medical experience of Septimus Smith, were drawn from Virginia Woolf's life. The original intention to have Clarissa kill herself—in the pattern of Woolf's own intermittent, despair—was rejected in favor of a "dark double" who would take that act upon himself. Creating Septimus Smith led directly to Clarissa's mystical theory of vicarious death and shared existence, saving the novel from a damaging imbalance on the side of darkness. Virginia Woolf's success in using her own madness as a subject for fiction, evidently provided the necessary confidence for attempting the equally delicate naterials of her next novel, *To the Lighthouse,* which concerned her unhappy childhood and the memories, still sensitive, of her parents.

Source: Manly Johnson, *"Mrs. Dalloway,"* in *Virginia Woolf,* Frederick Ungar Publishing Co., 1973, pp. 52–63.

Sources

Forster, E. M., *Aspects of the Novel,* Harcourt, Brace & Co., 1927.

———, *Virginia Woolf,* Cambridge University Press, 1942.

Hawthorn, Jeremy, *Virginia Woolf's "Mrs. Dalloway": A Study in Alienation,* Sussex University Press, 1975.

Henke, Suzette A., *"Mrs. Dalloway:* the Communion of Saints," in *New Feminist Essays on Virginia Woolf,* edited by Jane Marcus, University of Nebraska Press, 1981, pp. 125–47.

Jensen, Emily, "Clarissa Dalloway's Respectable Suicide," in *Virginia Woolf: A Feminist Slant,* edited by Jane Marcus, University of Nebraska Press, 1983, pp. 162–79.

Page, Alex, "A Dangerous Day: Mrs. Dalloway and Her Double," in *Modern Fiction Studies,* Vol. VII, No. 2, Summer 1961, pp. 115–24.

Woolf, Virginia, *The Diary of Virginia Woolf,* edited by Anne Olivier Bell with Andrew McNeillie, 5 vols., Hogarth Press, 1977–1984.

———, "Mr. Bennett and Mrs. Brown," in *The Gender of Modernism,* edited by Bonnie Kime Scott, Indiana University Press, 1990.

For Further Study

Abel, Elizabeth, *Virginia Woolf and the Fictions of Psychoanalysis,* University of Chicago Press, 1989.

The brilliant chapter on *Mrs. Dalloway* from Abel's book examines the way in which Woolf's novel responds to and contests Freud's theories about women.

Daiches, David, *Virginia Woolf,* James Laughlin, 1942.

Daiches book gives an excellent, highly readable overview of Woolf's art and fictions.

Edwards, Lee R., "War and Roses: The Politics of *Mrs. Dalloway,*" in *The Authority of Experience: Essays in Feminist Criticism,* edited by Arlyn Diamond and Lee R. Edwards, University of Massachusetts Press, 1977, pp. 161–77.

This essay provides an important and informative aspect on the politics of *Mrs. Dalloway.*

Fussell, Paul, *The Great War and Modern Memory,* Oxford University Press, 1975.

Fussel's text is a definitive book on WWI—its life in the popular imagination, the way soldiers experienced it, and the poetry of its soldiers.

Lee, Hermione, *Virginia Woolf,* Alfred A. Knopf, Inc., 1996.

Lee presents a recent and highly readable biography of the author.

Thomas, Sue, "Virginia Woolf's Septimus Smith and Contemporary Perceptions of Shellshock," in *English Language Notes,* Vol. 25, No. 2, December 1987, pp. 49–57.

Thomas offers an examination of the literature and attitudes about shell shock in Woolf's time.

Zwerdling, Alex, *Virginia Woolf and the Real World,* University of California Press, 1986.

Zwerdling's book discusses the social and political contexts and arguments of Woolf's novels.

The Octopus

Frank Norris

1901

The Octopus: A Story of California, first published in 1901 by Frank Norris, presents modern readers with a view of a specific time and place in American history when California was a new, open land of promise. The country's ability to produce agricultural abundance seemed endless, threatened only by greed and the interference of laws that serve the rich. The novel takes place in the San Joaquin valley, in the middle of the state. Wheat farmers struggle to grow crops and send them to market for a profit, while being beleaguered by the inflated prices of the giant railroad conglomeration—the "octopus" referred to in the title. This novel was the first one in what Norris planned to be a "Trilogy of Wheat," examining every aspect of the modern world through the progression of wheat, from seed to consumption. The second novel was *The Pit: A Story of Chicago,* about the commodities market. The third novel, *The Wolf,* was intended to follow what happened to the wheat crop once it was exported to Russia, but Norris died of a burst appendix before that book was written.

The novels of Frank Norris are considered to be clear and powerful examples of the literary movement that took place around the turn of the nineteenth century: American naturalism. As a response against the inflated prose and romantic ideals that marked most American novels that came before them, there rose a generation of writers who tried to focus their work on the harsh realities of modern life. By today's standards, Norris' characters may seem idealistic, and his plot lines might

seem contrived, but, as a reaction to novels that steered clear of sexuality and the degrading effects of capitalism, Norris' works were groundbreaking.

Author Biography

Benjamin Franklin Norris Jr.—Frank Norris, to his readers—is remembered for being one of the founding figures of American naturalism, a literary movement that flourished at the end of the nineteenth century and the start of the twentieth. His novels reflected the places that he had lived and his view that the world was changing for the worst, with humanity's baser instincts overrunning its nobility.

Norris was born on March 5, 1870, in Chicago, Illinois, to a wealthy and artistic family. His father was a wholesale jeweler, and his mother, who had once been an actress, encouraged her children toward cultural affairs. When he was fourteen, his family moved to San Francisco, which is a prominent setting in *The Octopus,* as well as several of his other novels. He was educated at private schools, and in 1887 he moved to Paris, to attend the famous Académie Atelier Julien art school. In 1890, he returned to the United States, enrolling in the University of California in a course of studies aimed at preparing him to take over his father's jewelry business. Norris published his first book, a long, romantic narrative in verse called *Yvernelle: A Legend of Feudal France,* in 1892, when he was still an undergraduate.

His parents' divorce while he was in college relieved Norris of the pressure of going into a business career. He left school without a degree, deficient in mathematics credits. He transferred to Harvard as a special student and studied under Lewis E. Gates, learning to appreciate the works of European naturalists such as Émile Zola. During that time Norris produced *McTeague,* a novel about the social and moral descent of a San Francisco dentist and his wife that is considered one of the great works of naturalism. He was hired by S. S. McClure to work as a journalist for *McClure's Magazine* and as a reader for McClure & Doubleday Publishing Company, and Doubleday published his first few novels.

In 1899, Norris began work on an "epic of wheat," which would trace the cycle of America's wheat crop, from production in California to distribution in the Chicago Board of Trade to its con-

Frank Norris

sumption in Europe. The first of these books was *The Octopus,* finished in 1901; the second, *The Pit,* was finished in 1902. The third book of the trilogy was never finished because an attack of appendicitis overcame Norris soon after *The Pit* was finished, and he died at the young age of thirty-two on October 25, 1902, in San Francisco.

Plot Summary

Book One

The first chapter of *The Octopus* starts with Presley riding his bicycle across the countryside, from the Los Muertos ranch to the seed farm past the mission, encountering various key characters along the way: Hooven, Harran, Dyke, Annixter, and Vanamee. It ends with an ominous event: the sheep that Vanamee was supposed to be watching are run over by a train. It is here, at the end of the first chapter, that the book's title is alluded to for the first and only time. Presley imagines that the sheep scattered around the tracks were run over by "the leviathan, with tentacles of steel clutching into the soil, the soulless Force, the iron-hearted Power, the monster, the Colossus, the Octopus."

The next day, Magnus Derrick arrives back at his ranch from San Francisco. An argument ensues with S. Behrman, the railroad's agent, when Magnus sees some ploughs he has bought on a flatbed at the train station. Because of regulations, the ploughs must ship all of the way through to San Francisco and back out to Guadalajara before he can take possession of them. Magnus arranges to have some of the local wheat growers come over to his house that night to discuss the railroad's rate increase. At the same time, Annixter, on the Quien Sabe ranch, notices that Hilma Tree, the daughter of a couple that works for him, is attractive. Annixter finds himself thinking about her, even though he is a confirmed woman-hater. He sees her flirting with Delaney, one of the ranch hands, and in an inexplicable fit of anger he fires Delaney.

At Derrick's ranch that evening, the discussion among the wheat growers is about the railroad "grading" the land. Years ago, when the railroad first came through, growers were given rights to all of the odd-numbered parcels within a twenty-mile radius of the track. The government owned the even-numbered parcels. The farmers had bought the government's parcels. They had farmed the even parcels and made improvements to them with the understanding that after they were graded, the railroad would sell the land to them for about two and a half dollars an acre. Some of the ranchers believe that since the railroad has bribed the Railroad Overseeing Commission, the farmers should bribe commission members. Magnus Derrick insists that he will not be involved in dirty politics.

In chapter four, Vanamee, whose true love was killed by an unidentified assailant eighteen years ago, has returned to the valley. He works as a shepherd among the laborers at Annixter's ranch and at night stalks the Mission where he used to meet his lover every night.

Annixter, still enchanted by Hilma Tree, shows interest in her work on his farm's dairy. When he is alone with her, he tries to kiss her, clumsily stepping on her foot in the process. She flees, and he curses himself for frightening her away. He devises a plan to throw a party upon the completion of the gigantic barn that he is having built. When he goes to the railroad office to buy off his land, he is told that the price has not been set. He also hears Dyke being told that the rate for shipping hops is two cents per pound.

At the dance when the barn is finished, the farmers all have a merry time, interrupted only by the intrusion of Delaney, whom Annixter had fired. Delaney shows up drunk on a stolen horse, wielding a pistol. Annixter sees in Hilma's eyes that she

is concerned about him, and he draws his own gun. Circling each other, he and Delaney shoot at each other until Delaney leaves, making Annixter a hero. The dance continues.

A messenger arrives at the dance, having ridden his bicycle from the telegraph company in town, with envelopes for each of the major ranchers in the valley. The telegraphs, from the railroad, contain the prices for their parcels of land. Instead of the two dollars and fifty cents per acre they are expecting, the prices range from twenty-two to thirty dollars an acre, which most of them cannot afford to pay.

Book Two

Book two opens with Lyman Derrick, Magnus's son, in his law office in San Francisco. He has been elected to the railroad commission with the help of money spent by his father and the other wheat growers, pledged to an average 10 percent in the rates for grain shipments. Lyman tells his father and brother that it will not be done easily or quickly. Presley visits with wealthy friends, who discuss the possibility of shipping California wheat oversees to China, giving Magnus Derrick grand plans for the future of his empire.

Annixter meets with Hilma and explains that he wants her with him all of the time. When she mentions marriage, he says that he is not the marrying kind. Horrified that he is suggesting something improper, she leaves, and the next day her family moves away from the ranch. He realizes that he actually could be a marrying man and vows to find her.

Dyke finds out at the railroad office that the rates have changed since he planted his crop, from two cents to five cents per pound. His profit wiped out, he becomes an alcoholic.

After seeing the way that the railroad has destroyed the farmers in the area, Presley writes a poem, "The Toilers," which gains nationwide attention. It is a poem about the exploitation of laborers. Throughout the rest of the book, rich people bring it up in conversations with him, amused but not threatened by his words.

On the way back to the valley from San Francisco, where Annixter has found Hilma and persuaded her to marry him, their train is robbed by an armed bandit, who is identified almost immediately as Dyke.

Lyman Derrick meets with the committee of wheat growers to report that the promised 10 percent cut in shipping rates for wheat has been enacted. But the cuts are averaged across the state: deep cuts in the rate were made in areas that do not even grow wheat. Where they live, and where most of the wheat is grown, there is no rate cut. The board members turn on Lyman and accuse him of selling out to the railroad. Later, Genslinger, who runs the local newspaper, blackmails Magnus for his part in bribing the commissioners, saying that he knows all about it because Lyman has worked for the railroad for years and took the farmers' money with no intent to help them. Magnus pays him ten thousand dollars to keep quiet.

Dyke arrives at Annixter's ranch, pursued by a posse of men hired by the railroad. He borrows a horse and water, and tries to run, but is captured.

During a huge round-up and slaughter of jackrabbits, word comes that the railroad has started evicting farmers from their land, putting their possessions out and putting in new tenants to live there. There is a shoot-out between the farmers and the railroad employees, during which Harran Derrick, Hooven, Osterman, Annixter and others are killed.

Presley goes to San Francisco, where he meets the president of the railroad and finds that he is not an evil man. He meets Hooven's daughter Minna, whom poverty has driven to prostitution. Chapter seven alternates scenes of a splendid, opulent dinner in the home of a railroad vice president with scenes of Hooven's widow starving on the city street. In the end, Behrman, the cold-hearted railroad agent who destroyed so many wheat ranchers, is buried under tons of wheat being dropped into the hold of a ship on which Presley is sailing. The ship is one that the wealthy people of San Francisco have arranged, with charitable contributions, to take wheat to the starving people of India.

Characters

Annixter

Annixter is Presley's best friend, a gruff man who is bad at social relations, especially with women. He is the proprietor of the Quien Sabe ranch, where he lives a simple lifestyle, often reading *David Copperfield*. Like Presley, Annixter is college-educated, with his degree in civil engineering. The responsibility of the ranch has given him chronic stomach troubles.

Annixter finds himself attracted to Hilma Tree, the daughter of a couple who live and work on his farm. His only other significant relationship with a woman, a clerk in a glove-cleaning establishment in Sacramento, ended poorly, driving Annixter to declare himself a woman-hater. With Hilma, he is awkward, and several times his attempts to develop a relationship with her are misinterpreted as lewd suggestions. Finally, after she and her family move away from the ranch after he has offended her, he follows them to San Francisco and proposes marriage.

After Hilma Tree marries him, Annixter becomes a much more thoughtful and generous man, suggesting moderation in situations where he previously might have advocated violent action. At the shoot-out between the farmers and the railroad employees at the irrigation ditch, Annixter is killed.

S. Behrman

Behrman, whose full first name is never given, is the villain of the piece. He is the banker in Bonneville, but that is just one of his jobs:

> He was a real-estate agent. He bought grain; he dealt in mortgages. He was one of the local political bosses, but more important than all this, he was the representative of the Pacific and Southwestern Railroad in that section of Tulare County.

As the railroad representative, Behrman is responsible for the ruin of Dyke, first because of his layoff and later because he changes the rates Dyke would have to pay to get his grain to market. Dyke tries to kill Behrman as a last desperate act before he is captured, but his gun misfires. Frustrated, Presley throws a bomb through the window of Behrman's house, but it does not injure him.

The railroad gives him Magnus Derrick's farmland for a cheap price in exchange for his loyalty, and he ends up taking possession, evicting all of the characters that have survived the tragic gunfight. To add insult to injury, he humbles Magnus by offering him an assistant clerk position if he will swear allegiance to the railroad. After getting Magnus to grovel, Behrman says that he will think it over and get back to him, adding, "you're getting pretty old, Magnus Derrick."

Behrman's end comes when he is looking over a ship that is to take his grain to India. Too cheap to spend four cents a bag to have the grain packaged, he instead has it poured into the ship's hold, but, tripping, he falls in with it and is smothered under tons of wheat.

Bismark

See Hooven

Media Adaptations

- While adaptations of *The Octopus* are scarce because of the novel's sprawling nature, Norris's book *McTeague* is available on an audiocassette recording from L.A. Theater Works, published in 1989.

Caraher

Saloon owner and communist, Caraher encourages his customers to stand up against the railroad with violence. Dyke spends weeks at Caraher's bar, drinking and listening to his ideas, before he becomes a train robber; Presley learns from Caraher how to build a bomb.

Cedarquist

One of Presley's connections among the social elite of San Francisco, Cedarquist owned the Atlas Iron Works, but closed it because it was not making enough money. By the end of the book, he has started a new venture, exporting American wheat to other countries.

Annie Payne Derrick

Annie is Magnus' wife, the mother of Lyman and Harran. She is a cultured woman, educated at the State Normal School in the teaching of literature, music, and penmanship. Annie insists that Magnus stay out of the League's blackmail scheme, but he eventually joins them anyway. In the end, Annie is left—somewhat reluctantly—to watch over her half-insane husband, supporting him by teaching literature at the seminary where she worked long ago.

Harran Derrick

Harran is Magnus and Annie's son; he looks and acts more like his father than his mother. He has a great share of the responsibility for managing the day-to-day operations at Los Muertos. He is one of Presley's closest friends. Harran's main problem is that he is a little excitable, jumping at the opportunity to bribe the Board of Railroad Commissioners, and all too willing to engage the opposition from the railroad in a gun battle. When shooting does occur at the irrigation ditch, Harran is shot, and he later dies in his parents' home.

Lyman Derrick

Magnus and Annie's younger son is seldom present in the novel. He lives in San Francisco, and is active in political circles. When the league of wheat growers needs someone to represent their interests on the Railroad Commission, they pay to get Lyman elected. They feel cheated by him when he announces the new reductions in shipping rates and find out that, despite their support, none of the reduced rates apply to them. At the meeting announcing this, he denies it. Later, though, when he is threatening to blackmail Magnus, Genslinger explains that Lyman had been on the railroad's payroll for two years, that he was the person that they wanted elected to the board, even though it had been the farmers' money that had elected him. After all of the death and misery caused by the railroad's pressure on the San Joaquin Valley farmers, Lyman ends up as a candidate for governor of California.

Magnus Derrick

One of the novel's key figures, Magnus is a proud, successful wheat farmer, the proprietor of the Los Muertos ranch. He comes from the old school of California gold miners, having been a prospector in his younger days. Magnus sold his share in the Corpus Christi mine just before the famous Comstock Lode of 1859, one of the richest mining deposits ever found. Magnus' mining background has formed his character, making him a man who is willing to take risks, and to sink all that he has into an uncertain prospect if there is a possibility of a huge payoff at the end. He is a leader of men, and he called "the Governor" by the people who know and respect him.

Having lost money on bad crops in the past two years, Magnus gambles heavily that the current year's crop will more than make up his losses. He invests in irrigation ditches and equipment. When the railroad threatens to take the property that he has cultivated, he finds himself faced with two horrible prospects; either lose his land, or compromise his moral standing by involving himself in a shady bribery scheme. Under pressure, he opts for bribery. His sufferings increase when the people whom he bribed, one of them being his own son Lyman, tell Genslinger the newspaper editor about the bribes. Genslinger blackmails him for a huge sum of money. After Magnus' other son Harran and others are killed in a shoot-out with railroad officials, Genslinger prints the truth about the bribe. Magnus ends up scorned by the people who had once looked up to him. He becomes penniless, half-insane, babbling, and unable to think.

As the ultimate indignity, S. Behrman, the railroad employee who takes over the Los Muertos ranch, offers Magnus a humiliating job as an assistant in the freight manager's office.

Dyke

At the beginning of the book, Dyke is an engineer for the railroad, but he receives news that he has been fired. He shifts his focus to growing hops, which he has heard would be a good, profitable crop to grow in the region. He leases a field and plants a crop, checking with the railroad to determine the rates for shipping his product, feeling assured that he can make a decent profit. Dyke is concerned about money because he has a daughter, Sydney, that he dotes on, and he wants to send her to a good school. When the crop is ripe, he prepares for the harvest and he goes to the railroad, only to be told that in the six months since he asked, the rate for shipping hops has more than doubled. At those rates, his profit margin is ruined, and he does not even bother to harvest the hops.

Devastated, Dyke takes to hanging around in Caraher's saloon, drinking and listening to the bartender's talk about anarchy. He eventually robs the Pacific and South Western train, using his knowledge of railroad operations to take over the engine and to go straight to the safe. For weeks, Dyke is a fugitive from justice, with a high reward on his head. He is finally chased down by a posse. Before they take him into custody, he draws aim on S. Behrman, the railroad agent who is most responsible for his ruin, but his gun misfires. They take Dyke into custody, and word later comes to Presley that Dyke had been sentenced to life imprisonment.

Genslinger

Genslinger is the editor of the local newspaper, the *Mercury*. It is well known that Genslinger is on the railroad payroll, that he will report news in a way that is favorable to the railroad. After Magnus Derrick arranges to bribe members of the Board of Railroad Commissioners, Genslinger goes to him and explains that the commissioners have given signed affidavits, explaining Derrick's crime. Genslinger agrees to not print the news in his paper for ten thousand dollars. After the shoot-out, which leaves Magnus' son Harran and others dead, Genslinger destroys Magnus' reputation by printing the information about the bribes in his newspaper anyway.

The Governor

See Magnus Derrick

Hooven

Hooven is a character of German origin, easily recognizable when he speaks because his dialogue is written with a thick accent. He is a tenant on the Los Muertos ranch who is able to keep his position because he asks Harran Derrick if his family can stay when the other tenants are dismissed. He dies during the gun fight between the farmers and the railroad employees.

Minna Hooven

Much earlier in the novel, when he and Harran are discussing Minna, Presley observes, prophetically, that she is the kind "who would find it pretty easy to go wrong if they lived in a city." In fact, Minna does "go wrong": she goes to San Francisco after the death of her father to find her mother and sister and, after spending her last nickel, becomes a prostitute.

Osterman

Osterman is one of the wheat farmers. He is a man with a sense of humor who dresses peculiarly and is willing to act like a buffoon for a laugh.

Presley

Presley is the most prominent character in the book: he is not really the protagonist because much of the action has nothing to do with him, but he is the novel's conscience, observing what happens and understanding the significance of it. Presley is the character at the beginning and at the end of the story, first travelling across the countryside to neighboring ranches in a sequence that introduces other main characters and finally leaving on a wheat-laden ship bound for India. Because he has connections in San Francisco high society, he is able to see characters on both sides of the central dispute.

Presley is thirty years old and is a poet who graduated with honors from an Eastern college. He came to live on the Los Muertos ranch for his health after nearly dying of consumption (tuberculosis). At the beginning, his artistic inspiration is dried up:

> He was in search of a subject; something magnificent, he did not know exactly what; some vast, tremendous theme, heroic, terrible, to be unrolled in all the thundering progressions of hexameters.

After witnessing Dyke's destruction because of the railroad company, Presley returns to his room at Los Muertos and works on "The Toilers," a poem that he started once and abandoned. When it is finished, he sends it to a San Francisco newspaper, which publishes it; it is then reprinted in other newspapers around the country and in a glossy national magazine, making Presley's name famous nationwide. Shelgrim, the railroad president, is familiar with the poem and is unimpressed with it, not because it takes a pro-labor stand, but because he finds the painting that inspired it to be more complete. Mrs. Gerard, the wife of the railroad vice president at whose home Presley has an extravagant meal, is also familiar with the poem and says that she was inspired to join with other society matrons to start a relief organization for the starving people of India. She is oblivious to the suffering of the farmers in the San Joaquin Valley that provide her with the chance to be extravagant and generous.

Frustrated with all the suffering and distraught over the ruin and imprisonment of Dyke, Presley briefly decides to take matters into his own hands. With the help of Caraher, he builds a bomb, which he throws into S. Behrman's house. The railroad employee is unharmed. Later, when he takes over the Los Muertos ranch, Behrman mentions in a condescending way that he knows Presley threw the bomb.

Shelgrim

Shelgrim is the president of the Pacific and South West Railroad. He is the man ultimately responsible for the farmers' misery. When Presley goes to Shelgrim's office, however, he finds Shelgrim to be a compassionate man. When an aid suggests firing an employee who constantly misses work because of alcoholism, Shelgrim wants the man's salary raised instead. He is a cultured man, with intelligent opinions about art and a philosophical attitude toward the problems between the railroad and the farmers. His attitude is that the wheat will grow and the trains will move, regardless of the sufferings of individual people.

Hilma Tree

Hilma is the nineteen-year-old daughter of a couple that lives on Annixter's ranch, Quien Sabe. Annixter notices her beauty one day, and he tries to kiss her, but she runs away, embarrassed, thinking that he was just making a pass at her. After a few months, he explains that he did not mean anything disreputable, and that he would like to be-

come involved with her, but when she mentions marriage he complains that he has no intention of marrying, leaving her once more believing that he intended to use her sexually. Hilma and her parents leave the ranch and move to San Francisco, where Annixter finds her and convinces her that, after her rejection, he became convinced that he loves her and wants her to be his wife.

They have a loving marriage, but it is ruined when he is killed in a gun battle with the railroad people. In her grief, Hilma loses the baby that she is carrying.

Venamee

Venamee is a strange, mystic figure who has been away from the San Joaquin Valley for years. He is able to summon Presley to him by sheer mental energy, and later in the novel he does the same with Father Sarria, a mission priest. His supernatural powers help Venamee cope with the grief of losing the one great love of his life.

Eighteen years earlier, when he was a young man, Venamee was involved with a girl, Angéle Varian. They would meet at night, by the old Mission. One night, when he arrived to meet her, Venamee found Angéle raped and beaten. No one ever found out the identity of the man who did it to her, and she died months later, giving birth to the daughter of her assailant.

Throughout the story, Venamee tries to use his power of mental conjuring to bring Angéle back from the dead. He finally achieves it when his dead lover returns to him in the form of her daughter, who was born at the same time that Angéle died. Venamee finds happiness, and he is able to cope with all of the suffering of his life. His final advice to Presley is helpful in putting the whole tragedy of the wheat farmers in a larger perspective: "Evil is short-lived. Never judge of the whole round of life by the mere segment you can see. The whole is, in the end, perfect."

Themes

Culture Clash

The Octopus appeared at a time when the character of American life was assumed to be defined by the opportunity for endless growth, symbolized by the millions of acres of hearty grain that grew abundantly from the country's fertile soil. Literature has traditionally used California to represent the country's growth potential because European settlers arrived on the eastern shores and expanded westward, making the west coast the last area to be developed. Whenever it seemed that America's natural potential was in any danger of facing limitations, there was always the promise that California had to offer. From mineral richness to agricultural bounty, California remained, time and again, a land that promised greatness.

In this novel, the farmers represent a natural culture. Not only do they work with soil and seed to produce nutritious wheat, but they also have a close-knit, moral society, willing to lend a hand to others who are temporarily down on their luck and careful to maintain traditional moral behaviors. Their society is presented as being almost perfect, but it is threatened from without by heartless and amoral aggression of the railroad.

The railroad, in this novel, represents a culture driven solely by profit, with no human concern. It is a product of technology, which allows it to be run from edicts passed far away, by people who make decisions affecting lives that they will never encounter. Norris does not try to present this money-hungry culture as being inherently evil, or controlled, in all cases, by evil people. Most railroad employees, such as S. Behrman and Genslinger, are in fact liars, driven by greed and the head of the railroad, Shelgrim, is overly generous in the case of an employee whom he knows personally. He proves to be a cultured, thoughtful man who is powerless to stop the personal destruction that his railroad might cause: "Blame conditions," he explains to Presley, "not men."

The destruction of the farmers is thus presented as the destruction of a culture of honor and truth by a senseless machine that devours culture in the name of profit. In this novel, there is no hope offered for the finer things in life: they are doomed to lose in an unfair struggle.

Moral Corruption

The economic destruction brought about by unchecked greed forces a decay of morals in this novel. Minna Hooven, for instance, is left with no recourse after the financial destruction of her family. She starts out a sweet, bright-eyed country girl, but when her money runs out and she is faced with starvation, Minna sells herself as a prostitute. Having made the decision to do so, she embraces her new, wicked ways: "Oh, *I've* gone to hell," she says scornfully. "It was either that or starvation." Another case of economic ruin leading to moral ruin is Dyke. At the start of the story, he is a loving

Topics for Further Study

- Airplanes and trucks, neither of which existed when this story took place, have significantly changed the influence of rail freight. Research the different types of shipping used to move grain today, explaining what power each has.

- Which states produce the most American wheat today? Which countries consume the most American wheat? Which countries produce the most wheat in the world?

- California is not associated with wheat production today. Research the decline of the California wheat industry and report on how other concerns have taken its place.

- Aid agencies to help people stranded without money are common in most big cities. Report on what a person like Mrs. Hooven, alone with her little girl and penniless in a city, could do today.

- Magnus Derrick sees his plows on a railroad car at his local station, but he cannot have them until they travel all of the way to San Francisco and back. Report on modern-day examples of laws that require actions that contradict common sense.

- Frank Norris chose to write a three-novel series about wheat because he saw it as one product that has an impact on every aspect of social life. Choose one product that you think is as universal today and write an outline for three books that are each independent, but tell the whole story.

family man, entirely devoted to the upbringing of his young daughter, but when his dream of financial independence is shattered by the railroad's reorganized rate structure, he becomes a desperado, killing innocent railroad men for money. He ends up hunted and humiliated, crazed with thirst, fighting like an animal who has lost any semblance of humanity.

The most obvious and disappointing example of moral corruption is Magnus Derrick, who begins the novel as a leader of men with uncompromising principles and ends up, after losing his ranch, a broken man. The first huge step in Derrick's moral corruption comes when he decides to participate in the League's plan to bribe the railroad commissioners. His initial reaction to this scheme is to dismiss it immediately, as the sort of thing that is beneath him. Faced with the railroad's almost certain victory in the matter of rate hikes, he eventually gives in to pressure from his cohorts, who insist that bribery is a necessary evil, preferable to letting the railroad progress without any opposition. Magnus' "temporary" moral lapse has a continuing effect, however, as the bribery leaves him vulnerable to blackmail by Genslinger, making him spend any money he has left after his legal battles to pay for the newspaperman's silence. After the shoot-out between the farmers and the railroad employees, his moral corruption is made public, and the supporters who had stood by him when they admired his self-control leave him almost immediately. The worst part of his downfall is that Magnus has no way of justifying his behavior to himself, even though a less moral person might easily excuse the moral complications that he goes through as being beyond his personal responsibility.

Politics

A political system can be seen as an equalizing force, gathering the electoral power of the masses to protect them from those who have all of the economic power. This is not, however, the vision presented in *The Octopus.* When the wheat growers feel that the railroad is taking advantage of their situation, they openly mock the idea that politicians might offer any help because they know that the railroad controls the state's political structure. The only way they seriously consider political involvement is through bribing the politicians themselves. Any possibility of an honest judgement from the political forces is unthinkable. Political corruption is so bad that Lyman Derrick betrays the wheat ranchers, in spite of both the fact that they have bribed him and that his father, Magnus, is the president of the ranchers' commission.

For a long time, the wheat growers hold out the hope that the United States Supreme Court will rule in their favor and put an end to the railroad's battle to take away their land. The court is not a regional body so it would not be under the influence of the California railroad the way that most of the politicians considering the case are. It is expected to be beyond corruption, impartial of the merits of the case. The fact that the Supreme Court rules against them indicates that, legally, the farmers' case is indeed weak, that the moral right that they see so clearly does not translate to a political system organized for the benefit of the rich.

In the novel's conclusion, Presley, one of the few surviving characters, notices that Lyman Derrick is running for governor of California with a good potential for winning. He has the support of the Republican party and the financial support of the railroad. He is also the man who betrayed his father and brother, sending them to ruin and to death, respectively, to support the railroad, which has him on the payroll. The book's final word on this subject, then, is that the relationship between politics and wealth is both undeniable and unstoppable.

Style

Naturalism

Frank Norris' writings, especially his earlier novel *McTeague,* are considered by literary critics to mark the very first experiments in the American strain of naturalism. Naturalism is often spoken of along with realism because both came about as reactions to the same trends. Realism developed first, in the mid-1800s, a rejection of the unearned optimism that the romantic movement proposed. If romanticism showed humans as innately kind and sympathetic, naturalism focused on the harsher elements of life. Realistic literature reminded its readership of the many social ills that humanity created for itself. Artists of the realist movement tried to capture all of the details of their subject, regardless of how unpleasant they may be, with a sharp focus that modern audiences take for granted because of the wide-spread ease of photography. Writers who were realists strove to shock audiences with their frankness and honesty about the unappealing aspects of human behavior. Charles Dickens' descriptions of poverty and pollution in London in his day present a good example of realism, as do Mark Twain's willingness to record the moral ambiguity that plagued his character Huckleberry Finn.

Realistic writers presented misery while commenting on the ways that human suffering is terrible. The difference that naturalism added was to step back from making any moral commentary whatsoever. Naturalism started in the mid 1800s with French writers such as Edmond Louis Antoine de Goncourt and especially Émile Zola, a particular favorite of Norris'. At the same time that Charles Darwin's theories showed human evolution as a mechanical progression of broader rules, and Karl Marx wrote about economical evolution that followed *its* own established rules, novelists tried to describe human behavior without judgement. These writers assumed that every movement was neither bad nor good, just a reaction to the environment it occurred in. In *The Octopus,* the head of the railroad tries to make Presley see that his behavior is not his own, but the fulfillment of forces beyond his control. The place where Norris drifts away from naturalistic principles is in portraying other railroad functionaries, such as S. Behrman, as conniving and evil, giving them free will instead of showing them as products of nature.

Setting

A generation earlier, *The Octopus* may have been set in one of the plains states when the railroad was just crossing the center of the country and impeding on the land used for farming. There are several reasons why California is a more powerful location. California is located at the end of the country where economic development has nowhere to turn, backed by the Pacific Ocean. A novel of this type taking place in Nebraska or Iowa would implicitly offer the downtrodden farmers open land to the west, where they could move and be free. In *The Octopus,* there is no free place to escape to, making the hard situation the farmers find themselves in more hopeless. Because California marks the end of westward expansion, an air of fatalism persists about the possibility for a fair settlement. If, as the book presents, the interests of the farmers are inherently at odds with those of the railroad, then there can only be one winner. With the opportunity for expansion, both interests could go their separate ways, but locked in battle at the end of the continent like this means that there is only going to be one winner. The farmers lose because they are simple, land-loving people who are stranded in the middle of a big state with their crops, and they need the railroads to move their crops to distant consumers.

Symbolism

This novel follows the actions of its characters in full details, but it also uses large symbols. While not central to the human emotions that drive the story, these symbols still tell readers much about the characters' overall positions in the world. One clearly symbolic segment is the slaughter of jackrabbits at the Osterman ranch. Coming in the chapter following the capture of Dyke by railroad employees, and before the gun fight between the

farmers and the authorities, it is clearly meant to raise readers' sense of frustration with the unfair way that the farmers are being driven off of their land. The details of the rabbit hunt, and the language that is used, are more weighty than this segment would deserve if it were considered just for its significance to the plot of the story. The sheer scope of the rabbits, who are never mentioned as a significant part of the environment anywhere else in the book, gives them meaning beyond their role in the story. Suddenly, they are everywhere:

> A panic spread; then there would ensue a blind, wild rushing together of thousands of crowded bodies, and a furious scrambling over backs, till the scuffing thud of innumerable feet over the earth rose to a reverberating murmur as of distant thunder, here and there pierced by the strange, wild cry of the rabbit in distress.

Men and boys, armed with clubs, go into the corral to beat the animals to death. It is a scene of horrifying violence, and it has nothing to do with the story except as a parallel to the merciless killing of the farmers by the railroad.

The other segment that is clearly symbolic is the "drowning" of S. Behrman at the end of the book. This character's general villainy makes readers wish for his destruction, but when he gets away from all of the other characters it seems that this wish will go unfulfilled. The reason that his death is appropriately symbolic is that it does not come at the hands of another person: he performs his job in a soulless, mechanical way, and it is in just such a way that he dies. Also, the image of Behrman being buried under a pile of wheat presents a neat reversal, since he has symbolically been "burying" the wheat farmers with bureaucracy throughout the whole story. Unlike the jackrabbit segment, this aspect is fully integrated into the story: the torrent of wheat that falls on him happens because Behrman is too cheap to put the wheat in bags, and cheapness is a trait of his character that is clearly established throughout the book.

Historical Context

Big Business

The American economic system is based on the principle that anyone with enough determination can start a business, regardless of size, and with luck make a living out of it. At first, the government encouraged Americans to settle in the West by giving away land, which in turn gave people an incentive to fight against the people who already lived there:

Compare
&
Contrast

- **1901:** The automobile has been invented, but few people can afford them. Under 20,000 motor cars are sold in the United States this year. Henry Ford, chief engineer for the bankrupt Detroit Automobile Company, starts his own company. He goes on to change the face of industry with his methods of mass production.

  Today: Car ownership among Americans of all ages and social classes is common. Eight and a half million cars are sold in the United States each year.

- **1901:** The president of the United States, William McKinley, is shot to death by a Polish-American anarchist.

  Today: Because of the threat of assassination, the president is kept separated from the people and surrounded by security guards.

- **1901:** Males born this year are expected to live 48.2 years. Females have a life expectancy of 51.1 years.

  Today: Males born today have an average life expectancy averaging around 73 years; for females, the figure is around 79 years.

- **1901:** 45.1 million Americans live in rural locations while only 30.2 million live in urban locations.

Today: 75 percent of America's population of 260 million people live in urban area. Of the 25 percent in rural areas, only 7 percent live on farms.

- **1901:** Meats and vegetables have to be served near where they are grown. Refrigerated railcars are available for long-distance shipping, but most households can keep things fresh for just a few days, using boxes cooled by ice.

  Today: Food chemists have developed methods of packaging perishable meals so that they can sit on shelves for months without refrigeration.

- **1901:** A temperance crusade, led by Carry Nation, attempts to stop the sale and distribution of alcohol in the United States.

  1920: Alcohol becomes illegal in the country with the passage of the eighteenth amendment, also known as the Volstead Act.

  1933: The twenty-third amendment is passed to repeal the eighteenth amendment, making alcohol legal again.

  Today: Alcohol is still legal, despite the fact that science has found many more adverse physical effects associated with it than were known in 1901.

---

poor families who owned practically nothing could cultivate a piece of free or cheap land and build their fortune. Similarly, in urban areas, a person starting with little could open a small business or a small manufacturing concern and make ends meet. This was the ideal of a capitalist democracy.

By the year 1901, the small business model had given way to corporate growth. Investors found that they could pool their money in the stock market to create powerful industrial entities that would have greater control over all spheres of their business operation, including government. One good example is U.S. Steel: when it was incorporated in 1901, it

had investment capitol of over one billion dollars, more than twice the annual budget of the federal government that year. The people who benefited from this growth were the people who were already rich. These people had extra money that they could invest. Small entrepreneurs, on the other hand, found themselves squeezed out of business by giant companies that could consolidate services, getting better prices from related businesses. For instance, a company that owned mining or growing concerns, manufacturing businesses, shipping and retail businesses could absorb deep discounts from one step of the process to the next, and offer lower prices to consumers. Small businesses that lacked such connections were driven into bankruptcy.

By the turn of the century, Americans were already worried that consolidation into bigger and bigger businesses was damaging to their way of life. John D. Rockefeller created the first trust company in 1882. This sort of legal corporation was meant to drive out competition by owning all of the manufacturers in any given industry, creating a monopoly. For instance, Rockefeller's Standard Oil Company at one time owned 90 percent of the oil refineries in America, giving it the power to set pricing at will. In 1890, the Congress of the United States passed the Sherman Anti-Trust Act, prohibiting any company from owning a monopoly in one field or from actively seeking to bar others from competing in that industry. To this day, the line between healthy competition and ruthless monopolistic tactics is unclear, as is evident from the split in public opinion over the government's charges of unfair trade against Microsoft Corporation.

Law Breakers

At the time this book was published, America had already been through its age of expansion. The West, as it is presented in books and movies with stereotypical cowboys and Indians, had been settled by farms and businesses. That age was not far enough in the past, though, to have been forgotten. Jesse James, the celebrated gunfighter, had died less than twenty years earlier, in 1882; William Bonney (Billy the Kid) was shot down in New Mexico a year earlier. At the same time, the nation saw a rise of a new class of "criminal"—the notorious "Robber Barons" of the 1880s and 1890s. This name was given to the rich industrialists who presided over the nation's largest industries such as J. P. Morgan (railroads), Andrew Carnegie (steel), John D. Rockefeller (oil), and Cornelius Vanderbilt (shipping). As the country became less rural and more urban, the threat of stagecoach robbers seemed tame, almost quaint, beside the economic threats posed by huge industries that could fire workers, increase their hours, lower their pay, or even have them relocated from their land.

The Mussel Slough Affair

Norris alluded to real-life events in *The Octopus,* such as the Mid-Winter Fair in San Francisco in 1894 and the famine that hit India in 1897. His main source of inspiration, however, was the Mussel Slough Affair of 1880, an event that happened in the San Joaquin Valley almost exactly as described in the novel's fictionalized account.

In the mid-1800s, the railroads grew at a tremendous pace, from twenty-three miles of track in the United States in 1830 to 30,000 miles thirty years later—a jump of over a 1000 percent. In another ten years the distance of track had increased to 53,000 miles. Much of this growth was due to government assistance. For the federal government, encouraging the railroads' growth meant increasing the country's wealth, since new roads spread out into areas with untapped resources.

In California, the government granted the Southern Pacific and Central Pacific Railways the rights to odd-numbered parcels of land along their tracks as a reward for laying the track. The two companies operated under one board of directors, and were, in effect, one company. When the line through the San Joaquin Valley was completed in 1872, the Central Pacific sent out flyers telling farmers that they would be able to buy the land from the railroad. The flyers named no particular price, but they implied that the land would be made available for just a little over the $2.50 per acre that the government charged for the even-numbered parcels. Farmers came, even though the land was dry and not good for farming, and they erected irrigation methods that made it more usable. In addition, they built houses and barns. The railroad circulars indicated that the price of the land would not be raised because of improvements that the farmers made.

As in the novel, the farmers found, when they tried to buy the land they were living on, that the railroad wanted considerably more than they had indicated would be the price. The farmers fought it in court, but, also as in the novel, the railroad moved to evict farmers while the court suit was in progress. Most of the farmers in the Mussel Slough area were at a countywide picnic to celebrate a new irrigation canal when railroad officials and marshals arrived to take possession of the lands. There are differing reports of what happened that day— of what was said, who fired first at whom. There were five deaths among the farmers, with two more dying later. A plaque was erected at the scene of the battle, and for years the name "Mussel Slough" was mentioned among opponents of the railroad to remind each other of the struggle they faced.

Critical Overview

Today, critics find it easy to agree that Frank Norris' novels hold a significant place in the history of American literature, even though there is little agreement about their worth as pieces of fiction.

The Octopus *was originally conceived as the first volume of Norris' proposed "Trilogy of Wheat," in which he hoped to focus on wheat as a life-force.*

Norris usually ends up being grouped with such naturalistic writers as Theodore Dreiser and John Dos Passos despite the fact that they both produced their most significant works more than twenty years after his death. His works fit so strongly in with the writers that followed him that critics who are not careful tend to forget what his world was actually like, and they obscure his true importance as a forerunner and visionary.

From the very start, there has been little agreement among critics about the value of Norris' works. Some critics found his characterizations moving, while others found them trite. Some felt that he changed the nature of intellectual discourse with his philosophy, but still more thought that he was only borrowing from works that came before, that were clearer and more coherent. Most found it easy to agree, though, that Norris had brought to America the sort of fiction that Émile Zola, one of his heroes, had outlined in his 1880 essay "The Experimental Novel." In his first published novel, *McTeague,* critics recognized the power of Norris' naturalist style, even though the crass brutality offended their sensibilities, which were cultivated in a genteel tradition of romanticism. Many critics took the work seriously. In *The Literary World,* John D. Barry noted that the book seemed "worthy to rank among the few

great novels produced in this country." However, many lamented the book's unpleasantness. A reviewer for the *Outlook* in 1899 hoped "that Mr. Norris will find subjects better worthy of his power," while the *Review of Reviews* echoed that, saying it was "to be hoped he may henceforth use [his ability] in the writing of books that will be not less true but a good deal more agreeable."

After the groundbreaking start of *McTeague,* critics took Frank Norris as a major literary force, and they accepted his subsequent literary works in terms of their expectations. The novelist Jack London, whom critics similarly chided when his realistic style led to sentimental plot lines and characterizations, recognized that Norris may have added excessive details in *The Octopus* that dilute the story, but he felt the end justified the means. He *has* produced results," London wrote in *American Literary Realism 1870–1910* upon the book's release in 1901.

> Titanic results. Never mind the realism, the unimportant detail, minute description . . . Let it be stated flatly that by no other method could Frank Norris or anybody else have handled the vast Valley of the San Joaquin and the no less vast-tentacled *Octopus.*

William Dean Howells, who was one of Norris' earliest supporters, saw a clear maturation from

McTeague to *The Octopus,* but he was also willing to see the later book without holding it up to its predecessor. "He is of his time," Howells wrote, "and, as I have said, his school is evident; and yet I think he has a right to make his appeal in *The Octopus* irrespective of the other great canvases beside which that picture must be put." Looking at the novel in its own right, Howells praises it, commenting that "[t]he play of an imagination fed by rich consciousness of the mystical relations of nature and human nature, the body and soul of earthly life, steeps the whole theme in an odor of common growth." Just because Howells appreciated the realism of Norris' early works did not mean that he could not accept the later work's broader, mystical, perspective.

As the years passed, critics could look at Norris' works as a lifetime progression, and they could take a broader perspective on the literary movement that Norris preceded. It did not help the reputation of *The Octopus* that the second book in his proposed trilogy, *The Pit,* was considered a weak effort, marred by the fact that he was writing about a world that he did not know well, and that the third novel was never written. Granville Hicks noted in 1935 that *The Octopus* "can scarcely be called a great book; it is too confused, and in the end too false." By that, he meant that the philosophy that dominates the novel, about the wheat and the railroad being bigger things than the humans whose lives are built and ruined around them was not enough to justify the suffering that is presented. "The thoughtful reader, however, finds Presley's (final) rhapsody the most disturbing kind of anticlimax. As a theory, it is ridiculous, and it destroys the emotional effect of the book, for it means that the contemptible Behrman has worked as surely for the good as the noble Derrick, the impulsive Annixter, or the violent Dyke.. . . How many problems Norris leaves unsolved: Magnus Derrick's ethical dilemma, the whole question of the use of violence, and the place of the poet in such a struggle as that between the railroad and the ranchers! And how far he is from a consistent interpretation of character!"

Contemporary critics tend to appreciate the advances that Norris made in *The Octopus,* even as they realize that he was not nearly as advanced as he might seem. The author, who considered himself a hard-nosed realist, might have flinched at Alfred Kazan's 1942 description of him, although many modern writers would accept it as true:

> [T]he key to Norris' mind is to be found in the naive, open-hearted, and essentially unquenchable joy as radiant as the lyricism of Elizabethan poetry, a joy that is like the first discovery of the world, exhilarating in its directness, and eager to absorb every flicker of life. Norris wrote as if men had never seen California before him, or known the joy of growing wheat in those huge fields that can take half a day to cross, or of piling enough flour on trains to feed a European nation.

Detractors may emphasize the naiveté mentioned in Kazan's assessment, but Norris' supporters, of which there are many, see mostly the joy in his sad work.

Criticism

David Kelly

Kelly is an instructor of creative writing and literature at two community colleges in Illinois. In the following essay, he argues that, in spite of the apparent simplicity of the novel's presentation of good and evil, there are morally complex characters who make readers question their own assumptions.

Reading a progressive, muckraking novel like Frank Norris' *The Octopus* tends to lead readers toward anger and indignation, of course; that is what novels of this type are supposed to do. These are books that call for change, and anger leads to change. There is a problem, though, when readers can tell that they are supposed to feel angry about matters that simply do not excite strong feelings. As years pass, the issues involved are not as outrageous as they once were. In a way, this is a natural and even desirable part of the muckraking process: if novels that are meant to incite change are effective, then the social situations they cover will in fact change, and in a few generations, if all goes well, nobody will have direct experience with the issues that once seemed so crucial.

As fiction writers, though, social novelists have a responsibility to create characters who stir up readers' emotions by the ways they interact within their own worlds. The best characters since the first recorded literature have remained untouched by time because they carry with them, in the stories that surround them, all that they need for making their own glory or failure. If the farmers of *The Octopus* are treated unfairly, then readers today should be able to empathize with their suffering; if the railroad officials in the book are abusing power, they should still make readers indignant in a far-off future when railroads have

> "What makes Norris' novel a lasting piece of fiction is that it truly examines the varieties of good and evil, and doesn't just use these concepts to further its social agenda."

ceased to be. Too often, though, novels have been used to elicit social change by using thin, disposable characters that have no more lasting power than the day's headlines.

What makes Norris' novel a lasting piece of fiction is that it truly examines the varieties of good and evil, and doesn't just use these concepts to further its social agenda. This fact, though, is not always clear, and it almost seems as if Norris was consciously working to sabotage readers' sense of his own fair-mindedness. It is almost too easy to pick out the heroes and villains in this novel: all of the railroad people are bad, some from ignorance rather than from evil hearts, and all of the people who work the soil are good, if sometimes misunderstood.

What makes this book more worthy of serious consideration than standard melodramatic fare is that, within the two camps, good and evil, there are whole spectra of guilt and innocence. In general, readers are encouraged to forgive the transgressions of "the good guys," no matter how bad; such as Annixter's vulgar approaches toward Hilma Tree or even Dyke's spree of robbery and murder. At the same time, the bad people are obscene throughout the book, even in such morally neutral matters of S. Behrman's having an annoyingly pretentious single initial. A few characters go beyond their general categories, though, and they raise difficult questions about what is and is not right.

The most obvious of these morally tangled characters is Magnus Derrick, whose struggle seems to be about determining what is best when his duty to the people of his community pushes him to do something that his conscience knows is wrong. When the idea first comes up to bribe politicians to get sympathetic members seated on the railroad commission, Magnus is staunch in his refusal; practical though the scheme is, his moral sense is such that he is not even willing to think

over its benefits. That changes, though, as it becomes more likely that the railroad might actually succeed in taking the land the farmers believe is theirs. For pages and pages of the novel, Magnus deliberates, with a motion that Norris actually describes as a pendulum swinging from one side to the other. On one side is the chance to crush his enemies, to defeat the injustice of their aggression against the farmers. On the other side is an admirable but impractical moral stance. By the time that he chooses to act, readers are so angered by the railroad's heartlessness that Magnus is forgiven any breach of ethics. His action to save his land and the people on it is presented as an act of self-defense, and is therefore justifiable.

In a traditional, shallowly-conceived progressive novel, a farmer might be excused any measure necessary to defend his land, just as the customs of self-defense are usually seen to extend beyond a person's body to cover his or her family. But Magnus Derrick is not a traditional farmer who works the land he loves: he is a profiteer, with no more claim to moral righteousness than the people who have designs on the land that he calls his. He certainly does not have the mystical bond to the soil that true farmers can claim. In his first scene in the book, Annixter speaks maliciously about the greedy agricultural practices that take place on Derrick's farm: "Get the guts out of the land; work it to death; never give it a rest. Never alternate your crop, and then when your soil is exhausted sit down and roar about hard times." This is not even a case of Derrick's being an inept farmer who is bound, by his talent for leadership, to fight for his land on the behalf of the good people who farm on it; at the beginning of the book, he has dismissed all of his tenants.

The best indicator of Magnus' moral right to keep Los Muertos, a right that supposedly is more important than his own moral law against bribery, is found in his plans for post-bribery life. An act of desperation is excusable; an act of selflessness, even more so; but there is no doubt that Magnus is bribing politicians to regain some of his lost power and, mostly, to make money. When it is suggested that this bribe will only affect shipping rates during the current railroad commission's term, and that the rates will rise with the next commission, Magnus answers, with a twinkle in his eye, "By then it will be too late. We will, all of us, have made our fortunes by then."

That one statement realigns the book's entire moral structure. Up to that point, throughout the

What Do I Read Next?

- Norris' novel *McTeague,* published in 1899, is considered by some to be his greatest work and one of the most influential pieces of American naturalism. It concerns a San Francisco dentist and his wife who slide into moral degradation when he loses his job and they both are forced to live on the streets.

- *The Pit: A Story of Chicago* by Norris is the second part of a trilogy about wheat that started with *The Octopus.* It examines the financial exchanges in Chicago, where the decisions regarding the value of wheat are made. The third part of the trilogy was never finished before Norris died.

- Upton Sinclair's classic 1904 novel *The Jungle* takes a cold, unflinching look at the brutal conditions in the Chicago beef processing plants. Like this novel, it examines the ways in which the social order corrupts and destroys ordinary, well-meaning people.

- Norris is usually mentioned along with Hamlin Garland, another master of American realism. Hamlin Garland's short-story collection, *Main-*

Travelled Roads, captures the same sense of rural America in the late 1800s and gives readers a basic, moving example of this literary genre.

- One of Norris' most important influences was the French writer Émile Zola, whose novels movingly capture the dehumanizing effects of the industrial age. Of all of Zola's books, *Germinal* is most similar to *The Octopus:* it concerns the suppression of coal miners.

- Many students know of Stephen Crane because of his book *The Red Badge of Courage,* which is one of the great war books of all time. He is also a prominent figure of American naturalism. Crane's novel *Maggie: A Girl of the Streets,* created a panic upon its first publication in 1893, due to its frank portrayal of sexuality.

- John Dos Passos' novel *Manhattan Transfer* was written much after Norris's time, in 1925, but it shows the same naturalistic tendencies that Norris pioneered, telling a broad, panoramic story of city lives following nature's laws.

---

entire first book of the novel, the struggle is presented as one between the farmers' natural rights against the railroaders' heartless greed. Once it is revealed that farming is just a money-making venture, like shipping, then there is hardly any reason for the farmers to become indignant about getting the worst in their land deal. Presley, the novel's closest thing to a protagonist, is shocked by Magnus' words, and after mulling them over, ends up attributing his attitude to his past as a wildcatter, a miner who is used to gambling with his fortune. Almost a half a page after Magnus' frank admission that greed is his motive, Norris, through Presley's musings, is able to regain some semblance of nobility by desperately appealing to the same patriotism that had previously been implied.

It was the true California spirit that found expression through him, Presley thinks, the spirit of the West,

unwilling to occupy itself with details, refusing to wait, to be patient, to achieve by legitimate plodding; the miner's instinct of wealth acquired in a single night prevailed, in spite of all.

What he is unable to explain is why this "instinct" is any more worth defending with guns than the greed of the railroad barons.

Dyke, the dismissed railroad man, is also presented as being on the side of good, even though his actions are clearly bad. In Dyke's case, the reason behind his immoral action is a little stronger: he does not just want profit for its own sake, or, as Magnus does, for the thrill of acquisition, but instead is trying to care for his little daughter, who is the focus of all that he does. But even though his motive is purer, his crime is much worse than bribery, and the railroad's provocation does not really deserve a bloody rampage. The railroad fired him from his job; the freight rates changed within half a year; are these supposed to be reasons enough to justify robbery and murder? Is the railroad supposed to take care to keep jobs open for employees based on how much they adore their children, or to raise rates only when everyone they deal with understands the principle of rate hikes?

At the very top of the railroad's evil empire is Shelgrim, who is at least as guilty by association as Magnus is innocent. Given Norris' ruthlessness in describing his evil characters, from S. Behrman's "great stomach" and "tremendous jowls" to the gruesomely narcissistic display of bourgeois wastefulness at the dinner thrown by Gerard, his presentation of Shelgrim is surprisingly mild. The sympathy Norris permits him is, after Magnus, the second clearest evidence of the novel's openness toward morals.

Norris quickly stops readers' expectations that Shelgrim will be a monster by having him double the salary of a troubled employee with three children, a man who could properly be fired for missing work while drunk. This act of mercy by him immediately separates Shelgrim from the heartless railroad bureaucracy that caused Dyke's dismissal. Shelgrim turns out, in his subsequent conversation with Presley, to have intelligent opinions about poetry and painting, and a humble philosophy about his own place in the grand scheme of life. Faced with a threat to his future like the one facing Magnus, it is difficult to tell how Shelgrim might behave, but in the moments Presley spends in his office, the railroad president proves, unlike the social machinery he controls, to have some sense of decency.

It seems that *The Octopus* has no great moral lesson, if all it is teaching is that people are individually better or worse than their circumstances. This is a lesson that literature often displays. The point stands out here, though, because so much of this book deals with generalizations, playing into the way readers generalize about morality and immorality. It might have been a stronger novel if it did not offer such easy, broad categories with which to judge its characters, but the fact that Norris takes care to complicate a few of the main moral dilemmas is a sign that readers are encouraged to question their own assumptions.

Source: David Kelly, Critical Essay on *The Octopus*, in *Novels for Students*, The Gale Group, 2001.

Alice R. Bensen

In the following essay, Bensen provides an overview of The Octopus, *including discussing Norris' inspiration for the novel.*

The Octopus was the sixth of the seven novels that Frank Norris wrote before his sudden death, at 32, in 1902. It is in most respects his best. In writing it, Norris was determinedly filling a gap in American literature: America had no adequate non-imitative "American novel" and no epic of the winning of the west.

By 1899 Norris had conceived an adequate subject: "the Wheat." Raised in the vast San Joaquin Valley of southern central California, it involved the labor of inhabitants of every ethnic and economic group. Then in "the Pit" in Chicago it was bought and resold to "the People" of the world. Finally, this product of American soil and labor sustained populaces of the farthest countries. *The Octopus* would be the first volume of a trilogy; *The Pit,* the second; and there would be a third, to have been called *The Wolf,* which Norris did not live to write.

The title *The Octopus* refers not, of course, to the wheat, but to the spoiling force, the railroad. The valley's fecundity gave rise to the railroad and made possible the abuses perpetrated by it. By the mid-1890s Norris had come to value and use various aspects of Zola's realism and naturalism—contemporary topics, careful documentation, close observation, recognition of natural forces—after a rather prolonged youthful period of captivation with medieval romance. The "Mussel Slough Massacre," the armed battle that had taken place between the agents of the Southern Pacific Railroad and the wheat farmers of Tulare County in May 1880, was the documented fact on which the action of *The Octopus* was based. In choosing to treat of the abuses of the railroad company, Norris was not taking a daring stand or even breaking new ground. The "unanimous hatred of the people of California toward the Southern Pacific Railway" already existed. The novel is more an epic than a work of propaganda.

The wheat and the need to transport it organize almost all of the action. The wheat grows on the new soil in generous abundance, ready to be used, but the railroad tycoons require farm machines to be moved by circuitous routes, raise rates prohibitively for small producers, cut wages despite high profits, fire those who protest, govern the local newspapers, and finally renege on the contracts made with the ranchers who have leased and improved the land. The company has bought the state government and the courts; the valley people are too disorganized to make a stand. Norris follows Zola in seeing the railroad as a living monster; it is a gigantic octopus with its tentacles clutching all.

Presley, an educated outsider and a poet, who has come to the west with the hope of writing a vaguely conceived grand romantic epic of the Indian and Spanish epochs, follows Norris's own development in jettisoning this plan and studying to depict the present valley situation. This observer is a friend of the young ranchers, drawn from friends of Norris: Harran Derrick, whose stately father Magnus had lost his bid for governorship rather than engage in corrupt politics; Annixter—truculent but admirable—the most fully presented character; the sophisticated Osterman. And there is Vanamee, an educated man, a strange mystic rover, temporarily a farm laborer, whose ethereal sweetheart, Angele, raped by an intruder, had died in childbirth; his friendship with the old Spanish priest at the mission church sustains in the novel the Spanish background of the region. Many of the workmen are of Spanish or Portuguese descent. And there is the old German farmer, the anarchist bar-owner, and a scattering of womenfolk.

Memorable set scenes, Norris's forte, dramatize the life of those who tend the wheat: the big barn dance, the jackrabbit drive, the annual plowing: "The ploughs, thirty-five in number, each drawn by its team of ten, stretched in an interminable line, nearly a quarter of a mile in length.... Each of these ploughs held five shears, so that when the entire company was in motion, one hundred and seventy-five furrows were made at the same instant. At a distance, the ploughs resembled a great column of field artillery." Further animating the meticulous details of the scene is the metaphor of the earth—"the uneasy agitation of its members, the hidden tumult of its womb, demanding to be made fruitful, to reproduce, to disengage the eternal renascent germ of Life that stirred and struggled in its loins."

The wheat is the living witness of the evolutionary force. When Annixter, after a night of internal struggle, finally recognizes his total love for Hilma—herself a type of Love—he sees in the dawn light the young wheat that has burst through the ground: "the Wheat, the Wheat . . . an exulting earth gleaming transcendent with the radiant significance of an inviolable pledge."

Though the struggle with the corrupt railroad causes the loss of Magnus Derrick's honor and the lives of Annixter, Harran, several other ranchers, and Hilma's baby, the promise of "life out of death" is sustained by the coming of the dead Angele's daughter the night of the first wheat, and by the unusually splendid harvest of the wheat itself. The

> " Though the struggle with the corrupt railroad causes the loss of Magnus Derrick's honor and the lives of . . . several other ranchers. . ., the promise of 'life out of death' is sustained by the coming of the dead Angele's daughter the night of the first wheat. . . ."

book ends with an ambiguous passage in which the leading railroad tycoon justifies the railroad as itself being ruled by forces beyond it. Unambiguously, the railroad's local petty tyrant, S. Behrman, as he is exulting at seeing his wheat rushing down the chute into a ship for India, is himself caught into the downward rush.

Norris's exact descriptions, his recording, like Zola's, of scenes, sounds, and smells, produced a vibrant and memorable novel, despite some overwriting and unclear logic.

Source: Alice R. Bensen, "*The Octopus:* Overview," in *Reference Guide to American Literature*, edited by Jim Kamp, St. James Press, 1994.

Warren French

In the following essay, French examines critical response to The Octopus, *and measures the consistency of the social theories presented in the novel.*

The traditional interpretation of *The Octopus* (1901) is summarized in the description of the novel in *The Oxford Companion to American Literature* as "dealing with the raising of wheat in California, and the struggle of the ranchers against the railroads." Coming as it did when the abusive practices of the railroads and the agitation of the enraged farmers were about to lead to major reform legislation, *The Octopus* has often been identified as either a result of the powerful Populist movement of the 1890's or a foreshadowing of the muckraking books of the early twentieth century—a kind of companion piece of Upton Sinclair's *The Jungle*.

Although Norris in 1899 wrote to a Mrs. Parks that he was firmly "enlisted upon the other side"

An early American Southern Pacific Sunset Limited locomotive

from the railroad trust and did not consider the Southern Pacific "legitimate or tolerable," there is no evidence that he was actively interested in the Populist movement. The only specific political reference in the novel is a derogatory mention of Lyman Derrick as the candidate of the "regular Republican" party, and in both *The Octopus* and *A Man's Woman,* Norris offers encomia to enterprising, dynamic San Francisco businessmen. There is little evidence of any very liberal political leanings on the part of a writer who allows a sympathetically presented manufacturer to say of himself and an editor, "I don't think his editorial columns are for sale, and he doesn't believe there are blow-holes in my steel plates . . . also it appears that we have more money than Henry George believes to be right". Ernest Marchand wondered why Norris had suddenly become interested in sociological questions when he came to write *The Octopus,* for "not a whisper" of such occurrences as the Homestead and Pullman strikes are heard in his earlier books. The answer very probably is that Norris was not so much interested in specific problems as in finding illustrations for his general theories of the proper conduct of life. We shall see that he does not really sympathize with either side in the struggle he depicts in *The Octopus.* He appears to have embraced Populist causes only when these chanced to

coincide with his preconceived notions; and, although Norris was associated with *McClure's,* one of the magazines most closely connected with the muckraking movement, he left its employ and New York without regret before the movement had gotten up full steam.

As early as the socially conscious 1930's, in fact, reform-minded critics began to doubt if *The Octopus* was even the work of the socially enlightened determinist that Norris was sometimes reputed to be. Granville Hicks pointed out in *The Great Tradition* that it was impossible to reconcile a strict determinism with a faith in all things working inevitably toward the good, and others were quick to seize his point and to charge Norris with being "confused." That critics might have been confused and Norris perfectly consistent but misunderstood seems not to have occurred to anyone until the vogue for social reform literature had begun to wane with the passing of the worst of the Depression.

The road to a greater understanding of Norris' "lost frontier" epic was paved in 1940 by "Norris Explains *The Octopus,*" an article in which H. Willard Reninger compares the novelist's critical theories with his practice. Citing the shepherd Vanamee's important conversation with the poet

Presley near the end of the novel, Reninger points out that the whole work demonstrates the viewpoint Vanamee enunciates when he tells his listener that if he looks at disaster "from the vast height of humanity . . . you will find, if your view be large enough, that it is *not* evil, but good, that in the end remains." Thus Reninger explains that the "alleged inconsistencies" in the novel are reconciled by an all-encompassing philosophy:

> The novel dramatizes the doctrine that although men in a given locality can be temporarily defeated by combined economic and political forces, which in themselves are temporary and contigent on a phase of civilization, the *natural forces,* epitomized by the wheat, which are eternal and resistless, will eventually bring about the greatest good for the greatest number.

Reninger's analysis is helpful, but not sufficiently critical of Norris' failure to carry out his theories. Reninger cites the novelist's demand that artists probe deeply into the motives of those "type men" who stand for the multitude, but he does not observe that Norris understood little about underlying human motives and that he usually brushes aside hard-to-analyze behavior as instinctive. Reninger takes Norris' ideas too much at their author's declared value; and since he dismisses Vanamee's mysticism as "merely a technique" Norris used, he fails not only to ask why only the shepherd is triumphant in his quest but also whether Norris was really conscious of all the ideas that influenced his interpretation of the events he employed.

Weaknesses of previous interpretations of the novel, including Reninger's, are well demonstrated in George Mayer's "New Interpretation." Meyer is the first to point out that Norris' opinion of the ranchers in the novel has been misconstrued and that he saw them not as "poor folks"—like the migrants in *The Grapes of Wrath* or victims of the system like the workers in *The Jungle*—but as "reckless would-be profiteers, as speculators so unfortunate as to be less powerful and ingenious than their competitors in a ruinous struggle for economic power."

He also corrects a long-standing misapprehension of the book by identifying Shelgrim, the railroad president who talks of nature in order "to rationalize his own irresponsibility," and not Norris as the fatalist. He also points out that the poet Presley is not a self-portrait of the author and that the tragedy depicted here need not invariably be repeated, because the reader can learn from the misfortunes of others. He recognizes, too, that the novel is a kind of transcendentalist tract illustrating Nor-

> **When we strip away the naïve arguments and the blatant attempts to titillate the reader's sentiment, we uncover a remarkable panorama of the life of a confused society torn between its desires. . . ."**

ris' "conviction that Americans wrought unnecessary evil by supporting an economic system that clashed violently with the facts of nature," the principal one of which is that "the wheat will flow irresistibly from the field where it is grown to mouths that need to be fed" and that the natural force of the movement "injures or destroys many individuals unlucky enough to be standing in its path."

Meyer's article might have provided a definitive reading of the novel if he had not considerably overestimated the author's capacity for abstract thinking. When he insists that Norris thought that, if men would cooperate with one another, they might eliminate the disastrous role that chance plays in human affairs, he fails to see the significance of the Vanamee subplot (he treats the shepherd only as a mouthpiece for certain views), and he ignores Norris' frequently reiterated preference for *doing* over *thinking,* since cooperation with other men (although not with the "forces of nature") requires even more thought than action.

A careful, thorough, rational scholar himself, writing during a period of grave international crisis, Meyer fails to give sufficient emphasis to the mystical elements in Norris' thought, his pre-occupation with "sixth senses," and his disdain for liberal education. The critic tries too hard to make the novel fit the pattern of the traditional reformist tract because he does not see that Norris was as suspicious of cooperation between individual men as he was of conflict between them.

Both Reninger and Meyer are correct in perceiving that *The Octopus* is internally consistent, but neither pays sufficient attention to the extent to which irrational elements influenced Norris' thought. Only by careful examination of the Vanamee subplot is it possible to observe the extent to which Norris tried to incorporate a good example, as well as several horrible ones, into the first volume of his epic trilogy.

This subplot has not always received the attention it deserves, because in *The Octopus*—as in other works—Norris' skill as a reporter caused the depiction of specific evils that were not his essential concern to overshadow the general moral he wished to convey. Although the book has been often reprinted and summarized, we should perhaps before beginning an analysis recall the major events of the involved plot Norris built around the notorious Mussel Slough affair, in which the exploitative practices of the railroads led to armed rebellion.

It is not always sufficiently acknowledged that the novel is an exercise in point of view. What it contains is what Presley, a poet somewhat reminiscent of Edwin Markham, sees during a summer that he spends in the San Joaquin Valley trying to discover a purpose and a direction for his own work. He is a guest of Magnus Derrick, an ex-governor who farms one of the largest ranches in the valley. Unfortunately Derrick—like most of his neighbors—does not have clear title to his property. Much of it belongs to the Pacific and Southwestern Railroad, "The Octopus," which has promised—but not contracted—sometime to sell the land to the ranchers at a low price. A crisis is precipitated when, at the height of a party, news arrives that the railroad demands that the ranchers either pay an exorbitant price for the properties they have improved or be evicted. When the railroad attempts to have a Federal posse evict the ranchers, an armed battle ensues in which six of the ranchers—including Derrick's son and his neighbor, Annixter—are killed. Derrick is further discredited when it is revealed that he has used bribery to buy a position on the state railroad commission for his son Lyman, who sells out to the railroads anyway. Like Curtis Jadwin in *The Pit,* Magnus Derrick speculates desperately and is utterly shattered.

Others suffer as well. Dyke, a loyal employee whom the railroad unjustly discharges and then bankrupts, turns train robber and goes to prison. Mrs. Hooven, widow of one of the ranch-hands killed in the skirmish, starves to death in San Francisco. Even Behrman, the principal agent of the railroad, who seems immune to human justice, is—in one of Norris' most spectacular scenes—finally smothered in the hold of a ship that is being loaded with his own wheat. Presley survives, but he leaves California, saddened by the death of his friends and

convinced that he is ineffectual as either poet or man of action.

The only major character to survive the holocaust is Vanamee, a shepherd who some years before the story begins had withdrawn from society after his sweetheart was mysteriously assaulted and died in childbirth. Living close to nature, he has developed mysterious telepathic powers, and he is finally rewarded for his renunciation of self-destructive ambition by winning the love of his former sweetheart's daughter.

All of these events are usually interpreted as adding up to an attack upon the railroad and to a paean of praise for the wheat—the irresistible life-force that frustrates those seemingly beyond the reach of human justice. Such an interpretation does not, however, satisfactorily explain all of the novel—especially the concluding sentiment that "in every crisis of the world's life . . . if your view be large enough . . . it is *not* evil, but good, that in the end remains."

A good approach to the matters needing attention is through Donald Pizer's recent "Another Look at *The Octopus,*" which restates Meyer's interpretation of Norris' attitude toward the ranchers as "speculators" and adds two further observations that aid understanding of the novel. First, Pizer shows that the story essentially concerns educating the poet Presley into a recognition of the insignificance of the individual in comparison to the operation of the great, benevolent forces of nature. Then he points out the novel's relationship to transcendental thought.

Basically, Pizer maintains, Norris is looking not confidently forward but nostalgically backward, since his "faith in individual perception of Truth and in the concomitant dependence upon a benevolent nature in discerning this Truth found its most distinctive statement in the transcendental movement." Pizer argues, as I do throughout this study, that Norris—driven by fear and distrust of contemporary civilization—sought principally to turn back the clock.

Ironically, Norris might have produced a more impressive work if he had been less nostalgic. As an angry plea for the rectification of specific evils, *The Octopus* is one of the most powerful tracts ever penned. Those who exract the story of the struggle between the ranchers and the railroad from the rest of the book are to a certain extent justified by the result. Judged, however, on the basis of what the author, and not posthumous editors, considered essential, the work fails to convey its full message convincingly not because of internal inconsistencies—since the final pages advance arguments that reconcile seeming internal contradictions—but because of the lack of examples to support these arguments adequately. In the long run evil may be less enduring than good, but Norris as a journalist depicts the short-range victory of evil more convincingly than as a novelist he demonstrates the ultimate triumph of good.

But about the supposed inconsistencies—charges that the novel is confused have generally centered upon two passages: Presley's incredible interview with Shelgrim, a railroad president apparently modeled on Collis Huntington of the Southern Pacific, and the concluding statement that "all things, surely, inevitably, resistlessly work together for the good."

Certainly the Shelgrim episode distorts the structure of the novel and begins to make us suspect the artistic integrity of a writer who peremptorily introduces a new viewpoint into a nearly completed work. To claim, however, as Ernest Marchand does, that after the interview "Norris walked arm in arm with [Presley] and shared his bewilderment" is to continue the unjustified identification of author and his character and to miss the real point of the incident.

During the interview, Shelgrim makes the often quoted statement, "You are dealing with forces, young man, when you speak of Wheat and the Railroads, not with men. . . . If you want to fasten the blame of the affair at Los Muertos on any one person, you will make a mistake. Blame conditions, not men." Presley regains the street "stupefied." He cannot refute this new idea, which "rang with the clear reverberation of truth" and he asks if anyone were "to blame for the horror at the irrigating ditch" where so many of his friends died.

These doubts, however, are Presley's, not Norris'. What has happened here—as elsewhere—is that Norris has botched the writing. The book is easily misread not because it expresses subtle ideas—the thinking is often quite simple-minded—but because Norris' writing about ideas is often muddy, and it is not easy to distinguish between what he thinks and what his characters think. We must recall, however, that despite the furore over his poem "The Toilers," (a work similar to Edwin Markham's "The Man with the Hoe"), Presley—as shown by an unsuccessful speech he delivers to a group of ranchers and by his abortive bombing of the villain's house—is not effective as either

thinker or doer, as a handler of either symbols or things.

Far from identifying himself with Presley (although they share some ideas), Norris throughout the book treats the poet with mild contempt as a "type" illustrative of the ineffectiveness of the literary man in coping with the violent forces in the world.

That Norris was also not taken in by the arguments he assigns Shelgrim is demonstrated later when at a society dinner he depicts Presley beginning to think things over and—in what Maxwell Geismar calls "the intellectual climax of the novel"—realizing that he has been duped by the fast-talking Shelgrim:

> The railroad might indeed be a force only, which no man could control and for which no man was responsible, but his friends had been killed, but years of extortion and oppression had wrung money from all of the San Joaquin, money that had made possible this very scene in which he found himself. . . . It was a half-ludicrous, half-horrible "dog eat dog," an unspeakable cannibalism Presley foresees that some day the people will rise and in turn "rend those who now preyed upon them." As George Meyer points out, Shelgrim uses "natural forces" as a rationalization for his own irresponsibility. Despite his high position, the railroad president is simply a confidence man, one who overwhelms counter-argument by a skillful use of question-begging and of faulty dilemmas (irresponsible operation or bankruptcy.)

Norris puts his finger on the real trouble when he says that "No standards of measure in [Presley's] mental equipment would apply to [Shelgrim] . . . not because these standards were different in kind, but that they were lamentably deficient in size." The forces at work are not necessarily uncontrollable (Marchand points out that "the growing of wheat is not a cosmic process, but a purely human activity"), but they cannot be controlled by the characters Norris has created.

To dwell on the insufficiency of his characters' mental equipment, however, would defeat the author's purpose, for it would conflict with the uncritical enthusiasm he expresses elsewhere when he asks about his "sturdy American" actors: "Where else in the world round were such strong, honest men, such strong, beautiful women?". The question is intended to be rhetorical; but it might be answered, "Anywhere that people are strong-minded enough to control the forces civilization has created." Norris has not proved that these forces cannot be controlled, but only that he cannot conceive the characters who could control them. He then proceeds to display unfounded confidence in himself by assuming that he knows as much about human capability as anyone.

This unwarranted confidence is responsible for what many readers consider the dogmatism of the conclusion. How did Norris know that "all things surely, inevitably, resistlessly work together for the good"? Why, he just knew it, and the reader who will not take his word for it is obviously as much out of harmony with the secret forces of nature as the ill-fated ranchers of the San Joaquin Valley. Part of the strength of Norris' work is that he never felt any doubt about his own perspicacity.

Probably more as model or "type" than proof of his theories, Norris did weave into his epic tale of the fall of the foolish, the tale of Vanamee as a kind of counter-narrative to guide those who seek the right road. This story is not usually credited with its proper importance in the over-all design of the novel, for the lonely shepherd is often ignored or mentioned only as spokesman for the philosophy that colors the final pages of the book. Yet even if Norris had not especially spoken in a letter to Isaac Marcosson of this subplot as "even mysticism . . . a sort of allegory," the amount of space he lavished upon the story and the fact that it is Vanamee's philosophy that is repeated at the end of the book should alert readers to the significance of the only major character in the story who emerges triumphant.

The shepherd enunciates the philosophy that "in every crisis of the world's life . . . if your view be large enough . . . it is *not* evil, but good, that in the end remains." We need not, however, take his word for this; his own story is supposed to illustrate the truth of the premise just as much as the story of the ranchers and their struggle against the railroad is supposed to illustrate the truth of the premise that those who stand in the way of irresistible forces will be destroyed.

Vanamee is a kind of latter-day Thoreau, "a college graduate and a man of wide reading and great intelligence, [who] had chosen to lead his own life, which was that of a recluse." Unlike Thoreau, however, his withdrawal from society is not an experiment, but a permanent policy. In view of the final contrast between what happens to him and to the others in the novel, we must conclude that Norris thought that the sensitive, introspective person could regain harmony with nature only by completely rejecting civilized society.

Vanamee loved Angèle Varian, who lived on a flower ranch near the mission where he met her nightly. One night, however, Angèle was met by a never identified "other," who raped her. When she died in childbirth, "the thread of Vanamee's life had been snapped."

As a result of his long isolation from society, Vanamee has developed a strange power to call other people to him. ("If I had wanted to, sir, I could have made you come to me from back there in the Quien Sabe ranch," he tells a priest.) He does not understand this power himself ("I understand as little of these things as you," he tells the priest, when asked about the power). Finally after eighteen years he returns to the scene of Angèle's rape and begins calling for her, demanding that God answer with "something real, even if the reality were fancied" Through a succession of scenes, we see the answer to this totally irrational call gradually materialize until at last "Angèle was realized in the Wheat."

The "answer" is Angèle's daughter, who has come in response to Vanamee's mysterious calls and who even more mysteriously loves him as her mother did. Her coming demonstrates specifically how good—in the large enough view—comes out of evil. The rape and death of Angèle were evil, but the child born of this bestiality is good. Norris even has Vanamee make this point specifically: "I believed Angèle dead. I wept over her grave; mourned for her as dead in corruption. She has come back to me, more beautiful than ever."

Does this example prove the sweeping generalization Norris makes at the end of the book? Probably many critics have overlooked the whole business because few could concede that it did. Even if we were willing to grant that one example might be enough to support a theory about the operation of the Universe, we could not overlook the extraordinary aspects of the particular situation— Vanamee's mysterious ability to use a kind of telepathic hypnosis (he speaks of a "sixth sense" or "a whole system of other unnamed senses" experienced by "people who live alone and close to nature"), and Angèle's daughter's remarkable duplication of not only her mother's appearance, but also her feelings.

What is Norris trying to say here? We cannot, of course, disprove telepathy, "sixth senses," and the transmigration of souls that he seems to be hinting at any more than he can prove their existence with this wild romance that most critics of the book have apparently found too embarrassing to discuss. But what we can say is that it is hard to imagine what Norris does mean if not that we must either put up with injustice and abuse, temporary "evils" of civilization, or else reject civilization altogether and take to the woods where we can develop "unnamed senses." If man's problem is to improve conditions in the world he has made, Norris is no help. He is rather like the man who, unable to do something himself, announces that it cannot be done and sits scoffing at those who try. Although he lived in a society full of worshippers of progress, with whom he is sometimes confused, he himself is a self-appointed propagandist for "hard" primitivism.

Another indication of the backwardness of Norris' thought is the really most remarkable part of the interview with Shelgrim, the railroad president—not the blatant sophistries about "forces," but the vignette of Shelgrim granting another chance to a drunken bookkeeper, an act that shatters Presley's concept of the executive as a bloodsucker. The reader may well ask along with Presley how the man who can handle an erring underling so intelligently and humanely can have treated so inhumanely the ranchers and Dyke, a once faithful employee whom the agents of the "octopus" drive to robbery, murder, and death.

The answer is that Shelgrim, as Norris conceives of him, is not really a competent administrator of a vast business, even though Norris may have drawn the incident from his own knowledge of the railroad executives. Actually the behavior that it illustrates can best be analyzed in the light of a passage from Steinbeck's *The Grapes of Wrath,* in which a dispossessed tenant ponders:

> "Funny thing, how it is. If a man owns a little property, that property is him, it's part of him, and it's like him. . . . Even if he isn't successful, he's big with his property. . . . But let a man get property that he doesn't see, or can't take time to get his fingers in, or can't be there to walk on it—why, then the property is the man. He can't do what he wants, he can't think what he wants. The property is the man, stronger than he is. And he is small, not big. Only his possessions are big—and he's the servant of his property."

This is a classic statement of the view of the "thing-handler" as opposed to the "symbol-handler"—that man can understand only that which he can actually see and feel. The tenant has grounds for his observation, because many men who have actually only the education and intelligence to be "thing-handlers" have been forced into or have taken upon themselves the roles of "symbol-handlers," with the distressing result that conditions occur like those depicted in both *The Octopus* and *The Grapes of Wrath.*

Actually Norris foreshadows part of Steinbeck's tenant's speech in his analysis of Magnus Derrick, the elder statesman among the ranchers:

> It was the true California spirit that found expression through him, the spirit of the West, unwilling to occupy itself with details, unwilling to wait, to be patient, to achieve by legitimate plodding. . . . It was in this frame of mind that Magnus and the multitude of other ranchers of whom he was a type, farmed their ranches. *They had no love for their land.* They were not attached to their soil. . . . To get all there was out of the land, to squeeze it dry, to exhaust it, seemed their policy. When, at last, the land worn out, would refuse to yield, they would invest their money in something else; by then, they would all have made their fortunes. They did not care. "After us the deluge" (italics mine).

The charge here is the same as that against the bankers in *The Grapes of Wrath,* and those who have supposed that Norris was as critical of the ranchers as of the railroads have been right as far as they have gone; but they should have gone further. He is actually more critical of the ranchers, because the point of the incident of Shelgrim's kindness is to suggest that he does actually love those around him—those with whose problems he is personally acquainted.

What Norris failed to see is that a man of such limited vision would be incompetent to operate successfully a vast railroad or any comparable enterprise since he would be unable to do what competent administrators of vast affairs must do if they are not to court disaster—set up and administer equitably and impartially uniform regulations for those with whom they deal directly and those with whom they do not. Of course such competent administrators were uncommon in the nineteenth century (they are still not especially abundant), but commercial disasters were fairly common. Many businesses and institutions (including the railroads) are still paying for the incompetence of the "self-made" administrators of the Gilded Age. Norris' shortcoming was that he reported ably enough what he saw, but he failed to perceive what was wrong. He stepped into the trap that awaits many uncritical admirers of the empire builder—the assumption that those who have the force and energy to put together an empire necessarily have the intelligence and patience to administer it adequately. A reporter, of course, would not be handicapped by making such an erroneous assumption, but it is likely to prove crippling to a man seeking to formulate rules for the conduct of life.

Ernest Narchand is right when he says that the real struggle in *The Octopus* is between "two types of economy"—the old, vanishing agricultural, and the rising industrial; but he does not see that both economies are administered in this novel by the same type of chieftain, since the author had no concept that a more complicated economy demands a new, more thoughtful type of leadership.

Norris got close enough to the ranchers to see their weaknesses, but he did not get as close to the managers of the railroad. *The Octopus* has often been called one-sided, but it has not been pointed out that the result of the oversimplified treatment of the railroad's role in the controversy is that it actually comes off better than it might because Norris was too busy looking for evil to notice incompetence. Shelgrim easily rationalizes away charges of malfeasance by blaming evils on forces rather than men, but he could not so easily dispose of charges of misfeasance or non-feasance.

Norris' naïvetè in the presence of empire builders recalls that the one striking exception to his attack upon civilization is his praise in *A Man's Woman* and "The Frontier Gone at Last" of those conquerors of the physical frontier who are now tackling the economic frontier. In "The True Reward of the Novelist," he had also observed that the "financier and poet" are alike, "so only they be big enough." He was probably dazzled enough by Huntington, who supported the *Wave,* to suppose him a truly great and good financier, just as he probably supposed himself a great and good artist.

An illustration of his susceptibility to the word-magic of the business titan occurs in *The Octopus* when Cedarquist, a prominent industrialist, after denouncing San Francisco's failure to support *his* iron works, which he calls an "indifference to *public* affairs" (my italics and shades of Charlie Wilson!), goes on:

> The great word of the nineteenth century has been Production. The great word of the twentieth century will be—listen to me, you youngsters—Markets. As a market for our Production . . . our *Wheat,* Europe is played out. . . . We supply more than Europe can eat, and down go the prices. The remedy is *not* in the curtailing of our wheat areas, but in this, we must have new markets, greater markets. . . . We must march with the course of empire, not against it. I mean, we must look to China.

What Cedarquist advocates is not spreading civilization, but simply disseminating stuff—things not ideas. He simply seeks to exert some mysterious power over others, and he is no more willing than Vanamee to accept responsibility for it. His talk of "marching with the course of empire" simply advocates doing rather than thinking—action

for its own sake, like the irresistible action of unthinking nature.

From this passage we can see how Norris can speak of nature at times as indifferent and yet at others as good. By *indifferent,* he does not mean what a non-teleological thinker would. He probably could not even conceive of the universe without "a sense of obligation" that Stephen Crane personifies in a poem. *Indifferent* to him simply means *unconscious.* Nature, he feels, does good without thinking about it—but it does do good in the long run. Indeed his opinion is that most of the trouble begins when people start thinking instead of feeling. Without thought, of course, one can have no sense of responsibility; but this did not disturb Norris, for he assumed that one who acted according to the proper "natural" feelings could do no wrong and would not need to worry about consequences.

We should not be surprised, however, that Norris does not insist that his characters be responsible for their actions, since he is irresponsible himself. His lack of responsibility, in fact, accounts for some of the most striking features of *The Octopus.* An example is a section of the novel which some critics have praised in which glimpses of Mrs. Hooven starving to death outside are alternated with glimpses of the guests of a railroad magnate gorging themselves on fancy food inside. Actually this is one of the most meretricious pieces of writing in the novel since it directly contradicts Norris' principle of writing about representative situations in order to lead to general statements about the operation of the universe. Here he uses a most extraordinary coincidence to agitate the reader's feelings. The point is not that readers should not be moved by Mrs. Hooven's sufferings and infuriated that they can occur in such a place, but that—if Norris' main point that everything works inevitably for the good is true—the sensations provoked by this incident are gratuitous. Such material has a place in the novel of social protest, but here Norris appears merely to be exploiting misery in order to display his talent. He is obliging the reader to indulge in the worst kind of sentimentality—to revel in feeling for its own sake, a kind of emotional masturbation. It is not surprising that the man capable of producing this passage completely failed to understand Harriet Beecher Stowe's motives in writing *Uncle Tom's Cabin.*

Another big scene—that in which S. Behrman, the agent of the railroad whose principle is "all that the traffic will bear," suffocates in the hold of a wheat ship—is suspect for different reasons. Com-

ing near the end of the novel, the scene at first appears a masterpiece of ironic symbolism: Behrman,
seemingly impervious to any attack by man, is
overwhelmed at last by the irresistible force of the
wheat he had hoped to exploit. The fat, rich man
is killed by the very substance that promises life to
starving Asiatics. The scene very well demonstrates
Norris' doctrine that men, "motes in the sunshine,"
might perish while the WHEAT remains (capitals
Norris').

Yet once again in creating this scene, Norris
was gambling—quite successfully—that the reader
would respond uncritically, unthinkingly. Behrman
had been depicted in such a way that the reader
would wish to see him punished for his offenses
and would view the suffocation as a punishment—
the wheat operating not as an indifferent force, but
as a *deus ex machina*. To see what is wrong with
the scene we need to remember that the incident
could have happened to anyone; there is nothing
earlier in the novel nor in the scene itself that justifies interpreting Behrman's death as retribution,
except our own feelings.

As Charles Walcutt points out in *American Literary Naturalism,* Behrman is an unsatisfactory
character anyway, since "his actions could be explained only by a deep-seated hatred which he is
not shown to harbor." In medieval literature, he
would be a stock figure—Mephistopheles, a manifestation of complete evil, immune to human attack; but in "naturalistic" fiction, he is incredible
unless the work is intended primarily as a morality play.

Perhaps, however, Norris was being truly naturalistic and emphasizing the irony of the coincidence that Behrman, invulnerable to other men,
was killed during a moment of triumph by natural
forces beyond his control. Why then have the
wheat—which in this book has been endowed with
a special symbolic significance as a *creative
force*—do the dirty work? It would be far more nat-
uralistically ironic to have this self-controlled,
scheming man inconspicuously killed in a situation
he had no part in creating—by a bullet intended for
another or a falling object. Actually Norris is trying to provide further evidence that things work inevitably, irresistibly for the good by having benevolent natural forces dispose of Behrman, but he
forces his point. Sending the forces of nature to do
a man's specific job both overly sentimentalizes nature and excuses man's irresponsibility—includ-
ingthe artist's when he falls back on gothic ma-

chinery to dispose of behavioral problems he has
raised.

Earlier in this chapter, I questioned Norris'
artistic integrity. The scenes I have just discussed
are further evidence that defending this book
against its earlier critics does not vindicate it but
simply brings to light more serious flaws. But lest
it appear that my only aim is to "debunk" *The Octopus,* I must make it clear that the novel is a magnificent imaginative achievement, one of the few
American novels to bring a significant episode
from our history to life in such a way that the reader
feels he is participating in the ponderous events.
Like *McTeague, The Octopus* compensates for its
defects with vivid reporting. When we strip away
the naïve arguments and the blatant attempts to titillate the reader's sentiment, we uncover a remarkable panorama of the life of a confused society torn between its desires, on the one hand, to
return to the irresponsible, formless life of the frontier and, on the other, to move on to a state that
might be more stable but also more chafing because
one's rights and responsibilities would be spelled
out by regulations.

Norris was consciously trying to produce an
epic. He called his work "The epic of the Wheat,"
and he twice insists on comparisons with Homer.
Despite his avowed lack of interest in style, he experimented with epic devices in this novel. The
long scene in Annixter's barn was obviously influenced by the description of revels in the Home-
ric poems, and it even pretends to poetry through
the use of refrains ("Two quarts 'n' a half. Two
quarts 'n' a half." "Garnett of the Ruby Rancho,
Keast from the ranch of the same name"), and they
are justified only as they tie together the whirl of
scenes composing this long, climactic chapter.

In a great measure, Norris himself wrote the
work that he demands in "A Neglected Epic," the
tale of the conquest of the West that would "de-
volve upon some great national event" and depict
a hero who "died in defense of an ideal, an epic
hero, a legendary figure, formidable, sad," who
"died facing down injustice, dishonesty, and crime;
died 'in his boots.'" Annixter meets the requirements—the clumsy misogynist who learns to love
first his own wife, then "others," until his love expands to embrace the whole world on the very day
that he rides to his death in defense of his homestead.

Curiously, most epics appear not at the zenith
of the societies they celebrate, but in their dying
days. Milton definitively stated a theology that was

just losing its grip on the minds and hearts of men; Dante gave final form to the neat pigeonholes of medieval cosmology just as this rigidly structured era was about to collapse into the Renaissance; and that even Homer wrote during the last days of the patriarchal society he depicts is suggested by the mildly satirical treatment of those gods who must earlier have been fervently worshipped. By the time a way of life has become clearly enough defined and seriously enough threatened to need defending, it has usually lost its impetus and is about to collapse from physical, intellectual or moral defects.

The Octopus is the epic of the conquest of the frontier by powerful, undisciplined forces. *Doing* rather than *thinking* was needed to overcome vast and often hostile geographical forces. But with the frontier gone, the kind of freedom it had permitted and even demanded for its conquest could only either disappear too, or turn upon itself self-destructively as it does in the battle between the rancher and the railroad here celebrated. Not long after the publication of *The Octopus,* both sides were to find that because they had failed to discipline themselves they were subjected to increasing external regulation, and "frontier psychology" was to become an anachronism after the last claims were staked. Some have speculated that *The Octopus* helped to bring about the regulation of the conditions it describes, but it is more likely that the regulation was already imminent, since, like many epics, the novel dealt with conditions that could not have persisted much longer.

Like *McTeague, The Octopus* is a valuable document because it expresses a philosophy that is not a lesson to its time, but a reflection of it. Norris could not achieve the detachment of a Conrad or even a Crane, because his own ideas, fears, and prejudices were too much like those of his characters. His lack of artistic integrity is not the result of hypocrisy, but of inadequate self-analysis. In his behalf it must be pleaded that he was not like the artistic prostitutes of Madison Avenue and Hollywood who cynically manipulate the public for their own temporary advantage. Rather he was like his own characters—especially Shelgrim and Magnus Derrick, the leaders of the contending parties, who were giants in their own time—whose offense was not that they deliberately did wrong but that because of adolescent self-infatuation, they failed to perceive the limitations of their own powerful gifts.

Norris did not really know how to cope with the evils of his times; he could only advise flight. Yet he enables us to see why his contemporaries could not cope with these evils. *The Octopus* is quite unintentionally a powerful tract, because the author who trusted action over thought shows us the dangers of sharing his beliefs.

Source: Warren French, "A Large Enough View," in *Frank Norris,* Twayne's United States Authors Series, Twayne, 1962.

Sources

Barry, John D., "New York Letter," in *Literary World,* March 18, 1899.

Hicks, Granville, "The Ears of Hope," in *The Great Tradition: An Interpretation of American Literature since the Civil War,* MacMillan Publishing Company, 1935, pp. 164–206.

Howells, W. D., "Frank Norris," in *North American Review,* Vol. 175, No. 6, December 1902, pp. 769–78.

Kazan, Alfred, "Progressivism: The Superman and the Muckrake," in *On Native Grounds: An Interpretation of Modern American Prose Literature,* Harcourt Brace Jovanovich, 1963, pp. 91–126.

London, Jack, "On Norris' *The Octopus,*" in *American Literary Realism 1870–1910,* Vol. 6, No. 1, Winter 1973, pp. 66–69.

Review of *McTeague* in *Outlook,* March 18, 1899.

Review of *McTeague* in *Review of Reviews,* June 1899.

For Further Study

Hochman, Barbara, *The Art of Frank Norris, Storyteller,* University of Missouri Press, 1988.
  Hochman's area of expertise is the age of American Realism: here she drives home Norris' importance to the development of American literature.

Hussman, Lawrence E., *Harbringers of a Century: The Novels of Frank Norris,* Modern American Literature series, Vol. 21, Peter Lang Publishing Company, 1999.
  This major new work examines Norris' philosophy, especially as it regards materialism, and puts his thoughts into the context of the facts of his life.

Orsi, Richard J., "*The Octopus* Reconsidered: The Southern Pacific and Agricultural Modernization in California, 1865–1915," in *California Historical Quarterly,* Vol. 54, No. 3, 1975.
  Orsi uses the perspective of time to see how the events of the novel reflected the situation in California at the turn of the century.

West, Lon, *Deconstructing Frank Norris' Fiction: The Male-Female Dialectic,* Peter Lang Publishing Co., 1998.
  West's book goes beyond the standard examinations of Norris as a Realist, to look at Jungian psychology behind the development of some of his characters. The book is based on West's Ph.D. dissertation at the University of Maryland.

The Painted Bird

Jerzy Kosinski
1965

Jerzy Kosinski's harrowing narrative, *The Painted Bird,* earned accolades from critics, yet also stirred a great deal of controversy when it was published in the United States in 1965. The novel, based on Kosinski's own experiences in Poland during World War II, centers on a young, unnamed boy's struggle to survive during the war by hiding in several remote villages in an Eastern European country. His parents had sent him to live with a foster mother while they hid from the Nazis, but when the foster mother dies, the boy is forced to wander alone from village to village. Due to his dark eyes and complexion, the villagers suspect he is a Jew or a gypsy and so continually torment him.

While some critics have found the novel's violence excessive, most applaud its realistic depiction of the horrors of World War II. Andrew Field in *Book Week* defends the novel, admitting:

> So awful . . . is this book that I can scarcely 'recommend' it to anyone, and yet, because there is enlightenment to be gained from its flame-dark pages, it deserves as wide a readership as possible.

Kosinski suffered years of torment after the novel's publication. The book was banned in Poland, his homeland, and he and his family suffered continual verbal and physical attacks by Eastern Europeans who considered the book slanderous to their culture. The novel endures, however, because of its powerful statement on the nature of cruelty and survival. In the Afterward of the second edition of *The Painted Bird,* Kosinski notes the impetus for the novel and for much of his writing:

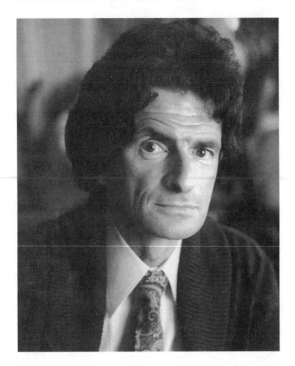

Jerzy Kosinksi

when his parents described their experiences during the war and their witnessing of "young children being herded into the trains," he writes, "it was therefore very much for their sakes and for people like them that I wanted to write fiction which would reflect, and perhaps exorcise the horrors that they had found so inexpressible."

Author Biography

When referring to his novel *The Painted Bird* in an "Afterword" published in its second edition, Jerzy Kosinski insists that he "remained determined that the novel's life be independent of mine." Yet scholars note that Kosinski's life closely echoed that of the unnamed boy in his first novel. Kosinski was born on June 14, 1933, in Lodz, Poland. His father, a scholar of the classics, and mother, a concert pianist, provided him with a sheltered childhood until Nazi Germany invaded Poland at the outbreak of World War II, when Jerzy was six years old. In an effort to save his life, his parents sent him to live with a foster mother while they went into hiding. After his foster mother's death a few months later, Jerzy was forced to find shelter and food in various peasant villages in Poland until he was re-

united with his parents at the end of the war. The traumatic events he suffered through during this period caused him to become mute when he was nine. In an interview with Barbara Leaming for *Penthouse,* Kosinski commented, "Once I regained my speech after the war, the trauma began. The Stalinist [system in Poland] went after me, asking questions I didn't want to hear, demanding answers I would not give."

Kosinski studied sociology and political science at the University of Lodz and earned a bachelor's degree in 1950. He also earned two master's degrees there, one in history in 1953 and the other in political science in 1955. While studying for his Ph.D. in sociology at the Polish Academy of Sciences, he and his family tried to gain permission to immigrate to the United States, but they were denied. Soon after, Kosinski created an elaborate plot to gain his freedom from his Communist-controlled homeland. He invented four scholars who he claimed were sponsoring research that needed to be completed in the United States. As a result, more than two years later, in 1957, he arrived in New York City—without finances or connections.

He soon learned English and continued his graduate studies at Columbia University. In his first book, *The Future Is Ours, Comrade: Conversations with the Russians,* a collection of essays written under the pseudonym Joseph Novak, Kosinski outlines the injustices of the Communist system. The work became an immediate bestseller. In 1965, he became a naturalized citizen, the same year his first novel, *The Painted Bird* was published, and it gained him more notoriety. Other successful novels followed, including *Steps,* which won the National Book Award in 1969 and *Being There,* which was made into a critically acclaimed film in 1979—earning him an Academy Award for best screenplay. Kosinski is also noted for his photography, which he exhibited throughout the world, and for his portrayal of Grigory Zinoviev in the 1981 film, *Reds.* On May 3, 1991, while suffering from severe heart disease and depression, Kosinski committed suicide in New York City.

Plot Summary

Part One

The Painted Bird starts in a large Eastern European city, in the fall of 1939. A six-year-old Jewish boy is sent by his parents to live in a village, while the parents go into hiding. World War II has just begun and Jews in German-occupied countries are being executed or sent to concentration camps. Within two months, Marta, the woman who is taking care of the boy, dies, leaving him alone to fend for himself. He is soon taken in by a farmer, who beats him. One day, an elderly woman called Olga the Wise One buys him and takes him to her hut. She teaches him valuable survival skills, including how to build and use a "comet," a can filled with slow burning materials that provide a constant heat source. She is the first one to tell him an evil spirit possesses him. Others in the village fear him because of his dark hair and eyes and so often set their dogs on him. One day, one of the villagers throws him into the river and he drifts miles away from Olga and the village.

He survives, due to the skills Olga has taught him, and comes to another village. A miller, nicknamed Jealous, who often quarrels with his wife and "mercilessly" beats her for her suspected infidelities, takes the boy in. One evening at dinner, the miller, his wife, and his plowboy watch two cats mating. When the miller asks the plowboy if he lusts after his wife, the plowboy does not answer. The miller gouges out the plowboy's eyes, and the stunned boy runs away. Lekh, a young man who sells birds in neighboring villages, takes the boy in. Lekh is in love with Stupid Ludmila, a wild, lustful woman who often seduces the village men. One day, a mob of village women savagely beat Ludmila and she dies. The boy finds Lekh inconsolable and leaves.

The boy then lives with a carpenter and his wife, who are convinced that his black hair will attract lightning to their farm. As a result, during thunderstorms, the carpenter takes the boy out to the middle of a field, away from his home. The boy comes to believe he has this power when, during one storm, he stays in the barn and sees it catch on fire after being struck by lightning. When the carpenter catches him, the boy pleads for his life and lures the carpenter to an old, abandoned military bunker, which is full of ravenous rats. After the carpenter accidentally falls in, he is ravaged by the frenzied rats.

Part Two

The boy moves to a village that is regularly occupied by German soldiers—who take the villagers' food and materials needed for their army. He lives with a well-respected blacksmith and his family, who treat him relatively well. Sometimes partisans come to the village and the house demanding assistance. One night, some partisans accuse the blacksmith of helping "enemies of the Fatherland" and beat the family. The partisans find the boy and turn him over to soldiers at a German outpost. One soldier is ordered to lead the boy off and kill him, but the soldier allows the boy to escape into the forest.

The boy then moves in with a farmer in another village, where he sees trains full of Jews and Gypsies headed toward concentration camps. The peasants tell him that the Germans' extermination of the Jews is God's punishment for the crucifixion of Christ. The boy wonders "whether so many Jews were necessary to compensate God for the killing of His son" and worries whether God will punish him, too. He decides that fair-haired, blue-eyed people are God's favorites and tries to think of ways people could change their looks so they could avoid the ovens.

One day, Germans capture the boy and a Jew who has also been hiding in the village, and transport them to a nearby police station. As they travel, groups of peasants beat them. A priest intervenes, but the Jew is killed. The boy is enthralled with a German officer's clean, hard appearance and becomes ashamed of his own by comparison. The boy declares, "I had nothing against his killing me." The soldier, however, hands the boy over to the priest, who finds a farmer named Garbos in the nearby village to take him in.

Garbos has a "dead, unsmiling face," and often beats the boy for no reason or sets his vicious dog on him. When the priest notices the boy's bruises and welts, he tells Garbos to bring the boy to the church. There, the boy begins preparations to become an altar boy and learns the rituals and beliefs of the Catholic Church. He decides that prayers will save him from harm, but Garbos finds new ways to torture him. While serving as an altar boy at a church feast, the boy accidentally drops the missal during an important moment in the service. Angry peasants throw him into a large manure pit, insisting the boy is a Gypsy vampire who will bring evil to the village. When the boy emerges, he discovers that he has become mute.

Later, the head of the village gives the boy to a farmer, Makar, who has been shunned by the village. The farmer lives with his son and daughter on the outskirts of town. Ewka, the nineteen-year-old daughter, teaches the boy how to sexually please her. When the boy botches the killing of a rabbit, Makar kicks him so hard in the stomach that he is immobilized for several weeks. One night he sees Ewka have sex with a goat under the direction of her father, and determines that the family "is in league with the Devil." Later, he decides that he will call on powerful evil spirits to help him survive. When he sees Ewka having sex with her brother, the boy leaves.

Part Three

In another village, Labina, a woman who works as a domestic to some of the richer peasants, takes him in. He feels safe with her, although he is disgusted by her sexual activities with the men in the village. As the Germans begin to lose the war, the front comes close. Soon Kalmuks, Soviet deserters who had fought with the Germans, invade the village, raping and murdering the inhabitants. The boy decides that God has not helped him because he is of the same tribe as the savage, black-haired and black-eyed Kalmuks. Soon, the Red Army saves the village.

The boy stays with the Red Army regiment that encamps near the village. The soldiers provide him with a safe, "calm and well-ordered" life. One of the soldiers, Gavrila, teaches him to read and explains the role of the Communist Party. Another soldier, Mitka, introduces the boy to poetry and sings songs to him. Through their influence, the boy accepts the Party's doctrine and determines to live as a communist. When drunken villagers kill some of Mitka's friends, Mitka takes revenge by perching in a tree and randomly shooting several villagers. The boy decides that revenge is a responsibility one must take.

When the war ends, the soldiers send the boy to an orphanage to await a reunion with his parents. There the boy pretends to be Russian and refuses to learn reading and writing in his own language. He makes a friend there, called "the Silent One," who is also mute. One day, the two visit a marketplace where the boy accidentally knocks down a table with produce on it. The farmer who owned the produce beats the boy savagely. In retaliation, the Silent One reroutes a train he thinks the farmer is travelling on, which causes the death of several people. Both the Silent One and the boy are devastated when they discover that the farmer was not on the train.

The boy's parents eventually find him at the orphanage and take him home. He, however, feels "smothered by their love and protection" and resents having to give up his freedom. His parents have adopted a war orphan who becomes "a nuisance" to him. One day, the little boy annoys him so much that the boy squeezes the orphan's arm

until it breaks. Feeling restless, the boy falls in with people who roam the streets at night, gambling, drinking, and having sex.

Doctors advise his parents to send the boy to the mountains for his health, and he moves in with an old ski instructor. One day while skiing, the boy falls and is sent to the hospital. When he answers the phone he thinks, "somewhere at the other end of the wire there was someone who wanted to talk with me . . . I felt an overpowering desire to speak." The novel ends as he regains his speech.

Characters

Anton

Villagers call Makar's twenty-year-old son, Anton, "Quail," "because he was like that bird in his habit of speaking only to himself and never answering other voices." The villagers shun him as much as they do his father.

A Blacksmith

The boy lives with a well-respected blacksmith and his family, who treat him relatively well. The boy admits, "the blacksmith liked to slap my face when he was tipsy and I got in his way, but there were no other consequences." One day, partisans come to the house and beat the blacksmith and his family unmercifully, then turn the boy over to German soldiers.

A Boy

The narrator and central character is a six-year-old Jewish boy at the beginning of the novel. He chronicles his life for the next six years as he struggles to survive on his own during the harrowing years of World War II. When he first arrives at a remote village, an elderly woman named Marta cares for him. He desperately misses his parents and continually wonders when they will come for him. After she dies and he is left alone to fend for himself, his fears are compounded. At this point he has no survival skills and so must depend on other villagers to keep him alive.

The boy quickly learns valuable survival lessons from Olga the Wise, a woman he lives with for a time, proving himself to be quick-witted and resourceful. He applies these skills throughout his frequently traumatic experiences with various villagers. Through these experiences, he also learns to adapt himself to any situation or to flee to survive. Norman Lavers, in his article on Kosinski for

Twayne's United States Authors Series Online, comments on the boy's "extraordinary ability to survive, noting,

> although he experiences some very low ebbs, he never curses the world itself or finds it unfair or unjust to him. He accepts it on its own terms, and continually tries to learn its rules, its central principles, so that he can function effectively in it. The key to his psychic health is his acceptance: his assumption of the normality of his situation.

Yet the atrocities that he witnesses and endures eventually become too much for him to bear and he is struck mute.

When others persecute him for his appearance, he gains a sense of inferiority that is only alleviated when the Russian soldiers take him in. Lavers concludes, "the boy is immediately, visibly different, arousing suspicion and fear. The lesson of being the odd man out, of the danger of being noticeable, is brought home to him over and over again." His initial feelings of inferiority make him a prime candidate for the indoctrination into the Communist Party, as directed by his Russian friends.

By the end of the novel, the boy has lost his innocence.

A Carpenter

A superstitious carpenter and his wife, who take the boy in, are convinced that his black hair will attract lightning to their farm. In an effort to avoid this, the carpenter leaves the boy shaking in fear in the middle of a field during thunderstorms. During one storm, the boy stays in the barn and it is struck by lightning. After the barn burns down, the carpenter beats him savagely and prepares to drown him. The boy, however, pleads for his life and lures the carpenter to an old, abandoned military bunker, which is full of ravenous rats. After the carpenter accidentally falls in, he is eaten by the frenzied rats.

The Cuckoo
See Mitka

Ewka

Makar's nineteen-year-old daughter, Ewka, avoids her father and brother, fearing they will force her to spend the afternoon with them in the goats' stable, where she hints that they enjoy themselves sexually. The villagers shun her because they think that she has evil powers. Ewka teaches the boy how to sexually please her, and they often en-

gage in sexual activities. Enjoying the physical contact with her, the boy says,

> there was nothing I would not do for her. I forgot my fate of a Gypsy mute destined for fire. I ceased to be a goblin jeered at by herders, casting spells on children and animals. In my dreams I turned into a tall, handsome man, fair-skinned, blue-eyed, with hair like pale autumn leaves. I became a German officer in a tight, black uniform. Or I turned into a bird-catcher, familiar with all the secret paths of the woods and marshes.

When the boy sees her mating with a goat and engaging in sexual activities with her father and brother, he leaves. Later, he bitterly recalls how gentle and loving he had been with Ewka, and that she had preferred "a stinking hairy goat" to him.

Garbos

Garbos is one of the cruelest men the boy lives with. He has a "dead, unsmiling face," and often beats the boy unmercifully for no reason or sets his dog on him. Garbos often taunts the boy by letting his snarling dog come within inches of him. At these times, the boy admits, "my terror was such that it nearly transported me to the other world." He often tortures the boy by screaming him awake or by throwing the dog on top of him as he sleeps, so that soon he would get no rest. He also hangs the boy by his arms from the ceiling, which causes him excruciating pain. The boy suggests that Garbos's extreme cruelty stems from his bitterness over the death of his son.

Gavrila

Gavrila is a political officer from the Red Army regiment that encamps near the boy's village. After the regiment arrives, the boy stays with them and is cared for by Gavrila and his fellow officer Mitka, who provide him with a safe, "calm and well-ordered" life. Gavrila spends long hours with the boy, teaching him to read and explaining the role of the Communist Party. Gavrila is a loyal member of the Party, and so tries to teach the boy Communist politics.

The boy adopts Gavrila's atheism when he accepts the soldier's theory that "the order of the world had nothing to do with God, and that God had nothing to do with the world" because "God did not exist. The cunning priests had invented Him so they could trick stupid, superstitious people." Gavrila plainly feels superior to the peasants that the boy has lived with. He convinces the boy that

> "there was no God . . . no devils, ghosts, or ghouls rising from graves. . . . These were all tales for ig-

norant people who did not understand the natural order of the world, did not believe in their own powers, and therefore had to take refuge in their belief in some God.

Gavrila tells the boy that "people themselves determined the course of their lives and were the only masters of their destinies." He plays on the boy's feelings of inferiority when he insists that under Stalin's leadership, "the Red Army was bringing to the liberated peoples a new way of life, which made all equal." There would be no rich and poor, no exploiters and no exploited, no persecution of the dark by the fair, no people doomed to gas chambers. When Gavrila shows him a picture of Stalin, the boy admits "he looked more of a Gypsy than I did." Ultimately, the boy concludes,

> Gavrila's lessons filled me with a new confidence. In this world there were realistic ways of promoting goodness, and there were people who had dedicated their whole lives to it. These were the Communist Party members.

Gavrila's influence has become so strong on the boy that he determines to find a way to continue living with him. After he goes to the orphanage, the boy wears a Soviet uniform that had been made for him and, under Gavrila's direction, reads the Soviet newspaper, *Pravda,* on a daily basis. He also pretends to be Russian and refuses to learn reading and writing in his mother tongue.

A German Officer

The boy catches his first glimpse of a German officer when he is captured by soldiers and brought to a nearby police station. This officer comes to represent all Germans to him and a standard against which he measures everyone else, including himself.

The Handsome One

See Laba

Jealous

Jealous is the nickname of a quiet miller the boy comes to live with. The miller often quarrels with his wife and "mercilessly" beats her for her suspected infidelities. He gouges out a plowboy's eyes when he assumes the boy lusts after his wife.

Laba

Labina tells the boy about her husband, Laba, the handsomest man in Labina's village. He was also, however, the poorest. Labina ruined her health and her looks when, after marrying Laba, she was forced to do a great deal of physical work. One day,

Laba left and did not return for more than a year. When he finally came back to the village, he brought with him beautiful clothes that impressed everyone. His dazzling dress greatly improved his stature in the community, and all the important people of the village vied for his attention. When his clothes were stolen, he hung himself, realizing he would no longer be highly regarded in the village.

Labina

A peasant woman who takes the boy in, Labina works as a domestic to some of the richer peasants. The boy feels safe with her although he is bothered by her frequent sexual contact with men from the village. When she engages in sexual activities with these men, the boy looks on with "disappointment and disgust at the two intertwined, twitching human frames" and decides, "so that's what love was: savage as a bull prodded with a spike." Labina had been beautiful, but she married a handsome, poor man, Laba, and so was forced to work constantly to support them.

Lekh

Lekh, who raises and sells birds, takes the boy in and teaches him about different species of birds. Lekh also teaches him about cruelty when he takes out his frustrations on the birds. When Stupid Ludmila, the woman he loves, does not come to him for a long time, he becomes "possessed by a silent rage." He then tortures one bird at a time by painting it bright colors and then returning it to the flock. The other birds reject the brightly colored one and attack it until it dies.

Makar

The boy lives for a time with a man named Makar and his son and daughter. Makar raises rabbits and goats and is treated as a stranger in the village since he has been there only a few years. The boy hears rumors about him having sexual relations with his son and daughter, which prove to be true. When the boy botches the killing of a rabbit, Makar kicks him so hard in the stomach that the boy is immobilized for several weeks.

Marta

The boy's parents send him to live with Marta when they go into hiding. Marta is a sick, elderly, peasant woman with a foul-smelling body due to infrequent washing. She, like the other villagers, is very superstitious, claiming that "evil forces nested [in the braids in her hair] twisting them and slowly inducing senility." She is the first to explain to him that his black eyes are Gypsy or witches' eyes and could, when looked at directly, cause crippling illness, plague, or death. When she dies of heart failure, the boy accidentally lights her on fire and burns down the cottage.

Mitka

Mitka is a sharpshooting instructor and a crack sniper from the Red Army regiment that encamps near the boy's village. He, along with his friend Gavrila, takes care of the boy and influences his views on life. Mitka introduces him to poetry and often entertains him by singing songs. The boy notes that Mitka is "one of the best liked and respected men in the regiment" and that he has "a fine military record." He considers Mitka to be a man "who worked for a better and safer world, not by praying at church altars, but by excelling in his aim." Mitka teaches him this doctrine as he takes revenge on the village after some men kill his friends. The boy watches while Mitka climbs a tree and randomly picks off several villagers and shoots them.

As a result, the boy decides that revenge is a responsibility one must take to regain the natural order and for personal satisfaction. He concludes that Mitka

> "had meted out revenge for the death of his friends, regardless of the opinions of others, risking his position in the regiment. . . . If he could not revenge his friends, what was the use of all those days of training in the sniper's art . . . of what value was the rank of Hero, respected and worshiped by tens of millions of citizens, if he no longer deserved it in his own eyes?"

From that point, the boy determines to live by Mitka's words and adopt his ruthlessness.

Olga the Wise One

Olga is a well-respected, elderly woman in the second village the boy comes to. She buys the boy from a farmer who had taken him in, and she teaches the boy how to survive on his own. She administers to the sick in the village with her homemade remedies. The boy greatly admires her for her talents.

Quail

See Anton

The Silent One

The Silent One is a young boy who has chosen to be mute and who befriends the boy at the orphanage. The Silent One tries to take revenge on the farmer who beat the boy, but he kills several innocent people instead, an act that devastates both him and the boy.

Stupid Ludmila

Stupid Ludmila is a woman who lives on her own in the forest outside of one of the villages and who lures men into sexual encounters. As a result, women often set dogs on her. When she was young, she refused to marry a man her parents had chosen for her. Infuriated, he enticed her outside the village where an entire herd of drunken peasants raped her until she lost consciousness. As a result, her mind became "addled." She is eventually killed by a mob of jealous women.

Themes

Coming of Age

The main focus of this semi-autobiographical novel is the tracing of the main character's coming of age in an Eastern European country during World War II. After the war begins and he is separated from his parents, he spends the remainder of the book trying to survive the brutal conditions he faces in various villages in which he lives. During this journey, he learns important lessons about himself and human nature in general.

Change and Transformation

As Kosinski unfolds this coming-of-age process, he reveals the changes and transformations the boy experiences. The biggest change occurs when the boy is wrenched from his parents and his comfortable life in a large city before the war and forced to live, as do many of the villagers, with deprivation and the constant threat of death. The boy also experiences internal transformations as he discovers necessary survival skills.

Alienation and Loneliness

One thing the boy learns to cope with is the alienation and loneliness that result when he is separated from his parents. He bonds to some degree with Marta, the first woman he stays with, but she soon dies, leaving him alone again. After that, the boy can only occasionally find a comforting relationship in his chaotic and dangerous world. Most of the comfort he finds is through women, but that comfort is always short-lived, as some outside force disrupts it. Olga the Wise teaches him valuable survival skills, including how to build and use a comet.

Topics for Further Study

- One of the charges against the book is that it presents Polish peasants as barbarians. Research the culture of Polish villages during the war years and compare your findings to descriptions of peasant life in the novel.

- Study the psychological effects of war trauma on children and compare your findings to the behavior of the main character.

- Investigate the efforts to reunite children separated from their parents during the war years. How successful were these efforts?

- Write a poem that expresses what it feels like to be an outcast.

The boy soon becomes separated from her, however, and again must find new shelter. Ewka provides him with physical comfort and introduces him to the mysteries of sexual love, but his time with her is cut short by her sexually deviant father, who forces Ewka to have sex with animals and with her brother. The Russian soldiers who take the boy in provide the most prolonged respite from his feelings of loneliness and alienation. He finds himself becoming part of a group and so begins to establish a sense of self.

In "Jerzy Kosinski's East European Self," Thomas S. Gladsky argues that the novel indicts Poland "for its part in the Holocaust" through the boy's lack of connection to his homeland. Gladsky comments, "So alienated is Kosinski's young narrator that he will not identify his own cultural-religious background, refer to his ethnic traditions, or even mention the name of the country despite the obvious Polish setting."

Strength and Weakness

The boy's ability to cope with his harsh surroundings reveals his strength of character and the nature of human adaptability. To survive, he learns how to fend for himself in his harrowing environment and to win over the villagers. When he can-

not turn a villager into an ally, he learns to avoid him or her. Cameron Northouse, in his article on Kosinski for the *Dictionary of Literary Biography,* notes that the boy also learns that "merely to react to the world is to be at its mercy," and that "the only important service is the service of survival."

Norman Lavers, in his article on Kosinski for *Twayne's United States Authors Series Online* concurs with this point, insisting that the boy survives by his wits rather than relying on "pure chance" to save him. He also adds that when the boy finds himself "in a situation of unremitting violence and deprivation," his strength and his need to carry on saves him. Lavers notes that the boy never allows himself to wallow in self-pity. He instead tries to adapt to his world and "continually tries to learn its rules, its central principles, so that he can function effectively in it."

One example of the boy's adaptability occurs when he is traveling to another village in order to find shelter and food. At one point he comes across a wounded horse and decides to bring him back to his owner, hoping to be rewarded with food or shelter for returning the man's property. When the owner decides the horse is no longer any use to him, the boy is able to shift gears and to convince the man that he is not Jewish or a Gypsy and is an "obedient worker," and so he is given a place to stay.

Violence and Cruelty

Through his experiences, the boy learns about the capacity for violence and cruelty in others as well as himself. He observes and endures constant brutality and horror as he struggles to survive. In his search for some measure of control over his life in this atmosphere, he discovers his own ability for cruelty. He comes to the realization that to survive in his harsh environment, he must become as vulgar as the others in his world. Paul R. Lilly, Jr., in his article for *The Literary Review,* notes that like most of Kosinski's characters, the boy's natural impulse is:

> to transform [himself] from victim to oppressor. . . .
> In the world of Kosinski, there are no other options open to the victim: he must seize power through deception or remain powerless.

The boy has transformed himself by the end of the novel into the oppressor as evidenced when he breaks his stepbrother's arm.

Style

Point of View

The main character narrates *The Painted Bird* from his point of view, which enables readers to more fully gain insight into the devastating consequences his nightmarish experiences have on him. The structure of the work creates a "Bildungsroman," which is a novel that focuses on the development of a young person, often symbolized as a movement from innocence to experience. Through the episodic structure of *The Painted Bird*, Kosinski plots the boy's development from a young, naïve, essentially helpless young boy to a mature, capable teenager who can survive on his own—and who has been forced to see the dark side of human nature within others as well as within himself.

Symbol

The title *The Painted Bird* refers to a ritual practiced by Lekh, one of the villagers with whom the boy lives for a time. When Stupid Ludmila, the woman Lekh loves, does not come to him for several weeks, he becomes "possessed by a silent rage." He then tortures one bird at a time by painting it bright colors and returning it to the flock. The other birds reject the brightly colored one and attack it until it dies. This cruel game provides the novel's dominant metaphor in its relationship to the boy's tormenting experiences during World War II. Like the painted bird, the boy is considered different when he is thrown in with his fellow human beings. Since he has dark eyes, complexion, and hair, the villagers, typically blue-eyed blondes, consider him an outsider. Their superstitious nature compounds their stereotype of the boy because they regard him as either a Jew or a gypsy with "evil powers."

The villagers treat the boy with the same cruelty as the flock that persecutes the bird. Because the villagers perceive him as different, they feel justified in harassing and ostracizing him. Some of the more cruel villagers consider it their right to beat and torture him.

Norman Lavers, in his article on Kosinski, argues that the boy's comet, a can filled with slow burning materials that provide a constant heat source, becomes a symbol of his developing strength and independence. Lavers writes that the comet is:

> a manifestation of the inner spark. It is the outward glow of the boy's determination to survive. But it is still more, it is his apartness itself, his individuality, that which is essential to survival 'without human help.' It is his essential aloneness, which is his independence and freedom. . . . With the comet to fend off the dark, the animals, the other humans, he 'felt perfectly safe.'

Historical Context

World War II

The world experienced a decade of aggression in the 1930s that culminated in World War II. This Second World War resulted from the rise of totalitarian regimes in Germany, Italy, and Japan. These militaristic regimes gained control as a result of the Great Depression experienced by most of the world in the early 1930s and from the conditions created by the peace settlements following World War I. The dictatorships established in each country encouraged expansion into neighboring countries. In Germany, Hitler strengthened the army during the 1930s. In 1936, Benito Mussolini's Italian troops took Ethiopia. From 1936 to 1939, Spain was engaged in civil war involving Francisco Franco's fascist army, aided by Germany and Italy. In March of 1938, Germany annexed Austria, and in March of 1939, occupied Czechoslovakia. Italy took Albania in April of that same year. On September 1, 1939, one week after Nazi Germany and the USSR signed the Treaty of Nonaggression, Germany invaded Poland and World War II began.

The Polish people suffered greatly during the war. A large part of the population of Poland was massacred or starved or placed in concentration camps. Polish Jews were almost eliminated from the country. Before the war there were more than 3 million Jews; after the war, there were only about one hundred thousand left.

German troops completed their withdrawal from Poland in early 1945. The socialization of Poland would soon begin. In 1947, Boleslaw Beirut, a Communist Pole and citizen of the USSR, was elected president by the Polish parliament. Soviet Marshall Konstantin Rokossovsky became minister of defense and commander in chief of the Polish army. In 1952, the constitution made Poland a model Soviet republic with an identical foreign policy to that of the USSR. The government cut off relations with the Vatican and religious leaders became chief targets of persecution.

The Holocaust

The Holocaust is the period during World War II when European Jews were persecuted and ex-

Compare
&
Contrast

- **1926:** Joseph Stalin becomes dictator of the Soviet Union. His reign of terror lasts for close to three decades.

- **1991:** On December 17, President Mikhail Gorbachev orders the dissolution of the Soviet Union, and a new Commonwealth of Independent States is formed by the countries that formerly made up the USSR.

- **1939:** Germany invades Poland and World War II begins.

1947: The socialization of Poland begins with the election of Boleslaw Beirut, a Communist Pole and citizen of the USSR.

1989: Lech Walesa is one of the architects of Solidarity, the first independent trade union in a Communist country. After months of labor unrest that threaten the stabilization of Poland's economy, the Polish government does not block the creation of Solidarity.

terminated by Nazi Germany. The impetus for this persecution came before the war, in the early 1930s, when Adolf Hitler came into power in Germany. In the years before the war, many European Jews immigrated to other countries in an effort to save themselves. After the war started, however, those who did not escape were sent to concentration camps. The persecution stemmed from Hitler's determination to exterminate Jews in every country invaded by Germany during the war years. Six million Jews were killed during the Holocaust.

The Cold War

Soon after World War II, when Russian leader Joseph Stalin set up satellite communist states in Eastern Europe and Asia, the "cold war" began, ushering in a new age of warfare and fear triggered by several circumstances: the United States' and the USSR's emergence as superpowers; each country's ability to use the atomic bomb; and communist expansion and the United States' determination to check it. Each side amassed stockpiles of nuclear weapons that could not only annihilate each country, but also the world. Both sides declared the other the enemy and redoubled their commitment to fight for their own ideology and political and economic dominance. As China fell to the Communists in 1949, Russia crushed the Hungarian revolution in 1956, and the United States adopted

the role of world policeman, the cold war accelerated.

The Cold War induced anxiety among Americans, who feared both annihilation by Russians and the spread of communism at home. Americans were encouraged to stereotype all Russians as barbarians and atheists who were plotting to overthrow the United States government and brainwash its citizens. The fear that communism would spread to the United States led to suspicion and paranoia, and the lives of many suspected communists or communist sympathizers were ruined. This "Red Scare" was heightened by the indictment of ex-government official Alger Hiss and Julius and Ethel Rosenberg for passing defense secrets to the Russians. Soon, the country engaged in a determined and often hysterical witch-hunt for communists, led by Senator Joe McCarthy and the House of Representatives' Un-American Activities Committee (HUAC). (In 1954, McCarthy was censured by the Senate for his unethical behavior during the Committee sessions.) By the time of McCarthy's death in 1957, almost six million Americans had been investigated by government agencies because of their suspected communist sympathies, yet only a few had been indicted.

This paranoid atmosphere provided Americans with an impetus for conformity. Many felt safety could be ensured only by submitting to the traditional values of church, home, and country. Yet, during this time, voices of protest began to emerge. Some refused to succumb to the anti-communist fervor and thus would not cooperate with the Senate hearings despite the threat of prison or exile from the United States. Others rebelled against a system that they thought encouraged discrimination and social and economic inequality.

Critical Overview

The critical response to the publication in 1965 of Jerzy Kosinski's *The Painted Bird* has been overwhelmingly positive but at the same time, extremely volatile. Many critics favorably compare the harrowing intensity of this novel to works by Franz Kafka and Albert Camus. Parallels are also made to *The Diary of Anne Frank.* Yet, the novel's graphic violence and bleak vision of humanity disturb some readers. The most vocal criticism came from Eastern Europe, where the book was banned for several years.

Oleg Ivsky applauded the novel in the *Library Journal,* commenting, "No matter how exaggerated and tendentious the horrors may seem in retrospect (especially cumulatively)—they all ring true. The simple, direct prose is as timeless as folklore." Ivsky "highly recommends" the novel for "discriminating readers with cast-iron stomachs." Andrew Field in *Book Week* echoes Ivsky's assessment when he writes, "So awful . . . is this book that I can scarcely 'recommend' it to anyone, and yet, because there is enlightenment to be gained from its flame-dark pages, it deserves as wide a readership as possible." Field also praises the novel's style, even though he finds "isolated incidents in the book that are rather strained and archly described," citing the motif of the painted bird, which he claims appears too often. He comments that "the overall performance is marked by a sureness of emphasis and tone of voice that has high literary merit."

Critics like Irving Howe in *Harper's,* wrote that "finally one wonders whether there is in this book a numbing surplus of brutality." Kosinski responded to the attention over the book's violence in his Afterward to the second edition:

Whether the reviews praised or damned the novel, Western criticism of *The Painted Bird* always contained an undertone of uneasiness. Most American and British critics objected to my descriptions of the boy's experiences on the grounds that they dwelt too deeply on cruelty. Many tended to dismiss the author

as well as the novel, claiming that I had exploited the horrors of war to satisfy my own peculiar imagination. . . . In point of fact, almost none of those who chose to view the book as a historical novel bothered to refer to actual source materials. Personal accounts of survivors and official War documents were either unknown by or irrelevant to my critics.

Anne Halley, in her review for the *Nation,* praises the novel's themes. She writes:

[This] survivor's story . . . belongs to that 20th-century genre which teaches us that . . . human life, the cheapest thing there is, can be maintained and has been for centuries in the midst of chaos, brutality, organized and disorganized ill will. . . . The various episodes, no doubt based on experience, seem to embody and play on recognizable folk-tale motifs, always with that 'realistic' twist, or reversal, which shows that there is neither justice, nor reason, nor black or white magic to help one in extremity.

Kosinski suffered years of torment after the novel's publication. In an article for *The American Spectator,* John Corry notes that the novel was "the making of Jerzy Kosinski, just as it was his undoing." Corry explains that after the novel came out:

Warsaw had set out to hurt him. He was not an ordinary anti-Communist émigré Pole; he was a celebrated anti-Communist Pole, and so he had to be discredited. *The Painted Bird,* the propagandists said, slandered Poland. In fact, it did not, but since the novel was banned, who in Poland would know?

In his "Afterward," Kosinski describes how the Polish government responded to *The Painted Bird.* Poland's state-controlled publications insisted that he had agreed to write the novel "for covert political purposes" as sanctioned by governmental authorities in America. Other Poles accused the book of being "a libelous documentary of life in identifiable communities during the Second World War." Some critics attacked him "for distorting native lore, for defaming the peasant character, and for reinforcing the propaganda weapons of the region's enemies." Kosinski was also criticized by anti-Communists, who claimed that he portrayed the Soviet soldiers in a positive light in order to justify Soviet influence in Eastern Europe.

The campaign to destroy Kosinski's name continued as accusations surfaced that he had employed ghostwriters; wrote the book for the CIA; and was part of a Zionist conspiracy. Cameron Northouse, in his article on Kosinski for the *Dictionary of Literary Biography,* explains,

since the book was completely distorted in the Communist press to depict it as an anti-Polish document that slandered the people of Kosinski's homeland, the local citizenry was aroused to violence. At one point, Kosinski's mother was defamed in the newspapers as

Polish prisoners at a Nazi concentration camp

the 'mother of a renegade' and crowds were incited to attack her house.

Kosinski also suffered physical and verbal attacks, as he notes in his "Afterward":

> On several occasions I was accosted outside my apartment house or in my garage. Three or four times strangers recognized me on the street and offered hostile or insulting remarks. At a concert honoring a pianist born in my homeland, a covey of patriotic old ladies attacked me with their umbrellas, while screeching absurdly dated invectives.

Despite the controversy surrounding its publication, most scholars consider *The Painted Bird* to be one of the best works to emerge from World War II.

Criticism

Wendy Perkins

Perkins is an associate professor of English at Prince George's Community College in Maryland and has published several articles on British and American authors. In the following essay, she examines the theme of survival in Kosinski's novel.

In *The Painted Bird* Jerzy Kosinski creates a dominant metaphor that reflects an unnamed young boy's harrowing experiences in an Eastern European country during World War II. Norman Lavers in an article on Jerzy Kosinski notes that when the boy's parents send him to live in a remote village while they go into hiding, his dark hair, eyes, and complexion make him "immediately, visibly different, arousing suspicion and fear. The lesson of being the odd man out, of the danger of being noticeable, is brought home to him over and over again." Kosinski symbolizes this lesson in one of the novel's episodes when the boy observes a cruel ritual practiced by Lekh, one of the villagers who takes him in. Lekh chooses the strongest bird from those that he raises and paints it with bright colors. When he sees a flock of birds in the sky, he releases his painted bird, which soars "happy and free, a spot of rainbow against the backdrop of clouds." When the bird joins the flock, the other birds, "dazzled by its brilliant colors," kill it.

Like the painted bird, the boy is considered unusual when he is thrown in with his fellow human beings, and so they harass and often attack him. Yet, unlike the bird, the boy learns to survive his harsh world through his remarkable ability to adapt to his surroundings.

Cameron Northouse, in his article on Kosinski for the *Dictionary of Literary Biography,* argues that the boy becomes a survivor "who has been altered by his experience, who has learned that to merely react to the world is to be at its mercy." The boy's ability to adapt to his environment by altering his personal philosophies becomes the key to his survival.

Reflecting on the boy's survival skills in *Twayne's United States Authors Series Online,* Norman Lavers concludes that even while confronted with continuous experiences of "unremitting violence and deprivation," the boy's instinct for survival becomes paramount. Lavers notes that the boy never becomes consumed with self-pity; instead he accepts his position in his world and "continually tries to learn its rules, its central principles, so that he can function effectively in it."

The first adaptation the boy makes is his acceptance of his otherness. Olga the Wise One, a kind, elderly woman who takes him in and teaches him crucial survival skills, informs him that an evil spirit possesses him. He soon notes that other villagers also believe this to be true, and as a result, they ostracize and torment him. Eventually, the boy comes to accept his uniqueness, acknowledging that he must be "possessed by an evil spirit," that crouched in him "like a mole in a deep burrow."

The boy quickly adapts to his new vision of himself and uses it to his advantage. He reasons that since an evil spirit possesses him, and others could recognize this fact by looking into his "bewitched black eyes," he could gain a certain power over them. He could accomplish this by casting spells over them through his stare. Adopting another valuable survival skill, he employs this perceived power whenever necessary. Sometimes, in an effort to cast spells on those who try to harm him, he shouts and glares at them. His belief in his special powers enables him to cope with the beatings he receives from Garbos, a cruel farmer with whom he comes to live for a time. He repeatedly glares at Garbos, who also believes in the boy's "evil powers" and so will not beat him to the point of death.

When he periodically escapes Garbos' beatings at a local Catholic church where he is training to be an altar boy, he begins to adopt some Catholic doctrine. Because he had tried to think of various ways to cast a spell on Garbos, "but nothing seemed feasible," he turns to what he considers to be the

> The boy never becomes consumed with self-pity; instead he accepts his position in his world and 'continually tries to learn its rules, its central principles, so that he can function effectively in it.'"

power of prayer. The priest teaches him that those who say more prayers "earn more days of indulgence, and this was also supposed to have an immediate influence on their lives." After this discovery, he insists that he has discovered the pattern of life. He states, "I understood why some people were strong and others weak, some free and others enslaved, some rich and others poor." As a result, he stops blaming others and takes responsibility for his misfortunes. His refusal to wallow in self-pity and his determination to adapt to his world gives him the strength to survive his harrowing experiences.

After he begins his daily prayer ritual, he concludes, "until now I had been a small humble bug that anyone might squash. From now on the humble bug would become an unapproachable bull." His belief that his prayers will earn him enough "days of indulgence" and so a deliverance from Garbos' brutality helps him withstand beatings and torture sessions where he is forced to hang from his arms for hours. Lavers notes that while the boy leaves himself open to new philosophies, he is "always an empiricist, always testing his theories against the facts of his world." When he discovers that the priest has become ill, he becomes confused, admitting, "I was astonished. The priest must have accumulated an extraordinary number of days of indulgence during his pious life, and yet here he was lying sick like anybody else." He leaves himself open to new interpretations of his experience in an effort to understand and thus cope with his world.

When he eventually escapes from Garbos' cruelty, he moves to a new farm where he gains a different type of education. Ewka, the nineteen-year-old farmer's daughter, teaches him how to sexually

What Do I Read Next?

- Kosinski's *Steps* (1968), a sequel to *The Painted Bird,* won the National Book Award for fiction. This work focuses on the boy as an adult who becomes fixated on retaliation for what he suffered as a child.

- *The Empire of the Sun* (1984), written by J. G. Ballard, chronicles the semi-autobiographical experiences of an eleven-year-old British boy named Jim living in Shanghai, China, during World War II. When the war comes to Shanghai, Jim is separated from his parents and sent to a prison camp, where he faces the harsh realities of war and learns important lessons about human nature.

- In *Night* (1958), Elie Wiesel's semi-autobiographical tale focuses on a teenager's internment in a Nazi concentration camp, and his overwhelming feelings of guilt for having survived when so many others, including his family, did not.

- *Anne Frank, The Diary of a Young Girl,* published in 1947, chronicles the courageous life of its author, a gifted Jewish teenager, after she and her family went into hiding in Nazi-occupied Amsterdam. Anne later died in a German concentration camp.

---

pleasure her. He finds comfort in his physical relationship with her. Yet when he sees her coupling with a goat, his vision of the world again makes a radical transformation. At first, he admits, "something collapsed inside me. My thoughts fell apart and shattered into broken fragments like a smashed jug."

He then makes a radical change in his perception of the nature of good and evil. Reflecting on what he has just observed, he determines that there are some, like Ewka, who are "in league with the Devil" and begins to think about the power of evil in relation to his own survival. He decides that by

"signing a pact with the Devil," and committing oneself to inflict "harm, misery, injury, and bitterness" on those he encounters, he could become stronger. Responding to others with "love, friendship, and compassion" would only weaken and subject him to more suffering. He concludes that those committed to "hatred, greed, revenge, or torture to obtain some objective" would receive help from the Devil.

Focusing on his own situation, he admits, "I felt annoyed with myself for not having understood sooner the real rules of this world. The Evil Ones surely picked only those who had already displayed a sufficient supply of inner hatred and maliciousness." In his newfound philosophy, the worse the act, the better the reward. Thus, he notes, "simply beating up an innocent man was worth less than inciting him to hate others. But hatreds of large groups of people must have been the most valuable of all." Reflecting on the suffering he has endured because of his "otherness," he notes, "I could barely imagine the prize earned by the person who managed to inculcate in all blond, blue-eyed people a long-lasting hatred of dark ones." He determines that because the Germans are "endowed with all their splendid abilities and talents" and are "invincible," "every German must have sold his soul to the Devil at birth. This was the source of their power and strength."

This newfound philosophy is reinforced when the villagers throw him into a manure pit after he drops the missal during an important church service. This experience causes him to lose his speech, and soon his thoughts turn toward revenge. He notes that he has often dreamed of punishing those who have made him suffer. Admitting that he has "already been recruited by the powers of Evil and had made a pact with them," he concludes that he now needs "their assistance for spreading evil." His commitment to revenge makes him feel "stronger and more confident," and so he declares, "the time of passivity was over; the belief in good, the power of prayer, altars, priests, and God had deprived me of my speech." He dreams of being as powerful as the Germans, which would enable him "to destroy others in the subtlest ways."

These ruminations fill him with a new sense of confidence and strength, and as a result, he admits, "I did not feel pain any more." As he wanders through the forest he hears whisperings and moans swirling around him in the darkness and decides, "the Evil Ones were interested in me at last.

He concludes that they had made him suffer in the past, only "to train [him] in hatred."

The boy's powerful desire to survive ebbs, however, during his experience with the Kalmuks, who invade the village toward the end of the war and torture, rape, and murder the inhabitants. Initially, the boy identifies with the warriors, noting that they are as darkly complexioned as he is. Yet when he witnesses their unremitting brutality, he withdrawals into himself, "overwhelmed by dread and disgust." At this point, he again alters his worldview to cope with the dangers of his new surroundings. He now concludes that his extraordinary suffering results from his ethnicity. Since his hair and eyes look similar to those of the Kalmuks, he determines, "Evidently I belonged with them in another world. There could be no mercy for such as me."

Lavers notes that this is the boy's "very lowest moment" spiritually as well as physically because a Kalmuk had just severely injured his chest. When Russian soldiers capture the Kalmuks and hang them from trees, the boy finds death in the air and almost gives into it, but his will to live becomes stronger than his need for peace.

After the boy is rescued by the Russian soldiers, and enjoys, for a time a safe, "calm and well-ordered" life, he readopts his belief in the power of revenge. Through his experiences, he has learned about the capacity for violence and cruelty in others. In his search for some measure of control over his life in this atmosphere, he also discovers his own facility for cruelty. Paul R. Lilly, Jr., in his article for *The Literary Review,* notes that like most of Kosinski's characters, the boy's natural impulse is "to transform [himself] from victim to oppressor," for at this point, there are no other options. He must seize the power of the oppressor and consider everyone and everything an enemy that must be controlled or destroyed. By the end of the novel, the boy has transformed himself into the oppressor as evidenced when he breaks his stepbrother's arm, probably in an effort to assert a position of dominance in the family.

The novel closes with an ambiguous portrait of the boy's emotional state. After he reunites with his parents, he finds it difficult to adapt to his new life because he feels that his parents inhibit his freedom. Lavers notes that he finds their restrictions "suffocating and unbearable." As a result he goes out only at night, when he can find other lost souls. Lavers argues, "He is coming now to what he believes is his final philosophical stance, his ultimate

picture of the world." The boy now decides, "Every one of us stood alone, and the sooner a man realized that all Gavrilas, Mitkas, and Silent Ones were expendable, the better for him." Yet he cannot sustain this dark pessimism. At the end of the novel, as he recuperates from a skiing accident and answers a ringing phone, he has an overwhelming desire to communicate to the person who has called him. He admits, "Somewhere at the other end of the wire there was someone, perhaps a man like myself, who wanted to talk with me." As a result he has "an overpowering desire to speak" and eventually he does. His overwhelming need to survive prompts him to try to reestablish a connection with others.

In an interview with Ben Brown in the *Detroit News,* Kosinski claims,

> The whole didactic point of my novels is how you redeem yourself if you are pressed or threatened by the chances of daily life, how you see yourself as a romantic character when you are grotesque, a failure.

In *The Painted Bird,* Kosinski illustrates the strength of the human spirit and its overwhelming will to survive the harsh nature of reality.

Source: Wendy Perkins, Critical Essay on *The Painted Bird,* in *Novels for Students,* The Gale Group, 2001.

John Corry

In the following essay, Corry traces Kosinski's life and career, calling The Painted Bird *"the making of Jerzy Kosinski, just as it was his undoing."*

When I heard that Jerzy Kosinski had killed himself, I was furious and then I cried, a not uncommon reaction, I suspect, among so many people who knew him. "I'm about to put myself to sleep," he said in a note to Kiki, his wife, and then lowered himself into a bathtub half-filled with water, tied a plastic shopping bag around his head, and died. What a whole gallery of twentieth-century thugs had been unable to do to Jerzy, Jerzy had done to himself. The author of *The Painted Bird, Steps, Being There,* and eight other books, was dead at 57. Jerzy, I thought, how could you?

Well, he could because he believed it was the correct thing to do. Jerzy was his own master. His heart condition had worsened and, as he said in the note to Kiki, he feared he might one day be a burden. He was the most considerate of men, and the possibility of becoming pitiable must have appalled him. Besides, his writing had not been going well, and if his health got worse he would be unable to write at all. That would have been the same as death. Words meant more to Jerzy, perhaps, than to any other writer.

> "Words meant more to Jerzy, perhaps, than to any other writer."

His life and his art testified to that. He was concerned with language and the mystical property of words, and what words and language could do. He once described Poland, which he fled in 1957, as a cage of words that had been placed around him by the world's most malevolent author. "I saw myself imprisoned in a large house of political fiction," he said, "persecuted by a mad bestselling novelist, Stalin, and a band of his vicious editors from the Kremlin, and, quite logically, I saw myself as a protagonist of his fiction."

Indeed he did, and he saw himself as the protagonist of his own fiction, too, although he could never quite come out and say it. Critics said his works were autobiographical; he said they were novels. Declare the works pure fiction, however, and he would insist everything in them was true. No other novelist of his time so joined his life and art, and no other novelist had his life so confused with his art. That was the Kosinski conundrum. His inner landscape was no secret—you had only to read the books to know thats—but the outside topography was mysterious.

Who was this exotic, hawk-faced man who aroused so much speculation? To begin with, he was witty and charming, and utterly bereft of malice. He was also a pain in the ass. He would badger friends about what he thought were matters of high importance, and keep badgering until he wore them out. He was fastidious, punctilious, and elegant. On the other hand, he made fun of himself. He mimicked his accent, ridiculed his physique, and laughed at his own eccentricities. He was a trickster, joker, and con man who was incapable of telling a lie. He was a casualty, mishap, and survivor who always feared he might hurt someone himself. He was, in short, one of the best men I knew.

I first met him in the late 1960s, just after he had won the National Book Award for *Steps.* Late at night he would nurse a glass of wine at a literary bar on Second Avenue and talk, firing words in bursts and ricocheting sentences and whole paragraphs off the walls and floor. Then he would fall silent and suddenly be out the door, taking his puns, epigrams, and dark humor with him. The other drinkers would speculate about where he had gone, though mostly, I suspect, he just went home to bed. Once he and Kiki invited me and my wife to dinner at their apartment on West 57th Street. After dinner, he told us he had a secret hiding place. If we left him alone for thirty seconds and then came back, he said, we would not be able to find him.

My wife and I stepped into the hallway, walked as far as the elevator, and then came back to the apartment. We looked under the bed and in the closets; we examined the furniture, windows, and doors. Kosinski had vanished. I remember being uncomfortable; for some reason I felt embarrassed. Finally, a cupboard door popped open and Jerzy unfolded from a shelf, where he had been lying behind some books. No matter where he lived, he said, he always had a hiding place. I had never met a Holocaust survivor before.

It was unpleasant, however, to think of that; in those days it was better to think of Jerzy as the subject of outrageous, appalling, but somehow amusing stories. Everyone knew them. Kosinski had missed a connecting flight to Los Angeles, where he was to stay at the home of Sharon Tate and Roman Polanski, because the airline had misplaced his luggage. That night, the Charles Manson gang invaded the household and butchered Miss Tate and her friends. The next day, Kosinski called the airline to complain again about the luggage. There were many stories about Jerzy Kosinski. You believed some, dismissed others, and treated a few as sly jokes. There were two running jokes in particular: Kosinski worked for the CIA and ghostwriters wrote his books.

That the jokes might have political purpose never occurred to me; that sleazy bureaucrats and Communist party hacks wanted to discredit a writer was unthinkable. I could not imagine that commissars had set slanders adrift like noxious fumes in their own stale air and then waited for cultural winds to disperse them. Kosinski's life was unimaginable enough already.

At age six, he had been separated from his parents and sent to live in the countryside when Germany invaded Poland. Everything afterwards, I think, always came back to that. His life as a child on the run from the Nazis became the basis for *The Painted Bird,* his first and most enduring novel. The boy in the novel is brutalized by villagers, but that is not its point. When Elie Wiesel reviewed *The Painted Bird* in the *New York Times,* he noted the "terrifying elements" in the "metamorphosis of the boy's mind." The boy discovered evil and learned the world was a dangerous place. He learned "every one of us stood alone." Wiesel was sensitive to that, but mistaken when he thought the narrator, the boy, was a Christian. "And their victim was neither Jew nor Gypsy," he wrote, "but a forlorn Christian child of good Christian parents." Of course, Jerzy Kosinski was Jewish.

Wiesel had read something that wasn't there; others would do that, too. Jerzy had not characterized the boy in *The Painted Bird,* other than saying the villagers thought he might be a Gypsy. Indeed, Jerzy had not even identified the boy as Polish. There was an artistic rationale for this— Jerzy once wrote a booklet explaining it—but a simpler one will do. Jerzy purposely had made his own outline obscure; if he could exist in the shadows, so to speak, it would be harder to track him down. The villagers, wherever they might turn up, would not be able to find him.

In Poland, Jerzy had taught sociology at the Academy of Sciences in Warsaw. In New York in 1958, he received a grant to do post-graduate work at Columbia. In 1960 he published *The Future Is Ours, Comrade,* and two years later *No Third Path,* both under the pseudonym Joseph Novak. They were nonfiction works about life in the Soviet Union—Jerzy had gone to school in Moscow in the early 1950s—but they suggested the novels later: the nearly anonymous Novak reported what he saw, expressing no viewpoint overtly. "The descriptions contained in this book do not propose moral codes and involve no judgments," Jerzy wrote in an epilogue to *No Third Path.* "They are sketches."

That wasn't true; Jerzy was just being slippery. The sketches showed a Communist society made up of oppressed and oppressor, and plainly Jerzy had made judgments. Years later, when the left got serious about discrediting him, it said the CIA had sponsored the publication of Jerzy's Novak books. It produced no evidence, of course, and in truth the spooks had had nothing to do with them, although it might have been nice if they had. The Novak books had literary merit, and they presented a more telling picture of the moral bankruptcy of Soviet life than the clunky memoirs Langley then seemed to favor.

The Painted Bird was published in 1965; *Steps* came three years later. "Celine and Kafka stand be-

hind this accomplished art," the *Times* review said then. It was extraordinary, really. A man who escaped Hitler and Stalin had published four books in ten years in a language he had not grown up speaking. The *Times* of London compared him to Conrad, and certainly that was apt. His searches for just the right English word had been prodigious. In the beginning, he would even call telephone operators late at night and try out words on them: Excuse me, miss, but I am a foreigner, and I do not know what this means. Later *The Painted Bird* went through nine full drafts; Jerzy made sixteen or seventeen copies of each draft and passed them on to friends. "I chose some people whose language was not English, and some who were Americans," he once explained. "I asked them to make a little cross next to anything that didn't sound right. If enough people marked a sentence, I knew something was wrong with it."

An eccentric technique, perhaps, and one not likely to be taught at, say, the University of Iowa's celebrated writing classes or the earnest poetry hutches of the New School; but Jerzy, as I said, was his own master, and for him it worked wonderfully well. *The Painted Bird* will survive after most other books are forgotten. Surely, it was the making of Jerzy Kosinski, just as it was his undoing. That, however, came later, and for years Jerzy thrived. In 1970 he received the American Academy of Arts and Letters award for literature. In 1973, he was elected president of the American chapter of PEN, the international association of poets, playwrights, editors, essayists, and novelists. The next year he was re-elected, serving the maximum time allowed.

He was an incongruous choice. PEN was approximately as politically diverse as the Soviet Writers Union, an organization with which it eerily shared some positions. (A few years after Jerzy left office, world PEN, with its American chapter applauding, sanctimoniously expelled the Chilean chapter, while allowing chapters from all Communist and Third World countries to remain.) Jerzy put PEN to actually doing something useful. He led it in a campaign to free writers imprisoned by tyrants of both the left and right. The key word here is "both." Before Jerzy, PEN had recognized only one kind of tyrant. When he left office, PEN's board of directors passed a resolution that said he had "shown an imaginative and protective sense of responsibility for writers all over the world," and that the "fruits of what he has achieved will extend far into the future."

I did not see Jerzy often in the years after that, although I did hear things about him. Whatever the fruits of his achievement at PEN, he was growing suspect in literary circles. He was too raffish, too prominent, and too likely to turn up as a guest on David Letterman. Warren Beatty had cast him in the movie *Reds*. Jerzy seemed to know everyone important. He referred to Henry Kissinger as Henry, an indictable offense in itself. His real sin, though, was that he was still his own man in a world where everyone else was the same.

There was, for example, the incident with Jack Abbott. Abbott, an imprisoned murderer, had corresponded with prominent writers, passionately pressing them to adopt his Marxist-Leninist worldview. Norman Mailer and others detected a rare literary talent in Abbott's letters and campaigned to have him released. Kosinski declined to join the campaign; he called Abbott a "misguided leftist." Mailer and his friends persisted, however, and Abbott won his freedom, a beneficence he repaid by immediately stabbing to death a young actor in the East Village. In the aftermath, Kosinski spoke of "criminal chic," and said the writers who supported Abbott had been drawn by his ideas and not by his talent. A few months later, the *Nation* magazine sponsored a conference of something called the American Writers Congress. It was a wholly anti-American gathering—financed by the usual foundations and the National Endowment for the Arts—and Jerzy said it reminded him of Eastern Europe. Eventually, it was only a matter of who would mug Jerzy first.

As it turned out, it was the *Village Voice*. It ran a long story that said Jerzy had hired editors and ghostwriters to write his books, and that he was connected to the CIA. This, it said, was his "dirty little secret." The story was trash, full of evidence that purported to prove one thing, but which, read carefully, proved nothing at all. It was nasty, venomous, and sly, a paradigm of the distasteful, and had no purpose other than to discredit Jerzy and take his identity away. The terrible thing was that it was successful. The story in the cheesy little New York weekly was picked up all over the world. The *Times* of London even put its account on page one. Italian, French, and West German publications repeated the accusations, and an imaginative few made up some of their own. (*Les Nouvelles Littéraires* in Paris asked why Kosinski carried a gun, had dozens of false identities, and kept tear gas bombs in his car.) The story turned up in daily papers in Turkey and Japan and Malaysia. And in Poland, where each innuendo and outright fabrica-

tion about Jerzy had come from in the first place, the Communist press quoted European and American articles about the story in the *Village Voice* as proof of what the government had been saying all along: that Jerzy Kosinski was an inveterate liar.

It was *The Painted Bird*. As I said, everything in Jerzy's life always came back to that. Even the headline in the *Voice*—"Jerzy Kosinski's Tainted Words"—had been a reminder. (How nasty that was; Jerzy had bled over those words.) When Jerzy published *The Painted Bird* years before, Warsaw had set out to hurt him. He was not an ordinary anti-Communist émigré Pole; he was a celebrated anti-Communist Pole, and so he had to be discredited. *The Painted Bird,* the propagandists said, slandered Poland. In fact, it did not, but since the novel was banned, who in Poland would know? The campaign went on for years: Jerzy used ghostwriters; he worked for the CIA; he plagiarized other novels; he was part of a Zionist conspiracy; nothing he said could be trusted. It was all fantastic, but in its way it worked quite well. Over time Warsaw's emissions spread like swamp gas and the *Voice* missed only the Zionist conspiracy.

After the *Voice* published its story, I told my editors at the *New York Times* I wanted to investigate its charges against Jerzy. Fine, they said, and I wrote a long article, carefully documented, tracing Warsaw's involvement. When it was published, however, it had an unexpected effect. Other publications attacked the *Times*. The best the other publications could say about Jerzy was that the charges against him were not proved. He deserved better, but he was not really surprised because he knew how treacherous words could be. It meant the villagers had finally caught him.

Source: John Corry, "The Most Considerate of Men," in *American Spectator,* Vol. 24, No. 7, July 1991, pp. 17–18.

Sources

Corry, John, "The Most Considerate of Men," in *American Spectator,* Vol. 24, No. 7, July 1991, pp. 17–18.

Field, Andrew, Review in *Book Week,* October 17, 1965, p. 2.

Gladsky, Thomas S., "Jerzy Kosinski's East European Self," in *Critique: Studies in Contemporary Fiction,* Vol. XXIX, No. 2, Winter 1988, pp. 121–32.

Halley, Anne, Review of *The Painted Bird* in *Nation,* Vol. 201, November 29, 1965, p. 424.

Howe, Irving, Review of *The Painted Bird* in *Harpers,* October 1965.

Ivsky, Oleg, Review of *The Painted Bird* in *Library Journal,* Vol. 90, October 1, 1965, p. 4109.

Kosinski, Jerzy, "Afterward," in *The Painted Bird* Grove Press, 1975, pp. ix–xxvi.

Lavers, Norman, "Jerzy Kosinski," in *Literary Review,* G. K. Hall, 1999.

Lilly, Paul R., Jr., "Vision and Violence in the Fiction of Jerzy Kosinski," in *Twayne's United States Authors Series Online,* Vol. 25, No. 3, Spring 1982, pp. 389–400.

Northouse, Cameron, "Jerzy Kosinski," in *Dictionary of Literary Biography,* Vol. 2: *American Novelists Since World War II, First Series,* edited by Jeffrey Helterman, Gale Research, 1978, pp. 266–75.

For Further Study

Sheehy, Gail, "The Psychological Novelist as Portable Man," in *Psychology Today,* December 11, 1977, pp. 126, 128, 130.
   Sheehy explores the novel's psychological themes and includes an interview with Kosinski.

Sloan, James Park, *Jerzy Kosinski: A Biography,* Dutton, 1996.
   Sloan provides details of Kosinski's life that parallel the boy's experiences in the novel.

Teicholz, Tom, ed., *Conversations with Jerzy Kosinski,* University Press of Mississippi, 1993.
   In this collection of interviews, Kosinski talks about his life in Poland, the themes in his novels, and his writing style.

Pilgrims in Aztlán

Miguel Méndez
1974

Miguel Méndez, in his novel *Pilgrims in Aztlán,* tells many different stories. Heralded as a "landmark in Chicano literature" by critic Roland Walter in the *Americas Review,* the stories in this novel are hard to read. The difficulties are based on many factors; one of the most prominent is Méndez's creative use of time—there is no straightforward linear progression. Another challenge is keeping track of the long list of characters. A third factor is the subject matter. There is no easy way of reading about the lives of oppressed and constantly hungry people. Underneath all this, there is also another factor. Juan D. Bruce-Novoa, in his article "Miguel Méndez: Voices of Silence," states that

> Méndez never trusts the lazy reader who would take advantage of the novel to amuse himself without committing anything in return. Méndez is not interested in entertaining [the reader] but moving [the reader] emotionally to compassion and intellectually and socially to action. In another respect, as in all rituals, complexity and even confusion are codes hiding and protecting the secrets of a culture from the outsider.

Another way that Méndez protects the secrets of his culture is to write only in Spanish. In addition, his complex writing style makes translating his books very difficult. His writing style is based on the oral tradition of storytelling. Méndez is very concerned about the loss of the oral tradition, especially in the lives of the Mexican people who, like him, have immigrated to the United States. Bruce-Novoa explains that the oral tradition has been used to pass down stories from one generation to the other. It is through this tradition that children learn from their elders. But in the United States, the children of these immigrants are growing up speaking English, encouraged by the educational system to abandon their traditional language. This creates a huge gap between the generations when the children speak English and their grandparents speak only Spanish. "The oral tradition is in danger of disappearing into the silent past," says Bruce-Novoa, "and the Chicano, cut off from this door to his heritage, could lose his cultural identity, his place in the present, and thus, disappear in the future as well." It is for these reasons that Méndez continues to write in a style that reflects his culture and the oral traditions of his people. His stories speak out for the growing silences in his traditions. Bruce-Novoa concludes that Méndez's writing "is the voice of silence crying for justice in the desert."

Miguel Mendez

Author Biography

There are so many remarkable things about Miguel Méndez that he himself has, at times, looked into the mirror and wondered who he was. He was born on June 15, 1930, in Bisbee, Arizona, a town that sits on the border between the United States and Mexico. Shortly after his birth, his family moved to El Claro, Mexico, where his father found work in a government-owned farming community. It was from his father that Méndez would learn the significance of the storyteller. His father's stories were conveyed to him in the traditional oral style. From his mother, who spoke both Spanish and English, Méndez would receive his love of language and reading.

Méndez attended school only through the sixth grade. This fact might have restricted someone with less determination, but Méndez used this circumstance to inspire himself to conquer the use of language. Throughout his years of working as a hired hand picking fruit and vegetables in the desert lands along the American-Mexican border, Méndez wrote prodigiously. He completed his first novel when he was only eighteen years old. During his years of farm work, he was to meet many of the characters that would people his future novels.

The borderland between the United States and Mexico has been the setting not only of Méndez's novels but also of his life. In 1946, he settled in Tucson, Arizona, where he became a bricklayer, a profession that he would practice for the next

twenty-four years. He continued writing during this time. With the advent of the popularity of Chicano literature in the 1960s, he published his first short story after fifteen years of writing.

Méndez writes his stories in Spanish, his language of choice, and only a few of his works have been translated into English. Méndez prefers writing in Spanish as it better reflects his cultural roots. His profound fascination with language and imagery and his sophisticated writing style make it difficult to translate his works into English.

Until 1970, Méndez continued working in the construction field. He then began teaching Spanish, Hispanic literature, and creative writing at Prima Community College. Méndez also began teaching at the University of Arizona in Tucson. It was during this new transition in his life that Méndez reworked *Peregrinos de Aztlán* (the title translates as *Pilgrims in Aztlán*) and eventually had the novel published.

Méndez's autobiography *Entre Letras Ladrillos* (the title translates both as *Among Letters and Bricks* and *From Labor to Letters*) was published in 1996.

Plot Summary

If there is a plot associated with *Pilgrims in Aztlán,* it existed, at one time, only in the author's head as careful foresight in planning a complicated scheme. In the book itself, there is only story. More definitively, there is a collage of stories. That is not to say, however, that there is no action.

The novel begins with an introduction to Loreto Maldonado, a former revolutionary, who is now eighty years old and a Tijuana car washer. Loreto is also a very proud Yaqui Indian whose main goal in each remaining day of his life is to maintain his dignity and to find some way of making enough money to keep himself from starving.

The reader will meet all the various characters who people this novel through Loreto as he mingles in the dust and noise of the busy Tijuana streets, bumping into people whose stories he unfolds. If there is a protagonist, Loreto is it.

Within the first few paragraphs, the author lets the reader know that this story is not going to be an easy one to read. He uses words and phrases such as bad luck, anger, aching, dirt, furious, poisonous, and brutalizing. He also foreshadows the types of characters that Loreto is about to introduce by stating that the foul-smelling city in which the story is about to be told "bore the curses of so many frustrated individuals: veterans of the dirty wars, whoring and the unemployed rumbling with chronic hunger."

Don Mario Davalos de Cocuch is the first character that Loreto runs into. Don Mario and his wife are on their way to church. Sundays are the time when they walk among the poor, offering alms before they pray for more money. When they offer Loreto some money, he refuses it. Loreto is not a beggar; he works for his money. Don Mario, on the other hand, was more likely to make his wife work, especially back in her youth when she did not have to hide her age under heavy applications of makeup. Don Mario, whom Loreto describes as a "bastard prince," made his fortune by bedding his wife to politically prominent officials. He is also the owner of a brothel.

Next, Loreto meets a woman who goes by the name of Malquerida. She is one of Don Mario's prostitutes, bought by him after she was, in essence, kidnapped from her country home as a young girl and brought to the city under the pretence of being given a legitimate job and, perhaps, finding a benevolent husband. "Her harsh character was nothing other than a deep bitterness that occupied the place of her large congenital tenderness."

The story then shifts back to Loreto who, the reader is told, has not eaten for three days. Out of this bitter hunger comes rage. As he walks to the corner where he usually stops cars in the midst of Tijuana traffic, asking the owners if he can wash their vehicles, Loreto sees a group of very young boys. In the group is Chalito, an ambitious child whose mission is to save his family from poverty. Loreto yells at the children, trying to scare them away. But the children hold their ground. They, too, are hungry. In a short few days following this encounter, Loreto learns that Chalito has died. After hearing the sad news, Loreto has trouble forgiving himself for being so harsh with Chalito.

Loreto next tells the story of Tony Baby, an American who has inherited his grandmother's wealth. He comes to Tijuana to spend the money, buying the favors of prostitutes. Later, when Loreto expands on the story of Tony's grandmother, the reader learns the cruelties of her former business practices. Tony's grandmother thought of herself as a good Christian who gave undocumented Mexican workers jobs. If it had not been for her, she rationalized, these people would be living out in the desert without water and food. In this way, she justifies paying them four dollars a day to cover their ten hours of labor. Eventually, when angered by the workers' decision to organize and ask for more livable wages, she turns them all in to the immigration officials.

The next few scenes personify Tijuana as a whore who postures itself in front of the American tourists, enticing them to leave their money in exchange for a few hours of being treated as emperors. Then Méndez moves in for a more intimate scene inside one of Tijuana's bars where dialogue, without attribution to specific characters, is read. After a brief interlude that announces the death of the little boy Chalito, the dialogue at the bar continues, and the reader meets Chuquito, the champion cotton picker whose reputation is the only remaining marker that he was once good. Chuquito is a broken man who, at the age of forty-five, has lost his agility and straight spine and spends most of his time swallowing liquor.

Loreto, in the meantime, eases in and out of dreams in which he remembers his friend and former military leader, Colonel Rosario Chayo Cuamea. Colonel Cuamea was a brave and forthright Yaqui Indian who lead his people during the Mexican Revolution. The Revolution gave Loreto a sense of self-respect, and he goes back in his memories to those times to recapture it. Colonel Cuamea will become a lasting character to whom Loreto will return throughout the story.

Little Jesus of Bethlehem is another character who appears mostly inside Loreto's memories. He was a childhood friend of Loreto who, because of his name and determination to speak the truth, became known as a healer. Little Jesus, also known as Chuyito, is another character who will appear at the end of the story in more detail.

The story, at this point, takes on a more general view of its characters, describing the plight of unnamed "pilgrims" as they cross the desert in search of work in the United States. Méndez also portrays the hardships of the lives of several prostitutes, before zooming in on two specific men in the desert. Lorenzo and Vate are poets who are struggling in the lethal heat of the sun in an attempt to save their families, back home, from starving. The author fills the reader's mind with images, putting faces on the seemingly unlimited throngs of immigrants by giving vivid details of these two young men. Lorenzo will not make it to the border, and Vate will have to bury him.

By the end of part two, Méndez will reintroduce all the characters he has created. They will wind in and out of the story, coming and going like dreams. In part two, he will expand on some of their stories, introducing minor characters to emphasize the contrasts between the rich and fully fed and the poor and destitute. Part two will stop with a young man, Frankie Perez, who stumbles into Loreto's arms. Only later will the reader realize that Frankie dies as a soldier in Vietnam.

Part three fills in the background information on Colonel Cuamea, details about his youth, his family, and his rise to power in the Mexican Revolution. Méndez finishes this section on Cuamea with the observation: "Being Indians meant being forgotten, being censored, being scorned, receiving the iniquitous sentence of the worst kind of poverty and insulting disdain for their dark skins." Immediately after this sentiment, Méndez writes about Loreto's death.

Méndez then returns briefly to Colonel Cuamea's death, and closes with the announcement of Frankie Perez's death in a letter sent to his parents. Frankie's father goes crazy with the news, but this gives Méndez a chance to lift the father up off the ground as a bird so that he can encompass the entire landscape of his people. The last page of the novel is the voice of Méndez, thinly veiled as two

different voices of a narrator. In the first voice, Méndez says, "We are descended to the bottom of the sea, where the stars descend to their nests, to ask if the heavens know where we are headed or where we come from." In the second voice, he says, "Break the silence of the centuries with the agony of our screams."

Characters

Chalito

Representative of all poverty-stricken street children, Chalito is a feisty little boy who thinks that he can make more money than anyone else can. He loves the sound of coins in his pockets and goes out early each day to work the streets. In his bid to free his family from poverty, he stays out too long one day, works too hard, gets drenched in the water that he uses to wash cars, and comes down with a serious chest cold. His family is unable to pay for medicine, let alone a visit to the doctor's office, and Chalito eventually dies.

Chalito's family is representative of most poor families living in Tijuana. His mother has given birth every year for ten years to nine children (including two sets of twins). His father is boastful and talks in "pretentious and ready-made sentences like politicians." The family survives due to the work of the mother, who sells tortillas; the older children, who shine shoes; and the younger ones, who wash cars. Lencho, Chalito's father, takes the money from the children and often gets drunk while his children go without food. They "were so hungry you could look right through to their souls."

When Chalito dies, his father goes crazy with grief, swearing never to touch alcohol again and to make sure that none of his children ever goes without food again. Rumor has it, says the narrator, that Lencho eventually breaks his promises and ends up in jail.

Chuco

See Chuquito

Chuquito

"If the work in the farm fields had been classified as an Olympic sport, how many gold medals ol' Chuco would have won!" Chuquito, called Chuco, is a champion picker. His reputation for picking over five hundred pounds of cotton in one day is legendary. Chuco is skinny and on the small side and moves "around with an agility so prodigious that it made you think of a dancer or boxer or some feline."

Chuco began working in the fields when he was twelve years old. By the time he reaches his thirty-fifth year, he is a broken man. The long days of backbreaking work have crippled him. When an old friend bumps into him in Los Angeles, Chuco is described as being "wrinkled like a raisin" at the age of forty-five. The friend finds Chuco squatting on the sidewalk with a big hat pulled down around his nose. He resembles a neon sign of a Mexican man in the same posture, leaning against a cactus, advertising one of Tony Baby's hot dog stands. Chuco tells his friend:

> You know what, pal? You see that pal there, leaning against the cactus? These people, pal, say that he's lazy, that he doesn't work, you know, but that guy's there, really, because he's all beat and all sad. The fellow was the harvest champion, you know. He's there because he's all tired out with no one to help him . . . [he's] just like a shovel or worn out pick that's not worth a damn anymore.

Other business people passing on the sidewalk are bothered by Chuco, calling him lazy, then sending for the police who take Chuco to jail.

Chuyito

Chuyito is a medicine man and a Yaqui Indian like Loreto. He is also a childhood friend of Loreto. He lived most of his life in the mountains, hiding from the federal troops who sought to slaughter all Yaqui Indians. He is called Little Jesus of Bethlehem because rumor has it that he has performed miraculous healings. It is often reported that he can speak in several languages, and when he is seen walking, from a distance he looks like he is floating.

When a man finds Chuyito in a bar, he goes over to his table and, calling him Little Jesus, tells Chuyito that he wants to follow him. Chuyito responds: "You want to follow me because you think this mission is a gringo movie in glorious Technicolor. But it isn't. Saving people is like dying over and over again."

Chuyito claims that he was, in some ways, cursed by having been baptized with the name of Jesus. He says that most of the people he healed had made themselves sick through all their greed and lying. All he did to cure them was to tell them to follow a path of truth.

But not all people wanted to follow him, government officials wanted to see him dead. They persecuted him because he went through towns and cities yelling "that the workers must be paid what is just." At one point when the police had caught

him, they beat him and threatened to hang him "but a storm with lightning came up suddenly," Chuyito says, and "the cowards thought that I had supernatural powers, and [the police] let me go." In the end, Chuyito is turned over to the police by a Judas-like character who is paid "fifty cents" to point Chuyito out to them.

Colonel Rosario Chayo Cuamea

Colonel Cuamea comes to life in Loreto Maldonado's dreams. Chayo, a Yaqui Indian like Loreto, is remembered not only as a great leader of the Yaqui people during the Mexican Revolution but also as the "man who deflowered death."

The narrator eases Colonel Cuamea into the story in quick glimpses through Loreto's dreams and memories. Some of his memories, Loreto admits, may be corrupted by stories he's seen on television. But toward the end of the novel, a fuller scene of Cuamea is presented, a story that is entangled in a more modern story of a young, Mexican veteran of another war, in Vietnam.

Cuamea represents a sort of Pancho Villa-type heroic character, one who fights against the four-hundred-year history of Indian suppression by white settlers (who steal Yaqui Nation land). In his youth, Cuamea makes a commitment to dedicate his life to fighting for his people. "With his whole life as a guerrilla fighter, tanned to the core by the rigors of the bloodiest of battles, fighting in the Revolution came naturally to Rosario Cuamea."

The author personifies death by giving it the name Skinny Lady and states that Cuamea is in love with her. In the scene of his death, Cuamea is portrayed as raping the Skinny Lady.

Don Mario Davalos de Cocuch

Don Mario Davalos de Cocuch has "the dapper appearance of a bastard prince." He is a poor boy who makes good by "combining the activities of politicians and thieves." He works his way up the ladder by "bedding his wife with prominent men in order to win promotions." During the Revolutionary War, he fights with the Federal Army against Pancho Villa. In the war, he is given a horse to ride that has a sharp spine. Don Mario leaves the war a wounded man not from battle but from having ridden the horse. He comes away with an "injury of his sphincter." Because of this, he must wear diapers for he has lost control of his bowels. Don Mario represents the greed and corruption of the men who made their fortunes after the war. He owns a brothel, and in the end, he is stabbed to death by the brother of a young woman whom he had bought as a prostitute.

Bobby Foxye

On the sidewalk sitting next to him one day, Loreto sees a young, raggedy man with long hair dressed in hippie fashion. This young man is Bobby Foxye. Over the course of the novel, the reader hears Bobby's story that is filled with details of a child raised by parents whose main goal in life was to make money. Bobby represents the restless American youths of the early 1970s who were, for the most part, both spoiled by the capitalistic society in which they were raised and disgusted by it. In attempts to rebel against the ways of their parents, these youths took on the role of feigned poverty.

Bobby's family is very rich, and he was not neglected financially. He was sent to boarding schools that "could not offer the warmth of the home," but Bobby preferred these schools because at home all his parents did was talk about money. "They swam furiously in an enormous sea of numbers," the narrator states.

Eventually, Bobby is sent to law school because his father wants to retire and then have Bobby take over the management of his business. For two years, Bobby stays away from his family, accepting their money but not attending any classes. One day, he comes home, wearing dirty and smelly clothes. He tells his parents that he does not want to be a lawyer. All he wants is "to live, love and not bother anyone." His father is furious with him and slaps him across the face saying: "You've been stealing my trust, exploiting me through deceit." Bobby's response to his father is: "Haven't you gotten rich by deceiving the whole world?"

La Malquerida

La Malquerida (whose real name is Rosenda Perez Sotolin) is a pretty, young woman who was tricked into becoming a prostitute. Méndez uses this character to put a face on the several somewhat faceless prostitutes that he mentions. La Malquerida is the only prostitute who is given any type of history. Her story includes having been lured to Tijuana on the pretense of finding a legitimate job, but once there, she is locked in a hotel room and sold to Tony Baby, who rapes her. Méndez also uses La Malquerida to emphasize that there is justice only for those who have money.

Lorenzo Linares

In the desert, Lorenzo, one of two poets in this story, loses his life. He is walking across the desert to find work on the other side of the border in the United States. He has, like most of the immigrants, a family that is depending on him to find work so that they might eat. On his way across, Lorenzo dies of thirst.

Everyone else in the group who is crossing the desert with Lorenzo makes it to the border. Only Lorenzo must be buried in a shallow grave in the sand. Vate, Lorenzo's buddy, believes that Lorenzo became so enraptured with the beauty of the desert landscape and the brilliance of the desert moon that he forgot that "he was conditioned to the time of his flesh and bones and became a part of the picture he was contemplating." Lorenzo fails to rest one night in the middle of his journey. He stays up all night, running over the sand dunes, captured by the deep desert silence. Vate says that Lorenzo "believed he was at the bottom of an enchanted sea."

The author uses Lorenzo to express his concept of the pilgrim. The narrator tells the reader that people like Lorenzo "come from the south, in the opposite direction from their forebears, in a pilgrimage without priests or prophets, dragging along a history without any merit for the one telling it, ordinary and repetitive in its tragedy."

Vate continues across the desert after Lorenzo's death. Toward the end of the novel, Vate, who never got over Lorenzo's death, writes an elegy, or funeral poem, to Lorenzo. Then Vate commits suicide.

Little Jesus of Bethlehem
See Chuyito

Loreto Maldonado

The narrator of *Pilgrims in Aztlán* describes Loreto Maldonado, in the beginning of the story, as a man who "lived with his soul turned like a telescope toward the living things of the past." Loreto is 80 years old and has more of a past than a future. But that is not the only reason that Loreto has turned his soul to things of the past. In Tijuana, Mexico, a border town where the poor and the destitute live in hunger and squalor amidst a steady flow of tourist money from the north, life is painful. For Loreto to focus on the present takes tremendous energy, not because he is old, tired, and hungry, but because the cruelties that one person is capable of afflicting on another sucks away all of Loreto's energy. Loreto is a proud, old man. He is also disciplined. His valor and dignity fill his soul even when his stomach is three days empty.

It is through Loreto that Méndez weaves his story. As Loreto walks the streets of his city, looking for cars to wash so that he might make fifty cents with which to buy food for the day, he bumps into the various characters of this story. When he is tired and sits down on the sidewalk to rest, his dreams take on visions from his past. Through these visions, the stories of the lives of warriors, healers, prostitutes, drunken fathers, Vietnam veterans, corrupt politicians, malnourished children, and unnamed emigrants on their way to the promised land of greenback dollars are all told. The stories are all filled with misery and wanting. Loreto collects these tales like a storyteller who retrieves the details of people's lives to save them "from oblivion by remembering them," as Salvador Rodriguez del Pino says in *Reference Guide to American Literature.* Loreto represents the oral tradition, a key element in Méndez's plea to protect and thus save the Mexican culture.

In reflections of his dreams and his daily visions, there are many times when Loreto feels that only purpose in his people's being alive is "to bear witness to how everybody else was fortunate." The poor and desolate are the mirror through which the fortunate ones refuse to see their own human likeness. Loreto's struggle, like the struggle of all the poor and hungry characters in this story, is "to reach a satisfying consciousness of self-worth, of his identity as a human being," says Oscar U. Somoza in his article "The Mexican Element in the Fiction of Miguel Méndez."

Sometimes Loreto's dreams are so vivid that upon waking, he barely remembers himself. At one point, as he stares into a store window, he jumps back when he focuses on his reflection. All he sees is an old, ugly man with a face that "revealed the wounds that his people had suffered. . . . he was the complete antithesis of feigned dignity." When Loreto's stomach churned with hunger, he "cocked his ears with intense curiosity, thinking that he was hearing his guts speaking in imploring voices that begged for food with a piteous tone." This embarrasses Loreto, and he becomes very upset with himself "because he had violated his own code of honor." But he goes on living, "dreaming that he's on an unknown planet and confined to oblivion like a foreigner without a country, ashamed of taking up someone else's space." However displaced he might feel, Loreto refuses to concede his "honor

which was in direct conflict with his chronic hunger."

Loreto is a Yaqui Indian who fought in the Mexican Revolution with Pancho Villa. He represents the ancient history of Mexico, the aboriginal people of the land who are caught between two harsh worlds: the one where they have been relegated to the non-fertile lands of the arid mountains; the other where they live in the ghettos of the cities. Their choices are few: either die of hunger staying put in their hostile territories or take a chance of dying of thirst as they cross the desert in search of migrant work in the farmlands of the United States. It is through Loreto that the reader sees and hears the stories of his people as they make these choices. The consequences of their choices are played out in the streets, the bars, and, sometimes, right in Loreto's lap as when he cries, while holding a Vietnam soldier.

In the end, Loreto dies. His body is found in a decrepit shack that was made out of empty cans and beer bottles, old advertisements for food, and a large box showing a child eating bread. "The front part of Loreto's house and more than half the door . . . were covered with a . . . picture of a steak that was so real that you could almost smell the aroma." If dignity were the only element holding together Loreto's final years, it becomes totally dismantled in his death. His body is wrapped in a rotten tarp and tossed into the back of an old garbage truck.

Frankie Perez

The author has Frankie Perez stumble down the sidewalks of Tijuana toward Loreto and then collapse in Loreto's arms. Later, the reader discovers that Perez dies in the Vietnam War. Perez represents the Mexican male youths who move with their families to the United States in search of a better life. They work in the fields with their parents and attend school as often as possible. The cost of their education, however, is often the loss of their language and culture. Then, in the era of this novel, when they reach the age of eighteen, they are drafted in droves and shipped to Asia where they play out their short lives as pawns in a war without victory or dignity.

When Frankie is drafted, he is proud to serve his newly adopted country. "He had a sacred duty to defend his country. His beloved country, so just and generous with all its sons." But when Frankie finds himself in the middle of the Vietnam jungle, and after he has witnessed so many atrocities of war, he fears that even the animals must know through their instincts "that the earth was inhabited by a being that was all cruelty and viciousness." In the telling of the story, Loreto intertwines Frankie's war with Colonel Cuamea's revolution. Both men were war heroes and brave soldiers. But the great difference between them was that Cuamea fought a war for his own native people on his own native land, while Perez fought in Asia for an adopted country that exploited him.

The novel ends with Frankie's family receiving the news that their son has been killed in Vietnam. His father looses his grasp on reality:

> The bosses said that he had gone crazy because he was a real drunk. In part that was true . . . but he also went mad from working like an animal . . . for seeing his family . . . sunken in the cruelest of poverties . . . and because of the death of his Frankie.

Tony Baby

Tony Baby is described as a "libidinous gringo" who hates to work. Tony is from the northern side of the border, or the United States, and he says, work "is for burros, oxen and fools." His grandmother, "a hairy chested woman," gains her fortune by selling hot dogs with chili sauce on top, calling them chili dogs to attract the Mexican-American population that lives in southern California.

Tony hates his grandmother, who makes him haul hot dogs around in a cart and work inside a huge refrigerator, stacking boxes of food. But Tony isn't the only one who hates her. When the men who work for Tony's grandmother try to organize to demand better wages, she calls in the immigration officials and has two hundred of the men arrested and sent back to Mexico.

The grandmother eventually dies, and Tony inherits her money. He then marries a woman who doesn't love him. Once his wife has gained a secure grasp on Tony's wealth, she refuses to go to bed with him. That's when Tony becomes a "dedicated frequenter of the border whorehouses, lost in the illusion that he was a rapist who couldn't be caught."

Rosenda Perez Sotolin

See La Malquerida

Vate

Vate is a poet and friend of Lorenzo Linares. While walking across the desert in an attempt to reach the United States to find work, Vate witnesses his friend's death and never gets over it. He

feels responsible for Lorenzo, having promised Lorenzo's wife that he would watch over his friend to make sure that Lorenzo would return to his family safely. After Lorenzo's death, Vate's "mind became a falling star dragging along a tail of orphan words." The only thing he can think about is how he could not save his friend. In an attempt to make sure that people do not forget his friend, Vate writes an elegy, or long funeral poem, about Lorenzo. Then Vate commits suicide.

Themes

Pilgrimage

The pilgrimage to Aztlán is a dominant theme in Méndez's novel. To understand the pilgrimage, the concept of Aztlán itself must be grasped. As a myth, Aztlán has symbolized "the existence of a paradisiacal region where injustice, evil, sickness, old age, poverty, and misery do not exist," says Luis Leal writing in the *Denver Quarterly*. In the essay "Myth, Identity and Struggle in Three Chicano Novels," the writer and poet Alurista states that Aztlán represents "a myth of origin" and has "at least three traditions in distinct historical periods. First there is the ancient "Pre-Mexica" version that "dates back to the arrival of the first settlers" of Mexico. This version states that Aztlán was an island now lost in the Atlantic Ocean "where an advanced civilization" once lived. The second version, dating back to the time before the Spanish invasion of Mexico, holds that Aztlán was located somewhere around the present-day southwestern region of the United States.

The third version, says Alurista, is "the Chicano version" that was drafted by the "delegates to the first national Chicano youth conference held in Denver, Colorado," in 1969. "Here, again . . . Aztlán is used as a metaphor which unifies . . . [but] . . . is referred to as being more than a geographical location." This third interpretation adds more significance to the original meaning of the symbol. "Aztlán is no longer just an origin, a source, a motherland, a testimony to an ancient heritage and tradition. Aztlán has become a mission and a state of mind, a way of facing contemporary reality and social conditions . . . [it] speaks of reclaiming that which once belonged to its original inhabitants."

For Méndez, says Alurista, Aztlán is a land that is in the hands of capitalists from both north and south of the Mexican-American border. Aztlán no longer represents a utopian land, but rather it is a

Topics For Further Study

- The Mexican Revolution is said to have been won but without a real victory for the Yaqui Indians. Research the cause that lay behind the uprising of the Yaqui Indians. Then find out where and to whom the spoils of the victory went if not to the Yaquis.

- The character of Colonel Rosario Cuamea is likened to the heroic figure of Pancho Villa. Research the biographical details of Villa's life and compare them to the story of Colonel Cuamea. How are they the same? How do they differ?

- The main characters in *Pilgrims in Aztlán* are predominately male. Look at Méndez's portrayal of women. What roles do they play? What types of females does Méndez emphasize? Is he sympathetic to their plight? Do they fare any better than the men?

- In an article written in the *Denver Quarterly,* Oscar U. Somoza states that Loreto Maldonado (the protagonist in *Pilgrims in Aztlán*) "must struggle within himself to reach a satisfying consciousness of self-worth." Study the passages in this book that detail Loreto's daily routines and experiences. How does Loreto, amidst his poverty and hunger, satisfy his need to find self-worth? How does he maintain a sense of dignity?

- In 1992, the president of the United Sates signed the North American Free Trade Agreement (NAFTA) with Mexico. This agreement was created to stimulate trade between the two countries. Through the years since that signing, there has been mounting criticism on both sides of the border concerning the loss of jobs and critical environmental pollution. Research current topics on this agreement. What are the major arguments in favor of NAFTA? What do the opponents argue? Discuss ways that these issues might be resolved.

- The word *Aztlán* in the title of this novel refers to an ancient, utopian land of the Aztecs. Historians do not know if this land actually exists, but in the past few decades the concept of Aztlán has become a focus of some politically active groups. Some groups claim that Aztlán is territory that was ceded to the United States through the Guadalupe Hidalgo Treaty in 1848 and is located in the southwestern portion of the United States. Some groups are suggesting that this area be returned to Mexico. Others suggest that the border area in both the United States and Mexico be set aside as a separate country all its own. Develop arguments for or against any, or all, of these suggestions.

"place of toil and misery for those who have recently returned. And, for those who have been in the territory for generations, it is a place where their labor is exploited and their dignity stripped away." If these people in Méndez's novel are on a pilgrimage, Alurista concludes, at best it is a pilgrimage toward a national ideal "to be sought and fought for by a new generation yet to come."

In the novel, an anonymous voice (although it bears resemblance to the voice of one of the poets, either Lorenzo or Vate) calls out from the depths of the desert:

> I was overtaken by imagination, and I saw in my pilgrimage many Indian peoples reduced by the torture

of hunger and the humiliation of plunder, traveling backwards along the ancient roads in search of their remote origin . . . I was hurt by the despair of feeling that utopia is ever a burning coal in consciousnesses tortured by the denial of sublime aspirations, and I fell to my knees begging for mercy.

War

Two wars are mentioned in detail in *Pilgrims in Aztlán:* the Mexican Revolution and the Vietnam War. In reference to the Mexican Revolution, "Méndez does not chronicle events about the conflict," says Oscar U. Somoza in his article "The Mexican Element in the Fiction of Miguel Méndez," instead he approaches it "and confront[s] it in a direct manner, letting [the characters] develop within the conflict but always with the freedom to return to the present moment when it is supposed that the Revolution has 'triumphed' and 'borne its fruits.'" The Revolution was not a success for the Yaqui people. Méndez's characters, says Somoza, like Colonel Cuamea and Loreto Maldonado, "are among that group of Mexicans who fought so their families could progress, yet even though their side won the battles, they came out of it with nothing."

In the novel, this outcome often puzzled Loreto who found himself going over "his experiences again and again, as if searching for the deficiency that by some misfortune might have turned things about, converting what could have been sublime into something awry, absurd." On the other hand, it is his experiences in the Revolution that stand out as some of his most vivid memories. By reflecting on these memories, it seems that Loreto is able to endure the terrible, undignified circumstances in which he finds himself as he struggles through each day. "This situation," Somoza states, "turns out to have been the reality for many of the surviving revolutionaries. If they were noble or idealistic they fell by the wayside like Loreto Maldonado. If not, they got ahead and became types such as . . . Davalos de Cocuch [a character who makes his money off of prostitution]."

The Mexican Revolution was a noble fight. The Yaqui people fought for a noble cause. But for what cause did the young men in the Vietnam War fight, especially the young men who were descendents of the Yaqui Indians? Méndez brings in the Vietnam War through the character of Frankie Perez. Frankie represents all the young men who were drafted by the thousands and sent to Asia to fight in a war that had no victory, no noble cause. The tone of voice used by the narrator as Frankie's experiences are told is coated in sarcastic irony. Here is a young man who is sent to the front lines to fight for a country whose long history includes the subjugation, if not attempted annihilation, of his own ancestral population. With an acerbic tongue in cheek, the narrator makes a list of American heroes for Frankie to turn to for inspiration. Instead of Villa and Zapata, Frankie has Superman, Batman, and, finally, the "Great Cowboy" to use as guides to bolster his courage when facing his Asian enemy.

> Alone, relates the narrator, mounted on his spirited horse, with a pistol in each hand, he [the "Great Cowboy"] had vanquished and eliminated thousands of Indians, liberating territories and caravans of religious men and women predestined by God our Lord

to colonize these lands, as fertile as they were vast. What is more, he had punished all of the evil Mexicans, killing them like rabbits or humiliating them just by looking at them askance.

The Vietnam War, the narrator concludes gave these young Mexican-American men "a great privilege! They had the distinction of dying, in a higher percentage, sacrificing themselves thus for their noble country."

Displacement

The results of the Mexican Revolution created a huge disparity between the corrupt politicians and businesspeople and the lower economical class. Opportunities for a major portion of the population were few, and poverty forced them "to leave their places of origin," says Somoza, "and set themselves up elsewhere." They leave their rural homes behind to search for work in the cities. Unfortunately, there are few jobs to be found in their own country. And thus begins the great emigration from their homeland.

Méndez depicts this emigration in small pieces, sharing brief moments throughout the novel with the great flood of humanity in its trek north across the desert in search of food.

> The only hope, says Somoza, that remains for these individuals, men as well as women, is to form part of a group that crosses the border toward a country that is not their own and that treats them as slaves . . . the few that manage to establish themselves in the United States find themselves . . . disoriented as . . . they discover no entry into a socio-economic ambience that rejects them and denies them the opportunities that belong to the Anglo-American group.

The character Vate, after burying his friend Lorenzo in the desert, says:

> I know that in the storybooks, the poor young man goes out to seek adventures, and he comes back rich and marries the daughter of the king. But now I also know that to be a Chicano or a wetback is to be a slave and to live scorned. It's been a century since I left my village, and someday I'll return to cry for my dead.

Style

Form

The form of *Pilgrims in Aztlán* might be considered new and inventive when compared to traditional concepts of written literature. However, when compared to oral tradition, an age-old process of handing down cultural stories from one generation to the next, the form of Méndez's novel is commonplace, as old as language itself. The first requirement in transposing oral tradition to the printed word is to create an orator or storyteller. In this novel, that role goes to Loreto Maldonado. Although it is not always clear where and how Loreto gets these stories, he is "the center for the loose voices of the novel," says Juan D. Bruce-Novoa in *Contemporary Chicano Fiction*. While the voices of the rich and powerful are written in public records such as newspapers and history books, the voices of the poor go unrecorded, says Bruce-Novoa. Their stories, if not passed down through oral tradition, are permanently lost. That is why Méndez tries to capture the form of oral storytelling in writing this book, a collection of stories about the poor.

In the telling of these seemingly random stories, the form becomes somewhat fractured. Chronological time exists but only as a jigsaw puzzle exists when broken in pieces. Jumps from the past to the present, from one story to the next, from poetic metaphor to vulgar slang challenge the reader to take an active part in the story. Who is talking now? Whose story is this? What is this new setting? Why is this voice so different? What time is it? Where is this story going? These questions buzz in the reader's head as the story progresses.

Bruce-Novoa states that this fracturing of form is also Méndez's way of reflecting the fracturing of the society of which he is writing. He says,

> . . . the fragmentation of the narrative reflects the confusion and disorganization of the people, whereas a chronological, orderly structure would reflect more the supposed order of society into which the Chicano is being pushed. The structural tensions of the novel reflect the structural tensions of the socio-cultural (and economic) struggle.

For the reader who is willing to face the challenge, Bruce-Novoa continues, Méndez has provided a surprise. If the reader has listened carefully, "the voice [at the end of the novel] reveals the purpose of the voyage. The reading has been an initiation rite in which the reader becomes [the pilgrim in Aztlán] worthy of the revelations to be made to him."

Figurative Language

The use of metaphor and personification begin on the first page of this novel and continues through the last pages. As if the story did not provide enough color in all the various voices, characters, time lines, and themes, Méndez splashes figurative language on each page as colorful as tropical flowers. His images take the ordinary, flat, black and white, printed pages and paint three dimensional murals that pull the reader into his imaginary landscapes.

On the first page alone, Méndez has a string of metaphors that begin with "the bucket was foaming like an angry camel," and end with a description of Loreto's difficulty in walking as that which is "experienced by ants after someone's sadistic footstep has stepped on them." On the second page, Méndez has Loreto's heart leaping around "like a rock-and-roll toad;" his brain is bubbling; his soul is a telescope; and he was "navigating like a falling star." Loreto's whole life, Méndez writes "meant struggling with death, as if the fluidity of his temporal condition were a black colt, the wildest of the wild, determined to whip him off his slippery back against the outcroppings of rocks."

Death, in Méndez's hands, is personified as the "Skinny Lady." In the desert, the landscape takes on human form as he talks about the "throat of the canyons," and the moon as a "tangible bride into whose ear he could speak beautiful things and who would cling tenderly to his arms."

The long lines of pilgrims crossing the desert become "a ladder of questions without answers, voices born of the bowels of the earth." The United States is a "Mecca for the hungry;" and the starving Mexican people are described as "skeletal women with tits like dry wells," children who look like "skin and bone pinatas," and their dogs are "so skinny they look like stringed instruments."

Two extended metaphors occur in part three of the novel. The first involves Colonel Cuamea and the Skinny Lady of Death. As Loreto tells the story, Colonel Cuamea was in love with Death and determined to "deflower" her. She taunts him through most of his adult life, but as an old man, he sees her and "without thinking" takes off his clothes, lies down, and prepares to meet her.

For her part, Death is torn between meeting him and turning away, postponing the inevitable. But she cannot resist. She approaches and sits astride him and is surprised to "feel a sharp object like a dagger tear at her insides." Angered, she digs into Cuamea and "yank[s] out the roots from which life hangs. Then she leaves his body lying there "rotting like an animal. Protruding eyes like large tomatoes adorned the carrion banquet."

The second extended metaphor involves Panfilo Perez, a man who has lost a son in the Vietnam War. Perez goes crazy at the news of his son's death and in his madness, he imagines himself "an enormous bird with black wings." In this form, Panfilo's eyes fill with a downpour that "was so thick that it was as if his soul had turned into a sea." He then flies so high that he can see "the teeth in the man in the moon." He also discovers that the stars "are pinatas . . . [and] . . . not phosphorescent billiard balls." The earth, through Panfilo's eyes, has rivers that look "just like varicose veins," and forests sit "thick on the cheeks of the ravines." When Panfilo flies up to talk to the sun, "he felt his beak warp as though it were made of molasses," then his claws become "soft like the hands of a newborn baby and his eyes as brilliant and fiery as two white-hot coals."

Historical Context

The late 1960s saw a rise in Mexican-American political activity as well as a substantial increase in the publication of Mexican-American literary works. While for other ethnic groups, these were years of protests against the Vietnam War and marches for women's liberation and civil rights, for Mexican-Americans it was a time of searching for and reclaiming an identity. During this same period in California, Colorado, and Texas, thousands of Mexican-American students were boycotting their schools, refusing to accept the Americanized versions of history, especially in terms of the historical supposition that Columbus had discovered America. They also demanded the creation of Chicano studies programs. It was a time of protests against working conditions in the agricultural fields and the disproportionate numbers of Mexican-American men fighting in Vietnam. Also during this time, David Sanchez helped organize the Brown Berets, a group that promoted Mexican pride.

One of the Mexican-American mottos of this era came from former professional boxer and poet Rodolfo Gonzales' "I am Joaquin," an epic poem chronicling four hundred years of Mexican history. The phrase that turned into a motto was "I will never be absorbed." It incited a move against enculturation. It was also at this time that the first Chicano Youth Liberation Conference was held. At the conference, The Spiritual Plan of Aztlán was drafted and legitimized by the delegates. It was in this plan that Aztlán, the mythical utopian symbol of Mexico, was used as a unifying metaphor for Mexican-Americans. It was also at this conference that a renewed interest in Aztlán changed the symbol to include not only a geographical location but also a state of mind. One of the final statements in

the Spiritual Plan declares, "We are Aztlán." With this statement, the poet Alurista says in his article "Myth, Identity and Struggle in Three Chicano Novels," "Aztlán has become a mission and a state of mind, a way of facing contemporary reality and social conditions."

During the 1970s, there was a flourishing of Mexican-American literature. Some of the more popular literature included Oscar Zeta Acosta's *The Autobiography of a Brown Buffalo,* Rudolfo Anaya's *Heart of Aztlán* and *Bless Me, Ultima,* Ernesto Galarz's *Barrio Boy,* and Jose Antonio Villarreal's *Pocho.* In this same time frame, Mexican-American studies programs were inaugurated in American colleges and universities.

On the other side of the border during this same period, student protests were on the rise. Mexico was in the grasp of a very strong governmental force that made several unpopular political arrests, suppressed several labor strikes, and annulled several controversial local elections. It was the time of the Mexico City-sponsored Summer Olympic Games, and the leaders of the country wanted to make sure that the international spotlight did not expose any signs of political or economic instability. Despite the crackdown on protests, the students' voices grew louder, and, in August of 1968, students convened in the largest antigovernment demonstration ever held. The police arrested the leaders of the protest and announced a ban on any further protests. This did not, however, stop the student activity. In October, another student protest was organized. Although the crowd was much smaller, the police did not waste any time. They came in with helicopters and tanks, and by the end of the skirmish, it was estimated that four hundred students were dead.

The 1970s brought a new Mexican president to power. In an attempt to de-radicalize the young leftists and intellectuals, the new president gave them posts in the government. As a matter of fact, this president, Echeverria, became a champion of leftist causes in Latin America. He began a redistribution of power and wealth through massive public-spending programs and was responsible for heavy state investment in the promotion of consumption and social welfare for the middle and lower classes. Echeverria was also responsible for programs that redistributed land and increased the number of schools and health clinics in the rural areas. Unfortunately, the combination of government spending and Echeverria's poor relationship with the national business community lead to a 450

Compare & Contrast

- **1970:** Hispanics make up 12 percent of California's population.

  1990: Hispanics make up 30 percent of California's population, and 9 percent of the total population of the United States.

  Today: It is estimated that there are six million undocumented workers in the United States.

- **1986:** The U.S. government signs the Immigration Reform and Control Act that confers legal status to three million people who came to the United States before 1982. This law also imposes legal sanctions on employers who are found to have employed undocumented workers.

  1994: Proposition 187, which denies state aid to illegal immigrants, is approved by voters. But, it is blocked by state and federal courts. Hispanic voter turnout rises seventeen percentage points in the following election.

  1996: The number of Hispanic registered voters reaches 6.6 million.

  Today: The AFL-CIO reverses its position on immigration and sponsors a rally in Los Angeles' Sports Arena where twenty thousand immigrants march, demanding unconditional amnesty.

- **1970:** Sixty-one percent of all urban dwellings in Mexico have access to running water. Fifty-nine percent have electricity. Forty-one percent have dirt flooring. Forty-one percent have indoor plumbing.

  1990: Seventy-nine percent of all urban dwellings in Mexico have access to running water. Eighty-seven percent have electricity. Twenty percent have dirt flooring. Sixty-three percent have indoor plumbing.

- **1960:** Seventy-six percent of Mexico's population live below the poverty level.

  1980: Forty-five percent of Mexico's population live below the poverty level.

  Mid-1980s: Poverty rate explodes as Mexico's economy tumbles.

- **1983:** United States and Mexico sign the La Paz Agreement on Cooperation for the Protection and Improvement of the Environment in the Border area.

  1991: Texas chooses a dumping site for radioactive waste: a small, poor, rural border county whose population is 70 percent Hispanic. Eleven more dumps are planned.

  Today: Life-threatening pollution increases along the border and is said to be caused by American-owned factories on the Mexican side of the border.

---

percent rise in Mexico's national debt and subsequent devaluation of the peso. A dramatic rise in the number of immigrants to the United States soon followed.

Critical Overview

Although only a few of Miguel Méndez's works have been translated into English, his writing impressed enough English-speaking, literary personages to win him a teaching position at a university. Not only that, it won him an honorary college degree. Although his writing is not well known to the general non-Hispanic population in the United States, the Hispanic community admires him as one of the finest, contemporary writers.

Méndez's novel *Pilgrims in Aztlán* was published around the same time that Mexican-American youths were beginning to organize a political movement whose basic premise was the resistance of enculturation. The students were refusing to give up their use of the Spanish language in school. They were rebelling against American history texts in

Mexican farm workers on a truck

which Christopher Columbus, for instance, was honored as the person who discovered America. Also at this time, the symbol of Aztlán, the mythical homeland of the Aztec people, was a rallying point for the students who were searching for a cultural identity. A reawakening need for symbols of their traditions found a home in this mythical symbol. This symbol seems to have arisen from some deep, collective passion and was found in the title of many literary works at the time. Méndez's book was one of the first. The symbol helped to unite the Hispanic community, and Méndez's book furthered the concept.

For these and other reasons, most critics view Méndez's book as a landmark in Hispanic literature. Oscar U. Somoza in "The Mexican Element in the Fiction of Miguel Méndez," says that with this novel Méndez "solidified his position as an outstanding representative of Chicano literary expression." Somoza adds that Méndez "emerges as a proponent of a deep moral approach toward socio-economic issues." Roland Walter, writing in the *Americas Review* calls Méndez's novel "a sociological document of high aesthetic standard."

Pilgrims in Aztlán, says Juan D. Bruce-Novoa in his "Miguel Méndez: Voices of Silence," is a story about the poor who have, without Méndez, no voice. He also admits that Méndez's book is hard to read. It is complicated by a fractured timeline and complex structure. It is a novel that "waits for someone capable of listening to and actualizing the voices." Despite its challenging style "the strong reader, the faithful, persistent reader will prove himself in the arduous reading by understanding Méndez's real message." That message waits for the reader at the end of the book, and like a rite of passage, says Bruce-Novoa, the reader must make his way through.

The book is a "wealth of oral tradition," continues Bruce-Novoa, and

> Méndez achieves the purpose of converting the oral tradition into fixed images: Méndez creates a synthesis of the voices of the poor and a written text that can compete in complexity and beauty with contemporary literature.

One of Méndez's deepest concerns is the loss of oral tradition in the Mexican-American culture. Because the younger generations are losing their language, the gap between their generation and the generation of their grandparents is widening. Since oral tradition is handed down from the older generation to the younger one, the oral stories of the older generation are being lost.

Although there is agreement that Méndez's text requires an active reader who is willing to record the names behind the voices and keep track of the histories behind the names, most critics also support Bruce-Novoa's statement that "what seduces us is not simply what is said [in Méndez's novel], but how it is said." Méndez's use of metaphor and his poetic appreciation of language makes the pilgrimage from the first page to the last well worth the effort.

Criticism

Joyce Hart

Hart is a freelance writer and former director of the Mentors Writing Conference. In this essay, she looks at the protagonist, Loreto Maldonado, as metaphor for the oral tradition and its role in the Mexican-American culture as interpreted in Méndez's novel.

The word *pilgrim* has several different connotations. From the Latin root, *peregrinus,* the word means "foreigner." A more descriptive definition translates as "one who travels to a foreign or sacred place." When the word is extended to *pilgrimage,* it encompasses the journey itself; and at its most philosophical extension can refer to the actual journey through life on earth. Underlying all these various interpretations of the word is the sense of movement. Someone is moving somewhere for some consciously or unconsciously determined reason.

This movement, or pilgrimage, is a theme that runs through all the many stories in Méndez's *Pilgrims in Aztlán.* But because there are so many stories, so many voices, and so many journeys, the reading of the novel can be challenging. The fragmentation of time and form demands greater attention than an easy-reading novel. This fragmentation, says Juan Bruce-Novoa in his article "Miguel Méndez: Voices of Silence," is done on purpose. Méndez wants to challenge the reader to take an active part in the stories, but he also wants the chaos to reflect the confusion that his characters are experiencing. This confusion also confronts the lives of Mexican-Americans, today, who, in Méndez's point of view, are losing their sense of their culture. This loss is reflected in the loss of the oral tradition, the process by which the older generation passes down stories to their children. The power of the oral tradition is that it holds the culture together by making sense out of the chaos of all of life's stories.

In the novel *Pilgrims of Aztlán,* the character who represents the oral tradition is the storyteller

Loreto Maldonado; he is the one who holds things together. Bruce-Novoa says that

> The oral histories, unacknowledged in society's official records vibrate in the head of the protagonist Loreto . . . Loreto is the center for the loose voices of the novel. Believing that the history of the poor is found in the oral tradition, Méndez needs a human center to contain it, to be its focus.

By not only listening to Loreto's stories but by also studying Loreto's pilgrimage (his movement through this novel), the reader is given a tool to help understand all the other stories. If Loreto were real and sitting in front of the reader, his tone of voice and facial expression, his past history with the reader, as well as his creativity in altering the insinuation of the story as it relates to the present time would all give more food with which to fuel the reader's imagination. It would fill in the gaps between all the stories. Because it is impossible to provide this set of circumstances, the reader must work to understand Loreto by studying the clues that Méndez provides in describing Loreto's actions, his motives, his thoughts, and his pilgrimage. The reader needs to ask: What drives Loreto? What is he looking for? Where is he going? Where has he been?

One of the first interesting facts the reader learns about Loreto is that, although he represents the oral tradition as the storyteller, he is, for the most part, silent. The histories of the poor may vibrate in his head, but "the complicated need to arrange his memories in a chronological order was now of no use to him. He lived with his soul turned like a telescope toward the living things of the past." This does not prevent him from seeing and hearing the stories of the present unfold in front of him, but they act only as catalysts to stir his memories. Another fact that the reader learns about Loreto in the opening pages of the novel is that he has, despite his current appearance and economic status, a "code of honor." Keeping this in mind, the reader can see through his eyes as Loreto reflects on the moral disposition of all the forthcoming characters. Knowing that Loreto is a noble man also helps to better understand his journey.

As Loreto walks down the streets of Tijuana each morning, what is he looking for? The casual reader might suggest that the old Yaqui Indian is looking for money with which to buy food. But is that all that his life is worth? Is Loreto only looking for survival? Loreto is a proud man with a proud past, but sometimes, in his present state, he does not recognize his own image.

How many times had he seen his reflection in the panes of glass of those buildings, where so many things are for sale, without recognizing himself, until after a few seconds it would strike him that that blackened and wrinkled face was his own?

Loreto is a man who is suffering from a lack of self image. He knows his past very well, but his present is unrecognizable. With this information, the reader might assume that Méndez is reflecting on his fears that his people, because they are losing their oral tradition, are also losing their identity, losing their sense of culture and place. Méndez strengthens this assumption in another description of Loreto as a man who "goes on living, or better, dreaming that he's on an unknown planet and confined to oblivion like a foreigner without a country."

Loreto is also a little mischievous. "He was amused by the parade of gringos buying souvenirs," Méndez writes. But then, a few paragraphs later when Méndez turns the point of view from the old man to the tourists, Loreto is fast asleep, snoring and sounding like "a serenade of pigs in heat calling for their females." Whether Loreto is feigning sleep, as well as his loud snoring, remains unknown. But the scene, at first, does invoke a sense of comedy. On another, more serious level, however, this is a foreshadowing of a scene yet to come. Point of view is very significant to Méndez, as is misinterpretation. The other scene in the story between a group of "gringos" that is walking past a Mexican man, Chuco, who is lying on the sidewalk, ends up with Chuco being thrown in jail. Although he is not sleeping, but rather contemplating a picture of a Mexican man sleeping, the white people, nevertheless, call him lazy. "All they think of is booze and sleep!" In fact, Chuco has worked all his life in the fields. He was known as the champion of all pickers because he worked so fast and so hard. His prone figure, like the prone figure of the Mexican man in the sign, is easily misinterpreted by people who have stereotypical identities of the Mexican man.

In the course of the novel, Loreto has direct confrontations with three young men. One is a young child, Chalito, whom Loreto tries to chase off his street corner where the child is washing cars. The child's precise age is unknown, but it can be deduced that his age is less than nine years. This child will haunt Loreto in future scenes. Chalito will die, not from anything that Loreto did, but for something he could not do. In a later dream, Loreto sees Chalito and puts his hands into his bulging pockets and pulls out handfuls of money that he

> **The reader needs to ask: What drives Loreto? What is he looking for? Where is he going? Where has he been?"**

gives to the child. Chalito is transformed, and Loreto recognizes himself as that child. It is through children that Loreto shows his strongest emotions. "They looked on him with the fresh eyes of children which are like fresh, unused film." Children are the future of the culture, "the dawn of another generation." This is Méndez talking as he worries about the loss of tradition for the future generations.

The next young man that Loreto encounters on the sidewalk is a white man from the United States. This young man is a college dropout. He is the product of a marriage blessed with money ("wealth based on the suffering of others") but bothered by having produced a child. The hippie represents the antithesis of the young boy Chalito's story. The hippie has chosen filth and is feigning poverty. However, Méndez may well be using the hippie as a warning. Mexican-American youths may be losing their culture, but what, if any, culture do the Anglo-Americans have? The irony goes further when Méndez has the hippie "speak with the lucidity of a Spanish university professor." Méndez contends that one of the main reasons for the disappearance of oral tradition in his culture is that the young children no longer speak their grandparent's language.

The third man that Loreto meets on the sidewalks is Frankie Perez. When Loreto first sees him, he makes the mistake, as Méndez says most all of us do, of prejudging him. "Loreto saw him coming out of a brothel . . . and knew he was going to fall. Later, his soul would become afflicted with the blackest anguish when he learned the enormous tragedy of the little drunk." Furthermore, Loreto thinks that Frankie is a young child, "he looked fifteen at the most." In truth, Frankie turns out to be a Vietnam veteran home on leave.

When Frankie stumbles and falls into Loreto's arms, it is the first scene in the book where the reader actually sees Loreto touching someone. Loreto holds him up and that's when he notices

What Do I Read Next?

- Oscar Z. Acosta's *The Autobiography of a Brown Buffalo* tells the story of a young Mexican-American man who becomes disillusioned with American culture and returns home to Juarez, Mexico. There he wastes away his life with prostitutes and alcohol until he is thrown into jail and told by a judge to go home and learn his father's language. The question for the protagonist to answer at this point is, Where is home?

- Another classic book by Oscar Z. Acosta, *The Revolt of the Cockroach People,* continues with the character Brown Buffalo after he has led Mexican-Americans through the revolts in Los Angeles during the late 1960s. Tired from the struggles, he goes back to Mexico, where he stays with his brother. In Mexico, Brown Buffalo sees another side of revolution, and he learns that the revolt against oppression is more widespread than he thought.

- *Bless Me, Ultima,* by Rudolfo A. Anaya, tells the story of a young boy who makes friends with a local healer who works magic among the people of the rural community where the boy and the healer live.

- *Heart of Aztlán,* by Rudolfo A. Anaya, is a novel about a family that leaves their rural home in New Mexico to find work in the city of Albuquerque. This moves means that the family has to sell their land, leaving them feeling unrooted and without a clear identity. The change strains family relations that are finally resolved by a blind musician and a witch.

- Raymond Barrio's *The Plum Plum Pickers* follows the life of a family of migrant workers and tells the harsh story of the oppressive working environment and the squalid living conditions in which they must live, as well as the greedy employer under whom they must work.

- Miguel Méndez's *The Dream of Santa Maria de las Piedra* is a story seen through the eyes of a group of old men who gather each day to share their memories and to gossip about the lives of the people in their small, rural village in the Sonora Desert in Mexico.

- Richard Vasquez's *Chicano* is another classic Chicano novel. Four generations of a Mexican-American family are portrayed. In one of the generations, a young girl, Maria Sandoval, falls in love with a young Anglo boy. The boy's head is filled with stereotypical versions of the young girl who must struggle to define her Mexican-American identity.

- Jose Antonio Villarreal's novel *Pocho* is considered a vanguard in the renaissance of Chicano literature in the early 1960s. It tells the story of a Mexican family's migration to the United States and their problems dealing with assimilation, racism, and a denial of their culture.

"that [Frankie] was dark, with a big nose and the features of a Yaqui. The old man trembled, shaken by a burst of tenderness." In this scene, it appears that Frankie dies while Loreto holds him. The truth is that Frankie dies in Vietnam, but Loreto senses Frankie's death coming, and the narrator confirms it. "The draw of life . . . it was fate that old Loreto Maldonado hold a symbolic wake over the body of Frankie, because nine months later, when he fell in Vietnam, no one accompanied his lifeless body."

Loreto, in some sense, is holding on to his own progeny, a descendent of his ancient culture—and his child is dying. What's more, he is dying because he went to fight in a foreign war, defending a country that does not honor him. In his stupor, Frankie relives his short life in bits and pieces of dialogue. "He, his family, the war, prejudice, slavery, school. Spanish is not to be spoken! Hunger. Spanish, no! The grapes, the cantaloupes, cucumbers, cotton. Without medications! I told you. Don't speak Spanish. Dark people are worthless. Get to working hard, hard, hard. Listen. Speak English. The war, the war, ah, ah, the war . . . . ''

While Loreto holds Frankie, Méndez plays a sort of duet with the memories of war between the two men. Loreto has his Mexican Revolution, the war that cost him his leg, the war in which he fought with his buddy Colonel Cuamea. Frankie has Vietnam. Back and forth like gunfire, Méndez mixes up the two wars, sometimes in the same paragraph. The Mexican Revolution, in name, was a victory for the Yaqui Indians as they were able to get rid of a despotic dictator and technically win back their lands. But where did the Revolution get Loreto? How did he end up living in the back streets of Tijuana? Was he any better off than Frankie? The only hint that Méndez offers as the difference between the two men is that at least Loreto fought on and for his own land.

> There has never existed a race that fought with such determination and courage for its land as the Yaquis did. Ready to die for their soil . . . Neither women nor old people were excluded from the struggle to death for the land that the white men grabbed from them like pulling their nails out.

"The Yaqui Loreto survived the unfortunate Frankie by two years," the narrator tells the reader. His body was discovered in the "little house that he had constructed in the neighborhood alongside the dried-up river." The river has been damned, obviously watering someone's lush fields. Garbage men find Loreto's body. They wrap it up and toss it into the back of their truck. Irony reigns again when the narrator describes Loreto's shack. It is constructed out of empty cans and bottles of food and drink. It is papered with posters of people eating and drinking. The only piece of furniture is a small chest inside of which is a picture. It is a picture of Loreto with Colonel Cuamea. There is also a document, one that states that Loreto, during the Mexican Revolution, had been a general.

Bruce-Novoa states that Loreto's "role as the custodian of oral history is underscored by the fact that only Loreto knows and remembers the semi-mythical deeds of Colonel Cuamea." But after his death "Loreto will not be included in the official accounts of the Revolution . . . like all members of the poor class, Loreto disappears, and with him all those oral histories he would have passed on to a younger generation if the oral tradition still functioned as it should." Loreto's death symbolizes the death of the oral tradition.

Source: Joyce Hart, Critical Essay on *Pilgrims in Aztlán*, in *Novels for Students*, The Gale Group, 2001.

Salvador Rodriguez del Pino

In the following essay, Rodriguez del Pino reviews Méndez's contributions to Chicano literature.

The craft of writing is a demanding skill. Not many are able to achieve it. Most of us spend all of our young years—from elementary school through college—learning it, and yet some of us graduate almost illiterate. If this is true, for learning the craft of writing, how much more difficult is it to be a good writer of literature? Until very recently, the writer or novelist needed good training in literature, money to support himself or herself, and time to write. Writing was an endeavor of the upper classes or of individuals willing to give up everything for the love of art. It certainly was not for the working classes, for the poor, or for the uneducated. Very few with these drawbacks ever succeeded. In 1971, Edward Simmens wrote: "At any rate, neither the upper-class Mexican-American nor the lower-class laborer has produced literature: the former is not inclined; the latter is not equipped." Yet, there are always exceptions. Miguel Méndez, a Mexican American bricklayer with a sixth-grade education, has produced some of the most polished Chicano literature written in Spanish and has received an honorary doctor's degree from the University of Arizona where he holds a position as professor of Latin American and Chicano literatures.

In my book *La novela chicana escrita en espanol: cinco autores comprometidos* (*The Chicano Novel Written in Spanish: Five Committed Authors*), I define Méndez's commitment as a commitment to the people, to the Chicano people, to be exact. His commitment, in the sense of being engagé, is a commitment he made to the nascent Chicano literary movement in order to rescue its oral history and to create the necessary images to document Chicano history, culture, and presence through the vehicle of the Chicano's ancestral language. Some of the other committed writers included in the book have abandoned their commitment of writing in Spanish. Only Méndez has continued to do so, and I am sure that Tomás Rivera would have also continued to do so had he lived. But the reason Méndez continues to write in Spanish is that he has not been able to master the English language well enough to use it as a literary medium. Some readers are glad, I suppose, because—whether for this reason or another—Méndez continues to preserve Spanish as an important factor in Chicano literature. And this is one of the important characteristics that distinguish Chicano

> " This literature demands that the reader be bilingual, as the corpus of Chicano literature cannot be divided into Spanish and English; each of the two languages is part of the same vital experience, and most of the time, they are intertwined in the same text. The bilingual factor sets Chicano literature apart as unique among national literatures."

literature as such, even though it still creates problems for English and Spanish departments in universities and for students as well. This literature demands that the reader be bilingual, as the corpus of Chicano literature cannot be divided into Spanish and English; each of the two languages is part of the same vital experience, and most of the time, they are intertwined in the same text. The bilingual factor sets Chicano literature apart as unique among national literatures.

Méndez's commitment stems from personal conviction and a cultural legacy that carries within itself the necessary and important need to preserve itself through oral history transmitted through the ritual of storytelling. Méndez has enhanced this ritual with the art of writing. Yet, while transmitting this cultural and historical legacy through literature, Méndez has not forgotten that contemporary Chicano culture is a symbiosis and amalgamation of three cultural heritages: indigenous, Hispanic, and Anglo American.

Ever since his two seminal stories, "Tata Casehua" and "Workshop for Images: Come in," appeared in *El Espejo* in 1969, Miguel Méndez has continued to keep his commitment to rescue the voices of silence and to create images that reflect and interpret the elusive reality and history of the Chicanos. In "Tata Casehua," Méndez sets forth his obsession to rescue the forgotten history and legacy of the people born under the sign of omega. These

are the descendants of the conquered peoples of America, who, according to Méndez, were doomed to extermination and oblivion by the arrival of the Europeans on the American continent. One must listen, he said, to the dispersed voices and histories of these peoples, carried by the wind that forever writes forgotten symbols on the ever-shifting sand dunes of the Sonora Desert—voices, he assures us, that whisper to the chosen ones the mystery of the ancient symbols that must be rescued from their silence. And Méndez is one of those initiated, as Bruce-Novoa explains in his article "La voz del silencio: Miguel Méndez."

In his other story, "Workshop for Images: Come In," Méndez tells us how reality is represented by the many broken pieces of a mirror that reflect a different perspective of the same reality and how people cling to the image of a certain reflection as the only true representation of reality. In order to grasp the essence of reality, he tells us, we must accept and realize that each broken piece is but part of the whole, and that the myriad reflections must be put together so we can comprehend and actually see the total image of reality. That is why, he tells us through examples in the story, each generation reacts and rebels against the perspective of reality held by the generation in power. This also works for the group that holds power in any society. The power group's view of reality is the basis for its interpretation of history, its rationale for oppressing other groups, and its obligation of imposing its own values and behavior. One of the examples Méndez uses to illustrate this concept in "Workshop for Images" is the older generation in power ordering the younger generation to fight and die and suffer the ravages of war in a conflict conceived by and based on the reality of the power group.

Méndez continues to use this personal concept of reality in his works and to present its many variations in order to capture the whole. *Peregrinos de Aztlán* is a case in point. The fragmented stories, anecdotes, and lives he presents in the text poignantly reflect the whole spectrum of the border reality that Méndez wants to portray. He would not have achieved this objective so thoroughly had he taken a more conventional and traditional approach with a single protagonist within a one-dimensional view of reality. Méndez, a voracious reader of world literature, could have used techniques and styles encountered in his readings, such as the fragmentation used in Dos Passos's *Manhattan Transfer* or Fuentes's *La región más transparente,* which in a sense he did. But he takes this approach a little further by presenting a physical and psychological reality fragmented even in its components, a reality that is contradictory, perverse, and arbitrary. One example of contradiction in the text is the description of the millions of tourists who visit Tijuana every year and of Rudolph H. Smith, the judge, who seem to be attracted to and cherish the Mexican culture and decorate their houses with Mexican designs and themes but, at the same time, cannot tolerate the presence of a dark Mexican in their home. This is a very contradictory but acceptable view of reality when practiced by those in power.

Méndez is also adept and sensitive when rescuing the indigenous and folk stories that appear in many of his works as well as in the transculturation process of introducing stories from the *Calilia et Dimna* into the Chicano world view. The stories or fables from the *Calila et Dimna* can be traced to India and Persia; they were written and preserved by the Arabs and translated into medieval Spanish in 1251 by order of the Castilian king Alfonso X, El Sabio. Méndez takes these stories inherited from the Hispanic legacy and turns them into Chicano literature through the process of bilingualism, Chicano psychology, and relocation to the border region of Arizona. Another Chicano writer who has drawn from Spanish literature is Rolando Hinojosa. Two of his sources for his Klail City Death Trip Series have been *Claros varones de Castilla* and *Generaciones y semblanzas,* Spanish masterpieces from the medieval period.

Méndez also draws from Latin American literature, another source of the literary legacy of the Chicano. His use of magical realism in his latest novel, *The Dream of Santa María de las Piedras,* is an extension of the Latin American propensity to mix the fantastic and the real, which is the mixture of the magical, spiritual, and physical reality that truly represents the holistic interpretation of Latin American reality. This is the result of the *mestizaje* of the magical and spiritual world of the indigenous people of America and the pragmatic, but mystic, reality of Spain. The desert seems an appropriate location for a Chicano version of Latin American magical realism, as the constant mirages and images produced by the heat and reverberations of the local elements create a fantastic atmosphere where both realities, the physical and the psychological, converge in a dramatic display presenting different levels of perception. Hallucinations? Illusions? Reality? All of these and more. That is the nature of the desert and of the land of Aztlán: a mixture of magical realism and mythol-

Three Yaqui Indian chiefs

ogy. A study of Méndez's use of magical realism in *The Dream of Santa María* can be found in the eloquent article by Alfonso Rodríguez in the proceedings from the conference in Barcelona on Culturas Hispanas de los Estados Unidos de América.

Méndez, again, juxtaposes both realities, as if to pit one against the other, in his epic poem *Los criaderos humanos y Sahuaros* (*The human breeding grounds and Sahuaros*). Poetic language, it seems, was the only vehicle for dramatizing the profound pain and grief that invade like a cancer the lives and circumstances of the downtrodden, the unwanted, the pariahs. These, according to Méndez, are the indigenous Americans, the people of the desert, of Aztlán, people who are not only victimized by "the terrible mother," the desert, but also by their fellow human beings, the powerful, the elite, entrenched in the cities. The desert and the city become the entities that breed their oppressors. The desert and the city emerge as constant leitmotifs in Méndez's works just like the dual representation of reality from "Tata Casehua" to *The Dream of Santa María de las Piedras,* these two elements are constant in his work no matter what the themes are or what genre he uses.

Another characteristic of Méndez's style is the reappearance of protagonists in his works. These characters are prototypes found along the border:

"Méndez M. employs a fragmented style of storytelling in order to include the many stories that the city harbors, and he anchors them in the feverish mind of Loreto, an old car washer, who retrieves them from oblivion by remembering them."

streetwise kids, wetbacks, gossipy old men, prostitutes, and Indians, people Méndez knew and lived with during his youthful pilgrimage through the Southwest. To anybody who has lived in any of the border cities, Tijuana, Juárez, Nogales, or Brownsville, Méndez's characters seem like old friends. The Mexico-United States borderland is unlike any other region in the world. It is a two-thousand-mile stretch of land where the first world confronts the third world, creating some kind of utopia (a good place or no place, depending on your interpretation of the term). It is the dumping ground of two countries where the people who live there must forever scheme and invent daring strategies for survival. A place where on one side people are constantly looking for ways to cross the borderline, while on the other they are constantly looking for more brutal ways to stop them. Yet, it is a place full of life and energy. A place where races and languages mix freely together, and whose economic strength relies upon the creativity of the people, with no holds barred. Anything goes, as long as you don't get caught. In spite of its dynamics, Mexico and the United States disassociate themselves from the borderland. They argue that it is a place completely created by a bad press in order to embarrass both governments and that the border represents neither Anglo American values nor the traditions of Mexican culture. Méndez does not describe this world any differently in his work. In fact, he adds that it is a place where greed, injustice, and discrimination pervade. Yet, despite the harshness of the situation and the hostility of the environment, it is the people struggling for survival in this place that make the border the last frontier in America.

And Miguel Méndez continues to tell the world their story.

Source: Salvador Rodriguez del Pino, "Miguel Méndez: The Commitment Continues," in *Miguel Méndez in Aztlán: Two Decades of Literary Production*, edited by Gary D. Keller, Bilingual Review/Press, 1995, pp. 89–91.

Salvador Rodriguez del Pino

In the following essay, del Pino presents an overview of Peregrinos de Aztlán, *stating that Méndez "indicts the perverse political systems converging on the border by rescuing stories that were never officially told."*

Peregrinos de Aztlán, Miguel Méndez M.'s first novel, was a long awaited literary event in Chicano literature. Méndez M. had already achieved recognition through his short stories "Tata Casehua" and "Taller de imagenes: pase" (Shop of Images: Come In), which had been written in a very polished prose and innovative imagery in the Spanish language. *Peregrinos* came to verify the masterful use of language by a Chicano construction worker who had not finished high school and who, by reason of class, education, and resources, was considered incapable of writing literature. The novel did not disappoint anyone. Instead, it added new dimensions to the Spanish language by including apocryphus dialects such as Border Spanish, Chicano Spanish and "pachuco calo" (a hybrid street Barrio jargon) into a literary text. In other words, Méndez M. gave genuine expression to the different characters that inhabit the Mexican and Chicano world of "the Border."

The Border is a region where Méndez M. lived and experienced the injustice and oppression perpetrated by two political systems that converge and confront each other along one of the longest borders in the world: the U.S./Mexico border. The microcosm is Tijuana, a city on the California-Mexico border. Within this city one finds representatives of almost all suppressed classes as well as oppressors whose stories converge and confront each other by their need to be told. Méndez M. rescues these stories about ordinary people who are neither heroes, personalities, nor famous. These are stories about the downtrodden, the helpless, the poor, and the unwanted whose only crime seems to be their skin color and their Indian race.

Méndez M. employs a fragmented style of storytelling in order to include the many stories that the city harbors, and he anchors them in the feverish mind of Loreto, an old car washer, who retrieves them from oblivion by remembering them. The Anglo hippie, the white-slaver, the prostitute, the corrupt judge, the cynical bureaucrat, and the hapless undocumented worker are some of the characters that find voice through Méndez M., who lets them speak in their own language. Reading the text is a tour de force in linguistic expertise as the reader must be knowledgeable in various levels of Southwestern dialects in order to fully appreciate the richness of the text.

Méndez M. structures the novel in three parts: in the first part Loreto introduces the many characters to the reader as he meets these characters while walking the streets looking for cars to wash; the second part elaborates and details their stories and develops their personalities; and the third centers on Colonel Cuamea, an old Yaqui warrior, and Frankie Pérez, who dies in Vietnam. Revolution and war are the scenarios in the third part where the lives of Cuamea and Frankie are compared through a personal struggle of ideals.

The procession of deaths throughout the text, some of them tragic, others ironic, intensify the contrast of forgotten heroic stories with the uninspiring and useless lives of the people in power. Méndez M. creates here a novel of thesis where he indicts the perverse political systems converging on the border by rescuing stories that were never officially told or were too banal to be considered. One of these is the story of Pedro, the brother of Rosenda, who kills Mario Miller de Cocuch for selling his sister into prostitution. The local papers report the incident by presenting the vilest character in the novel as a "very distinguished citizen in city politics and business who is suddenly and without provocation assaulted and stabbed by an unknown evildoer who, without a word and driven by his criminal instinct, kills him and rapidly flees." The honor and dignity of the poor is constantly reviled by those in power who seem to be the only ones to command respect by reason of wealth or political power. The stories succeed one another as Loreto guides us through the streets of the city introducing us to characters who seem to be invisible and insensible to the feelings of the foreign tourist or the wealthy passerby. The lives and histories of these city outcasts are retrieved from history's garbage pile and brought to life to remind us that their lives are also important and serve as counterparts to the stories of heroes and great persons that official history chooses, through a perverse system of values, as worthy of remembrance. Méndez M. reminds us that most of these outcasts and unwanted people are heroes themselves as the

struggle for survival in the border is a heroic act in itself.

It took almost twenty years for *Peregrinos* to be translated into English. It was no easy task for translator David Foster to plunge himself into a linguistic labyrinth of converging dialects and levels of meanings and to come forth with a substantially good translation. While there may be detractors and critics who will find fault with it, they all have to agree that it was a difficult project and that its greatest achievement so far is that it made available, for the first time, an example of Chicano literature that had been kept away from English-speaking readers.

Source: Salvador Rodriguez del Pino, "*Peregrinos de Aztlán:* Overview," in *Reference Guide to American Literature,* edited by Jim Kamp, St. James Press, 1994.

Sources

Alurista, "Myth, Identity and Struggle in Three Chicano Novels: Aztlán . . . Anaya, Méndez and Acosta," in *European Perspectives on Hispanic Literature of the United States,* edited by Genvieve Fabre, Arte Publico Press, 1988, pp. 82–90.

Bruce-Novoa, Juan D., "Miguel Méndez: Voices of Silence," in *Contemporary Chicano Fiction,* edited by Vernon E. Lattin, Bilingual Press, 1986, pp. 206–14.

Leal, Luis, "In Search of Aztlán," in *Denver Quarterly,* Vol. 16, No. 3, Fall 1981, pp. 17–23.

Rodriguez del Pino, Salvador, "*Peregrinos De Aztlán:* Overview," in *Reference Guide to American Literature,* edited by Jim Kamp, 3d ed., St. James Press, 1994.

Ryan, Richard, "Border Towns Face Pollution Crisis Two Years into NAFTA," in *Detroit News,* January 2, 1996.

Somoza, Oscar U., "The Mexican Element in the Fiction of Miguel Méndez," translated by Leland H. Chambers, in *Denver Quarterly,* Vol. 17, No. 1, Spring 1982, pp. 68–77.

Walter, Roland, "Social and Magical Realism in Miguel Méndez' *El Sueno de Santa Maria,*" in *Americas Review,* Vol. 18, No. 1, Spring 1990. p. 103.

For Further Study

Bacon, David, *LA Weekly: News Feature: Immigrant Workers,* www.laweekly.com/ink/99/46/news-bacon.shtml (October 8–14, 1999).

> Bacon's article is a news story about the plight of Mexican-American workers at an L.A. furniture store. When the workers tried to organize to ask for higher wages, the employer insisted on seeing their green cards in an attempt to squelch the unity of the group.

Bruce-Novoa, Juan D., "Mexico in Chicano Literature," in *Retrospace,* Arte Publico Press, 1990, pp. 52–62.

Bruce-Novoa, one of the leading literary critics of Chicano literature, writes a brief history of the various ways that Mexico is presented in literature throughout Chicano renaissance. It provides the reader with references to some of the more influential writings of the times.

Illegal Alien Resident Population, www.ins.usdoj.gov/ graphics/aboutins/statistics/illegalalien/index.htm (July 23, 2000).

For more detailed information about the trends of illegal migration in the United States, this website, sponsored by the U.S. government agency Immigration and Naturalization Service, breaks down this population into various categories. The categories include the country of origin, the state of residence, and the total population.

Leal, Luis, "The Problem of Identifying Chicano Literature," in *Identification and Analysis of Chicano Literature,* edited by Francisco Jimenez, Bilingual Press, 1979, pp. 2–6.

This article provides an interesting background and summary of the current literary theory in reference to Mexican-American literature. Leal tries to answer the question, What makes a literary work Chicano Literature? Leal mentions Méndez's work as well as the writings of several other authors who were involved in the Chicano literary renaissance.

Profile of Illegal Border Crossers, http://gort.ucsd.edu/mw/ tj/profile.html (July 23, 2000).

This website offers an overview of would-be illegal border crossers as developed from research conducted by San Diego Dialogue in the San Ysidro Port of Entry in partnership with the University of California, San Diego. It is an interesting observation about the kinds of people who cross at a particular entry at the border between Mexico and California.

Rabbit, Run

John Updike

1960

"Who likes Rabbit, apart from his author?" Hermione Lee asks in *The New Republic*.

> Sexist, dumb, lazy, illiterate (he spends the whole novel not finishing a book on American history), a terrible father . . . an inadequate husband, an unreliable lover, a tiresome lecher, a failing businessman, a cowardly patient, a typically "territorial" male: What kind of moral vantage point is this?

But, she writes, "What redeems Rabbit is that, inside his brutish exterior, he is tender, feminine, and empathetic."

Set in Brewer, Pennsylvania, a fictional counterpart of the real-life city of Reading, *Rabbit, Run* examines the experiences of a young man who is trapped in an unfulfilling life and his equally unfulfilling attempts to leave his family and find a new life. When the book was first published, it shocked many readers with its explicit descriptions of sexuality, and according to Robert Detweiler in *John Updike,* some reviewers even speculated that Updike wrote a scandalous novel on purpose to capture the attention of the reading public. However, Detweiler notes, in the ensuing decades, standards of what was appropriate and acceptable in novels have been greatly relaxed, and "it can now be appraised much more objectively in terms of its artistic qualities."

Since writing *Rabbit, Run,* Updike has written three other novels about Rabbit, at approximately ten-year intervals: *Rabbit Redux* (1971), *Rabbit Is Rich* (1981), and *Rabbit at Rest* (1990). Rabbit Angstrom has become Updike's most well-known

John Updike

character, and *Rabbit, Run* is his most recognized book title. He has won numerous awards and honors and is widely regarded as one of America's great novelists.

Author Biography

"I'm a publishing fool, so anything I did not publish must be pretty bad," John Updike told Michael Rogers in *Library Journal,* and indeed, Updike is widely regarded as one of America's most prolific novelists.

John Bemrose wrote in *Maclean's,* "For almost 40 years, Updike has catalogued the growing and aging pains of America's middle class with such tireless virtuosity and boyish effervescence that it sometimes seems he has drunk from the fountain of youth." Updike, who was born on March 18, 1932, in Shillington, Pennsylvania, had what Bemrose called a "secure, slow-paced upbringing there." His father was a high school teacher who was bored and disenchanted with his work and had the urge to move on but never left his family. "There was a lot of complaining," Updike told Bemrose. "My father had an appetite for moving on. But it wasn't indulged to the point where he walked out and left me fatherless."

Updike currently lives in Beverly, Maryland, with his second wife, Martha; they were married in 1977, and Updike has four grown children from his first marriage. He spends three hours daily writing but does not usually use a word processor. "You can sneak into your imagination a little easier with pencil and paper," he told Bemrose.

"It was a friendlier time when I started out, certainly," Updike told Rogers. "Would my first novel, *The Poorhouse Fair* . . . even be published now, or would it get published by one of those gallant little university presses that's trying to fill the gap [in publishing and literature]? There is a relative lack of playfulness and experimentalism in the lists of the increasingly corporate publishers."

"Although a character like Rabbit Angstrom and I don't have the same sociological circumstances, a lot of my thoughts go into his brain," Updike told Rogers.

Updike has no thoughts of retiring. He told Rogers, "There's obviously a time when you should hang it up, but I don't feel I'm there yet. I still have things I'm trying to do, and I still get pleasure out of the challenge."

Plot Summary

Section One

As *Rabbit, Run* opens, twenty-six-year-old former high school basketball star Harry "Rabbit" Angstrom is on his way home from his unfulfilling job as a demonstrator of a kitchen gadget, the MagiPeel vegetable peeler. He spots some kids playing basketball and joins their play, fantasizing about his lost glory days, then runs home to his tiny, squalid apartment. His wife, Janice, who is pregnant, is home watching television and drinking. She asks Rabbit to go get their car, pick up their son, Nelson, and get her some cigarettes. This string of errands weighs on Rabbit, who feels trapped and bored in his job, his marriage, and his life. He sees his son through the window of his in-laws' house and decides to leave him in their care. On impulse, he gets in the car and starts driving south, away from his old life.

Turning onto smaller and smaller roads, Rabbit gets lost, stopping for directions but receiving only enigmatic answers: one man tells him, "The only way to get somewhere, you know, is to figure out where you're going before you get there." Eventually, demoralized, tired, and lonely, he turns around and finds his way back home. He does not want to go back to his wife and son, so he hides out with his former coach, Marty Tothero.

Tothero, who has a young girlfriend, arranges for her to bring a friend, Ruth, and the four of them go out to dinner. Rabbit goes home with Ruth, who is a part-time prostitute and impulsively decides to move in with her. He sneaks back to his own apartment to get his clothes. Although his wife is not there, the minister of Janice's parents' church, Jack Eccles, sees him and tries to convince him to return to his family. Although he does not succeed, he sets a date for Rabbit to meet him for golf the next week. Rabbit knows this is so that Eccles, and through him his wife's family, can keep tabs on him and perhaps persuade him to go home, but he agrees to show up.

Section Two

Rabbit has quit his job for the MagiPeel company, and Eccles arranges for him to work as a gardener. Rabbit finds out that Ruth is pregnant, and Rabbit is the father of her child. Janice is angry at Rabbit for being irresponsible and dense. When Rabbit goes out with Ruth, they run into one of Ruth's former boyfriends, and Rabbit is filled with jealousy: he asks her to do everything for him, sexually, that she did for her other boyfriends, a demand she finds demeaning and humiliating.

That night, Eccles notifies Rabbit that Janice is in the hospital, giving birth to their baby. Rabbit runs out on Ruth and goes to the hospital where he is reunited with Janice. Back in their apartment, he and Nelson wait for Janice to come home from the hospital.

Rabbit begins working for Janice's father at his used-car lot, and Janice comes home with the baby. Rabbit goes to church but only because he has seen Eccles's wife who is pretty and who flirts with him, and he's interested in her. That night, Janice pushes him away, and he leaves, wandering around town and looking for Ruth. He still feels trapped, bored, and frustrated with life; none of these women are the answer.

When Rabbit abandons her again, Janice is hurt and depressed, and she starts drinking to dull the pain, drinking all night and all the next day. Her mother is coming to visit her, and she tries to give the new baby a bath before the visit, but she is so drunk that she unintentionally lets the baby drown in the bath.

Section Three

Rabbit, horrified and guilt-stricken over his child's death, goes back to Janice, feeling that the death is his fault: if he had not left Janice, it would never have happened. At the baby's funeral, however, he begins to believe that the child is now in heaven. He is buoyed up by this thought, almost happy, but Janice doesn't share or understand his sense of peace and release. He tries to explain to her that he now understands that she, like the baby, is a victim, but no one else knows what he's talking about—including Janice. At the burial, he runs away from the graveyard, which is at the foot of a mountain, and flees into the forest that covers its slopes. He wanders, alienated and lost, and eventually returns to town and goes to Ruth.

As the novel ends, Rabbit is running again—this time, from Ruth, still feeling trapped, looking for a new life, a way out.

Characters

Harry Angstrom

A twenty-six-year-old former high school basketball star, Rabbit is now unhappily married to Janice, who is pregnant. He has a young son, Nelson, and a boring and unfulfilling job selling kitchen gadgets for the Magipeel vegetable peeler company. He is restless and unhappy, unable to regain his former glory as a sports star, and he feels trapped by the mundane demands of being a husband and father. Rabbit leaves home, looking for something—he doesn't know what—that will show him there is meaning in life. He senses that there must be something greater and more meaningful than the world he lives in, but he doesn't know what that is.

Although Rabbit is a seeker, in a religious sense he is naïve. He has been raised Christian but only has a limited, Sunday-school awareness of what this means, in the sense that he knows some things are considered sinful, such as alcohol, gambling, and cigarettes. He is also aware that cheating on his wife and leaving his family are sinful, but this awareness does not stop him from doing so; his feeling that he needs to find himself takes precedence over these rules. "If you have the guts to be yourself, other people'll pay your price," he says at one point. His spiritual shallowness is shown in one scene, in which he is lying in bed with his girlfriend Ruth, a prostitute, and he prays.

Media Adaptations

- *Rabbit, Run* was filmed by Warner Bros. in 1970 and starred James Caan as Rabbit.

As Rachael C. Burchard wrote in *Yea Sayings,* this prayer doesn't change his actions, but "it comforts and reassures him, allowing him to ignore responsibility."

Rabbit is also naïve about women; although he is twenty-six years old, he seems unable to see women as people who exist apart from his sexual desire for them. He seems incapable of seeing a woman, any woman, without having sexual fantasies about her, and he thinks all these women are equally interested in him, despite evidence to the contrary. His inability to contain his immature sexual impulses leads him to act irresponsibly and to hurt others. He is also constantly on the lookout for a new conquest and compares sexual relationships to his high school success in sports:

> I once played a game real well. I really did. And after you're first-rate at something, no matter what, it kind of takes the kick out of being second-rate. And that little thing Janice and I had going, boy, it was really second-rate.

Janice Angstrom

Rabbit's wife, who is pregnant with their second child in the beginning of this novel, is also bored and disillusioned but fills up the void in her life with alcohol and television. She simply wants Rabbit to behave like an ordinary husband and can't understand why he has the urge to run. In the morning, Updike writes,

> She feels the workday approaching like an army of light, feels the dark ridged houses beneath her as potentially stirring, waking, opening like castles to send forth their men, and regrets that her own husband is unable to settle into the rhythm of which one more beat is about to sound. Why him? What was so precious about him?

Like Rabbit, Janice is not very articulate and is inclined to avoid problems rather than discuss them and make changes. After a nasty fight, in which she and Rabbit curse and demean each other,

she goes into the kitchen and calls, "And honey pick up a pack of cigarettes, could you?" as if everything is normal. Of course it isn't, and she drinks to dull her emotional pain. At the end of the book, this avoidance has disastrous consequences when she gets very drunk and accidentally drowns her new baby.

Jack Eccles

Eccles is Janice's parents' clergyman, an Episcopal minister. Although he professes to be religious, he does not have any faith. He plays golf with his churchgoers so he can be a pal to them and hangs out at that corner soda shop with teenagers, again being a pal. His wife is aware of the self-serving nature of these actions, however, and she remarks that he does not particularly want to help the teenagers; he is merely titillated by the teenagers' questions about how far you can "go" on a date without being sinful. He is similarly chastised by another minister, Reverend Kruppenbach, who tells him, "[You are] a minister of God selling his message for a few scraps of gossip and a few games of golf."

Unlike Rabbit, who places his own search for meaning above conventional religious and moral rules, Eccles is more interested in getting people to follow the rules than in the meaning behind them. Eccles believes actions are more important than meaning and belief, and in fact does not seem to have much belief in anything. When Rabbit asks Eccles, "Remember that thing we used to talk about? The thing behind everything?" meaning the source of meaning in life, Eccles says, "Harry, you know I don't think that thing exists in the way you think it does."

Because Eccles is more interested in behavior than belief, he tries to get Rabbit to go back to his wife and get a respectable job. Similarly, he meddles in other people's lives, trying to get them to behave as society says they should, without reflecting on the meaning of their lives. As Donald J. Greiner wrote in *John Updike's Novels,* he is "more a social worker than a man of faith."

This conflict between Eccles' lack of faith and the demand of his profession that he have faith is evident in Eccles' every move. Updike writes, "Eccles wrestles in the pulpit with the squeak in his voice. His eyebrows jiggle as if on fishhooks. It is an unpleasant and strained performance, contorted; somehow; he drives his car with an easier piety."

Lucy Eccles

Lucy is Eccles' wife. She flirts with and teases Rabbit. Although she's a pastor's wife, she is not particularly religious and is more interested in the psychosexual theories of Sigmund Freud than in the church. She feels trapped and bored with the "nice" behavior enforced on her by the role of minister's wife and is immediately attracted to Rabbit and his similar rebellion against accepted behavior. She flirts with Rabbit and asks him to walk her home, but then when he approaches her, she is insulted and won't do anything with him.

Ruth Leonard

Ruth is a no-nonsense kind of woman; she is realistic about her life. A part-time prostitute, she is protective of her own heart and is naturally suspicious of Rabbit's motives when he sleeps with her and almost instantly demands to be her husband, though he is still married to Janice. Secretly, she knows he will go back to his wife, but she is charmed by him. She is heavy, solidly built, and her solidity is comforting to Rabbit, who uses Ruth as a kind of anesthetic against the demands of life: "If he can just once more bury himself in her he knows he'll come up with his nerves all combed."

Rabbit

See Harry Angstrom

Marty Tothero

Tothero is Rabbit's old coach, a washed-up old man who lives in a shabby room above a men's club. When Rabbit first leaves Janice, he goes to Tothero, who takes him in, gets him to go out on a double date, and introduces him to Ruth Leonard. Updike writes of Tothero, "He looks like a big tired dwarf. He seems foreshortened; a balding big head and a massively checkered sports coat and then stubby legs in blue trousers that are too long . . ." Tothero is what Rabbit might become if he doesn't take care: a broken-down old man who was once a sports hero and still reminisces sadly about his former glory.

Themes

The Quest

In *John Updike,* Susan Henning Uphauser wrote that "many critics have identified Rabbit's running as a religious quest, a search for meaning beyond the natural world." Of all the characters in

Topics for Further Study

- Harry "Rabbit" Angstrom, like Holden Caulfield in J. D. Salinger's *The Catcher in the Rye,* rebels against his life. Read *The Catcher in the Rye* and write about how these two characters are similar and how they differ.

- In the late 1950s, when the book was written, the feminist movement had not yet occurred. All of the women in the book are wives or are otherwise dependent on men, with no careers or work of their own. How do you think the feminist movement affected relationships between women and men, and how do you think it might affect the relationships of the couples in Updike's book?

- When Rabbit goes on his road trip, he is surprised to find that all of America is not the same—that people can tell he is from somewhere else simply by looking at him. Do you think the different regions of America have become more similar to each other since the late 1950s, or are there still places that are very different from each other? In your own travels, what have you noticed that makes other people and places seem different from those where you live?

- Rabbit feels compelled to find a meaningful life, even if his search hurts others. Do you think this is right? Why or why not?

- Rabbit was a 'big man' in high school but has not done anything notable since then. Because athletic skill is dependent on physical factors that usually change with age, most athletes have to face the fact that at some point, they must enter a different career and find success in another area of life. For example, some athletes, such as young Olympic gymnasts, reach their peak in their early teens. After this, their athletic ability declines and they must find new careers or work in a different area of their sport. Research the life of a young athlete you admire and discuss how he or she dealt with this change, or how he or she plans to continue to be successful.

the novel, he is the only one who senses that there is meaning hidden somewhere in life, that "somewhere behind all this . . . there's something that wants me to find it." In 1950s American society, which Uphauser characterized as "spiritually suffocating," of course, he cannot find this meaning. Thus, she wrote, "Updike conveys the confusion, meaninglessness, and uncertainty in American society today."

As Uphauser points out, Updike makes the image of the quest clear in each of the three sections of the book: in the first section, he and Ruth climb the mountain, which is called Mount Judge, hoping to find a truth at the top. They don't find anything, and Rabbit turns to Ruth as if she is the truth he seeks. In the second section, Rabbit goes to church but is again distracted by sexual desires when he sees the minister's wife, who flirts with him. In the third section, he climbs the mountain again but is frightened by the lonely, alienated feeling he experiences at the top, so he runs back to town and to Ruth.

Updike does not present any answers to Rabbit's quest; readers don't have any sense that he will ever find what he's looking for or that he will solve his difficulties with women, with trust, with finding fulfillment and happiness and a home that doesn't strangle him. In this, Updike is extremely honest, since for many people, this is how life is. Many people feel bored, disillusioned, and trapped, and just as Rabbit is not comforted by traditional religious views (in the form of Jack Eccles), many Americans are similarly not comforted by traditional religion. Unlike older societies and those in which traditions are still strong, American society does not offer any absolute answers to those seeking meaning in their lives. Like Rabbit, many people wander from job to job, state to state, and relationship to relationship, in search of the same "something" that Rabbit seeks.

A Complicated Hero

Rabbit evokes conflicting feelings in most readers. Many readers are angered by Rabbit's desertion of his family, his philandering, and his sleazy attitude toward women: this is not what is expected from the hero of a book. On the other hand, some of Rabbit's other qualities are admirable. He wants his life to be meaningful, and will settle for nothing less. He is driven to seek a meaningful life, and resists the common life that everyone else in the book accepts unquestioningly. He questions his job, his marriage, his past, his choice of girlfriends, and sees his whole life, and

other people's lives, as examples of hypocrisy. He refuses to settle, thinking "somewhere there was something better for him than listening to babies cry and cheating people in used-car lots." When Jack Eccles tells him to be a man, act "mature," and take care of his family, Rabbit is horrified, since to him, being "mature" is "the same as being dead." As Uphauser notes, "And indeed, maturity, settling 'into the nationwide rhythm' of meaningless and monotonous work, devotion to family, the acquisition of material objects, *may* imply spiritual death."

Like many readers, other characters in the novel deplore and admire these same qualities in Rabbit. Ruth hates how irresponsible he is but admires him because, she says, "in your stupid way you're still fighting," and Eccles wants Rabbit to go back to his family but admires his spiritual questioning, his odd faith in God, and his sense of a supernatural level of reality beyond the stale grind of daily life.

Updike's Emphasis on Sex and Sports

One aspect of the novel that offends many critics and readers is Updike's emphasis on sex. Rabbit sees every woman he meets in sexual terms, and he uses the exhilaration he feels in sex as an attempt to come closer to the meaningful, intense, spiritual side of life that he's seeking. However, his sexual experiences are all ultimately unfulfilling and don't lead him any closer to the "something" he wants to reach.

As an ex-star athlete, Rabbit sees his chosen sport of basketball in sexual terms: the two kinds of physical achievement are the same in his mind. Sports are like sex, sex is like sport, and all of them are allied to religion in his mind: his actions are an attempt to come in contact with something greater than the self.

Style

Updike's Use of Metaphor

As Hermione Lee pointed out in the *New Republic,* in Updike's work, everything becomes a metaphor: every ordinary object and event can be seen as signifying something else, often a larger truth. "This is the most metaphorical writing in American fiction, except for Melville's," she wrote. Rabbit sees everything as meaningful but also as strange. Lee commented on Updike's comparisons of Rabbit's heart to many things: it's described as "a fist, an amphitheater, a drum, a galley slave, a ballplayer waiting for the whistle." In Updike, she noted, "no object, no creature, is too ordinary or too technical to be subjected to metaphor."

Rich Detail

Updike's work is notable for its rich, precise, and accumulated detail of ordinary life. Lee quoted other reviewers, who loved Updike's "meticulous taxonomy" of "the material nature of the world," and admire his "saluting and memorializing American superabundance." Updike spends the same amount of energy on details of passing scenes that he does on crucial moments, so every moment in the book, no matter how small and fleeting, is extraordinarily vivid. For example, when Rabbit stops at a roadside cafe for coffee late at night, Updike writes,

> Somehow, though he can't put his finger on the difference, he is unlike the other customers. They sense it too, and look at him with hard eyes, eyes like little metal studs pinned into the white faces of young men sitting in booths three to a girl, the girls with orange hair hanging like wiggly seaweed or loosely bound with gold barrettes like pirate treasure. At the counter middle-aged couples in overcoats bunch their faces forward into the straws of gray ice-cream sodas.

In another scene, Updike describes a street corner: "Tall two-petalled street-sign, the cleat-gouged trunk of the telephone pole holding its insulation against the sky, fire hydrants like a golden bush: a grove." This level of detail is continued throughout the book and combines with Updike's use of present tense to make the book as vivid and immediate as a movie. In addition, it gives readers a rich sense of life in middle-class America in the second half of the twentieth century. Anthony Quinton wrote in a *Times* (London) review that "what [the Rabbit books] amount to is a social and, so to speak, emotional history of the United States over the last twenty years or more."

Use of the Present Tense

Rabbit, Run, unlike many other novels, is written entirely in the present tense. Instead of presenting Rabbit's story as something that is over-and-done with, Updike uses present tense to give the story an immediate, "this-is-happening-now" quality, which has the effect of making readers feel they are right there in the action. For example, when he is driving south to get away from his home, Updike writes, "The road twists more and more wildly in its struggle to gain height and then without warning sheds its skin of asphalt and worms on

in dirt. By now Rabbit knows this is not the road but he is afraid to stop the car to turn it around. He has left the last light of a house miles behind."

According to Alice and Kenneth Hamilton in *The Elements of John Updike,* the author deliberately chose this technique to give his prose a cinematic quality. They quote author Jane Howard, to whom Updike said,

> I originally wrote *Rabbit, Run* in the present tense, in a sort of cinematic way. I thought of it as *Rabbit, Run: A Movie.* Novels are descended from the chronicles of what has long ago happened, but movies happen to you in the present, as you sit there.

In *John Updike,* Robert Detweiler wrote that Updike "composes the whole novel in the historical present to provide a precarious dramatic immediacy—a short-story technique that functions very well in this long narrative."

Historical Context

According to Erik Kielland-Lund in *New Essays on Rabbit, Run,* "John Updike has said that the book is a product of the fifties and not really in a conscious way *about*" the fifties. However, Kielland-Lund noted, the book aptly reflects the American world at that time, in often dazzling detail. Even when it was published, Kielland-Lund noted, the book was recognized as reflecting "characteristics of society at that time": individualism, immaturity, religiosity, and love of sports. Donald J. Greiner wrote in *John Updike's Novels* that, as Updike himself noted in the foreword to the Modern Library edition of the book, it was written in 1959, in the present tense. The time of its writing contained the time of its action. Thus, the songs Rabbit hears on the radio, the news he hears, and the styles he sees were typical of the late fifties. According to Greiner, Updike has also said, "My fiction about the daily doings of ordinary people has more history in it than the history books."

The 1950s were known as the age of conformity because of the widespread emphasis on behaving according to rather strict, and preferably unexamined, social mores. People were urged to go to church, to be patriotic, to work hard, and to raise families, without really questioning whether they truly wanted to do these things.

During the 1950s, family stability was highly valued. Divorce rates dropped and birth rates rose. Men and women were taught to see getting mar-

Compare
&
Contrast

- **1950s:** In 1959, the average American yearly income is $5,016.

  Today: In 1999, the average yearly income is $53,350.

- **1950s:** In 1959, there are 3,287 AM radio stations, 578 FM stations, and 509 television stations in the United States.

  Today: In 1999, there are 4,782 AM radio stations, 5,745 FM radio stations, and 1,599 television stations in the United States.

- **1950s:** In 1959, the cost of a new car averages $2,132.

Today: In 2000, the average cost of a new car is over $20,000.

- **1950s:** In the 1950s, when fathers abandon their children, as Rabbit does in the case of both Janice and Ruth, it is difficult for the children's mothers to force them to pay child support, or even to prove that the children are the man's offspring.

  Today: Legislation helps mothers force fathers to pay child support, and DNA testing can be used to prove that a man is the father of a child.

ried and having a family as the ultimate attainment of respectability and adult status, a sort of happily-ever-after Cinderella story of domestic bliss, and they married younger than people do today: Rabbit, at twenty-six, remarks that he married relatively late. Men were expected to be the sole providers for their families, preferably through working in business, while their wives stayed at home taking care of children. For those who found that this dream was a nightmare, however, there was little opportunity for constructive escape.

Some people, like Rabbit's wife Janice, found escape in alcohol and tranquilizers, which Kielland-Lund noted have been called the "American housewife's answer to what [Betty Friedan] calls 'the problem that has no name.'" Separated from the chance to engage in productive work, these women often suffered from low self-esteem and used tranquilizers and alcohol to get through the day.

During this decade, television became for the first time the dominant medium of communication and entertainment, and millions of Americans watched situation comedies, family shows, and game shows, such as the one Rabbit watches in Janice's hospital room:

> The idea is all these women have tragedies they tell
> about and then get money according to how much

applause there is, but by the time the M.C. gets done delivering commercials and kidding them about their grandchildren and their girlish hairdos there isn't much room for tragedy left.

Other popular television shows such as *Leave It to Beaver* and *The Mickey Mouse Club* showed wholesome families and youngsters who suffered only minor, amusing problems, furthering the view of the normal family as a father, a mother, and children, as well as the idea that divorce was uncommon and shameful.

In the 1950s an increasing number of Americans began attending college: this boom in enrollment was largely funded by the GI Bill, a government scholarship program that gave low-cost student loans to soldiers who had fought in World War II.

At that time, the feminist revolution was still a couple of decades away, and the contemporary attitudes toward women are reflected in the book. Women were supposed to be mothers, wives, or girlfriends; they were not considered to have much of an existence apart from men. The pinnacle of a girl's life was supposed to be the day she married, and other contributions of women to society were downplayed.

Because Updike is a realist, he shows the dark side of this dream: restriction always leads to some

James Caan as Rabbit and Carrie Snodgrass as Janice in the 1970 film version of the novel

form of rebellion, and the fifties were no exception. Despite being an age of conformity, as Sanford Pinsker pointed out in *New Essays on Rabbit, Run*, "the 1950s were also anxious . . . jumpy, and filled with rebelliousness." Rabbit Angstrom personifies this rebelliousness as he struggles against the traps of family, work, and social expectation.

Critical Overview

"The novels of John Updike have spawned a criticism remarkable in its contentiousness," Bernard

A. Schopen wrote in *Twentieth Century Literature.* "His books have evoked critical outrage, bewilderment, condescension, commendation, and an enthusiasm approaching the fulsome. The same novel might be hailed as a major fictional achievement and dismissed as a self-indulgence or a failure." In *John Updike,* Susan Henning Uphauser wrote,

> *Rabbit, Run* has elicited a spectrum of responses so varied that it is difficult to believe that critics are writing about the same novel. Many first reviewers admired Updike's style but repudiated the novel, emotionally offended. Recent criticism identifies *Rabbit, Run* as the most powerful of Updike's novels. Yet its ability to offend remains.

And in *John Updike's Novels,* Donald J. Greiner wrote that it "continues to upset the unprepared reader." It does so for several reasons: chief among these are its explicit sexuality and its moral ambiguity.

Explicit Sexuality

Many reviewers have been deeply offended by Updike's explicit descriptions of sexual scenes. Eliot Fremont-Smith wrote in the *Village Voice,*

> It must have been the sexuality that so upset the respectable critics. . . . Their consternation had to do with what seemed a great divide between John Updike's exquisite command of prose . . . and the apparent no-good vulgar nothing he expended it on.

Alfred Chester, one of the earliest reviewers of Updike, wrote, "A God who has allowed a writer to lavish such craft upon these worthless tales is capable of anything," according to Sanford Pinsker in *New Essays on Rabbit, Run.*

In many cases, these critics seemed to be allowing their disgust with Updike's descriptions of sex to color their perception of his work as a whole. Robert Detweiler wrote in *John Updike,* "As frequently happens, the furor accompanying the depiction of sexual amorality increased the difficulty of judging the novel's artistic quality. Most of the reviews appeared to be impulsive reactions to the subject matter rather than measured assessments." However, even in today's more permissive atmosphere, the novel still offends some readers, largely because of Rabbit's (and, some reviewers believe, Updike's) obsession with sex.

Despite this, those who are not offended have found depth and meaning in the novel that escaped some earlier critics. Donald J. Greiner wrote in *John Updike's Novels* that in the decades since the book's publication, as the furor over sexual explicitness has subsided, it has become apparent that in the book Updike

> . . . takes a common American experience—the graduation from high school of a star athlete who has no life to lead once the applause diminishes and the headlines fade—and turns it into a subtle expose of the frailty of the American dream. . . . It is now clear that he has written a saga of middle-class America in the second half of the twentieth century.

Moral Ambiguity

Because Updike does not offer a clear moral perspective in his books, some readers have asserted that Updike is unwilling or unable to deal with serious moral issues, that his books are self-indulgent rambling, and that he has nothing substantial to say. However, other critics see this ambiguity as a positive feature of the novel, contributing to its depth. As Erik Kielland-Lund noted in *New Essays on Rabbit Run,* "Updike's fiction consistently opens more doors than it closes and asks many more questions than there are simple answers to," and "Whether it is a question of freedom versus commitment, alienation versus belonging, faith versus skepticism, or egotism versus altruism, Updike manages to convey both the difficulty and the seriousness of the human condition."

Susan Henning Uphauser wrote that in her opinion these wildly differing but fervently held convictions about the worth—or worthlessness—of the novel prove its artistic success, since, she wrote, Updike intended to jar his readers, to make them feel as uncomfortable and ambivalent about their lives as Rabbit feels about his. "Faced with irreconcilable conflicts, our first response may be, like Rabbit's, to run," she wrote, and she noted that this response proved Updike's success in getting readers to identify with Rabbit's situation.

Use of Language

Whether they believe his work is moral or immoral, pointless or deeply meaningful, many of Updike's critics agree that he has great command of the English language. Rachael C. Burchard wrote in *Yea Sayings* that "His style is superb. His work is worth reading if for no reason other than to enjoy the piquant phrase, the lyric vision, the fluent rhetoric." In *John Updike,* Susan Henning Uphauser commented, "In the midst of diversity there are certain elements common to all Updike's writing. Most important, there is Updike's remarkable mastery of language."

However, like almost all commentary on Updike, this area is also controversial. In *Time to Murder and Create: The Contemporary Novel in Crisis,* John W. Aldridge wrote that Updike

> . . . has none of the attributes we conventionally associate with major literary talent. He does not have an interesting mind. He does not possess remarkable narrative gifts or a distinguished style. In fact, one of the problems he poses for the critic is that one has real difficulty remembering his work long enough to think clearly about it.

Sanford Pinsker remarked in *New Essays on Rabbit Run* that those who dislike his work

> . . . often count up the references to popular culture—from newspapers and magazines to radio and television—and conclude that he says far too much about far too little. One would be hard pressed to think of

a subject, however inconsequential, which Updike's prose would *tinge* with purple.

Readers Love It

Whatever the critics say, many readers love the book. In 1998, readers of *Library Journal* included *Rabbit, Run* in their list of their favorite books of the twentieth century, but it was not included on the more highly regarded Modern Library List of the twentieth century's greatest novels. "I did feel a little hurt," Updike told *Library Journal* interviewer Michael Rogers. "You like to be on lists as long as they exist."

Criticism

Kelly Winters

Winters is a freelance writer and editor and has written for a wide variety of academic and educational publishers. In the following essay, she discusses the theme of the quest in John Updike's novel.

In *The Elements of John Updike,* Alice and Kenneth Hamilton wrote,

> Updike directs us to those aspects of earth which can speak to us of heaven and show us how to relate ourselves qualitatively to it. He gives us . . . specific scenes set in one particular place at one particular time . . . concrete situations confronting us from day to day. And he lets us see that, behind the shifting surface of the experiences life brings us, there is one constant question which each of us must answer for himself: Does the universe, blindly ruled by chance, run downward into death; or does it follow the commands of a Living God whose Will for it is life?

Throughout the book, Rabbit looks for the answer to this question although he does not consciously think of it in religious terms. He is on a quest for meaning, and his story is in some ways the oldest story in the world: people have been telling tales of quests for thousands of years.

Dean Doner wrote in *John Updike: A Collection of Critical Essays* that the novel is successful because Rabbit is symbolic of us all, and his search for meaning and purpose in his life reflects a uniquely twentieth-century view of this search. The things Rabbit flees from are the things that oppress many people in modern society: Doner summed them up as

> an economy which traps a man into mean, petty, lying hucksterism; tenement-apartment housing which traps a man and his family into close, airless, nerve-

shattering 'togetherness'; unimaginative, dirty cities which offer no release for the spirit; the ugly voices of advertising and television.

The book is also different from many older quest stories because, traditionally, the person on a quest is a purer soul than Rabbit is. Rabbit has a rudimentary awareness of sin—he thinks of smoking, gambling, and drinking as sins, in a Sunday-school sort of way—but does not connect the facts that he's cheating on his wife and abandoning his child with the notion of sin. In his mind, his own search for self overrides the concept of sin: if he is truly being himself, everything's okay, and he even says, "If you have the guts to be yourself, other people'll pay your price." This makes him a complex and often annoying character to the reader, who simultaneously admires Rabbit's insistence on finding himself and is disgusted by how Rabbit goes about doing so. In the classical quest, the hero is a "hero" in every sense of the term: someone who is admirable, or who is at least conscious of his or her own shortcomings.

The book begins with an actual, physical quest: Rabbit hops in his car and takes off, heading south, which to him is a kind of promised land of milk and honey:

> He wants to go south, down, down the map into orange groves and smoking rivers and barefoot women. It seems simple enough, drive all night through the dawn through the morning through the noon park on a beach take off your shoes and fall asleep by the Gulf of Mexico. Wake up with the stars above perfectly spaced in perfect health.

Significantly, he can't get there as easily as he imagined. The road turns. "But he is going east, the wrong direction, into unhealth, soot, and sting, a smothering hole where you can't move without killing somebody." Although he temporarily escapes this trap, for the rest of the book, Rabbit will not be able to do anything without hurting someone: his wife Janice, Ruth, himself, and, indirectly, his new baby.

Not realizing that the trap he's in is more spiritual than physical, he keeps on driving. He has no map, and when he gets one, it only confuses him. An old gas station attendant, who picks up on his confusion, tells him, "The only way to get somewhere, you know, is to figure out where you're going before you go there." Of course, he has no idea exactly what he wants out of life, or even this road trip, and this advice only makes him aware of his confusion and angers him. He wanders, apparently almost in circles and ends up on a road that grows more and more narrow as it steeply climbs. "By

> The road turns. 'But he is going east, the wrong direction, into unhealth, soot, and sting, a smothering hole where you can't move without killing somebody.' Although he temporarily escapes this trap, for the rest of the book, Rabbit will not be able to do anything without hurting someone: his wife Janice, Ruth, himself, and, indirectly, his new baby."

now Rabbit knows this is not the road but he is afraid to stop the car to turn it around. He has left the last light of a house miles behind." The road ends in a lovers' lane, where everyone has someone except him. The map, far from being helpful, is now a trap: "a net, all those red lines and blue lines and stars, a net he is somewhere caught in." He rips up the map, is frightened when another car comes up behind him, and drives blindly off. He knows he must go back home and face his life, instead of running away from it, but he doesn't go home; he keeps on running from his family.

This sequence foreshadows the track of the whole novel; throughout the book, Rabbit encounters various people and then runs from them: his wife, Ruth, Eccles. He is looking for "something that wants him to find it," something beyond the physical reality of his life, the cluttered apartment, the "tightening net" of his empty marriage and meaningless job. As Rachael C. Burchard wrote in *Yea Sayings,* Rabbit's story is intended to show that people need "some undefined element which modern American culture—specifically twentieth-century Christianity, small Pennsylvania town version—has not provided." Rabbit's "misdirected and uncharted search" is symbolic of the inner search many people must undergo when they realize that modern culture does not satisfy their need for meaning, purpose, and connection.

Whenever Rabbit follows social customs, or does what others want him to do, he gets in trouble. He is the kind of man who should not have married when he did, should not have "settled down" and had a child before he was ready, but that was simply what everyone did. In fact, whenever Rabbit does what other people, or society, require from him, he only gets deeper in trouble; as Dean Doner wrote in "Rabbit Angstrom's Unseen World," "The road map—the way laid out for him by other people—always leads Rabbit further into the net" of confusion, staleness, and despair.

Rabbit, like characters in other Updike novels, is experiencing a midlife crisis—perhaps a little early, given that he is only in his mid-twenties, but it is at this point that people often examine their lives, reassess what they have done, and find it lacking; life is not fulfilling, and something must be done before it's too late. Updike is interested in middles: as he told Jane Howard in *Life* magazine,

> There is a great deal to be said about almost anything. Everything can be as interesting as every other thing. An old milk carton is worth a rose. . . . The idea of a hero is aristocratic. Now either nobody is a hero or everyone is. I vote for everyone. My subject is the American Protestant small town middle class. I like middles. It is in middles that extremes clash, where ambiguity restlessly rules.

In keeping with Updike's interest in ambiguity, there is no clear answer to Rabbit's search. Bernard Schopen wrote in *Twentieth Century Literature* that "Updike has said that the central theme of each of his novels is meant to be a moral dilemma, and that his books are intended as moral debates with the reader." However, Schopen also noted, Updike "believes there are no solutions" to the moral dilemmas he presents and "specifically rejects the notion that literature should inculcate moral principles or precepts." Updike creates a "morally ambiguous" world, in which the characters are complex and in which they cannot be easily divided into good and bad people.

In his encounters with others, Rabbit often seems on the verge of breaking through to finding some source of meaning, but ultimately, these things are shown to be empty. Chief among them are the church, in the person of the minister Jack Eccles, who, far from being inspiring, is if anything more shallow and morally flawed than Rabbit, who at least has belief in "something"—which the minister lacks.

Unlike many other quest stories in which the hero (or heroine) finds what he or she was looking for and is transformed, Updike's story has no clean ending. At the end of the book, Rabbit is still seeking, and the church has provided no answers. He runs from Ruth's demand that he marry her and out in the street "lifts his eyes to the church window. It is, because of church poverty or the late summer nights or just carelessness, unlit, a dark circle in a limestone facade." There is no light, or guidance, for him there.

There is light, however, "in the streetlights," a sign that the only real answer to his quest is to continue seeking. "He decides to walk around the block, to clear his head and pick his path." At least, although he's still seeking, he's finally beginning to follow the old gas station man's advice to "figure out where you're going before you go there." However, although he tries, he still doesn't really know what he's doing and walks blindly. Updike writes,

> His hands lift of their own and he feels the wind on his ears even before, his heels hitting heavily on the pavement at first but with an effortless gathering out of a kind of sweet panic growing lighter and quicker and quieter, he runs. Ah: run. Runs.

Source: Kelly Winters, Critical Essay on *Rabbit, Run,* in *Novels for Students,* The Gale Group, 2001.

Hermione Lee

In the following review of Rabbit at Rest, *Lee analyzes the character of Rabbit Angstrom as presented by Updike through the four "Rabbit" novels.*

When *Rabbit at Rest* was recently published in Britain, John Updike made an appearance on television. Smiling urbanely in a solid tweed jacket, and looking like a priest disguised as a banker, he seemed to identify uncomplicatedly with Harry "Rabbit" Angstrom as a "good person"—"good enough for me to like him." In *Rabbit, Run,* we were told, he acted out Updike's unfulfilled desire to have been a six-foot-three basketball hero. In *Rabbit Redux,* he reflected Updike's own "conflicted" conservatism. In *Rabbit is Rich,* his own happiness. In *Rabbit at Rest,* his mixed feelings of being worn-out and ill-at-ease and yet still in love with his country.

An epitaph for Rabbit? "Here lies an American man." This neat formulation went unchallenged by his interviewer, but probably Updike's statements as a smiling public man should be distrusted. For what goes on in the Rabbit books is much stranger than he makes out. Rabbit is certainly solid and "real," a very thick fictional entity. Part of the joke of the name (more easily recognized, I suppose, in 1960, when people still read Sinclair Lewis) is its echo of Babbitt, whose idea of the

> *An epitaph for Rabbit? 'Here lies an American man.' This neat formulation went unchallenged by his interviewer, but probably Updike's statements as a smiling public man should be distrusted."*

ideal citizen ("At night he lights up a good cigar, and climbs into the little old bus, and maybe cusses the carburetor, and shoots out home") is one of the epigrams for *Rabbit is Rich,* the smuggest book of the four. When Rabbit supports Nixon and Vietnam in *Rabbit Redux,* or hangs around the wife-swapping clubhouse types in *Rabbit is Rich,* he seems a stable enough piece of the American booboisie, a spokesman (though in a language he would never use himself) for the American dream: "America is beyond power, it acts as in a dream, as a face of God. Wherever America is, there is freedom, and wherever America is not, madness rules with chains, darkness strangles millions. Beneath her patient bombers, paradise is possible."

But Rabbit as ideal citizen has always been a problem. His years of glory as a 1940s high school basketball champion in Mt. Judge, a suburb of Brewer, Pennsylvania, are well past by the time the first book begins, when he is 26. Right from the start, then, he is looking back on lost virtue. What takes place inside his continuing present is mostly dismal, squalid, or banal. In *Rabbit, Run,* trapped by parents, parents-in-law, local minister, and his miserable small family, Rabbit runs out on his alcoholic wife, Janice, who accidentally drowns their baby while their small son Nelson looks on. Then Rabbit leaves his pregnant mistress Ruth (a lapsed hooker) and returns to Janice. Ten years on in *Rabbit Redux,* the book of the '60s, Janice goes off to have an affair, and Rabbit takes Jill and Skeeter, a rich lost hippy girl and her black revolutionary friend, into his house. Teenaged Nelson observes their sexual and political skirmishing. One night (while Rabbit is next door making love to the mother of Nelson's best friend) the house is burned down by racist neighbors, and Jill is killed. In the '70s Rabbit gets "rich" in his wife and mother-in-law's Toyota business. He buys gold, and he and Janice make love covered in Krugerrands, but out there in Carter's America the gasoline is running out and the hostage crisis is running on.

Now, in *Rabbit at Rest,* the greedy Rabbit of the Reagan years has become hugely overweight. On a quarrelsome family holiday in Florida, where he and Janice now have a condominium, he takes his granddaughter out sailing and has a heart attack and an operation—not a bypass, which terrifies him, but an angioplasty, to unclog his arteries from all "the old grease I've been eating." Meanwhile the wretched Nelson is stealing from the Toyota franchise to feed his cocaine habit and is beating up his wife, and Janice is becoming increasingly independent. (Rabbit "preferred her incompetent.") Nelson's secrets come out and she gets him to a rehabilitation center, from which he emerges talking in an "aggravating tranquilized nothing-can-touch-me tone." But Rabbit alone refuses to be cured of junk food and irresponsible desires, and out of the hospital he finds himself unexpectedly making love to his daughter-in-law. When she tells on him, he runs away to Florida, where, after a last pathetic attempt at a basketball game with a group of black kids, Rabbit has another, probably terminal, heart attack.

Rabbit reaches the climax of his career as "an American man" in *Rabbit at Rest* by playing Uncle Sam in his hometown July Fourth parade, his heart Babbittishly thumping at the feeling that "this is the happiest f—ing country the world has ever seen." Are we supposed to take this seriously? The episode has an uneasy tone, partly ironic (his goatee is coming unstuck with sweat, he is having to stay back from the lead car in the parade "so Uncle Sam doesn't look too associated with the police"), but also embarrassingly mawkish, as Rabbit's eyes burn at the strains of "God Bless America." Even here, Rabbit's Babbittry is not stable or comfortable: like the disastrous family barbecue he decides to have in Florida, "it sounds ideally American but had its shaky underside."

When Rabbit starts out, in *Rabbit, Run,* making the journey south that the older Rabbit finally completes, he stops at a wayside café and looks around at the other customers. They all seem to him to "amplify his strangeness." "He had thought, he had read, that from shore to shore all America was the same. He wonders, is it just these people I'm outside, or is it all America?" There are times when Updike wants to put him inside, to make the overweight ex-sports-champ car salesman a voice for

the American dream, a paradigm for an American era. In *Rabbit at Rest* he seems to be doing this more, but it's equivocal.

The analogies between a Rabbit reduced by illness, who has lost domestic authority and is being pushed out of the Toyota business, and America under Bush ("we're kind of on the sidelines. . . . doing nothing works for Bush, why not for him") are explicit enough to be acknowledged by the other characters, and by Rabbit himself. There's no doubt that Rabbit's compulsive junk snacking, Nelson's addiction, the ruin of the business, even granddaughter Judy's compulsive flicking between TV channels ("an impatient rage . . . a gluttony for images") are meant as figures for American waste and greed: "Everything falling apart, airplanes, bridges, eight years under Reagan of nobody minding the store, making money out of nothing, running up debt, trusting in God."

This would just be dull, post-Reagan disapproval (sometimes it *is* a bit dull) if Rabbit weren't so oddly ambivalent. He is the emblem of the obnoxious age, but he is also outside it, minding about it, alienated by it. A lonely Rabbit. Nelson and Janice are more at home in America than Rabbit, and he distrusts the language they use. "Faux," he notices, seeing tourist signs on Route 27 for museums and antiques ("Old, old, they sell things as antiques now that aren't even as old as he is, another racket") is itself a false word: "*False* is what they mean." Rabbit spends a lot of time skeptically listening to (brilliantly travestied) "faux" languages, from Nelson's rehabilitated sermons on low self-esteem and Janice's women's group pieties, vindictively ridiculed ("all those patriarchal religions tried to make us feel guilty about menstruating"), to the health-speak of heart surgeons ("For my money, not to keep beating about the bush, the artery bypass is the sucker that does the job") and waitresses ("it's wonderful if you're going macrobiotic seriously and don't mind that slightly bitter taste, you know, that seaweed tends to have"). These languages are all about getting yourself cleaned up and becoming a better product. Unlike everyone else in the novel, the salesman Rabbit is losing faith in sales talk.

And in other American myths, too. Harry and Janice take their bored grandchildren on a tour of the Edison house in Florida (one of the novel's dazzling set pieces), but Harry doesn't buy the guide's sickly spiel about Edison as "the amazing great American." "It was all there in the technology, waiting to be picked up," says Harry. "All this talk about his love for mankind, I had to laugh!" Edison was just another greedy American consumer. Money is all anything is about. When they close Kroll's, the big downtown Brewer department store, "just because shoppers had stopped coming in," Rabbit understands that

> the world was not solid and benign, it was a shabby set of temporary arrangements rigged up for the time being, all for the sake of the money. You just passed through, and they milked you for what you were worth. . . . If Kroll's could go, the courthouse could go, the banks could go. When the money stopped, they could close down God Himself.

God Himself another American artifact, and no one to trust, after all.

And so Updike has it both ways. Harry is Uncle Sam, but he's also Ishmael. He is all too American and he is alienatedly un-American. He fits in with that long line of Hs, from Huck to Holden to Humbert to Herzog, who carry the freight of American history but are outside of it, looking on. But there is a difference. Harry lacks charisma.

Who likes Rabbit, apart from his author? Sexist, dumb, lazy, illiterate (he spends the whole novel not finishing a book on American history), a terrible father (for Nelson he's "a big dead man on his chest"), an inadequate husband, an unreliable lover, a tiresome lecher, a failing businessman, a cowardly patient, a typically "territorial" male: What kind of moral vantage point is this? Here is Rabbit, for instance, shaking hands with a dying homosexual:

> Squinting, Harry takes the offered hand in a brief shake and tries not to think of those little HIVs, intricate as tiny spaceships, slithering off onto his palm and up his wrist and arm into the sweat pores of his armpit and burrowing into his bloodstream there. He wipes his palm on the side of his jacket and hopes it looks like he's patting his pocket.

This awful joke brilliantly caricatures the lowest common denominator of reactions to AIDS, implicating readers who pride themselves on being too liberal and informed to think like this. There is even a kind of charm to the episode, in Harry's anxiety not to offend, and in the gap between what his mind and his hand are doing. The charm of Rabbit, such as it is, has to do with the distance between his feelings and his behavior, or with his own surprise at what he seems to be like:

> Though his inner sense of himself is of an innocuous passive spirit, a steady small voice, that doesn't want to do any harm, get trapped anywhere, or ever die, there is this other self seen from the outside, a six-foot-three ex-athlete weighing at least two-thirty . . . a shameless consumer of gasoline, electricity, news-

papers, hydrocarbons, carbohydrates. A boss, in a shiny suit.

What redeems Rabbit is that, inside his brutish exterior, he is tender, feminine, and empathetic, like Leopold Bloom, the more intelligent and complex character who inspired him. Lying in the hospital, he "thinks fondly of those dead bricklayers who bothered to vary their rows at the top of the three buildings across the street . . . these men of another century up on their scaffold." Sometimes, eating meat, he can even imagine how it felt to be that animal before it was killed, can apprehend "the stupid monotony of a cow's life" in the taste of beef. He is curious, inquiring, not bigoted—or at least his bigotry is benign, as in his Protestant envy of the chosen people: "Harry has this gentile prejudice that Jews do everything a little better than other people, something about all those generations crouched over the Talmud and watch-repair tables, they aren't as distracted as other persuasions, they don't expect to have as much fun." It must be a great religion, he thinks, "once you get past the circumcision."

This is affable and easy-going compared with that other long-running fictional American, Nathan Zuckerman, who is unable to make light of prejudice in Rabbit's way. They are opposites, of course: famous author vs. obscure salesman, relentlessly eloquent taboo-breaker vs. muddled consumer, thin Jew vs. fat Protestant. The nearest thing to a Roth character in the Rabbit books is Skeeter, who speaks with all the rage and the obsessive energy of a black Portnoy. Yet both Angstrom and Zuckerman are heart cases. In *Rabbit, Run* Harry's unforgiving mother has been taught at church that "men are all heart and women are all body," and Harry's heart, where "guilt and responsibility slide together like two substantial shadows," beats loudly through the book. Now it is clogged, vulnerable, a second self exposed. In *The Counterlife,* Nathan's (and/ or his brother Henry's) hearts are their manhood; only a heart operation will renew their potency. Maybe this coincidental anxiety about heart disease is just an inevitable phase for middle-aged male American writers. But both, in their dramatically different fictional ways, are speaking about the difficulties of life as an American man. To "have a heart" is to be unmanly; and both feel acutely the dangers of being unmanned, whether by surgery, loss of libido, feminism, or oblivion.

Zuckerman, though, like Herzog or Humboldt, speaks his author's language, whereas Rabbit

What Do I Read Next?

- In *Rabbit Redux* (1971), Updike continues Rabbit's story, as Janice turns the tables and cheats on Rabbit.

- *Rabbit is Rich* (1981), by Updike, shows Rabbit making it big in the car sales business.

- In Updikes' *Rabbit at Rest* (1990), Rabbit faces getting old.

- In Philip Roths' *Portnoys Complaint* (1969), a Jewish man talks to his psychiatrist and provides a commentary on 1960s America.

- Lorrie Moores' *Self-Help: Stories* (1995) explores the pleasures and pains of modern relationships.

- Alice Munro's *The Love of a Good Woman* (1994) examines love and betrayal in a small town.

doesn't sound like Updike. This makes life easier for Updike, since people don't go around accusing him of losing his Toyota franchise or making love to his daughter-in-law. But it also adds to our sense of Rabbit's unmanly helplessness—he seems to be caught inside a language that is strange to him, but by which he is defined. It is a virtuoso operation, even to those readers who feel, inappropriately I think, that Rabbit is being socially condescended to by his author. But what is it for?

It's quite clear that Updike can write in any version of American he chooses. Why has he returned so often, in between novels of immense erudition and sophistication like *Roger's Version,* to this elaborate, even perverse match of dumb subject and lyrical, fastidious text? The voice of the Rabbit books, so unlike Rabbit's, is wise, mournful, elegiac, telling us wry truths: "Life is noise," or "Within a hospital you feel there is no other world," or "We grow more ins and outs with age." Rabbit as Everyman? That's easy enough. But the voice does something stranger still. Everything it looks at—and how much it looks at!—changes its shape as it gets put on the page. This is the most

metaphorical prose writing in American fiction, except for Melville's.

And like Melville's, Updike's metaphors are born of that old American transcendentalist desire that the things of this world should stand for something, and not be mere junk. "And some certain significance lurks in all things," Melville's Ishmael hopes, "else all things are little worth, and the round world itself but an empty cipher." In the debate over belief in *Roger's Version,* the god-fearing computer scientist complains about the arguments of a skeptical Jewish bacteriologist: "This is all metaphor." "'What isn't?' Kriegman says. 'Like Plato says, shadows at the back of the cave.'"

Rabbit's Platonism makes us see everything as meaningful, but also as shadowy and strange. His heart, of course, has the star role as shape-shifter: it can be a fist, an amphitheater, a drum, a galley slave, a ballplayer waiting for the whistle. But the solid world outside is also undone by images of floating and drowning, so that Rabbit's tumble into the Gulf of Mexico, an incident itself rich with metaphor ("Air, light, water, silence all clash inside his head in a thunderous demonstration of mercilessness"), spills out into the rest of the book as a figure for his mortality: "His heart floats wounded in the sea of ebbing time."

No object, no creature, is too ordinary or too technical to be subjected to metaphor. Things used to being treated figuratively—birds, trees—get a new treatment, always cunningly connected to what Rabbit might observe: birds call "like the fluttering tinsel above a used car lot," a pink dogwood blooms "like those old photos of atomic bomb-test clouds in the days when we were still scared of the Russians." Even Harry's uncircumcised hard-on makes an American poem: "You can feel the foreskin sweetly tug back, like freezing cream lifting the paper cap on the old-time milk bottles."

Updike is rightly admired for the dazzling thinginess of the Rabbit books. British readers of *Rabbit at Rest* especially love getting so much American stuff, and praise Updike most for "his meticulous taxonomy" of "the material nature of the world" and for his "everywhere saluting and memorializing American superabundance." Where Updike is dispraised by British critics, it's for doing too much American materialism, "pigging out" on it, just like Rabbit. But such a criticism misses the point. For Updike, as for Rabbit, there is no such thing as too much of what is called (in *Roger's Version*) "the irrepressible combinations of the

An image of the quintessential 1950s nuclear family

real." Rabbit's last word, "Enough," is carefully preceded by "Maybe."

But whether it is too much or enough, Updike's America is surely there: Brewer and its suburb, Mt. Judge, are accepted as Pennsylvanian places historically surveyed from the 1940s to the 1990s. Neither reader nor author feels any embarrassment about identifying Brewer as Reading, Berks County, Pennsylvania. Like William Carlos Williams's Paterson, Rabbit's Brewer is a real, recognizable place—and it keeps posing the question of whether there are no ideas but in things.

Still, how peculiar these metaphorladen, metamorphosing, cluttered landscapes are! Nobody can

"do" the strangeness of American places better, not David Lynch or Sam Shepard or Nathanael West or Don DeLillo. Look at the lovingly horrified attention he gives to what for anyone else would be a nonspace, the corridor outside the Angstroms' door in "Valhalla Village," 59600 Pindo Palm Boulevard:

> The corridor is floored in peach-colored carpet and smells of air freshener, to mask the mildew that comes into every closed space in Florida. A crew comes through three times a week vacuuming and the rug gets lathered and the walls worked once a month, and there are plastic bouquets in little things like basketball hoops next to every numbered door and a mirror across from the elevator plus a big runny-colored

Basketball is a recurring theme throughout the novel

green and purple vase on a table shaped like a marble half-moon, but it is still not a space in which you want to linger.

Rabbit's final run through Southern poverty and north Florida theme parks to this out-of-season condo is a masterpiece of verisimilitude; but this is verisimilitude hovering on the borders of the surreal. When Rabbit turns the key into the empty apartment, "There are no cobwebs to brush against his face, no big brown hairy spiders scuttling away on the carpet." But even without tipping it over into American Gothic, this place, with its shell collection and its formica and its fake-bamboo desk and its dead TV screen, is scary enough: "a tight structure hammered together to hold a brimming amount of fear."

Florida is made for surreality, but even in solid old Brewer, Pennsylvania, there is something untrustworthy about the landscape. Updike has Rabbit drive through his "boyhood city" over and over again, minutely noting the changes from industrial energy to postindustrial decay and renewal: mills turned into factories, railroads into garbage dumps, music stores into running-shoe emporiums, churches into community centers, hotels into Motor Inns. Defunct movie houses and retitled restaurants haunt Rabbit's wary vision of the present:

"Johnny Frye's Chophouse was the original name for this restaurant on Weiser Square, which became the Cafe Barcelona in the Seventies and then the Crepe House later in the decade and now has changed hands again and calls itself Salad Binge." And in the course of this poetry of naming, appearances come adrift.

So Rabbit's memory, which cuts a deep, narrow slice into the American past, fuses with the narrative's metaphors to make an elegy for our world. Even the tastelessly caricatured Japanese Toyota representative, who has come to pass stern judgment on the Angstroms' American mismanagement of the franchise ("Too much disorder. Too much dogs—t."), ends up sounding like Tasso, in a transformation only Updike could bring about: "'Things change,' says Mr. Shimerda. 'Is world's sad secret'" *Il mondo invecchia, E invecchiando intristisce.*

If everything is flux, what becomes of our selves? Rabbit's sensuality, materialism, greed, and fear—his ordinariness—have been necessary to Updike because they embody so powerfully his discussion of the soul's relation to the body. Because Rabbit is so fleshy and gross, so tender and frightened, he brings home the human condition. In *Rogers's Version,* whose debate on science and belief could be read as a chilling scholastic commentary on the Gospels according to Rabbit, Roger considers the heresy of Tertullian, who believes "that the flesh cannot be dispensed with by the soul," and will be resurrected. An Angstromian version of his proposition would read: "Dear Flesh: Do come to the party. Signed, your pal, the Soul." Roger can see the attraction:

> In our bodily afterlife, are we to know again ulcers and wounds and fevers and gout and the wish for death? . . . And yet, my goodness, pile on the cavils as you will, old hypothetical heretic or pagan, we do want to live forever, much as we are, perhaps with some of the plumbing removed, but not even that would be strictly necessary, if the alternative is being nothing, being nonexistent specks of yearning in the bottomless belly of *nihil.*

Under surgery, Rabbit is queasily aware of the peculiar relationship between the self, the soul, "the me that talks inside him all the time," and "this pond of bodily fluids and their slippery conduits." Where does the "me" that talks go, if it is separated from its home of flesh? Rabbit has a terrible fear of falling into the void. The Lockerbie disaster preoccupies his imagination, very much as space travel did in *Rabbit Redux.* The dread of the unsleeping universe is picked up from that novel; in *Rabbit*

Redux he thinks: "The universe is unsleeping, neither ants nor stars sleep, to die will be to be forever wide awake." Here, again: "Stars do not sleep,
but above the housetops and tree crowns shine in
a cold arching dusty sprinkle. Why do we sleep?
What do we rejoin?"

Rabbit resents the little space he has to occupy,
penned round within the limits of his life. But he
hunkers down into it too, like a creature in his burrow. Outside is what met the passengers on the
plane over Lockerbie. "It is truly there under him,
vast as a planet at night, gigantic and totally his.
His death. The burning intensifies in his sore throat
and he feels all but suffocated by terror." His fear
is our fear; Updike makes us know it.

Source: Hermione Lee, "The Trouble with Harry," in *New
Republic,* Vol. 203, No. 26, December 24, 1990, pp. 34–37.

Sources

Aldridge, John W., *Time to Murder and Create: The Contemporary Novel in Crisis,* McKay, 1966.

Bemrose, John, "Culture of Speed," in *Macleans,* February
26, 1996, p. 70.

Burchard, Rachael C., *Yea Sayings,* Southern Illinois University Press, 1971.

Detweiler, Robert, *John Updike,* Twayne Publishers, 1984.

Doner, Dean, "Rabbit Angstrom's Unseen World," in *New
World Writing 20,* J. B. Lippincott Co., 1962, pp. 63–75.

Fremont-Smith, Eliot, Review, in *Village Voice,* September
30, 1981.

Greiner, Donald J., *John Updike's Novels,* Ohio University
Press, 1984.

Hamilton, Alice, and Kenneth Hamilton, *The Elements of
John Updike,* Wm. B. Eerdmans, 1970.

Howard, Jane, Interview, in *Life,* November 4, 1966.

Kielland-Lund, Erik, "The Americanness of *Rabbit, Run:* A
Transatlantic View," in *New Essays on "Rabbit Run,"* edited
by Sidney Trachtenburg, Cambridge University Press, 1993,
pp. 77–93.

Lee, Hermione, "The Trouble with Harry," in *New Republic,* December 24, 1990, pp. 34–37.

Pinsker, Sanford, "Restlessness in the 1950s: What Made
Rabbit Run?" in *New Essays on "Rabbit Run,"* edited by
Sidney Trachtenburg, Cambridge University Press, 1993,
pp. 53–75.

Quinton, Anthony, Review, in *Times* (London), January 14,
1982.

Rogers, Michael, "The Gospel of the Book: 'LJ' Talks to
John Updike," Interview, in *Library Journal,* February 15,
1999, p. 114.

Schopen, Bernard A., "Faith, Morality, and the Novels of
John Updike," in *Twentieth Century Literature,* Winter
1978, pp. 523–35.

Uphauser, Susan Henning, *John Updike,* Frederick Ungar
Publishing Co., 1980.

For Further Study

Plath, James, ed., *Conversations with John Updike,* University Press of Mississippi (Jackson), 1994.
Plath presents a collection of interviews with Updike.

Thorburn, David, and Howard Eiland, eds., *John Updike: A
Collection of Critical Essays,* Prentice-Hall, 1979.
This text provides critical essays that examine John
Updike's work from a variety of viewpoints.

Rebecca

Daphne du Maurier

1938

"Last night I dreamt I went to Manderley again." This opening line from *Rebecca* is one of the most powerful, most recognized, in all of literature. For more than sixty years, audiences around the world have praised Daphne du Maurier's novel as a spell-binding blend of mystery, horror, romance, and suspense. In this book, readers can see the traditions of romantic fiction, such as the helpless heroine, the strong-willed hero, and the ancient, imposing house that never seems to unlock its secrets. Using elements familiar to audiences of romances through the ages, from the moody and wind-swept novels of the Brontë sisters in the 1840s to the inexpensive entertainments of today, *Rebecca* stands out as a superb example of melodramatic storytelling. Modern readers considered this book a compelling page-turner, and it is fondly remembered by most who have read it.

The story concerns a woman who marries an English nobleman and returns with him to Manderley, his country estate. There, she finds herself haunted by reminders of his first wife, Rebecca, who died in a boating accident less than a year earlier. In this case, the haunting is psychological, not physical: Rebecca does not appear as a ghost, but her spirit affects nearly everything that takes place at Manderley. The narrator, whose name is never divulged, is left with a growing sense of distrust toward those who loved Rebecca, wondering just how much they resent her for taking Rebecca's place. In the final chapters, the book turns into a detective story, as the principal characters try to re-

veal or conceal what really happened on the night Rebecca died.

Author Biography

Daphne du Maurier was born in London, on May 13, 1907. Her grandfather was artist and novelist George du Maurier, who drew cartoons for the satiric humor magazine *Punch* and illustrated books, including a few of Henry James' novels; his own novel *Trilby* included a mystic character named Svengali, which has since become a common word in the English language. Her father was Sir Gerald du Maurier, one of the most famous actors on the English stage in the 1910s and 1920s, who first performed the role of Captain Hook in *Peter Pan.* Daphne, along with her sisters, was educated at home. She began publishing short stories in 1928, with the help of her uncle, who was a magazine editor, and her first novel, *The Loving Spirit,* was published in 1931. The following year, she married Major-General Sir Frederick Arthur Montague Browning II. Literary success came quickly. In 1936, she achieved international success with *Jamaica Inn,* a tale of smuggling along the Cornish coast. It was followed in 1938 by *Rebecca,* which became a huge bestseller. Alfred Hitchcock filmed both novels in 1939 and 1940, respectively. Hitchcock also made one of his best-known films, 1963's *The Birds,* from a 1952 du Maurier short story.

For more than twenty-five years, du Maurier lived at Menabilly, a country estate that was the inspiration for Manderley. Her marriage to Browning was a friendly one but not a loving one, and she kept herself occupied by writing and entertaining friends. The couple's social circle included some of the most famous people of the day, including Sir John Gielgud, Douglas Fairbanks, Jr., and the actress Gertrude Lawrence, who was rumored to have been her lover. Browning's death in 1965 came as a blow to her. She moved from Menabilly to another famous house, Kilmarth, which dated back to the 1300s. The novel *The House on the Rock* is about Kilmarth.

In addition to novels and short stories, du Maurier also published biographies of Branwell Brontë (the brother of Anne, Charlotte, and Emily), of her father and grandfather, and of Sir Francis Bacon. She wrote several plays, including a three-act adaptation of *Rebecca.* Among her autobiographical works is *Myself, When I Was Young* and *The "Rebecca" Notebooks, and Other Memories.* She also

Daphne du Maurier

wrote several books of local history about Cornwall, where she lived.

Daphne du Maurier died in Par, Cornwall, England, on April 19, 1989, at age of eighty-one. She had not written anything in years, and it was decades since her last important piece of fiction, *The House On the Strand,* was published in 1969.

Plot Summary

The Future

The first two chapters of *Rebecca* take place at some undetermined time in the future. The narrator remembers events that happened in the past at Manderley, an English country estate. She and an unidentified male companion are traveling around foreign countries, reminding themselves of the life they once lived by reading the English news in newspapers. This section gives readers a description of Manderley and vaguely mentions other characters that will be important as the story progresses: Mrs. Danvers, Favell, and, of course, Rebecca.

The final paragraphs of the second chapter take the action back in time, to the very start of the story, when the narrator was a companion to Mrs. Van

Hopper and was staying at the hotel Cote d'Azur at Monte Carlo.

The Hotel Cote d'Azur

Mrs. Van Hopper is presented as a greedy, vain, patronizing woman who likes to think of herself as entering European high society, although she clearly is too ill-mannered to do so. Her companion is a poor young woman who could never afford to be in such an expensive resort by herself. When Mrs. Van Hopper sees Maxim de Winter, she recognizes him and asks to sit at his table, using the excuse that he and her nephew know each other. She does not recognize his impatience with her, although the narrator does. Later, after they have gone back to their room, de Winter sends a note to the narrator, apologizing if he has been rude.

The next morning, Mrs. Van Hopper becomes ill, and her companion finds herself with free time. She has lunch with de Winter, and then they start meeting regularly for rides in the country in his car. She tells him about her life, but he hardly talks about his. From Mrs. Van Hopper's gossip, she knows that his wife died in a boating accident about eight months earlier, and that he owns the estate known as Manderley.

When Mrs. Van Hopper decides that she wants to return to America, the narrator tells de Winter. He returns to Mrs. Van Hopper's room with her and explains that her companion will not be going with her, that they are in love and going to be married.

The Uncomfortable Months

After a few weeks of honeymooning in Italy, Maxim de Winter returns to Manderley with his wife. Not having come from a wealthy background, she is intimidated by the responsibilities of being the mistress of a huge estate. She is uncomfortable with giving orders to the servants. They respond to her discomfort in different ways. Frith, the senior butler, is patient with her uncertainty and is willing to offer polite suggestions as to ways that she might want to handle things, if she wishes, always making it clear that domestic situations are hers to command. On the other hand, there is Mrs. Danvers, who came to Manderley when de Winter was first married to his first wife, Rebecca. Mrs. Danvers does not allow anything to be changed in Rebecca's bedroom, keeping it exactly as it had been when she was alive. She also corrects the new Mrs. de Winter when she tries to change the way that Rebecca did things. Maxim is hesitant to talk about

Rebecca, and so the narrator assumes that he is tortured by the memory of their love.

Once, while walking out near the shore, her dog (who had been Rebecca's dog) leads her to a cottage that is falling apart in disrepair. There, she meets Ben, a retarded young man who talks in mysterious half-sentences, frightening her. When she tells Maxim that she met Ben in the cottage, he is upset to hear that the cottage was unlocked, making her suspect that he wants it to remain unchanged, the way Rebecca left it.

One afternoon, while Maxim and the other servants are away, she finds Mrs. Danvers with a strange man, who introduces himself as Jack Favell. He is loud and aggressive, although he asks her not to tell Maxim that he was in the house. Later, from Maxim's sister, she finds out that Favell was Rebecca's cousin. Maxim finds out that Favell was there and reprimands Mrs. Danvers, who, walking away, gives Mrs. de Winter a scornful, piercing stare.

The Masquerade

After local people keep asking Mr. and Mrs. de Winter if they are going to have the grand costume ball, which has been a long-standing tradition at Manderley, Maxim agrees to go ahead with it. Mrs. Danvers suggests to Mrs. de Winter that she might want to have her costume patterned after one of Maxim's ancestors, pictured in an oil portrait in the hall. She agrees and draws a sketch of the picture of Caroline de Winter, which she sends to a costume maker in London that Mrs. Danvers has recommended. She waits with growing excitement for the day of the ball, certain that it will be her chance to show off as the mistress of the house.

Before the party begins, she walks downstairs in her costume, only to find Maxim and her close friends horrified: the costume is the same one that Rebecca wore to the last ball at Manderley. Maxim, in a rage, shouts at her to go upstairs and change. She thinks about staying in her room all night, but Maxim's sister Beatrice convinces her to attend the ball in a regular dress and explain to the guests that the costume makers had sent the wrong package. Throughout the whole evening, Maxim stays away from her, and when he does not come to bed that night, she becomes convinced that he hates her for desecrating the memory of Rebecca.

The Sunken Boat

The next day, while she and Mrs. Danvers are arguing, word comes that a ship has run aground in the bay. The divers who are sent to assess the damage find a greater surprise: at the bottom of the sea is Rebecca's boat, with a dead body in it. That night, Maxim explains to his wife that he lied when he identified Rebecca's body, miles upshore, months after her disappearance. The body in the boat is hers. He put it there after he killed her, and then he sank the boat. He was not, after all, living with grief over Rebecca because she was a cruel, spiteful, promiscuous woman. His love for his new wife is true.

When the body is identified as Rebecca's, there is an inquest. Just before the case is closed, with the finding that she became trapped in the boat when it sank, it is revealed that the boat would not have sunk on its own, that someone pounded holes into it from the inside. Mrs. de Winter, fearing Maxim's exposure, leaves the courtroom in a faint, but she later finds out that the verdict was that Rebecca committed suicide.

Favell shows up that night with a letter that Rebecca sent him on the day she died, asking him to meet her that night; he says that it proves that she did not plan suicide. When Maxim refuses to pay blackmail, the local magistrate is called. He does not believe Favell's claim that he and Rebecca were lovers, and when Ben is called in to testify about seeing them together, he refuses to say anything, afraid that they mean to commit him. The next day they all drive to London to see the doctor that Rebecca had consulted. He tells them that she had cancer and was going to die a painful death. The magistrate accepts this as evidence of her suicide, and on the drive home, Maxim guesses to his wife that Rebecca goaded him into killing her.

The narrator explains that they later found out that Mrs. Danvers received a long-distance call, probably from Favell, and that she packed her belongings and left Manderley in a hurry. The last paragraph of the book describes the closing scene in which, returning from London, Mr. and Mrs. de Winter come around a corner to find the house engulfed in flames.

Characters

Ben

Ben is a mentally retarded man who lives near Manderley and spends his time near the cove where Rebecca kept her boat. When he first shows up, speaking in riddles that she does not understand, he frightens Mrs. de Winter. When Favell is trying

Media Adaptations

- In 1977, as part of the celebration of her seventieth birthday, Daphne du Maurier participated in a television biography about her life. This rare interview by Cliff Michelmore, entitled *The Make Believe World of Daphne du Maurier,* is available in VHS cassette from Banner Films in London.

- *Rebecca* is one of director Alfred Hitchcock's most celebrated films, made in 1940 with Laurence Olivier and Joan Fontaine.

- *Rebecca* was also adapted to a television series on the British Broadcasting System in 1978 starring Jeremy Brett, Joanna David, and Anna Massey, with direction by Simon Langson.

- A 1996 adaptation of the book, co-produced by Carlton-UK television and WGBH-TV in Boston, stars Charles Dance, Diana Rigg, and Faye Dunaway. This version is directed by Jim O'Brien with a screenplay by Arthur Hopcraft.

- A 1993 abridged audiocassette version of the book, read by Jean Marsh, is available from Audio Renaissance.

- There is an unabridged audiocassette version, released in 1999 by Audio Partners Publishing Company, which is read by Anna Massey, who played Mrs. Danvers in the 1978 British television version.

to prove that he and Rebecca were lovers, he sends for Ben as a witness that he was a frequent night visitor to the cottage where she often slept. Ben is confused, however, and afraid that the authorities have sent for him to put him in an asylum, and he refuses to say anything about what he knows.

Frank Crawley

Frank is the manager of business affairs at Manderley, an efficient and faithful employee who, though boring, is always extremely tactful about what he says in social situations. Soon after she meets him, Mrs. de Winter feels that she can trust Frank. When she is uncomfortable about how Maxim might feel about his dead wife, Frank assures her that she is just what Maxim needs, making him one of her first friends at Manderley. She even feels comfortable enough with him to ask him directly if Rebecca was beautiful, and he replies: "I suppose she was the most beautiful creature I ever saw in my life." From this she assumes that he, like everyone else, was in love with Rebecca. Later, when Maxim tells her the truth about Rebecca, he explains that Frank had wanted to quit his job because she kept pestering him sexually and would not leave him alone. When Maxim is accused of killing her, it becomes clear that Frank knows he really is guilty and probably knew all along, although he has remained quiet.

Mrs. Danvers

Mrs. Danvers came to Manderley as Rebecca's maid soon after Rebecca and Maxim were married. She is very formal and intimidating toward the new Mrs. de Winter, showing her how things are done at the house and practically insisting that the traditions that Rebecca started be continued. She has two encounters with Mrs. de Winter that are particularly odd. In the first, Mrs. de Winter goes for the first time to the rooms that Rebecca occupied after seeing Mrs. Danvers in the window with a strange man, who turns out to be Jack Favell. While she is in the room, Mrs. Danvers comes in and, as if she is a curator in a museum showing off a prized collection, shows her Rebecca's belongings. She touches the bed, the clothes, and the hair brushes adoringly. She says that she allows no one else into Rebecca's rooms, that by keeping them intact it is like Rebecca has never really left, remarking that "It's not only in this room.. . . It's in many rooms in the house. In the morning-room, in the hall, even in the little flower-room. I feel her everywhere. You do too, don't you?"

It is Mrs. Danvers who suggests the costume for the ball that makes Maxim angry with his wife because it is the same one that Rebecca wore. The evening of the ball, she sees Mrs. Danvers in the hall, an evil smile on her face: "The face of an exulting devil."

On the day after her humiliation at the masquerade ball, Mrs. de Winter finds Mrs. Danvers in Rebecca's room. Mrs. Danvers tells her directly that she should never have come to Manderley, and, recognizing her misery, stands beside her at the window, urging Mrs. de Winter to jump and kill herself before they are interrupted.

Later, it becomes clear to Mrs. de Winter that it was Mrs. Danvers, with the help of Favell, who set Manderley afire before disappearing.

Maxim de Winter

When he first appears at Monte Carlo at the beginning of the novel, Maxim is the mysterious, handsome forty-two-year-old stranger who has suffered the tragic loss of his wife eight months earlier. After a brief courtship, he asks the book's narrator to marry him, and he takes her back to his country estate, Manderley, which is famous all over the world. Whenever his late wife, Rebecca, is mentioned, he becomes excessively emotional. He and his new wife move into a wing of the house on the far side of the one he occupied with Rebecca. He encourages her not to do things that Rebecca did. She assumes this to mean that he still mourns the memory of his late wife and is not willing to let Rebecca's place in his heart be taken by another.

Once the boat that Rebecca died in is found, Maxim confesses the truth to his wife: Rebecca was, in spite of the glowing praise of almost everyone who knew her, a spiteful, bitter woman who threatened to make him responsible for her child by another man, and in a fit of rage he killed her. The most incriminating piece of evidence against him is that he identified a body that washed up on the shore far away, months after her disappearance, as Rebecca. Because he is well liked in the community, the officials are willing to accept that his identification was a mistake. There is no evidence of foul play on the corpse that they find on the sunken boat because Maxim's shot passed through her heart without touching any bone.

For several of the book's final chapters, Rebecca's cousin, Jack Favell, questions Maxim's innocence, first trying to blackmail him and then, when Maxim calls his bluff, insisting that the authorities investigate further. Maxim does not lose his composure by denying Favell's accusations or trying to prove them wrong; instead, he risks exposure by agreeing to any steps that might prove him guilty. In the end, when it is found out that Rebecca was not pregnant but that she was, in fact, dying of cancer, he guesses that she actually wanted him to kill her, that she wanted to die without suffering and to leave him with the guilt of her murder.

Mrs. de Winter

The narrator of this book is never called by her given name. Not until she is married to Maxim de Winter is she directly referred to by name. She was a poor orphan, whose parents both died within five weeks of each other. She took a job as companion to the wealthy American, Mrs. Van Hopper, with whom she is staying at Monte Carlo in the south of France when they meet Maxim de Winter.

After Maxim marries her and takes her back to his estate, Manderley, she feels self-conscious about her position as mistress of the house. In her embarrassment, she leaves the details of the house to the servants, thus permitting them to continue with the patterns they had become used to under Maxim's late wife, Rebecca. She allows herself to be bullied by Rebecca's personal maid, Mrs. Danvers, who continually corrects her about how things should be done, remarking that "Mrs. de Winter," meaning Rebecca, arranged things. Mrs. Danvers is always ready to embarrass the new Mrs. de Winter by pointing out her timidity; however, the other servants and laborers at Manderley, as well as people who live nearby and stop there, are kind to her.

When Maxim agrees to throw a grand costume ball at Manderley, his wife, at the suggestion of Mrs. Danvers, orders a costume that reproduces the gown and wig worn by a de Winter ancestor in one of the mansion's oil paintings. As the party approaches, her childish excitement rises to a fevered pitch, but when Maxim sees her costume, he loses his temper and tells her to take it off—it is identical to the one Rebecca wore at the last ball before her death. She hides in her room, but eventually comes out in an ordinary dress from her closet and performs her duties as a hostess although she feels that she has insulted Maxim and has been humiliated by him.

It is the day after the ball that the boat in which Rebecca died is found. A series of events, which include accusations of murder aimed at Maxim and a formal inquest, follows. Throughout the rest of the book, the narrator relates the action and describes her concern, but her involvement is minimal.

Jack Favell

When the narrator first encounters Favell, he has been sneaked into Manderley by Mrs. Danvers. He is there on a day when the other servants are off, and his car is hidden behind the house. He is a bold, annoying man, who makes leering, suggestive remarks, offering Mrs. de Winter cigarettes and asking her to go for a ride in his car. He is obviously familiar with the estate: the young dog, Jasper, knows him, and he refers to Mrs. Danvers as "old Danny." She later finds out that he is Rebecca's cousin and that Maxim does not want him

in the house. In addition, he and Rebecca were lovers; Favell contends that at the time of her death, Rebecca was planning to run away with him and marry him.

Favell is the driving force for the action in the book's later chapters. Upset that an inquest has determined that Rebecca died by suicide, he shows up at Manderley with a note that she sent him on the afternoon of the day she died, asking him to meet her that night as she had something important to tell him. Using this as proof that she did not intend to kill herself, he attempts to blackmail Maxim, and when that does not work, he insists that the authorities be called to investigate, leading them to call Ben as a witness, to go through Rebecca's diary, and, finally, to drive to London to interview her doctor. At last, Favell gives up. Outside of the doctor's house, he is feeling sick. Maxim and his wife find out later that Favell actually returned to Manderley to take Mrs. Danvers away, starting the house on fire before they left.

Frith

Frith has been a servant at Manderley since Maxim was a child. He is faithful, performing his duties without ever letting any opinions or suspicions be known.

Colonel Julyan

The Colonel is the magistrate of Kerrith, the leading law official in the county. He is a guest at the masquerade ball, and, two days later, he dines at Manderley after Rebecca's sunken boat has been raised and her skeleton found. In spite of the tension in the room, the Colonel makes small talk with Mrs. de Winter until the servants have left the room, and it is only then that he is open about the sunken boat.

When Favell makes accusations against Maxim, Colonel Julyan is brought in to investigate. At first, he is obviously disgusted by Favell's drunken state, but he weighs the evidence carefully. His eventual determination is that there is plenty of evidence for believing that Rebecca committed suicide and little reason to think that she did not. Maxim de Winter, however, believes in the end that the Colonel can tell he is guilty but content to let the matter be forgotten.

Beatrice Lacy

Maxim's sister, Beatrice, is the opposite of his wife. She is tall, athletic, and outspoken. At first, she seems intimidating, and the narrator does not think that they will get along. Still, Beatrice (or

"Bee," as her friends call her) is fond of the narrator. Her wedding present to the couple, a set of books about the history of art, is chosen because one of the few things she knows about her new sister-in-law is her interest in drawing. She takes Maxim's wife along with her when she goes to see their grandmother, to introduce her to the only other member of Maxim's family.

When Mrs. de Winter mistakenly upsets Maxim by wearing the same costume to the Manderley ball that Rebecca once wore, Beatrice helps her get over her humiliation, picking out an ordinary dress from her closet and telling her that it will look fine on her. Although her assertiveness in social affairs is useful in that case, it becomes dangerous later. After a coroner's inquest finds that Rebecca committed suicide, Beatrice, not knowing that Maxim killed her, tells her sister-in-law to insist that they open the case again because she thinks that a suicide verdict is a humiliation to her brother. At the time, her son is home from school with the measles, and no one is allowed to leave the house, so she is not able to raise a fuss that could have exposed her brother's guilt in the crime of Rebecca's murder.

Major Giles Lacy

Beatrice's husband is something of a stereotype: a big, dull, jovial man, who recedes into the social background behind his brash, domineering wife. When Maxim discloses the truth about Rebecca, he mentions that it was obvious from Giles' loud, boisterous manner when he and Rebecca came back from an afternoon of boating that they had had a fling.

Robert

Robert is the assistant butler at Manderley. He performs the duties, such as going to the post office, that Frith is incapable of doing.

James Tabb

Tabb is the shipbuilder who performed yearly maintenance on Rebecca's boat. After it is pulled from the harbor, people said that he had not maintained it properly, and Tabb, to save his professional reputation, inspected it. He testifies at the inquest that the boat sank because of holes deliberately put in it from the inside, a fact that nearly causes great trouble for Maxim before the coroner declares it an act of suicide.

Mrs. Van Hopper

At the beginning of the book, the narrator is employed as a companion to Mrs. Van Hopper, a rich and pretentious American woman. She is a social climber, trying to ease into upper-class European society by introducing herself to its finest members. In the case of Maxim de Winter, she uses snapshots that some mutual friends have sent her from their vacation as an excuse to sit at his table and have lunch with him. After de Winter tells her that he is in love with her companion and is taking her away to marry her, Mrs. Van Hopper offers her congratulations, but when he leaves, she raises doubts in the narrator's mind:

> "Of course," she said, "you know why he's marrying you, don't you? You haven't flattered yourself he's in love with you? The fact is that empty house got on his nerves to such an extent he merely went off his head. He admitted as much before you came into the room. He just can't go on living there alone. . ."

Themes

Loyalty

The driving force behind the actions of this book's characters is loyalty. This is seen most clearly in the characters of Frank Crawley, the business manager of Manderley, and Frith, the head butler. Crawley expresses his loyalty by being congenial, never shying away from a topic of conversation and yet never expressing exactly what he thinks either. Mrs. de Winter can sense that Crawley is on her side, but she also knows that he will not be completely honest about what he thinks of Rebecca because his sense of loyalty to Maxim would forbid it. Frith is just as deeply loyal, but it is easier for him to keep up his attitude of detachment because, as a servant, he is not involved in family matters nor expected to know about the de Winters' affairs anyway.

Like Frith, Mrs. Danvers is a family servant, but her sense of loyalty makes her negligent in her duty. She is loyal to Rebecca, the dead member of the family, and, in her attempt to preserve Rebecca's memory, she is disrespectful to the current Mrs. de Winter. At first, her loyalty appears as just an annoying, but almost respectable, personality tic, as when she tells the narrator that certain practices are followed because "that is the way Mrs. de Winter wants it done," ignoring the fact that the person she is talking to is now Mrs. de Winter. After the costume ball, her hostility becomes open, and she tries to capitalize on the narrator's grief at her inability to fit in by urging her toward suicide, because "You tried to take Mrs. de Winter's place."

In the end, her loyalty to Rebecca's memory makes it impossible for Mrs. Danvers to accept that the new Mrs. de Winter and Maxim can be happy together, so she burns Manderley down.

The narrator's greatest concern, however, is her suspicion that, despite having married her, Maxim is loyal to the memory of Rebecca. She reads his moodiness to mean that he is still grieving over his lost wife. His refusal to use the bedroom that he used with Rebecca, his refusal to go near the cottage Rebecca used, and his anger at seeing her wear the same costume Rebecca wore all seem like signs that he is not willing to give up the memory of her. In the end, when he admits to having actually hated Rebecca and killed her, the narrator does not even think of leaving him because he is a murderer; she stays loyal to him throughout the investigation because she loves him.

Flesh versus Spirit

Part of the narrator's sense of inferiority results from the fact that she is competing with the memory of a dead woman. Her sense of what Rebecca was like builds up slowly from isolated clues: the inscription in a book, her formal agenda left in her desk, Mrs. Danvers' description, and the descriptions of all of the people who knew her. The most uncomfortable comparison comes from Maxim's grandmother who, at eighty-three, is senile and unpredictable: in the middle of their conversation, she loses touch with reality and calls out, "I want Rebecca, what have you done with Rebecca?" There are several practical reasons that the narrator feels she cannot compete with Rebecca, as she finds out about her beauty and social grace. She also is unable to compete because Rebecca is just a memory and therefore is incapable of doing wrong, while she, being human, is quite fallible. Rebecca's continuing presence in Manderley is manifest in the way she decorated it, in her schedules and customs (such as the daily approval of the menu), and in the words of praise visitors have for her. She haunts the narrator as much as if she actually occupied the house like a ghost. "Sometimes I wonder," Mrs. Danvers tells her, as they are looking at Rebecca's belongings. "Sometimes I wonder if she comes back here to Manderley and watches you and Mr. de Winter together."

The ironic thing is that the ghost of Rebecca that haunts Manderley is more a result of terror than of grief. Maxim de Winter remembers her as a mean-spirited woman who put on a sickly sweet image before the public. If he is haunted by her, it is because of his own internal struggle with the guilt

Topics for Further Study

- Monte Carlo is still recognized around the world as a vacation spot for the rich. Research what it was like in the 1930s: what sort of people went there, what sort of activities were available, and so forth.

- Using the descriptions in the novel, draw sketches of various locations at Manderley.

- Write a short story about where Maxim de Winter and his wife will eventually end up after they finish traveling, as described in the very first chapters. Bear in mind that this novel ends at just about the time that World War II begins.

- The novel describes how Rebecca threatened to have someone else's child and make Maxim de Winter raise it as his own. Research British law and try to find out how difficult it would have been, in the 1930s, for him to divorce her.

- Several times in the novel, the characters predict what the weather will be like, with observations such as "the glass is dropping." Explain how a barometer works and how accurate its predictions are likely to be.

- *Rebecca* is still popular today. Find out the sales figures throughout the years. Try to explain at least one period of high or low sales.

he feels for killing her, not because he misses her at all. Frank Crawley's elusiveness about Rebecca, which the narrator thinks is because of his suppressed love for her, is actually discomfort, because she put him in an awkward position by making sexual advances toward him. Beatrice and Giles cannot speak of her memory clearly because they both know that she seduced Giles, and so, unsure of how to speak of her, they end up talking about her with polite praise. In the formal British setting of this novel, people find it better to speak well of the dead than of the living.

Guilt and Innocence

One of Daphne du Maurier's greatest achievements in this novel is to convince readers of the innocence of the murderer and the guilt of the murder victim. There are several reasons why, according to the novel's moral structure, Rebecca deserved to die. For one thing, she was cruel and a liar: as Maxim explains it, "They all believed in her down here, they all admired her, they never knew how she laughed at them behind their backs, jeered at them, mimicked them." Mrs. Danvers repeats Rebecca's falseness when she bursts Favell's delusion that she loved him: "Love-making was a game with her, only a game. She told me so. She did it because it made her laugh." Another reason Rebecca deserved her fate is the fact that she was promiscuous: when the truth comes out about her, the list of men she was with or tried to seduce includes Favell, Crawley, Giles, and, presumably, a lot of others, first in London, and then, increasingly, at her cottage at Manderley, where she would invite men for "picnics." In addition, there are perversities that are not described in the book, things that she told to Maxim that he says, with a shudder, "I shall never repeat to another soul." The ultimate offense, the one that drives him to shooting her, is that she threatens to have another man's child and tell everyone that it is Maxim's so that the child would be raised bearing his name: "And when you died Manderley would be his. You could not prevent it. The property's entailed."

Maxim's innocence in killing Rebecca stems from the fact that it is a selfless act: he is not protecting himself, but the good name of Manderley, which her exploits threaten to destroy. To the narrator, Maxim's pureness of heart, his love for her, and his devotion to Manderley are more important than the fact of the murder he committed. They find out in the end that Maxim was even less guilty than they had assumed him to be because Rebecca had cancer and was going to die anyway. One last factor in mitigating Maxim's responsibility for what he did is his guess that Rebecca goaded him into shooting her, so that she could die a quick and painless death and make him feel guilty about doing what cancer would have done in a few months anyway. Readers are left with the impression that Rebecca is guilty and that Maxim, who actually killed her and buried her at sea, is a victim of circumstances.

Style

Setting

There are two main settings for this novel. The first is the resort of Monte Carlo on the southern coast of France. Since 1862, when the first gambling casino was opened there, the town has been famous around the world as a playground for Europe's rich. Starting the book in this setting serves to establish the wealthy social class of these characters. It also helps to raise readers' curiosity about Manderley, which is talked about constantly, even by characters who have never been there but who know it by reputation. The narrator buys a postcard of Manderley in a shop in Monte Carlo.

Most of the book tales place at Manderley, the English country estate that has been owned by the de Winter family for generations. The house itself is imposing to a young girl who was not raised in this wealthy social environment. It is so large that she gets lost, so large that one entire wing can be shut off with Rebecca's personal belongings with little effect. Ancient portraits hang on the walls, reminding the narrator of the responsibility of becoming part of a well-established dynasty. The place is decorated with expensive things that Rebecca put there, constantly reminding her of the presence of the first Mrs. de Winter.

The house is surrounded by trees, which can be inviting on a sunny day but frightening on a dark, rainy one. Past the trees is the bay. Manderley's proximity to the sea is important because it adds to the beauty of this rich estate but also because the sea hides the corpse of the murder victim, but hides it in a way that it can be found again. One other significant aspect of Manderley is the mysterious cottage where the narrator encounters Ben: this place is left to decay, obviously because Maxim cannot bring himself to go there, raising the prospect of mystery until the end, when it turns out to be central to the horrible events of the past.

Structure

Most of *Rebecca* follows a chronological path, from the time the narrator meets Maxim de Winter at Monte Carlo to the night that Manderley burns down. There is, however, a prelude that takes place some time after the events in the novel. There is no way to tell when this beginning section, which comprises the first chapter and a half, takes place, only that the events that happened at Manderley still haunt the narrator and her male companion, who is left unidentified.

The function of this beginning is to foreshadow events that the reader is going to read about. Mrs. Danvers is mentioned, and so are Jasper the dog and Favell. They are all brought up in the natural way that they might pass through the mind of someone thinking about the past. Because readers do not know what these names refer to, however, they serve in these first chapters to focus attention, to keep readers alert for the story that is about to unfold. The most important element of this introduction is the fact that the man travelling with the narrator is not identified: while reading the main story, readers have to be alert to signs that her love affair with Maxim de Winter might end and to look for clues that hint who her true love might turn out to be.

Gothicism

The true flowering of the gothic novel was during the late eighteenth and early nineteenth centuries when it was a sub-category of the much broader romantic movement in literature. While romanticism explained humanity's relationship with nature as one of mutual benefit, with nature providing an escape from the rules of society and offering artistic souls a chance to express themselves creatively, Gothicism stressed the frightening, dark, unsure aspects of nature. The most powerful example of the gothic novel is Mary Wollstonecraft Shelley's *Frankenstein,* which is concerned with the tragic results that can occur when humans tamper with nature.

Gothic novels usually include elements of the supernatural, mystery, and horror. In *Rebecca,* all of the events end up being explained within the realm of commonly understood reality, but the haunting "presence" of Rebecca's personality gives the book a Gothic mood. Another key element of these works is their setting in ancient castles, usually decaying, which is an element that shows the romantic movement's fascination with ancient history along with the Gothic interest in death and decay. The short stories of Edgar Allan Poe contain many of the most recognizable Gothic elements. Many of the novels that modern readers associate with romance and horror use elements of Gothicism.

Narrator

Readers are often so comfortable with the narrative voice used in this novel that they can finish the entire book without realizing how little they know about the woman who is telling the story. Du Maurier does not even provide a name for this person. She is described as being small and girlish, with a pageboy haircut. (Frank Crawley suggests that she might be Joan of Arc at the masquerade because of her hair.) The book does not, however, tell how old she is nor where she was raised nor how she came to work for Mrs. Van Hopper, her employer when the story begins. She does like to

draw, but not so much that she practices her interest within the story, and she seems perplexed by the books on art history that Beatrice gives her. It is not until the seventh chapter that any of the other characters addresses her directly, and then it is as "Mrs. de Winter," a title that identifies her in relation to her husband.

Du Maurier manages to keep her readers from being curious by having this narrator describe the things around her with such fascination and loving detail that all attention is drawn to them. The people and events that she encounters fill her imagination, and she in turn fills the reader's imaginations with her descriptions. Maxim de Winter, in particular, is so important to her that she focuses her story on him. Furthermore, this narrator has such a complete, believable personality, which comes out through her telling of the story, that readers find that they are not curious about her past.

Historical Context

Post World War I

During the 1800s, Britain had built its empire by adding colonies, dominions, and protectorates. These were the great years of the British Empire: Queen Victoria, reigning for over sixty years, gave the nation a sense of stability and progress. Her conservative social views created the stiff-lipped, formal stereotype of the British citizen that is known today and that is portrayed in *Rebecca:* strict rules of behavior between the sexes, tea at four-thirty each day, and a fascination with wealth that was suppressed by the good taste not to talk about it. When Victoria died in 1901, her son Edward succeeded her to the throne. The Edwardian age in England is considered a time of international stability, owing to Edward VII's talent for negotiations. Like the Victorian era, Edward's reign from 1901 to 1910 was marked by domestic stability and social formality.

World War I shattered the tranquility of Europe, especially of Great Britain. Previous military conflicts, such as the Crimean War and the Boer War, had been marked by the civility of the participants. In the previous battles, the British class system had been clearly maintained, separating officers from soldiers, keeping the former far from the fighting, in deference to their ranks. World War I, on the other hand, brought new technology that destroyed any sense of class in battle. Long-range cannon, portable machine guns, and, especially, the use of poisonous gas forced the genteel tradition

Compare & Contrast

- **1938:** The first nuclear fission of uranium is achieved by German scientists. This is the physical reaction that leads to the nuclear bomb.

  1945: Nuclear bombs are dropped on the Japanese cities Hiroshima and Nagasaki, hastening the end of World War II by killing nearly two hundred thousand people.

  Today: After decades of international fear about the devastation that nuclear weapons can cause, no other nuclear bombs have been used during wartime.

- **1938:** Cancer is barely understood. The first cancer-causing agents, known as "carcinogens," have been isolated in England just five years before.

  Today: Cancer is the number two cause of death in the United States, but millions of dollars are spent on research each year, and much progress has been made in understanding causes and treatments.

- **1938:** The first steps in photocopy technology are made, as inventor Chester Carlson develops a method to reproduce an image on paper using electrostatic attraction.

  Today: Image reproduction has progressed to the point that computer users are transferring scanned images from one machine to another, without ever using paper to transmit them.

- **1938:** Orson Welles presents his radio program about an alien invasion, *War of the Worlds,* in the style of a news program. Across America, hundreds of listeners believe that Martians are really invading Earth, and become panicked.

  Today: Audiences are used to radio and television programs that use the same style as the news, and few people would take such a preposterous story seriously.

- **1938:** Radio and motion pictures are the main forms of entertainment in America. People living in urban areas attend live theater productions. Television technology is invented, but TV ownership is not widespread until after World War II.

  Today: Most homes own at least one television, many with the possibility of access to over five hundred channels at a time through cable and satellite systems.

- **1938:** Air travel is still an uncertain proposition. In 1937, aviator Amelia Earhart is lost at sea in the Pacific Ocean while trying to circumnavigate the globe. In 1938, Douglas Corrigan flies illegally from New York to Dublin, giving the excuse that his compass had led him in the wrong direction and earning him the nickname "Wrong-Way Corrigan."

  Today: International flights are routine, and all flight paths are monitored by the Federal Aviation Administration.

---

to wake up to the inhumane horrors of modern warfare.

Being with the winning forces, Britain benefited at the end of the war; colonies that had been under German control became British mandates. For a short while, there was a post-war economic boom as laborers returned and industry grew. The old social class system, though, with the type of rigid structure that du Maurier presents in *Rebecca,* was on its last legs as modern technology made the feudal system that great estates like Manderley were built upon seem increasingly pointless.

The Approach of World War II

Like America and many other countries around the world, Great Britain suffered through an economic depression in the 1930s. The country, which had started the century as the most powerful on Earth, was forced to take measures that would assure its continued economic stability. In 1931, for instance, the British government, which had been borrowing money from France and the United States to get by, imposed a heavy tariff on items that were brought into the country. This helped to control the economy, forcing British citizens either to buy goods that were made within the British Empire or to add tax money to the general revenue base. Although it helped the economic situation, British self-esteem suffered from this sign of economic weakness. The country's free trade policy had been a source of pride for Britain, and this forced abandonment of that policy was a clear sign that Great Britain no longer dominated the world the way it once had.

At the same time, Adolf Hitler and the Nazi party were rising to power in Germany. To a large extent, Hitler was able to gain power because of the same worldwide economic stagnation that was affecting America, Britain, and other countries. Germany was hit particularly hard, with prices of basic foods and supplies sometimes doubling within a week. Hitler was able to appeal to the suffering people, and he also addressed the matter of German pride, convincing the German people that the country was being mistreated by the international community. The Treaty of Versailles, which established the conditions for Germany's surrender in 1918, separated the states that had made up the German Republic, and placed restrictions on the country's armed forces, leaving Germany economically and militarily vulnerable. The Nazi party was voted into power in 1933 because the electorate believed that they could end the country's suffering and humiliation.

Almost immediately, Hitler's government began its program of military expansion. In the following years, German forces were used to absorb Yugoslavia, Czechoslovakia, and Poland, all of which it had given up to end the war. Looking back on it, many people wondered why the countries that had led the winning force in World War I did not stop Germany when it first started to violate the Treaty of Versailles. For one thing, many people across the world agreed with the German view that the treaty had been too confining and had caused the citizens of Germany to suffer more than they should have, and so there was not strong opposition to the steps Germany took to "correct" the situation. Another reason was that the economic crisis made countries in Western Europe, such as England and France, reluctant to fight if they did not have to. Hitler signed new treaties with London, agreeing to limit the size of the German military, giving those who wanted to avoid war a

chance to argue that it would be unnecessary. The forces opposing intervention into German affairs were so strong that the world ignored the stories that escaped from German territories of concentration camps where, it has been proven, millions of Jews, gypsies, and homosexuals were mutilated and killed.

Great Britain eventually did enter into war with Germany in 1939, after Hitler broke a nonaggression pact with Poland and attacked that country. By that time, it was clear that he intended to continue endless expansion and that treaties made no difference. At the start of the war, the brunt of opposing Hitler fell upon France, which was defeated by the Germans in 1940, and England, which was hammered by German bombing raids. Seventy thousand British civilians died during the war, which lasted until 1945.

Critical Overview

Rebecca is one of those novels that critics have a difficult time disrespecting. On the one hand, it does have excessive, overblown language in places, and its plot is far from original. On the other hand, the book's overwhelming approval by the general public, from its first printing in 1938 up through today, has made it in some respects immune to negative criticism, forcing reviewers to think twice before dismissing it as just one more popular romance. In general, critics have tended to take the time to find out what is effective in this novel and why it works, rather than just dismissing it because of its weaknesses.

Basil Davenport, reviewing *Rebecca* for the *Saturday Review* when it was first published, identifies the book as a mystery about who Rebecca really was and what happened to her, but he also credits du Maurier for writing so well and so compellingly that she does not have to rely on the murder mystery plot: "The book is skillfully contrived so that it does not depend only on knowledge of it for its thrill; it can afford to give no hint of it till two-thirds of the way through." Davenport goes on to explain that *Rebecca* is, after all, melodrama: the heroine, for one thing, is "at times quite incredibly stupid," such as when she takes advice from the housekeeper whom she knows hates her. He also points out "a forced heightening of the emotional values," a disreputable trick that melodrama relies on. Still, Davenport finds the novel "as absorbing a tale as the season is likely to bring."

As time went on, critics saw *Rebecca* outlive the usually short life cycle of popular romances, elbowing its way into a position in literary history. John Raymond, writing about it in the *New Statesman* in 1951, identifies du Maurier as "a poor woman's Charlotte Brontë" of the 1930s. He goes on to note, "Her *Rebecca*, whatever one's opinions of its ultimate merits, was a *tour de force.*" He further suggests that du Maurier's fame may have made her a force for the literary world to reckon with but that her writing had become twisted by her commercial success so that she was then writing prose that was ready to be adapted to movies. Raymond's review of *My Cousin Rachel,* which came at the tail end of du Maurier's prolific period of one romantic bestseller after another, describs the book:

> . . . a honey for any Hollywood or Wardour Street tycoon. Slick, effective, utterly mechanical, the book is a triumphant and uncanny example of the way in which a piece of writing can be emasculated by unconsciously "having it arranged" for another medium.

Like Raymond, critics of the 1950s tended to cloud their judgments of du Maurier's writing with the tremendous financial success that it brought the author.

In the 1950s, du Maurier's style shifted as she focused on supernatural elements, particularly in her collection *Kiss Me Again, Stranger.* The short stories in that book were met with mixed enthusiasm. John Barkham's review in the *New York Review of Books* simply captures the acceptance of her style at the time by noting of the eight stories, "None of them is bad, and several are very good indeed." In particular, he points out the excellence of "The Birds," which was adapted years later to one of Alfred Hitchcock's most famous movies.

Throughout the 1950s and 1960s, du Maurier became better known as a writer of the supernatural, rather than as a romance writer who used supernatural elements to build suspense, as she had been after the success of *Rebecca.* Susan Hill, writing in 1971 about another collection of scary stories called *Not After Midnight,* notes that it was:

> . . . a good read, and most likely, a bestseller. If only the quality of the prose matched up to her inventiveness, if only the dialog were not so banal and the descriptions so flat, we might have something more than holiday reading on our hands.

With her popularity clearly established, and the reading public jumping at the chance to buy new novels from her, du Maurier moved, in later life, to writing about real-life subjects: her father, her grandfather, her early life, the countryside where she lived, and the occasional historical figure, such as Sir Francis Bacon. Critics tended to ignore her non-fiction works, or, if they did look them over, they approached them with a polite, patronizing attitude, suggesting that they viewed them as signs of a popular writer dabbling in a hobby. Of her book about Bacon, for instance, historian Pat Rogers notes, "Daphne du Maurier has many literary gifts, but I am not sure that this book has fully enlisted them." It is likely that a review of a book by a true historian would not have been so congenial and non-critical.

Criticism

David Kelly

Kelly is an instructor of creative writing and composition at two community colleges in Illinois. In the following essay, he examines whether the lack of information about the narrator of du Maurier's story is a legitimate artistic device or just an amusing but ultimately pointless trick.

No one could ever reasonably question the popularity of British romance and mystery writer Daphne du Maurier. An author who sells books in the millions is rare enough, but her fans took their enthusiasm beyond simple purchases. In an age before the internet made conversing with fellow enthusiasts as easy as sitting down at a keyboard, there were several societies devoted to her, like the fan clubs that movie stars tend to attract. Most of this cult of du Maurier centers around one book: her 1938 neo-Romance, *Rebecca.* The book attracts new fans every year, with thoughtful readers of literature beaming about how hard they found it, after the last page, to shake off their involvement in the lives of the dashing Maxim de Winter, the repressed Mrs. Danvers, catty Bee, and all of the rest of the larger-than-life characters who roam the halls of Manderley.

It is tempting to give in to du Maurier, to congratulate her posthumously for creating a world that has lasted over a half of a century. There is, however, another side of the argument, a side that would describe *Rebecca* as nothing more than a work of really competent trash, which owes its popularity to its appeal to the least common denominator in literary tastes. To critics of this inclination, the book's continuing popularity is no sign of the author's talent, but of her willingness to corrupt her

Joan Fontaine as the second Mrs. de Winter and Laurence Olivier as Maxim de Winter in the 1940 film version of the novel, directed by Alfred Hitchcock.

considerable skills to be all things to all people, ending up with nothing particular to say.

It is an age-old debate: is it mere snobbery to say that what sells is trash, or is it delusional to say that what sells is art? One way or the other, in the case of *Rebecca,* it seems impossible to separate the book's overwhelming popularity from its merit.

The question becomes even more compelling when the focus of inquiry is narrowed to one particular aspect of the book, such as du Maurier's handling of the narrator. For the first third of the book, she has no name, a mystery that the author is clearly willing to go out of her way to preserve. It is not as if there are no opportunities to have the character's name revealed in dialog, or in a memory of something once said to her, or any of the countless other tricks that authors use to reveal such information. Du Maurier knows that she is teasing readers about it, and she makes her teasing quite clear. "But my name was on the envelope," the narrator says of a letter de Winter sends her in chapter 3, "and spelled correctly, an unusual thing." This story takes the time to draw attention to something, without going on to say what that something is.

Artistically, this coy act should not work. It usually does not. Beginning writers often try leav-ing out specific details about crucial characters, hoping that, without names or faces, it will be eas-ier for readers to relate to the characters, as if anonymity is the same thing as universality. Usu-ally, avoiding the obvious just results in weak writ-ing because readers tend to feel less, not more, in-volved when details are left out. The book may work because of this technique, or it might work in spite of it. The general rule against obscurity just might be wrong, but anyone who has read much amateurish writing that tries to stir up suspense by leaving out facts will swear that it is right. The other two likely explanations are difficult to unwrap from one another: either du Maurier just happened to find that one-in-a-million recipe of the precise amount of characterization needed, without one atom over, or else readers are willing to let her get away with underwriting her main character because the rest of the book is just so much fun.

There is plenty of reason to believe the first option, the one about du Maurier's precision in molding a credible human being of the second Mrs. de Winter. It is, after all, not as if the character is *entirely* left up to readers' imaginations. Some facts are given about her. She is supposed to have artis-tic talent, although this is always brought up in the negative, in terms of the sketching that she has *not* been working at. She is young, as the other characters always point out, with short black hair and pale skin. At Monte Carlo, talking about her father, she thinks of herself as "so much of a schoolgirl still," which is an attitude readers see reflected in the way others behave around her.

The narrator's father, in fact, is considered by her to be her "secret property," but readers never really find out why. All that is explained is that she has told Maxim de Winter about her childhood, but the facts of that childhood, and what made it special, are not shared with the reader. A critical reader has to wonder why du Maurier chose to provide, as an indicator of the narrator's past life, only a shell of a father, without filling in the details. If readers feel that they know this narrator, then the author's work is done, but if they are being asked to accept the relationship between de Winter and the narrator as a standard father fixation, with stereotyped behaviors from a psychology text taking the place of true characterization, then the author has not done her job but is getting away with cheating. Throughout the book, details about Mrs. de Winter seem to indicate that she is oversimplified, an incomplete character type. Readers are not given enough facts to consider her as a person.

One more consideration makes it even more difficult to judge how well Daphne du Maurier has rendered this very important character: offsetting the lack of details provided is the full richness of her voice, which readers hear from the first page to the last. So well is the voice rendered, through word choices, sentence structure, and the nature of the specific details she chooses to dwell on, that it is easy to know her feelings about any particular issue mentioned, whether she explains her thoughts or not. In effect, the entire book is a trip taken from within her mind. There may not be much said about her past, nor is there much reflection on her own identity because she simply is not the introspective kind. If this is her intention, then du Maurier actually defines this character's personality by refusing to say much about it, by letting her exist in the present rather than being the sum of her past.

The other way that it is possible to say that the book's imprecision about this one character works would be to consider the narrator's place in the book as a whole. Whether it was du Maurier's intention or not, this character seems to take up just the right amount of place, proportionally, in the overall story. If one looks at *Rebecca* as a whole world, and not as the story of this one character,

then too much about her might take away from another part of the story and throw the whole finely-tuned machine out of balance. For instance, there is obviously a balance between the first Mrs. de Winter, Rebecca, and the second, the book's narrator. More about the narrator and she might overshadow Rebecca; if more were said about Rebecca to keep her equal to the narrator, the secret of de Winter's feelings about her might fail to surprise. Knowing too much about the narrator might make her sympathetic, thereby making readers less likely to believe that de Winter could love Rebecca's memory more than his wife. More about her past could help readers decide whether her uneasiness about Rebecca is paranoia or legitimate fear, which would diminish the book's overall effect. This is not like most literature, which is character-driven; it is suspense. Just knowing the narrator's name could potentially wake readers out of the trance that du Maurier's writing casts so successfully, making the situation too real, even though the book relies on taking them away from common reality.

Rebecca's detractors call the book mechanical, pointing to the wooden characters and situations that could exist nowhere except Manderley. It is true that these characters are not filled in as great authors can do, not given lives of their own. They exist as tools. Mrs. Danvers, for instance, is unimaginable beyond her job in the book, which is to react to Maxim de Winter and his new wife. She could hardly be imagined with an existence outside of that setting because she has no real personality. This may be the author's intent in creating her; if so, it is not necessarily a well-chosen plan. Even Maxim de Winter, moody and tortured, is such a non-entity that readers, like the narrator, can ignore his shooting down a pregnant woman. What he does matters very little because he has such little substance.

The other characters may or may not be put together sketchily, but one cannot think of du Maurier as doing sloppy work in creating the narrator. She obviously chose to direct attention away from this character, rather than letting readers know who she is and what she thinks. Rebecca, the character, is a mystery because the narrator knows little about her and is too overwhelmed by the grandeur of Manderley to find out more. *Rebecca* the novel is effective to the extent that readers are just as willing to forget their questions about the new Mrs. de Winter.

Literature often relies on readers playing an active role, and the measure of *Rebecca*'s success might just be found in how one defines "active." If being distracted, if having one's curiosity stifled and not fed, is active, then the book works as literature. On the other hand, there is much to be said for the charge that hiding Mrs. de Winter's personality is a trick, one that might be amusing but does not make for good, lasting fiction. Sales records do not establish a book's true value, but the continued admiration of wave after wave of fans just might be enough to prove that Daphne du Maurier's unorthodox presentation of Mrs. de Winter is effective.

Source: David Kelly, Critical Essay on *Rebecca,* in *Novels for Students,* The Gale Group, 2001.

Jane S. Bakerman

In the following essay, Bakerman discusses du Maurier's romantic suspense novels, noting her inventiveness, and that "the many, many, modern gothics which echo Rebecca*" are good evidence that du Maurier tends to set trends rather than to follow them.*

During her long, distinguished career, Daphne du Maurier has tried her hand successfully at both fiction and nonfiction—biography, autobiography, historical romance, short stories and celebrations of place—but her auctorial reputation rests most firmly upon six romantic suspense novels whose plots stem from some crime or crimes. The novels are *Jamaica Inn, Rebecca, Frenchman's Creek, My Cousin Rachel, The Scapegoat,* and *The Flight of the Falcon.*

Central to the du Maurier tradition are sound, exciting, workable plots: an orphan seeks refuge in her aunt's home only to find it the center of a smuggling ring; a young wife lives under the shadow of her predecessor and of her husband's secret; a noblewoman abandons family responsibilities to become lover and cohort of a pirate; a youth falls in love with a distant relative who is not only his beloved cousin's widow but also a suspected poisoner; an Englishman exchanges identities with a Frenchman and lives his double's life for a time; and an aimless young man finds his long-lost brother who is engaged in what may be a diabolical scheme. All of these basic plots are thrilling, all allow for abundant complication and all offer good possibilities for quick pace and great suspense.

Though even so swift a summary of the plots reveals variety, there are elements of commonality shared by all six titles under discussion here. For critics, that commonality has sometimes been dismissed as "formula fiction," and this term (often perceived as demeaning) has contributed to some

> Beginning writers often try leaving out specific details about crucial characters, hoping that, without names or faces, it will be easier for readers to relate to the characters, as if anonymity is the same thing as universality."

misapprehension of the skill with which the author combines formulaic elements with experiments in established literary forms, especially variations of the *Bildungsroman,* to create the freshness and innovation which account for so much of her appeal. Indeed, the many, many modern gothics which echo *Rebecca* are good evidence that du Maurier tends to set trends rather than to follow them.

Certainly, it is no disgrace either to establish or to follow a popular, even beloved, literary formula. Du Maurier has done both; she tends to capitalize on some very old, established patterns (some reaching back into folk literature)—the worried, self-conscious second wife, the dangerous dark-haired beauty, the ineffectual male seeking self-definition and power, the dark, mysterious male—and bend them to her will and to her skill.

The cultural images and symbols du Maurier employs in her romantic adventures are very closely allied with the cultural myths or themes which she explores. *Rebecca,* for instance, opens with one of English fiction's most famous lines, "Last night I dreamt I went to Manderley again." Manderley, the named house which has become so indispensable to modern gothic fiction, is a very important socio-cultural symbol in the novel, for it represents all the pleasures, perquisites, comfort and standing of the powerful upper class to which Maxim de Winter belongs. Manderley is Maxim's heritage both in fact and in symbol and he will do almost anything to protect it.

Similarly yet differently, Jamaica Inn is the central sociocultural symbol of the novel named after it. Normally, an inn represents a safe harbor for the weary traveler. Jamaica Inn, however, is an

What Do I Read Next?

- The script for Arthur Hopcraft's 1996 adaptation of *Rebecca* for television has been published in paperback by Andre Duetsch Ltd.

- Readers who enjoy the sweeping romance of *Rebecca* generally like du Maurier's previous novel, *Jamaica Inn* (1936), about a young woman who moves out to a house on the British moors and is faced with mystery and romance there.

- Susan Hill wrote a sequel to *Rebecca* called *Mrs. de Winter* (1993). Hill's book carries on where du Maurier's novel left off. Die-hard fans of the original book should beware that reviewers generally find Hill's version to be a disappointment.

- One of the most interesting and in-depth biographies of Daphne du Maurier is Martyn Shallcross' *The Private World of Daphne du Maurier,* published in 1992.

- While *Rebecca* is a good example of romantic literature, the supreme example of the genre is Emily Brontë's 1847 novel *Wuthering Heights,* which also has a female protagonist in love with a cruel, strong male figure, living in a big, secluded English house.

- The novel's plot, about a second wife who is haunted by the memory of the glamorous first wife, is clearly in debt to another classic romance: *Jane Eyre,* also published in 1847, by Charlotte Brontë, Emily's sister.

- Kazuo Ishiguro's 1989 novel *Remains of the Day* is about the life of a faithful old-time English butler, a type that disappeared quickly after World War II. It gives excellent insight into the mind of a man like *Rebecca*'s Frith.

ironic symbol: there, plans for theft and bloodshed are laid; there, the spoils of shipwreckers (criminals of the lowest class) are stored. Not only the seat of criminal activity, the inn is also personally dangerous for Mary Yellan, the young woman who seeks refuge there. The emotional impact of both Manderley and Jamaica Inn is very great, for one represents a form of "the good life" any reader can recognize (and many desire) and the other represents all the false hopes and failed refuges most human beings encounter during the short journey between the cradle and the grave.

The cultural materials du Maurier most frequently employs in her romantic crime fiction also indicate elements of social convention. The British class system conflicting with the concept of upward mobility (for females via marriage; for males by assertion of control over lands and money); the idea that outside marriage a young woman has almost no identity; and the importance of retaining one's good name (no matter what reputation one deserves) are all central to these works. In *Rebecca* for example, Maxim de Winter resorts to extreme violence to preserve his reputation and it is the consensus among those of his peers privy to his secret that he acted properly in doing so. Mrs. de Winter and Mary Yellan desire upward mobility and believe that marriage is their vehicle to security and status. Philip Ashley, the narrator of *My Cousin Rachel,* genuinely mourns Ambrose, the cousin from whom he inherits a vast estate, yet Philip is aware that as the master of the family holding, he enjoys power and position which would have been unattainable in a secondary or even a shared mastery.

Beyond those socio-cultural images and symbols lie others, even more pervasive and more powerful than those based upon class, property and reputation. Du Maurier also explores universal problems which take on the aura of cultural myth. The difficulty of distinguishing between good and evil and the impossibility of purging certain kinds of guilt are important in almost every story. Mary Yellan nearly falls prey to a very wicked man because she mistakes cultural trappings for his real nature. Armino Donati (*The Flight of the Falcon*) wants to trust his brother's charm, poise, and attractiveness, but he suspects that vicious intent lies beneath Aldo's attractive exterior, and John, the protagonist-narrator of *The Scapegoat,* must learn that even the most crass codes of behavior can generate redemptive action.

Maxim de Winter not only hides his crime successfully but also involves his current wife and others in the concealment; he pays with years of misery, the loss of almost everything he sought to protect, yet guilt remains a constant in his life. Philip Ashley weighs the evidence against Rachel, his beloved, judges her—and lives out his years pondering his own guiltiness. Like Maxim de Winter, he has been both judge and jury; like Maxim, he must forever bear the memory and the weight of his actions.

The universal, mythically proportioned problems lying at the heart of du Maurier's most important novels are, indeed, basic. They are also, however, problems with which most human beings are expected to make their peace fairly early in life. One of the most important lessons learned by the very young is the ability to look behind disguise and to discover the essential decency or corruption of others, and very early on, people generally learn to assuage, ignore, or expiate guilt. Though these lessons may well have to be relearned or modified as maturing individuals confront new problems, people and situations, the groundwork, the basic principles of choice and evaluation, ought to be established during adolescence.

Though the du Maurier characters are no longer teenagers, they are, nevertheless, curiously immature for their years. Preoccupied by hard work and secluded in a small, friendly community, Mary Yellan has missed the experiences she needs to develop her judgment. Carefully protected, Philip Ashley has depended upon his cousin Ambrose for guidance. Both Armino Donati and John, the surnameless hero of *The Scapegoat,* have simply abdicated responsibility; they refuse to act. Maxim de Winter, seemingly an adult in full control of his powers, is caught in the grip of an obsession, Manderley and all it stands for, and is actually the most immature character of the lot. And Dona St. Columb, protagonist of *Frenchman's Creek,* a wife, mother, noblewoman, is frozen into unmaturity, for she has substituted social activity and petulant rebellion for awareness and growth. Thus, these important characters are, for all narrative purposes, youngsters, and in her stories, du Maurier exposes them and many of their fellows to the maturation tests and experiences most commonly found in stories about adolescents. This device adds considerably to the novels' suspense, for it is, in a sense, a plot within a plot. Not only do readers wonder when and if the dangers and courtships will be resolved happily, but they also wonder if the characters will be able to come to terms with the worlds in which they must live. Readers are keenly interested in discovering whether or not the characters will ever resolve the question of who they really are.

This question is also linked to another cultural artifact du Maurier exploits widely. She uses one of the oldest of western European tales, the Cin-

 Certainly, it is no disgrace either to establish or to follow a popular, even beloved, literary formula. Du Maurier has done both; she tends to capitalize on some very old, established patterns (some reaching back into folk literature)—the worried, self-conscious second wife, the dangerous darkhaired beauty, the ineffectual male seeking self-definition and power, the dark, mysterious male—and bend them to her will and to her skill."

derella story, in various ways throughout these six novels. Almost mythic itself, it becomes the vehicle for the ethical questions (of good and evil, of guilt) upon which the plot complications turn. Various elements of the Cinderella story appear in each of the novels under discussion here and all of them hinge upon the character's discovery of who he or she really is, the discovery at the heart of Cinderella's adventures.

In du Maurier's romantic suspense novels, as in *Cinderella,* the major question is not detection but justice. It is important that Cinderella's triumph include the public humiliation of her wicked relatives because, in the eyes of many people, public punishment is equated with justice. Because the evils which Cinderella confronts, overt cruelty, jealousy and selfishness, are easy to identify and are subject to social disapproval, the wicked are punished; justice, seemingly, is served.

But the evils which the du Maurier protagonists confront are more complex; simple, obvious punishment is not always meted out. Instead, the irony which colors du Maurier's social commentary also affects her portrayal of justice, for while justice is always imposed, it is often served secretly, privately. To du Maurier, the impact of a crime is of far greater interest than the solution of a puzzle and this interest demands sophisticated modes of punishment.

The crime motif in du Maurier's novels is also enriched by another element of the Cinderella story, the disguise pattern. Frequently, the novels' protagonists appear in disguise; Lady Dona St. Columb, for instance, dresses as a boy when committing piracy. To her bitter dismay, Mrs. de Winter unwittingly disguises herself as Rebecca, her predecessor, for she is tricked into duplicating the costume Rebecca once wore to a fancy-dress ball and this scene lays the groundwork for the revelation of Maxim's crime. These disguises are fascinating and useful plot complications, lending action, adventure, or ironic foreshadowing to the stories.

Even more useful, however, are the disguises worn by the other characters, and these disguises exacerbate the difficulty of separating evil from goodness, one of the mythic themes which pervades these works. In each of the novels, at least one very powerful personality is examined and explored; these characters are charismatic, mysterious, disguised. Several are not what they seem to be and are unmasked. Frances Davey, the Vicar of Altarnum (*Jamaica Inn*), is not really a devout pastor ministering wholeheartedly to his flock but a dangerous criminal. Maxim de Winter is not a man emotionally crippled by the death of his beloved but rather a man tortured by guilt and the refusal to pay for his crime.

Others among these disguised charismatics are better than they first seem. Jean-Benoit Aubéry, the French pirate, *is* actually a criminal, but he is more decent, caring and nurturing than all the nobles among whom Dona St. Columb has lived. Jem Merlyn (*Jamaica Inn*) who makes no attempt to hide his career as petty criminal and horse thief, is far more honest with Mary Yellan than are the other inhabitants of the Bodmin area.

A third group, most notably Rebecca de Winter and Rachel Sangalletti Ashley, are essentially unknowable—one is never sure just which guise is mask, which reality. The world perceived Rebecca as the epitome of feminine grace and beauty, the perfect mistress for Manderley. To Maxim, her husband, she seemed a corrupt monster. To Mrs. Danvers, the housekeeper, and to Jack Favell, Rebecca's lover and cousin, she appeared to be a free spirit, capable of commanding devotion even from beyond the grave. Though most of the characters choose to believe Maxim's interpretation of Re-

becca's character, the puzzle is never resolved. Nor is the mystery surrounding Rachel's character dispelled; she may be tragically accused of and punished for a crime she did not commit, a crime which was, indeed, never committed by anyone, or she may be a grasping poisoner who kills for wealth and position. These characters not only drive forward the action, but they also complicate the process of distinguishing between good and evil, sometimes beyond the capacity of the protagonists (and some readers). Unlike the disguises of the Cinderella figures, these enigmatic masks are meant to be impenetrable.

The disguise motif, then, establishes the most difficult tests the Cinderella figures must pass in order to win better lives. Further, because the enigmatic figures may mislead the protagonists, the element of disguise also strengthens the other fictional pattern du Maurier exploits. The education or maturation novel, the *Bildungsroman* (for which *Cinderella* is one of several important prototypes), is deeply embedded in both "serious" and popular fiction throughout western culture. Itself enormously popular, it is prime material for a writer like du Maurier who seeks a very wide audience.

In the traditional *Bildungsroman,* a young person who has great faith in his own power and potential tests his mettle as a means of initiation into maturity. He often takes a journey, acquires mentors of varying levels of reliability and engages in dangerous adventures. Ultimately, he emerges sadder but wiser, ready to take his place in adult society. He has compromised with the ideal and settled for pragmatism. Du Maurier uses this treatment of the *Bildungsroman,* most commonly found in "high culture" novels, very successfully in both *Jamaica Inn* and *Frenchman's Creek.*

In *Jamaica Inn,* Mary Yellan dreams of security and hopes to find peace and opportunity living with her aunt and uncle at the inn. Instead, she finds danger to her life and honor and a host of false mentors. Among them is her criminal uncle, Joss Merlyn, who presents a sexual threat; he finds Mary attractive and to her dismay, she is somewhat drawn to him. For relief, advice and comfort, Mary turns to a local minister, one of du Maurier's masters of disguise, who does, indeed, advise her but who is actually also a false mentor.

Because of his abusive treatment of her aunt and because of his criminal activity, which she slowly comes to recognize, Mary has little trouble recognizing Joss as an evil person; indeed, he represents the worst that life can offer her: sexual excess, constant danger, shared criminal behavior. Dark, mysterious, violent, Joss symbolizes trouble and degeneration. The Reverend Mr. Davey, however, seems to represent redemption until his mask is finally stripped away during a melodramatic series of events that include an abduction and wild chase over the moors.

Not only does the final unmasking of Davey leave Mary without a functioning mentor, it also forces her to question the basic rules of social convention. She has hoped to establish a very normal, secure life on the Cornish coast, and obviously one means of doing so would have been to marry well, preferably, like most of the Cinderellas, to marry *up*. The revelation of Davey as villain and exploiter removes him from the ranks of potential mates and also, importantly, calls into question the viability of Mary's dreams of security and status.

A poor girl with modest dreams, Mary is barred, finally, from upward mobility by the rules of the class system. Tainted by her low birth, her poverty, her association with criminals (she is even an unwilling spectator and thus marginally a participant in one raid), Mary cannot change her status. She shares in the guilt for this last raid because she was there and because willful blindness as well as circumstance have stopped her from preventing it.

Though Mary has learned not to trust outward appearances, her fate lies, finally, in the hands of yet another masquerader. Jem Merlyn, Joss' younger brother, is an enigmatic man who reveals little of his true emotion, a sexually attractive person who prefers liason (when he can get it) to marriage. Nevertheless he loves Mary and is the only individual who acts effectively to save her from rape or murder. Despite the tensions which exist between them in the early days of their acquaintance, Mary "believes" that she loves Jem, that he is her true mate and she rides off with him, " 'Because I want to: because I must; because now and for ever more this is where I belong to be.' "

The real world for which Mary, chastened and tempered, settles is a marginal world in which she will always hover between poverty and security, social acceptance and rejection, love and danger. Ironist that she is, du Maurier gives no guarantees that for this young woman there will be any "happily ever after." Though Mary is a successful *Bildungsroman* protagonist (she has learned, she has matured, she has compromised), she is a failed Cinderella; the class system prevails and Mary Yellan is frozen into the fringes of accepted society. She

has love but little else, and du Maurier refuses to promise that that will be enough.

On the surface of her life, Dona St. Columb is, at the opening of *Frenchman's Creek,* Cinderella leading an enchanted life after the glass slipper has slid smoothly onto her foot. Chronologically an adult, Dona is nevertheless a rebellious child. Disgusted with her dull husband, often irritated by the demands of motherhood, and bored with London life, Dona disguises herself and engages in dangerous, illegal pranks, "playing at" highway robbery, until, restless and annoyed with herself as much as with her world, she runs away to Navron House, the family estate, fleeing both her obligations and her escapades.

There, however, she moves even more deeply into disguise and danger, for she comes to love a French pirate who is raiding the Cornish coast. A kind of nautical Robin Hood, Aubéry, the Frenchman of the title, teaches Dona what love and sexual satisfaction really are, and she revels in the relationship. Initially disguised as chic matron, polished noblewoman, Dona believes she has found her true nature when disguised as a thieving boy or sensual lover and she discovers that she is not only a competent thief but also a clever schemer when she undertakes to save her lover from imprisonment and death. During this period, Navron House continues to stand for the positive qualities of whatever is decent in Dona's public life, everything opposed to the corruption symbolized by London. The nearby creek where the Frenchman moors his ship and *La Mouette* itself symbolize freedom, love, the right to break—social codes in order to achieve happiness—everything children imagine that adulthood allows.

Eventually, Dona must choose between life with the Frenchman and life as Lady St. Columb and in the end, social convention and family obligation claim her. For her, life as a constrained, postball Cinderella *is* reality whereas life on the fringes of society is dream. Except in memory, she will truly become,

> a gracious matron, and smile upon her servants, and her tenants, and the village folk, and one day she will have grandchildren about her knee, and will tell them the story of a pirate who escaped.

Dona will not live happily ever after, but she will live responsibly.

She, too, has been tempered and chastened and like Mary, she responds, however hesitantly, to the lessons she has learned. If Mary Yellan cannot penetrate respectable levels of English society, no more can Dona St. Columb abdicate the upper classes. These young women come to know themselves very well; they find out precisely who they are, but they are, finally, defined by the social roles assigned by birth. Their very traditional *Bildungsroman* journeys, culminating in compromise and pragmatic acceptance, are complete.

In popular fiction, two variations of the traditional *Bildungsroman* occur frequently and du Maurier experiments with these varieties just as she does with the traditional pattern in *Jamaica Inn* and *Frenchman's Creek.* As feminist critics have pointed out, the modern gothic novel is a form of the *Bildungsroman* whose youthful protagonists, usually females, are, either consciously or unconsciously, engaged in a quest for advancement as well as for adulthood. They want power, selfhood, love and maturity and much of the time, they tend to perceive these desirables as interchangeable if not synonymous.

In a sense, they feel that they will be forever unworthy if they are not loved by some greatly desirable person, but also, secretly or even unconsciously, they feel themselves to be the equal—if not the superior—of most of the characters surrounding them. This conflicting sense of self-worth (obvious in *Cinderella*) is often painful and almost always results in the protagonists' maintaining a kind of public guise of meekness which hides a fiery, judgmental, or even arrogant personality. Cinderellas, they are not only disguised initially by their lowly positions, but also they actively parade a mask of humility.

The second Mrs. de Winter, the protagonist-narrator of *Rebecca,* is precisely this sort of person and because of the confessional nature of the novel, readers are privy to the seemingly meek, the genuinely humble and the bitingly judgmental elements of her nature from the outset. Though she maintains a quiet, obedient exterior, she denounces thoroughly (and with some good cause) Mrs. Van Hopper, an American of abundant financial means and absolutely no taste, whom she serves as companion. She feels distinctly superior to the Van Hopper world but too inexperienced, uninteresting and plain to be a likely helpmeet of Maxim de Winter. Both attitudes cause her considerable trouble. Ironically, she accepts Mrs. Van Hopper's evaluation of her personality and assumes that to Maxim she is merely a toy, a pet, that she can never truly be his equal. Yet, inwardly, she weeps and rages, for she yearns to be his true companion, to move beyond the shadow of Rebecca and into promi-

nence as the mistress of Manderley, with which she has been entranced since childhood.

Maxim, enigmatic, preoccupied with keeping secret the crime he has committed, withholds a large part of himself from his second wife even though he senses and deplores her unhappiness. In turn, Mrs. de Winter, unaware of Maxim's true thoughts, assumes he is still grieving for Rebecca. Both marriage partners maintain disguises, acting out a "happy" married life, refusing to share, pretending before outsiders and one another.

This Cinderella temporarily acquires both her prince and her castle, but she can genuinely enjoy neither, and when truth does finally prevail between the de Winters, it is too late. The prince, the princess and the marriage survive, but the castle, Manderley, symbol of all the perks of upper-class life, is destroyed. Once again, du Maurier's irony intrudes and the class system prevails. Mrs. de Winter deserves her tainted prince *only if* they are exiled from the social circles to which Maxim was born and to which Mrs. de Winter aspires. Cinderella finds that compromise dominates adulthood and the real world; she acquiesces and endures the consequences of fallen pride. Society has preserved its aura of respectability by protecting Maxim from disclosure of his crime, but nevertheless, it has firmly punished the de Winters. Though this *Bildungsroman* hero has learned her lessons all too well, there is nowhere to use her education.

> We can never go back again, that much is certain. The past is still too close to us. The things we have tried to forget and put behind us would stir again, and that sense of fear, of furtive unrest, struggling at length to blind unreasoning panic—now mercifully stilled, thank God—might in some manner unforseen become a living companion, as it had been before.

Instead, the de Winters drift through Europe, maintaining the social façade, marking time until death releases them.

In traditional adventure-suspense fiction, the protagonist takes a slightly different view of himself than do gothic heroes such as Philip Ashley and Mrs. de Winter. They do not perceive themselves as better than others and they do not yearn for status. Usually, these characters have seen something of life, have become aware of its stresses and pitfalls and, as protection, have disguised themselves as "small," inconsequential persons. Each must stretch his capacity, admit his own potential, abandon insignificance, *expand* in order to meet and conquer some criminal threat. Doing so will signify emergence from a willfully chosen, prolonged adolescence into full maturity. Generally, they pass their exacting tests and emerge stronger, more confident, no longer hiding their capabilities from the world.

Du Maurier's experiments with this variant of the *Bildungsroman, The Flight of the Falcon* and *The Scapegoat,* allow their protagonists much more promising futures than do her treatments of the traditional *Bildungsroman* or of the modern gothic, even though the events are just as melodramatic, the assessments of human nature just as uncompromising. Furthermore, in these novels, the questions of guilt and evil are expanded considerably, a fact underscored by the use of non-English settings.

Though matters of social class and its privilege remain important in *The Scapegoat* and are echoed by allusions to earlier times in *The Flight of the Falcon,* these novels are allegories and du Maurier uses St. Gilles, the French village dominated by the de Gué family of *The Scapegoat,* and Ruffano, the Italian university city in which *The Flight of the Falcon* is set, as microcosms. In the first novel, she examines the political and economic impact of one man's criminality, selfishness and arrogance. In the second, she explores the effects of a clever, ambitious man's manipulation of oppressive political systems.

Because du Maurier is chiefly a storyteller and not a philosopher, dramatic action dominates theme in these novels; the political implications are not particularly profound and they are certainly not unique. However, these implications intensify the suspense in both books, just as they later intensify her futuristic political study, *Rule Britannia* (1972) and they continue du Maurier's examination of the conflict between personal ambition and one's duty to others which is the subject of such novels as *I'll Never Be Young Again* (1932) and *The Progress of Julius* (1933), novels outside the boundaries of romantic suspense fiction.

Du Maurier complicates the problems of distinguishing between good and evil and of guilt and emphasizes the allegorical nature of *The Flight of the Falcon* and *The Scapegoat* by using Christian symbolism in both. Crucial action in *The Flight of the Falcon* takes place during Easter Week, for instance, and a priest, a character in *The Scapegoat,* states the theme of both books:

> 'There is no end to the evil in ourselves, just as there is no end to the good. It's a matter of choice. We struggle to climb, or we struggle to fall. The thing is to discover which way we're going'.

Daphne du Maurier (far right) at home with her husband, Major-General Frederick Browning, and children at Menabilly Estate in Cornwall, England

Both novels also depict Satanic and Christlike figures who are very much alike: in *The Scapegoat,* the men are identical in appearance and in *The Flight of the Falcon,* they are putative brothers. Further, the Donati brothers share a kind of *Doppelgänger,* the spirit of Claudio, a long-dead Duke of Ruffano, who is depicted as both tempted and tempter in an old painting, "The Temptation of Christ." These devices help du Maurier move beyond questions of personal complicity and individual destiny around which *Rebecca, My Cousin Rachel, Frenchman's Creek* and *Jamaica Inn* center and focus attention, instead, upon the basic duality of human nature.

An examination of her treatments of the Cinderella story and of her experiments with various forms of the *Bildungsroman,* then, indicate that Daphne du Maurier brings a rich imagination, a sound sense of story line and action, and a great willingness to experiment to her fiction. Though individually the novels considered here—*Jamaica Inn, Frenchman's Creek, Rebecca, My Cousin*

Rachel, The Flight of the Falcon and *The Scapegoat*—match Cawelti's definition of formula fiction, together, they demonstrate that any formula—or any literary convention—can be reinvented fruitfully. In the hands of a true storyteller, the old is always new and the "du Maurier Tradition" demands bold inventiveness, intelligence and a special awareness of the roots, artifacts, strengths and weaknesses of the culture from which it springs, toward which it is directed. Du Maurier blends all of these requirements into the heady compounds of the expected and the surprising which are so pleasurable to her readers. In achieving these ends, she surpasses her competitors and her imitators. Others may emulate Daphne du Maurier, but she remains dominant.

Source: Jane S. Bakerman, "Daphne du Maurier," in *And Then There Were Nine,* edited by Jane S. Bakerman, Bowling Green State University Popular Press, 1985, pp. 12–29.

Basil Davenport

In the following review, Davenport calls Rebecca a quality melodrama, comparing it with Jane Eyre.

So Cinderella married the prince, and then her story began. Cinderella was hardly more than a school-girl, and the overworked companion of a snobbish woman of wealth; the prince was Maximilian de Winter, whom she had heard of as the owner of Manderley in Cornwall, one of the most magnificent show places in England, who had come to the Riviera to forget the tragic death of his wife Rebecca. He was twice the little companion's age, but she conceived a starved girl's adoration for him when he was kind to her, and there was something about her freshness that seemed to please him. Then to her astonished rapture, he proposed marriage to her, and carried her off to the splendors of Manderley, in its forest of azaleas, sloping down to the sea that had drowned Rebecca, the first Mrs. de Winter—"Mrs. de Winter," simply, as every one still calls her. For slowly and subtly the girl's dream changes to a nightmare. The great house where she cannot find her way, the first wife's shuttered bedroom, the servants who say that in Mrs. de Winter's time there were no complaints, and above all the old housekeeper, who keeps for the first Mrs. de Winter the ghoulish devotion of Phaedra's nurse or Electra's old slave—they all close in on her, like the monstrous azaleas. There was some mystery about Rebecca's death, too, as the village idiot knows; but the book is skillfully contrived so that it does not depend only on knowledge of it for its thrill; it can afford to give no hint of it till two-thirds of the way through. But the revelation, when it comes, leads to one of the most prolonged, deadly, and breathless fencing-matches that one can find in fiction, a battle of wits that would by itself make the fortune of a melodrama on the stage.

For this is a melodrama, unashamed, glorying in its own quality, such as we have hardly had since that other dependant, Jane Eyre, found that her house too had a first wife. It has the weaknesses of melodrama; in particular, the heroine is at times quite unbelievably stupid, as when she takes the advice of the housekeeper whom she knows to hate her. But if the second Mrs. de Winter had consulted with any one before trusting the housekeeper, we should miss one of the best scenes in the book. There is also, as is almost inseparable from a melodrama, a forced heightening of the emotional values; the tragedy announced in the opening chapter is out of proportion to the final outcome of the long battle of wits that ends the book. But it is as absorbing a tale as the season is likely to bring.

Source: Basil Davenport, "Sinister House," in *Saturday Review of Literature,* Vol. XVIII, No. 22, September 24, 1938, p. 5.

Sources

Barkham, John, Review in *New York Review of Books,* March 8, 1953, p. 8.

Davenport, Basil, "Sinister House," in *Saturday Review,* September 24, 1938, p. 5.

Hill, Susan, Review in *New Statesman,* July 23, 1971.

Raymond, John, Review in *New Statesman,* August 11, 1951.

Rogers, Pat, "Saving Her Bacon," in *Spectator,* Vol. 237, No. 7727, July 31, 1976, p. 20.

For Further Study

Auerbach, Nina, *Daphne du Maurier: Haunted Heiress,* University of Pennsylvania Press, 1999.

This recent critical examination of du Maurier defends her against criticism that finds her work superficial.

Forster, Margaret, *Daphne du Maurier: The Secret Life of the Renowned Storyteller,* St. Martin's Press, 1994.

This is the biography that was authorized by du Maurier's family. It has some probing information because the author had more access to papers and interviews than many du Maurier scholars.

Horner, Arvel, and Sue Zlisnik, *Daphne du Maurier: Writing, Identity and the Gothic Imagination,* St. Martin's Press, 1998.

This relatively new study of the author's works concentrates on the supernatural elements with which she worked.

Vickers, Stanley, *The du Maurier Companion,* edited by Diana King, Fowey Rare Books, 1997.

This reference work lists all of the novels, plays, films, and autobiographical works by du Maurier and other literary members of her family.

The Slave Dancer

Paula Fox

1973

Paula Fox did not begin writing until 1962 when she was thirty-nine years old, but since then she has enjoyed critical acclaim and praise from the many readers of her books. She writes fiction for children and novels for adults, and of all her books, *The Slave Dancer* has been the most widely praised and recognized. The book tells the story of thirteen-year-old Jessie Bollier, who in 1840 is kidnapped from his New Orleans home and forced to play his fife on a slave ship while the slaves are "danced," or exercised. The book won the Newbery Medal in 1974, and Fox has also won the Hans Christian Andersen medal for her work.

Despite this praise, the book has also been the subject of controversy. Some critics believed it was racist and that it portrayed slaves unfairly, as despairing, weak people unable to fight for themselves, and, indeed, as responsible for their own enslavement. In addition, several characters in the book are racists, and their language and attitudes offended some readers.

However, most reviewers agree that Fox has impeccable control of the English language; *The Slave Dancer,* like her other books, has been widely praised for the poetry of Fox's prose, her rich imagery, and her mythic storytelling, as well as her deft handling of a topic many people previously considered too horrific for children to read about.

Author Biography

Paula Fox was born in New York City, on April 22, 1923. When Fox was five, her parents sent her to live with a minister and his bedridden mother in upstate New York while her parents traveled. They were busy with her father's career as a writer of plays and films and did not have time to raise her. The minister shared his love of reading, poetry, and history with her. At age five, she had her first experience with the thrill of writing when she suggested to the minister that he write a sermon about a waterfall, and he agreed. She told a *New York Times* writer, "I grasped . . . that everything could count, that a word, spoken as meant, contained in itself an energy capable of awakening imagination, thought, emotion."

When she was six, she moved to California for two years and then was sent to live with her grandmother on a sugar plantation in Cuba, where she went to school in a one-room schoolhouse and quickly learned to speak Spanish. Three years later, the revolution in Cuba forced her to leave, and she returned to New York City with her grandmother. By the time she was twelve, she had already attended nine different schools and hardly knew her parents. Of her parents, she told Sybil Steinberg in *Publishers Weekly* only that her mother was very young and was unable to take on the responsibility of a child. What she did know—and took strength from—was books. In every place she lived, except Cuba, there was a library, and Fox always found it.

Fox had to leave high school early, and she worked a wide variety of jobs, including salesperson, rivet-sorter, and machinist to support herself. When she was sixteen, she got a job in California, reading books for Warner Brothers, and when she was twenty-one, a lucky break led her to a job as a journalist in Poland. She eventually returned to Manhattan, married, and had two sons, but the marriage ended in divorce.

Despite her lack of formal education, Fox was accepted into Columbia University, and for almost four years, she studied, worked full time, and raised her sons until lack of money forced her to quit the school. She then took various teaching jobs and began to write. She told Steinberg that she had "an ineradicable tendency to tell stories and listen to them. Reading was everything to me."

Fox married again, and when her new husband won a Guggenheim award, they went to Greece where she wrote her first novel, *Poor George,*

Paula Fox

which was accepted by Harcourt Brace. Thus began her prolific career as a writer of books for both children and adults. *The Slave Dancer* won the Newbery Medal, and her other books have won her a Newbery Honor, the American Book Award, and the Hans Christian Andersen Medal. She has also received awards from the National Institute of Arts and Letters and the National Endowment of the Arts, as well as a Brandeis Fiction Citation.

Plot Summary

The Errand

Thirteen-year-old Jessie Bollier, his widowed mother, and his sister live in a one-room home in a poor quarter of New Orleans in 1840. His mother makes a meager wage sewing dresses, and Jessie plays his fife to make a few pennies. He dreams of being rich someday, and although he is curious about the lives of slaves he sees, he is forbidden to visit the slave market and knows little about their daily existence. His mother tells him that despite his family's grinding poverty,

> there were souls whose fates were so terrible in comparison to ours, that we should consider ourselves among the fortunate of the earth. I knew she was

thinking of the slaves who were sold daily so close to where we lived.

When his mother has to make a dress in a hurry, she sends Jessie out to his aunt's house to get some candles so she can stay up late to sew, but on the way home from this errand, two sailors who have seen him playing his fife kidnap him.

The Moonlight

Their ship is *The Moonlight,* a ship bound for Africa, under Captain Cawthorne, a man so brutal that when he meets Jessie, he bites Jessie's ear hard enough to draw blood. Captain Cawthorne tells Jessie that *The Moonlight* is a slave ship, involved in a "lucrative and God-granted trade," and that anyone who tries to interfere with it is a pirate. Jessie will play his fife to make the slaves "dance" once they are on board; this exercise will keep them strong and fit so that they will bring in more money when they are sold. In addition, he is expected to help around the ship.

Jessie meets Ned Spark, the ship's carpenter and occasional doctor, who professes to be a Christian but who will profit from the slave ship's voyage as much as the rest of the crew, including the ill-tempered cook; Nick Spark, the Mate, who is as cruel as the captain; and Ben Stout, who says he is sorry for Jessie's kidnapping, talks kindly to him, and gives him extra clothes and a piece of bread.

Once Jessie settles in, he notices that Purvis, who is a good sailor despite his rough manners and teasing sense of humor, is always busy, and he realizes that even though Purvis is one of the men who kidnapped him, he can trust him. Purvis tells Jessie that other ships will try and stop the slave ship from completing its journey. The British, who are against slavery, will board the ship and confiscate the slaves and the profits.

The Shrouds

Until now, Jessie has been confused by the crew, who defend the trade, saying that so many ships are involved in it that the laws against it don't matter. Claudius Sharkey, a crewmember, tells Jessie that in addition to the British cruisers that make the trade dangerous, American ships also patrol against importers of slaves. However, the possible profit from these voyages outweighs the danger: "He spread his arms as wide as he could to show me the money the smugglers made after they'd taken the slaves inland and sold them."

Although Ben Stout has been kind to him, Jessie doesn't trust him. Instead, he likes Purvis:

"Purvis, with his horrible coarse jokes, his bawling and cursing, Purvis, whom I trusted."

One morning, at dawn, he sees a sailor sneaking forward on the ship, and returning with an egg—part of the captain's private food supply. He is not sure who the sailor is, and soon Purvis is named as the culprit, tied up by Ben Stout and another sailor, and brutally flogged and then hung from the rigging. Later, he finds out that Stout stole the egg, and was happy when Purvis was blamed. When he asks Purvis why he didn't deny being the thief, Purvis says, "The officers of this ship would not care what the truth was."

The Bight of Benin

When the ship arrives off the coast of Africa, all the preparations for taking on slaves are completed. They go up and down the coast, and the captain goes out at night in a small boat and deals with the African chiefs who are selling the slaves.

Jessie is sick of being on the ship, sick of what he learns about the slave trade, and when Purvis asks him to help set up a tarp to provide shade for the slaves when they eat their meals, he refuses: "nearly senseless with rage. . . . I considered casting myself over the side and confounding them all!" But he gives in because he believes that no one on the ship would save him, and he would die. "I went slowly toward Purvis, feeling a shame I'd never felt before," he says.

> Later, when he protests against the slave trade, Purvis becomes violently angry, and tells Jessie that his own Irish ancestors came to America in ships no better than the slave ships—"locked up in a hold for the whole voyage where they might have died of sickness and suffocation. . . . Do you know my father was haunted all his days by the memory of those who died before his eyes in that ship, and were flung into the sea? And you dare speak of my parents in the same breath with these [slaves]!

Jessie wonders how Purvis can be so angry about the conditions his parents traveled under, and at the same time fail to see how it's wrong to treat the slaves like this. But Jessie realizes that he can't talk to any of the crew about this; whenever he is upset about slavery, he is beaten.

The slaves arrive. Two of them die, Jessie notes, "and Stout dumped their bodies over the side as I dumped waste." Then a little girl dies and is tossed over the same way. Jessie is horrified, and his punishment when the sailors notice it is observed by one of the slaves, a young boy the same age as Jessie. An instant, unspoken bond forms between Jessie and the young slave boy though they don't speak the same language.

Nicholas Spark Walks on Water

They set sail, back toward America. Every other day, groups of slaves are brought on deck where Jessie plays the fife and Stout whips them to make them "dance," or exercise. He is filled with self-loathing, and also, to his horror, he realizes that he hates the slaves, the symbol of his own slavery on the ship.

> I hated their shuffling, their howling, their very suffering!" he says. "I hated the way they spat out their food upon the deck, the overflowing buckets, the emptying of which tried all my strength. . . . I would have snatched the rope from Spark's hand and beaten them myself! Oh, God! I wished them all dead! Not to hear them! Not to smell them! Not to know of their existence!

He drops his fife on the deck and runs to his sleeping quarters, but he is brought back to the deck and flogged by Stout for his disobedience.

> But as the blows fell," he says, "I became myself again. I was a thirteen-year-old male, not as tall as, though somewhat heavier than, a boy close to my own age, now doubled up in the dark below, not a dozen yards from where I was being beaten.

The beating changes him, makes him more aware; he observes the sailors "with as little pity as they observed the blacks." He feels pity for the slaves, realizing he is in the same position as they: all of them are on the ship against their will. He says, "I hated what I did [playing the fife]. I tried to comfort myself with the thought that, at least, it gave them time out of the hold. But what was the point of that or anything else?"

As the ship travels on, discipline degenerates; the ship is filthy, the men are filthy and are often drunk. Jessie separates himself from them, stepping away mentally, remembering every object in his home, dissociating himself from the horrible present. During this time, he becomes aware that the slave boy is watching him every time he is on deck. He points to himself with the fife, saying his name: "Jessie."

When a slave attacks the mate, Nicholas Spark, Spark guns him down and is immediately bound with a rope and thrown overboard: by killing the African man, he has destroyed the profit that would come from selling him, and Spark's own life is not worth that much. "Don't you see?" Purvis asks, "There went the profit!"

The Spaniard

By this time, the slaves are all sick, and so are most of the crew. Stout is still trying to make friends with Jessie, who ignores him. To get revenge, Stout steals Jessie's fife and tosses it into the hold where Jessie must walk over the bodies of the slaves to look for it—or be flogged if he doesn't find it. The young slave boy finds it and hands it to Jessie, saving him from the horrendous task and the punishment.

They reach the coast of Cuba, and Captain Cawthorne begins bargaining with a Spaniard to sell the slaves. On the following day, they will be unloaded and sold.

Ben Stout's Mistake

The sailors arrange a party, bringing out rum and chests of clothes, dressing up the slaves like women, and getting drunk. Jessie is ordered to play his fife while the sailors dance and slap the slaves around. A sail appears, indicating a ship is approaching. Stout claims that he knows it, and it won't harm them. Cawthorne, who doesn't believe him and thinks the ship is a threat, orders all the slaves and the evidence of slavery to be thrown over the side, and the sailors begin tossing men, women, and children over the rail. Cawthorne, believing the ship is English, hoists the American flag, and, too late, realizes the ship is American.

The other ship approaches and a battle ensues, perceived only dimly by Jessie, who is in mortal terror. At the same time, a storm breaks over both vessels. Jessie grabs the young slave boy, and both of them crawl to the hold where they hide. While they are down there, a sailor up above closes the hatch, which is always closed in storms.

They remain trapped for several days during the storm. Finally, they hear a violent crash: the ship has run aground. The hatch cover falls away, and they crawl out, finding everyone dead except Captain Cawthorne, who is dying, the slaves gone, and the ship wrecked. Land is nearby, and they swim to it.

The Old Man

The two boys are taken in by an old man, an escaped slave who lives deep in the woods of Mississippi. He feeds them and helps them regain their strength, and he arranges for others to take the slave boy, whose name is Ras, north where he can be free. He tells Jessie how to walk the three-day journey back to New Orleans and asks him not to tell anyone because if Jessie tells anyone about the old man, he may be recaptured and taken back to slavery.

Home and After

Jessie walks home and finds his mother and sister, but he doesn't settle easily back into his old life. He has lost his old dreams of becoming rich since he does not want to do anything that is connected in any way with slavery. He has discovered that "everything I considered bore, somewhere along the way, the imprint of black hands." Eventually, he decides to become an apothecary—the 1840s equivalent of a pharmacist—and moves to Rhode Island where there are no slaves. He sends for his mother and sister and lives a quiet life. He misses the South, and for the rest of his life, he wonders what happened to Ras, but he never finds out. When the Civil War breaks out, he fights on the Northern side.

As the years pass, the horror of the voyage recedes in his consciousness, and he doesn't think about it every day. He marries and has a family. One thing, however, remains from the voyage: he cannot stand the sound of music because it reminds him of dancing the slaves:

> For at the first note of a tune or a song, I would see once again as though they'd never ceased their dancing in my mind, black men and women and children lifting their tormented limbs in time to a reedy martial air, the dust rising from their joyless thumping, the sound of the fife finally drowned beneath the clanging of their chains.

Characters

Agatha Bollier

Agatha is Jessie's aunt (the sister of his father) and is more well-to-do than the Bolliers. They turn to her in times of trouble, asking for small things, such as extra candles so that Jessie's mother can stay up late working on dresses. Since Jessie's father's death, Agatha has been irritable and withdrawn, and she is also fussy and demanding, telling Jessie how to walk and warning him not to be clumsy with her furniture whenever he enters her house. Jessie says, "I had no other memory of Aunt Agatha except as a woman who especially disliked me." Agatha dislikes the fact that Jessie makes a living playing the fife and tells him he should be apprenticed and learn a respectable trade, saying that she doubts he would gain any benefit from school. However, she is generous with her candles and other gifts, and although Fox never says this

directly, the reader senses that Agatha does care about Jessie; She wants his life to be better than it is but can't express this wish in a positive way. When Jessie eventually returns from his long and harrowing journey, she treats Jessie with affection and kindness and no longer accuses him of being a "bayou lout."

Betty Bollier

Betty is Jessie's sister. She is four years younger than he and has little part in the story. She is quiet and kind, and he thinks of her often during the voyage. When he comes back, she is even nicer to him, treating him like an invalid. When he moves to Rhode Island, he sends for her and his mother and takes care of both of them financially.

Jessie Bollier

Thirteen-year-old Jessie Bollier makes a few pennies each day by playing his fife in the rougher districts of 1840s New Orleans. He, his mother, and his young sister Betty are very poor, and they own almost nothing, living in a single damp room on Pirate's Alley where his mother works as a seamstress for the wealthy women of New Orleans.

Until this point, Jessie has largely been protected from experiencing the horrors of slavery because his family is too poor to own slaves and because his mother has forbidden him to loiter near the slave market. He dreams of being rich one day, "in a fine suit, with a thousand candles to hand if I needed them instead of three grudgingly given stubs. I imagined the splendid house I would live in, my gardens, my carriage and horses." He is intrigued by the slaves he sees, curious about their lives.

In January of 1840, while he is walking along daydreaming, Jessie is abducted by sailors who have seen him playing his fife. They carry him off to a slave ship called the *Moonlight,* and tell him that after the ship reaches Africa and they take on slaves, his job will be to play for the slaves so that they will "dance" and thus keep themselves strong, fit, and profitable.

The voyage is a living hell for Jessie, who sees the slaves treated worse than animals and who finds depths of ugliness within himself that he never dreamed existed. Forced to have his whole existence revolve around the slaves, he is shocked to find himself hating them, hating the entire ship's crew, hating himself. He sees men, women, and children die, sees them thrown over the side of the ship, and sees the crewmembers mercilessly flogged. When the ship is overtaken by an American anti-slavery vessel, the crew begins throwing the slaves overboard, but at the same time, a ferocious storm hits. Jessie and a slave boy, Ras, go hide in the hold, and the two of them become friends. When the ship founders on a reef, everyone but Jessie and Ras dies. They make their way to shore and are taken in by an escaped slave, Daniel, who tells Jessie how to walk back to New Orleans, three days' journey away.

Later, Jessie's earlier dreams of becoming rich have been tempered by reality as he realizes that all the wealth he saw around him was either the result of slaves' work or was somehow connected with the slave trade because slavery is so deeply ingrained in his culture. He eventually is apprenticed to an apothecary and moves to Rhode Island where there is no slavery and brings his mother and sister there, too. Despite his new life, he is still homesick for the South—the Mississippi, the tropical smells—and for his friend Ras, whom he never sees again.

During the Civil War, he fights for the North and spends some time in a horrendous prisoner-of-war camp, which he survives, he believes, because he was prepared for its horrors on the *Moonlight.*

Eventually, he largely forgets his terrible voyage; he has a family and a peaceful life, except for one legacy of that trip that remains: for the rest of his life, he cannot stand hearing music because it reminds him of the slaves' tormented dancing.

Mrs. Bollier

Mrs. Bollier is Jessie's mother, a young widow who was originally from Massachusetts. She makes her living by sewing dresses for the wealthy ladies of New Orleans. One of the only beautiful things in their one-room home is her wooden sewing box, which has a winged fish carved on the top and beside which sits her basket of spools of bright thread. Jessie says, "By candlelight, the warmth of the colors made me think the thread would throw off a perfume like a garden of flowers." Sometimes, their home is filled with her work—rich swathes of damask or silk. She is harried and worried, always struggling to make enough money to feed her children. Even after Jessie returns from his voyage, his mother still sometimes weeps at the thought of what he has been through and at the thought of what happened to the slaves. Perhaps because of her Northern upbringing, she is against slavery. She warns Jessie to stay away from the market where slaves are sold and is shocked to hear of a slave called Star by her owner: "It's not a human name," she says.

Captain Cawthorne

Captain of the *Moonlight,* he is a ruthless man with a capricious temper, who, when he first meets Jessie, picks him up and bites his ear hard enough to draw blood, as a sort of warning about who's boss on the ship. His crew is afraid of him, although they know that on other ships there are captains who are worse. He lives in relative luxury on the ship, with private quarters, good food, and plenty of water, when the others do without, and he does not hesitate to flog Purvis when he is accused of stealing an egg from the captain's hen. He is single-mindedly devoted to profit and despises the anti-slavery British ships that run down slavers and confiscate their slaves and their profits. He also despises the African chiefs who sell their own people to the slavers. Eventually, Jessie realizes, "I was on a ship engaged in an illegal venture, and Captain Cawthorne was no better than a pirate."

Adolph Curry

Adolph is the ship's cook. Jessie describes him as "the thinnest man I'd ever seen. . . . His skin was the color of suet except for uneven salmon-colored patches along the prominent ridges of his cheekbones." He is in a perpetual bad temper, and Purvis explains that this is habitual with ships' cooks: "It's the smoke that maddens them, and whatever good humor they start with is fried to a crisp by the head."

Daniel

Daniel is an escaped slave who has found a safe haven deep in the woods near the coast of Mississippi. When Jessie and Ras swim to shore, he finds them, takes them in, and takes care of them until they are strong enough to leave. Although it is dangerous for him to shelter Jessie since Jessie is white and may tell others where he is, Daniel treats him kindly and trusts him to keep his secret. Daniel is resourceful, living entirely on the produce of his small garden and a few farm animals. Daniel arranges for friendly people to take Ras north where he can be free and tells Jessie the route back to New Orleans, three days' walk away. He gives him food for the journey and wishes him safe travel. As Jessie says, "Daniel had saved my life. I couldn't expect more than that."

Ned Grime

Grime is an older man who serves as the ship's carpenter (and, occasionally, the surgeon). He is not a sailor and knows little about running the ship. He holds himself apart from the crew, "as if he lived a mile from the earth and had nothing to do with the idiot carryings on of the human race," Jessie says. He is against taking boys and men on as sailors against their will, and he is religious and talks about the evils of slavery, saying "It's all the Devil's work," but Jessie stops listening when he finds out that like all the crew, Grime will eventually profit from the voyage. When Ned says of slavery, "My heart's not in it," Jessie says, "I wondered about his heart, imagining it to be something like one of the raisins Curry used to slip into the plum duff."

Jessie's Father

Jessie's father died when Jessie was four. He worked on a snagboat, which cleared away the tree stumps and other debris that blocked steamboat navigation on the river. His small boat was caught by a current, he lost his balance, fell, and was sucked underwater before anyone could help him. He appears in Jessie's dreams, mostly as a voice crying, "Oh, swim!" and Jessie still grieves his loss.

Clay Purvis

Purvis is an Irishman and one of the two sailors who abduct Jessie and carry him off to the *Moonlight*. Purvis has seen Jessie playing his fife in the market earlier and has even given him money. "Don't you remember a man who gave you money?" he asks Jessie. "I'm about to do even more for you. I'm going to take you on a fine sea voyage." Purvis is a big, rough man with a mocking sense of humor, and though he is uneducated and loutish, he has a soft spot for Jessie, disguised under his rough treatment of him. For example, one day when Jessie begins to cry with homesickness, Purvis picks him up, shakes him, and threatens to hang him up in the rigging—in an attempt to take his mind off it. He is a good sailor, never idle, skilled at many tasks on board, and a good teller of sea tales. When Ben Stout steals an egg from the captain's private supply, Purvis is blamed and takes the flogging that results without protest.

Purvis is a man of his time, and he does not have much sympathy for the slaves, regarding them as less than human and noting that his own Irish ancestors crossed the sea in conditions just as bad as theirs. When Jessie shows any sympathy for the slaves, Purvis is enraged, as if sympathy for them somehow lessens his ancestors' suffering. He asks Jessie, "Do you know my father was haunted all his days by the memory of those who died before his eyes in that ship, and were flung into the sea? And you dare speak of my parents in the same breath with these [slaves]!" Jessie rightly thinks it's senseless of Purvis to protest how his parents were treated but not to object to the same treatment when it is applied to Africans, but he can never talk sense into Purvis about this topic. Despite this, he trusts Purvis over Ben Stout. "It was Purvis whom I was eager to see when I woke up in the morning," he says, "Purvis with his horrible coarse jokes, his bawling and cursing, Purvis whom I trusted."

Ras

Ras is a slave boy on the ship who is fascinated by Jessie. Jessie is also intrigued by him because they are the same age and they are both on the ship against their will. When Stout throws overboard a young slave girl who has died, Jessie cries out, and Ned Sharkey smacks him so hard he falls down. Jessie says, "When I got up, I saw a boy close to my own age, staring at me from among the group of silent slaves squatting beneath the tarpaulin. I could not read his expression." When the two of them are the only survivors of a raid and shipwreck of the *Moonlight,* they are taken in by an escaped slave, and Ras is thrilled, thinking he has found a piece of home until he realizes the old man is wearing white people's clothes. Eventually, Daniel, the escaped slave, helps Ras escape, too, sending him to the North with allies.

Claudius Sharkey

Sharkey is the other sailor involved in Jessie's abduction. He explains the facts of the slave trade to Jessie: that British cruisers made it dangerous by watching out for illegal American slavers, pursuing them, confiscating their cargo, and arresting their crews. The trade was also made dangerous by American ships that patrolled, looking for privateers like the *Moonlight.*

Nicholas Spark

Spark is the Mate, who, Jessie says, "kept to the Captain's side like a shadow. He had a brooding look on his face, and when he spoke, his voice sizzled like a hot poker plunged into water." He does whatever the Captain orders, usually brutally. Although he is obviously evil, Jessie finds that he is easier to deal with than someone like Stout, whose evil is hidden at first.

Benjamin Stout

At first, Ben Stout appears to be trustworthy; the first thing he says to Jessie is, "I'm sorry for what's been done to you." Unlike the other sailors, he is quiet and polite. Like Jessie, he was forced to become a sailor but eventually came to like it and quickly becomes bored and restless on land. He takes Jessie in hand, shows him around the ship, and gives him clothes to wear, as well as a chunk of bread, and tells him what chores to do. Other than Purvis, he is the only crewmember who takes much notice of Jessie at all. Although he seems kind, this is only a thin veneer over an untrustworthy and sly heart: Stout steals an egg, blames Purvis, and then, at the Captain's orders, assists in flogging Purvis for the crime Stout did. He speaks the slaves' language and talks softly to them, saying things that Jessie cannot understand but which seem to drive the slaves mad with fear or sadness. He seems to take pleasure in tormenting people in this subtle, sly way. Jessie stops trusting him and regards him with deep mistrust and fear. Stout is bothered by this since he wants to influence Jessie. "I've been so good to you," he says. "I don't understand your ingratitude. They've all talked against me. I suppose that accounts for it." Jessie does not answer him. Purvis later tells Jessie, "He is dead. He's been dead for years." He tells Jessie there is someone like him on almost every ship: someone spiritually, morally dead, "and no one's the wiser until two weeks at sea when one of the crew says to another, 'Ain't he dead? That one over there by the helm?' and the other says, 'Just what I was thinking—we've got a dead man on the ship.'" When Jessie won't speak to him, Stout steals his fife and drops it in the hold where Jessie has to scramble over the bodies of the slaves to look for it, or else be punished by the captain for losing it. The slave boy, Ras, finds it and hands it to him.

Themes

Freedom and Imprisonment

From the very beginning of *The Slave Dancer,* themes of imprisonment and escape run through the book. In the opening chapter, Jessie and his family live in one tiny room, little more than a cell, with a few meager possessions, and Jessie feels crowded there, particularly in bad weather: "I hated the fog," he says. "It made me a prisoner." When he visits his Aunt Agatha to ask for a few candles, he is ordered about like a prisoner: "'Don't walk there!' she would cry. 'Take your huge feet off that carpet! Watch the chair—it'll fall!'"

Soon after this visit to his aunt, Jessie is captured and taken to the slave ship—a fate that will soon be paralleled in the fates of the slaves he must play his fife for. Like them, he is beaten; like them, he eats horrible food; like them, he has no option for escape other than jumping over the side and

drowning. However, no matter how much he suffers, their suffering is always worse, a fact of which he is always aware.

The sailor Purvis, whose parents came from Ireland under conditions similar to those of the slaves, resents any pity Jessie feels for the slaves, because somehow, to him, it dishonors his parents' suffering when anyone cares about how the Africans are treated.

Jessie's physical imprisonment is bad enough, but Fox also shows how he becomes mentally imprisoned—how, from feeling sorry for the slaves, Jessie enters a time when he hates them—for they are the reason he was taken from his home, the reason for his own servitude on the ship. Also, as David Rees noted in *The Marble in the Water,* Jessie, after being abused by the crew, briefly becomes one of them, one of the abusers. He is only woken from this terrible state of mind by a beating.

Although the sailors are technically free men, they are not mentally free: limited by their lack of education and their brutally difficult lives, they can only muster up compassion for the slaves for a short time, and only when the voyage is going well. Some, such as Nicholas Spark and Ben Stout, never do; Stout is described as "dead," in an emotional or spiritual sense, and Jessie says that Spark is "entirely brainless and evil only in the way that certain plants are poisonous": he is mindlessly, ruthlessly evil, not even human.

Even after Jessie returns home, he is never completely free again. He has been deeply marked by his experiences and they shape everything he does, from his choice of a career, to his decision to move to Rhode Island, and his fighting for the North in the Civil War. He is never truly carefree again: for the rest of his life, he cannot bear to listen to music because it brings up memories of the slaves' suffering.

The only truly free person in the book is, ironically, Daniel, the escaped slave who has created a small farmstead deep in the Mississippi forest. However, his freedom is precarious: if anyone finds him, or even if Jessie tells anyone about him, he may be recaptured and forced into slavery again. Interestingly, Daniel constantly risks his hard-won freedom: the book implies that he is involved with the Underground Railroad and has a network of contacts who lead slaves to freedom.

Hypocrisy Versus Integrity

Jessie's mother is religious, and she warns him to stay away from the slave market and from tav-

Topics For Further Study

- Create a map and draw the route that Jessie took from his kidnapping in New Orleans to Africa and then to the shipwreck in the Gulf of Mexico and his walk home to New Orleans. Also, calculate how many miles Jessie traveled.

- Jessie and Ras feel very close to each other even though they don't speak the same language. Many years later, Jessie is still looking for Ras and hoping that someday he will see him. Why do you think this is the case? How did the boys communicate with each other on the ship, during the shipwreck, and at Daniel's house?

- In the book, the slaves on board *The Moonlight* do not rebel against their captors. However, on a real ship named the *Amistad* in 1839, the slaves did rebel under the leadership of a slave named Cinque and took control of the ship for some time until it landed in Long Island. Research the *Amistad* uprising and compare and contrast it to events in *The Slave Dancer.* What eventually happened to the slaves on the *Amistad?*

- Jessie spends three days and nights walking alone through the woods from Mississippi to New Orleans. If you were hiking alone in the woods for that time, what would you need to survive? Jessie had very little. What is the smallest amount of food and gear that you think you would need to survive? What would you be most afraid of and why?

- Ras is sent north with friends of Daniel's, presumably to freedom. Jessie looks for him but never finds him. What do you think happened to Ras? Write a story telling what his life was like, starting from the time he left Daniel's hut in the forests of Mississippi.

- In New Orleans in 1840, poor children were expected to work. If you lived in 1840 and had to work at age thirteen, what work could you have done to help your family survive?

- In *Interracial Books for Children,* Binnie Tate wrote that "through the characters' words, [Fox] excuses the captors and places the blame for the slaves' captivity on Africans themselves. The author slowly and systematically excuses all the whites in the story for their participation in the slave venture and by innuendo places the blame elsewhere." Do you agree with this statement? Why or why not?

---

erns. She is also aware that no matter how poor she and her family are, "there were souls whose fates were so terrible in comparison to ours, that we should consider ourselves among the fortunate of the earth," meaning the slaves.

Purvis tells Jessie a story of a captain of a slave ship that started out with 500 slaves and 30 crewmembers, and ended with 183 slaves and 11 crewmembers alive; most were killed by disease, some by violence.

> The Captain took his Bible and left that ship—and the sea. I've heard tales that he's a walking preacher now, goes to towns and villages and gets up on a box and tells people the world is going to end any day and if there ain't no people he tells the trees and the stones." This story parallels the real life of John Newton, a slave ship captain who quit his work, became

a preacher, and wrote the well-known hymn "Amazing Grace."

However, there are more hypocrites than truly religious people in the book. Like Jessie's mother and the reformed captain, Ned Grime, the ship's carpenter, professes to be religious. However, he holds himself aloof from the rest of the crew, and talks "as if he lived a mile from the earth and had nothing to do with the idiot carryings on of the human race." He has a chilly view of God, stating, "God has no wish to share his secrets with Adam's descendants." When Purvis is flogged and Jessie, upset, leans against Ned, Ned not only does not console him, but also "made not the slightest accommodation of his body to my weight," Jessie says. Ned talks about religion often, but when Jessie discovers that he will make just as much profit as the rest of the crew from the voyage, he discounts him.

Captain Cawthorne, who is in charge of the slave ship, mentions in the same breath that the slave trade is both "lucrative and God-given," and the sailors justify it by saying that everyone else is doing it. So many ships are transporting slaves that the laws against such transport are meaningless.

In fact, the book implies that most people are hypocrites as bad as Cawthorne, if not as obvious, and that, as Jessie realizes later, almost every job, profession, or source of income available is connected in some way with the transport, sale, or labor of slaves. Almost everyone, no matter what he or she does, is living off slave labor, however distantly. With this realization, the book becomes an indictment of almost everyone in white society. As David Rees wrote in *The Marble in the Water,* "It is a savage indictment of a whole society, intensely political in its overtones which ring down through the ages to the present day."

Style

Poetic Prose

"The distinction and beauty of the words she uses and her absolute command of subtlety and nuance in rhythms and sentence structure place Paula Fox above almost all other children's writers," Rees states in his book. Other critics agree: Fox's use of language has brought her the Newbery Medal, the Hans Christian Andersen Award, and recognition in both the United States and England. Fox's prose is spare but poetic, filled with rich imagery grounded in intense physical detail, rhythm, and cadence. For example, when Jessie is captured and taken by a small boat to the ship, Fox writes:

> We passed a small island. I saw the glimmer of a light in a window—only that solitary, flickering yellow beacon. I felt helpless and sad as though everyone in the world had died save the three of us and the unknown lamplighter on the shore. Then, as if daylight was being born inside the boat itself, I began to make out piles of rope, a wooden bucket, a heap of rusty looking net, the thick boots of my captors.

In passages like these, Fox juxtaposes accurately drawn emotion with exact detail of place, time, and people, making the events—and the emotions—seem absolutely real.

Emotional Accuracy

Throughout the book, Fox describes Jessie's mixed emotions with stunning clarity, even when they are shocking in their intensity and negativity, or when they are not what the reader expects. Soon after he is captured, Jessie experiences a surge of happiness as the ship speeds on, and even he is surprised by this. "When I remembered the wretchedness of my situation, I wondered if there was something about a ship that makes men glide from one state of mind to another as the ship cuts through water."

Later, forced to play for the slaves, forced to be a part of their suffering, he is shocked to find that he hates them—hates their shackled shuffling, their groaning, hates their suffering—and hates himself for hating them. Because the sailors have abused him, he now takes it out on them, seeing them as the cause of his captivity on the ship. Although this state of mind is short-lived, and ends when Jessie himself is beaten, Fox does not shy away from depicting it. Like other people in intolerable situations, Jessie develops the ability to mentally retreat from the situation: "I found a kind of freedom in my mind, I found how to be in another place." However, unlike Ned Grime, the hypocritical carpenter, he can't sustain this, and is soon slapped back to reality and to awareness of his place in the tormenting of the slaves.

When Jessie and Ras are rescued by Daniel, the escaped slave, Fox shows Jessie's wistful desire to be as close to Daniel as Ras is, and his awareness that because he is white, Daniel will never trust him in the same way.

Long after the voyage and for the rest of his life in Rhode Island, Jessie is marked by the experience, like all people who have been through intense suffering. Although outwardly he is like his neighbors, inwardly he retains the memory of the short voyage, and he can never enjoy music as he did when he was still a child.

First Person

The book is told in first person—an excellent choice since the reader can "hear" Jessie telling his story, and it seems far more alive and realistic than if the same story was were told in third-person. Like the spellbinding sea stories Purvis tells, readers are right there in the story with Jessie as he describes the ship, the crew, the slaves, and the horrifying events. By the end of the book, the reader knows Jessie intimately: he has shared every thought and feeling as honestly as if he were in the same room

Compare & Contrast

- **1840s:** Slavery is legal in the southern part of the United States, and African Americans have no rights.

  Today: African Americans are legally entitled to all the same rights as other Americans, although American society is still struggling against racism.

- **1840s:** It takes a ship four months to travel from North America to Africa and back, and the journey is extremely hazardous.

  Today: Airplanes can safely make the trip from North America to Africa and back in just a matter of hours.

- **1840s:** Children are not required to attend school, but they are expected to work to help their families make a living, and they often work long hours.

  Today: Child labor is against the law, and all children must attend school.

- **1840s:** The area around New Orleans is forest, farms, and swamps. Jessie could walk toward the city for three days and see almost no people and few signs of human habitation.

  Today: Large–scale urban growth and development of highways have made wilderness like the one Jessie walks through increasingly rare, especially around large cities such as New Orleans.

with the reader, confessing the terrible story that has weighed on his mind for most of his life.

Historical Context

The Slave Trade

Paula Fox is a contemporary writer, but *The Slave Dancer* is set in 1840, in New Orleans, and on the slave ship *The Moonlight.* Fox brings this time to life through Jessie's eyes: the reader learns that although it was illegal to import slaves from Africa, this trade went on, and that the sale of American-born slaves was open and accepted. As a *World Book* article on the trade noted, by the early 1800s, more than 700,000 slaves lived in the southern United States, and by 1860, there were about four million slaves in these states. Although Jessie's family is too poor to own slaves, he sees them in the streets and in the homes of the wealthy, and it is understood that anyone who has any money owns servants, and that most occupations are directly or indirectly related to the work of slaves. Until Jessie sees the truth about slavery, it doesn't occur to him to question whether this is

right or wrong—it's just the way things are in his time and place. Attitudes toward people of African descent were also affected by the common racist conviction among whites, as Jessie notes, that "the least of them was better than any black alive."

Because the sole motive of the slave trade was profit, some captains of slave ships tried to pack as many people as possible into their ships and transport them for the lowest possible cost. Others believed in "loose packing"; they did not take on as many slaves, and allowed them more room on the ship, hoping that this would cut down on sickness and death among the captives. (In the book, Captain Cawthorne is called "a tight packer" by his crew.) On all ships, the slaves were kept chained in the hold at all times except when they were brought on deck to exercise. This crowding, and the complete lack of any sanitary facilities, led to disease and death on all slave ships, whether tightly or loosely packed. The slave trade across the Atlantic, between the Americas and Africa, lasted from the 1500s to the mid-1800s, and although no one knows for sure how many Africans were taken from their homeland, most sources estimate that around 10 million people were transported, according to the *World Book.*

Group of slaves being herded onto a ship by British soldiers

The Underground Railroad

The Underground Railroad was not a railroad, and it was not underground. It was a network of people who helped slaves escape and find freedom in the northern United States and in Canada where slavery was illegal. The slaves traveled mostly at night, on foot or any other way they could, and hid during the day in secret places or in the homes and buildings of anti-slavery activists. Because running away and helping slaves to run away was illegal in the South, people involved in this mission used code words, often from the railroad, so that others would not know what they were doing. For example, the people who helped the slaves were called "conductors," and the hiding places were called "stations." In *The Slave Dancer,* Daniel, and the two men who come to help Ras to escape, are conductors. Because their work endangers them, they are concerned that Jessie might tell others about them.

The Underground Railroad mainly operated from 1830 until the 1860s and helped many thousands of people escape from slavery. Although these people made it to the North, some were recaptured by slave hunters and taken back to the South. Because of this, many people fled even to Canada, particularly Ontario, where they were safer. In 1850, the U.S. Congress passed a fugitive slave law against returning escaped slaves to bondage.

The most famous conductor on the Underground Railroad was Harriet Tubman, who had run away from slavery. Not content with finding her own freedom, she returned to the South 19 times and helped about 300 people to escape.

Sailors' Hard Lives

As Fox makes clear, it was common for men and boys to be "pressed," or kidnapped, onto ships to become sailors as Jessie is. Benjamin Stout confides, "I was pressed too, although when I was older than you, and for a much longer voyage than this will be." Taken against their will, these sailors served under the iron command of captains who, like Cawthorne, used violence and punishment to enforce discipline on board their ships. Being a sailor was a dangerous occupation: death from illness and shipwreck was common, and for slavers, so was the threat of prosecution by British or American forces if they were caught.

Critical Overview

A Widely Praised Writer

Paula Fox has been praised by many critics for the beauty, clarity, authority, and subtle poetry of her prose, as well as the depth of her ideas and her execution of them in fiction. *The Slave Dancer* is generally considered one of her finest works. For example, John Rowe Townsend wrote in *A Sounding of Storytellers* that *The Slave Dancer* "is a historical novel of weight and intensity which stands on its own, at a distance from [Fox's] other books," and called the book her "finest achievement."

Controversy Over the Book

Although the book has been widely praised, some critics have objected to it, claiming that it is racist. In *Interracial Books for Children*, Binnie Tate wrote that:

> through the characters' words, [Fox] excuses the captors and places the blame for the slaves' captivity on Africans themselves. The author slowly and systematically excuses all the whites in the story for their participation in the slave venture and by innuendo places the blame elsewhere.

Binnie Tate, quoted in *Cultural Conformity in Books for Children*, wrote that the book "perpetuates racism . . . [with] constantly repeated racist implications and negative illusions," and in the same volume, Sharon Bell Mathis called the book "an insult to black children."

In the case of *The Slave Dancer*, some have objected to the fact that the slaves are portrayed as nonresistant, demoralized, nameless victims. However, Hamida Bosmajian wrote about this namelessness in *Nightmares of History*, commenting that "both the point of view of the novel and the circumstances of history make it impossible to name the slaves. Only after the shipwreck can Jessie exchange names with Ras, the sole black survivor."

Controversy over the novel's possible racist undertones extended to the ceremony in which Fox received the Newbery Award for the book where there were demonstrations against the book. Fox was shaken by this news but gave her speech; afterward, some of the demonstrators came up to her and let her know that she was "forgiven."

Emotionally Accurate

In *Nightmares of History*, Hamida Bosmajian wrote that Fox "is accurate in portraying the psychology of human beings in extreme situations," referring to the changing and conflicting emotions Jessie experiences, from apathy to rage to detachment, and even occasional happiness. Bosmajian, who analyzed books dealing with historical traumatic events and their survivors, noted that in these situations, people often do not behave admirably, or as we would like them to behave. Bosmajian also wrote that we

would like our children to sing songs of innocence, but it is difficult to delude children who have intimations of nuclear war. By breaking with the convictions of children's literature, [books such as *The Slave Dancer*] open spaces or blanks for the young readers' thoughts.

Uncompromising Moral Integrity

In an essay in *Horn Book*, Alice Bach described *The Slave Dancer* as "one of the finest examples of a writer's control over her material. . . . With an underplayed implicit sense of rage, Paula Fox exposes the men who dealt in selling human beings." In the *New Statesman*, Kevin Crossley-Holland wrote that the book is "a novel of great moral integrity. . . . From start to finish . . . Fox tells her story quietly and economically; she is candid but she never wallows." And Bob Dixon, in *Catching Them Young: Sex, Race and Class in Children's Fiction*, praised the book as "a novel of great horror and as great humanity . . . [approaching] perfection as a work of art."

Bach also wrote that what sets Fox apart from other writers

> who are knocking out books as fast as kids can swallow them, is her uncompromising integrity. Fox is nobody's mouthpiece. Her unique vision admits to the child what he already suspects: Life is part grit, part disappointment, part nonsense, and occasionally victory. . . And by offering children no more than the humanness we all share—child, adult, reader, writer—she acknowledges them as equals.

David Rees wrote in *The Marble in the Water* that

> the way [Fox] constructs her plots and the way she uses the English language make her second to none. And in *The Slave Dancer*, she has given us a masterpiece, the equal of which would be hard to find.

Criticism

Kelly Winters

Winters is a freelance writer and editor who has written for a wide variety of academic and educational publishers. In the following essay, she discusses themes of truth and moral questions in Fox's story.

As John Rowe Townsend pointed out in *A Sounding of Storytellers*, children's literature in the 1950s and early 1960s tended to promote a gentle, reassuring view of children, their families, and their role in society. He wrote, "Childhood was part of a continuing pattern—the orderly succession of the generations—and [in the accepted view] children were growing up to take their place in a known and understood world." By the late 1960s, however, people were becoming aware that this notion of childhood as a safe, protected time was just that—a notion—and it did not reflect the reality of children's lives. Children, like adults, suffer, experience trauma, and live through conflicting emotions about events they cannot control or justify.

As Townsend noted, Fox was one of the first writers to wake up to this reality. He wrote that she "was one of the small number of writers who brought quick sharp perceptions to the new and in many ways uneasy scene, and also an instinctive sympathy for the young who . . . had to deal with it." In her early works, children and adults fail to understand each other: there is no cozy bond between the generations. In *The Slave Dancer,* Fox takes a larger step and looks at a terrifying time in human history through the eyes of a boy who, like the slaves, is taken captive and experiences the horrendous reality of *The Moonlight.* Even worse, he must help others mistreat the slaves, using his gift for music as an instrument of torment. As Townsend wrote, the presence of a child in this setting is an alarming and awakening touch of truth. In *The Slave Dancer,*

> The 'young eye at the centre' is no mere convention of the adventure story for children; it is the one perspective from which the witnessing of dreadful events can be fully and freshly experienced, and at the same time the moral burden be made clear.

Some reviewers have questioned whether this exposure to horrendous events is appropriate for children and whether books like *The Slave Dancer* can be considered children's literature, despite the presence of the "young eye at the center." In her essay, "Nightmares of History," in *Children's Literature Association Quarterly,* Hamida Bosmajian wrote that such books not only can but should be included in the canon of writing for young people. Bosmajian wrote that for children who are personally experiencing trauma such books can have "therapeutic value" and can "raise the consciousness of youngsters whose environment is stable."

As Bosmajian points out, historical "nightmares" created by adults, such as the Nazi Holocaust, nuclear war, or the enslavement of Africans, always include children since they affect whole societies. It is impossible to pretend, given the reality of these circumstances, that all children live the protected lives that earlier books portrayed. Bosmajian wrote that perhaps some adults object to stories about these events because "we fear that to depict the children within the nightmare of history

> *This loss of a certain amount of joy, this tempering of the soul and of hope, is only natural in someone who has seen what Jessie has seen. To write a book in which someone saw the suffering of slaves and who then went home and 'recovered' from the experience would be shallow and false."*

will both taint our own image of innocence and deny young readers trust in the future we shape." However, she notes, telling children about these events and letting them discuss their concerns about them "cannot but be therapeutic."

Paula Fox obviously supports the view that writers should not shy away from portraying real pain and notes that some contemporary books may pretend to look at the dark side of life but in the end try to make readers believe that everything will be all right. Fox told Sylvia Steinberg in *Publishers Weekly,* "The American idea is that everything can be solved. Our lives are not problems to be solved! They're to be lived! . . . Children are given liar's clothes early on. It's a way of not looking." And, more heatedly she said, "At the core of everything I write is the feeling that the denial of the truth imprisons us even further in ourselves." In her essay "Some Thoughts on Imagination in Children's Literature" in *Celebrating Children's Books: Essay on Children's Literature in Honor of Zena Sutherland,* she described such books as "tract literature" and as

> stories that strain to teach children how to manage life by merely naming such "problems" as disease, physical anomalies, and even death and by assuring them there is nothing to be afraid of, nothing to suffer about, nothing complex.

Clearly, *The Slave Dancer* is not that kind of book. The book contains disease, physical (and moral) anomalies, death, and a host of other frightening things: Jessie's father is dead, his family is extremely poor, he is kidnapped, he is beaten and

What Do I Read Next?

- In *Western Wind* (1993), by Paula Fox, a lonely young girl is sent to live with her grandmother on a remote island off the coast of Maine.

- Paula Fox's *Monkey Island* (1991) tells the story of a homeless boy, Clay Garrity, who lives on the streets and is eventually helped by two other homeless men.

- In *Up From Slavery,* originally published in 1901 and reprinted in 2000 by Signet, Booker T. Washington tells the story of his early life as a slave and how he rose to become president of Tuskegee Institute in Alabama.

- *To Be a Slave* (1988), by Julius Lester, is a collection of reminiscences of ex-slaves about their experiences, from leaving Africa, through the Civil War, and into the early twentieth century.

- *Narrative of the Life of Frederick Douglass: An American Slave,* by Frederick Douglass, originally published in 1845 and reprinted by Signet in 1997, relates his life as a former slave who eventually became a minister, orator, and leader of his people. The book talks of his days as a slave and describes how he gained his freedom.

- *The Narrative of Sojourner Truth* (1997), by Sojourner Truth (d. 1883) and Olive Gilbert, is a partial autobiography of a slave woman who became a pioneer in the struggles for racial and sexual equality.

---

sees others beaten, he sees slaves thrown over the rail of the ship—both dead and alive—after being starved, exposed to disease, and tormented—and he doesn't know if he will ever make it home alive. Worse, he not only has to witness the torment of the slaves but he is forced to become one of their oppressors as he plays his flute; he is aware that, even though he is like them in the sense that he is a prisoner on the ship, when they reach land, he will be free to go home to his mother and sister, a choice that will forever be denied to the slaves. In addition, he is aware that because he is white, the crew automatically regards him as "human," whereas they don't see the slaves as human at all. For Jessie, who has noted his kinship with the slave boy Ras, this false dichotomy is troubling: he knows that, at bottom, there is no difference between them, but the sailors beat him whenever he shows compassion for the slaves' humanity and their suffering.

Jessie cannot find an easy solution to these moral questions and to the questions of why people are cruel and why people suffer. Even after Jessie makes it home, he is changed permanently. Although he grows up and manages to make a modestly successful life, with a decent career, a wife, and a child, the scars of the voyage are always with him. His decisions to become an apothecary, move to the North, and fight for the Union side during the Civil War are all direct results of his harrowing childhood experience. For his whole life, he avoids or fights against anything that helps the cause of slavery. For his whole life, he struggles against the memory of his own brief captivity on the ship and the marks it has left on his psyche. Even though he appears normal and well adjusted to his neighbors and even when he rarely thinks consciously about the ship, he is unable to hear any music—no matter how simple—without pain. His musical gift, which was once so lighthearted and free, has become a continuing symbol of the slaves' torment, and of his own.

This loss of a certain amount of joy, this tempering of the soul and of hope, is only natural in someone who has seen what Jessie has seen. To write a book in which someone saw the suffering of slaves and who then went home and "recovered" from the experience would be shallow and false. In "Some Thoughts on Imagination in Children's Literature," Fox wrote of books that bring up social problems and then provide easy answers: "The implicit instructions of contemporary 'realistic' books may vary . . . but they have the same sequel: they smother speculation, they stifle uncertainty, they strangle imagination." In these books, she wrote, "We present children with cozy books about desertion and death and sex, promising them that, in the end, everything can be made all right. Thus we drown eternal human questions with contemporary bromides."

Although Fox's work is painfully realistic, it is not pessimistic. Jessie does manage to create a good life; he is not scarred to the point of being unable to contribute positively to the world. As John Rowe Townsend wrote in *A Sounding of Sto-*

rytellers, "Ultimately the book is not depressing; the human spirit is not defeated."

Fox's insistence on telling the truth is allied to her sense that writing for adults is no different from writing for children. She once stopped to write a children's book in the middle of writing a novel for adults and says that she does not write differently for her two audiences. John Rowe Townsend, in *A Sense of Story,* quoted Fox as having said, "I never think I'm writing for children when I work. A story does not start for anyone, nor an idea, nor a feeling of an idea; but starts more for oneself." Unlike other writers, who "write down" for children or try to teach some moral lesson, Fox follows her instincts and tells the truth about events, believing that the truth is inherently interesting and that only by exploring it can readers, and writers, grow as human beings.

In her acceptance speech for the Newbery Award, reprinted in *Newbery and Caldecott Winners, 1966–1975,* Fox wrote that writing helps us "to connect ourselves with the reality of our own lives. It is painful; but if we are to become human, we cannot abandon it."

Source: Kelly Winters, Critical Essay on *The Slave Dancer,* in *Novels for Students,* The Gale Group, 2001.

John Rowe Townsend

In the following essay excerpt, Townsend calls The Slave Dancer *Fox's "finest achievement," and says children "ought not to grow up without it."*

I have left until last the book which, so far, is Paula Fox's finest achievement. I do not think it could have been predicted from her earlier work that she would write such a book as *The Slave Dancer.* It is the story of Jessie Bollier, a boy who is pressed into the crew of the slave ship *Moonlight* in 1840 for a voyage to Africa, picking up a cargo of blacks to be sold in Cuba. This is a case where the discipline of writing for the children's list has been wholly to the benefit of the book as a work of art. The 'young eye at the centre' is no mere convention of the adventure story for children; it is the one perspective from which the witnessing of dreadful events can be fully and freshly experienced, and at the same time the moral burden be made clear. Jessie is horrified by the treatment of the slaves, but he is powerless to prevent it; moreover he is young, white, and one of the crew, and the oppressors are his fellow-countrymen.

Jessie plays the fife, and his job is to make music to which, for brief periods daily, the slaves can exercise. This is called dancing the slaves. The aim

"Is such knowledge fit for children? Yes, it is; they ought not to grow up without it. This book looks at a terrifying side of human nature, and one which—in the specific manifestation of the slave trade—has left deeply-planted obstacles in the way of human brotherhood."

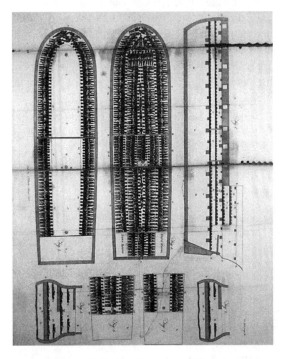

Diagram of a British slave ship, showing the layout for stowing 292 slaves lying down in the lower deck

is to keep them (relatively) healthy and therefore marketable, in spite of the crowded and filthy conditions in which they live. A slave has no human value but has a financial one: a dead slave is a lost profit. As the voyage goes on, the slaves, crammed together in the reeking hold, become sick, half-starved and hopeless, most of them suffering from 'the bloody flux', an affliction that makes the latrine buckets inadequate. And Jesse finds that 'a dreadful thing' is happening in his mind:

> I hated the slaves! I hated their shuffling, their howling, their very suffering! I hated the way they spat out their food upon the deck, the overflowing buckets, the emptying of which tried all my strength. I hated the foul stench that came from the holds no matter which way the wind blew, as though the ship itself were soaked with human excrement. I would have snatched the rope from Spark's [the mate's] hand and beaten them myself! Oh, God! I wished them all dead! Not to hear them! Not to smell them! Not to know of their existence!

The Slave Dancer is not a story solely of horror. It is also a novel of action, violence and suspense, culminating in shipwreck (which was indeed the fate of a slaver called *Moonlight* in the Gulf of Mexico in 1840; the actual names of her crew are used). Jessie and a black boy named Ras with whom he has made a precarious friendship are the only survivors; they reach land and there is a limited happy ending. Ras is set on the road to freedom; Jessie gets home to his mother and sister, is apprenticed, lives an ordinary, modestly-successful life, and fights in the Civil War on the Union side.

> After the war my life went on much like my neighbors' lives. I no longer spoke of my journey on a slave ship back in 1840. I did not often think of it myself. Time softened my memory as though it was kneading wax. But there was one thing that did not yield to time.
>
> I was unable to listen to music. I could not bear to hear a woman sing, and at the sound of any instrument, a fiddle, a flute, a drum, a comb with paper wrapped around it played by my own child, I would leave instantly and shut myself away. For at the first note of a tune or of a song, I would see once again, as though they'd never ceased their dancing in my mind, black men and women and children lifting their tormented limbs in time to a reedy martial air, the dust rising from their joyless thumping, the sound of the fife finally drowned beneath the clanging of their chains.

Those are the closing sentences of *The Slave Dancer*. Ultimately the book is not depressing; the human spirit is not defeated. But it is permeated through and through by the horror it describes. The casual brutality of the ordinary seamen towards the slaves is as fearful in its way as the more positive and corrupt cruelty of the captain and mate and the revolting, hypocritical crew member Ben Stout. For the seamen are 'not especially cruel save in their shared and unshakable conviction that the least of them was better than any black alive'. They are merely ignorant. Villainy is exceptional by definition, but dreadful things done by decent men, to people whom they manage to look on as not really human, are a reminder of our own self-deceit and lack of imagination, of the capacity we all have for evil. There, but for the grace of God, go all of us.

Is such knowledge fit for children? Yes, it is; they ought not to grow up without it. This book looks at a terrifying side of human nature, and one which—in the specific manifestation of the slave trade—has left deeply-planted obstacles in the way of human brotherhood. The implication was made plain by Paula Fox in her Newbery acceptance speech in 1974. We must face this history of evil, and our capacity for evil, if the barriers are ever to come down.

Source: John Rowe Townsend, "Paula Fox," in *A Sounding of Storytellers: New and Revised Essays on Contemporary Writers for Children,* J. B. Lippincott, 1979, pp. 55–65.

Sources

Bach, Alice, Review in *Horn Book,* August 1974.

Bosmajian, Hamida, "Nightmares of History: The Outer Limits of Children's Literature," in *Children's Literature Association Quarterly,* Winter 1983, pp. 20–22.

Crossley-Holland, Kevin, Review in *New Statesman,* November 8, 1974.

Dixon, Bob, *Catching Them Young: Sex, Race and Class in Children's Fiction,* Pluto Press, 1977.

Mathis, Sharon Bell, "*The Slave Dancer* Is an Insult to Black Children," in *Cultural Conformity in Books for Children: Further Readings in Racism,* edited by Donnarae MacCann and Gloria Woodard, Scarecrow Press, 1977.

Rees, David, "The Colour of Saying," in *The Marble in the Water: Essays on Contemporary Writers of Fiction for Children and Young Adults,* in *Horn Book,* 1980, p. 114–27.

Steinberg, Sybil, "Paula Fox: Writing for Two Genres, She Has Earned a Reputation for High Quality Novels and Books for Young People," Interview, in *Publishers Weekly,* April 6, 1990, p. 99.

Tate, Binne, "Racism and Distortion Pervade *The Slave Dancer,*" in *Cultural Conformity in Books for Children: Further Readings in Racism,* edited by Donnarae MacCann and Gloria Woodard, Scarecrow Press, 1977.

Townsend, John Rowe, *A Sense of Story: Essays on Contemporary Writers for Children,* J. B. Lippincott, 1971.

———, *A Sounding of Storytellers: New and Revised Essays on Contemporary Writers for Children,* J. B. Lippincott, 1979, pp. 55–65.

For Further Study

Fox, Paula, "Some Thoughts on Imagination in Children's Literature," in *Celebrating Children's Books: Essay on Children's Literature in Honor of Zena Sutherland,* edited by Betsy Hearne and Marilyn Kaye, Lee and Shepard Books, 1981.

In this essay, Fox discusses how books fuel the imagination of children.

Hamilton, Virginia, *Her Stories,* Scholastic, 1995.

Hamilton offers a collection of African-American folktales, fairy tales, and true stories. The book won the 1996 Coretta Scott King award.

Kingman, Lee, *Newbery and Caldecott Winners, 1966–1975,* Horn Book, 1975.

This contains Fox's acceptance speech for the Newbery Medal, which she won for *Slave Dancer.*

Marcus, Leonard S., "An Interview with Phyllis J. Fogelman," in *Horn Book,* March, 1999, p. 148.

Editor Fogelman discusses young adult literature about African Americans.

Myers, Walter, *Now Is Your Time: The African-American Struggle for Freedom,* HarperCollins Juvenile Books, 1992.

Myers tells the history of African Americans through the narratives of outstanding individuals.

Too Late the Phalarope

Alan Paton

1953

Following his successful debut with *Cry, the Beloved Country,* Alan Paton wrote a second novel set in South Africa, *Too Late the Phalarope.* This second novel continues to be overshadowed by its predecessor, despite considerable critical opinion that it is the more polished of the two. Both books carry Paton's imprint in their portrayal of unfairness in a system designed to keep the races separate. As a dedicated political activist, Paton saw his writing as a means to a higher end. *Too Late the Phalarope* clearly exhibits the author's disgust with injustice in a supposedly "moral" society.

Cry, the Beloved Country centers on the black experience in South Africa, while *Too Late the Phalarope* depicts the lives of Afrikaners (descendants of Dutch settlers who traveled to South Africa three hundred years ago). Specifically, Paton depicts a heroic protagonist, Pieter van Vlaanderen, grappling with private issues in the face of a strict law forbidding interracial sexual relationships. Pieter's internal struggles are intensified by the fact that, as a top-ranking police officer, he represents lawfulness and duty. His inability to resolve his dilemma with self-control leads to his ruin.

Numerous critics regard *Too Late the Phalarope* as a modern-day Greek tragedy. The story features an extremely virtuous and upright hero whose downfall comes about as the result of his own tragic flaw. Further, secondary characters (such as Pieter's family) are destroyed by forces outside themselves and over which they have no control. The narrator, Sophie, is somewhat re-

moved from the rest of the characters because of her disfigurement, and thus serves as the chorus, commenting on the action of the plot. By updating the Greek tragedy, Paton refers to the universality of human suffering and weakness while demonstrating the dangers of an unjust social structure.

Author Biography

Alan Paton is remembered as an exceptional writer, a passionate activist, and a compelling educator. He was born on January 11, 1903, in Pietermaritzburg in Natal, a province of South Africa. Paton's father, like Jakob van Vlaanderen in *Too Late the Phalarope,* was a domineering, harsh, and religious man. Although he was a tyrant at home, James Paton also passed along his love of literature and writing to his children. Alan Paton married in 1928, had two children with his wife, and was widowed in 1967. He remarried two years later.

After completing his education at Pietermaritzburg College and Natal University, Paton taught for three years in rural Ixopo, which would later serve as the setting for *Cry, the Beloved Country.* In 1935, he became the principal of Diepkloof, a school for delinquent boys. Paton changed the dynamics in the school from force and conflict to trust and respect. This experience prompted him to travel around the world to study prison systems. He wrote his first novel during these travels. Upon his return to South Africa, Paton went to live on the south coast of Natal, where he wrote articles about issues pertinent to South Africa. In the early 1950s, he became a founder of the liberal Association of South Africa, which would later evolve into a political party. In the 1960s, the South African government attempted to control Paton's actions by revoking his passport, so that if he left the country he would not be allowed to return. This did not, however, slow him down in his fight against racism and apartheid on his native soil.

In 1948, Paton published his first and best-known work, the novel *Cry, the Beloved Country.* *Too Late the Phalarope* was published in 1953, and although most critics regard it as his best work, Paton's reputation as a writer rests largely on his first novel. Both novels reflect the author's anti-apartheid sentiment and his hope for a brighter future for South Africa. Paton also wrote poetry and short stories, but felt too strongly about remaining

Alan Paton

politically active to devote all of his time to writing.

Critics admire Paton's fiction for messages that are clear without being heavyhanded and for his sympathetic portrayal of black characters suffering exploitation. For a short while, members of the South African black community criticized Paton for depicting black characters as either victims of uncontrollable passions or as members of a beaten-down race. This controversy soon subsided, and the continued popularity of his works today suggests that readers around the world are still responsive to his writing.

Paton died of throat cancer on April 12, 1988, at his home in Natal, South Africa.

Plot Summary

Chapters 1–13

The narrator, Sophie van Vlaanderen, begins by describing her nephew Pieter's childhood. Because Sophie has lived with her brother and his family for many years, she has known Pieter his entire life. His relationship with his father has always been strained because his father is harsh and distant. Sophie believes that Pieter has his father's strength and masculinity and his mother's gentleness and caring nature.

From the very beginning, Sophie refers to the family's eventual destruction and how she might have saved Pieter from his fall. Because she tells the story in past tense, she often foreshadows events to come.

Pieter has grown up and was a decorated soldier in the war, after which he was given a high-ranking position with the police. As second-in-command, he is resented by Sergeant Steyn, who is older and more experienced than Pieter, and yet must report to him.

Pieter is a well-known rugby player who often plays with the younger men in the town. One night, he catches one of the players pursuing a young black woman. Because of the Immorality Act of 1927, which forbids sexual relationships between blacks and whites, the young man could face serious charges. Instead, Pieter talks to him and allows him to go free.

The next day, Pieter visits his friend Matthew Kaplan ("Kappie"), with whom he shares an interest in stamp collecting. While Pieter is looking over some stamps for purchase, Pieter's father, Jakob, enters Kappie's store. Because of past incidents related to stamp collecting, Pieter becomes uncomfortable in his father's presence, and finishes his business quickly. This interaction brings about one of his "black" moods that haunts him throughout the story.

A man named Smith is sentenced to hang for murder. He had impregnated one of his black servants, and knew that it would be obvious that he was the father. To avoid punishment under the Immorality Act, he and his wife killed the girl and cut off her head so that the body could not be identified if it was found. The crime is discovered, however, and Smith faces murder charges, of which he is found guilty and sentenced to hang.

Pieter is sent to find Stephanie, a young woman who makes a living for herself and her illegitimate child by brewing and selling illegal liquor. She is often arrested and seems unaffected by serving jail time. When Pieter finds her, he experiences a strange attraction to her, which he terms "the mad sickness." He denies it to himself and takes the girl to town to face charges. The judge warns her that if she does not find legal work, she may lose her child. She reacts strongly; this threat pierces her veil of nonchalance.

A new minister arrives in town and everyone comes to see him, having heard that he is an impressive speaker. Pieter's sister, Martha, blushes as she looks at the new minister, as do all the young unmarried women.

A large party is planned for Jakob's birthday. Pieter gives his father a book, which is a bold gesture because Jakob only reads from the family Bible. Pieter gives him *The Birds of South Africa* and Jakob is so pleased that the entire family is proud of Pieter.

Chapters 14–26

Nella leaves with the children to visit her parents for an extended stay. Her marriage to Pieter has been tense; both are relieved but also anxious at the prospect of being apart for a while. Stephanie stops by Pieter's house to tell him that she has gotten legitimate work, and Sophie notices a look pass between them. She senses danger and from here on is nervous for her nephew.

Plagued by his attraction to Stephanie, a woman who should repulse him, Pieter decides to talk to Kappie about his problem. However, he cannot bring himself to confess the desire that shames him. Kappie can tell that something is wrong, but does not try to push Pieter into telling him.

A few days later, Pieter meets with his cousin Anna, and they talk and drink brandy. Pieter does not usually drink, so the brandy takes effect and he goes to a place where he knows he will see Stephanie. He finds her, and they sleep together, and when Pieter returns home there is a note on his door that reads, "I saw you." Overwhelmed by guilt and terror, he becomes paranoid. He imagines that everyone has found out about his crime and judged him until Kappie tells him off-handedly that he left the note because he saw Pieter drinking brandy with his cousin.

Deeply relieved, Pieter returns to his routine. Sergeant Steyn leaves on vacation with his family, where his daughter picks up small seashells as souvenirs. Sophie mentions this in a mysterious, foreshadowing way.

Nella returns home with the children and she and Pieter enjoy a very romantic evening that rekindles their love. The joy is only temporary, however, because they soon return to their old habits and patterns. As a result, Pieter's "black mood" returns, and he seeks Stephanie out and has sex with her a second time.

Chapters 27–39

Once again filled with guilt, Pieter feels profoundly ashamed of himself. The young minister visits, asking Pieter if he thinks Jakob will allow him to marry Martha. In a lightened mood, Pieter assures him that Jakob will approve and gives the young man advice on dealing with Jakob.

Pieter, Jakob, Sophie, and the rest of the family go on a picnic. Sophie describes it as the last time they were all truly happy before they were destroyed. In an unusual moment of togetherness, Jakob takes Pieter on a walk to show him some of the birds from his book, most notably the phalarope.

Back at work, Pieter learns that Stephanie has lost her job. She is distraught at the thought of losing her child, and when she runs into him in the street, she explains that she needs a lawyer but has no money. He offers to give her some money, but they must meet privately so as not to arouse suspicion. They agree to meet at night, and when they do, she seduces him, even though he promised himself he would not have sex with her again.

The next day, he is called into the captain's office. The captain is the highest-ranking police authority and he tells Pieter that a charge has been made against him of violating the Immorality Act. Pieter denies it repeatedly until evidence mounts against him. The final proof is a small seashell placed in Pieter's pocket by Stephanie. Steyn has given it to her for that very purpose. Stephanie's knowledge that there is a seashell in Pieter's pocket, and her accurate description of it, are proof that she has been intimate with him.

Jakob disowns Pieter, crossing his name out of the family Bible. He demands that Pieter's name never be mentioned in the house again. He changes his will, removing Pieter and adding Nella and the children on the condition that they never have anything more to do with Pieter. When Jakob's wife says she must see her son Pieter once more, he tells her that if she leaves the house, she cannot return. Sophie chooses to see her nephew, even though she will no longer be allowed in her brother's house.

Pieter loses his job and faces imprisonment, but his aunt, Kappie, and the captain stay by his side. As it turns out, the captain is the father of Stephanie's child. Martha is forced by the scandal to break off her engagement to the minister, who leaves town shortly thereafter. The townspeople whisper about the incident, and soon after, Jakob dies. Before he goes to prison, Pieter gives Sophie his diary that tells the story of his downfall. He says

it is for Nella to read, in hopes that she will come back to him. It is the diary that enables Sophie to tell the story of the novel.

Characters

Anna

Anna is Pieter's cousin. She claims that she is not married because the only man she would have married was Pieter, and he married someone else. Anna is a modern woman who smokes and wears "yellow trousers" that Sophie detests.

Esther

Esther is the elderly woman with whom Stephanie and her child live. Esther is reportedly the oldest woman in the village—more than a hundred years old—and claims to remember when the Boers first came to the area although Sophie doubts this.

Japie Grobler

Japie is a childhood friend of Pieter's who grows up and becomes a social worker. He and Pieter attended school and college together before their careers took them in different directions. When the new Social Welfare Department opens in Venterspan, his hometown, Japie is sent to run it. This delights him, as he holds fond memories of Pieter, Frans, and Tante Sophie (Aunt Sophie), who still live there. Japie is always joking, so Jakob does not take him seriously.

Japie works hard to try to help Stephanie find a job when she is threatened with losing her child. While Pieter pushes him to find work for her, Sophie (suspecting trouble for Pieter, her nephew) encourages Japie to send her away, which he cannot do because there is no law for it.

Matthew Kaplan

Kappie is a good friend of Pieter's, with whom he shares an interest in stamp collecting. A friendly Jewish man, Kappie respects Pieter and enjoys having him for coffee and to listen to music.

When Pieter considers telling someone about his strong attraction to Stephanie, he chooses Kappie as his potential confidant because he knows that instead of being judgmental, Kappie will be sympathetic and supportive. Pieter cannot bring himself to talk about his problem, however, although Kappie is sensitive enough to see that something is troubling his friend. At the end of the story, Kap-

Media Adaptations

- *Too Late the Phalarope* was adapted as a play by Robert Yale Libott, first produced on Broadway at the Belasco Theater on October 11, 1956.

- An audio adaptation was made by Books on Tape in 1982.

---

pie is one of the few people who stays by Pieter's side.

Captain Massingham

The only man of higher authority than Pieter, the captain is a respectable and wise man who thinks highly of Pieter. He is a serious man who respects duty above all else. He does not joke or laugh, having lost his son in gunfire and his wife soon afterwards. He lives with his mother, and although he is English, he speaks Afrikaans like a Boer.

When the captain behaves toward Pieter almost as a loving father, Pieter comes close to telling him about his crime. Pieter eventually learns that Stephanie's illegitimate child was fathered by the captain, who would have helped Pieter if he had known what Pieter was experiencing.

Mr. Smith

Smith is introduced as an example of how seriously the Immorality Act of 1927 is taken in Venterspan. Having impregnated one of his servant girls, he panics because he knows that it will be obvious that he is the child's father. To avoid punishment and shame, he and his wife murder the girl, cutting off her head so the body cannot be identified if discovered. The crime is found out, however, and Smith is tried and sentenced to hang.

Stephanie

Stephanie is a black woman in her mid-twenties who becomes the object of Pieter's sexual obsession. On three different occasions, she has sexual relations with him. Stephanie is a mysterious woman whose constantly alternating smiles and frowns do not seem to reflect her true feelings in any given situation. In chapter 2, Sophie remarks, "She took her sentences smiling and frowning, and would go smiling and frowning out of the court to the prison, and would come out from the prison smiling and frowning, . . ." She seems completely unaffected by anything except the threat of losing her illegitimate child.

Stephanie lives with Esther and brews and sells illegal liquor to support herself. As a result of her lifestyle, she is well-known by the police, who have arrested her often. When she is threatened with having her child taken away from her, she seeks out legal work, but is unable to hold onto such a position, so she returns to earning money illegally. Faced with the reality of losing her child, she goes along with Sergeant Steyn's plan to destroy Pieter, and betrays him.

Sergeant Steyn

Because Pieter is given the high-ranking position of lieutenant in the police force, Sergeant Steyn is resentful at being made subordinate to a man who is younger than he is. Steyn's resentment is made worse by a few incidents in which Pieter is harsh to him, and he resolves to destroy Pieter. He conspires with Stephanie to trap Pieter into sleeping with Stephanie a third time so that evidence can be collected, including a shoe print and a seashell placed in Pieter's pocket by Stephanie.

Emily van Vlaanderen

Emily is one of Pieter's three sisters. She is the middle sister and is married to a man from Johannesburg.

Frans van Vlaanderen

Frans is Pieter's younger brother.

Henrietta van Vlaanderen

Henrietta is the eldest of Pieter's three sisters. She is married to a quiet man who is afraid of Jakob.

Jakob van Vlaanderen

Jakob is Pieter's harsh and distant father, whose physical stature matches his strong personality despite his limp. He is cold, intimidating, and intolerant, and is unable to understand Pieter, who is equally comfortable riding and shooting with the neighborhood boys, or admiring flowers or collecting stamps alone. He is the chairman of his political party although he rarely appears for meetings, feeling that the members of the party are his "oxen." His prized possession is the family Bible brought over by his ancestors from Holland, and he often reads from "the Book." In fact, until Pieter gives him a book of pictures of South African birds, the only book Jakob ever reads is the Bible. When he learns of his son's crime, the first thing he does is cross Pieter's name out of the family Bible.

Jakob is depicted as a rigid and religious man who demands control in his home. Many critics claim that his sudden death at the end of the story is the result of his shame and hurt over his son's act.

Koos van Vlaanderen

Koos is Frans's ten-year-old son, who idolizes his uncle Pieter and hopes to become a police officer. When Pieter is shamed by his crime, Koos loses all affection for Pieter and becomes withdrawn.

Martha van Vlaanderen

Martha is Pieter's youngest sister. She and the new minister fall in love, and she anticipates great joy in married life. Because of Pieter's crime, however, she coldly breaks off the engagement, hiding her pain from the world as she resigns herself to life as a spinster.

Mrs. van Vlaanderen

Pieter's mother's first name is never revealed in the story although her personality is described on several occasions. She is a warm and compassionate woman who loves her family unconditionally. In chapter 1, Sophie notes, "If ever a woman was all love, it was she, all love and care." Sophie believes that Pieter inherited his father's masculinity and his mother's sweet temperament. Even when Mrs. van Vlaanderen learns of her son's crime, her first instinct is to run and see him, but Jakob forbids it. As a widow, however, she is free to see her son, whom she tries to comfort as best she can.

Nella van Vlaanderen

Pieter's wife, Nella, is a sweet, shy woman who is afraid of the roughness present in the world. Not only does she fear the big city of Johannesburg, she also fears such things as the coarse laughter of men in bars. She is a loving mother and a dutiful wife although she and her husband are sexually incompatible. After her husband's crime is revealed, her response is unknown because Jakob sends Nella and the children away from Pieter.

Pieter van Vlaanderen

The novel's main character, Pieter, is the lieutenant of the police. He breaks the law forbidding sexual contact between whites and blacks. Depicted as a divided personality from childhood, he suffers an internal struggle between what he knows to be moral and legal, and what he finds himself uncontrollably compelled to do. The strife within Pieter manifests itself as "black moods" that are described as falling upon him, almost as if they are separate from his true self.

Pieter is a charming, virtuous, and athletic man who is a pillar in his community of Venterspan. He is respected for being tender and understanding toward blacks as well as whites, an attitude he developed at a young age. Pieter enjoys reading on a variety of subjects, even though his father only reads the Bible. Like his father, he is tall and radiates an imposing presence. Pieter regularly attends church and is a well-known rugby player who is admired by many. He has a wife, Nella, and children, and lives near his parents, aunt, and siblings. His relationship with his father has always been strained, a situation that temporarily lightens just before Pieter's crime is discovered.

Sophie van Vlaanderen

Sophie is the narrator of the story. She is Pieter's aunt, who, because of her facial disfigurement, lives with her brother and his family although she remains a bit of an outsider. Having never married, she regards Pieter as the son she never had, and dotes on him shamelessly. Her position in the family is subordinate to that of both Jakob and Pieter; she loves both, but feels overpowered by them. She is a religious woman who attends church regularly and reads the Bible often.

A keen observer of those around her, Sophie notices that something is wrong with her nephew early in the novel and, based on a look that passes between Stephanie and Pieter, she becomes very anxious for him. Even before this, she realizes that Pieter is a deeply divided person in many respects. Throughout the book she remarks that if she had only been more assertive with her nephew, she might have prevented the tragedy that befell the family.

Mr. Vorster

Vorster is a young man who works in the police station. He admires Pieter greatly until Pieter falls from grace after which Vorster completely turns on him.

Dominee Vos

Vos is the young minister who arrives in town amidst great anticipation. The townspeople have heard that he is a wonderful speaker, and he upholds this reputation with his first sermon. Also an avid rugby player, he is thrilled to meet Pieter, whose reputation as an athlete is well-known. Before long, the minister and Martha fall in love and plan to marry. He leaves the town, however, after Martha breaks their engagement.

Themes

Morality

In *Too Late the Phalarope,* Paton depicts morality as something that resides within and also as something that is imposed by external forces, such as church and government. Pieter's fall suggests that morality, when imposed on individuals by outside forces, is merely a façade. Despite Pieter's position in law enforcement, the external morality imposed by the law is inadequate to prevent him from breaking the very law he is sworn to uphold and enforce.

In contrast, Stephanie's sense of morality is wholly internal, directed only by her maternal drive to keep her child. To this end, she is comfortable brewing and selling illegal liquor, seducing Pieter, and later betraying him. She has no difficulty breaking the law forbidding sexual relations between white men and black women because she sees it as an opportunity to gain the favor of a powerful man. Her duty is to herself and her child, so she is easily recruited by Sergeant Steyn to deceive Pieter to better her chances of keeping her child.

Justice and Consequences

Paton is very clear in his message that breaking political and moral laws brings severe consequences, just or not. Even before Pieter meets privately with Stephanie, he understands the ramifications of acting against the Immorality Act of 1927. Not only has he seen the terror of men who violate it (like Smith), but in chapter 16, his diary reveals his thoughts when Stephanie visits him briefly at his home:

> I should have said to her, let them take your child, and send you to prison, let them throw you into the street, let them hang you by the neck until you are dead, but do not come to my home, nor smile at me, nor think there can be anything between you and me. For this law is the greatest and holiest of laws, and

if you break it and are discovered, for you it is nothing but another breaking of the law. But if I break it and am discovered, the whole world will be broken.

Pieter indeed suffers greatly when his crime is discovered: He loses his position as lieutenant of the police; he loses the respect of many of his friends; his father, Jakob, disowns him and forbids the very mention of his name; and his wife and children are sent away. He endures shame, humiliation, and imprisonment. Additionally, his family suffers for Pieter's actions. His young sister, Martha, must break her engagement to the minister, after which she resigns herself to life as a spinster. His mother is forbidden to see him. His aunt, by choosing to see him again, is permanently cast out of Jakob's home. Jakob lives in a state of rage and sorrow after his son's crime is revealed, and he dies shortly thereafter.

The case of Smith portrays the seemingly inescapable nature of justice. Smith tries to cover up his crime of impregnating a servant girl by murdering her. The crime is found out, however, and Smith is sentenced to hang for his actions. His attempt to sidestep justice only brings it upon him more harshly as he faces a charge of murder, along with the contempt of the townspeople who know him as a man who has murdered a young girl and an unborn baby to avoid just punishment.

The Divided Self

Sophie frequently refers to Pieter's divided self. At the beginning, she describes him as a child who could out-ride and out-shoot other boys, and at the same time enjoy delicate things like flowers and stamps. She considers him both a boy and a girl for this reason, and explains how disturbed Jakob is about his son's softer side.

Later in the story, when Pieter is a man, Sophie describes the battle raging within him as a struggle between what he knows is good and right and what he finds repulsive. She adds that his struggle is intensified because he cannot control his attraction to that which repels (or should repel) him. Ultimately, he gives in to his "evil" side and indulges his attraction to Stephanie on three different occasions. Sophie remarks in chapter 4, "Darkness and light, how they fought for his soul, and the darkness destroyed him, the gentlest and bravest of men." Much later, after having sex with Stephanie the third time, Pieter bathes while

> trembling with the secret knowledge of the abject creature that was himself, that vowed and could not keep his vows, that was called to the high duty of the law and broke the law, that was moved in his soul

by that which was holy and went reaching for that which was vile, that was held in respect by men and was baser than them all.

Sophie is not alone in her view of Pieter as divided; he sees himself that way, too. He refers to his attraction to Stephanie as the "mad sickness," and views it as something that comes to him of its own will. He sees it as a force separate from him, and yet one he cannot cast out of himself. Pieter's "black moods" are portrayed the same way—each one is a separate entity that shrouds him and refuses to be wished away.

Guilt

Once Pieter has broken the law, he is overwhelmed with guilt. He perceives his whole world differently, imagining that everyone around him knows what he has done. Immediately following his first offense, he prays with deep humility, hoping not to offend God by being presumptuous in thinking He will hear his prayer. Pieter imagines:

> that a trumpet had been blown in Heaven, and that the Lord Most High had ordered the closing of the doors, that no prayer might enter in from such a man, who knowing the laws and the commandments, had, of his own choice and will, defied them. As he makes his way home, he is covered with the smell of the kakiebos (a weed with a pungent smell) he had lain down in, and he feels that he is stinking with corruption, with a smell that will travel through the entire town, notifying everyone of his deed. Watching a group of oxen, he envies them because they are "holy and obedient" animals.

Reflecting on how other men his age tell raunchy jokes, Pieter writes in his diary in chapter 15 (when he is only thinking of committing the crime but has not yet done so), "Yet they were all cleaner and sweeter than I. That is a thing I never understood." When Vorster, the young man who works at the police station, is in low spirits, Pieter suspects it is because he has found out what Pieter has done and no longer admires him. The captain's distant mood makes Pieter wonder if he has heard of the crime. When a neighbor sees Pieter and spits and turns away, Pieter can think of no other reason for such behavior than that he, too, knows what Pieter has done. In his relationship with his wife, Pieter becomes more helpful and thoughtful, speaking kind words because of his desire to be with his loving family. At the same time, he is less physically affectionate to his wife because even a kiss on the lips tears him apart. In chapter 21, Pieter's diary reads:

> And what madness made a man pursue something so unspeakable, deaf to the cries of wife and children and mother and friends and blind to their danger, to

Topics for Further Study

- In *Too Late the Phalarope* Alan Paton depicts a racially divided society in which laws govern relationships between individuals of different races. Can you think of other historical instances of racism supported or encouraged by laws or government leaders? Prepare a chart that compares and contrasts such situations with the one Paton describes.

- Throughout the novel, Sophie refers to "the door." How does Paton use the door as a symbol, and what does it symbolize? Prepare a brief lecture as if you were explaining symbolism to young students unfamiliar with the concept. As an illustration, refer to Paton's use of door imagery.

- Read Edgar Allan Poe's short story "The Tell-Tale Heart." How does Poe's depiction of guilt compare to Paton's depiction of Pieter's guilt after the first time he meets with Stephanie? How can you account for the different outcomes?

- Research the life of Nelson Mandela and his fight against apartheid in South Africa. What do you think are the three most important things he has done for the cause? Then speculate on how the course of history might have been different without his efforts.

- Review the climate, resources, and population of South Africa, along with its history since the arrival of the Dutch. Now look at a map and consider what geographical factors are significant to the tumultuous past of this country.

- Pieter's awkward relationship with his father is typical of many families. Take into account psychological, sociological, and personality factors, and provide an explanation for the distant relationship of the father and son in the novel. Can your conclusions be generalized to other people's situations? Why or why not?

grasp one unspeakable pleasure that brought no joy, ten thousand of which pleasures were not worth one of the hairs of their heads?

Readers are less sympathetic to Pieter when, after his first offense goes unnoticed, he repeats it. The first time, his guilt is fueled by terror that the note on his door ("I saw you") was from someone who had seen him with Stephanie. The second time, his guilt is fueled completely by his own shame and feelings of weakness.

Style

First-Person Narrator

Paton's use of Sophie as the story's narrator is unusual because she is a secondary character yet has special knowledge of Pieter's thoughts and feelings by virtue of having Pieter's diary as a resource. Consequently, she is in a position to tell the reader about events and conversations that happened outside her personal experience.

Although she is a secondary character, Sophie is a reliable narrator for three reasons. First, she includes excerpts from Pieter's diary to support what she is saying. Second, she explains early in the novel that because of her facial disfigurement, she has always been slightly apart from everyone else, even in her own family. This unique position has enabled her to become an especially keen observer of those around her. It is Sophie, after all, who suspects something is happening between Pieter and Stephanie simply because of a look she notices that Stephanie gives to Pieter. Third, Sophie is honest and never claims to fully understand everything in the story. She readily admits it when there is something she does not understand, as in chapter 4 when she tells about the stamps that Kappie shows Pieter. She says that they are particularly expensive, but since she is not a stamp collector, she cannot say why: "If you cannot understand it, I cannot explain it, never having understood it myself." Rather than omit this passage from the story, she includes it, despite her admittedly limited knowledge in the area.

Biblical Allusions

Paton's father was a very religious man who conducted his own church service every Sunday in the Paton home. From the early age of five, Alan Paton preached on biblical subjects to his family, as he was assigned to do by his father. In *Too Late the Phalarope,* the author's familiarity with the

Bible is evident in various passages that draw on biblical language or passages. His application of biblical ideas indicates an ability to draw from the Bible excerpts applicable to a variety of situations.

Chapter 26 contains a paraphrase of Ecclesiastes 3:1–5; Sophie remarks

> For I know there is a time to weep and a time to laugh; a time to mourn and a time to dance; a time to cast away stones and a time to gather stones together; a time to embrace and a time to refrain from embracing.

At the end of the same paragraph, she adds that "to have a feast is good, and to eat and drink and be merry, but one cannot live on feasting." This is a clear reference to Matthew 4:4 and Luke 4:4 in which Jesus says that man cannot live by bread alone. At the end of the novel, Jakob is found dead, "bowed over the Book of Job." This is significant because in the Bible, Job is a righteous man who suffers and endures much.

Simile

Sophie frequently uses similes to illustrate her points. This may be a result of her observational skills, which would enable her to see similarities between images or experiences that may not occur to those around her. Sophie regards Stephanie, for example, as being like a tigress in protecting her child. In chapter 26, Nella's sexual distance from her husband is offered as a partial explanation for Pieter's seeking out Stephanie's company. Pieter is compared to a man who loses a jewel and then seeks it out among filth and garbage. After Pieter confesses to his transgression, Sophie says in chapter 35 that she expects the dreadful news to "go like fire from every house to every house, and from every farm to every farm in the grass country."

In chapter 23, Pieter notices that Vorster seems withdrawn. Because Pieter imagines that the boy knows about the crime, the narrator describes Vorster as having "a drawn and unhappy face, like a man who has taken great steps for God and has publicly given his life and his possessions, and then finds that he no more believes in Him." As Kappie tries to make sense of Pieter's changing moods, Sophie notes in chapter 25, "Kappie sat there like a man with a puzzle with a hundred pieces, with a picture all but complete, with six or seven pieces that would not fit at all." In the same chapter, she recalls the family's momentary return to happiness as she comments, "And I remember that time, for our happiness came back again, like a moment of sunshine from a heavy sky."

Foreshadowing

Because she is telling the story in past tense, Sophie occasionally holds the reader's interest by the use of foreshadowing. By interspersing intriguing "teasers" throughout he novel, she keeps the reader engaged in the action of the plot. At the end of chapter 6, for example, Sophie describes Neila as sweet and innocent, adding, "Then the hard hand of Fate struck her across the face, and shocked her into knowledge, but only after we had been destroyed." The destruction to which Sophie refers occurs much later in the book, when the family is torn apart by Pieter's crime. Similarly, in chapter 15, Sophie comments on sudden changes in weather, concluding, "So did my summer turn, not into quietness and peace, but to the dark black storm that swept us all away."

Hinting at how Pieter's crime would eventually be discovered, Sophie notes in chapter 25 that Sergeant Steyn went on vacation with his family, and his daughter picked up bits of seashell. Sophie concludes that the girl "collected them in her innocence, and put them in a box, and brought them back to Venterspan; and by one of them collected in innocence, the house of van Vlaanderen was destroyed."

Historical Context

Jan Christiian Smuts

A statesman and philosopher, Jan Christiian Smuts was a well-known military leader in South Africa during the early twentieth century. He was a Dutch-speaking Boer whose family originally arrived in South Africa in 1692 as farmers. Smuts grew up in the hostile political climate in which the British and the Dutch were fighting for control of South African land. Educated in law, Smuts adhered to the idea that to cultivate the continent, compromise and peace were necessary between the warring European nations. After the Jameson Raid (an effort by the British to provoke a war), however, Smuts sided with the Boers and proclaimed his loyalty to Afrikaner nationalism.

When the Boer War erupted in 1899, Smuts was still hoping to achieve peace between the British and the Dutch, but was consistently disappointed by efforts to negotiate. Smuts distinguished himself as a military leader during the war, and he and General J. H. de la Rey organized resistance against opposing forces in western Transvaal (one of the two Afrikaner republics).

When the war was over, Smuts returned to law and was the principal designer of the constitution of the Union of South Africa. As he delved deeper into politics, he made enemies of miners and politicians on the far right. Chief among his opponents were members of the National Party. In both world wars, Smuts led South Africa against Germany; in World War I, he led troops as a military leader; during World War II, he was prime minister, and under his leadership South Africa entered the war.

Segregation in South Africa

As British and Dutch forces fought for control of South African land, the native populations were subject to new laws governing their social and political separation from the white citizens. In the early twentieth century, both Jan Christiian Smuts and his political opponent, J. B. M. Herzog, supported racial segregation in South Africa, although Smuts did not favor abolishing all rights for blacks.

The first parliament was established in South Africa in 1910, and one of the first decisions made was to restrict blacks to purchasing land within designated reserves. The reserves, however, accounted for only seven percent of the total land. This extreme limitation ensured that migratory labor would continue to be available for white landowners and that blacks would be forced to work for low wages in mines and other industries. When World War II ended in 1945, political leaders realized that South Africa was rapidly becoming an industrialized nation, which meant that the black population was gaining freedom and importance. To address this, the Boers (white South Africans of Dutch descent) adopted a policy of apartheid, the aftereffects of which continue to be a dominant political issue in South Africa.

Even before apartheid, there were laws governing the social interactions of blacks and whites. An example of this is the Immorality Act of 1927, which is at the center of *Too Late the Phalarope*. This Act outlawed sexual relationships between blacks and whites, and later the Act would be expanded to forbid sexual relationships between whites and any other race. Toward the end of the twentieth century, as apartheid began to crumble, so did these laws.

Compare
&
Contrast

- **1920s:** Among the laws governing social behavior in South Africa is the Immorality Act of 1927, forbidding sexual relations between blacks and whites. While originally designed to protect helpless servant women from being exploited by powerful bosses, the law eventually comes to represent the pursuit of racial purity by European settlers. The punishments for violating this Act are severe, and the social consequences are staggering.

  Today: In 1991, 74 percent of Americans say they view interracial marriage as acceptable. In 1994, the number of black-white interracial marriages in America has risen to 1.2 million, compared to only 651,000 in 1980.

- **1920s:** Education for native South Africans is lacking, and illiteracy is the norm. In a culture with a strong oral tradition, little emphasis is placed on learning to read, despite efforts by missionaries. This is reflected in *Too Late the Phalarope,* in which the black children marvel at Pieter's ability to read any book he picks up.

  Today: According to the *United Nations Statistical Yearbook,* the literacy rate in the United States is 99.5 percent.

- **1920s:** Because political power is held by whites, segregation is a way of life throughout South Africa. As a result, blacks have little control over their social, political, or financial lives until the latter part of the century, when apartheid begins to crumble.

  Today: Effects of the racial segregation that once dominated U.S. society still linger. Because of a strong civil rights movement in the 1950s and 1960s, American laws supporting segregation are no longer in effect, but racial tension persists in social interactions, art, film, music, and other elements of culture.

- **1920s:** Smallpox is an often-deadly disease feared by people in South African villages. Even into the 1960s there are ten to fifteen million cases reported every year.

  Today: Thanks to the discovery by Edward Jenner of a vaccination against smallpox, and a worldwide vaccination effort in 1967, smallpox is nonexistent today. As of 1979, the disease was declared extinct, with only controlled samples of the virus kept in a few laboratories.

Modernist Period in Literature (1914–1965)

World War I ushered in the literary movement known as Modernism. While the term is primarily applied to British literature, critics generally consider Paton to have been a modernist author at the time *Too Late the Phalarope* was published. Some of his later work is considered postmodernist.

The Modernist Period is characterized by lost optimism following the horrors of the war and the beginnings of experimentation as writers intentionally broke with tradition and conventions regarding literary form and content. Literature written during this time often focuses on social issues, attempting to raise the consciousness of readers and introduce them to new realities. Much modernist work emphasizes the individual experience over the larger social context and contains psychological, philosophical, or political elements. Many works, such as T. S. Eliot's *The Waste Land,* reflect a sense of fragmentation and despair. *Too Late the Phalarope* is an example of a modernist work that depicts self-awareness and the dark side of human nature.

Critical Overview

Critics generally agree that *Too Late the Phalarope,* while often overshadowed by *Cry, the Beloved Country,* is Paton's best work. At the time

A "Whites Only" sign in South Africa

of publication, reviewers were already recognizing it as superior to its predecessor.

In his 1953 review, Harold C. Gardiner wrote that the novel is a "much more tautly drawn tale" than the first. He added that it is compassionate, while remaining "strong and manly, and manifests . . . a deeply felt realization of the moral plight, of the agony of soul of others." Nicholas H. Z. Watts of *Durham University Journal* commented that *Too Late the Phalarope* "matches the elegiac beauty and power of the earlier novel and the intensity of Paton's most recent one [*Ah, But Your Land Is Beautiful*] and deserves greater recognition than it has yet received." Similarly, Kirsten Holst Petersen observed in *Reference Guide to English Literature,* "Paton is . . . at his very best when he explores the Calvinist Boer mind as he does in *Too Late the Phalarope,* an excellent but much ignored book."

Stylistically, Paton's novel is scrutinized both favorably and unfavorably. Sheridan Baker of *English Studies in Africa* found the use of Sophie as a narrator to be a too-obvious and old-fashioned literary device. Further, he regarded her as ineffective, commenting, "Paton brings Sophie a long way into reality, but he cannot make her narrative mechanics natural." Baker suggested that Paton uses Sophie as a narrator to avoid dealing with the black-white sexual relationship head-on. He remarked,

"Sophie enables him to stop short." In contrast, other critics have commended Paton's stylistic ability in the novel, with special praise for the character of Sophie. In *International Review,* Irma Ned Stevens named the point of view in *Too Late the Phalarope* as one of the novel's notable strengths, adding that Sophie's telling of the story is carried out in wisdom and love. F. Charles Rooney wrote in *Catholic World* that Paton skillfully uses the narrator to express his own beliefs, adding that Sophie "becomes such a real person to the reader that there is never a question of sermonizing. In her, Paton has created his only really well-defined woman; this portrait is a work of technical mastery and avoids a potential sore spot."

Numerous critics point to the biblical elements present in *Too Late the Phalarope,* as well as to the novel's similarities to a Greek tragedy. In his *Books with Men behind Them,* author Edmund Fuller refers to Sergeant Steyn as a Judas figure, who betrays Pieter and then disappears from the story. Commenting on the novel's religious language and content, Rose Moss of *World Literature Today* remarked:

> Paton's liturgical style and its clear connections with the Bible and Christian practice offer a way to connect individual virtue with the virtue and sufferings of others, with the history and hopes of devout peo-

ple in other times and places and, finally, with the story of Christ, whose suffering and death demonstrate that the end of the story is not despair but hope.

Along with many other critics, Fuller commented on Paton's use of the classical tragedy form. In *Too Late the Phalarope,* he explained, the author creates a relatively simple story featuring a virtuous protagonist whose tragic flaw destroys his life. The hero ultimately grasps what has happened and understands his responsibility for the outcome. Watts described four classical elements in *Too Late the Phalarope:* well-known themes, such as the inevitable fall; unity of time, place, and action; the presence of an almost sexless, detached narrator; and a heroic central figure. Generally speaking, critics admire Paton's use of classical techniques in a modern setting, and maintain that, as in the Greek tragedies, these techniques give the story a broad-based appeal and relevance.

While some scholars find the novel lacking in universality, others counter that universal themes are the book's strength. To a small group of critics, the setting is too specific in time and place, and the culture of the community is too foreign, to be applicable to contemporary life. Because Pieter is presented as such a noble and charming man at the beginning of the book (in fact, Sophie compares him to a god), they deem him inaccessible to readers, and they are not particularly sympathetic to his guilt and weakness. On the other hand, critics such as Gardiner regard the novel as universally meaningful. He commented, "It is infinitely more than a mere tale of misguided passion. The great passion that emerges in the pages is of Mr. Paton's own hatred of racial discrimination." Commenting on Paton's fiction, Fuller wrote,

> The measure of his books is that while distilling the essence of South Africa, they speak to many aspects of the condition of the whole world. He has struck universal notes, and the world outside his own land honors him for his art, his humanity, and his integrity.

Despite disagreement over where *Too Late the Phalarope* fits in the context of world literature, most scholars commend the novel as Paton's most polished fiction. Articulating this sentiment, Watts concluded:

> This, Paton's finest novel, thus operates with great success on several levels. It is a convincing story of crime and punishment. It is a strong study of individuals who, despite their pronounced characteristics, are always more than stereotypes. As a psychological novel, it is a powerful depiction of the corrosive effect of guilt and the destructive power of a repressed subconscious. . . . And it turns out to be what we perhaps first expected: a devastating critique of

apartheid and the spirit that underlies it. Paton's commitment to social justice and compassion, which rises so movingly from the pages of *Cry, the Beloved Country,* here finds such unity of composition, such austerity of expression, such integrity of faith and such universal meaning that *Too Late the Phalarope* stands as an exceptional book.

Criticism

Jennifer Bussey

Bussey holds a master's degree in interdisciplinary studies and a bachelor's degree in English literature. She is an independent writer specializing in literature. In the following essay, she considers the power of words in Paton's novel.

The first sentence of *Too Late the Phalarope* is, "Perhaps I could have saved him, with only a word, two words, out of my mouth." Alan Paton establishes from the onset that in this novel, the power of words will be substantial and will play an important role in the plot. Words are in some cases considered as immutable as if written in stone; in other cases they have the potential to bring about life-changing outcomes.

Pieter uses the power of the written word by writing a secret diary, which he gives to his aunt at the end of the book. Readers must remember that it is the diary that allows Sophie to know everything that has happened. Without Pieter's diary, there is no novel.

As an officer of the law, Pieter understands the authority of the written word, especially in the forms of laws and charges. Before he breaks the law, he feels drawn to Stephanie, yet he knows that acting on his impulse is very dangerous. He seems less concerned with the moral weight of his decision to break the law than he does with the legal consequences of doing so. He has sexual relations with Stephanie on three different occasions, and yet the word "adultery" never enters his mind. He feels guilt and behaves more lovingly toward his family, but what frightens him is the thought of being exposed and subjected to legal punishment. This indicates that his psyche is terrorized by the law rather than the ideology behind it; by the letter of the law, not its spirit.

In two instances, the inviolable nature of charges, once written, is emphasized. In chapter 21, Pieter fears that Sergeant Steyn has discovered his crime and will, at any moment, come forward with the charges against him. Pieter thinks:

Then there could be no mercy, for when a charge is made, a charge is made, and once a thing is written down, it is written down; and a word can be written down that will mean the death of a man, and put the rope around his neck, and send him into the pit; and a word can be written down that will destroy a man and his house and his kindred and his friends, and there is no power, of God or Man or State, nor any Angel, nor anything present or to come, nor any height, nor depth, nor any other creature that can save them, when once the word is written down.

This passage is repeated almost verbatim at the end of chapter 35, after Pieter has confessed his crime to the captain. At this point, of course, the charge has been made and, as stated in the passage, Pieter will soon be destroyed along with his family, and will lose most of his friends.

Perhaps the most striking example of the power of written words is the note left on Pieter's door, which he discovers when he returns home after the first time he sleeps with Stephanie. The note says, "I saw you," and all Pieter can think of is the cracking sound he heard just after he and Stephanie finished making love. At the time, Pieter had feared it was a "watcher," who saw everything and would soon destroy Pieter's life by revealing his crime. The note on the door seems to confirm this, and Pieter is engulfed in panic and fear, waiting for his doom. In chapter 21, Sophie writes that he "thought only of the note, the note, with the three small words and the seven letters that could destroy a man." In the next chapter, Pieter looks at the note again, "but it told him no more than it had told him before, that he was in peril greater than any death." The note haunts him to the extent that he becomes paranoid, wondering who knows about him and who does not. He interprets his coworkers' bad moods as intentional distancing from him, and he imagines that a neighbor's unfriendly behavior is a sign of disgust at Pieter's crime. Each day is progressively worse until he learns that Japie innocently left the note after he saw Pieter having drinks with his cousin Anna. He only meant to tease his friend, and as soon as Pieter realizes that nobody saw his crime, his entire reality changes.

The book uses another case of misunderstood words to move the plot forward at a key juncture. In a bad mood, Pieter notices a prisoner while on inspection with Steyn one afternoon. Pieter knows that this prisoner is supposed to be in court, and asks Steyn why the prisoner is in the wrong place. When Steyn answers that he thought the prisoner's court date was the next week, Pieter orders him to get the written instructions that Pieter himself had made out for Steyn. Sheepishly, Steyn returns, ex-

> "Each day is progressively worse until he learns that Japie innocently left the note after he saw Pieter having drinks with his cousin Anna. He only meant to tease his friend, and as soon as Pieter realizes that nobody saw his crime, his entire reality changes."

plaining that he made a mistake and read the date wrong. Pieter is enraged, and asks Steyn if he is unable to read. Because of this incident, Steyn is humiliated and vows to destroy Pieter. Although he already disliked and resented Pieter, this episode fortifies Steyn's resolve to be rid of Pieter for good. While it may be argued that Steyn was already so close to committing himself to Pieter's ruin that any similar incident would have achieved the same outcome, Paton chose to set Pieter's fate in motion because of a few misunderstood words.

The tragedy of misunderstood words resurfaces when Sophie laments in chapter 31 that she did not act when she could have to save her nephew. She explains:

> And now as I write I am like a woman whose man is dead, because of some accident that was not foreseen, or because of some doctor that was not called, or because of some word that sounded like another; and she reproaches herself, and thinks that if for years she had not said . . . let's go tomorrow, or if she had said, let's go by the lower road, perhaps her man would be alive again.

By equating a misunderstood word with an accident or the failure to call a doctor, Sophie expresses the seriousness of the power of words. Moreover, this passage makes a point that, like the accident and the decision not to call the doctor, misunderstood words are preventable, yet often result in tragedy.

In *Too Late the Phalarope,* there is also an underlying belief in the action value of words, meaning that written or spoken words have the power to change people's feelings and opinions (and, by extension, other people's fates). Early in the story, in

What Do I Read Next?

- Athol Fugard's play *Master Harold . . . and the Boys* (1983) examines the extremes of racial tension in South Africa. Written by a South-African playwright, it is a story that addresses the human capacity for hate and fear in a drama that is emotionally wrenching.

- Nobel Prize-winning author Nadine Gordimer's *July's People* (1981) tells the story of a liberal white family in South Africa who are rescued by July, their servant, and taken to his village. The story reveals the profound differences and similarities between July's people and the white family.

- *The Scarlet Letter* (1850) is Nathaniel Hawthorne's classic novel of guilt, repentance, and vengeance. It tells the story of Hester Prynne, an unmarried woman whose baby is fathered by the town's young minister.

- Alan Paton's *Cry, the Beloved Country* (1948) is the story of Zulu priest Stephen Kumalo, who travels to hostile Johannesburg, where his son is on trial for murdering a white man. This book is Paton's most famous work.

- Robert Ross's *A Concise History of South Africa* (1999; Cambridge Concise Histories) provides an overview of the last 1500 years of development, turmoil, and triumph in South Africa.

chapter 1, Sophie explains why she is telling the story:

> And I write it all down here, the story of our destruction. And if I write it with fear, then it is not so great a fear, I being myself destroyed. And if I write it down, maybe it will cease to trouble my mind. And if I write it down, people may know that he was two men, and that one was brave and gentle.

Sophie hopes that her writing will not only change her feelings about her painful experience, but that it will also change people's minds about what kind of man her nephew is.

When Pieter commits his crime, he becomes very prayerful and engages in bargaining with God. He makes vows and repeats them, hoping that his words will travel to heaven and change the consequences of his actions. He recalls a story of a man surrounded by enemies who dropped to his knees and prayed, and when the man opened his eyes, he was alone. Pieter hopes that, by praying and making promises, his imagined (at this point) enemies will also disappear.

The act of reading figures into the lives of the characters in very different ways. Pieter turns to his books in search of a way to cleanse his spirit of evil, or, at the very least, to learn some way to find peace and relief from his turmoil. Certain the answers are somewhere in his books, "He went into his study, and looked there amongst his learned books that told all the sins and weaknesses of men, hoping to find himself, though this he had already done, finding nothing." Jakob reads the cherished family Bible exclusively until his son gives him a book of South African birds as a gift. This book becomes a temporary bridge between the two men, as the father takes the son on a picnic to show him the phalarope, one of the birds misidentified in the book. After Pieter's crime is exposed, Jakob's first act is to take the family Bible and cross Pieter's name off the family list. This is a symbolic act meant to remove Pieter and his shameful ways from the family. As for Sophie, she reads very little but says at the end of the book that though she is gradually getting past the pain of the events told in the novel, when she reads of a man who has broken "the iron law" (the Immorality Act), her grief returns.

It is not surprising that Paton, a writer, would believe so strongly in the power of words. Indeed, as an activist, he relied on his words to change people's minds, inform his readers, and challenge existing ideas. Today he is still considered one of South Africa's most influential and important writers, which is a testament to the power of his own words on subjects that were so meaningful to him.

Source: Jennifer Bussey, Critical Essay on *Too Late the Phalarope*, in *Novels for Students*, The Gale Group, 2001.

Edward Callan

In the following essay, Callan examines Too Late the Phalarope *by comparing and contrasting it with Paton's first novel,* Cry the Beloved Country.

Paton's second novel, *Too Late the Phalarope*, is similar in certain respects to *Cry, the Beloved Country,* but, for the most part, the novels differ strikingly. But works have similarities of style and dramatic method, and each relates a comparatively simple story. *Too Late the Phalarope* tells the story of Pieter van Vlaanderen, a young police lieutenant decorated in war and also nationally famous as a football player. He is a married man with two children, highly respected in the rural Afrikaner community and, indeed, the kind of man in whose presence other men feel constrained to subdue loud talk or off-color jokes. Yet Pieter van Vlaanderen transgresses the strict prohibitions of the South African Immorality Act which forbids sexual relations between members of different races, and thereby brings tragic destruction on himself and his family.

But the differences between the two novels are more significant than the similarities. *Too Late the Phalarope* concentrates on the inner struggles in the soul of one man in the South African social situation; for the clamor of many voices and the broad overview, it substitutes an inner dialogue between two aspects of a divided personality. Furthermore, while the theme of restoration is still fundamental in the second novel, it is approached indirectly, and its attendant note of hope is muted. This is due in part to its literary method, which resembles the method of Greek tragedy more closely than does that of the earlier novel, but it also may be due to the changes that meanwhile took place in South Africa's political climate.

The note of hope in *Cry, the Beloved Country* had some real basis in fact. There were signs in the months immediately following World War II that South African society was prepared to accept progressive change in relations among the races. In 1946 Prime Minister J. C. Smuts had appointed a commission to look into South Africa's urban conditions and the problems of migratory African labor—the very conditions and problems that impelled Paton to write *Cry, the Beloved Country*. It was generally expected that this commission, known as the Fagan Commission, would present liberal recommendations to Parliament. It was also generally anticipated that any such recommendations would be implemented by Parliament through the influence of the Deputy Prime Minister Jan Hofmeyr, who then seemed likely to succeed General Smuts as Prime Minister.

In 1948, the same year that *Cry, the Beloved Country* appeared, the typical rhythm of South African politics reasserted itself, for any suspicion that the Liberal Spirit is working among parliamentary leaders starts a ground-swell for racial intolerance among the white voters, particularly in

> " *Too Late the Phalarope* concentrates on the inner struggles in the soul of one man in the South African social situation; for the clamor of many voices and the broad overview, it substitutes an inner dialogue between two aspects of a divided personality."

rural areas. And in the general elections of that year, Dr. Malan's Nationalist Party received an unexpectedly large plurality for its policy of *apartheid*. This policy denies Africans the right to permanent residence in the towns, and emphasizes ineradicable cultural differences between their tribal heritage and the heritage of "Western Civilization," which is thought to be the birthright of whites only. Jan Hofmeyr died a few months after this election, and with him went much of the hope of powerful, outspoken opposition to the new government's policies. In these respects at least, the hope of going forward in faith implicitly present in *Cry, the Beloved Country* was diminished.

By 1952, the year that Paton wrote *Too Late the Phalarope* during a three-month period in London and in an English seaside boarding house, the new Nationalist government in South Africa had begun implementing its policies of *apartheid* with little regard for opposition views. Paton did not, however, turn his new novel into an attack on *apartheid*, nor into propaganda for any political cause. His choice of the magnanimous Afrikaner woman Tante Sophie as the narrator proves to be a valuable device in this respect. He does not even set the novel with any obviousness in the post-1948 period, and he ignores the immediate social and economic manifestations of *apartheid*. Instead he probes penetratingly into its roots in the ideal of Pure Race; and makes manifest the extent to which this ideal—placed above all other considerations—constitutes a false deity, or "heretical Christianity," as he calls it elsewhere. It is this pride in Pure Race, set up as an ideal, that the narrator, Tante Sophie, has in mind in her summing up: "I pray we shall not walk arrogant, remembering Herod whom an Angel of the Lord struck down, for that he made himself a God." Sophie's view implies that this racial arrogance has affinities with the Greek concept of *hybris*—the special manifestation of pride that incurs tragic retribution. *Hybris* is the arrogation by men of attributes proper only to the gods, and tragedy is the inevitable destruction meted out to *hybris*.

Too Late the Phalarope is a Greek tragedy in modern South African dress. It is set in a small town in the eastern Transvaal—a district populated almost wholly by Afrikaans-speaking white farmers who cherish the four fundamental and inseparable tenets of Afrikaner Nationalism: *Volk, Kerk, Taal, Land.* The *Volk* is the separate and unique Afrikaner People descended from the Voortrekkers; the *Kerk* is the Afrikaner branch of the Dutch Reformed Church to which, ideally, all the *Volk* adhere; the *Taal* is the Afrikaans language which, in place of a national boundary, identifies their nationhood; and the *Land* is the soil of South Africa, sacred to the Afrikaner *Volk* in almost the same sense that the Promised Land was sacred to the Israelites.

These fundamental ideals are summed up in the novel by the Afrikaner patriarch, old Jakob van Vlaanderen, when he rebukes the besotted Flip van Vuuren who persisted in demanding, "what's the point of living, what's the point of life?": "So Jakob van Vlaanderen stood up from his chair, and said in a voice of thunder, the point of living is to serve the Lord your God, and to uphold the honour of your church and language and people, take him home." Jakob van Vlaanderen represents the attitude of those Afrikaans-speaking South Africans who refused to accept Louis Botha's ideal of bringing all white South Africans together in a common patriotism. His wife and his sister, Tante Sophie, adhere to Louis Botha's ideal discussed in Chapter 1, above; his son Pieter, in the finer aspects of his character, might be said to personify Botha's ideal.

This difference in their estimates of where the duties of patriotism lie constitutes one of the causes of friction between Jakob and his son Pieter. At the outbreak of World War II, the South African Parliament was divided on the question of entering the war against Hitler's Germany on Britain's side, or remaining neutral, and General Smuts carried his motion for participation by a very narrow majority. The people were similarly divided. So it was found expedient to agree that men already in the armed forces and police should be permitted either to retain their positions at home or to volunteer for service abroad. Those who so volunteered were identified by orange tabs on their shoulderstraps, which, unfortunately, sharply distinguished them from those who did not; the oath taken by these volunteers came to be known as "the red oath" from the color of the tabs. Jakob van Vlaanderen was one of those who saw the war as "an English war" in which no true Afrikaner should participate: "And when his son Pieter took the red oath and had gone to war, he would bear no mention of his name. . ." When Pieter returned, Jakob would refer to his service medals and decorations, which included the Distinguished Service Order, as "foreign trash."

Pieter's volunteering for war service was later to play a large part in his tragic downfall. Since he had attained the rank of major in the army, he returned to the local police force as an officer. He therefore outranked Sergeant Steyn, who had longer service, but who, agreeing with Jakob's Afrikaner patriotism, had refused to take "the red oath." This is the source of the enmity that makes Sergeant Steyn the instrument of Pieter's destruction. Steyn is something of an Iago, but his hatred is not motiveless.

This general climate of nationalism lying behind the conflicts of *Too Late the Phalarope* is one of the elements that makes it an authentic portrait of an important segment of South African life. As he did in *Cry, the Beloved Country,* Paton adds to this general authenticity by weaving certain actual events of the time into the action of his plot. In his hands these actual events become dramatic properties inseparable from the action of the story.

One of these "properties" is the book that Lieutenant Pieter van Vlaanderen gives as a birthday gift to his father. The non-fictional model for this fictional book was *The Birds of South Africa*—a comprehensive work with fine color illustrations like the Audubon series in the United States, published in South Africa in 1948. For Paton, one of whose hobbies is birdwatching, this would have been a memorable event, made even more memorable by the fact that its author, the respected naturalist Austin Roberts, died that year. The title of this book pleases old Jakob van Vlaanderen, to whose intense nationalism the name South Africa borders on the sacred, but the name of the author repels him. He will not even mention it, and he always refers to the author as "the Englishman." Since Paton does not reveal the author's name, readers are left to assume that old Jakob's repugnance is a measure of his hostility to Englishmen in general. But there would be good reason for Jakob's special repugnance toward the name Roberts, for the British general whose armies invaded the Transvaal across the very terrain of the novel's setting, and who for a time during the Boer War virtually ruled South Africa, was General Lord Roberts.

It may be the touch of obscurity resulting from Paton's reluctance to extend to his readers a clearer motive for Jakob's repugnance that leads some to seek symbolic significance in the book of birds and, in particular, in the elusive little bird, the phalarope. The book of birds does affect the relations between Jakob and his son, but it is not a symbol in any exact sense. Neither is the phalarope a symbol. It is an actual bird about whose habits old Jakob, in fact, knew more than "the Englishman" who wrote the book. In *The Birds of South Africa,* Austin Roberts has some hesitation in classifying the phalarope as a South African bird, because he has only one recorded observation of each of the two species of phalarope, the "Grey" and the "Red-necked," on South African coasts. Jakob knew the phalarope as a fairly common inland bird also, and the Englishman's ignorance was a topic, therefore, that he was happy to discuss even with his son Pieter, with whom he had never before achieved rapport.

Another actual event of the period—or an account closely based on it—helps Paton to establish the atmosphere of obsession with racial purity in a society where the most unforgivable thing is to break "the iron law that no white man might touch a black woman"; and that the most terrible thing in the world is to have such a transgression discovered. This is the case of "the man Smith," modeled on an actual contemporary case of a white farmer who murdered an African servant girl who was pregnant by him. In the hope of preventing the discovery of his victim's identity, which might lead to his own discovery, "the man Smith," with his wife's complicity, cut off and hid the murdered girl's head. In Paton's account, this gruesome crime by an otherwise mild-mannered man is interpreted principally as a consequence of his fear that his illicit sexual relations across the racial line would be discovered.

This account of "the man Smith" provides a dramatic instance of the general air of intense concern with the issue of race-mixture that followed the Nationalist Party election victory of 1948. There was then a law in force against illicit sexual relations between white and non-white. This was Act 5 of 1927, under which Lieutenant Pieter van Vlaanderen is charged in the novel *Too Late the Phalarope.* In 1949 and 1950 there were further extensions of this basic law: the Prohibition of Mixed Marriages Act of 1949, and the Immorality Act Amendment Act of 1950. The basic law may at one time have had the merit claimed for it of protecting African women from the whims of white overlords, but the extensions of the basic Act reveal the essence of the new Nationalist ideal. By prohibiting interracial marriage even at a church ceremony, and by extending the Act to cover any racial mixing, as for example, between Indian and Cape Colored communities, the emphasis is clearly focused on the ideal of Pure Race, and not on justifiable protection of vulnerable women. One may find interesting corroboration of this attitude in textbooks widely used in Transvaal schools. In the chapter "Race Relations: White and non-White" in one junior high school textbook in social studies, there is a subheading "The Sin of Race Mixture" which argues that God wills separate races. This account culminates in a long quotation from someone identified only as "one of our great statesmen," that begins with what is tantamount to a summary of *Too Late the Phalarope:* "We must all keep our people white. Great is the pain for blood-relatives and friends if anyone sins against this highest law; greater still is the scandal when a people sins against its own blood."

It is in this context of an ideal of racial purity that classified race-mixture as the ultimate sin—the sin "against this highest law" as the textbook puts it—that Paton sets the tragedy of Pieter van Vlaanderen.

Finally, one should recall in this connection Paton's own account of the times in the Public Affairs pamphlet *South Africa Today.* This pamphlet, intended for American audiences unfamiliar with the complexities of race relations in South Africa, is a scrupulously fair appraisal of the trend of events in South Africa in 1951—a year or so before he set to work on *Too Late the Phalarope.* As a contemporary account, *South Africa Today* provides a very useful background to Paton's novels. It gives a brief historical sketch of the origins and development of South Africa's racial groups, and indicates the current status of each. Its account of "Modern Industry and Tribal Life" with a subsection on "Crime and Disintegration" gives, in small space, the social record dramatized in *Cry, the Beloved Country.* Its account of "The Immediate Situation," more relevant to *Too Late the Phalarope,* points out that racial separation was not a new concept introduced by the Nationalist Party.

What was new was the strengthening of the framework of laws requiring the compliance of all with the ideals of *apartheid.* At this early stage, much of this framework of laws was still only 'projected,' but among those already passed into law, Paton notes: "The present Government has amended and widened the Immorality Act of the Hertzog Government . . . It has passed a Mixed Marriages Act which now forbids marriages between whites and non-whites."

Paton makes one statement in *South Africa Today* about his own attitude to Afrikaner nationalism that has a significant bearing on the tone of *Too Late the Phalarope,* and of his other works, particularly the biography of Jan Hofmeyr. He concludes *South Africa Today* at the point where he feels he has written enough for his readers to grasp "the complexity and tragedy" of South Africa's situation, saying:

> This situation is more tragic for the Afrikaner Nationalist than for the English-speaking South African, for although both know no other home, this is true in a different sense of the Afrikaner. In this I feel for him painfully and deeply. That is why, for example, I never use hurtful language in giving any account of Nationalist policies. But the world will take no account of his fierce devotion . . . nor of my compassion.

It is this attitude, including its compassion, that Tante Sophie brings to *Too Late the Phalarope,* and to that extent her fictional character incorporates something of Paton himself.

Various characters in *Too Late the Phalarope* embody contrasting attitudes to this sin against the highest law. Some, representing a majority view in the town of Venterspan, uphold the law with iron determination. These include Pieter's father, old Jakob van Vlaanderen, and his father-in-law, who declares he would shoot the offender like a dog. The proponents of this kind of justice include also his fellow policeman, Sergeant Steyn, and the previously admiring young recruit, Vorster. Others view Pieter's transgression with greater compassion. But these are a minority, represented by his aunt, Tante Sophie; his mother; the English-speaking police officer, Captain Massingham; and the Jewish storekeeper, Matthew Kaplan, who is affectionately known by the Afrikaans diminutive, "Kappie." It is chiefly through the contrasting attitudes of old Jakob and Tante Sophie that we see the opposing themes of destruction and restoration brought into confrontation; and here the sacrificial justice demanded by the iron law outweighs the compassionate justice exhorted by Christ to his fol-lowers. Ironically, this victory of vengeance over compassion is exactly what the novel propounds as the greatest of all offenses from a Christian standpoint. Pieter's superior officer, Captain Massingham, sums this up when he says: "An offender must be punished, *mejuffrou,* I don't argue about that. But to punish and not to restore, that is the greatest of all offences." And Tante Sophie, significantly, responds, "Is that the sin against the Holy Ghost?"

These contrasting attitudes, pitting what amounts to the acceptance of inexorable fate against the impulse toward forgiveness and restoration, bear significantly on the status of *Too Late the Phalarope* as a tragedy in the literary sense. It may, therefore, be useful to look more closely at Jakob and Sophie, the two chief embodiments of these attitudes.

Jakob van Vlaanderen, as his name suggests, combines some of the qualities of an Old Testament patriarch with the Afrikaner's elemental Flemish roots. Enshrined in his Transvaal home is the great family Bible in the Dutch language version, containing the names of the van Vlaanderens for 150 years. His forebears had brought it with them from the Cape Colony when they trekked inland to set up their independent Boer republics beyond the reach of British laws and their equal application to white and black. Jakob van Vlaanderen was a strong-willed giant of a man who understood the word obedience "better than he understood the word love." He was an upright man, just in accordance with his own unwavering principles. He believed that his duty to God demanded that he uphold the separateness and racial purity of the Afrikaner people. As befitted his exclusive nationalism, he was a lover of all things South African, including the birds of the veld.

Jakob understood strength and determination in a man, but not sensitivity; he treated the sensitive side of his son's character—his pleasure in such fragile beautiful things as flowers and stamps—with harshness and suspicion. Eventually, prompted by his son's gift of a book of South African birds, he took hesitant steps toward reconciliation. He arranged to show Pieter the phalarope, the little wading bird about whose habits the author of the book was mistaken; and, although perplexed by the whole thing, he even purchased some expensive stamps for him.

This thaw in the iciness of his attitude toward his son adds great poignancy to the novel by suggesting what might have been; but it is not the fact

A South African village

that father and son recognized a common interest too late that supplies the essential element of tragedy. An essential element of tragedy, in addition to the flaw in the hero's character, is that the fate of those enmeshed in its web is determined, like that of King Oedipus, by a power outside their control. This external determining element is present in *Too Late the Phalarope* as a form of historical determinism attendant upon the fundamental assumption that the Afrikaner people are a Pure Race set apart. Therefore, when Jakob hears that his son has "sinned against the race," he knows exactly what his duty to the race demands of him: "So he took the pen and ink, and he crossed out the name of Pieter van Vlaanderen from the book. . ." Then, referring to Pieter's gift of the book of birds: "You will take the book, he said, and the pipe, and everything that the man ever gave to me, and every likeness of him, and everything in this house that has anything to do with him, and you will burn and destroy them all." This ritual of denial culminates in prayer to God for the destruction of his son's soul; for Jakob solemnly opened the family Bible and read "the most terrible words that man has ever written" from the Hundred and Ninth Psalm, beginning: *"When he shall be judged, let him be condemned; and let his prayer become sin."* And old Jakob read on, blind to the irony that "the most ter-

rible words" of the Psalm are explicitly directed against the man who *"who remembered not to show mercy."*

Old Jakob's actions are predictable. The reader, in fact, accepts them as the inevitable expression of his character. But they are ultimately dictated by an impersonal force outside himself rather than by a father's response to a son's transgression. For Old Jakob could not act otherwise and still maintain the purity of race as the highest law.

The contrasting qualities of mercy and compassion are embodied in Jakob's maiden sister, Tante Sophie van Vlaanderen, who relates Pieter's story. Sophie is a watcher set apart from normal family life and love by a severe facial disfigurement. She has lived all her life in Jakob's house, and she has lavished on her young nephew, Pieter, all the affection of her own unfulfilled maternal instincts. We therefore see both father and son from her sympathetic viewpoint. Her concern for these men, and indeed for all men, is deeply Christian; her Christianity, based on love, contrasts strikingly with Jakob's narrower, puritanical Christianity that respects obedience above all. As narrator, Sophie presents the other characters in all their human frailty; but she refrains from passing judgment on them. She is at pains, for example, to show the human side of Jakob: "For some said he was a hard and love-less man, and would ride down any that stood in his way without pity or mercy. But I tell you it was not true." Yet she is not a party to Jakob's extreme devotion to exclusive Afrikaner nationalism; she prefers to retain her allegiance to Louis Botha's policy of reconciliation.

Sophie has other advantages as a narrator besides her magnanimity of outlook. Having lived all her life with the van Vlaanderen family, she can link her knowledge of Pieter's childhood relations with his father to the events of his tragedy. She recognizes that his downfall is not brought about wholly by momentary temptation, but that it is a consequence of accumulated life experience. Her ability to reveal how past events foreshadowed destruction intensifies the element of tragic inevitability in the novel.

Although Sophie is an observer set aside, with little power over events, she is emotionally involved in the fortunes of Pieter and Jakob. This appears to be one of Paton's main motives in creating her. Speaking of the vitality of the South African novel in English, particularly in the hands of writers of English or Jewish extraction, or Colored writers like Peter Abrahams, Paton has remarked that in South Africa, where the racial struggle primarily pits African against Afrikaner: "It is the Englishman, the Jew and the Coloured man, who are, even when they are drawn into the struggle, the observers. It is they who are better placed than either Afrikaner or African . . . to see the real drama that history has unfolded, even when they are deeply or emotionally involved."

In *Too Late the Phalarope,* Tante Sophie fills an analogous role. She is presented to us as being clearly aware of her own powers of observation. She knows that she developed these powers because she was set apart from the ordinary stream of life by her disfigurement: "I have learned to know the meaning of unnoticed things, of a pulse that beats suddenly, of a glance that moves from here to there. . ." It was she who rightly suspected the marital difficulties between Pieter and his wife Nella; it was she who correctly interpreted Stephanie's sensual invitation to Pieter; it was she who felt uncomfortable about the flirtatious Cousin Anna, who wore the yellow trousers. Paton's device of the secret diary as one source of her information may be an arbitrary one, but it proves useful in establishing her reliability as an observer; for, at key points, she is able to quote from the diary to confirm her original intuition.

Whatever her technical limitations, one must admit that only a narrator of Tante Sophie's qualities of mind could provide a suitable vehicle for the religious theme of the novel: namely, that it is not the judgment of God but the judgment of men that is a stranger to compassion.

As has already been remarked, *Too Late the Phalarope* resembles *Cry, the Beloved Country* in certain aspects of its artistic method. It is similarly arranged in dramatic sequences depending largely on effective dialogue and the support of a modified chorus. Furthermore its plot has a similar double action. The plot of *Too Late the Phalarope* is divided almost exactly into two complementary movements. The first gradually unfolds the events leading to Pieter van Vlaanderen's temptation and sin; the second reveals him enmeshed in a web of tragedy and destruction. Chapters 1 through 19 may be said, therefore, to comprise The Book of Temptation; Chapters 20 through 39, The Book of Retribution. The two complementary actions of the plot imply an ironic contrast; namely, that even though Pieter's adultery transgresses the laws of God, it is not God, but an idol—the false deity of Pure Race—that exacts the terrible retribution of Pieter's destruction, and the destruction of all belonging to him.

It should perhaps be noted, too, that just as *Cry, the Beloved Country* superimposes a religious theme on a primary social one, *Too Late the Phalarope* superimposes a religious theme on a psychological one. Both novels may therefore be read on more than one level.

In what is here termed The Book of Temptation, Paton represents Pieter van Vlaanderen's temptation and sin as a consequence of several interrelated causes, no one of which is singled out as dominating him so completely that he cannot resist it. Ultimately, he deliberately chooses to seek out the black girl Stephanie; without this element of deliberate choice there would be no intentional offending against the laws of God, and therefore no sin in the Christian sense. The web of contributive causes includes elements that we may tentatively distinguish as psychological, spiritual, physical, and instinctive.

One psychological cause of Pieter's transgression is deeply rooted in the duality of his own nature. He is aware of two conflicting sides to his character: the one, brave and upright; the other possessed by an elemental urge attracting him, he says, to what he most hated. He conceals this side of his character behind a mask of cold reserve, and when this urge takes hold of him he calls it "the mad sickness." Evidently this "mad sickness" is a strong, but unwanted, sexual attraction to women outside his marriage. His comment on his father's simple, matter-of-fact statemen that he had never touched a woman other than his wife is: "I felt . . . a feeling of envy too, and wonder that I was otherwise." Since Pieter also envies those fellow students at the university who spoke of their physical revulsion to the touch of a non-white person—a revulsion he does not share—it seems clear that by "the mad sickness" he means a sexual desire forbidden by the iron law of his people "that no black woman should be touched by a white man."

The novel suggests that the psychological conflict in Pieter's character has roots in his childhood relations with his father. Pieter, referring to his father's anger at his interest in stamp collecting, says bitterly to Matthew Kaplan: "There was trouble long before the stamps . . . I was born before the stamps." In this respect Pieter's desire for Stephanie can be explained as a psychological impulse to revolt against all his father stood for. But Paton does not rationalize Pieter's action to the extent of lifting the burden of responsibility from his shoulders and transferring it to old Jakob. Pieter was conscious of his problem, and could have sought help. Indeed, his successive attempts to reveal himself to the young clergyman, Dominee Vos, to Kappie, and to Captain Massingham, constitute one link between the theme of temptation, which he can choose to resist, and the web of tragedy manipulated by forces outside his power. There is tragic irony in his successive failures to unburden himself; on each occasion that he attempts to do so, the regard in which others hold him—their worshipful attitude towards him as their hero—intervenes. Even though he had but one thought in his mind—"to tell one human soul of the misery of my life, that I was tempted by what I hated"—a fatal flaw prevents him from doing so; and he asks, but leaves unanswered, "Was it pride that prevented me?"

Another source of Pieter's psychological conflict is the tension between him and his wife Nella, arising from her attitude to married love. However, it would be more relevant to Paton's wider purpose, embracing the problem of love at several levels, to note the possibility of spiritual, in addition to psychological, roots for Nella's attitude. In her marriage, Sophie tells us, Nella had "some idea that was good and true but twisted in some small place, that the love of the body, though good and true, was apart from the love of the soul." In so describing

Nella, Paton seems to be pointing beyond such commonplace categories as prudery or Puritanism, to the classic Christian heresies of the Manicheans and the Gnostics. The extreme Manichean doctrine holds that man's body is the work of the Devil and that the soul is engaged in eternal war with it; it is akin to the Gnostic rejection of man's material nature in favor of an idealized abstraction comparable, for example, to the concept of Pure Race. Nella's attitude to married love may be, partly, a heritage from the religious Puritanism of her people; but her extreme revulsion at hearing that the boy Dick had attempted to accost the black girl, Stephanie, suggests that her other heritage, the ideal of Pure Race, is inextricably entwined with her religious outlook. Since Paton has elsewhere referred to the ideal of Pure Race as "a Christian heresy," Nella's attitude may well embody the view that the racial ideals enshrined in the theories of Pure Race constitute a modern Manichean or Gnostic outlook. The point need not be insisted upon, but it provides, like Book Three of *Cry, the Beloved Country,* another instance of Paton's distrust of abstract utopian, or totalitarian, schemes that substitute an inhuman perfection for the flesh and blood realities of the human condition.

If Nella's part in Pieter's susceptibility to temptation is remote, the part played by Anna is immediate and physical. Anna occupies Tante Sophie's thoughts to a surprising extent—wholly out of proportion to her two brief appearances in the novel. Anna, who is described as "a kind of cousin," works in the city and has acquired city attitudes towards fashions in dress and social drinking. She says openly that Pieter was the only man she ever wanted to marry. When Sophie reveals her dislike of those city women who wear trousers of various colors, she dwells on the point that "it is the yellow trousers that anger me most of all." Later, she tells us that Anna "smokes and wears the yellow trousers that I most dislike." Not really wicked, Anna is flashy, bored by the small town, and slightly vulgar. She is, ultimately, the temptress who, partly unwittingly, is the immediate instrument of Pieter's destruction. At the critical psychological moment when his black mood is deepest as a consequence of Nella's obtuse letter, Sergeant Steyn's mistake, and the high emotional temperature that caused him to write his letter of resignation, Anna waylays him with feminine wiles and the plea "I'm dying for a drink." So, in the Royal Hotel, they have brandy after brandy, "more than he had every drunk before." Aroused by the brandies, Anna's company, and her parting kiss, he goes to meet Stephanie in the vacant ground. Paton implies, nevertheless, that Pieter's choice is deliberate; for whatever forces the underlying psychological drives, the brandies, and Anna's company may have released, his final preparations for the encounter with Stephanie are calculated.

In contrast to Pieter's agonized struggles to avoid temptation, the black girl Stephanie has a simple, uncomplicated purpose for seeking him out. Her life in and out of prison, where she has been sent for brewing illicit liquor, is devoted to the single-minded aim of retaining her sole possesson—her illegitimate child. In her instinctive preoccupation with the safety of her child, she seizes on the only possibility she can think of for recruiting this great man's protection; it is for the same reason—to avert danger to her child—that she later carries out Sergeant Steyn's plan to destroy him.

The second movement of the plot of *Too Late the Phalarope,* The Book of Retribution, reaches beyond the interesting psychological and moral aspects of temptation toward the pity and terror of tragedy. The opening episodes of this second movement parallel those opening chapters of the first movement that establish the social atmosphere in which transgressing the prohibitions of the Immorality Act constitutes the most terrible thing in the world. In this case Paton skillfully intensifies the atmosphere, and involves the reader's emotions in the pity and terror that Aristotle identifies as the characteristic effect of tragedy. Pity draws out our sympathy for the tragic character so that we share in his dread of impending evil; terror, in Aristotle's view, is the powerful sense of the utter destructiveness of the impending evil.

First, however, we should note the simple ease with which Paton solves a literary problem that many critics have declared to be insurmountable: the problem of reconciling a Christian viewpoint with tragedy as a literary form. These critics argue on various grounds. One ground is that the Christian conception of free will cannot admit of determined, inescapable fate. Another is that Christianity can admit only one possible form of tragedy, namely, damnation. Paton undercuts the dilemma by building his tragedy, not on the consequences of Pieter van Vlaanderen's act understood as a sin against God (he leaves this as an inner, private matter), but on the consequences of his act understood as a "sin against the race."

Paton therefore disposes of the sin against God's law in a single paragraph, in which Pieter prays to God in Heaven, partly for forgiveness for

his act, and partly for forgiveness for presuming to pray at such a moment. This short paragraph closes with a striking metaphor for the theological assertion that sin cuts man off from God's love:

> For he had a vision that a trumpet had been blown in Heaven, and that the Lord Most High had ordered the closing of the doors, that no prayer might enter in from such a man, who knowing the laws and the Commandments, had, of his own choice and will, defied them.

From this point on, Paton's literary concern is not with Pieter's guilt, but with his terror of discovery. For even while Pieter was praying he heard a twig crack, and he suspected a watcher in the dark. Thereafter he prays repeatedly, not for forgiveness, but that he might not be discovered: "but now it was another mercy that he sought, not to be saved from sin but from its consequences." In the first movement of the plot we encountered "the man Smith" driven by the same terror to a desperate act. But whereas Smith's terror is merely implied, Paton builds up Pieter's mounting terror in great detail, and skillfully involves the reader. After an account of Pieter's ritual cleansing of himself in Chapter 20, Paton devotes four chapters to his three days of terror. Chapters 21 and 22 concern the first day of terror. Chapter 23 begins: "The second day of terror was as bad as the first. . ."; Chapter 24 begins: "And the third day of terror was the worst. . . ." The significance of these episodes goes beyond their immediate value as instruments of suspense; for only by demonstrating the intensity of the tragic character's terror of the impending evil, can Paton assure the reader that the tragic blow, when it comes, is tantamount to total annihilation.

But the blow does not fall on Pieter immediately, and for a time he feels assured that his prayers to avoid discovery have been answered. Therefore when the blow does fall, it comes suddenly and from an unexpected quarter. The events he interpreted as signs that his transgression had been discovered turn out to be mere coincidence or the shallow practical jokes of the welfare worker, Japie Grobler. Pieter's endurance of terror brings a full recognition that the consequences of his act, if discovered, will involve not only himself but Nella and his children and all who bore the name van Vlaanderen. There is hope that his determination to avoid bringing destruction on them will strengthen him against the desire for Stephanie.

These glimmerings of hope seem to point toward a new dawn when old Jakob arranges the family picnic where he and Pieter watch for the phalarope together. Their discovery of a shared interest opens a breach in the wall of hostility between them. If it was this hostility that nourished the psychological roots of Pieter's compulsion to rebel against the iron laws his father represents, the discovery of a common interest in the phalarope could imply that unconscious motivation would no longer drive Pieter into the arms of Stephanie.

But the growing inner determination, the picnic, and the phalarope come too late. Sergeant Steyn, like Iago in his enmity, takes a hint of suspicion for surety. He sets a trap for Pieter, and Stephanie, out of fear for the security of her child, carries out Steyn's purpose. She plants the evidence on Pieter and turns witness against him, and he is convicted and sentenced to prison for contravening the Immorality Act, No. 5 of 1927.

Pieter's destruction as a public man is more complete and enduring than his prison sentence. As he had once explained to young Dick: "It's a thing that's never forgiven, never forgotten. The court may give you a year, two years. But outside it's a sentence for life." In the society that made the iron laws there is no hope of public forgiveness or restoration. The characters representing the forces of arrogant pride in race treat the transgressor with supreme contempt. Therefore, in *Too Late the Phalarope,* as in *Cry, the Beloved Country,* the theme of restoration centers around the acceptance of personal responsibility by those who, while detesting the sin, continue to love the sinner and forgive him. These characters, representing the forces of love, try in their various ways to restore Pieter. His friend Kappie, the Jewish storekeeper, suffers mutely with him, but acts with courage to dissuade him from suicide. Captain Massingham is able to put the theme of restoration into words. It is he who recognizes that to destroy and not to restore is the greatest of all offenses, and it is his words that make Sophie understand that Pieter's future rests with Nella, the injured wife: "There is a hard law, *mejouffrou,* that when a deep injury is done to us we never recover until we forgive." The most meaningful forgiveness must come from Nella, for she is the person most wronged by Pieter's action.

As Sergeant Steyn's hatred was an agent of Pieter's destruction, his mother's love is the agent of the measure of restoration possible to him. Sophie attributes Nella's return to stand by Pieter during his trial to the agency of his mother's love: "the girl came back, silent but steadfast, borne on the strong deep river of the mother's love." The love personified by Pieter's mother contrasts with the intense self-concern underlying total devotion of others to pride in Pure Race. We learn little of her in the novel beyond Sophie's estimate that "if ever a woman was all love, it was she. . . ." Her unselfish love is set as a healing spring in the desert of destructive racial pride. Significantly, in her personal relations with people and her humanitarian concern for the welfare of others, she shares the characteristic unselfishness of Arthur Jarvis in *Cry, the Beloved Country.* Thus she provides another fictional parallel for the qualities of Edith Rheinallt Jones that Paton describes in "A Deep Experience." Sophie's final summing up suggests this when she says that Pieter's story would be better told by her sister: "And I wish she could have written it, for maybe of the power of her love that never sought itself, men would have turned to the holy task of pardon, that the body of the Lord might not be wounded twice, and virtue come of our offences."

Source: Edward Callan, "The Pride of Pure Race: *Too Late the Phalarope,*" in *Alan Paton,* Twayne, 1999.

Sources

Baker, Sheridan, "Paton's Late Phalarope," in *English Studies in Africa,* Vol. 3, No. 2, 1990, pp. 152–59.

Fuller, Edmund, "Alan Paton: Tragedy and Beyond," in *Books with Men Behind Them,* Random House, 1962, pp. 83–101.

Gardiner, Harold C., "Chapter Three: Alan Paton's Second Masterpiece," in *In All Conscience: Reflections on Books and Culture,* Hanover House, 1959, pp. 12–16.

Moss, Rose, "Alan Paton: Bringing a Sense of the Sacred," in *World Literature Today,* Vol. 57, No. 2, Spring 1983, pp. 233–37.

Petersen, Kirsten Holst, "Alan Paton: Overview," in *Reference Guide to English Literature,* St. James Press, 1991.

Rooney, F. Charles, "The 'Message' of Alan Paton," in *Catholic World,* Vol. 194, No. 1160, November 1961, pp. 92–98.

Stevens, Irma Ned, "Paton's Narrator Sophie: Justice and Mercy," in *International Review,* Vol. 8, No. 1, Winter 1981, pp. 68–70.

Watts, Nicholas H. Z., "A Study of Alan Paton's *Too Late the Phalarope,*" in *Durham University Journal,* Vol. 76, No. 2, June 1984, pp. 249–54.

For Further Study

Gordimer, Nadine, "Unconfessed History," in *New Republic,* Vol. 186, No. 12, March 24, 1982, pp. 35–37.
    South African Nobel Prize-winning author Gordimer discusses the voice in *Too Late the Phalarope* as it compares to the voice in Paton's later novel, *Ah, But Your Land Is Beautiful.*

Hooper, Myrtle, "Paton and the Silence of Stephanie," in *English Studies in Africa,* Vol. 32, No. 1, 1989, pp. 53–63.
  Hooper reviews the story of *Too Late the Phalarope* with special attention to the causes, purposes, and outcomes of Stephanie's silence.

Paton, Alan, *Journey Continued: An Autobiography,* Scribner, 1988.
  This is the second part of Paton's autobiography, completed just before his death in 1988.

———, *Towards the Mountain,* Scribner, 1980.
  This is the beginning of Paton's intriguing autobiography that describes the author's upbringing and political activism in his native South Africa.

Thompson, J. B., "Poetic Truth in *Too Late the Phalarope,*" in *English Studies in Africa,* Vol. 24, No. 1, 1981, pp. 37–44.
  Thompson examines the novel outside of its obvious historical scope in order to reveal the contemporary relevance and universal themes.

The World According to Garp

John Irving
1978

Although John Irving's first three novels were relatively well-received by the critics, he was basically unknown to the general public until *The World According to Garp* became an international bestseller when it was published in the United States in 1978. The novel features the memorably eccentric characters, outlandish situations, and moments both joyous and heartbreaking that so many readers cherish. It is the tragicomic life story of author T. S. Garp, son of the controversial feminist Jenny Fields. Garp's world is filled with "lunacy and sorrow." His mother is a radically independent nurse who conceives him by taking advantage of a brain-damaged soldier. His best friend is a transsexual who was formerly a tight end for the Philadelphia Eagles. Garp struggles vainly to protect the people he loves. His life is both hilarious and ultimately tragic.

Irving's novel was especially popular on college campuses across the nation because of its youthful energy, and the novelist was applauded for creating realistic and strong female characters. *Garp* is an intricately plotted novel, and its themes are universal: love, sex, death, art, gender roles. The book shares many of the characteristics of Irving novels published before and after it. For example, in several Irving novels, children grow up without one or more parents, as in *The Hotel New Hampshire* (1981) and *The Cider House Rules* (1985). *Garp* is also influenced by Irving's experiences in Austria in the 1960s, as are *Setting Free the Bears* (1968) and *The 158-Pound Marriage* (1974).

John Irving

For the most part, critics gave the novel excellent reviews. Millions continue to read Irving's books, and thus he remains one of the most popular and successful American writers of the last twenty-five years.

Author Biography

John Irving was born in Exeter, New Hampshire, on March 2, 1942. Although Irving has said that *The World According to Garp* is not autobiographical, there are many similarities between the novelist and the title character. Irving, like Garp, has never met his biological father. (However, Irving's mother gave him some letters his father had written during World War II and he used his father's experiences for a character in *The Cider House Rules*. "Being a novelist," Irving once said, "is never throwing anything away.") Irving also grew up at a prep school, Exeter Academy, where his stepfather taught Russian history. He eventually attended the school himself and there acquired his lifelong interests of wrestling and writing. He was an average student, but he later discovered that one of the reasons he struggled was because he was dyslexic.

Irving was disenchanted during his brief time as a student at both the University of Pittsburgh (1961) and the University of New Hampshire (1962). He traveled to Austria in 1963 to attend the University of Vienna and the decision profoundly affected him. He lived in Vienna off and on through much of the 1960s, and the city's influence is seen in his fiction. He also married painter Shyla Leary while he was in Austria. He became the father to two boys, Colin and Brendan. He earned his M. F. A. at the University of Iowa Writers Workshop in 1967 where Kurt Vonnegut, Jr. was one of his mentors. In 1969, he stayed with director Irvin Kershner in a castle built by Charlemagne while they vainly worked on an unproduced screen adaptation of Irving's first novel, *Setting Free the Bears* (1969). His next two novels, *The Water-Method Man* (1972) and *The 158-Pound Marriage* (1974) didn't share his first book's modest success. During this period, Irving was awarded a Rockefeller Foundation grant (1971–1972), a National Endowment for the Arts fellowship (1974–75), and a Guggenheim fellowship (1976–77).

The publication of his fourth novel, *The World According to Garp,* changed everything for him. Irving left publishing giant Random House for E. P. Dutton because he was unsatisfied with the publicity for his second and third novels. *Garp* was a huge critical and popular success. The novel was nominated for a National Book Award in 1979 and won an American Book Award in 1980. The book was made into a moderately received film version starring Robin Williams as Garp.

All of Irving's novels since Garp have been critically acclaimed bestsellers, including *The Hotel New Hampshire* (1981), *The Cider House Rules* (1985), *A Prayer For Owen Meany* (1989), *Son of the Circus* (1994), and *A Widow For One Year* (1998). Irving has been both an English professor and wrestling coach through the years. A collection of his fiction and some essays, *Trying to Save Peggy Sneed,* was published in 1996. Two volumes of his memoirs, *The Imaginary Girlfriend* (1996) and *My Movie Business* (1999), have also been published. Since *The World According to Garp* was adapted to film in 1982, film versions of two of his other novels have been made: *The Hotel New Hampshire* in 1984 and *The Cider House Rules* in 1999. Irving won the Academy Award for Best Adapted Screenplay for *The Cider House Rules* (Michael Caine won the Best Supporting Actor award for his portrayal of Dr. Larch). Irving divorced his first wife in 1981. He remarried in 1987 his Canadian agent, Janet Turnbull. He currently lives with Turnbull and their son, Everett, in southern Vermont.

Plot Summary

Garp's Conception, Birth, and Childhood

Irving's novel opens in Boston, 1942, with the introduction of T. S. Garp's mother, Jenny Fields. Jenny is an independent woman ahead of the times. She quits college to become a nurse when she decides that higher education for women is meant to groom them for marriage. Jenny has little tolerance for the behavior of men, as demonstrated by the incident that opens the book. A soldier in a movie theater attempts to fondle Jenny. She uses a scalpel she carries in her purse to slice his arm from shoulder to wrist. She is perturbed when the authorities, as well as her own brothers, suggest that she has some kind of relationship with the man. She is released when it is discovered that the man has a wife and child in New York. The incident, along with the treatment she receives from her wealthy family, reinforces her beliefs about men, women, and relationships:

> In this dirty-minded world, she thought, you are either somebody's wife or somebody's whore—or fast on your way to becoming one or the other. If you don't fit either category, then everyone tries to make you think there is something wrong with you. But, she thought, there is nothing wrong with me.

Thus, Jenny becomes something of a maverick for the time: A single, working woman, living alone, with no use for men. However, while working in the obstetrics ward at Boston Mercy, she comes to realize that, although she doesn't care for men, she *does* like babies. Jenny informs the other nurses that she intends to find a man to make her pregnant, "just that, and nothing more." The hospital administration moves her to the intensive care unit in an effort to discourage her. Instead, she finds the answer to her dilemma in the form of Technical Sergeant Garp, a soldier whose wounds have severely damaged his brain. T. S. Garp can still function sexually, however, and Jenny takes advantage of this. Garp eventually ends up dying from his wounds, but Jenny becomes pregnant. After she loses her job, she moves in with her parents until the baby, a nine-pound boy, is born; she names the boy T. S. Garp (she never learned the soldier's first name).

Jenny takes a job as a nurse at Steering School, a private school for boys. The young Garp enjoys his life growing up at Steering. The hospital becomes his home, and he has a near-death experience at the age of five when he attempts to capture pigeons on the roof with a lacrosse stick. He becomes friends with the numerous children of the Percy family although Stewart and Midge Percy (heirs to the Steering fortune) look down their noses at Jenny and Garp. Jenny, of course, is unafraid to show her disdain for them. She becomes especially contemptuous of the Percys when their dog, Bonkers, bites off a large chunk of Garp's ear, and Stewart refuses to put the dog to sleep. Garp survives his childhood and eventually attends Steering himself.

Garp's Adolescence

With his mother's help, Garp becomes a competent student. He has difficulty, however, choosing a sport. He dislikes any of the sports using balls. One day while Garp is sick in bed, Jenny visits the gymnasium where she meets Ernie Holm, the wrestling coach, and his daughter Helen. Helen's mother was a nurse who abandoned the family when Helen was a small child. Helen mistakenly identifies Jenny as her mother, embraces her, and is embarrassed when she learns the truth. Jenny signs Garp up for wrestling. Garp is at first hesitant, but then discovers that he loves the sport. He also becomes interested in Helen. After Helen tells him that she plans to marry a writer ("a *real* writer"), Garp is determined to become an author.

Garp writes a short story every month from the end of his freshman year in high school until graduation. Mr. Tinch, Garp's English teacher, encourages him. Garp shows Helen his first story during his junior year. She is kind in a letter she writes to him reviewing the story, but she is nonetheless unimpressed. Garp becomes a champion wrestler in his senior year. He and his mother decide to travel to Austria to write after he graduates. Garp has his first sexual encounters with Cushie Percy. On his graduation night, Cushie sneaks out of her house to meet Garp. They are confronted by the old, but still vicious, dog Bonkers. The dog lunges; Garp pins the dog down and bites off its ear, thus avenging himself.

It is 1961 when Garp and Jenny arrive in Vienna. Jenny begins to write her autobiography; Garp has less success with his short story. He spends the beginning of his stay in Vienna wandering through the city. Garp and his mother discuss the nature of lust. Jenny cannot understand it;

the eighteen-year-old Garp is of course overwhelmed by it. They run into some prostitutes while on a walk one day and Jenny pays one of them, a woman who calls herself Charlotte, to sit and chat. Garp becomes one of Charlotte's regular customers. After cancer kills Charlotte, he discovers that she was old enough to be his mother. He eventually finds enough inspiration to begin his first serious short story: "The Pension Grillparzer." Helen reads the finished story and knows that Garp is truly a writer. She agrees to marry him. Jenny sends her manuscript to a brilliant editor, John Wolf, and he publishes her autobiography. Wolf becomes Garp's editor as well.

Garp's Adult Life

Jenny becomes a famous and controversial figure when her autobiography, *A Sexual Suspect,* is published. After her parents die, she uses their New Hampshire mansion as a women's counseling center. Garp is mystified by her success, and he dislikes some of the people that begin to associate with Jenny. He especially detests a group of woman known as the Ellen Jamesians. Named after a young girl who was beaten, raped, and horribly mutilated, the women surgically remove their own tongues as a protest against the awful treatment women sometimes receive from men. Jenny supports Garp and Helen as they begin their lives together. The young couple have their first child, a boy they name Duncan. Helen teaches at a university as Garp writes his first novel. *Procrastination,* a historical novel about Vienna during World War II, is published when Garp is twenty-four. Garp captures a child molester in the city park. He later feels like a child molester himself when he has a brief affair with one of Helen's students who baby-sits for Duncan.

Walt, Garp and Helen's second child, is born. They become friends with another young couple, Harrison and Alice Fletcher. The Fletchers are a mirror image of the Garps: Harrison is a teacher, and Alice is a writer. One night, Alice tearfully informs Garp that Harrison is having an affair. The betrayal prevents her from writing. Helen (who discovers Garp's previous indiscretions) proposes an unusual solution to the problem. She determines that if she were to have an affair with Harrison while Garp has an affair with Alice, the Fletchers marriage can be saved. Of course, this only makes matters worse: Harrison falls in love with Helen while Alice and Garp fall in love. Helen ends the relationships after six months, and the Fletchers move away because of Harrison's affair with a student. Garp uses the experience as inspiration for his

second novel, *Second Wind of the Cuckold.* The novel is an abysmal failure, and Garp finds himself unable to write. Meanwhile, he is surprised when he is able to befriend one of the people in his mother's entourage. Roberta Muldoon is a transsexual and former professional football player. She and Garp become very close friends.

Garp occupies himself with raising the family while he has writer's block. He has an odd encounter with the mother of Duncan's friend, Ralph. He chases down speeders and lectures them about the dangers of their behavior. He writes an essay about this practice in an effort to shake off his writer's block, but Helen is unimpressed by it. She begins to tire of Garp's irritable behavior and decides to have an affair with Michael Milton, one of her graduate students. One of Milton's ex-girlfriends reveals the affair to Garp. He is furious, and he demands that Helen end it immediately. Helen, who is still in love with Garp, agrees. Garp takes the children out so that Helen can call Milton and let him know that the relationship is over. Milton comes to the house to see Helen one last time. They are sitting in Milton's car parked in the driveway when Garp pulls up without his headlights on. In the car crash, Walt dies, and the rest of them are terribly injured.

Jenny nurses the physically wounded and heartbroken family back to health at the mansion at Dog Head's Harbor. As they heal, Garp and Helen decide to have another child, and they have a daughter named Jenny. Garp writes a lurid and tragic novel, *The World According to Bensenhaver,* to help him cope with the overwhelming sadness stemming from the loss of Walt. John Wolf can't believe that Garp expects him to publish it. However, Wolf gives the novel to the woman who cleans his office. Her opinion has proven to be valuable to Wolf in the past. Although she doesn't actually like Garp's novel, she is unable to put it down. Wolf decides to publish the novel, and he advises the Garps to leave the country to avoid the inevitable controversy. The book becomes a bestseller. Jenny gets involved in New Hampshire politics while the Garps are in Austria. She is assassinated during a political rally, forcing Garp's family to return home from Europe.

When the family arrives back in the United States, they stay at Steering. Funeral arrangements have already been made before Garp's arrival by his mother's followers, and no men are to be allowed. Garp dresses up like a woman to attend, but he is forced to flee when he is recognized by Pooh

Percy. He meets the actual Ellen James on his flight home and invites her to join his family. Ellen admires Garp and wants to become a writer as well. Upon his return to Steering, Garp discovers that Ernie Holm had a heart attack and has died. Garp becomes the new wrestling coach when he and Helen decide to raise their children at Steering. Roberta convinces Garp to use part of Jenny's estate to establish the Fields Foundation to help women in need. Ellen James writes an essay entitled "Why I Am Not An Ellen Jamesian" and Garp encourages her to publish it. After it is published, Garp publicly defends Ellen. Garp survives an assassination attempt by an Ellen Jamesian. He begins to write *My Father's Illusions*. Before he can finish, he is shot to death by Pooh Percy (now an Ellen Jamesian) inside the Steering gymnasium in front of Helen and his wrestling team. An epilogue summarizes what happens in the lives of the other characters after Garp's death.

Characters

Arden Bensenhaver

Arden Bensenhaver is the titular character in Garp's third novel, *The World According to Bensenhaver*. Bensenhaver is a police detective who works on the rape case of Hope Standish. His own wife was raped and murdered years earlier. Bensenhaver has no mercy for rapists, and he tampers with contradictory evidence in an effort to ensure that Hope's rape is seen exactly for what it is. Bensenhaver is forced to retire from the police force for his unorthodox methods, and Dorsey Standish, Hope's paranoid husband, hires the ex-detective as a bodyguard for his family. Hope forces her husband to make Bensenhaver leave their home after she tires of the bodyguard's intrusion on their family's life. Bensenhaver later has a stroke and returns to the Standish home. He mistakes Dorsey Standish for an intruder one night and shoots him. He lives the remainder of his life in an old-age home for the criminally insane.

Dean Bodger

Bodger is the gruff but caring dean of Steering School, an exclusive prep school for boys. He is one of the few people to befriend Jenny Fields, the school nurse, as she raises Garp at the school's infirmary. He drives around the school grounds at night, with a spotlight attached to his car, looking for students out past curfew. Garp attempts to cap-

ture pigeons on the infirmary roof one night and becomes dangerously trapped in a rusty gutter. Bodger shines his spotlight on the boy, startling the pigeons. The gutter breaks apart, but fortunately Jenny is there to catch the boy. One of the pigeons strikes Bodger in the chest and knocks the wind out of him. He regains consciousness thinking that he caught the falling Garp. He spends the rest of his life thinking that he has saved Garp's life. Later, he hires Garp to be the wrestling coach at Steering after Ernie Holm dies. Bodger remains dean long enough after Garp's death to see Duncan graduate from Steering. After his retirement, Bodger dies during a wrestling match.

Bonkers

Bonkers is the large, vicious Newfoundland dog owned by the Percy family. Jenny wants the dog put to sleep when it bites off a piece of Garp's ear, but Midge and Stewart Percy refuse to do it. Garp gets his revenge many years later on the night of his graduation as he is sneaking Cushie away from the Steering mansion. When Bonkers lunges at him, Garp uses a wrestling move to throw the old dog down and bites part of the animal's ear off.

Bonkie

See Bonkers

Florence Cochran Bowlsby

Florence Cochran Bowlsby is the seductive, divorced mother of Duncan's friend Ralph. Garp refers to her as "Mrs. Ralph" because he never learns her name. Garp's first close encounter with Florence occurs when he chases her down for speeding. Garp, although he is somewhat attracted to her, doesn't approve of her behavior. Florence recognizes this, and she assures him that Duncan, who is spending the night at her house, will be safe. Later that evening, the restless Garp decides to run by the woman's house to make sure that Duncan is secure. He finds the woman drunk and depressed; she asks him to make the young man in her bedroom leave. Garp forces the young man to leave. Florence then tries to seduce Garp, but Garp controls himself. He realizes that he has misjudged her before he leaves with Duncan. Florence ultimately obtains a Ph.D. in comparative literature. She corresponds with Helen after Garp's death, writing in a letter that "[Garp's] seduction [was a] non-occurrence I have always regretted but respected."

Media Adaptations

- *The World According to Garp* was adapted as a film written by Steve Tesich, directed by George Roy Hill, starring Robin Williams and Glenn Close, with music by David Shire, for Warner Brothers in 1982; it is available on Warner Brothers home video.

- An unabridged audio-book version of *The World according to Garp,* narrated by Michael Prichard, was released by Random House Audiobooks in 1998.

Charlotte

Charlotte is one of the prostitutes that Garp and Jenny meet in Vienna. Jenny pays the beautiful, older prostitute to sit with them and answer Jenny's questions about lust. Garp finds himself attracted to her and he eventually becomes one of her regular customers, as well as her friend. One evening, Garp cannot find her, and he discovers that she is sick in the hospital with cancer. He visits her often, telling the nurses that he is her son. Charlotte's death disturbs him. He later finds out that Charlotte has paid Tina and Wanga, two other prostitutes, to each give him a session for free.

Dickie

Dickie is the brother of Harriet Truckenmiller, the wife of Jenny's assassin. He is one of several men who were forced to shoot Kenny Truckenmiller after he murdered Jenny. He is very protective of his sister when Garp visits her incognito.

The Dream-Teller

The dream-teller is one of the members of the Circus Szolnok in Garp's short story, "The Pension Grillparzer." He was married to Herr Theobald's sister at one time. He accurately tells the disturbing dream of Johanna, the grandmother of the traveling family in the story. She is so upset that she slaps him. The dream-teller is institutionalized years later when he goes mad. His removal from the pension coincides with its return to a Class C rating.

Duna

Duna is the old, unicycle-riding bear in Garp's short story, "The Pension Grillparzer." He is owned by the sister of Herr Theobald, the pension's manager. Duna is part of a pathetic Hungarian circus troupe living at the Pension Grillparzer. The bear becomes senile and is forced to move into a zoo. He dies at the zoo, "embarrassed to death" when zoo officials must shave his chest to treat a rash.

Fat Stew

See Stewart Percy

Father

The father is one of the characters in Garp's short story, "The Pension Grillparzer." His job is to rate various hotels, restaurants, and pensions for the Austrian Tourist Bureau. He is a decent man who brings his family along on his travels. He constantly makes mental notes about the establishments he examines. His assignment in the story is to investigate the Pension Grillparzer's application to be upgraded from a Class C rating to a Class B. Despite his family's odd experience at the pension, he very kindly upgrades the rating.

Jenny Fields

Jenny Fields is the eccentric mother of Garp. She is a strong, independent woman who, as a young nurse in Boston during World War II, is ahead of her time. She lives alone, much to her family's chagrin. They believe that she must be leading a promiscuous lifestyle. Of course, nothing could be further from the truth; Jenny has no interest in sharing either her body or her life with a man. She is basically asexual, and perhaps somewhat aloof, but she is not without warmth or passion. In fact, she discovers that she loves children as she works in the obstetrics ward of Boston Mercy Hospital. She informs her colleagues that she is determined to use a man to impregnate her, no strings attached. The administration of the hospital learns of her plans and she is transferred to the intensive care unit. It is in the ICU that she is actually able to fulfill her wishes as she cares for the brain-damaged Technical Sergeant Garp. She uses the helpless, yet aroused, soldier to impregnate herself.

After Jenny gives birth to Garp, she gets a job as a nurse at the Steering School, an exclusive prep school for boys. Garp later notes that: "It's odd . . .

that my mother, who perceived herself well enough to know that she wanted nothing to do with living with a man, ended up living with eight hundred boys." Jenny raises Garp at the infirmary and cares for him through the various traumatic incidents of his childhood. She watches as Garp becomes a champion wrestler, falls in love with his coach's daughter, and nurtures his talent as a writer. She travels with him to Austria, where both plan to write. She is perturbed by the nature of lust, and her opinions on the subject play a large role in her autobiography, *A Sexual Suspect.*

The publication of Jenny's book makes her a celebrity and a feminist champion. She also becomes wealthy and is able to support Garp and Helen, who have married, as they pursue their respective careers. She attracts a wide variety of followers, including the Ellen Jamesians and transsexual Roberta Muldoon. She opens her family's mansion at Dog's Head Harbor as a retreat for troubled women. After the accident that kills Walt Garp and maims the rest of the family, Jenny nurses them back to health at Dog's Head Harbor. Helen and Garp have a daughter they name after Jenny. Garp writes *The World According to Bensenhaver* during his recovery and John Wolf, his editor, recommends that he leave the country before the book's release to avoid the publicity. Jenny becomes involved with the New Hampshire gubernatorial campaign while Garp and his family are out of the country. She supports a female candidate who is being demonized by her male rival. Jenny is assassinated when she appears to speak at a rally in support of the woman. Garp, as executor of Jenny's estate, agrees to establish the Fields Foundation. The foundation continues Jenny's work helping women in need.

Alice Fletcher

Alice Fletcher is the wife of Professor Harrison Fletcher. She is a frustrated writer with a speech impediment. She and Garp fall in love when Helen agrees to a swap of partners in an ill-conceived attempt to teach Harrison not to have affairs with students. Alice is heartbroken when Helen ends the swap after six months. Alice and Harrison are forced to move away because the university learns of his affair with the student. Alice later has a daughter who becomes a cello player. The daughter goes on a date with Duncan after a New York City performance. Alice and Harrison end up dying in a plane crash on a trip to Martinique.

Harrison Fletcher

Harrison Fletcher is a colleague of Helen Holm. The professor is married to a lisping writer named Alice. The Garps and the Fletchers become friends. Garp discovers that Alice cannot write because of Harrison's love affair with one of his students. When Helen finds out, she proposes that the couples swap partners in an effort to make Harrison forget his dalliance with the student. The swap is a disaster; Alice and Garp fall in love, and Harrison falls in love with Helen. Helen breaks the affair off when she realizes it is useless. Harrison is forced to take a job at another college when the university denies him tenure because of his affair with the student. He and Alice later die in a plane crash on the way to Martinique.

Duncan Garp

Duncan is the first son of Garp and Helen. Garp assumes the traditionally female role of primary caretaker in bringing up both Duncan and Walt. This allows him to write as Helen teaches. Garp is an extremely protective father, and both of the boys grow up in relative safety and comfort until the horrible car accident that kills Walt and maims Duncan. Duncan loses his right eye when his head is impaled on the knobless stick shift of Garp's Volvo. Duncan recovers at Dog's Head Harbor, and his artistic talents emerge when he begins to study photography. He illustrates a version of "The Pension Grillparzer." Duncan attends Steering School after Garp's death. He becomes a close friend to Roberta Muldoon and Ellen James, and he helps raise his younger sister, Jenny. He also becomes an accomplished painter and photographer. He survives a motorcycle accident, but loses one of his arms. After Roberta's death, he marries one of the former football player's transsexual friends. He helps Donald Whitcomb publish Garp's unfinished novel, *My Father's Illusions.* He lives a long life before choking to death on an olive as he laughs at one of his own jokes.

Jenny Garp

Jenny Garp is born after the death of Walt. She is named after her grandmother, Jenny Fields. She is a toddler when Garp is assassinated. She is brought up by Helen, Duncan, and Ellen James. While caring for Duncan during his recovery from a motorcycle accident, she decides to become a doctor. Jenny is married, twice, and gives birth to three children. She becomes a director of a branch of the National Cancer Institute. She orders copies of Garp's novels in stores across America in order to keep his books in print. After a long life, she dies of cancer.

T. S. Garp

The World According to Garp is the life story of T. S. Garp, bastard son of proto-feminist nurse Jenny Fields. Garp is reared by his loving, dangerously straightforward, and independent mother at an exclusive prep academy for boys, the Steering School. Jenny is a nurse at the school, and she lives with Garp in the school's infirmary. Garp is eventually old enough to attend the school and he becomes a champion wrestler. He falls in love with his wrestling coach's daughter, Helen Holm, and he works to become a writer to win her heart. After he graduates, he travels to Europe (joined by his mother) for inspiration. He writes his first serious short story, "The Pension Grillparzer," while living in Vienna. The story convinces Helen that he is a true writer and they marry. Meanwhile, to Garp's horror, Jenny's autobiography turns her into a celebrity.

Garp writes and cares for the children while Helen teaches at a university. The novel details Garp's many struggles with his art. He is forced to deal with a nonexistent audience for his work, irate readers, and writer's block. Garp and Helen love each other dearly, but their marriage is forced to survive many trials. First, they make an odd attempt to save another couple's marriage by swapping partners. Garp has affairs with babysitters and Helen takes a graduate student as a lover. Finally, their marriage faces the ultimate test when a tragic car accident kills one child and permanently disfigures another. They spend months physically and mentally healing at Garp's mother's home at Dog's Head Harbor. Garp and Helen finally forgive each other, and Garp purges the horror of the accident by writing *The World According to Bensenhaver,* a disturbing and violent novel.

Garp is often at odds with his mother throughout his life. He is irritated by her attitude toward lust and he dislikes many of the oddballs she attracts (with the exception of Roberta Muldoon, who becomes a good friend). However, in many ways, Garp is much like his mother. He shares her love for children; he is a good nurturer. He is also stubborn and fearlessly opinionated. It is these latter traits that doom both mother and son. Garp is murdered not long after his mother is assassinated. Perhaps the most succinct analysis of Garp's character is made at the beginning of chapter 11:

If Garp could have been granted one vast and naïve wish, it would have been that he could make the world *safe*. For children and for grownups. The world struck Garp as unnecessarily perilous for both.

Technical Sergeant Garp

Technical Sergeant Garp is the brain-damaged, ball-turret gunner that Jenny discovers in the ICU of Boston Mercy. A severe head wound causes the soldier to regress to infancy. Jenny nurses the man as the debilitating injury slowly but surely kills him. Although the man has the mind of an infant, Jenny realizes that he is potent enough for her to realize her dream of pregnancy and she uses him successfully. The soldier dies a short time later; Jenny never learns his first name.

Walt Garp

Walt is the second son of Helen and Garp. He dies tragically in the car accident that maims the rest of his family. Later in the book, the family discusses the origin of its code for an indefinable feeling of fear just beneath the surface of everyday life: the Under Toad. One day while swimming, Walt misunderstood his father's instructions to "watch out for the undertow" as "watch out for the Under Toad." Walt mistakenly believed that a creature lived in the water waiting to pull unwary swimmers underneath. In an afterword written twenty years after the original publication of *The World According Garp,* Irving admits that the idea of the Under Toad came from one of his own children.

Hathaway

Hathaway is the lacrosse player laid up in the Steering School infirmary with two broken legs when young Garp disappears. Hathaway tells the impressionable, five-year-old Garp that a lacrosse stick might be used to capture the noisy pigeons living on the roof. Garp almost falls off the roof when he steals Hathaway's stick in an attempt to catch the pigeons.

Herr Theobald's Sister

Herr Theobald's sister is the owner of Duna the bear in Garp's short story, "The Pension Grillparzer." She has, at one time or another, been married to each of the members of the Circus Szolnok. Her brother allows the circus to stay at his pension. She is forced to give Duna to the zoo after the bear grows senile. She is the only one left when the narrator of the story returns years later to visit the pension.

Ernie Holm

Ernie Holm is the wrestling coach at Steering and the father of Helen. Originally from Iowa, Ernie goes to New Hampshire to coach after his wife leaves him and abandons Helen. He turns the Steering wrestling team into state champions, and Garp becomes one of his star wrestlers. Ernie becomes friends with Jenny Fields after she signs Garp up for the team. He dies of a heart attack while reading pornography shortly after Jenny's assassination.

Helen Holm

Helen is the daughter of Steering School wrestling coach, Ernie Holm. Helen's father brought her to New Hampshire from Iowa after her mother abandoned them. Helen is a bright, studious girl who is always reading. Helen tells Garp she will only marry a real writer, and the lovesick Garp is determined to become one. He demonstrates his ability after he graduates from Steering and travels to Vienna to write "The Pension Grillparzer." For Garp, Helen is the quintessential audience, the ultimate reader. She agrees to marry him.

Their marriage triumphs over great adversity. Helen, usually sensible, makes a poor decision when she decides that swapping partners would be the best way to save the Fletchers' marriage. Helen, weary of Garp's egocentrism, takes a graduate student as a lover. This leads indirectly to the horrible car accident that kills Walt and maims Duncan. However, Helen and Garp are able to forgive each other while mourning, and they have another child. She cannot bring herself to read *The World According to Bensenhaver*, because she knows that Garp has used the writing of the lurid novel as a catharsis for the loss of Walt. Helen is incapable of restraining Garp from becoming a public figure after he publishes the novel and his mother is assassinated. Garp publishes a defense of an essay written by Ellen James against Helen's wishes. After Garp is murdered, Helen protects his memory by jealously guarding his journals and unpublished work. Donald Whitcomb, the young Steering English teacher who worships Garp, is the only outsider who is granted access to Garp's papers. Helen remains close to Roberta Muldoon and John Wolf. She lives a long life, and while there are other men, none can compete with the memory of Garp.

The Hungarian Singer

The Hungarian singer is one of the characters in Garp's short story, "The Pension Grillparzer." He is a member of the sad circus troupe living in the pension. He was once married to Herr Theobald's sister. He runs off with another woman at the end of the story.

Ellen James

Ellen James is the namesake of the radical feminist group known as the Ellen Jamesians. As a young girl, Ellen was beaten and raped by a group of thugs; her tongue was sliced off in an effort to prevent her from identifying them, but they neglected the young girl's ability to write. The members of the Ellen Jamesians purposely remove their own tongues as both a show of "support" for Ellen and a protest against the mistreatment of women by men. The Ellen Jamesians are major supporters of Jenny Fields, but Garp despises them. Garp meets the actual Ellen James as he returns from his mother's funeral. She resents the Ellen Jamesians as well. She admires Garp and hopes to one day be a writer as well. Garp invites her to join his family at Steering. Ellen writes an essay rejecting the Ellen Jamesians and Garp encourages her to publish it. Garp's defense of this essay leads to increased hostility between him and the Jamesians and, ultimately, to his assassination. Ellen stays with the Garp family after the novelist's death. She becomes a respected poet, and Roberta Muldoon often reads her work in public for her. She becomes an accomplished swimmer as well, but she drowns one day when the undertow is too strong.

Jenny's Brothers

Jenny's two unnamed brothers (one a law student, the other a legal professor) come to her rescue when she is arrested for stabbing a soldier who gropes her in a movie theater. They, like their parents, misunderstand Jenny. They mistake her independence for promiscuity. One of the brothers dies during World War II, and the other is killed in a sailboating accident.

Jenny's Father

Jenny's father is the wealthy owner of a shoe manufacturing company. Her father, like the rest of the family, doesn't understand her independence. He believes that Jenny is promiscuous, and Jenny's pregnancy convinces him that he was right. He allows her to live at the family's home while her pregnancy comes to term. He is disappointed when she takes a job at Steering School because he would rather she stay in hiding at Dog's Head Harbor until her bastard son grows up and moves away.

Jenny's Mother

Jenny's mother disapproves of Jenny's solitary lifestyle. Again, like the rest of the family, she believes that Jenny is promiscuous. She gives the young nurse dozens of what Jenny believes are water bottles. Later, Jenny discovers that her mother was really giving her dozens of douche bags.

Johanna

Johanna is the grandmother who travels with the family in Garp's short story, "The Pension Grillparzer." The father in the family works for the Austrian Tourist Bureau. He travels to critique the various hotels, restaurants, and pensions around the country. Johanna is described as a "regal dame" with little patience for some of the lower-class places the family is forced to stay. She is shaken and disturbed when a "dream-teller" at the Pension Grillparzer relates her mysterious dream to the family at dinner. The family leaves the circus-like atmosphere of the pension with the upset Johanna after only one night. Johanna dies in her sleep some time later.

The Man Who Could Walk Only on His Hands

The man who could walk only on his hands is one of the circus characters in Garp's short story, "The Pension Grillparzer." He can walk only on his hands because the Russians supposedly removed his shin bones. As with all the other (human) members of the Circus Szolnok, the man was at one time married to Herr Theobald's sister. He is killed when his necktie gets caught in an escalator.

Michael Milton

Michael Milton is the unlikable, arrogant graduate student taken as a lover by Helen. Milton is a pompous Francophile. He stubbornly refuses to accept Helen's break-up phone call as their final meeting and insists on going to her house while Garp takes the boys to the movies. He is horribly mutilated in the ensuing accident in Garp's driveway. Years later, he visits Duncan Garp, posing as a biographer and asking questions about the accident. Duncan, who does not recognize Milton because he never knew him, sends the man away.

Mother

The mother is one of the characters in Garp's short story, "The Pension Grillparzer." She travels with her family as her husband rates the hotels of Austria for the Austria Tourist Bureau. She grows tired of the pension because of the effect the visit is having on her mother, Johanna. Later, after Johanna dies, the mother begins having the same strange dream told by the dream-teller at the Pension Grillparzer.

Robert Muldoon

See Roberta Muldoon

Roberta Muldoon

Roberta Muldoon is the lovable transsexual who becomes a close associate of Jenny Fields and an intimate friend of the Garp family. Roberta is the former Robert Muldoon, a tight end for the Philadelphia Eagles of the National Football League. She admires Jenny and is extremely protective of the provocative nurse. Roberta and Garp become especially close; she often cries on his shoulder after breaking up with one of her many lovers. Roberta blames herself when Jenny is assassinated, and she is heartbroken when Garp is murdered as well. She remains close to the remaining members of the Garp family after Garp's death. She has an affair with Garp's editor, John Wolf. She dies while Duncan Garp is recovering from a motorcycle accident.

Narrator of "The Pension Grillparzer"

One of many characters in the stories within the novel is the narrator of Garp's short story "The Pension Grillparzer." The narrator of the story is the older of two brothers who travel with their family to hotels across Austria. The father works for the Austrian Tourist Bureau; he secretly ranks the hotels, pensions, and restaurants that the family visits. The narrator drives the car for the family and helps determine the rankings. His visit to the Pension Grillparzer deeply affects him and he visits the pension years later to discover its sad condition.

Bainbridge Percy

Bainbridge (Pooh) Percy is the odd and disturbed youngest child of the Percy family. She wears diapers until she is a teenager. For some strange reason, she bears a grudge against men in general and Garp in particular. She recognizes Garp at his mother's funeral and alerts the other women. Garp is forced to flee. Pooh later becomes an Ellen Jamesian and murders Garp. After being institutionalized for many years, Pooh is finally rehabilitated. She works with retarded children and, at the age of fifty-four, she has her own child. She dies of a stroke after a long life.

Cushie Percy

See Cushman Percy

Cushman Percy

Cushie Percy is the eldest daughter of Stewart and Midge Percy. She and Garp are childhood friends who become physically attracted to each other as teenagers. Garp shares his earliest sexual experiences with Cushie. They spend Garp's graduation night together in the Steering School infirmary. Several years later, Cushie dies during childbirth.

Midge Percy

Midge Percy is the heir to the Steering fortune. She and her husband Stewart live in the sprawling Steering mansion with their five children and a dog, Bonkers. Midge is a conceited woman who looks down her nose at Jenny and Garp. Although Jenny allows Garp to play with the Percy children, she is contemptuous of the adult Percys. Jenny is furious when Midge refuses to have Bonkers put to sleep after the dog bites Garp. Midge does not recognize Garp at the funeral of her husband.

Pooh Percy

See Bainbridge Percy

Stewart Percy

Stewart Percy is the boorish husband of Midge Percy (heir to the Steering fortune). He meets Midge Percy in Hawaii while he is in the service. Stewart teaches a ridiculous class at Steering called "My Part of the Pacific," which details the history of the two naval battles in which he was present. The students call him "Fat Stew" and "Paunch" behind his back. Stewart looks down on Jenny and Garp. Jenny, recognizing this disdain, dislikes him intensely. She gets a great deal of pleasure informing Stewart that "Garp bit Bonkie." Stewart dies soon after Jenny's assassination, and he and Ernie Holm are buried on the same day.

Benny Potter

Benny Potter is a cruel student who mocks the English teacher Tinch. Years after they graduate, Potter runs into Garp in the bar of a New York City hotel. Potter cavalierly informs Garp of Tinch's death. Garp angrily roughs Potter up.

Ralph

Ralph is Duncan's friend, the son of Florence Cochran Owlsby (known to Garp as "Mrs. Ralph").

He grows up to become a newspaperman and is killed in a war.

Mrs. Ralph

See Florence Cochran Bowlsby

Randy

Randy is the young hippie that "Mrs. Ralph" asks Garp to remove from her bedroom. Randy ignores the woman's commands to leave and Garp must use force to get him out of the house. Later, the police pick Garp up as he is carrying Duncan home, and Randy is in the car. After the accident, Randy appears briefly at Dog's Head Harbor and befriends Duncan. He leaves, discouraged by Garp's intolerance.

Oren Rath

Oren Rath is the ignorant brute who rapes Hope Standish and forever alters the course of her family's life in Garp's third novel, *The World According to Bensenhaver*. Hope kills him with his fishing knife while he is raping her.

Robo

Robo is the narrator's younger brother in Garp's short story, "The Pension Grillparzer." He travels with the family as they rate various hotels and restaurants. Robo's main concern is how well each establishment cooks its eggs. He is more entertained than frightened by the strange occurrences at the Pension Grillparzer; he actually enjoys his stay. Years later, he dies in an explosion at the university he attends.

Jillsy Sloper

Jillsy Sloper is an uneducated black woman who cleans the office of editor John Wolf. Occasionally, when the editor is determining whether or not to publish a particular book, he will give a manuscript to Jillsy. He first discovered that Jillsy had a knack for predicting popular success when he gave her *A Sexual Suspect*, the autobiography of Jenny Fields. He is astonished when Jillsy tells him that she couldn't stop reading Garp's lurid, violent novel, *The World According to Bensenhaver*. Garp dedicates the novel to Jillsy at Wolf's suggestion even though he has never met the woman. Garp finally does meet her on the day of his mother's funeral; she tells the surprised novelist that Jenny "was worth two or three of *you!*" Jillsy ends up dying of breast cancer.

Dorsey Standish

Dorsey Standish is one of the characters in Garp's third novel, *The World According to Bensenhaver*. His wife's horrible rape turns him into an overprotective, hopelessly paranoid man. He attempts to protect his family by hiring Bensenhaver, the ex-detective who worked on his wife's rape case, as a private bodyguard. His wife resents Bensenhaver's intrusion into the family's life and she forces her husband to make him leave. The couple loses their second child to a horrible accident while Dorsey is spying on Hope (he correctly believes she is having an affair). Dorsey becomes sterile and concocts an outlandish scheme for Hope to become pregnant by her lover so that they can have another child. Meanwhile, Bensenhaver has a stroke and he is allowed to return to the Standish home. One night, Bensenhaver mistakenly shoots and kills Dorsey as the man lurks about the house spying on his wife.

Hope Standish

Hope Standish is the woman who is brutally raped in the first chapter of Garp's third novel, *The World According to Bensenhaver*. She is forced to kill her rapist, Oren Rath, as he rapes her. Arden Bensenhaver is the detective who finds her after the ordeal. Hope is victimized not only by her rape, but by her husband's overwrought reaction to the rape. Although her husband hires Bensenhaver as a bodyguard, Hope resents the intrusion into her family's life and forces Dorsey to make the ex-detective leave. She suggests having a second child in an effort to counter her husband's anxieties. Unfortunately, the child accidentally chokes to death on a piece of gum when Dorsey leaves the two boys alone to follow his wife. Hope is having an affair because she can no longer bear her husband's idiosyncrasies. Dorsey, who becomes sterile, determines that Hope should try to become pregnant by her lover, but she should not see the man for any other reason. Dorsey is killed by Bensenhaver, who mistakes Dorsey for an intruder as Dorsey sneaks around the house. Hope does have another child. She and her family are now able to live a happy life, free from the anxieties of her dead husband.

Margie Tallworth

Michael Milton breaks off a relationship with college student Margie Tallworth when Helen agrees to have an affair with him. Margie sees Helen in Michael's car and writes a note to Garp informing him of the affair.

Herr Theobald

Herr Theobald is the owner of the pension in Garp's short story, "The Pension Grillparzer." He desperately desires to upgrade his pension's rating from a Class C to a Class B. However, he cannot bring himself to expel the Circus Szolnok from the pension's premises because of his sister's involvement with the odd troupe. The father in the story, a representative of the Austrian Tourist Bureau, pities the man and upgrades the pension from a C to a B. Herr Theobald dies years later while investigating strange noises in the night. He has a heart attack when he sees Duna the bear wearing the dream-teller's suit.

Tina

Tina is one of the prostitutes Garp meets in Vienna. She has a large scar on her forehead resembling a peach pit. Charlotte tells Garp that nothing is "too funny" for Tina. After Charlotte's death, Tina informs Garp that Charlotte has paid for two free "visits" with the prostitutes.

Mr. Tinch

Mr. Tinch is the stuttering, halitosis-cursed, English teacher who becomes a kind of mentor to Garp while he attends Steering School. His nickname among the students is "Stench." When Tinch asks Garp if his breath stinks in front of the class, Garp denies it to spare his teacher from embarrassment. It is Tinch who recommends that Garp and Jenny stay in Vienna when they travel to Europe. On his way home from a faculty party one winter night, Tinch slips, hits his head, loses consciousness, and freezes to death.

Harriet Truckenmiller

Harriet Truckenmiller is the divorced wife of the man, Kenny Truckenmiller, who assassinates Jenny Fields. She is a hairdresser in a small New Hampshire town. She is looked after by her brother, Dickie. Garp visits her, in disguise, to determine whether she deserves a grant from the Fields Foundation. He determines that she does indeed deserve a grant and tells the board to give her money.

Kenny Truckenmiller

Kenny Truckenmiller is the assassin of Jenny Fields. He is a deer hunter who blames Jenny for his divorce from his wife, Harriet. After shooting Jenny, he is gunned down by a group of men including Dickie, his brother-in-law.

Wanga

Wanga is one of the prostitutes Garp meets in Vienna. She has a disfigured lip from a cut obtained when she was a child. Garp later uses the free sessions paid for by Charlotte for "visits" with Wanga.

Donald Whitcomb

Donald Whitcomb is the young English teacher at Steering who worships Garp. He witnesses Garp's assassination in the gymnasium. He befriends Helen, and she chooses him to write Garp's biography. He waits until Helen's death to write the last chapter.

John Wolf

John Wolf is the editor whose company publishes both the autobiography of Jenny Fields and the novels of T. S. Garp. He has a sharp eye for work that has the potential to be a popular or critical success. However, he also listens to the opinion of his cleaning woman, Jillsy Sloper, whenever he is stumped. He becomes a friend and confidant to Garp. He ruthlessly, but cleverly, uses Garp's tragedy to publicize *The World According to Bensenhaver*. He has an affair with Roberta Muldoon after Garp's death. Wolf dies of cancer before he can see Garp's biography in print.

Themes

Gender Roles

Irving's novel examines the significance of gender roles in American society. Jenny's independence as a woman is frowned upon by both her family and society in general. Young women usually didn't live alone in the 1940s. For example, it is immediately assumed that Jenny has some relationship to the soldier she stabs in the movie theater. Jenny resents the idea that a woman has to be "either somebody's wife or somebody's whore." In fact, Jenny exhibits some traditionally masculine traits: she is strong, plainspoken, and willful. This is demonstrated when her lack of a husband doesn't prevent her from getting pregnant. Her refusal to allow society to pigeonhole her because of her gender stirs great controversy and ultimately leads to her assassination. Alternately, Jenny's son Garp reverses gender roles. Garp, although he is very masculine, assumes the traditionally female role of domestic caretaker. Helen works while Garp cleans, cooks, and cares for the children. Although the arrangement is simply a matter of convenience (Garp can also write as he performs the domestic

Topics for Further Study

- Irving has said that the *The World According to Garp* was not influenced by American political and social events of the sixties because he spent half of that decade in Austria. Write an essay using examples from the novel to contradict him.

- Duncan Garp illustrates a version of "The Pension Grillparzer" with his father. Using the media of your choice (pencils, paints, clay, etc.), illustrate a scene or scenes from Garp's short story.

- Near the end of the novel, Garp discusses his ideas for his next three novels: *My Father's Illusions, The Death of Vermont,* and *The Plot Against the Giant*. Write your own first chapter for one of these novels using information from the book.

- The Ellen Jamesians mutilate themselves in protest of violence against women. Do you think this is realistic? What are some of the extreme methods people have used throughout history to protest real or imagined injustices?

- Study and discuss the world of book publishing. What do you think makes one book a bestseller and another a failure? What are some examples of books that were both critical and popular successes, and what do these books have in common?

- Look up the official rules of high school and college wrestling. Compare these rules to what is currently known as "professional wrestling."

chores), the role of "house-husband" was unusual at the time. Finally, the character of Roberta Muldoon demonstrates the most drastic gender reversal in the novel. The former football player is obviously happy to be a female.

Death and Disfigurement

Irving's novel ends with the words, "in the world according to Garp, we are all terminal cases."

Irving seems almost obsessed with the absurdity and randomness of violence and death. The author often details the deaths of his characters in *The World According to Garp* almost immediately after introducing them. Garp himself is conceived amongst dying and disfigured men in the intensive care unit of Boston Mercy. He is disfigured as a child when Bonkers the dog bites off part of his ear. Garp is disgusted by the self-mutilation of the Ellen Jamesians; he is more sympathetic to the gender-changing mutilation performed on Roberta Muldoon by doctors. His family is traumatized by the car accident that kills Walt. Duncan loses one of his eyes in the accident, and Michael Milton is horribly injured. Late in the novel, the concept of the Under Toad is introduced. The Under Toad, a play on the word "undertow," is the code word the Garps use for a powerful feeling of dread. Garp "smells" the Under Toad when he receives the phone call in Austria informing him of Jenny's assassination. Garp himself is assassinated near the end of the novel. Finally, the epilogue details the various deaths of most of the remaining characters. Irving leaves very few loose ends.

Love and Lust

The World According to Garp is concerned with all the various types of love. The love between parents and children is demonstrated first by the relationship between Jenny and Garp and then by the relationship Helen and Garp have with their children. Garp loves his children so powerfully that he is overprotective. Irving also examines the love between husband and wife. Garp and Helen love each other so fiercely that their marriage is able to withstand several catastrophes. There are also many loving friendships in the book; for instance, Garp and Roberta Muldoon become extremely close and loving friends. The novel also examines the nature of lust. Garp believes that his mother is somewhat cold because she doesn't experience lust, but Jenny recognizes that lust can often be disastrous. She takes care of dozens of women at Dog's Head Harbor who have been victims of lust. Garp's own life is affected by lust. First of all, Garp contracts gonorrhea in Austria when he runs into a trio of American tourists and he can't control his baser instincts. Garp also threatens his marriage when he has brief flings with babysitters. Finally, Helen's lust leads her into an affair that almost destroys the family.

Art and Creativity

Garp's life as a writer is an important subject in the novel. He often struggles with his art. He has difficulty writing in Vienna as his mother churns out her autobiography. However, he is finally inspired enough to write a charming short story, "The Pension Grillparzer." Irving uses the device of fiction within fiction to display Garp's work in the novel. The complete texts of "The Pension Grillparzer" and the essay "Vigilance" are part of the novel. In addition, the entire first chapter of Garp's novel, *The World According to Bensenhaver,* is chapter 15 of *The World According to Garp.* The plots of novels both written and unwritten are discussed as well. Garp, like many authors, is cursed by writer's block at various moments in his career. He also uses his art as a catharsis for personal tragedy when he writes *The World According to Bensenhaver.* He appears to be entering a productive stage in his career, with plans for three novels, shortly before he is murdered.

Style

Bildungsroman

Bildungsroman is a German word meaning "novel of development." A *bildungsroman* is the study of the growth of a youthful character and thus it applies to Irving's novel. The novel concerns Garp's coming of age, and his maturation as a person and artist. The main character in a *bildungsroman* learns about life through all of its ups and downs and through his interactions with the variety of people he meets and relationships he forms. Garp learns about women through his relationships with his mother, Cushie Percy, Helen Holm, Charlotte the Austrian prostitute, Alice Fletcher, Mrs. Ralph, and Ellen James. His experiences as a husband and father teach him invaluable lessons about love, discipline, responsibility, pain, and hope. He encounters friendship with John Wolf and Roberta Muldoon, and he endures hatred from the Ellen Jamesians and Pooh Percy. Garp lives a full life in a mere thirty-three years.

Black Humor

Black humor, or comedy, can be defined as writing that displays elements of disillusionment and cynicism. *The World According to Garp* is a work of tragicomedy. The book moves from one moment to the next between "lunacy and sorrow." In his review published in the April 13, 1978, edition of *The New York Times,* Christopher Lehmann-Haupt perfectly describes the black humor of *The World According to Garp:*

This is not going to be easy to explain. At the climax of John Irving's fourth novel . . . a truly horrifying accident occurs. Bones are broken, flesh is torn, eyes are put out, and appendages are severed. It is highly realistic, too, and in order to explain exactly how it happens, one would have to sum up dozens of plot details, all the way down to why the knob on a Volvo's gear shift happens to be missing. Moreover, at the point in the story when the accident occurs, we have grown extremely attached to the characters involved . . . Yet one of our reactions to this catastrophe is to burst out laughing. There we are, numb with shock and sick with concern, and suddenly we are laughing. And not feeling all that guilty about doing so either.

Foreshadowing

Irving uses foreshadowing, a literary device that creates expectation or sets up an explanation of later developments, to great effect in *The World According to Garp*. One example is Garp's childhood confrontation with Bonkers the dog. The vicious Newfoundland bites off a piece of Garp's ear. This scene foreshadows Garp's retaliation when, as a teenager, Garp bites off a piece of the dog's ear. Another instance of foreshadowing involves the broken knob on the gearshift of the Garp family's Volvo. The Garps procrastinate replacing the knob, and Duncan ultimately loses an eye when his head is impaled on the knobless shifter in a car accident. Later in the novel, Duncan is spotting handicapped people from the windows of John Wolf's Manhattan office. The first person he notices is a man with no arm; after Garp's death, Duncan loses an arm in a motorcycle accident. Finally, Garp's death, in many ways, is foreshadowed by Jenny's assassination.

Irony

Irony in literature can be defined as the effect of language in which the intended meaning is the opposite of what is stated. This can also be applied to the actions of characters in a novel. For example, it is ironic that Garp, an otherwise loving and overprotective father, contributes indirectly to the death of one son and the injury of another when he smashes into Michael Milton's car. Garp's friendship with Roberta Muldoon is ironic in the context of his distaste for the self-mutilation of the Ellen Jamesians. It is also ironic that Garp is murdered in the Steering School gymnasium, a place he and Helen have associated with safety.

Setting

The various settings of *The World According to Garp* are important to the atmosphere of the novel. The importance of the academic setting of the Steering School is demonstrated in the following passage in which Dean Bodger invites Garp to stay as wrestling coach after the death of Ernie Holm:

> "Why don't you stay with us awhile?" Bodger asked Garp; with his strong, pudgy hand, sweeping the bleary windows in Buster's Snack and Grill, the dean indicated the campus of the Steering School. "We're not a *bad* place, really," he said.

> "You're the only place I know," Garp said, neutrally.

Garp is also deeply influenced by the weary decadence of Vienna. The setting directly influences his story, "The Pension Grillparzer." Hospitals and other places of rest, such as the mansion at Dog's Head Harbor, also play an important role in the novel.

Historical Context

Assassination in the Sixties and Seventies

Assassination can be defined as killing someone by sudden attack. The term assassin in the twentieth century generally refers to the hired or delegated killer of some politically important personage. Recent assassins have seem deranged and obsessed with notoriety. Although there have been many assassinations throughout history, it seems as if there was an epidemic of assassination in the last half of the twentieth century, especially in the United States. Irving has stated that the political events in the United States during the 1960s and 1970s had no effect on the writing of *Garp*. This is rather difficult to believe considering the important role assassination plays in the novel's plot.

There were four notorious American assassinations during the 1960s. These deaths dealt shocking blows to American idealism. The assassination of President John F. Kennedy on November 22nd, 1963, was the first of the four. The president was shot while riding in a motorcade through Dallas. Kennedy's assassination was the catalyst for a variety of conspiracy theories. However, the Warren Commission—a group of judges, senators, and representatives assigned by President Lyndon B. Johnson to investigate the assassination—determined that Lee Harvey Oswald acted alone when he shot President Kennedy. Oswald himself was murdered by Jack Ruby, a Dallas restaurant owner, the day after the assassination.

Just two years later, Malcolm X was assassinated on February 21, 1965 as he was speaking to an audience in a Harlem ballroom. Three men affiliated with the Black Muslim faith were convicted of the killing. It is generally held that Malcolm X was killed in an attempt to influence his followers to remain with the Black Muslims. Then, just three years later, the country was rocked by two more assassinations in quick succession. First, civil rights activist and minister Martin Luther King, winner of the Nobel Peace Prize, was shot while standing on the balcony of the Lorraine Motel in Memphis on April 4, 1968. Career criminal James Earl Ray was convicted of the murder, but years later the King family supported Ray because they believed that he was the scapegoat in a conspiracy against the Reverend King. On June 4, 1968, just two months after King's assassination, Senator Robert F. Kennedy, the younger brother of John, was shot while leaving a hotel in California after winning the state's Democratic presidential primary. Kennedy died a day later, and Sirhan B. Sirhan was later convicted of the murder.

The assassination of Jenny Fields in *The World According to Garp* is similar to the attempted assassination of segregationist, Alabama governor George Wallace. Wallace was shot by Arthur H. Bremer on May 5, 1972, while campaigning for the Democratic presidential nomination. There were two assassination attempts on President Gerald R. Ford (who was, ironically, a member of the Warren Commission) on separate trips to California in September of 1975. Both of the assailants were women: Lynette Fromme, a former devotee of Charles Manson, and Sara Jane Moore. Certainly, one might determine that the prevalence of assassination in public life influences (at least indirectly) the plot of *The World According to Garp*.

Feminism

Feminism and the women's liberation movement play an important role in *The World According to Garp*. Women's issues are explored in many of Irving's novels. The origins of feminism, the theory that women should have political, economic, and social rights equal to men, can be traced back to the late eighteenth century with the writings of Mary Wollstonecraft and the nineteenth century when women in Great Britain and the United States fought for property and voting rights. The invention of the birth control pill and the publication of Betty Friedan's *The Feminine Mystique* (1963) helped spur the rebirth of feminism and establish the modern women's liberation movement in the 1960s. Friedan, Gloria Steinem, and several other feminist leaders founded NOW, the National Organization for Women, in 1966. NOW, and many other feminist organizations, fought for such changes as abor-

tion rights; federally supported child care; equal pay for women; the occupational upgrading of women; and the removal of all legal and social barriers to education, political influence, and economic power for women. Since the U.S. Supreme Court case of *Roe v. Wade* in 1973, which legalized abortion in the first trimester, there has been somewhat of a backlash against feminism. However, the influence of the women's liberation movement of the 1960s and 1970s led to broad changes in American society.

Critical Overview

In the April 30, 1978, edition of the *Washington Post Book World,* William McPherson wrote that *The World According to Garp* is: "A wonderful novel, full of energy and art, at once funny and horrifying and Heartbreaking. . . . You know *The World According to Garp* is true. It is also terrific.

Many of the initial reviews for *The World According to Garp* were equally enthusiastic. Christopher Lehmann-Haupt, in a favorable review published in the *New York Times* on April 13, 1978, recognized the book as "what is easily [Irving's] best novel to date." Mark Stevens, in a brief review published in the March 2, 1979, issue of the *National Review,* wrote that "*The World According to Garp* is the work of an extravagant imagination." In a review published in the April 23, 1978, issue of the *New York Times Book Review,* Julian Moynahan stated that "[Irving's] instincts are so basically sound, his talent for storytelling so bright and strong, that he gets down to the truth of his time."

Several critics admired Irving's skillful blending of humor and tragedy. Lehmann-Haupt noted that "we find ourselves laughing throughout *The World According to Garp,* and at some of the damndest things." Stevens wrote that *Garp* is "richly comic, its dialogue and scenes sometimes filled with a riotous energy worthy of the Marx Brothers." Several critics also commented favorably on "The Pension Grillparzer," the first short story written by Garp in the novel. Moynahan wrote that "the utterly charming 'The Pension Grillparzer' . . . glows at the heart of *The World According to Garp.*" Michael Malone, in a review published in the June 10, 1978, issue of *The Nation,* wrote:

> The short story, 'The Pension Grillparzer,' which the novelist, Garp, rightly suspects is the best thing he ever wrote, and which I suspect is the best thing in *The World According to Garp*—and further suspect Irving may think so too—is a beautiful fiction.

There were, however, critics who did not find Irving's novel "utterly charming." For example,

John Lithgow as Roberta Muldoon, Glenn Close as Jenny Fields, and Robin Williams as T. S. Garp in the 1982 film version of the novel

critic Richard Gilman attacked what he believed was the novel's "fundamental insincerity." In the October 6, 1979, issue of the *Nation,* he wrote:

> *The World According to Garp* is a model of its kind, and its kind is a seductive imitation of literary seriousness, an elegantly perpetrated, if not wholly deliberate, hoax. Irving's book is an extremely instructive example of how to have it all ways, an impressive feat of having one's literary cake while eating off commercial success."

Even some of the favorable reviews found flaws in Irving's novel. Moynahan, in noting a publisher's blurb saying that the book was "rich, humorous, and wise," wrote: "The book is certainly rich and humorous but it is more confused than wise." Malone, in his generally positive review, questioned what he called the novel's tendency to "explicate rather than embody" the idea that "comedy and death may be intrinsically joined."

Many academic articles on the novel have been published in various journals through the years as well. For example, Raymond J. Wilson examined the postmodern construction of *The World According to Garp* in the Fall 1992, edition of *Critique: Studies in Contemporary Fiction.* Wilson compares Irving's fiction to the works of John Barth and Robert Coover. He demonstrates that Irv-

ing's novel has a number of characteristics that identify it as a postmodern novel. For example, in *The World According to Garp* there is a "zone of the bizarre, where fantasy best expresses our sense of reality" as well as "a propensity for metafiction, in which writing draws attention to the techniques and processes of its own creation."

In another essay, published in *Gender Studies: New Directions in Feminist Criticism,* Janice Doane and Devon Hodges analyze the female characters in *Garp.* They contend that the strong female characters in the novel only serve to cover the "patriarchal power inscribed in traditional narrative conventions." They claim that in *The World According to Garp* "truth is structured in such a way as to guarantee paternal authority and to silence women no matter how much they speak." Of course, Irving, and many of his readers, would disagree with this conclusion.

Criticism

Joyce Hart

Hart has degrees in literature and creative writing and focuses her published writing on literary themes. In this essay, she examines the possi-

> The scene is bloody and brutal with Jenny slicing through skin and muscle and attempting to cut off the man's nose . . . The tension that might have built up from this scene is released in comic style, as with the line from Jenny: "'If I'd wanted to kill him,' she told the police, later, 'I'd have slit his wrist. I'm a nurse. I know how people bleed.'"

ble reasons why the characters and storyline in Irving's novel, although fraught with tragedy, elicit very little sorrowful or distressing emotional responses.

John Irving's *The World According to Garp* is often referred to as a tragicomedy, a term that identifies a story as containing representations of both the lighter situations of life that cause laughter and the more sorrowful consequences of human actions that cause tears. Irving's novel definitely has large quantities of both types of these situations, spurred by unending strings of episodes that readers might conclude only Irving could successfully place into one novel. However, although the comic reactions to Irving's story are easily stirred, there is a hesitation or outright nonreaction to the more mournful circumstances and their consequences in Irving's story. Why is this true? How does Irving pull readers in and make them fascinated enough about his characters to keep his readers compelled to turn the pages to the end of his story, making them laugh at all the impossible situations, and yet barely move them or, worse yet, make them laugh at horrendous episodes of bloody and tragic circumstances?

Possible answers to these questions might be found in Irving's own definitions of his writing. For instance, in an article by Richard Bernstein in the *New York Times,* Irving is quoted as saying, "I've read about myself that I am not to be taken seriously because I am a shameless entertainer, a crowd pleaser.. . . You bet. I am." In other words, by Irving's own definition, he wants to keep his readers entertained, a pursuit that usually entails delving only lightly into the material of a story with the goal of making one's audience smile or laugh. From this definition, readers might conclude that even if Irving himself categorized his novel as a tragicomedy, he would lean toward the comedic portion of this labeling.

Later in the same *New York Times* article, Bernstein has another Irving quote: "I am a comic novelist," claims Irving. Then Irving adds, "It is my deliberate decision to create someone who is capable of moving you and then hurting him." So with this statement, Irving confirms that his emphasis is on the comedic side of life despite the fact that he also admits that he wants to stir other emotions—empathy, for example, for the suffering that he inflicts on his characters. But is empathy evoked in his readers? Does Irving move his readers in both directions, toward the comedy and the tragedy as the term tragicomedy implies? Or is this term misapplied in reference to Irving's writing?

In an attempt to examine this question, this essay will take up the condition that Mel Gussow describes in another *New York Times* article in which he describes Irving's writing with the statement, "Irving himself is expert at alternating scenes of zestful humor and deep sorrow, eventually knitting together all diverse narrative strands until there are no degrees of separation." If by this statement Gussow means that Irving knits his humor and sorrow together until there is no separation between the two, then it might be that this lack of separation is the clue as to why it is difficult to feel empathy for Irving's characters when they are suffering. Given the choice between laughing and crying, it seems only natural that readers would want to lean toward the humor in life. And maybe that is why readers of *The World According to Garp* find themselves laughing at the novel's scenes of death, mutilation, and rape.

At the beginning of *The World According to Garp,* the focus of the story is on Jenny Fields, Garp's mother. And the first blood drawn comes at the hands of Jenny in defending herself from a sexually aggressive male stranger who affronts her in a movie theater. The scene is bloody and brutal with Jenny slicing through skin and muscle and attempting to cut off the man's nose; and yet the reader feels very little sentiment, fear, or loathing for either the would-be assailant or for Jenny. The tension that might have built up from this scene is

What Do I Read Next?

- *The Hotel New Hampshire* (1981) was John Irving's follow-up to *The World according to Garp*. The novel details the misadventures of an eccentric family and it is controversial for its exploration of a consensual incestuous relationship between a sister and brother. Jodie Foster and Rob Lowe starred in the 1984 film version directed by Tony Richardson.

- Irving's *The Cider House Rules* (1985) is another story of a boy growing into adulthood. The novel is thoughtfully influenced by the works of Charles Dickens, yet it is thoroughly modern and controversial in its examination of twentieth-century society's treatment of women and children. It is the story of Homer Wells, an orphan who grows up in mid-century New England, tutored (and loved) by the ether-addicted abortionist, Dr. Wilbur Larch. The novel was made into an award-winning film in 1999; Irving also won the Academy Award for the screenplay adaptation of his novel.

- A new generation of readers joined Irving's longtime fans when *A Prayer for Owen Meany* (1989) was published. It is a deeply spiritual and moving story of a pint-sized young boy who hits a foul ball that strikes his best friend's mother in the head and kills her. It is a grand tale of friendship and fate.

- Wally Lamb's *She's Come Undone* (1992) is the funny, heartbreaking coming of age story of Dolores Price. The lovable, pathetic, and overweight Dolores almost buries herself in the guilt and grief of a painful childhood. Lamb has been lauded for his realistic portrayal of an abused young woman and her struggle with mental illness.

- One of Irving's favorite authors is Gunter Grass, the German novelist who won the Nobel Prize for Literature in 1999. Grass's best known work is probably *The Tin Drum*. The story of a three-year-old boy who refuses to grow up is a wise and savagely comic depiction of Nazi Germany.

- Like Irving, many novels written by Charles Dickens feature children who are orphaned or somehow abandoned by one (or both) of their parents. *Oliver Twist* (1838) is one of these. A gang of child pickpockets led by the sneaky adult, Fagin, takes in young Oliver, one of the most famous orphans from Dickens's works. *David Copperfield* (1850) details the trials and tribulations of the titular character. The boy, like Garp, is born without a father. However, young David loses his mother shortly after she marries and leaves the boy with a wretched stepfather. Both of these novels were tremendously successful in the nineteenth century, and they remain popular today because of the detailed plotting and memorable characters.

- In the late 1960s, one of Irving's mentors at the University of Iowa Writer's Workshop was the celebrated American novelist Kurt Vonnegut Jr. Although the writers have vastly different styles, they share a penchant for eccentric characters and odd situations. Perhaps Vonnegut's most famous work is *Slaughterhouse-Five* (1969), the story of Billy Pilgrim, a soldier snatched up during World War II by time-travelling aliens. Vonnegut based some of the scenes on his own experiences as a prisoner in Germany during the World War II firebombing of Dresden. Vonnegut uses dark humor in the novel to attack the barbarity of war.

---

released in comic style, as with the line from Jenny: "'If I'd wanted to kill him,' she told the police, later, 'I'd have slit his wrist. I'm a nurse. I know how people bleed.'" Lines like this, at the height of a dramatic moment, cause readers to snicker, a

response that comes out almost involuntarily like when witnessing someone falling down after slipping on a banana skin. The humorous aspects of the incident somehow wipe out empathy for the pain that is suffered. Forgotten in the laughter is

> " . . . John Irving has never been able to construct a believable plot, but he has always tried to make a virtue of this chronic deficiency. Which is to say that, like other formless novelists—Pynchon, Barth, Doctorow—he abandons any pretense at narrative (and therefore psychological) realism, and seeks instead to attract and maintain the reader's attention with random monstrosities and grotesque occurrences, chiefly sexual or violent in nature, frequently both."

the fact that Jenny was accosted and her assailant is in pain.

A little later in the story, Jenny meets Technical Sergeant Garp, (who is about to become the protagonist's father) whose brain has been accidentally mutilated by metal fragments, causing, in effect, a lobotomy (or severance of nerve fibers in the front part of his brain). The accident leaves the senior Garp in an imbecilic mental state, which gives Irving a chance to turn this bloody and horrific accident into another comedic scene. Irving does this by taking away all of Garp's abilities to function, except for one. Garp maintains an erection and is constantly masturbating. When Irving has Jenny taking advantage of Garp's erection by easing herself upon him, there is little thought of Jenny's inappropriateness. There is also little thought of defining Jenny as a rapist, which is what she is in essence; and had the sex of the characters been reversed, this scene might have been very controversial. Instead, this scene evokes laughter. Irving has not emotionally connected his readers to the senior Garp. He is just an almost-dead body, a casualty without family or loved ones to protect and

care for him. Jenny is the closest thing this soldier has to a friend. And although she cares for him (albeit in a very unusual nursing fashion), even Jenny has no emotional connection to him. Jenny wants to be pregnant, and this soldier's body is her solution to accomplishing this without the messiness of having an affair. The scene and final moments of this man's life are funny because of Jenny's nonconformity, her unusual determination, and her inappropriateness. No one is saddened by the death because the only thing that the senior Garp is remembered for is his erection.

Books like Ken Kesey's *One Flew over the Cuckoo's Nest* and Larry McMurty's *Terms of Endearment,* both of which were successful, popular novels that were eventually produced as movies, are also termed tragicomedies. But these two novels differ from *The World According to Garp* in that they make readers bond with the characters. The consequence is that readers feel the terror and loss as well as the humor as depicted in the character's fictional lives. Irving's novel continually comes up short on the tragic side. This is partly due to the fact that, as already described, Irving inserts comedy into every tragic scene, not allowing his readers to come to terms or even realize that other emotions may be at play. But there is another reason why Irving's novel does not inspire empathy for the tragedies that his characters endure.

Irving tends to create characters that appear to be more like issues rather than flesh and blood people. Infidelity, for example, is an issue that Irving dwells on. So, he creates characters that he can use to represent infidelity. One such character is the young graduate student, Michael Milton, with whom Garp's wife, Helen, has an affair. While attempting to end the affair, Helen offers Michael a final act of oral sex, which results in her biting off part of Michael's penis. Michael is a one-dimensional character at best. Even though Irving briefly describes the agony that Michael suffers, there is little if any emotional response in reading about it. Michael represents just one in a long line of issues, and the loss of part of his penis not only tickles the funny bone, it also feels somewhat justified. Infidelity disrupts or strains the marital bonds. Since this is an issue that Irving wants to explore, Michael's loss substantiates Irving's conclusion.

There are also several feminist issues in *The World According to Garp*. Some of these issues deal with rape, others with transgender concerns, physical abuse, and general empowerment and sexuality topics. In discussing these issues, Irving creates situations that end in physical mutilation (such as women cutting off their tongues) and death. One such death is Jenny Fields'. Garp learns of his mother's death via a long-distance phone call. His reaction to the news is to first ask who killed her. When he finds out it was a man, his next reaction is to reflect on how difficult it must have been for the character Roberta (a man who has gone through a sex change) to say the word *man*. At first Irving diverts the emotions that might be lurking behind the tragedy of losing a mother by going immediately to the feminist issue as espoused by Roberta's distaste for men.

In this same scene, Irving next has Garp ask Roberta if she is alone. Roberta responds that she is with a group of women, all of whom once lived with Garp's mother. Garp's second response to the death of his mother, instead of reflecting on his own sense of loss, is to go directly to this group of women: "And Garp could imagine them all, the wailing women at Dog's Head Harbor—their leader murdered." By doing this, Irving dismisses Garp's emotions completely. Rather than having lost a mother, Garp relates only to the issues of feminism and how the movement has lost a spokesperson. And then to cap off this conversation, Irving has Garp say, "She [Garp's mother] wanted her body to go to a med school." This discussion of Garp's mother's death is neither sad nor funny. Rather it is bland, leaving the reader with words without any emotion. The issue of feminism has been played out. The topic is now somewhat resolved or at least it is coming to some kind of conclusion in this story. The loss of Garp's mother is not felt because by the time she dies in the novel, she too has become only an issue.

There is only one incident in the novel that evokes empathy. It occurs at the end of chapter thirteen, "Walt Catches Cold." However, readers don't even know that the tragedy occurs until the next chapter. There is a strange silence surrounding this tragic event, the death of Garp's son Walt; and it is in this silence that empathy is born. Walt dies in a car accident. But Irving encloses this accident in a sort of sick humor. The results of the accident begin with the aforementioned incident in which Garp's wife bites off the grad student's penis. The consequences of the accident also include a broken jaw and arm and the loss of an eye. No one walks away from this accident unharmed and yet it is hard for the reader to know how to react to all the injuries. Irving points out the bodily harm done to Garp, his wife, their oldest son, and the grad student, but there is no mention of Walt. Walt is some-

> "[Is the tale told in *The World According to Garp*] implausible? Not nearly so implausible as the actual history we have been through in the time John Irving's fiction covers. . . ."

how skipped over. Readers are not even give a hint of this tragic consequence until the next chapter when Garp, his tongue swollen from having bitten it during the accident, says: "I *mish* him."

With these words, Garp opens up his heart to the reader. Irving has set the stage, having shown earlier in the novel Garp's love for his young son. As the details of Walt's death are slowly unfolded, so are the emotions. Walt's death has affected every member of the family. And in showing this, the reader is also affected. Irving does not use humor in this one incident. Neither does Walt represent anything other than a much-loved son. He is not an issue. He is a full-blown, flesh and blood character. If there is true tragedy in this story, it all centers on Walt. Irving has made a point to demonstrate how concerned Garp was for Walt's safety throughout the novel. Garp would run after cars that drove down his street too fast, admonishing the drivers to be more considerate for the safety of the children who lived on that block. Garp told Walt stories that had very pronounced moralistic endings so that Walt would be prepared to deal with the harsh realities of life. And yet, it was Garp himself who was responsible for Walt's death, because he played dangerously with his children, driving without the car's lights on, showing off.

Unfortunately, this tragedy is so embedded in a story filled with comic releases and issue-oriented characters that there is the possibility that this truly tragic moment is lost. Maybe if Irving had employed more silences around some of the other tragic events, his novel might not have been as entertaining, but the reading of it might have evoked stronger emotions. Instead, his novel is just as likely to be referred to as a comedy as it is a tragi-comedy, which is sort of a tragedy in itself.

> **"** Garp's world is so bizarrely and completely dangerous that while one nods how true, how true, one never quite suspends disbelief. Like the accident, everything awful could happen, but that it does is somehow too neat."

Source: Joyce Hart, Critical Essay on *The World According to Garp*, in *Novels for Students*, The Gale Group, 2001.

Bryan Griffin

In the following review, Griffin discusses The World According to Garp*'s lack of plot, vulgar comedy, and obsession with "kinky violence."*

The World According to Garp was, of course, 1978's *Ragtime*, which is to say that it is the most recent manifestation of the greatest-novel-of-the-decade. . . .

Mr. Irving's previous novels were much shorter than the *Garp* book, and they hadn't attracted a great deal of attention. True, the man was "one of the most imaginative writers of his generation" (Dutton), but then so was everybody else. Clearly it was going to take more than mere imagination to turn Mr. Irving into a major literary event. It was going to take greatness. Let's face it, it was going to take a little naked profundity. . . .

The World According to Garp does indeed have "extraordinary" qualities. Its plot, for one thing. Like so many extraordinary things, the story lacks, shall we say, credibility. That is not necessarily a criticism: John Irving has never been able to construct a believable plot, but he has always tried to make a virtue of this chronic deficiency. Which is to say that, like other formless novelists— Pynchon, Barth, Doctorow—he abandons any pretense at narrative (and therefore psychological) realism, and seeks instead to attract and maintain the reader's attention with random monstrosities and grotesque occurrences, chiefly sexual or violent in nature, frequently both. The idea, in other words, is to horrify or titillate the reader to such an extent

that he or she will be compelled to continue reading, even without the promise of any realistic development of story or explication of character. . . .

[Except] for numerous asides concerning art, genitalia, social diseases, and related subjects, it must be admitted that Mr. Irving writes mostly about (a) different ways of raping people and animals, and (b) different ways of killing people and animals. The novelist Garp is sometimes a participant, sometimes not.

Irving's talent is primarily comedic, and his purposes are best served by his dialogue, which is well done and often amusing. It is important to note at the outset that his style as a whole is *not* exhibitionistic, not even mildly tortured: it does not seek to function as a smokescreen for the author's views and perceptions. More than anything else, however, Irving's prose is the prose of a poorly educated man—his vocabulary is uninspiring, his knowledge of the grammatical proprieties is severely limited. He is a child of his time in his lack of respect for lucidity ("Garp was an excessive man," and "Garp felt a peculiar feeling of unfairness overwhelm him"). In Irving's case, however, the sporadic incoherence and the syntactical sloppiness seem to be simply the consequence of the author's unwillingness—or, perhaps, his inability—to polish his output, rather than a deliberate smog-policy. The carelessness, in other words, is in the expression, not in the sentiments which seek that expression. Like all other Major American Novelists, Irving says his ambition is to write "accessible" fiction, and he has done so. His style is simplistic, almost childlike—it is, in other words, what has come to be referred to as "readable." What *Garp* is, is a funny book. Or rather, it tries to be. But it is a low humor, based chiefly on the prepubescent assumption that conscientious vulgarity is by definition amusing.

The immature quality of John Irving's comedic sense is worth mentioning primarily because of its subsidiary effect, which is to conceal, or at least to disguise, the novel's more fundamental flaw. What we are talking about, of course, is Irving's obsession with kinky violence (or violent kinkiness, it is hard to say which), and what concerns us here is the perverse enthusiasm with which many American critics have embraced that eccentric quality. . . .

The assumption of profundity extends . . . to the moral arena, so that many of us automatically accept John Irving's apparent bloodlust as something more than that, simply because the author's native intelligence is so obvious; whereas, in fact, the bloodlust may be merely . . . bloodlust. . . .

Source: Bryan Griffin, Review of *The World according to Garp,* in *Atlantic Monthly,* June 1979, pp. 51–55.

Julian Moynahan

In the following review, Moynahan speculates on the relation of the Irving's fictional world to his real-world experiences.

The World According to Garp shows that John Irving is haunted by the high level of quotidian American violence and the vulnerability of American lives. He can't get the frequency of assassination as a method of settling our domestic political and social quarrels out of his mind; and he is tormentedly aware of something like a war on women going on in our society as women's struggle for real equality continues and intensifies. He has not, however, arrived at wisdom on any of these matters. Apart from Andrew Greeley and some other heavy-breathing pundits, who has?. . .

Through its formal convolutions and sinuosities this novel is . . . a sort of treatise on how reality is processed by fiction; it takes a sophisticated view of the relations in art between the imaginary and the actual. For example, Garp writes as his fourth book "The World According to Bensenhaver." It has a lurid plot entailing rape, manslaughter and other violence, and represents Garp's idiosyncratic attempt to deal with the trauma of a terrible, ridiculous accident. . . . The Bensenhaver narrative, an entire chapter of which is included, is obviously a parody of the work containing it. So we are left to ponder the following question: What traumas suffered by John Irving elicited *The World According to Garp,* as Garp's traumas elicited "The World According to Bensenhaver"? The fact that such questions are not really answerable, except in imagination, does not make them less interesting and important.

A bit more on this point of the relation of fiction and "reality." Jennie Fields's assassination while campaigning in a shopping plaza evokes the assassination attempt on George C. Wallace during the 1972 Presidential primaries. The woman gubernatorial candidate loses ground in her campaign when she bursts into tears during a public appearance, recalling the famous incident of Senator Edmund Muskie's "womanish" tears outside the newspaper office in Manchester, N.H. There is no doubt Mr. Irving wants us to make these connections. It's all part of his demonstration of how fiction, in creating a world of its own, remains tied

> "Lost tongues, lost ears, severed penises, blinded eyes, broken bones, Gothic nightmares, Jacobean melodramas, tasteless jokes about disability: it all sounds like a self-indulgent fantasy, the kind of clever creative-writing-school trick writing that one would go a long way to avoid. But it isn't that, at all."

by the lifeline of the writer's experience to the world we all share. . . .

[Is the tale told in *The World According to Garp*] implausible? Not nearly so implausible as the actual history we have been through in the time John Irving's fiction covers. . . .

All novelists, if they are any good, want to use their craft to tell the truth. But this aim was perhaps more difficult to keep in view during the last 10 or 15 years than at any comparable period in our literary history. There was the lurid and unending public melodrama, which seemed to put the merely private imagination into the shade unless it went out of its way to astonish and amaze. Academic modernists such as Robert Scholes and Tony Tanner plumped firmly for types of fictional "fabulation" that would outdo and ignore historical reality in the shaping of self-sufficient worlds. . . . No wonder then that a fairly typical young novelist of the late 1960's, Tom McHale, should have remarked. . ., "I am into exaggeration," and mentioned that several young writers in the University of Iowa Writing Program, when he was there, were into, or thinking of going into, the same racket.

The problem, of course, is to know when exaggeration becomes lying, emotional and mental lying, about the world one is struggling to discover and invent in one's fiction. This problem is not well handled in many fabulated works, and drastically limits their value. As for John Irving, who also did time at Iowa, I should say he was on the horns of the dilemma. That is, his new novel contains some febrile fabulations (the wrong sort of exaggeration) in its handling of the feminist theme, yet his instincts are so basically sound, his talent for storytelling so bright and strong, that he gets down to the truth of his time in the end. Especially in "The Pension Grillparzer," a touching work, as good as, and rather like the best of Buñuel, a work of love, realism and wild imagination that is both astonishing and true. . . .

Source: Julian Moynahan, "Truths by Exaggeration," in *New York Times Book Review,* April 23, 1978, pp. 1, 27–29.

Eliot Fremont-Smith

In the following review, Fremont-Smith describes the world of Garp as a "horrendous" but "marvelous" "invented contraption," in which Irving plays the role of master magician similar to that of the Wizard in the Wizard of Oz.

The World According to Garp is a book of dimensions. It is entertainment on a grand, anyway stylish, scale. It is bravado transfigured into bravery—or maybe the other way around. In fact, I think quite often the other way around—which is not to damn, but to wonder. . . .

Murder is a frequent occurrence in *Garp* (both Garp and his mother die in this fashion), but it isn't about murder really, it's about how to breathe life into life. Mayhem and mutilation are on every other page, but the theme of the book is addressed to making things whole. The Ellen Jamesians can't speak (and Garp himself smashes his jaw and must communicate by notes), yet the novel is concerned with articulation as perhaps the only saving grace. One of the most unforgettable characters is a football tight end turned trans sexual (there is homoerotic awareness everywhere), yet *Garp* is profoundly centered on heterosexual urges and itches and relationships and fulfillments, and, out of these *and* beyond them, on families and children. Garp is a true romantic hero: he wants the world safe, not for himself, but for them. . . .

One reads [the accident scene at the center of the book transfixed in horror. Also with the lips quivering to smile It's so awful, it's so funny. Perfect justice, and therefore farcical; its appropriateness (in New England yet) is raucous. . . .

Garp's world is so bizarrely and completely dangerous that while one nods how true, how true, one never quite suspends disbelief. Like the accident, everything awful could happen, but that it does is somehow too neat. Part of the manipulation

is disarmament by irony—for an awareness of ironic possibility accompanies every disaster, every shock. . . . Garp's second son was conceived as, in a sense a reserve—in case the first son became a victim of the unsafe world. It is the second who is killed.

So, the world (Garp's) is horrendous; yet his struggle to make it sensible—accountable, as it were, to a human sense of order—is strangely unnecessary. For the world (Irving's) works just fine: It is a marvelous invented contraption.

Another comparison comes to mind, *The Wonderful Wizard of Oz.* In Baum's tale, you will recall, Toto pulls aside a curtain in the Wizard's Emerald City palace to reveal the Wizard, not as he seemed to be to Dorothy and her companions, but as the former elixir salesman, now working his magic by manipulating a mechanical control board. Part of the lasting power of the *Oz* story is that while this magic is revealed, made rational, the greater magic (the cosmos of Oz) is left mysterious.

With *Garp,* however, it's the reader who pulls aside the curtain, and it is not Garp who is revealed at the controls but John Irving. He is a master magician, and the show is great. But we see too much, and both Garp's dread and Irving's optimism fade away into what one too sharply realizes is an illusion. A grand illusion, very powerful; the book can freak you out. But, in the end, the interest of *The World According to Garp* lies not in that world, but in the Wondrous mechanics of its invention and the deft manipulation—while the show goes on—of our awe and tears and laughter. . . .

Source: Eliot Fremont-Smith, "Blood and Ketchup on Mat," in *Village Voice,* May 22, 1978, pp. 77–78.

Margaret Drabble

In the following review, Drabble focuses both on the novel's presentation of the sense of insecurity and the nearness of death and violence in everyday life and on its counter to the theory of creative writing that sees personal tragedy as material for future stories.

[*The World According to Garp*] is not merely a book about writing a book: in the first chapters, [Irving's] defensive, distancing techniques strike more than the reality of the subject matter; it is only gradually that the meaning is released. This is just as well, for the book contains almost intolerable pain. It is a bloody package, and if he had flung this in front of us we would have backed away in horror. As it is, we read on, at first entertained, then puzzled, then trapped, wanting to look away, but by this time unable to avert our eyes . . . or at least, this is what happened to me. . . .

It is a baffling book in many ways. Beneath the surface lies a solid, suburban, everyday life. . . . Garp's perceptions of his children, his anxious protective love, his rebellion against and acceptance of this deadly anxiety, are beautifully done: there is a fine scene where, worried about the fecklessness of the mother who has invited his son to stay for the night, he creeps around to spy at one o'clock in the morning, and sees through a window in the lethal rays of the television

> crammed against the sagging couch the casual bodies of Duncan and Ralph, half in their sleeping bags, asleep (of course), but looking as if the television has murdered them. In the sickly TV light their faces look drained of blood.

This sense of death round the corner grows in the novel, and finally dominates it: the Garp family calls it the Under Toad, after a misapprehension of Garp's baby Walt about warnings against the undertow in the ocean. Every anxious parent knows the Under Toad, and I am not sure if anxious parents should be recommended to read this book, for the way in which the Toad gets Walt is really too much to bear, even dressed up as it is in such a macabre array of horror.

The macabre elaboration is, I imagine, designed to diminish rather than to intensify the book's message about the violent insecurity of the world we are forced to inhabit. But Irving's fantasies are so near the bone that three-quarters of the way through the novel I began to wonder whether perhaps there really *was* an American feminist society called the Ellen Jamesians, named after a child rape victim named Ellen James whose tongue had been cut out by her attackers. Lost tongues, lost ears, severed penises, blinded eyes, broken bones, Gothic nightmares, Jacobean melodramas, tasteless jokes about disability: it all sounds like a self-indulgent fantasy, the kind of clever creative-writing-school trick writing that one would go a long way to avoid. But it isn't that, at all.

For one thing, it does have a good deal to say about feminist movements and the changing roles of husbands and wives. . . . More important, to me, was the novel's commentary on what I have to call the creative process, pretentious though those words always sound. Irving has some sharp comments on reviewers who took for autobiography in fiction, and the quarrels of Garp's biographers after his death ought to make one pause, but they

don't. It is obvious that Garp/Irving is commenting in the novel on Irving's own literary career: his first novel, *Setting Free the Bears,* was set in Vienna and featured bears and the Vienna Zoo, as does Garp's first imaginative effort, "The Pension Grillparzer." . . .

The worlds of Bensenhaver and Garp and Irving are the worlds of the mid-thirties, of mid-career, when a crushing awareness of an accumulating store of memory, most of it unpleasant, threatens to warp and inhibit the imagination. Irving's account of this process is particularly interesting. Unlike poets, most novelists seem to look forward to middle age, and to the fund of experience and observation upon which the older writer can draw: after all, many major writers didn't even start until they were older than Irving now is. Moreover, most novelists tend to look upon personal tragedy as something that can eventually be made useful, turned into grist for the mill: the more the writer suffers, the more he has to write about.

Irving challenges this assumption. His protagonist looks back to the days of visionary gleam, when he could write purely, happily, from out of the air, not from out of himself. These days have gone. Garp, struck down by the death of his son, for which he bears terrible responsibility, looks back to the first sentence of his first book, and says:

> Where had it come from? He tried to think of sentences like it. What he got was a sentence like this: "The boy was five years old; he had a cough that seemed deeper than his small, bony chest." What he got was memory, and that made muck. He had no pure imagination any more.

This is finely said, though luckily untrue, for the novel itself contains muck, memory, and imagination, and the muck gives it a weight that *Setting Free the Bears* lacked. The zaniness has been replaced by stoicism, and the jokes are now black. But there are also tenderness, respect, humanity. I particularly liked publisher John Wolf, surely one of the most appreciative portraits ever drawn by a writer: he smokes himself to death, for his "deep restlessness and unrelieved pessimism could only be numbed by smoking three packs of unfiltered cigarettes per day." Forget the bears: the wolves will do fine. . . .

Source: Margaret Drabble, "Muck, Memory, and Imagination," in *Harper's Magazine,* July 1978, pp. 82–84.

Sources

Bernstein, Richard, "John Irving: 19th-Century Novelist for These Times," in *New York Times,* April 25, 1989, p. 13.

Doane, Janice, and Devon Hodges, "Women and *The World according to Garp*," in *Gender Studies: New Directions in Feminist Criticism,* Bowling Green University Popular Press, 1986, pp. 60–69.

Feron, James, "All About Writing, According to Irving," in *New York Times,* November 29, 1981, p. 4.

Gilman, Richard, "The Whole Earth Novel," in *Nation,* Vol. 229, October 6, 1979, pp. 310–12.

Gussow, Mel, "John Irving: A Novelist Builds out from Fact to Reach the Truth," in *New York Times,* April 28, 1998.

Irving, John, *My Movie Business: A Memoir,* Random House, 1999.

Lehmann-Haupt, Christopher, Review in *New York Times,* April 13, 1978, p. 53.

Malone, Michael, "Everything That Rises," in *Nation,* Vol. 226, June 10, 1978, pp. 707–10.

McPherson, William, Review in *Washington Post Book World,* April 30, 1978, p. E1.

Moynahan, Julian, "Truths by Exaggeration," in *New York Times Book Review,* April 23, 1978, p. 1.

Stevens, Mark, Review in *National Review,* Vol. 31, March 2, 1979, p. 313.

Wilson, Raymond J., III, "The Postmodern Novel: The Example of John Irving's *The World according to Garp*," in *Critique: Studies in Contemporary Fiction,* Vol. 34, No. 1, Fall 1992, pp. 49–62.

For Further Study

Carton, Evan, "The Politics of Selfhood: Bob Slocum, T. S. Garp, and Auto-American Biography," in *Novel,* Vol. 20, No. 1, Fall 1986, pp. 41–61.

Carton compares and contrasts the main characters of *The World According to Garp* and Joseph Heller's *Something Happened* (1974) in an examination of "the individual's uncertain identity and political complicity."

Friedan, Betty, *The Feminine Mystique,* Norton, 1963.

Friedan's well-known and widely-read book is the acknowledged text that inspired the women's liberation movement of the 1960s and 1970s.

McKay, Kim, "Double Discourses in John Irving's *The World According to Garp*," in *Twentieth Century Literature,* Vol. 38, No. 4, Winter 1992, pp. 457–75.

In this compelling article, McKay examines the two roles played by the narrator of *The World According to Garp:* the biographer and the fiction writer.

Miller, Gabriel, *John Irving,* Frederick Ungar Publishing Company, 1982.

Miller's work is an early biography of John Irving.

Reilly, Edward C., *Understanding John Irving,* University of South Carolina Press, 1991.

This later biography by Reilly not only offers background information on Irving, but also presents critical examination of his work.

Tolman, Rolf, ed., *Vienna: Art and Architecture,* with photos by Gerald Zugmann and Achim Bednorz, Konnemann, 1999.

Tolman's book is an excellent coffee table book displaying the art and architecture of the Austrian city.

Zavoral, Nolan, *A Season on the Mat: Dan Gable and the Pursuit of Perfection,* Simon & Schuster, 1998.

Zavoral's book presents the story of the final season of legendary University of Iowa wrestling coach and former Olympic champion, Dan Gable.

Glossary of Literary Terms

A

Abstract: As an adjective applied to writing or literary works, abstract refers to words or phrases that name things not knowable through the five senses.

Aestheticism: A literary and artistic movement of the nineteenth century. Followers of the movement believed that art should not be mixed with social, political, or moral teaching. The statement "art for art's sake" is a good summary of aestheticism. The movement had its roots in France, but it gained widespread importance in England in the last half of the nineteenth century, where it helped change the Victorian practice of including moral lessons in literature.

Allegory: A narrative technique in which characters representing things or abstract ideas are used to convey a message or teach a lesson. Allegory is typically used to teach moral, ethical, or religious lessons but is sometimes used for satiric or political purposes.

Allusion: A reference to a familiar literary or historical person or event, used to make an idea more easily understood.

Analogy: A comparison of two things made to explain something unfamiliar through its similarities to something familiar, or to prove one point based on the acceptedness of another. Similes and metaphors are types of analogies.

Antagonist: The major character in a narrative or drama who works against the hero or protagonist.

Anthropomorphism: The presentation of animals or objects in human shape or with human characteristics. The term is derived from the Greek word for "human form."

Antihero: A central character in a work of literature who lacks traditional heroic qualities such as courage, physical prowess, and fortitude. Antiheroes typically distrust conventional values and are unable to commit themselves to any ideals. They generally feel helpless in a world over which they have no control. Antiheroes usually accept, and often celebrate, their positions as social outcasts.

Apprenticeship Novel: See *Bildungsroman*

Archetype: The word archetype is commonly used to describe an original pattern or model from which all other things of the same kind are made. This term was introduced to literary criticism from the psychology of Carl Jung. It expresses Jung's theory that behind every person's "unconscious," or repressed memories of the past, lies the "collective unconscious" of the human race: memories of the countless typical experiences of our ancestors. These memories are said to prompt illogical associations that trigger powerful emotions in the reader. Often, the emotional process is primitive, even primordial. Archetypes are the literary images that grow out of the "collective unconscious." They appear in literature as incidents and plots that repeat basic patterns of life. They may also appear as stereotyped characters.

Avant-garde: French term meaning "vanguard." It is used in literary criticism to describe new writing that rejects traditional approaches to literature in favor of innovations in style or content.

B

Beat Movement: A period featuring a group of American poets and novelists of the 1950s and 1960s—including Jack Kerouac, Allen Ginsberg, Gregory Corso, William S. Burroughs, and Lawrence Ferlinghetti—who rejected established social and literary values. Using such techniques as stream of consciousness writing and jazz-influenced free verse and focusing on unusual or abnormal states of mind—generated by religious ecstasy or the use of drugs—the Beat writers aimed to create works that were unconventional in both form and subject matter.

Bildungsroman: A German word meaning "novel of development." The *bildungsroman* is a study of the maturation of a youthful character, typically brought about through a series of social or sexual encounters that lead to self-awareness. *Bildungsroman* is used interchangeably with *erziehungsroman,* a novel of initiation and education. When a *bildungsroman* is concerned with the development of an artist (as in James Joyce's *A Portrait of the Artist as a Young Man*), it is often termed a *kunstlerroman.* Also known as Apprenticeship Novel, Coming of Age Novel, *Erziehungsroman,* or *Kunstlerroman.*

Black Aesthetic Movement: A period of artistic and literary development among African Americans in the 1960s and early 1970s. This was the first major African-American artistic movement since the Harlem Renaissance and was closely paralleled by the civil rights and black power movements. The black aesthetic writers attempted to produce works of art that would be meaningful to the black masses. Key figures in black aesthetics included one of its founders, poet and playwright Amiri Baraka, formerly known as LeRoi Jones; poet and essayist Haki R. Madhubuti, formerly Don L. Lee; poet and playwright Sonia Sanchez; and dramatist Ed Bullins. Also known as Black Arts Movement.

Black Humor: Writing that places grotesque elements side by side with humorous ones in an attempt to shock the reader, forcing him or her to laugh at the horrifying reality of a disordered world. Also known as Black Comedy.

Burlesque: Any literary work that uses exaggeration to make its subject appear ridiculous, either by treating a trivial subject with profound seriousness or by treating a dignified subject frivolously. The word "burlesque" may also be used as an adjective, as in "burlesque show," to mean "striptease act."

C

Character: Broadly speaking, a person in a literary work. The actions of characters are what constitute the plot of a story, novel, or poem. There are numerous types of characters, ranging from simple, stereotypical figures to intricate, multifaceted ones. In the techniques of anthropomorphism and personification, animals—and even places or things—can assume aspects of character. "Characterization" is the process by which an author creates vivid, believable characters in a work of art. This may be done in a variety of ways, including (1) direct description of the character by the narrator; (2) the direct presentation of the speech, thoughts, or actions of the character; and (3) the responses of other characters to the character. The term "character" also refers to a form originated by the ancient Greek writer Theophrastus that later became popular in the seventeenth and eighteenth centuries. It is a short essay or sketch of a person who prominently displays a specific attribute or quality, such as miserliness or ambition.

Climax: The turning point in a narrative, the moment when the conflict is at its most intense. Typically, the structure of stories, novels, and plays is one of rising action, in which tension builds to the climax, followed by falling action, in which tension lessens as the story moves to its conclusion.

Colloquialism: A word, phrase, or form of pronunciation that is acceptable in casual conversation but not in formal, written communication. It is considered more acceptable than slang.

Coming of Age Novel: See *Bildungsroman*

Concrete: Concrete is the opposite of abstract, and refers to a thing that actually exists or a description that allows the reader to experience an object or concept with the senses.

Connotation: The impression that a word gives beyond its defined meaning. Connotations may be universally understood or may be significant only to a certain group.

Convention: Any widely accepted literary device, style, or form.

D

Denotation: The definition of a word, apart from the impressions or feelings it creates (connotations) in the reader.

Denouement: A French word meaning "the unknotting." In literary criticism, it denotes the resolution of conflict in fiction or drama. The *denouement* follows the climax and provides an outcome to the primary plot situation as well as an explanation of secondary plot complications. The *denouement* often involves a character's recognition of his or her state of mind or moral condition. Also known as Falling Action.

Description: Descriptive writing is intended to allow a reader to picture the scene or setting in which the action of a story takes place. The form this description takes often evokes an intended emotional response—a dark, spooky graveyard will evoke fear, and a peaceful, sunny meadow will evoke calmness.

Dialogue: In its widest sense, dialogue is simply conversation between people in a literary work; in its most restricted sense, it refers specifically to the speech of characters in a drama. As a specific literary genre, a "dialogue" is a composition in which characters debate an issue or idea.

Diction: The selection and arrangement of words in a literary work. Either or both may vary depending on the desired effect. There are four general types of diction: "formal," used in scholarly or lofty writing; "informal," used in relaxed but educated conversation; "colloquial," used in everyday speech; and "slang," containing newly coined words and other terms not accepted in formal usage.

Didactic: A term used to describe works of literature that aim to teach some moral, religious, political, or practical lesson. Although didactic elements are often found in artistically pleasing works, the term "didactic" usually refers to literature in which the message is more important than the form. The term may also be used to criticize a work that the critic finds "overly didactic," that is, heavy-handed in its delivery of a lesson.

Doppelganger: A literary technique by which a character is duplicated (usually in the form of an alter ego, though sometimes as a ghostly counterpart) or divided into two distinct, usually opposite personalities. The use of this character device is widespread in nineteenth- and twentieth-century literature, and indicates a growing awareness among authors that the "self" is really a composite of many "selves." Also known as The Double.

Double Entendre: A corruption of a French phrase meaning "double meaning." The term is used to indicate a word or phrase that is deliberately ambiguous, especially when one of the meanings is risqué or improper.

Dramatic Irony: Occurs when the audience of a play or the reader of a work of literature knows something that a character in the work itself does not know. The irony is in the contrast between the intended meaning of the statements or actions of a character and the additional information understood by the audience.

Dystopia: An imaginary place in a work of fiction where the characters lead dehumanized, fearful lives.

E

Edwardian: Describes cultural conventions identified with the period of the reign of Edward VII of England (1901-1910). Writers of the Edwardian Age typically displayed a strong reaction against the propriety and conservatism of the Victorian Age. Their work often exhibits distrust of authority in religion, politics, and art and expresses strong doubts about the soundness of conventional values.

Empathy: A sense of shared experience, including emotional and physical feelings, with someone or something other than oneself. Empathy is often used to describe the response of a reader to a literary character.

Enlightenment, The: An eighteenth-century philosophical movement. It began in France but had a wide impact throughout Europe and America. Thinkers of the Enlightenment valued reason and believed that both the individual and society could achieve a state of perfection. Corresponding to this essentially humanist vision was a resistance to religious authority.

Epigram: A saying that makes the speaker's point quickly and concisely. Often used to preface a novel.

Epilogue: A concluding statement or section of a literary work. In dramas, particularly those of the seventeenth and eighteenth centuries, the epilogue is a closing speech, often in verse, delivered by an actor at the end of a play and spoken directly to the audience.

Epiphany: A sudden revelation of truth inspired by a seemingly trivial incident.

Episode: An incident that forms part of a story and is significantly related to it. Episodes may be either self-contained narratives or events that depend on a larger context for their sense and importance.

Epistolary Novel: A novel in the form of letters. The form was particularly popular in the eighteenth century.

Epithet: A word or phrase, often disparaging or abusive, that expresses a character trait of someone or something.

Existentialism: A predominantly twentieth-century philosophy concerned with the nature and perception of human existence. There are two major strains of existentialist thought: atheistic and Christian. Followers of atheistic existentialism believe that the individual is alone in a godless universe and that the basic human condition is one of suffering and loneliness. Nevertheless, because there are no fixed values, individuals can create their own characters—indeed, they can shape themselves—through the exercise of free will. The atheistic strain culminates in and is popularly associated with the works of Jean-Paul Sartre. The Christian existentialists, on the other hand, believe that only in God may people find freedom from life's anguish. The two strains hold certain beliefs in common: that existence cannot be fully understood or described through empirical effort; that anguish is a universal element of life; that individuals must bear responsibility for their actions; and that there is no common standard of behavior or perception for religious and ethical matters.

Expatriates: See *Expatriatism*

Expatriatism: The practice of leaving one's country to live for an extended period in another country.

Exposition: Writing intended to explain the nature of an idea, thing, or theme. Expository writing is often combined with description, narration, or argument. In dramatic writing, the exposition is the introductory material which presents the characters, setting, and tone of the play.

Expressionism: An indistinct literary term, originally used to describe an early twentieth-century school of German painting. The term applies to almost any mode of unconventional, highly subjective writing that distorts reality in some way.

F

Fable: A prose or verse narrative intended to convey a moral. Animals or inanimate objects with human characteristics often serve as characters in fables.

Falling Action: See *Denouement*

Fantasy: A literary form related to mythology and folklore. Fantasy literature is typically set in nonexistent realms and features supernatural beings.

Farce: A type of comedy characterized by broad humor, outlandish incidents, and often vulgar subject matter.

***Femme fatale*:** A French phrase with the literal translation "fatal woman." A *femme fatale* is a sensuous, alluring woman who often leads men into danger or trouble.

Fiction: Any story that is the product of imagination rather than a documentation of fact. Characters and events in such narratives may be based in real life but their ultimate form and configuration is a creation of the author.

Figurative Language: A technique in writing in which the author temporarily interrupts the order, construction, or meaning of the writing for a particular effect. This interruption takes the form of one or more figures of speech such as hyperbole, irony, or simile. Figurative language is the opposite of literal language, in which every word is truthful, accurate, and free of exaggeration or embellishment.

Figures of Speech: Writing that differs from customary conventions for construction, meaning, order, or significance for the purpose of a special meaning or effect. There are two major types of figures of speech: rhetorical figures, which do not make changes in the meaning of the words, and tropes, which do.

***Fin de siecle*:** A French term meaning "end of the century." The term is used to denote the last decade of the nineteenth century, a transition period when writers and other artists abandoned old conventions and looked for new techniques and objectives.

First Person: See *Point of View*

Flashback: A device used in literature to present action that occurred before the beginning of the story. Flashbacks are often introduced as the dreams or recollections of one or more characters.

Foil: A character in a work of literature whose physical or psychological qualities contrast strongly with, and therefore highlight, the corresponding qualities of another character.

Folklore: Traditions and myths preserved in a culture or group of people. Typically, these are passed on by word of mouth in various forms—such as legends, songs, and proverbs—or preserved in customs and ceremonies. This term was first used by W. J. Thoms in 1846.

Folktale: A story originating in oral tradition. Folktales fall into a variety of categories, including legends, ghost stories, fairy tales, fables, and anecdotes based on historical figures and events.

Foreshadowing: A device used in literature to create expectation or to set up an explanation of later developments.

Form: The pattern or construction of a work which identifies its genre and distinguishes it from other genres.

G

Genre: A category of literary work. In critical theory, genre may refer to both the content of a given work—tragedy, comedy, pastoral—and to its form, such as poetry, novel, or drama.

Gilded Age: A period in American history during the 1870s characterized by political corruption and materialism. A number of important novels of social and political criticism were written during this time.

Gothicism: In literary criticism, works characterized by a taste for the medieval or morbidly attractive. A gothic novel prominently features elements of horror, the supernatural, gloom, and violence: clanking chains, terror, charnel houses, ghosts, medieval castles, and mysteriously slamming doors. The term "gothic novel" is also applied to novels that lack elements of the traditional Gothic setting but that create a similar atmosphere of terror or dread.

Grotesque: In literary criticism, the subject matter of a work or a style of expression characterized by exaggeration, deformity, freakishness, and disorder. The grotesque often includes an element of comic absurdity.

H

Harlem Renaissance: The Harlem Renaissance of the 1920s is generally considered the first significant movement of black writers and artists in the United States. During this period, new and established black writers published more fiction and poetry than ever before, the first influential black literary journals were established, and black authors and artists received their first widespread recognition and serious critical appraisal. Among the major writers associated with this period are Claude McKay, Jean Toomer, Countee Cullen, Langston Hughes, Arna Bontemps, Nella Larsen, and Zora

Neale Hurston. Also known as Negro Renaissance and New Negro Movement.

Hero/Heroine: The principal sympathetic character (male or female) in a literary work. Heroes and heroines typically exhibit admirable traits: idealism, courage, and integrity, for example.

Holocaust Literature: Literature influenced by or written about the Holocaust of World War II. Such literature includes true stories of survival in concentration camps, escape, and life after the war, as well as fictional works and poetry.

Humanism: A philosophy that places faith in the dignity of humankind and rejects the medieval perception of the individual as a weak, fallen creature. "Humanists" typically believe in the perfectibility of human nature and view reason and education as the means to that end.

Hyperbole: In literary criticism, deliberate exaggeration used to achieve an effect.

I

Idiom: A word construction or verbal expression closely associated with a given language.

Image: A concrete representation of an object or sensory experience. Typically, such a representation helps evoke the feelings associated with the object or experience itself. Images are either "literal" or "figurative." Literal images are especially concrete and involve little or no extension of the obvious meaning of the words used to express them. Figurative images do not follow the literal meaning of the words exactly. Images in literature are usually visual, but the term "image" can also refer to the representation of any sensory experience.

Imagery: The array of images in a literary work. Also, figurative language.

***In medias res*:** A Latin term meaning "in the middle of things." It refers to the technique of beginning a story at its midpoint and then using various flashback devices to reveal previous action.

Interior Monologue: A narrative technique in which characters' thoughts are revealed in a way that appears to be uncontrolled by the author. The interior monologue typically aims to reveal the inner self of a character. It portrays emotional experiences as they occur at both a conscious and unconscious level. Images are often used to represent sensations or emotions.

Irony: In literary criticism, the effect of language in which the intended meaning is the opposite of what is stated.

J

Jargon: Language that is used or understood only by a select group of people. Jargon may refer to terminology used in a certain profession, such as computer jargon, or it may refer to any non-sensical language that is not understood by most people.

L

Leitmotiv: See *Motif*

Literal Language: An author uses literal language when he or she writes without exaggerating or embellishing the subject matter and without any tools of figurative language.

Lost Generation: A term first used by Gertrude Stein to describe the post-World War I generation of American writers: men and women haunted by a sense of betrayal and emptiness brought about by the destructiveness of the war.

M

Mannerism: Exaggerated, artificial adherence to a literary manner or style. Also, a popular style of the visual arts of late sixteenth-century Europe that was marked by elongation of the human form and by intentional spatial distortion. Literary works that are self-consciously high-toned and artistic are often said to be "mannered."

Metaphor: A figure of speech that expresses an idea through the image of another object. Metaphors suggest the essence of the first object by identifying it with certain qualities of the second object.

Modernism: Modern literary practices. Also, the principles of a literary school that lasted from roughly the beginning of the twentieth century until the end of World War II. Modernism is defined by its rejection of the literary conventions of the nineteenth century and by its opposition to conventional morality, taste, traditions, and economic values.

Mood: The prevailing emotions of a work or of the author in his or her creation of the work. The mood of a work is not always what might be expected based on its subject matter.

Motif: A theme, character type, image, metaphor, or other verbal element that recurs throughout a single work of literature or occurs in a number of different works over a period of time. Also known as *Motiv* or *Leitmotiv*.

Myth: An anonymous tale emerging from the traditional beliefs of a culture or social unit. Myths use supernatural explanations for natural phenomena. They may also explain cosmic issues like creation and death. Collections of myths, known as mythologies, are common to all cultures and nations, but the best-known myths belong to the Norse, Roman, and Greek mythologies.

N

Narration: The telling of a series of events, real or invented. A narration may be either a simple narrative, in which the events are recounted chronologically, or a narrative with a plot, in which the account is given in a style reflecting the author's artistic concept of the story. Narration is sometimes used as a synonym for "storyline."

Narrative: A verse or prose accounting of an event or sequence of events, real or invented. The term is also used as an adjective in the sense "method of narration." For example, in literary criticism, the expression "narrative technique" usually refers to the way the author structures and presents his or her story.

Narrator: The teller of a story. The narrator may be the author or a character in the story through whom the author speaks.

Naturalism: A literary movement of the late nineteenth and early twentieth centuries. The movement's major theorist, French novelist Emile Zola, envisioned a type of fiction that would examine human life with the objectivity of scientific inquiry. The Naturalists typically viewed human beings as either the products of "biological determinism," ruled by hereditary instincts and engaged in an endless struggle for survival, or as the products of "socioeconomic determinism," ruled by social and economic forces beyond their control. In their works, the Naturalists generally ignored the highest levels of society and focused on degradation: poverty, alcoholism, prostitution, insanity, and disease.

Noble Savage: The idea that primitive man is noble and good but becomes evil and corrupted as he becomes civilized. The concept of the noble savage originated in the Renaissance period but is more closely identified with such later writers as

Jean-Jacques Rousseau and Aphra Behn. See also Primitivism.

Novel of Ideas: A novel in which the examination of intellectual issues and concepts takes precedence over characterization or a traditional storyline.

Novel of Manners: A novel that examines the customs and mores of a cultural group.

Novel: A long fictional narrative written in prose, which developed from the novella and other early forms of narrative. A novel is usually organized under a plot or theme with a focus on character development and action.

Novella: An Italian term meaning "story." This term has been especially used to describe fourteenth-century Italian tales, but it also refers to modern short novels.

O

Objective Correlative: An outward set of objects, a situation, or a chain of events corresponding to an inward experience and evoking this experience in the reader. The term frequently appears in modern criticism in discussions of authors' intended effects on the emotional responses of readers.

Objectivity: A quality in writing characterized by the absence of the author's opinion or feeling about the subject matter. Objectivity is an important factor in criticism.

Oedipus Complex: A son's amorous obsession with his mother. The phrase is derived from the story of the ancient Theban hero Oedipus, who unknowingly killed his father and married his mother.

Omniscience: See *Point of View*

Onomatopoeia: The use of words whose sounds express or suggest their meaning. In its simplest sense, onomatopoeia may be represented by words that mimic the sounds they denote such as "hiss" or "meow." At a more subtle level, the pattern and rhythm of sounds and rhymes of a line or poem may be onomatopoeic.

Oxymoron: A phrase combining two contradictory terms. Oxymorons may be intentional or unintentional.

P

Parable: A story intended to teach a moral lesson or answer an ethical question.

Paradox: A statement that appears illogical or contradictory at first, but may actually point to an underlying truth.

Parallelism: A method of comparison of two ideas in which each is developed in the same grammatical structure.

Parody: In literary criticism, this term refers to an imitation of a serious literary work or the signature style of a particular author in a ridiculous manner. A typical parody adopts the style of the original and applies it to an inappropriate subject for humorous effect. Parody is a form of satire and could be considered the literary equivalent of a caricature or cartoon.

Pastoral: A term derived from the Latin word "pastor," meaning shepherd. A pastoral is a literary composition on a rural theme. The conventions of the pastoral were originated by the third-century Greek poet Theocritus, who wrote about the experiences, love affairs, and pastimes of Sicilian shepherds. In a pastoral, characters and language of a courtly nature are often placed in a simple setting. The term pastoral is also used to classify dramas, elegies, and lyrics that exhibit the use of country settings and shepherd characters.

Pen Name: See *Pseudonym*

Persona: A Latin term meaning "mask." *Personae* are the characters in a fictional work of literature. The *persona* generally functions as a mask through which the author tells a story in a voice other than his or her own. A *persona* is usually either a character in a story who acts as a narrator or an "implied author," a voice created by the author to act as the narrator for himself or herself.

Personification: A figure of speech that gives human qualities to abstract ideas, animals, and inanimate objects. Also known as *Prosopopoeia*.

Picaresque Novel: Episodic fiction depicting the adventures of a roguish central character ("picaro" is Spanish for "rogue"). The picaresque hero is commonly a low-born but clever individual who wanders into and out of various affairs of love, danger, and farcical intrigue. These involvements may take place at all social levels and typically present a humorous and wide-ranging satire of a given society.

Plagiarism: Claiming another person's written material as one's own. Plagiarism can take the form of direct, word-for-word copying or the theft of the substance or idea of the work.

Plot: In literary criticism, this term refers to the pattern of events in a narrative or drama. In its simplest sense, the plot guides the author in composing the work and helps the reader follow the work. Typically, plots exhibit causality and unity and have a beginning, a middle, and an end. Sometimes, however, a plot may consist of a series of disconnected events, in which case it is known as an "episodic plot."

Poetic Justice: An outcome in a literary work, not necessarily a poem, in which the good are rewarded and the evil are punished, especially in ways that particularly fit their virtues or crimes.

Poetic License: Distortions of fact and literary convention made by a writer—not always a poet—for the sake of the effect gained. Poetic license is closely related to the concept of "artistic freedom."

Poetics: This term has two closely related meanings. It denotes (1) an aesthetic theory in literary criticism about the essence of poetry or (2) rules prescribing the proper methods, content, style, or diction of poetry. The term poetics may also refer to theories about literature in general, not just poetry.

Point of View: The narrative perspective from which a literary work is presented to the reader. There are four traditional points of view. The "third person omniscient" gives the reader a "godlike" perspective, unrestricted by time or place, from which to see actions and look into the minds of characters. This allows the author to comment openly on characters and events in the work. The "third person" point of view presents the events of the story from outside of any single character's perception, much like the omniscient point of view, but the reader must understand the action as it takes place and without any special insight into characters' minds or motivations. The "first person" or "personal" point of view relates events as they are perceived by a single character. The main character "tells" the story and may offer opinions about the action and characters which differ from those of the author. Much less common than omniscient, third person, and first person is the "second person" point of view, wherein the author tells the story as if it is happening to the reader.

Polemic: A work in which the author takes a stand on a controversial subject, such as abortion or religion. Such works are often extremely argumentative or provocative.

Pornography: Writing intended to provoke feelings of lust in the reader. Such works are often condemned by critics and teachers, but those which can be shown to have literary value are viewed less harshly.

Post-Aesthetic Movement: An artistic response made by African Americans to the black aesthetic movement of the 1960s and early '70s. Writers since that time have adopted a somewhat different tone in their work, with less emphasis placed on the disparity between black and white in the United States. In the words of post-aesthetic authors such as Toni Morrison, John Edgar Wideman, and Kristin Hunter, African Americans are portrayed as looking inward for answers to their own questions, rather than always looking to the outside world.

Postmodernism: Writing from the 1960s forward characterized by experimentation and continuing to apply some of the fundamentals of modernism, which included existentialism and alienation. Postmodernists have gone a step further in the rejection of tradition begun with the modernists by also rejecting traditional forms, preferring the anti-novel over the novel and the antihero over the hero.

Primitivism: The belief that primitive peoples were nobler and less flawed than civilized peoples because they had not been subjected to the tainting influence of society. See also Noble Savage.

Prologue: An introductory section of a literary work. It often contains information establishing the situation of the characters or presents information about the setting, time period, or action. In drama, the prologue is spoken by a chorus or by one of the principal characters.

Prose: A literary medium that attempts to mirror the language of everyday speech. It is distinguished from poetry by its use of unmetered, unrhymed language consisting of logically related sentences. Prose is usually grouped into paragraphs that form a cohesive whole such as an essay or a novel.

Prosopopoeia: See *Personification*

Protagonist: The central character of a story who serves as a focus for its themes and incidents and as the principal rationale for its development. The protagonist is sometimes referred to in discussions of modern literature as the hero or antihero.

Protest Fiction: Protest fiction has as its primary purpose the protesting of some social injustice, such as racism or discrimination.

Proverb: A brief, sage saying that expresses a truth about life in a striking manner.

Pseudonym: A name assumed by a writer, most often intended to prevent his or her identification as the author of a work. Two or more authors may work together under one pseudonym, or an author may use a different name for each genre he or she publishes in. Some publishing companies maintain "house pseudonyms," under which any number of authors may write installations in a series. Some authors also choose a pseudonym over their real names the way an actor may use a stage name.

Pun: A play on words that have similar sounds but different meanings.

R

Realism: A nineteenth-century European literary movement that sought to portray familiar characters, situations, and settings in a realistic manner. This was done primarily by using an objective narrative point of view and through the buildup of accurate detail. The standard for success of any realistic work depends on how faithfully it transfers common experience into fictional forms. The realistic method may be altered or extended, as in stream of consciousness writing, to record highly subjective experience.

Repartee: Conversation featuring snappy retorts and witticisms.

Resolution: The portion of a story following the climax, in which the conflict is resolved. See also *Denouement.*

Rhetoric: In literary criticism, this term denotes the art of ethical persuasion. In its strictest sense, rhetoric adheres to various principles developed since classical times for arranging facts and ideas in a clear, persuasive, appealing manner. The term is also used to refer to effective prose in general and theories of or methods for composing effective prose.

Rhetorical Question: A question intended to provoke thought, but not an expressed answer, in the reader. It is most commonly used in oratory and other persuasive genres.

Rising Action: The part of a drama where the plot becomes increasingly complicated. Rising action leads up to the climax, or turning point, of a drama.

Roman a clef: A French phrase meaning "novel with a key." It refers to a narrative in which real persons are portrayed under fictitious names.

Romance: A broad term, usually denoting a narrative with exotic, exaggerated, often idealized characters, scenes, and themes.

Romanticism: This term has two widely accepted meanings. In historical criticism, it refers to a European intellectual and artistic movement of the late eighteenth and early nineteenth centuries that sought greater freedom of personal expression than that allowed by the strict rules of literary form and logic of the eighteenth-century neoclassicists. The Romantics preferred emotional and imaginative expression to rational analysis. They considered the individual to be at the center of all experience and so placed him or her at the center of their art. The Romantics believed that the creative imagination reveals nobler truths—unique feelings and attitudes—than those that could be discovered by logic or by scientific examination. Both the natural world and the state of childhood were important sources for revelations of "eternal truths." "Romanticism" is also used as a general term to refer to a type of sensibility found in all periods of literary history and usually considered to be in opposition to the principles of classicism. In this sense, Romanticism signifies any work or philosophy in which the exotic or dreamlike figure strongly, or that is devoted to individualistic expression, self-analysis, or a pursuit of a higher realm of knowledge than can be discovered by human reason.

Romantics: See *Romanticism*

S

Satire: A work that uses ridicule, humor, and wit to criticize and provoke change in human nature and institutions. There are two major types of satire: "formal" or "direct" satire speaks directly to the reader or to a character in the work; "indirect" satire relies upon the ridiculous behavior of its characters to make its point. Formal satire is further divided into two manners: the "Horatian," which ridicules gently, and the "Juvenalian," which derides its subjects harshly and bitterly.

Science Fiction: A type of narrative about or based upon real or imagined scientific theories and technology. Science fiction is often peopled with alien creatures and set on other planets or in different dimensions.

Second Person: See *Point of View*

Setting: The time, place, and culture in which the action of a narrative takes place. The elements of setting may include geographic location, characters' physical and mental environments, prevailing cultural attitudes, or the historical time in which the action takes place.

Simile: A comparison, usually using "like" or "as", of two essentially dissimilar things, as in "coffee as cold as ice" or "He sounded like a broken record."

Slang: A type of informal verbal communication that is generally unacceptable for formal writing. Slang words and phrases are often colorful exaggerations used to emphasize the speaker's point; they may also be shortened versions of an often-used word or phrase.

Slave Narrative: Autobiographical accounts of American slave life as told by escaped slaves. These works first appeared during the abolition movement of the 1830s through the 1850s.

Socialist Realism: The Socialist Realism school of literary theory was proposed by Maxim Gorky and established as a dogma by the first Soviet Congress of Writers. It demanded adherence to a communist worldview in works of literature. Its doctrines required an objective viewpoint comprehensible to the working classes and themes of social struggle featuring strong proletarian heroes. Also known as Social Realism.

Stereotype: A stereotype was originally the name for a duplication made during the printing process; this led to its modern definition as a person or thing that is (or is assumed to be) the same as all others of its type.

Stream of Consciousness: A narrative technique for rendering the inward experience of a character. This technique is designed to give the impression of an ever-changing series of thoughts, emotions, images, and memories in the spontaneous and seemingly illogical order that they occur in life.

Structure: The form taken by a piece of literature. The structure may be made obvious for ease of understanding, as in nonfiction works, or may obscured for artistic purposes, as in some poetry or seemingly "unstructured" prose.

***Sturm und Drang*:** A German term meaning "storm and stress." It refers to a German literary movement of the 1770s and 1780s that reacted against the order and rationalism of the enlightenment, focusing instead on the intense experience of extraordinary individuals.

Style: A writer's distinctive manner of arranging words to suit his or her ideas and purpose in writing. The unique imprint of the author's personality upon his or her writing, style is the product of an author's way of arranging ideas and his or her use of diction, different sentence structures, rhythm, figures of speech, rhetorical principles, and other elements of composition.

Subjectivity: Writing that expresses the author's personal feelings about his subject, and which may or may not include factual information about the subject.

Subplot: A secondary story in a narrative. A subplot may serve as a motivating or complicating force for the main plot of the work, or it may provide emphasis for, or relief from, the main plot.

Surrealism: A term introduced to criticism by Guillaume Apollinaire and later adopted by Andre Breton. It refers to a French literary and artistic movement founded in the 1920s. The Surrealists sought to express unconscious thoughts and feelings in their works. The best-known technique used for achieving this aim was automatic writing—transcriptions of spontaneous outpourings from the unconscious. The Surrealists proposed to unify the contrary levels of conscious and unconscious, dream and reality, objectivity and subjectivity into a new level of "super-realism."

Suspense: A literary device in which the author maintains the audience's attention through the buildup of events, the outcome of which will soon be revealed.

Symbol: Something that suggests or stands for something else without losing its original identity. In literature, symbols combine their literal meaning with the suggestion of an abstract concept. Literary symbols are of two types: those that carry complex associations of meaning no matter what their contexts, and those that derive their suggestive meaning from their functions in specific literary works.

Symbolism: This term has two widely accepted meanings. In historical criticism, it denotes an early modernist literary movement initiated in France during the nineteenth century that reacted against the prevailing standards of realism. Writers in this movement aimed to evoke, indirectly and symbolically, an order of being beyond the material world of the five senses. Poetic expression of personal emotion figured strongly in the movement, typically by means of a private set of symbols uniquely identifiable with the individual poet. The principal aim of the Symbolists was to express in words the highly complex feelings that grew out of everyday contact with the world. In a broader sense, the term "symbolism" refers to the use of one object to represent another.

T

Tall Tale: A humorous tale told in a straightforward, credible tone but relating absolutely impossible events or feats of the characters. Such tales were commonly told of frontier adventures during the settlement of the west in the United States.

Theme: The main point of a work of literature. The term is used interchangeably with thesis.

Thesis: A thesis is both an essay and the point argued in the essay. Thesis novels and thesis plays share the quality of containing a thesis which is supported through the action of the story.

Third Person: See *Point of View*

Tone: The author's attitude toward his or her audience may be deduced from the tone of the work. A formal tone may create distance or convey politeness, while an informal tone may encourage a friendly, intimate, or intrusive feeling in the reader. The author's attitude toward his or her subject matter may also be deduced from the tone of the words he or she uses in discussing it.

Transcendentalism: An American philosophical and religious movement, based in New England from around 1835 until the Civil War. Transcendentalism was a form of American romanticism that had its roots abroad in the works of Thomas Carlyle, Samuel Coleridge, and Johann Wolfgang von Goethe. The Transcendentalists stressed the importance of intuition and subjective experience in communication with God. They rejected religious dogma and texts in favor of mysticism and scientific naturalism. They pursued truths that lie beyond the "colorless" realms perceived by reason and the senses and were active social reformers in public education, women's rights, and the abolition of slavery.

U

Urban Realism: A branch of realist writing that attempts to accurately reflect the often harsh facts of modern urban existence.

Utopia: A fictional perfect place, such as "paradise" or "heaven."

V

Verisimilitude: Literally, the appearance of truth. In literary criticism, the term refers to aspects of a work of literature that seem true to the reader.

Victorian: Refers broadly to the reign of Queen Victoria of England (1837-1901) and to anything with qualities typical of that era. For example, the qualities of smug narrowmindedness, bourgeois materialism, faith in social progress, and priggish morality are often considered Victorian. This stereotype is contradicted by such dramatic intellectual developments as the theories of Charles Darwin, Karl Marx, and Sigmund Freud (which stirred strong debates in England) and the critical attitudes of serious Victorian writers like Charles Dickens and George Eliot. In literature, the Victorian Period was the great age of the English novel, and the latter part of the era saw the rise of movements such as decadence and symbolism. Also known as Victorian Age and Victorian Period.

W

Weltanschauung: A German term referring to a person's worldview or philosophy.

Weltschmerz: A German term meaning "world pain." It describes a sense of anguish about the nature of existence, usually associated with a melancholy, pessimistic attitude.

Z

Zeitgeist: A German term meaning "spirit of the time." It refers to the moral and intellectual trends of a given era.

Cumulative Author/Title Index

Numerical

1984 (Orwell): V7

A

The Accidental Tourist (Tyler): V7
Achebe, Chinua
    Things Fall Apart: V2
Adams, Douglas
    The Hitchhiker's Guide to the
        Galaxy: V7
Adams, Richard
    Watership Down: V11
The Adventures of Huckleberry Finn
    (Twain): V1
The Adventures of Tom Sawyer
    (Twain): V6
The Age of Innocence (Wharton):
    V11
Alcott, Louisa May
    Little Women: V12
Alice's Adventures in Wonderland
    (Carroll): V7
Allende, Isabel
    The House of the Spirits: V6
Allison, Dorothy
    Bastard Out of Carolina: V11
All Quiet on the Western Front
    (Remarque): V4
Alvarez, Julia
    How the García Girls Lost Their
        Accents: V5
    In the Time of the Butterflies: V9
Always Coming Home (Le Guin): V9
The Ambassadors (James): V12
Anaya, Rudolfo
    Bless Me, Ultima: V12

Anderson, Sherwood
    Winesburg, Ohio: V4
Angelou, Maya
    I Know Why the Caged Bird
        Sings: V2
Animal Dreams (Kingsolver): V12
Animal Farm (Orwell): V3
Annie John (Kincaid): V3
Appointment in Samarra (O'Hara):
    V11
As I Lay Dying (Faulkner): V8
Atlas Shrugged (Rand): V10
Atwood, Margaret
    The Handmaid's Tale: V4
Auel, Jean
    The Clan of the Cave Bear: V11
Austen, Jane
    Pride and Prejudice: V1
The Autobiography of Miss Jane
    Pittman (Gaines): V5
The Awakening (Chopin): V3

B

Baldwin, James
    Go Tell It on the Mountain: V4
Ballard, J. G.
    Empire of the Sun: V8
Bastard Out of Carolina (Allison): V11
The Bean Trees (Kingsolver): V5
The Bell Jar (Plath): V1
Bellow, Saul
    Seize the Day: V4
Beloved (Morrison): V6
Betsey Brown (Shange): V11
Billy Budd, Sailor: An Inside
    Narrative (Melville): V9

Black Boy (Wright): V1
Blair, Eric Arthur
    Animal Farm: V3
Bless Me, Ultima (Anaya): V12
The Bluest Eye (Morrison): V1
Body and Soul (Conroy): V11
Bradbury, Ray
    Fahrenheit 451: V1
Brave New World (Huxley): V6
Breathing Lessons (Tyler): V10
The Bride Price (Emecheta): V12
Brontë, Charlotte
    Jane Eyre: V4
Brontë, Emily
    Wuthering Heights: V2
The Brothers Karamazov
    (Dostoevsky): V8
Brown, Rita Mae
    Rubyfruit Jungle: V9
Bulgakov, Mikhail
    The Master and Margarita: V8
Butler, Octavia
    Kindred: V8

C

The Caine Mutiny: A Novel of World
    War II (Wouk): V7
The Call of the Wild (London): V8
Camus, Albert
    The Stranger: V6
Candide (Voltaire): V7
Cane (Toomer): V11
Card, Orson Scott
    Ender's Game: V5
Carroll, Lewis
    Alice's Adventures in
        Wonderland: V7

Catch-22 (Heller): V1
The Catcher in the Rye
        (Salinger): V1
Cather, Willa
        My Ántonia: V2
Ceremony (Marmon Silko): V4
The Chocolate War (Cormier): V2
Chopin, Kate
        The Awakening: V3
The Chosen (Potok): V4
Christie, Agatha
        Ten Little Indians: V8
A Christmas Carol (Dickens): V10
Chronicle of a Death Foretold
        (García Márquez): V10
Cisneros, Sandra
        The House on Mango Street: V2
The Clan of the Cave Bear (Auel):
        V11
Clavell, James du Maresq
        Shogun: *A Novel of Japan:* V10
Clemens, Samuel
        The Adventures of Huckleberry
        Finn: V1
The Adventures of Tom Sawyer: V6
The Color Purple (Walker): V5
Cooper, James Fenimore
        The Last of the Mohicans: V9
Conrad, Joseph
        Heart of Darkness: V2
Conroy, Frank
        Body and Soul: V11
Cormier, Robert
        The Chocolate War: V2
Crane, Stephen
        The Red Badge of Courage: V4
The Crazy Horse Electric Game
        (Crutcher): V11
Crime and Punishment
        (Dostoyevsky): V3
Crutcher, Chris
        The Crazy Horse Electric Game:
        V11
Cry, the Beloved Country
        (Paton): V3

D

The Dead of the House (Green): V10
de Cervantes Saavedra, Miguel
        Don Quixote: V8
Defoe, Daniel
        Robinson Crusoe: V9
Deliverance (Dickey): V9
Democracy (Didion): V3
Dick, Philip K.
        Do Androids Dream of Electric
        Sheep?: V5
Dickens, Charles
        A Christmas Carol: V10
        Great Expectations: V4
        A Tale of Two Cities: V5

Dickey, James
        Deliverance: V9
Didion, Joan
        Democracy: V3
Dinesen, Isak
        Out of Africa: V9
Dinner at the Homesick Restaurant
        (Tyler): V2
Do Androids Dream of Electric
        Sheep? (Dick): V5
Doctorow, E. L.
        Ragtime: V6
Don Quixote (de Cervantes
        Saavedra): V8
Dorris, Michael
        A Yellow Raft in Blue Water: V3
Dostoyevsky, Fyodor
        The Brothers Karamazov: V8
        Crime and Punishment: V3
Dr. Jekyll and Mr. Hyde (Stevenson):
        V11
Dreiser, Theodore
        Sister Carrie: V8
du Maurier, Daphne
        Rebecca: V12

E

The Edible Woman (Atwood): V12
Ellen Foster (Gibbons): V3
Ellis, Bret Easton
        Less Than Zero: V11
Ellison, Ralph
        Invisible Man: V2
Emecheta, Buchi
        The Bride Price: V12
Empire of the Sun (Ballard): V8
Ender's Game (Card): V5
Erdrich, Louise
        Love Medicine: V5
Esquivel, Laura
        Like Water for Chocolate: V5
Ethan Frome (Wharton): V5

F

Fahrenheit 451 (Bradbury): V1
A Farewell to Arms
        (Hemingway): V1
Faulkner, William
        As I Lay Dying: V8
        The Sound and the Fury: V4
Fitzgerald, F. Scott
        The Great Gatsby: V2
The Fixer (Malamud): V9
Flagg, Fannie
        Fried Green Tomatoes at the
        Whistle Stop Café: V7
Flowers for Algernon (Keyes): V2
Forster, E. M.
        A Passage to India: V3
        A Room with a View: V11

        Howards End: V10
Fox, Paula
        The Slave Dancer: V12
Frankenstein (Shelley): V1
Fried Green Tomatoes at the Whistle
        Stop Café: (Flagg): V7
Fuentes, Carlos
        The Old Gringo: V8

G

Gaines, Ernest J.
        A Lesson Before Dying: V7
        The Autobiography of Miss Jane
        Pittman: V5
Giants in the Earth (Rölvaag): V5
García Márquez, Gabriel
        Chronicle of a Death Foretold:
        V10
        Love in the Time of Cholera: V1
        One Hundred Years of Solitude:
        V5
Gardner, John
        Grendel: V3
Gibbons, Kaye
        Ellen Foster: V3
The Giver (Lowry): V3
Go Tell It on the Mountain
        (Baldwin): V4
Golding, William
        Lord of the Flies: V2
Gone with the Wind (Mitchell): V9
Gordimer, Nadine
        July's People: V4
The Grapes of Wrath (Steinbeck): V7
The Grass Dancer (Power): V11
Great Expectations (Dickens): V4
The Great Gatsby (Fitzgerald): V2
Green, Hannah
        The Dead of the House: V10
Greene, Bette
        Summer of My German Soldier:
        V10
Grendel (Gardner): V3
Guest, Judith
        Ordinary People: V1
Gulliver's Travels (Swift): V6

H

Haley, Alex
        Roots: The Story of an American
        Family: V9
The Handmaid's Tale (Atwood): V4
Hardy, Thomas
        The Return of the Native: V11
        Tess of the d'Urbervilles: V3
Hawthorne, Nathaniel
        The Scarlet Letter: V1
The Heart Is a Lonely Hunter
        (McCullers): V6
Heart of Darkness (Conrad): V2

Heller, Joseph
   Catch-22: V1
Hemingway, Ernest
   A Farewell to Arms: V1
   The Old Man and the Sea: V6
   The Sun Also Rises: V5
Hesse, Hermann
   Siddhartha: V6
Hinton, S. E.
   The Outsiders: V5
   Tex: V9
The Hitchhiker's Guide to the Galaxy
   (Adams): V7
The Hobbit (Tolkien): V8
House Made of Dawn (Momaday):
   V10
The House of the Spirits (Allende):
   V6
The House on Mango Street
   (Cisneros): V2
How the García Girls Lost Their
   Accents (Alvarez): V5
Howards End (Forster): V10
Hugo, Victor
   Les Misérables: V5
Hurston, Zora Neale
   Their Eyes Were Watching
   God: V3
Huxley, Aldous
   Brave New World: V6

I

I Know Why the Caged Bird Sings
   (Angelou): V2
In Country (Mason): V4
In the Time of the Butterflies
   (Alvarez): V9
Invisible Man (Ellison): V2
Irving, John
   The World According to Garp:
   V12

J

James, Henry
   The Ambassadors: V12
Jane Eyre (Brontë): V4
The Joy Luck Club (Tan): V1
Joyce, James
   A Portrait of the Artist as a
   Young Man: V7
July's People (Gordimer): V4
The Jungle (Sinclair): V6

K

Kafka, Franz
   The Trial: V7
Kerouac, Jack
   On the Road: V8

Kesey, Ken
   One Flew Over the Cuckoo's
   Nest: V2
Keyes, Daniel
   Flowers for Algernon: V2
Kincaid, Jamaica
   Annie John: V3
Kindred (Butler): V8
Kingsolver, Barbara
   Animal Dreams: V12
   The Bean Trees: V5
   Pigs in Heaven: V10
Kingston, Maxine Hong
   The Woman Warrior: V6
Kitchen (Yoshimoto): V7
Knowles, John
   A Separate Peace: V2
Kogawa, Joy
   Obasan: V3
Kosinski, Jerzy
   The Painted Bird: V12

L

The Last of the Mohicans (Cooper):
   V9
Laurence, Margaret
   The Stone Angel: V11
Lee, Harper
   To Kill a Mockingbird: V2
The Left Hand of Darkness (Le
   Guin): V6
Le Guin, Ursula K.
   Always Coming Home: V9
   The Left Hand of Darkness: V6
Les Misérables (Hugo): V5
Less Than Zero (Ellis): V11
A Lesson Before Dying (Gaines): V7
Like Water for Chocolate
   (Esquivel): V5
Little Women (Alcott): V12
Lolita
   (Nabokov): V9
London, Jack
   The Call of the Wild: V8
Lord of the Flies (Golding): V2
Love in the Time of Cholera (García
   Márquez): V1
Love Medicine (Erdrich): V5
Lowry, Lois
   The Giver: V3

M

Machiavelli, Niccolo
   The Prince: V9
Mailer, Norman
   The Naked and the Dead: V10
Malamud, Bernard
   The Fixer: V9
   The Natural: V4

Mama Day (Naylor): V7
Marmon Silko, Leslie
   Ceremony: V4
Mason, Bobbie Ann
   In Country: V4
The Master and Margarita
   (Bulgakov): V8
McCullers, Carson
   The Heart Is a Lonely Hunter: V6
Melville, Herman
   Billy Budd, Sailor: An Inside
   Narrative: V9
   Moby-Dick: V7
Méndez, Miguel
   Pilgrims in Aztlán: V12
Mitchell, Margaret
   Gone with the Wind: V9
Moby-Dick (Melville): V7
Momaday, N. Scott
   House Made of Dawn: V10
Morrison, Toni
   Beloved: V6
   The Bluest Eye: V1
   Song of Solomon: V8
Mrs. Dalloway (Woolf): V12
My Ántonia (Cather): V2

N

Nabokov, Vladimir
   Lolita: V9
The Naked and the Dead (Mailer): V10
Native Son (Wright): V7
The Natural (Malamud): V4
Naylor, Gloria
   Mama Day: V7
   The Women of Brewster Place: V4
Night (Wiesel): V4
Norris, Frank
   The Octopus: V12

O

Oates, Joyce Carol
   them: V8
Obasan (Kogawa): V3
O'Connor, Flannery
   Wise Blood: V3
The Octopus (Norris): V12
Of Mice and Men (Steinbeck): V1
O'Hara, John
   Appointment in Samarra: V11
The Old Gringo (Fuentes): V8
The Old Man and the Sea
   (Hemingway): V6
On the Beach (Shute): V9
On the Road (Kerouac): V8
One Day in the Life of Ivan
   Denisovich (Solzhenitsyn): V6
One Flew Over the Cuckoo's Nest
   (Kesey): V2
One Hundred Years of Solitude
   (García Márquez): V5

Ordinary People (Guest): V1
Orwell, George
    1984: V7
    Animal Farm: V3
Out of Africa (Dinesen): V9
The Outsiders (Hinton): V5

P

The Painted Bird (Kosinski): V12
A Passage to India (Forster): V3
Paton, Alan
    Cry, the Beloved Country: V3
    Too Late the Phalarope: V12
The Pearl (Steinbeck): V5
Pigs in Heaven (Kingsolver): V10
Pilgrims in Aztlán (Méndez): V12
Plath, Sylvia
    The Bell Jar: V1
*A Portrait of the Artist as a Young
    Man* (Joyce): V7
Potok, Chaim
    The Chosen: V4
Power, Susan
    The Grass Dancer: V11
Pride and Prejudice (Austen): V1
The Prince (Machiavelli): V9

R

Rabbit, Run (Updike): V12
Ragtime (Doctorow): V6
Rand, Ayn
    Atlas Shrugged: V10
Rebecca (du Maurier): V12
The Red Badge of Courage (Crane):
    V4
Remarque, Erich Maria
    All Quiet on the Western Front: V4
The Return of the Native (Hardy):
    V11
Robinson Crusoe (Defoe): V9
Rölvaag, O. E.
    Giants in the Earth: V5
A Room with a View (Forster): V11
*Roots: The Story of an American
    Family* (Haley): V9
Rubyfruit Jungle (Brown): V9

S

Salinger, J. D.
    The Catcher in the Rye: V1
The Scarlet Letter (Hawthorne): V1
Seize the Day (Bellow): V4
A Separate Peace (Knowles): V2
Shange, Ntozake
    Betsey Brown: V11

Shelley, Mary
    Frankenstein: V1
Shogun: A Novel of Japan (Clavell):
    V10
Shute, Nevil
    On the Beach: V9
Siddhartha (Hesse): V6
Sinclair, Upton
    The Jungle: V6
Sister Carrie (Dreiser): V8
SThe Slave Dancer (Fox): V12
laughterhouse-Five (Vonnegut): V3
Solzhenitsyn, Aleksandr
    *One Day in the Life of Ivan
       Denisovich:* V6
Song of Solomon (Morrison): V8
The Sound and the Fury (Faulkner):
    V4
Steinbeck, John
    The Grapes of Wrath: V7
    Of Mice and Men: V1
    The Pearl: V5
Stevenson, Robert Louis
    Dr. Jekyll and Mr. Hyde: V11
The Stone Angel (Laurence): V11
Stowe, Harriet Beecher
    Uncle Tom's Cabin: V6
*The Strange Case of Dr. Jekyll and
    Mr. Hyde* (Stevenson): see *Dr.
    Jekyll and Mr. Hyde*
The Stranger (Camus): V6
The Sun Also Rises (Hemingway):
    V5
Swift, Jonathan
    Gulliver's Travels: V6
Summer of My German Soldier
    (Greene): V10

T

A Tale of Two Cities (Dickens): V5
Tan, Amy
    The Joy Luck Club: V1
Ten Little Indians (Christie): V8
Tess of the d'Urbervilles (Hardy):
    V3
Tex (Hinton): V9
Their Eyes Were Watching God
    (Hurston): V3
them (Oates): V8
Things Fall Apart (Achebe): V2
To Kill a Mockingbird (Lee): V2
To the Lighthouse (Woolf): V8
Tolkien, John Ronald Reuel
    The Hobbit: V8
Tolstoy, Leo
    War and Peace: V10
Too Late the Phalarope (Paton): V12
Toomer, Jean
    Cane: V11

The Trial (Kafka): V7
Twain, Mark
    *The Adventures of Huckleberry
       Finn:* V1
    The Adventures of Tom Sawyer:
       V6
Tyler, Anne
    The Accidental Tourist: V7
    Breathing Lessons: V10
    *Dinner at the Homesick
       Restaurant:* V2

U

Uncle Tom's Cabin (Stowe): V6
Updike, John
    Rabbit, Run: V12

V

Voltaire
    Candide: V7
Vonnegut, Kurt, Jr.
    Slaughterhouse-Five: V3

W

Walker, Alice
    The Color Purple: V5
War and Peace (Tolstoy): V10
Watership Down (Adams): V11
Wharton, Edith
    The Age of Innocence: V11
    Ethan Frome: V5
Wiesel, Eliezer
    Night: V4
Winesburg, Ohio (Anderson): V4
Wise Blood (O'Connor): V3
The Woman Warrior (Kingston): V6
The Women of Brewster Place
    (Naylor): V4
Woolf, Virginia
    Mrs. Dalloway: V12
    To the Lighthouse: V8
The World According to Garp
    (Irving): V12
Wouk, Herman
    *The Caine Mutiny: A Novel of
       World War II:* V7
Wright, Richard
    Black Boy: V1
    Native Son: V7
Wuthering Heights (Brontë): V2

Y

A Yellow Raft in Blue Water
    (Dorris): V3
Yoshimoto, Banana
    Kitchen: V7

Cumulative
Nationality/Ethnicity Index

African American

Angelou, Maya
  *I Know Why the Caged Bird
    Sings:* V2
Baldwin, James
  Go Tell It on the Mountain: V4
Ellison, Ralph
  Invisible Man: V2
Gaines, Ernest J.
  *The Autobiography of Miss Jane
    Pittman:* V5
Haley, Alex
  *Roots: The Story of an American
    Family:* V9
Hurston, Zora Neale
  *Their Eyes Were Watching
    God:* V3
Kincaid, Jamaica
  Annie John: V3
Morrison, Toni
  Beloved: V6
  The Bluest Eye: V1
  Song of Solomom: V8
Naylor, Gloria
  Mama Day: V7
  The Women of Brewster Place: V4
Shange, Ntozake
  Betsey Brown: V11
Toomer, Jean
  Cane: V11
Walker, Alice
  The Color Purple: V5
Wright, Richard
  Black Boy: V1

Algerian

Camus, Albert
  The Stranger: V6

American

Alcott, Louisa May
  Little Women: V12
Allison, Dorothy
  Bastard Out of Carolina: V11
Alvarez, Julia
  *How the García Girls Lost Their
    Accents:* V5
Anaya, Rudolfo
  Bless Me, Ultima: V12
Anderson, Sherwood
  Winesburg, Ohio: V4
Angelou, Maya
  *I Know Why the Caged Bird
    Sings:* V2
Auel, Jean
  The Clan of the Cave Bear: V11
Bradbury, Ray
  Fahrenheit 451: V1
Brown, Rita Mae
  Rubyfruit Jungle: V9
Butler, Octavia
  Kindred: V8
Card, Orson Scott
  Ender's Game: V5
Cather, Willa
  My Ántonia: V2
Chopin, Kate
  The Awakening: V3
Cisneros, Sandra
  The House on Mango Street: V2
Clavell, James du Maresq
  Shogun: A Novel of Japan: V10
Clemens, Samuel
  *The Adventures of Huckleberry
    Finn:* V1

  The Adventures of Tom Sawyer: V6
Conroy, Frank
  Body and Soul: V11
Cooper, James Fenimore
  The Last of the Mohicans: V9
Cormier, Robert
  The Chocolate War: V2
Crane, Stephen
  The Red Badge of Courage: V4
Crutcher, Chris
  The Crazy Horse Electric Game:
    V11
Dick, Philip K.
  *Do Androids Dream of Electric
    Sheep?:* V5
Dickey, James
  Deliverance: V9
Didion, Joan
  Democracy: V3
Doctorow, E. L.
  Ragtime: V6
Dorris, Michael
  A Yellow Raft in Blue Water: V3
Dreiser, Theodore
  Sister Carrie: V8
Ellis, Bret Easton
  Less Than Zero: V11
Ellison, Ralph
  Invisible Man: V2
Emecheta, Buchi
  The Bride Price: V12
Erdrich, Louise
  Love Medicine: V5
Faulkner, William
  As I Lay Dying: V8
  The Sound and the Fury: V4

Fitzgerald, F. Scott
  The Great Gatsby: V2
Flagg, Fannie
  Fried Green Tomatoes at the
    Whistle Stop Café: V7
Fox, Paula
  The Slave Dancer: V12
Gaines, Ernest J.
  A Lesson Before Dying: V7
  The Autobiography of Miss Jane
    Pittman: V5
Gardner, John
  Grendel: V3
Gibbons, Kaye
  Ellen Foster: V3
Green, Hannah
  The Dead of the House: V10
Greene, Bette
  Summer of My German Soldier:
    V10
Guest, Judith
  Ordinary People: V1
Hawthorne, Nathaniel
  The Scarlet Letter: V1
Heller, Joseph
  Catch-22: V1
Hemingway, Ernest
  A Farewell to Arms: V1
  The Old Man and the Sea: V6
  The Sun Also Rises: V5
Hinton, S. E.
  Tex: V9
  The Outsiders: V5
Hurston, Zora Neale
  Their Eyes Were Watching God:
    V3
Irving, John
  The World According to Garp:
    V12
James, Henry
  The Ambassadors: V12
Kerouac, Jack
  On the Road: V8
Kesey, Ken
  One Flew Over the Cuckoo's
    Nest: V2
Keyes, Daniel
  Flowers for Algernon: V2
Kincaid, Jamaica
  Annie John: V3
Kingsolver, Barbara
  Animal Dreams: V12
  The Bean Trees: V5
  Pigs in Heaven: V10
Kingston, Maxine Hong
  The Woman Warrior: V6
Knowles, John
  A Separate Peace: V2
Le Guin, Ursula K.
  Always Coming Home: V9
  The Left Hand of Darkness: V6

Lee, Harper
  To Kill a Mockingbird: V2
London, Jack
  The Call of the Wild: V8
Lowry, Lois
  The Giver: V3
Mailer, Norman
  The Naked and the Dead: V10
Mason, Bobbie Ann
  In Country: V4
McCullers, Carson
  The Heart Is a Lonely Hunter: V6
Melville, Herman
  Billy Budd: V9
  Moby-Dick: V7
Méndez, Miguel
  Pilgrims in Aztlán: V12
Mitchell, Margaret
  Gone with the Wind: V9
Momaday, N. Scott
  House Made of Dawn: V10
Morrison, Toni
  Beloved: V6
  The Bluest Eye: V1
  Song of Solomon: V8
Norris, Frank
  The Octopus: V12
Oates, Joyce Carol
  them: V8
O'Connor, Flannery
  Wise Blood: V3
O'Hara, John
  Appointment in Samarra: V11
Plath, Sylvia
  The Bell Jar: V1
Potok, Chaim
  The Chosen: V4
Power, Susan
  The Grass Dancer: V11
Rand, Ayn
  Atlas Shrugged: V10
Rölvaag, O. E.
  Giants in the Earth: V5
Salinger, J. D.
  The Catcher in the Rye: V1
Sinclair, Upton
  The Jungle: V6
Shange, Ntozake
  Betsey Brown: V11
Steinbeck, John
  The Grapes of Wrath: V7
  Of Mice and Men: V1
  The Pearl: V5
Stowe, Harriet Beecher
  Uncle Tom's Cabin: V6
Tan, Amy
  The Joy Luck Club: V1
Toomer, Jean
  Cane: V11
Twain, Mark
  The Adventures of Huckleberry
    Finn: V1
  The Adventures of Tom Sawyer: V6
Tyler, Anne

  The Accidental Tourist: V7
  Breathing Lessons: V10
  Dinner at the Homesick
    Restaurant: V2
Updike, John
  Rabbit, Run: V12
Vonnegut, Kurt, Jr.
  Slaughterhouse-Five: V3
Walker, Alice
  The Color Purple: V5
Wharton, Edith
  The Age of Innocence: V11
  Ethan Frome: V5
Wouk, Herman
  The Caine Mutiny: V7
Wright, Richard
  Black Boy: V1
  Native Son: V7

Asian American

Kingston, Maxine Hong
  The Woman Warrior: V6
Tan, Amy
  The Joy Luck Club: V1

Asian Canadian

Kogawa, Joy
  Obasan: V3

Australian

Clavell, James du Maresq
  Shogun: A Novel of Japan: V10

British

Adams, Douglas
  The Hitchhiker's Guide to the
    Galaxy: V7
Adams, Richard
  Watership Down: V11
Austen, Jane
  Pride and Prejudice: V1
Ballard, J. G.
  Empire of the Sun: V8
Blair, Eric Arthur
  Animal Farm: V3
Brontë, Charlotte
  Jane Eyre: V4
Brontë, Emily
  Wuthering Heights: V2
Carroll, Lewis
  Alice's Adventurers in
    Wonderland: V7
Chrisite, Agatha
  Ten Little Indians: V8
Conrad, Joseph
  Heart of Darkness: V2
Defoe, Daniel
  Robinson Crusoe: V9
Dickens, Charles
  A Christmas Carol: V10

Great Expectations: V4
A Tale of Two Cities: V5
du Maurier, Daphne
Rebecca: V12
Forster, E. M.
A Passage to India: V3
Howards End: V10
A Room with a View: V11
Golding, William
Lord of the Flies: V2
Hardy, Thomas
The Return of the Native: V11
Tess of the d'Urbervilles: V3
Huxley, Aldous
Brave New World: V6
Marmon Silko, Leslie
Ceremony: V4
Orwell, George
1984: V7
Animal Farm: V3
Shelley, Mary
Frankenstein: V1
Shute, Nevil
On the Beach: V9
Stevenson, Robert Louis
Dr. Jekyll and Mr. Hyde: V11
Swift, Jonathan
Gulliver's Travels: V6
Tolkien, J. R. R.
The Hobbit: V8
Woolf, Virginia
Mrs. Dalloway: V12
To the Lighthouse: V8

Canadian

Atwood, Margaret
The Edible Woman: V12
The Handmaid's Tale: V4
Kogawa, Joy
Obasan: V3
Laurence, Margaret
The Stone Angel: V11

Chilean

Allende, Isabel
The House of the Spirits: V6

Colombian

García Márquez, Gabriel
Chronicle of a Death Foretold: V10
Love in the Time of Cholera: V1
One Hundred Years of Solitude:
V5

Danish

Dinesen, Isak
Out of Africa: V9

Dominican

Alvarez, Julia
How the García Girls Lost Their
Accents: V5
In the Time of Butterflies: V9

European American

Hemingway, Ernest
The Old Man and the Sea: V6
Stowe, Harriet Beecher
Uncle Tom's Cabin: V6

French

Camus, Albert
The Stranger: V6
Hugo, Victor
Les Misérables: V5
Voltaire
Candide: V7

German

Hesse, Hermann
Siddhartha: V6
Remarque, Erich Maria
All Quiet on the Western Front: V4

Hispanic American

Cisneros, Sandra
The House on Mango Street: V2

Italian

Machiavelli, Niccolo
The Prince: V9

Irish

Joyce, James
A Portrait of the Artist as a
Young Man: V7

Japanese

Yoshimoto, Banana
Kitchen: V7

Jewish

Bellow, Saul
Seize the Day: V4
Kafka, Frank
The Trial: V7
Malamud, Bernard
The Fixer: V9
The Natural: V4
Wiesel, Eliezer
Night: V4

Mexican

Esquivel, Laura
Like Water for Chocolate: V5
Fuentes, Carlos
The Old Gringo: V8

Native American

Dorris, Michael
A Yellow Raft in Blue Water: V3
Erdrich, Louise
Love Medicine: V5
Marmon Silko, Leslie
Ceremony: V4
Momaday, N. Scott
House Made of Dawn: V10

Nigerian

Achebe, Chinua
Things Fall Apart: V3

Norwegian

Rölvaag, O. E.
Giants in the Earth: V5

Polish

Kosinski, Jerzy
The Painted Bird: V12

Romanian

Wiesel, Eliezer
Night: V4

Russian

Bulgakov, Mikhail
The Master and Margarita: V8
Dostoyevsky, Fyodor
The Brothers Karamazon: V8
Crime and Punishment: V3
Nabokov, Vladimir
Lolita: V9
Rand, Ayn
Atlas Shrugged: V10
Solzhenitsyn, Aleksandr
One Day in the Life of Ivan
Denisovich: V6
Tolstoy, Leo
War and Peace: V10

South African

Gordimer, Nadine
July's People: V4
Paton, Alan
Cry, the Beloved Country: V3
Too Late the Phalarope: V12

Spanish

Saavedra, Miguel de Cervantes
Don Quixote: V8

West Indian

Kincaid, Jamaica
Annie John: V3

Subject/Theme Index

*Boldface denotes discussion in *Themes* section.

A

Abuse
  Animal Dreams: 45
Adolescence and Identity
  Little Women: 123
Adultery
  The World According to Garp: 342
Adulthood
  Little Women: 134–137, 139
  Rebecca: 273–276
  The Slave Dancer: 293, 295
Adventure and Exploration
  The Ambassadors: 14–15, 17
  Little Women: 134, 136–139
  Pilgrims in Aztlán: 221–223, 228
  Rebecca: 271, 273–276
Africa
  The Ambassadors: 3–4, 7–10, 12, 17–22
  The Bride Price: 65–67, 72, 74–79
  The Slave Dancer: 282, 290
  Too Late the Phalarope: 298, 307–310, 313–316, 318
Alienation and Loneliness
  The Painted Bird: 201
Ambiguity
  The Ambassadors: 19–22
American South
  Rabbit, Run: 250, 253–254
American Southwest
  Animal Dreams: 24, 26–27, 30–31

Bless Me, Ultima: 47, 49, 53–55, 59–61
American West
  Animal Dreams: 45
  The Octopus: 168, 170, 174–177, 179, 181
  Pilgrims in Aztlán: 225–226
Anger
  Bless Me, Ultima: 49, 54
  Little Women: 133–136, 139
  The Painted Bird: 197–198, 203
  Pilgrims in Aztlán: 216, 224
  The Slave Dancer: 282, 287, 292
  Too Late the Phalarope: 319
Apartheid
  Too Late the Phalarope: 307–310
Art and Creativity
  The World According to Garp: 336
Atonement
  Bless Me, Ultima: 49
Authoritarianism
  The Painted Bird: 195, 203–205

B

Bildungsroman
  Bless Me, Ultima: 61
Bloomsbury Group
  The Ambassadors: 9, 12–13
  Mrs. Dalloway: 148, 157–158, 163, 166–167

C

Central America
  Animal Dreams: 25–27, 31–34, 38, 42, 45

Change and Transformation
  The Painted Bird: 201
Charity
  Little Women: 140, 143–144
Childhood
  Little Women: 133–135, 137, 139–140, 143–145
  The Slave Dancer: 292–294
Christianity
  The Bride Price: 74, 76–77
  Too Late the Phalarope: 313, 316–320
Clash of Cultures
  Bless Me, Ultima: 52
Classicism
  Too Late the Phalarope: 310
Colonialism
  The Bride Price: 67, 76
Comedy
  The Edible Woman: 110–111, 113–114
Coming of Age
  The Painted Bird: 201
  Little Women: 143–144
Communism
  The Painted Bird: 198, 203–206, 210–212
A Complicated Hero
  Rabbit, Run: 242
Consciousness
  Mrs. Dalloway: 153
Courage
  The Bride Price: 72, 87
  Little Women: 144, 146
Crime and Criminals
  The Ambassadors: 8–9, 12
  The Bride Price: 65, 68, 72, 74, 77, 84, 87, 89, 91

The Octopus: 170–171, 175–176, 179, 182–184, 188–189, 191–193

Rebecca: 271–272, 274–277

The Slave Dancer: 280, 282–283, 291

Too Late the Phalarope: 300, 304–307, 310–312

Cruelty

Animal Dreams: 45

Bless Me, Ultima: 60–62

Little Women: 119, 124–125

The Octopus: 169, 177, 180–181

The Painted Bird: 195, 197, 201–203, 205–209

The Slave Dancer: 282–283, 287–288, 291

The World According to Garp: 344

Culture Clash

Animal Dreams: 30

The Bride Price: 74

The Octopus: 174

Curiosity

The Edible Woman: 111–114

Rebecca: 264–265

D

Dance

Little Women: 143

The Slave Dancer: 280, 282–284

Death

Animal Dreams: 24, 26–27, 30–32

Bless Me, Ultima: 49–50

The Bride Price: 65, 67–68, 72, 74–75, 77, 84–90

Little Women: 119, 123, 125–127, 140–141, 144–146

Mrs. Dalloway: 150–151, 154–155, 157–158, 163–167

The Octopus: 168, 176–177, 179–180, 187–193

The Painted Bird: 195, 197–198, 201, 203, 205

Pilgrims in Aztlán: 216–217, 223–225, 229–231

Rabbit, Run: 251–252, 254–255

Rebecca: 256–259, 262–267

The Slave Dancer: 282–284, 287, 289–291

Too Late the Phalarope: 301, 304, 306, 310

The World According to Garp: 323, 325–327, 336–340, 342–343

Death and Disfigurement

The World According to Garp: 335

Defiance and Resistance

The Bride Price: 72

Devil

The Ambassadors: 14–15

Dialect

Pilgrims in Aztlán: 234–235

Dialogue

Pilgrims in Aztlán: 216

Too Late the Phalarope: 313, 318

Disease

The Ambassadors: 8, 11–12

Little Women: 118–119, 126

Disillusionment

The Ambassadors: 7

Displacement

Pilgrims in Aztlán: 223

Diversity

The Ambassadors: 9

The Divided Self

Too Late the Phalarope: 304

Drama

Too Late the Phalarope: 318

The World According to Garp: 325, 335, 340

Dreams and Visions

The Ambassadors: 20–22

Bless Me, Ultima: 48–49, 53, 56, 60–62

Little Women: 133–135, 137–139

E

Emotions

Animal Dreams: 31, 44

The Bride Price: 81, 86

The Edible Woman: 96, 113

Little Women: 129–130, 145–146

Mrs. Dalloway: 164–165

The Octopus: 177, 181, 192

The Painted Bird: 209

Pilgrims in Aztlán: 214

Rabbit, Run: 243, 245

Rebecca: 267, 272, 274–275

The Slave Dancer: 287, 289, 292–293

Too Late the Phalarope: 318–320

The World According to Garp: 340, 342–343

Epic

The Bride Price: 86–87, 90

The Octopus: 186, 188, 190, 193–194

Europe

The Ambassadors: 1–4, 7, 9–12

Little Women: 119, 124–125

Mrs. Dalloway: 148, 150–151, 154–156

The Painted Bird: 195, 202–205, 210–212

Rebecca: 258–259, 264–267

The World According to Garp: 323, 325–326, 336–338

Evil

The Ambassadors: 14–15

Bless Me, Ultima: 47, 52, 56

The Octopus: 171, 175–177, 181–182, 184, 187–190, 192–194

The Painted Bird: 207–209

Rebecca: 267, 271–275, 277

Too Late the Phalarope: 304–305, 319–320

Exile

The Bride Price: 84, 87, 90

F

Family Life

Little Women: 116, 129, 133, 137, 140–142, 144, 146

Too Late the Phalarope: 317

Farm and Rural Life

Animal Dreams: 26, 31–33, 38, 40–41, 45

Bless Me, Ultima: 48–50, 52–55

The Bride Price: 67, 76–77

The Octopus: 168–171, 174–177, 179–185, 187–192, 194

The Painted Bird: 197–198

Pilgrims in Aztlán: 223, 225–226

Too Late the Phalarope: 313–315

Fate and Chance

Animal Dreams: 38–41, 43–45

The Edible Woman: 110–113

Mrs. Dalloway: 159

The Octopus: 186–187, 189–193

Rebecca: 258, 264–265, 267–268

Too Late the Phalarope: 314, 316–318, 320

Fear and Terror

The Ambassadors: 14–17

The Bride Price: 67, 72, 76, 81–83

The Edible Woman: 112–113

Mrs. Dalloway: 151, 157

The Painted Bird: 197, 202, 204

Rabbit, Run: 251, 254–255

Rebecca: 256, 259, 263, 265–266

The Slave Dancer: 295–296

Too Late the Phalarope: 315, 320–321

Femininity

The Edible Woman: 109–114

Feminism

Animal Dreams: 25, 33–35

The Bride Price: 77–79

The Edible Woman: 94, 103–107, 109–110, 113–114

Little Women: 133–134, 136–140, 142–144, 146

The World According to Garp: 323, 338

Flesh Versus Spirit

Rebecca: 263

Folklore

The Ambassadors: 14–15, 17

The Edible Woman: 109, 114

Pilgrims in Aztlán: 214–215, 223–224, 227–229, 231

Foreshadowing

The Bride Price: 74

Little Women: 124–125
Too Late the Phalarope: 300, 307
The World According to Garp: 337
Forgiveness
Too Late the Phalarope: 316, 320–321
France
The Ambassadors: 7
Freedom and Imprisonment
The Slave Dancer: 287
Friendship
Little Women: 142, 144

G

Gender Roles
The Bride Price: 71
The Edible Woman: 101
Little Women: 122
The World According to Garp: 335
The Edible Woman: 102, 113–114
The World According to Garp: 323, 335
Generosity
Little Women: 139, 143, 146
Ghost
Rebecca: 256, 263
God
Bless Me, Ultima: 49–50, 52–53, 55, 57, 59
The Bride Price: 82–83
The Painted Bird: 197–198
Rabbit, Run: 249–252
The Slave Dancer: 282–283, 288–289
Too Late the Phalarope: 313–318, 320
Gothicism
Rebecca: 265, 271, 276–277
Greed
The Octopus: 168, 175, 182–183
Rabbit, Run: 250–251, 254
Grief and Sorrow
The Bride Price: 84–85, 89
Little Women: 139, 144, 146
The World According to Garp: 340, 342
Guilt
Too Late the Phalarope: 305
Rebecca: 263–264, 272–275, 277
Too Late the Phalarope: 300–301, 305–306, 310
Guilt and Innocence
Rebecca: 263

H

Happiness and Gaiety
The Bride Price: 82–83
Little Women: 118–119, 122, 125, 129–132

Too Late the Phalarope: 300–301, 306
Hatred
The Edible Woman: 111, 113
Little Women: 134, 136, 138
Mrs. Dalloway: 157, 165–166
The Painted Bird: 197–198, 204–206, 208–210, 212
Rebecca: 258–259, 262–263
The Slave Dancer: 283, 287, 289
Too Late the Phalarope: 298, 304, 307, 310, 314–315, 318–319, 321
The World According to Garp: 326, 336
Heaven
Animal Dreams: 45
The Bride Price: 67, 74–75
Heritage and Ancestry
The Bride Price: 67–68, 72–76, 84–86, 90
Heroism
The Bride Price: 83–87, 90
The Edible Woman: 107, 109
Little Women: 140, 144–145
Pilgrims in Aztlán: 234–235
Rabbit, Run: 247–248
Rebecca: 256, 267, 273, 276
Historical Periods
The Edible Woman: 110
Pilgrims in Aztlán: 221
History
The Ambassadors: 3, 8
Bless Me, Ultima: 56
The Bride Price: 79
The Edible Woman: 109–110
Mrs. Dalloway: 148, 150–151, 153–154
Pilgrims in Aztlán: 223–226
Rabbit, Run: 237, 243
Rebecca: 265, 268
The World According to Garp: 337
The Holocaust
The Painted Bird: 197, 202–205
Honor
The Octopus: 189, 193–194
The Slave Dancer: 292
Hope
The Octopus: 175–176, 180
Too Late the Phalarope: 301, 305, 307–310, 313, 315, 320–321
Humility
Rebecca: 275–276
Humor
The Bride Price: 84, 86
The Edible Woman: 110–113
Little Women: 119, 124–125, 140–141, 145
The Painted Bird: 210
The World According to Garp: 336, 338–344, 347
Hypocrisy Versus Integrity
The Slave Dancer: 287

I

Imagery and Symbolism
The Bride Price: 65, 75
The Edible Woman: 97, 101, 103, 105–107, 109–113
Mrs. Dalloway: 164–165
The Octopus: 174, 177, 180
Pilgrims in Aztlán: 221, 224–225, 228, 230–231
Rabbit, Run: 242–243, 252, 254
Rebecca: 275
Imagination
The Edible Woman: 109–112, 114
The World According to Garp: 347
Immigrants and Immigration
Pilgrims in Aztlán: 214–217, 226
The Individual and Society
The Bride Price: 89
Individualism and Community
Animal Dreams: 30
Insanity
Mrs. Dalloway: 163, 166–167
Irony
The Octopus: 193
Rebecca: 272–276
Too Late the Phalarope: 317–319
The World According to Garp: 337

J

Judaism
The Painted Bird: 195–197, 202–203
Too Late the Phalarope: 314, 316, 318, 321
Justice and Consequences
Too Late the Phalarope: 304

K

Killers and Killing
Animal Dreams: 27, 30, 33–34
Bless Me, Ultima: 48–50
Mrs. Dalloway: 150, 157, 165–167
The Octopus: 188–189, 193
The Painted Bird: 197–198, 203–204
Rebecca: 259, 263–264, 267
Too Late the Phalarope: 300
The World According to Garp: 326, 336–338
Kindness
Little Women: 143–146
The Octopus: 188, 190–193
Knowledge
The Ambassadors: 7, 12
Mrs. Dalloway: 159–161
Rebecca: 267

L

Landscape
  Animal Dreams: 26–27, 30–32, 34, 38–39, 44–45
  Bless Me, Ultima: 56, 58–59
  The Bride Price: 74–76, 87–89
  The Octopus: 168, 170, 175, 177, 179–181
  The Painted Bird: 195, 197–198, 205
  Pilgrims in Aztlán: 215–217, 222–225, 232–233
  Rebecca: 258–259, 264, 266
  The Slave Dancer: 282–283, 287–290
Law and Order
  The Bride Price: 72, 74–77, 84–85, 87, 89
  The Octopus: 168, 170–171, 176, 179, 182, 185, 188, 191
  The Painted Bird: 197, 202, 204–205
  Pilgrims in Aztlán: 215, 225–226
  Rebecca: 273, 275
  The Slave Dancer: 282, 289–291
  Too Late the Phalarope: 298, 300–301, 304–305, 307–321
Literary Criticism
  Bless Me, Ultima: 55, 59
  The Bride Price: 78
  The Edible Woman: 107, 110, 112
  Little Women: 128
  Mrs. Dalloway: 155
  The Octopus: 176
Loneliness
  The Bride Price: 89–90
  Little Women: 141–143, 146
  Mrs. Dalloway: 149, 154–155, 158, 163, 166–167
  The Painted Bird: 201–202, 205
Loss of Innocence and Quest for Understanding
  Bless Me, Ultima: 52
Love and Lust
  The World According to Garp: 336
Love and Passion
  The Ambassadors: 3–4, 7, 19, 21
  Animal Dreams: 38, 42–43, 45
  The Bride Price: 68, 71, 74, 78, 84–86, 90
  Little Women: 118, 122, 124–126, 129–141, 143–146
  Mrs. Dalloway: 150, 157–158, 163–167
  The Octopus: 170, 175, 177, 188, 191, 193–194
  Rabbit, Run: 249–252, 254
  Rebecca: 258–259, 263–266, 271–272, 274–276
  Too Late the Phalarope: 300, 304–305, 309–310, 316–321

  The World According to Garp: 323, 326, 336–337
Lower Class
  The Painted Bird: 197–198, 205
Loyalty
  Rebecca: 262–264
  Too Late the Phalarope: 316, 318, 320–321

M

Magic Realism
  Pilgrims in Aztlán: 233
Marriage
  The Bride Price: 65, 67–68, 71–72, 74–75, 77, 84–85, 87, 89, 91
  The Edible Woman: 96, 102–103, 106–107, 109
  Little Women: 119, 123–124, 126, 129, 133–135, 138, 142, 146
  Rebecca: 272, 275–276
  Too Late the Phalarope: 315, 318–319
  The World According to Garp: 325–326, 336
Memoir
  Too Late the Phalarope: 301, 304–306
Memory and Reminiscence
  Animal Dreams: 24, 26–27, 31–32, 34–38
  Mrs. Dalloway: 163–164, 167
  Rebecca: 258, 262–263
Mental Instability
  Mrs. Dalloway: 163
Middle East
  Mrs. Dalloway: 150, 154, 156
Modernism
  Mrs. Dalloway: 156
  Too Late the Phalarope: 308
Monarchy
  Mrs. Dalloway: 159–160
Money and Economics
  The Ambassadors: 10–12
  The Bride Price: 67, 72, 76–77
  Little Women: 116, 118, 123–124, 126–128, 140–142
  The Octopus: 170–171, 175–179, 186–187, 189, 191–192
  Pilgrims in Aztlán: 216, 223–225, 227
  Rebecca: 266–267
Mood
  Too Late the Phalarope: 300–301, 305
Moral Corruption
  The Octopus: 175
Morality
  Too Late the Phalarope: 304
Morals and Morality
  The Ambassadors: 18–21
  Animal Dreams: 45

  The Bride Price: 84–86, 89–90
  Little Women: 133–137, 139
  The Octopus: 175–177, 181–182, 184, 188, 193–194
  The Painted Bird: 207
  Pilgrims in Aztlán: 223, 227
  Rabbit, Run: 249, 251
  Rebecca: 264, 267, 273
  Too Late the Phalarope: 298, 304, 306, 309–310, 316, 320–321
Motherhood
  The Edible Woman: 111–112
  Little Women: 133–134, 136–139
Murder
  Rebecca: 263–264, 267
  Too Late the Phalarope: 300, 304
  The World According to Garp: 326–327, 335–338
Music
  Mrs. Dalloway: 163–167
  The Slave Dancer: 284, 287–291–296
Mystery and Intrigue
  The Octopus: 188, 190, 192–193
  Rebecca: 256, 258, 264–265, 267, 271–276
Myths and Legends
  Bless Me, Ultima: 47, 55–56, 60–61
  The Edible Woman: 109–111, 113
  Pilgrims in Aztlán: 221, 225, 227
  Rebecca: 271–274

N

Narration
  The Ambassadors: 9–10, 13, 20–21
  Animal Dreams: 24, 32, 34
  Bless Me, Ultima: 53, 55, 60–62
  The Bride Price: 67–68, 74, 80, 83–86, 88–91
  The Edible Woman: 95–96, 102, 105, 110–114
  Little Women: 124–125, 133–139
  Mrs. Dalloway: 148–151, 155, 158–161
  Pilgrims in Aztlán: 217, 223–224, 230,– 231
  Rebecca: 256–259, 262–265, 269–270, 272–273, 276
  Too Late the Phalarope: 298–299, 306, 309–310, 313, 317–318
Nationalism and Patriotism
  Too Late the Phalarope: 313–316, 318
Naturalism
  The Octopus: 168, 176–177, 180, 193
Nature
  Animal Dreams: 31–32, 35, 37–38

Bless Me, Ultima: 56, 60–61
The Bride Price: 68, 87–88
Little Women: 145
The Octopus: 177, 180–181,
188, 190, 192–193
The Painted Bird: 195, 201–203,
208–209
Rabbit, Run: 252
Rebecca: 265
Too Late the Phalarope: 318–319
The World According to Garp:
325, 336
Nightmare
Bless Me, Ultima: 60–61
1950s
Rabbit, Run: 242–245
1960s
The Edible Woman: 102–104,
106–107, 110, 114
The World According to Garp:
323, 337–338
North America
Bless Me, Ultima: 53–55
The Edible Woman: 103–104
The Octopus: 176, 179
The Painted Bird: 195, 204–205
Pilgrims in Aztlán: 214–215, 217,
221, 223–226
The Slave Dancer: 283, 287,
289–291
The World According to Garp:
323, 326, 337–338
Novel
The Ambassadors: 1–3, 8–10,
12–15, 17
Animal Dreams: 24, 31–36, 38, 45
Bless Me, Ultima: 47, 52–56,
58–63
The Bride Price: 65, 67, 72, 74,
78–79, 83–91
The Edible Woman: 103,
105–107, 109–111, 113–114
Little Women: 119, 123, 125,
127–137, 139
Mrs. Dalloway: 148–150,
153–155, 157–161, 163–164,
166–167
The Octopus: 168–169, 175–177,
179–190, 192–194
The Painted Bird: 195, 198,
201–203, 205, 210–212
Pilgrims in Aztlán: 214, 216–217,
221–229
Rabbit, Run: 237–239, 242–243,
245–247
Rebecca: 256, 263–265, 267–269,
271, 273–274, 276–277
Too Late the Phalarope: 298,
301, 306–307, 309–310,
312–316, 318–319, 321
The World According to Garp:
323–326, 335–340, 342–344,
347

Nuclear War
Bless Me, Ultima: 55
Rebecca: 266
Nurturance
Little Women: 135, 137–138

O
Old Age
Mrs. Dalloway: 163–165, 167

P
Painting
Rebecca: 257–258, 265
Parody
The Edible Woman: 110–111, 113
Perception
Bless Me, Ultima: 59–62
Rebecca: 271–274, 276–277
The Slave Dancer: 283, 287–289
Permanence
Little Women: 127–129, 132–135,
139
Rebecca: 265–266
Persecution
The Edible Woman: 110–112, 114
Mrs. Dalloway: 163–164, 166
The Painted Bird: 195, 203–205
Rebecca: 264
The Slave Dancer: 293–294
Personal Identity
The Edible Woman: 101
Little Women: 137–138, 140, 142
Personification
Pilgrims in Aztlán: 216, 224
Too Late the Phalarope: 314,
316–317, 319, 321
Philosophical Ideas
The Octopus: 187, 190, 194
Too Late the Phalarope: 319
Pilgrimage
Pilgrims in Aztlán: 221
Plants
Mrs. Dalloway: 149–151, 155
Plot
Animal Dreams: 30, 32, 34
Bless Me, Ultima: 60, 62
Little Women: 130–131
Mrs. Dalloway: 159–161
The Octopus: 168, 177, 180
Rebecca: 273–274
Too Late the Phalarope: 314,
318, 320
The World According to Garp:
337–338, 344
Poetry
The Octopus: 186–189, 192–193
Point of View
The Ambassadors: 10, 13
Animal Dreams: 26, 32
Bless Me, Ultima: 53

The Bride Price: 85, 88, 90
The Edible Woman: 102, 112–114
Mrs. Dalloway: 150, 155
Pilgrims in Aztlán: 228–229
Politicians
The Bride Price: 75–78
The Octopus: 171, 176, 179,
186–189, 191
The Painted Bird: 204
Pilgrims in Aztlán: 216, 225
The World According to Garp:
337–338
Politics
The Octopus: 176
The Ambassadors: 11–12
Animal Dreams: 24–25, 27,
32–35, 41–43, 45
The Bride Price: 76–78
The Edible Woman: 94, 103–104
Mrs. Dalloway: 154–158
The Octopus: 170, 176–179,
186–188
The Painted Bird: 197, 204–206,
210–212
Pilgrims in Aztlán: 216, 223,
225–226
Too Late the Phalarope: 298,
304, 307–308, 313–316
The World According to Garp:
326, 337–338
Postcolonialism
The Bride Price: 80
Poverty
Pilgrims in Aztlán: 216–217, 221,
223–224, 226–227
Pride
Little Women: 133–135, 137, 139
Too Late the Phalarope: 313–314,
319, 321
Prostitution
Pilgrims in Aztlán: 216–217, 223
Psychology and the Human Mind
The Ambassadors: 9–10, 13–17
Animal Dreams: 33, 35
Bless Me, Ultima: 59–62
The Edible Woman: 110, 112–114
Little Women: 136, 138
Mrs. Dalloway: 164, 166
Rebecca: 256, 264
Too Late the Phalarope: 318–321
Punishment
Rebecca: 273–274, 276

Q
The Quest
Rabbit, Run: 241

R
Race
Pilgrims in Aztlán: 214–215, 221,
223–225, 227, 231–234

The Slave Dancer: 283, 288, 290, 292
Too Late the Phalarope: 298, 300, 307–310, 313–321
Racism and Prejudice
The Slave Dancer: 280, 290, 292
Too Late the Phalarope: 307–310
Realism
The Octopus: 176, 180–181
Recreation
Rabbit, Run: 244
Religion and Religious Thought
Animal Dreams: 26, 32
Bless Me, Ultima: 47, 54–59
The Bride Price: 67, 74, 76–77, 80, 83, 86, 89
The Painted Bird: 202, 204
Rabbit, Run: 241–243, 250–251
The Slave Dancer: 287–288
Too Late the Phalarope: 306, 309, 314, 318–319
Religious Works
Too Late the Phalarope: 300–301, 306, 309
Remorse and Regret
Little Women: 118–119, 125
Revenge
The Painted Bird: 198, 208–209
Too Late the Phalarope: 314, 316, 318, 320
Roman Catholicism
Bless Me, Ultima: 53, 55–56

S

Science and Technology
The Ambassadors: 8–9, 12
Mrs. Dalloway: 159, 161
The Octopus: 175–177, 179–180
Rebecca: 265–266, 268
Search for Identity
Bless Me, Ultima: 52
Search for Knowledge
Little Women: 137, 139
Rabbit, Run: 247–249
Search for Self
The Edible Woman: 100
Selfishness
Little Women: 134–136, 139, 141–144
Selfless*
Little Women: 133–141, 144, 146
Sentimentality
Little Women: 132–134
Rebecca: 278
Setting
Bless Me, Ultima: 53–54
The Bride Price: 67, 78–79
Little Women: 125, 129
Rebecca: 263–265
The World According to Garp: 337
Sex and Sexuality
The Edible Woman: 109, 111–113

Little Women: 133–139
The Painted Bird: 197–198, 202
Rabbit, Run: 237, 239, 242, 246
Too Late the Phalarope: 298, 300–301, 304, 306–310
The World According to Garp: 323, 325–326, 336
Sickness
The Ambassadors: 3–4
Little Women: 118, 124, 126
The Slave Dancer: 282–283, 290–291
Sin
The Bride Price: 84, 86–87
The Octopus: 175–176, 182–184
Rebecca: 273–275
Too Late the Phalarope: 298, 300–301, 304–308, 313, 315–318, 320–321
Slavery
The Bride Price: 65, 67–68, 72, 74–75, 84–87
The Slave Dancer: 280–284, 287–296
Slavery and Oppression
The Bride Price: 72
Social Change
Mrs. Dalloway: 154
Social Order
Mrs. Dalloway: 154, 163–164
Solitude
Mrs. Dalloway: 150, 154
Soul
Too Late the Phalarope: 313, 317, 319
Spiritual Leaders
Bless Me, Ultima: 48–49, 52–53, 56–57, 59
Too Late the Phalarope: 300–301, 304, 307
Spirituality
Bless Me, Ultima: 56–58
The Painted Bird: 207–208
Too Late the Phalarope: 305, 309–310, 313, 317, 320
Sports and the Sporting Life
Rabbit, Run: 238–239, 242–243, 246, 249–251, 253
The World According to Garp: 325–327, 335, 337
Strength and Weakness
The Painted Bird: 202
Structure
The Ambassadors: 10, 12–13
Animal Dreams: 37
Little Women: 125, 127
The Sublime
The Ambassadors: 14
Suicide
Mrs. Dalloway: 149, 155, 157–158
Supernatural
Rebecca: 265, 268

Survival
The Painted Bird: 207–208
Suspense
Rebecca: 271, 273, 276–277

T

Things
The Ambassadors: 8
Time and Change
The Ambassadors: 20–22
Rebecca: 264–265
Tragedy
Too Late the Phalarope: 313–320
The World According to Garp: 340, 343
Trust
The Slave Dancer: 282, 289

U

Uncertainty
The Ambassadors: 17, 19–22
Understanding
Bless Me, Ultima: 60–61
The Bride Price: 83, 87–88, 91
Little Women: 134, 136–137
Updike's Emphasis On Sex and Sports
Rabbit, Run: 242

V

Vietnam War
Pilgrims in Aztlán: 222–225
Violence and Cruelty
The Painted Bird: 202

W

War
Pilgrims in Aztlán: 222
War, the Military, and Soldier Life
The Ambassadors: 1, 7, 11--12
Animal Dreams: 26, 33
Bless Me, Ultima: 48, 53–55
The Bride Price: 74, 76, 78
Little Women: 118–119, 123, 126–128
Mrs. Dalloway: 150, 154, 156–157, 163–164, 166
The Painted Bird: 195–198, 201–205
Pilgrims in Aztlán: 216–217, 222–224, 230–231
Rebecca: 265–267
The Slave Dancer: 284, 287, 292
Too Late the Phalarope: 300, 304, 307–309, 313–316, 319–321
The World According to Garp: 323, 325, 335

Wealth
  Little Women: 118, 123–124, 128
Wealth and Poverty
  Little Women: 123
Wildlife
  The Painted Bird: 197, 202–203,
    205–207

The Slave Dancer: 280, 287,
  289–295
Too Late the Phalarope: 315–317
The World According to Garp:
  323, 326, 336–338
World War I
  Rebecca: 265, 267

World War II
  Bless Me, Ultima: 47, 49, 53–55
  The Painted Bird: 195–196, 201,
    203–206
  Rebecca: 266–267